AMERICAN HITS
The Ones That Got Away

Contents

- Introduction
- Week by week listing of all records that made the Billboard 'Bubbling Under' chart and Cash Box 'Looking Ahead' chart from 1959 to 1985
- Records listed by artist

Introduction

The period from the late 1950s to the 1980s stands out as an exceptionally vibrant time in the realm of popular music, marked by unparalleled creativity, the emergence of highly revered songs, and the rise of legendary singers and groups. The era began when big bands and crooners dominated the charts. By the middle of the fifties a fusion of R&B, jazz and country was helping to form rock and roll. The 1960s saw dance crazes such as The Twist and The Locomotion becoming popular for a while after which The Beatles led the British Invasion and Motown, Atlantic and numerous other record labels brought us classic soul. The 1970s saw the emergence of singer-songwriters, glam rock and punk. The eighties brought the 'New Romantics and electronic music.

Our previous books have chronicled every hit from the first chart in July 1940 to the last one of the 1980s. These were the top 20s, top 30s and top 100s of this classic period of music. From June 1959, Billboard magazine began to list up and coming records that were outside of the Hot 100 each week. This section of the chart was called 'Bubbling Under'. In October 1959, Cash Box magazine began a similar listing which they called 'Looking Ahead'. The purpose of these additional chart placings was to show which records were gaining airplay and starting to sell in the shops with the expectation that some of them would become big hits. Many of the records that appeared on the 'Bubbling Under' and 'Looking Ahead' charts never made the top 100 and for many years have been forgotten and disregarded. These records are listed in this new book showing the date they entered the 'Bubbling Under' and 'Looking Ahead' lists and the highest chart position (outside of the top 100) that each one achieved. Billboard discontinued their 'Bubbling Under' charts in August 1985 while Cash Box continued with their additional chart placings until February 1993.

This book covers the period up to the end of Billboards additional chart in 1985. Within the pages of data, you can see which chart the record appeared in, either (BB) for Billboard or (CB) for Cash Box week by week.

Following that chronological data, there is an alphabetical list by artist which at last gives these record makers the recognition that they deserve.

DOE	Title	Artist	Peak	Chart
01/06/1959	Mama's Place	Bing Day	104	BB
01/06/1959	Getting Nearer	John Lester & Mello-Queens	105	BB
01/06/1959	My First Love	The Four Coins	106	BB
01/06/1959	Car Trouble	The Eligibles	107	BB
01/06/1959	I'm Confessin' (That I Love You)	Terri Dean	107	BB
01/06/1959	What Good Is Graduation	Graduates	110	BB
01/06/1959	Crying My Heart Out For You	Neil Sedaka	111	BB
01/06/1959	Souvenirs	Barbara Evans	111	BB
01/06/1959	When Your Love Comes Along	The Five Satins	112	BB
08/06/1959	I Know It's Hard But It's Fair	The "5" Royales	103	BB
08/06/1959	Sing Along	Jimmy Dean	106	BB
08/06/1959	Smile	Art Mooney And His Orchestra	107	BB
15/06/1959	You Are Everything To Me	Johnny Mathis	109	BB
22/06/1959	Time Has A Way	Sam Fletcher	103	BB
29/06/1959	A Very Precious Love	Hernando And The Orchestra	103	BB
29/06/1959	Pure Love	Sonny James	107	BB
06/07/1959	All Nite Long	Billy Vaughn And His Orchestra	102	BB
13/07/1959	Slow Motion	Wade Flemons	101	BB
13/07/1959	Let Nobody Love You	Little Willie John	108	BB
13/07/1959	Little Bitty Johnny	Travis & Bob	114	BB
13/07/1959	Bye Bye Baby Goodbye	Teresa Brewer	115	BB
20/07/1959	Misty	Sarah Vaughan	106	BB
20/07/1959	Big Surprise	The Four Preps	111	BB
27/07/1959	Happy Lonesome	Marion	102	BB
27/07/1959	Our Love	The Rivieras	103	BB
27/07/1959	Sweetie Pie	Bob Crewe	111	BB
27/07/1959	I Can't Begin To Tell You	Jane Morgan	113	BB
27/07/1959	Soldier's Joy	Jerry Reed	115	BB
03/08/1959	Romeo	The Cadillacs	105	BB

03/08/1959	Hold On	Ed Townsend	106	BB
03/08/1959	Roulette	Russ Conway	106	BB
03/08/1959	Love Me Now	Jules Farmer	112	BB
24/08/1959	You	Darlene Mccrea	103	BB
24/08/1959	Ronnie Is My Lover	The Delicates	105	BB
24/08/1959	Summertime (Part 2)	Sam Cooke	106	BB
24/08/1959	Island Of Love	The Sheppards	109	BB
24/08/1959	Miss Lonely Hearts	Dodie Stevens	111	BB
31/08/1959	Starlight	Lee Greenlee	102	BB
31/08/1959	I'm Confessin' (That I Love You)	Louis Prima & Keely Smith	115	BB
07/09/1959	Cute Little Ways	Hank Ballard And The Midnighters	106	BB
14/09/1959	Boys Do Cry	Joe Bennett And The Sparkletones	105	BB
14/09/1959	Pine Top's Boogie	Jo Stafford	105	BB
21/09/1959	Vacation Days Are Over	The Argyles	101	BB
28/09/1959	Are You Sorry?	Joni James	102	BB
28/09/1959	Broken Arrow	Chuck Berry	108	BB
03/10/1959	The Story Of Our Love	Johnny Mathis	104	CB
03/10/1959	Childhood Sweetheart	Chuck Berry	105	CB
03/10/1959	Are You Sorry?	Joni James	106	CB
03/10/1959	My Baby's Got Soul	Larry Williams	110	CB
03/10/1959	Double Eagle Rock	The Champs	111	CB
03/10/1959	Brightest Wishing Star	Pat Boone	112	CB
03/10/1959	Cloud Nine	Bill Justis & His Orchestra	113	CB
03/10/1959	Everything I Have Is Yours	Dorothy Collins	113	CB
03/10/1959	Growin' Prettier	Johnny October	113	CB
03/10/1959	Afraid	Sammy Salvo	114	CB
03/10/1959	Cute Little Ways	Hank Ballard & The Midnighters	118	CB
03/10/1959	Don't Leave Me	Marv Johnson	120	CB
05/10/1959	You're Mine	The Falcons	107	BB
10/10/1959	I Want You Forever	Brook Benton	103	CB

10/10/1959	My Heart Became Of Age	Annette With The Afterbeats	103	CB
10/10/1959	You Must Try	The Guides	103	CB
10/10/1959	Broken Arrow	Chuck Berry	111	CB
10/10/1959	The Way To My Heart	Valerie Carr	111	CB
10/10/1959	To A Young Lover	The Tassels	116	CB
10/10/1959	But Not For Me	Ella Fitzgerald	118	CB
10/10/1959	Take A Giant Step	Johnny Nash	119	CB
10/10/1959	That's All Right	Ray Smith	123	CB
17/10/1959	Little Queenie	Jerry Lee Lewis & His Pumping Piano	106	CB
17/10/1959	Liza Jane	Dale Hawkins	112	CB
17/10/1959	Dear Someone	Johnny Restivo	120	CB
19/10/1959	Cat Walk	Lee Allen	102	BB
19/10/1959	My Type Of Girl	The Memos	105	BB
19/10/1959	Sunrise Serenade	Roger Williams	106	BB
19/10/1959	All Nite Long (Part 1)	Robert Parker	113	BB
24/10/1959	He Needs Me	Nina Simone	107	CB
24/10/1959	Alice Blue Gown	Leroy Holmes & His Orchestra	113	CB
24/10/1959	Good Good Lovin'	James Brown & The Famous Flames	113	CB
24/10/1959	Lonely Moon	Johnny Wells	123	CB
26/10/1959	Piano Shuffle	Dave "Baby" Cortez	103	BB
26/10/1959	Growin' Prettier	Johnny October	106	BB
31/10/1959	Gilee	Sonny Spencer	102	CB
31/10/1959	Maybe It's Because (I Love You Too Much)	Sarah Vaughan	104	CB
31/10/1959	First Love	The Playmates Donny-Morey-Chic	109	CB
31/10/1959	Little Girl Blue	Nina Simone	117	CB
31/10/1959	Sunrise Serenade	Roger Williams	119	CB
02/11/1959	Mexican Joe	Mitchell Torok	102	BB
02/11/1959	It Might Have Been	Joe London	112	BB
07/11/1959	Cat Walk	Lee Allen	107	CB
07/11/1959	Have I Told You Lately That I Love You?	Jill Corey	107	CB

07/11/1959	Verdi Mae	Phil Phillips	114	CB
14/11/1959	Goodbye Little Darlin'	Johnny Cash & The Tennessee Two	106	CB
14/11/1959	Kookie's Love Song (While Dancing)	Edd "Kookie" Byrnes & The Mary Kaye Trio	108	CB
14/11/1959	I'd Climb The Highest Mountain	Keely Smith	116	CB
14/11/1959	I Was Wrong	Jerry Butler	118	CB
14/11/1959	The Great Duane	Ritchie Hart	124	CB
16/11/1959	(It's No) Sin	Billy Vaughn And His Orchestra	105	BB
21/11/1959	Drum Party	Sandy Nelson	101	CB
21/11/1959	Lil' Girl	Frank Gari	102	CB
21/11/1959	One More Chance	Rod Bernard	103	CB
21/11/1959	That Funny Feeling	Jaye P. Morgan	112	CB
21/11/1959	Years From Now	Della Reese	115	CB
21/11/1959	In The Still Of The Night	Della Reese	116	CB
21/11/1959	Only You, Only Me	Jackie Wilson	119	CB
21/11/1959	Riders In The Sky	Kay Starr	125	CB
21/11/1959	She's Alright	Bo Diddley	125	CB
28/11/1959	In The Still Of The Nite	The Five Satins	108	CB
28/11/1959	I Cried Like A Baby	Nappy Brown	117	CB
28/11/1959	Sweet Georgia Brown	Hutch Davie & His Honky Tonkers	117	CB
28/11/1959	Blue Jean	BoBBy Gee & The Celestials	121	CB
28/11/1959	Take Me Along	The Ames Brothers	124	CB
30/11/1959	EBB Tide	Roy Hamilton	105	BB
30/11/1959	Say Man, Back Again	Bo Diddley	106	BB
30/11/1959	I Laughed At Love	Joni James	108	BB
30/11/1959	Blues Get Off My Shoulder	Dee Clark	109	BB
05/12/1959	Candy Apple Red	Bonnie Guitar	103	CB
05/12/1959	Why Don't You Believe Me	The Kalin Twins	105	CB
05/12/1959	100 Years From Today	The Spaniels	123	CB
12/12/1959	Steady Eddy	Dodie Stevens	117	CB
12/12/1959	Blues Get Off My Shoulder	Dee Clark	118	CB

12/12/1959	Mairzy Doats	Dodie Stevens	119	CB
12/12/1959	I Laughed At Love	Joni James	123	CB
14/12/1959	Baghdad Rock (Part 1)	The Shieks	111	BB
19/12/1959	Babalu's Wedding Day	The Eternals	108	CB
19/12/1959	One More For The Road	Hank Leeds	111	CB
19/12/1959	Dynamite	Cliff Richard	115	CB
19/12/1959	Just For Your Love	The Falcons	125	CB
21/12/1959	Wistful Willie	Jimmie Rodgers	112	BB
21/12/1959	Wintertime	The Four Coachmen	113	BB
26/12/1959	Little Donkey	Patti Page	105	CB
26/12/1959	Mediterranean Moon	The Rays	113	CB
26/12/1959	Jack Of All Trades	Eugene Church	117	CB
26/12/1959	Big Hearted Me	Don Gibson	119	CB
28/12/1959	Earth Angel	The Penguins	101	BB
28/12/1959	How Will It End	Barry Darvell	110	BB
02/01/1960	I Really Do	The Spectors Three	121	CB
04/01/1960	Clap Your Hands - Part 1	The Wheels	102	BB
04/01/1960	One More For The Road	Hank Leeds	103	BB
04/01/1960	Waltzing Matilda	David Carroll	112	BB
09/01/1960	How Will It End?	Barry Darvell	101	CB
09/01/1960	One Mint Julep	Chet Atkins	101	CB
09/01/1960	The Whiffenpoof Song	Bob Crewe	101	CB
09/01/1960	Star Spangled Heaven	Conway Twitty	104	CB
09/01/1960	Twangy	The Rock-A-Teens	109	CB
09/01/1960	Since I Made You Cry	The Rivieras	112	CB
11/01/1960	No One (Can Ever Take Your Place)	Sam Cooke	103	BB
16/01/1960	What's Happening	Wade Flemons	116	CB
16/01/1960	Beloved	Bob Beckham	118	CB
16/01/1960	La Mer	Trade Martin	122	CB
16/01/1960	(You Gotta Be A) Music Man	Danny Valentino	123	CB

18/01/1960	Love Me, My Love	Dean Martin	107	BB
18/01/1960	Beautiful Brown Eyes	Judy, Johnny And Billy	110	BB
18/01/1960	You're The Only Star (In My Blue Heaven) (b-side)	Billy Vaughn And His Orchestra	110	BB
23/01/1960	A Closer Walk	Pete Fountain	101	CB
23/01/1960	Respectable	The Isley Brothers	123	CB
30/01/1960	Waltzing Matilda	Jimmie Rodgers	103	CB
30/01/1960	Waltzing Matilda*	Merrill Staton Choir	103	CB
30/01/1960	Bad Boy*	Robin Luke	105	CB
30/01/1960	Earth Angel	The Penguins	105	CB
30/01/1960	Beautiful Brown Eyes	Judy, Johnny & Billy	110	CB
30/01/1960	Love Me, My Love	Dean Martin	110	CB
30/01/1960	If You Need Me	Fats Domino	113	CB
01/02/1960	Chop Sticks	Billy Vaughn And His Orchestra	103	BB
01/02/1960	Let Me Go Lover	Carol Hughes	114	BB
06/02/1960	Little Sister	Cathy Carr	102	CB
06/02/1960	My Heart Belongs To Only You	The Twilights	104	CB
06/02/1960	Secret Of Love	Elton Anderson With Sid Lawrence Combo	111	CB
06/02/1960	You're The Only Star (In My Blue Heaven)	Billy Vaughn & His Orchestra	118	CB
06/02/1960	Some Enchanted Evening	Carl Mann	119	CB
06/02/1960	Are You Willing, Willie	Marion Worth	125	CB
08/02/1960	Home From The Hill	The Kingston Trio	102	BB
13/02/1960	Was It A Dream	Royal Teens	108	CB
13/02/1960	The Puerto Rican Pedlar	Norman Warren & The Warrentones	121	CB
13/02/1960	The Puerto Rican Pedlar*	Sid Feller & His Orchestra & Chorus	121	CB
15/02/1960	Work Out	Baby Washington	105	BB
15/02/1960	Little Sister	Cathy Carr	106	BB
15/02/1960	Magic Star	The Fleetwoods	113	BB
20/02/1960	Little Sister*	Connie Stevens With The Buddy Cole Trio	102	CB
20/02/1960	Honey Love	Narvel Felts	117	CB
20/02/1960	Have Love Will Travel	Richard Berry & The Pharaohs	122	CB

Date	Title	Artist	#	Chart
22/02/1960	Scandinavian Shuffle	The Swe-Danes (Alice Babs, Ulrich Neumann & Svend Asmussen)	101	BB
22/02/1960	Good Bye Kansas City	Wilbert Harrison	102	BB
22/02/1960	Summer Set	Mr. Acker Bilk And His Paramount Jazz Bandmr. Acker Bilk And His	104	BB
27/02/1960	This Is My Love	The Passions	105	CB
27/02/1960	Work Out	Baby Washington	109	CB
27/02/1960	Straight A's In Love	Johnny Cash & The Tennessee Two	115	CB
27/02/1960	I Remember When	Cameos	121	CB
27/02/1960	I Don't Regret A Thing	Mitzi Gaynor	124	CB
29/02/1960	Tamiami	Bill Haley And His Comets	101	BB
29/02/1960	What Do You Want To Make Those Eyes At Me For?	Ray Peterson	104	BB
29/02/1960	All Through The Night	The Mystics	107	BB
05/03/1960	Good Bye Kansas City	Wilbert Harrison	101	CB
05/03/1960	Scandinavian Shuffle	The Swe-Danes (Alice Babs, Ulrich Neumann & Svend Asmussen)	102	CB
05/03/1960	The Same Old Me	Guy Mitchell	103	CB
05/03/1960	All Is Well	Johnny Mathis	106	CB
05/03/1960	Anyway The Wind Blows	Doris Day	109	CB
05/03/1960	Water Boy	Bob Crewe	111	CB
07/03/1960	Cindy	Teddy Vann	104	BB
12/03/1960	Rockin' Charlie Part I	BoBBy Peterson Quintet	108	CB
12/03/1960	Gotta Get A Date	Van Strickland	111	CB
12/03/1960	Werewolf	The Frantics	113	CB
12/03/1960	Teen-Ex	The Browns Featuring Jim Edward Brown	114	CB
12/03/1960	All Through The Night	The Mystics	123	CB
12/03/1960	Don't Mess With My Man	Irma Thomas	124	CB
14/03/1960	If I Knew	The Cruisers	102	BB
14/03/1960	I Only Want You	The Passions	113	BB
19/03/1960	Jambalaya	BoBBy Comstock & The Counts	102	CB
19/03/1960	Two Thousand, Two Hundred, Twenty-Three Miles	Patti Page	103	CB
19/03/1960	Down By The Riverside (Qu'il Fait Bon Vivre)	Les Compagnons De La Chanson	107	CB
19/03/1960	Will You Ever Be Mine	Donnie Elbert	107	CB

19/03/1960	Come On Home	Sonny Til & Orioles	110	CB
19/03/1960	Is It Wrong (For Loving You)	WeBB Pierce	117	CB
21/03/1960	A Six Pack To Go	Hank Thompson And His Brazos Valley Boys	102	BB
26/03/1960	Rockin' Red Wing	Sammy Masters	101	CB
26/03/1960	Lovey	The Clovers	102	CB
26/03/1960	If I Knew	The Cruisers	110	CB
26/03/1960	Walk With The Wind	The Fidelitys	115	CB
26/03/1960	Never Let Me Go	Lloyd Price & His Orchestra	124	CB
28/03/1960	Come Dance With Me	Eddie Quinteros	101	BB
28/03/1960	You Belong To Me	100 Strings And Joni (James)	101	BB
28/03/1960	Rockin' Red Wing	Ernie Freeman	106	BB
02/04/1960	Dearest (Cara)	Al Martino	106	CB
02/04/1960	Chains Of Love	Joe Turner	118	CB
02/04/1960	'TIL Tomorrow	Janice Harper	121	CB
09/04/1960	Rockin' Red Wing	Ernie Freeman	101	CB
09/04/1960	Listen My Love	Rod Lauren	103	CB
09/04/1960	I'll Be Seeing You	The Five Satins	107	CB
09/04/1960	I Burned Your Letter	Ruth Brown	111	CB
09/04/1960	You Belong To Me	100 Strings & Joni (James)	114	CB
09/04/1960	Amigo's Guitar	Dodie Stevens	123	CB
16/04/1960	Poor Boy Needs A Preacher	The Untouchables	103	CB
18/04/1960	That's You	Nat "King" Cole	101	BB
18/04/1960	Our Waltz	Sarah Vaughan	103	BB
18/04/1960	What Will I Tell My Heart	Phil Phillips	108	BB
18/04/1960	Stolen Angel	Scott Bros.	110	BB
23/04/1960	Foot-Patter	The Fireballs	111	CB
23/04/1960	Old Black Joe	Jerry Lee Lewis With Gene Lowery Singers	121	CB
25/04/1960	Go On, Go On	Jivin' Gene	101	BB
25/04/1960	Roll Call Company "J"	The Balladeers	104	BB
25/04/1960	The Miracle Of Life	Robie Lester	107	BB

30/04/1960	That's You	Nat King Cole	104	CB
30/04/1960	You Understand Me	Sam Cooke	107	CB
30/04/1960	What Will I Tell My Heart	Phil Phillips	117	CB
30/04/1960	Just For A Thrill	Ray Charles & His Orchestra	123	CB
30/04/1960	What Has She Got	Carmen Mcrae	125	CB
02/05/1960	My Little Honey Dripper	Joe Turner	102	BB
02/05/1960	Please Don't Eat The Daisies	Doris Day	102	BB
02/05/1960	John Henry (The Steel Driving Man)	Buster Brown	105	BB
02/05/1960	You're Singing Our Love Song To Somebody Else	Jerry Wallace	115	BB
07/05/1960	No Time For Tears	Sam Hawkins	102	CB
07/05/1960	Please Don't Eat The Daisies	Doris Day	102	CB
07/05/1960	Roll Call Company "J"	The Balladeers	106	CB
07/05/1960	This Could Be The Start Of Something	Steve Lawrence & Eydie Gorme	113	CB
07/05/1960	Go On, Go On	Jivin' Gene	121	CB
07/05/1960	Deep Sea Ball	Clyde Mcphatter	123	CB
07/05/1960	The Sky Is Crying	Elmore James & His Broomdusters	123	CB
09/05/1960	Holy One	Freddie Fender	107	BB
09/05/1960	Biology	Sue Raney	109	BB
14/05/1960	Shadows Of Love	Lavern Baker	104	CB
14/05/1960	John Henry (The Steel Driving Man)	Buster Brown	112	CB
14/05/1960	The Little Matador	The Champs	113	CB
14/05/1960	Little By Little	Junior Wells	119	CB
21/05/1960	Ruby Baby	Ronnie Hawkins & The Hawks	112	CB
21/05/1960	Moon Dawg!	The Gamblers	117	CB
21/05/1960	Do You Think Of Me (Denkst Du Noch An Mich)	Cindy Ellis	124	CB
23/05/1960	Born To Be With You	The Echoes	101	BB
23/05/1960	Smiling Bill Mccall	Johnny Cash	110	BB
23/05/1960	One Last Kiss	BoBBy Vee	112	BB
28/05/1960	Tell It Like It Is	Eddie Bo	101	CB
30/05/1960	(I'll Be With You In) Apple Blossom Time	The Platters Featuring Tony Williams	102	BB

30/05/1960	Like Love	André Previn And His Piano And Orchestra	108	BB
30/05/1960	The Breeze And I	Santo & Johnny	109	BB
30/05/1960	Ooh! What A Day!	Sarah Vaughan	111	BB
04/06/1960	The Breeze And I	Santo & Johnny	102	CB
04/06/1960	Why, Why, Why	Steve Lawrence	110	CB
04/06/1960	My Own Fault	B.B. King	113	CB
04/06/1960	Rosie Lee	Jimmy Edwards	116	CB
04/06/1960	Big Rock Candy Mountain	Dorsey Burnette	118	CB
06/06/1960	Big Rock Candy Mountain	Dorsey Burnette	102	BB
06/06/1960	Three Steps To Heaven	Eddie Cochran	108	BB
06/06/1960	So Blue	The Vibrations	110	BB
11/06/1960	P.S. I Love You	The Starlets	104	CB
11/06/1960	Ooh! What A Day!	Sarah Vaughan	107	CB
11/06/1960	Dry Bones	Bill Black's Combo	115	CB
11/06/1960	Wild Weekend	The Rebels	115	CB
11/06/1960	Crawdad	Bo Diddley	117	CB
11/06/1960	Early In The Morning	Roy Milton	119	CB
11/06/1960	Tonto	The Noteables	122	CB
13/06/1960	Moonlight Cocktails	The Rivieras	103	BB
13/06/1960	Mule Skinner Blues	Rusty Draper	105	BB
13/06/1960	Crawdad	Bo Diddley	111	BB
18/06/1960	Mais Oui	Bob Beckham	102	CB
18/06/1960	So Blue	The Vibrations	105	CB
18/06/1960	Come Go With Me	The Chevrons	124	CB
20/06/1960	Mais Oui	Bob Beckham	105	BB
20/06/1960	P.S. I Love You	The Starlets	106	BB
20/06/1960	Look For A Star	Nicky Como	110	BB
20/06/1960	The Wind	The Jesters	110	BB
20/06/1960	It's Over, It's Over, It's Over	Frank Sinatra	111	BB
25/06/1960	Moonlight Cocktails	The Rivieras	105	CB

25/06/1960	That's My Kind Of Love	Marion Worth	110	CB
25/06/1960	Columbus Stockade Blues	Pete Fountain	118	CB
25/06/1960	Cruise To The Moon	The Chaperones	121	CB
27/06/1960	Miller's Cave	Hank Snow	101	BB
27/06/1960	My Babe	Little Walter And His Jukes	106	BB
27/06/1960	I'm With You	The "5" Royales	107	BB
27/06/1960	Your Memory	Five Satins	107	BB
27/06/1960	The Wind	The Diablos Featuring Nolan Strong	114	BB
02/07/1960	Honky-Tonk Girl	Johnny Cash	108	CB
02/07/1960	If I Look A Little Blue	Lloyd Price & His Orchestra	111	CB
02/07/1960	Theme From "THE Untouchables"	The Applejacks	117	CB
02/07/1960	She's Mine	Conway Twitty	119	CB
04/07/1960	Pardon Me	Billy Bland	102	BB
04/07/1960	I'll Fly Away	Lonnie Sattin And Orchestra	103	BB
04/07/1960	Lonely Little Robin	The Browns Featuring Jim Edward Brown	105	BB
04/07/1960	The Story Of A Broken Heart	Johnny Cash And The Tennessee Two	107	BB
04/07/1960	There's A Star Spangled Banner Waving Somewhere-1960	Betty Johnson And The Johnson Family Singers	111	BB
09/07/1960	Miller's Cave	Hank Snow	104	CB
09/07/1960	Sealed With A Kiss	The Four Voices	109	CB
09/07/1960	Four Little Girls In Boston	Jimmie Rodgers	116	CB
09/07/1960	Space Flight	Sam Lazar Trio	120	CB
09/07/1960	The Wind	The Jesters	121	CB
09/07/1960	The Wind*	The Diablos Featuring Nolan Strong	121	CB
09/07/1960	Church Bells May Ring	Sunny Gale	125	CB
11/07/1960	If The World Don't End Tomorrow (I'm Comin' After You)	Doug Warren And The Rays	107	BB
11/07/1960	A Perfect Understanding	Doris Day	111	BB
16/07/1960	Everything About You	Ty Hunter With The Voice Masters	120	CB
18/07/1960	If You're Lonely	Annie Laurie	104	BB
18/07/1960	If The World Don't End Tomorrow I'm Comin' After You	Carl Smith	107	BB
23/07/1960	If The World Don't End Tomorrow (I'm Comin' After You)	Doug Warren & The Rays	101	CB

23/07/1960	Lost Love	Scott Bros.	109	CB
23/07/1960	Madelina	The Four Preps	114	CB
23/07/1960	Your Memory	Five Satins	117	CB
30/07/1960	Songs By Ricky Ep	Ricky Nelson	105	CB
30/07/1960	I Know	The Spaniels	107	CB
30/07/1960	Sons And Lovers	Percy Faith & His Orchestra	110	CB
30/07/1960	Gonna Be Waitin'	Charlie Rich With Gene Lowery Singers	116	CB
30/07/1960	River Of Tears	Harold Dorman	119	CB
30/07/1960	If You're Lonely	Annie Laurie	123	CB
06/08/1960	If The World Don't End Tomorrow (I'm Comin' After You)*	Carl Smith	101	CB
06/08/1960	Killer Joe	The Jazztet Featuring Art Farmer & Benny Golson (Narration: Benny	101	CB
06/08/1960	Goodnight Sweetheart, Goodnight (Goodnight, Well It's Time To Go)	The Untouchables	102	CB
06/08/1960	Cholley-Oop	Hong Kong White Sox	103	CB
06/08/1960	Lonely Guy	The Gallahads	103	CB
06/08/1960	A Help-Each-Other Romance	Lavern Baker & Ben E. King	105	CB
06/08/1960	I Can't Stop Loving You	Tommy Zang	106	CB
06/08/1960	A Broken Vow	The Chordettes	117	CB
06/08/1960	We Know	Joni James	124	CB
08/08/1960	A Broken Vow	The Chordettes	102	BB
08/08/1960	One Wonderful Love	Ray Smith	103	BB
08/08/1960	Gee, But I'm Lonesome	Ron Holden	106	BB
08/08/1960	Sergeant Preston Of The Yukon	Ray Stevens	108	BB
08/08/1960	Hully Gully Cha Cha Cha	Skip And Flip And Their Orchestra	109	BB
08/08/1960	Sons And Lovers	Percy Faith And His Orchestra	111	BB
13/08/1960	My Shoes Keep Walking Back To You	Guy Mitchell	106	CB
13/08/1960	Sergeant Preston Of The Yukon	Ray Stevens	112	CB
13/08/1960	I Ain't Givin' Up Nothin' (If I Can't Get Somethin' From You)	Clyde Mcphatter	122	CB
15/08/1960	All I Could Do Was Cry (Part 2)	Joe Tex	102	BB
15/08/1960	Drifting Texas Sand	WeBB Pierce	108	BB
15/08/1960	I Can't Stop Loving You	Tommy Zang	108	BB

15/08/1960	Lonely Guy	The Gallahads	111	BB
15/08/1960	Over You	Aaron Neville	111	BB
20/08/1960	A Teenager Feels It Too	Denny Reed	108	CB
20/08/1960	Wait	Jimmy Clanton	111	CB
20/08/1960	Hully Gully Cha Cha Cha	Skip & Flip & Their Orchestra	123	CB
22/08/1960	Whiffenpoof Song	Browns Featuring Jim Edward Brown	112	BB
27/08/1960	Luck Of The Irish	Rusty Draper	108	CB
27/08/1960	Robot Man	Jamie Horton	112	CB
27/08/1960	All I Could Do Was Cry Part 1	Joe Tex	117	CB
03/09/1960	Speaking Of Her	Adam Wade	108	CB
03/09/1960	Way Over There	The Miracles	109	CB
05/09/1960	The Ghost Of Billy Malloo	Dorsey Burnette	103	BB
05/09/1960	Who Coulda' Told You (They Lied)	Lloyd Price And His Orchestra	103	BB
05/09/1960	Tell Tommy I Miss Him	Marilyn Michaels	110	BB
10/09/1960	Tell Tommy I Miss Him	Marilyn Michaels	102	CB
10/09/1960	I Never Knew (Till Now)	Dick Lee	113	CB
10/09/1960	Brighten The Corner Where You Are	The Browns Featuring Jim Edward Brown	114	CB
12/09/1960	Ee-I Ee-I Oh! (Sue Macdonald)	Jimmy Jones	102	BB
12/09/1960	What A Dream	Conway Twitty	106	BB
12/09/1960	Slipping Around	Betty Johnson	109	BB
17/09/1960	The Ghost Of Billy Malloo	Dorsey Burnette	102	CB
17/09/1960	Tonight's The Night	The Chiffons	103	CB
17/09/1960	Back To School	Ritchie Adams	108	CB
17/09/1960	Five Brothers	Marty RoBBins	112	CB
17/09/1960	Over You	Aaron Neville	112	CB
17/09/1960	Pretty Little Dancin' Doll	Dick Caruso	125	CB
19/09/1960	Blue Velvet	The Paragons	103	BB
19/09/1960	Going By The River (Part Ii)	Jimmy Reed	104	BB
19/09/1960	Old Cape Cod	Billy Vaughn And His Orchestra	111	BB
24/09/1960	Hello My Lover	Ernie K-Doe	102	CB

24/09/1960	Journey Of Love	The Crests Featuring Johnny Maestro	111	CB
24/09/1960	Stranger From Durango	Richie Allen	112	CB
24/09/1960	Hey, Hey, Baby!	Jon Thomas	121	CB
26/09/1960	Don't You Just Know It	The Fendermen	110	BB
01/10/1960	Old Cape Cod	Billy Vaughn & His Orchestra	102	CB
01/10/1960	Come Back, Silly Girl	Steve Lawrence	112	CB
01/10/1960	Don't Let Love Pass Me By	Frankie Avalon	124	CB
03/10/1960	Please Help Me, I'm Falling	Homer And Jethro	101	BB
03/10/1960	Itchin' (b-side)	Jimmy Jones	106	BB
08/10/1960	Blue Heartaches	Tommy Edwards	113	CB
08/10/1960	Ee-I, Ee-I Oh! (Sue Macdonald)	Jimmy Jones	117	CB
08/10/1960	There's Nothing On My Mind Part 1	The Teen Queens Betty And Rose	121	CB
08/10/1960	Cinderella	Classics	123	CB
10/10/1960	Theme From "The Dark At The Top Of The Stairs"	Percy Faith And His Orchestra	101	BB
15/10/1960	I Could Make You Mine	The Wanderers	102	CB
15/10/1960	My Hero	The Blue Notes	103	CB
15/10/1960	Dance With Me Georgie	The BoBBettes	104	CB
15/10/1960	On My Knees	Charlie Rich	105	CB
15/10/1960	The Girl With The Story In Her Eyes	The Safaris With The Phantom's Band	106	CB
15/10/1960	Stay With Me (A Little While Longer)	Ed Townsend With The Townsmen	108	CB
15/10/1960	Moved To Kansas City	Harold Dorman	111	CB
15/10/1960	I Hear My Baby	Larry Williams	114	CB
15/10/1960	Nobody Knows You When You're Down And Out	Nina Simone	115	CB
15/10/1960	Always, Always	Johnny Cymbal	118	CB
15/10/1960	High Time	Henry Mancini & His Orchestra	125	CB
17/10/1960	Theme From "The Dark At The Top Of The Stairs"	Chet Atkins	103	BB
17/10/1960	Shim Sham Shuffle	Ricky Lyons	104	BB
22/10/1960	Midnight Lace*	Sid Feller & His Orchestra & Chorus	102	CB
22/10/1960	The Big Time Spender, Parts 1 & 2	Cornbread & Biscuits	109	CB
22/10/1960	Before This Day Ends	George Hamilton Iv	113	CB

22/10/1960	The Chariot Race	Ben Blur	116	CB
22/10/1960	The Nervous Auctioneer	Robin Wilson	121	CB
22/10/1960	Harmony	Billy Bland	123	CB
24/10/1960	Stay With Me (A Little While Longer)	Ed Townsend With The Townsmen	101	BB
24/10/1960	Charming Billy	Johnny Preston	105	BB
29/10/1960	Last Date	Lawrence Welk & His Orchestra Featuring Frank Scott On Piano	103	CB
29/10/1960	Be My Love	Joni James	112	CB
29/10/1960	Be My Love*	Joanie Sommers	112	CB
29/10/1960	Little Tear	Gary Stites	112	CB
29/10/1960	Taking Care Of Business	Ruth Brown	119	CB
05/11/1960	Zing! Went The Strings Of My Heart	The Kalin Twins (Herbie & Hal)	103	CB
05/11/1960	Woman From Liberia	Jimmie Rodgers	108	CB
05/11/1960	Canadian Sunset	Gene Ammons Quartet	115	CB
07/11/1960	60 Minute Man	The Untouchables	104	BB
07/11/1960	Jaguar And Thunderbird	Chuck Berry	109	BB
12/11/1960	Can She Give You Fever	Ernie Tucker	104	CB
12/11/1960	When I Fall In Love	The Flamingos	107	CB
12/11/1960	Hurricane	Dave "Baby" Cortez	111	CB
12/11/1960	Before This Day Ends	Eddy Arnold	113	CB
12/11/1960	Hushabye Little Guitar	Paul Evans	116	CB
12/11/1960	In The Mood	The Hawk	117	CB
14/11/1960	Gee Whiz	BoBBy Day	103	BB
14/11/1960	Good News	Eugene Church	106	BB
14/11/1960	Brand New Heartache	The Everly Brothers	109	BB
19/11/1960	The King Of Holiday Island	Don Rondo	108	CB
19/11/1960	Valarie	Starlites	118	CB
19/11/1960	Hold Back The Dyke	Steve Lawrence	122	CB
19/11/1960	The Madison Twist	Charlie Hoss & The Ponies	124	CB
21/11/1960	Please, Please, Please	James Brown With The Famous Flames	105	BB
21/11/1960	Please, Please, Please	The "5" Royales	114	BB

26/11/1960	You Are My Sunshine	Johnny & The Hurricanes	112	CB
28/11/1960	Cinderella	Classics	109	BB
03/12/1960	I Need A Change	Miracles	114	CB
03/12/1960	Gee	Jan & Dean	119	CB
05/12/1960	Oh, Lonesome Me	Bob Luman	105	BB
05/12/1960	Zing! Went The Strings Of My Heart	The Kalin Twins (Herbie & Hal)	112	BB
05/12/1960	Round Robin	Donnie Brooks	115	BB
10/12/1960	Salvation Rock	Marv Meredith & His Orchestra	103	CB
10/12/1960	Sugar Bee	Cleveland Crochet & Hill Billy Ramblers	103	CB
10/12/1960	Happy, Happy Birthday	Wanda Jackson	106	CB
10/12/1960	Mean, Mean Man	Wanda Jackson	108	CB
10/12/1960	Free	Ty Hunter & The Voice Masters	113	CB
10/12/1960	Have You Ever Been Lonely (Have You Ever Been Blue)	Teresa Brewer	120	CB
12/12/1960	I'll Be Home For Christmas (If Only In My Dreams)	Bing Crosby	102	BB
12/12/1960	Rudolph, The Red-Nosed Reindeer	Paul Anka	104	BB
17/12/1960	Milk Cow Blues	Ricky Nelson	101	CB
17/12/1960	The Slide Part I	Googie Rene	104	CB
17/12/1960	Before I Fall In Love Again (I'll Count To Ten)	Clyde Mcphatter	106	CB
17/12/1960	The Birthday Card	Brooks Arthur	110	CB
17/12/1960	Confidential	The Fleetwoods	111	CB
17/12/1960	One More Chance	Clyde Mcphatter	117	CB
19/12/1960	Why, Why, Bye, Bye (b-side)	Bob Luman	106	BB
24/12/1960	The Jazz In You	Gloria Lynne	103	CB
24/12/1960	I Gotta Go ('Cause I Love You)	Brian Hyland	105	CB
24/12/1960	Steal Away	Sam Cooke & The Stars	113	CB
26/12/1960	I Ain't Down Yet	Dinah Shore	103	BB
26/12/1960	The Slide (Part 1)	Googie Rene	105	BB
26/12/1960	Dominick The Donkey (The Italian Christmas Donkey)	Lou Monte	114	BB
31/12/1960	I Gotta Go ('Cause I Love You)	Brian Hyland	101	BB
31/12/1960	I Remember (In The Still Of The Night)	The Crests With Johnny Mastro	102	BB

31/12/1960	Look Out	Ted Taylor	105	BB
31/12/1960	Lop-Sided Over-Loaded (And It Wiggled When We Rode It) (b-	Brian Hyland	105	BB
31/12/1960	What Are You Doing New Year's Eve	Danté And The Evergreens	107	BB
31/12/1960	Gee Baby	Joe & Ann	108	BB
31/12/1960	I Ain't Down Yet	Art Mooney And His Orchestra	108	BB
31/12/1960	Sing (And Tell The Blues "So Long")	Al Kasha	111	CB
31/12/1960	Take Me To Your Ladder (I'll See Your Leader Later)	Buddy Clinton	115	BB
31/12/1960	Yes, I'm Lonesome Tonight*	Ricky Page	122	CB
07/01/1961	Oh Lonesome Me	Johnny Cash	108	CB
07/01/1961	Oh, Lonesome Me	Bob Luman	108	CB
07/01/1961	If I Knew	Nat King Cole	109	CB
07/01/1961	Yeah Baby	Danté And The Evergreens	112	CB
07/01/1961	Gun Slinger	Bo Diddley	115	CB
07/01/1961	The World In My Arms	Nat King Cole	125	CB
09/01/1961	Yeah Baby (b-side)	Danté And The Evergreens	104	BB
09/01/1961	Because I Love You	Dee Clark	105	BB
09/01/1961	Don't Say You're Sorry	Paul Anka	108	BB
09/01/1961	The Misfits	Don Costa Orchestra And Chorus	116	BB
09/01/1961	There's More Pretty Girls Than One	WeBB Pierce	118	BB
14/01/1961	I Remember (In The Still Of The Night)	The Crests With Johnny Mastro	116	CB
14/01/1961	No Man Is King	Rufus (Mr. Soul) Beacham	118	CB
14/01/1961	Face Of An Angel	Joey Dee & The Starliters	122	CB
14/01/1961	What Brought Us Together	The Edsels	125	CB
16/01/1961	I'll Never Be Free	Lavern Baker & Jimmy Ricks	103	BB
16/01/1961	Free	Ty Hunter & The Voice Masters	110	BB
21/01/1961	Guess Things Happen That Way	June Valli	104	CB
21/01/1961	I Ain't Down Yet	Dinah Shore	105	CB
21/01/1961	I Love You So	The Chantels	117	CB
23/01/1961	We Belong Together	Robert & Johnny	104	BB
23/01/1961	We Belong Together	The Belmonts	108	BB

30/01/1961	Teenage Vows Of Love	The Dreamers	104	BB
30/01/1961	The Jazz In You	Gloria Lynne	109	BB
04/02/1961	We Belong Together	The Belmonts	103	CB
04/02/1961	Dream Boy	Annette With The Afterbeats	105	CB
04/02/1961	Matilda Has Finally Come Back	Cookie & The Cupcakes	109	CB
04/02/1961	There's A New Man In The White House	The Senators	117	CB
04/02/1961	Closer To You	Johnny Adams	120	CB
06/02/1961	I'm Tired	Ray Peterson	104	BB
06/02/1961	Pledge Of Love	Curtis Lee	110	BB
06/02/1961	Theme From "A Summer Place" (Wenn Der Sommer Kommt)	Lolita	112	BB
06/02/1961	In Jerusalem	Jane Morgan	115	BB
11/02/1961	Tunes Of Glory*	Mitch Miller With His Orchestra & Chorus	102	CB
11/02/1961	Theme From "A Summer Place" (Wenn Der Sommer Kommpt)	Lolita	105	CB
11/02/1961	Marie, Marie	Roger Williams	108	CB
11/02/1961	Marie, Marie*	Serino	108	CB
11/02/1961	Goodnight Mrs. Flintstone	The Piltdown Men	111	CB
11/02/1961	Funky	The Cavaliers	115	CB
11/02/1961	Golden Wildwood Flower	Tom & Jerry	115	CB
11/02/1961	When I Fall In Love	Etta Jones	118	CB
11/02/1961	Exotic	The Night Beats	119	CB
13/02/1961	Call Me Anytime	Frankie Avalon	102	BB
13/02/1961	Some Of Your Lovin'	Johnny Nash	104	BB
13/02/1961	Hold It	James Brown Presents His Band	109	BB
18/02/1961	In Jerusalem	Jane Morgan	102	CB
18/02/1961	Don't Let Him Shop Around	DeBBie Dean	103	CB
18/02/1961	Cherry Berry Wine	Charlie Mccoy	104	CB
18/02/1961	The World Is Waiting For The Sunrise	Don Gibson	104	CB
18/02/1961	A Lover's Question	Ernestine Anderson	108	CB
18/02/1961	Mojo Hand	Lightin' Hopkins	109	CB
18/02/1961	What'd I Say	Jack Eubanks, His Orchestra & Singers	114	CB

18/02/1961	The Secret	Clint Ballard Jr.	119	CB
18/02/1961	Green Stamps	The T-Birds	122	CB
18/02/1961	It Must Be Love	Eddie Bo	131	CB
18/02/1961	Theme From "CHECKMATE"	Johnny Williams & His Orchestra	135	CB
20/02/1961	Tomorrow Is A-Comin'	Clyde Mcphatter	103	BB
20/02/1961	A Night With Daddy "G" (Part 2)	The Church Street Five	111	BB
25/02/1961	Not Me	U.S. Bonds	105	CB
25/02/1961	You're My Baby	Ike & Tina Turner	111	CB
25/02/1961	Milord	Edith Piaf	121	CB
25/02/1961	Illusion	Nat King Cole	122	CB
25/02/1961	Sack O' Woe	Ray Bryant Combo	127	CB
25/02/1961	It Shouldn't Happen To A Dog	Gene & Ruth	130	CB
27/02/1961	Banned In Boston	Merv Griffin	101	BB
27/02/1961	Little Sad Eyes	The Castells	101	BB
27/02/1961	Hey! Look Me Over	The Pete King Chorale And Orchestra	108	BB
27/02/1961	I'm Jealous	Ike & Tina Turner	117	BB
04/03/1961	Tomorrow Is A-Comin'	Clyde Mcphatter	116	CB
04/03/1961	Raisin' Sugar Cane	The Untouchables	117	CB
04/03/1961	Vaya Con Dios (May God Be With You)	Tommy Edwards	119	CB
04/03/1961	Call Me Anytime	Frankie Avalon	120	CB
04/03/1961	A Night With Daddy "G" (Part 2)	The Church Street Five	124	CB
04/03/1961	Hokey Pokey	The Champs	125	CB
04/03/1961	My Foolish Heart	Nancy Wilson	132	CB
04/03/1961	Riot In Cell Block Number Nine	Wanda Jackson	134	CB
06/03/1961	Please Say You Want Me	Little Anthony And The Imperials	104	BB
06/03/1961	Illusion	Nat King Cole	108	BB
06/03/1961	The World Is Waiting For The Sunrise	Don Gibson	108	BB
06/03/1961	I'll Love You Til The Cows Come Home (b-side)	Clyde Mcphatter	110	BB
06/03/1961	Milord	Frank Pourcel And His Orchestra	112	BB
06/03/1961	Church Bells May Ring	Willows	114	BB

06/03/1961	Not Me	U.S. Bonds	116	BB
11/03/1961	Please Say You Want Me	Little Anthony & The Imperials	102	CB
11/03/1961	Kokomo	The Flamingos	107	CB
11/03/1961	I'll Love You Till The Cows Come Home	Clyde Mcphatter	112	CB
11/03/1961	Royal Whirl	The Royaltones	119	CB
11/03/1961	The Fuzz	Grady Martin & His Guitar	120	CB
11/03/1961	Do You Want It That Way	Dinah Washington	121	CB
11/03/1961	Battle Of Gettysburg	Fred Darian	127	CB
11/03/1961	I Met Him On A Sunday (Ronde-Ronde)	The Shirelles	127	CB
11/03/1961	The Slop	Chet Atkins	135	CB
13/03/1961	Louisiana Man	Rusty & Doug	104	BB
13/03/1961	Little Girl, Little Boy	Al Martino	109	BB
13/03/1961	Foolin' Around	Buck Owens	113	BB
13/03/1961	Trouble Up The Road	Jackie Brenston	118	BB
13/03/1961	Daddy, Daddy (Gotta Get A Phone In My Room)	Robin Clark	120	BB
18/03/1961	Bounty Hunter	The Nomads	107	CB
18/03/1961	Tara's Theme From Gone With The Wind	Ferrante & Teicher	110	CB
18/03/1961	Shadrach	The Viscounts	118	CB
18/03/1961	Cimarron	Bill Snyder & Dick Manning	123	CB
18/03/1961	Mood Indigo	Floyd Cramer	126	CB
18/03/1961	Sincerely, Your Friend	Benny Joy	130	CB
20/03/1961	Your Goodnight Kiss (Ain't What It Used To Be)	Guy Mitchell	106	BB
25/03/1961	A City Girl Stole My Country Boy	Patti Page	102	CB
25/03/1961	Louisiana Man	Rusty & Doug	104	CB
25/03/1961	Little Lonely One	Gary Stites	109	CB
25/03/1961	Little Lonely One	The Jarmels	109	CB
25/03/1961	Loch Lomand Rock	The Ramrods	119	CB
25/03/1961	The Very Thought Of You	Little Willie John	121	CB
25/03/1961	(Theme From) My Three Sons	Bob Moore & His Orchestra	132	CB
25/03/1961	The Water Was Red	Johnny Cymbal	133	CB

25/03/1961	Oh Mein Papa	Dick Lee	134	CB
25/03/1961	Greener Pastures	Stonewall Jackson	135	CB
27/03/1961	Everybody's Doin' The Pony	Fay Simmons	107	BB
27/03/1961	The Water Was Red	Johnny Cymbal	108	BB
27/03/1961	Sweethearts On Parade	Etta Jones	115	BB
27/03/1961	Bounty Hunter	The Nomads	116	BB
01/04/1961	Big Mr. C	The Link Eddy Combo	106	CB
01/04/1961	Daddy, Daddy (Gotta Get A Phone In My Room)	Robin Clark	121	CB
01/04/1961	Uh Huh	Mike Clifford	130	CB
01/04/1961	Whip-Poor-Will	Teresa Brewer	131	CB
01/04/1961	Little Star	Chuck Berry	134	CB
01/04/1961	Gidget Goes Hawaiian	Duane Eddy	135	CB
03/04/1961	Gidget Goes Hawaiian	Duane Eddy	101	BB
03/04/1961	Are You Sure	The Allisons	102	BB
08/04/1961	Who Will The Next Fool Be	Charlie Rich	102	CB
08/04/1961	Sparkle And Shine	The Four Coquettes	103	CB
08/04/1961	Come Along	Maurice Williams & The Zodiacs	104	CB
08/04/1961	Won'cha Come Home, Bill Bailey	Della Reese	105	CB
08/04/1961	My Blue Heaven	Frank Sinatra	108	CB
08/04/1961	One Hundred Percent	Lloyd Price & His Orchestra	125	CB
08/04/1961	Out Of A Clear Blue Sky	Lawrence Welk & His Orchestra	128	CB
08/04/1961	Dark As A Dungeon	Tennessee Ernie Ford	129	CB
08/04/1961	Lost The Right	Freddie Scott	129	CB
10/04/1961	African Waltz	Johnny Dankworth & His Orchestra	101	BB
10/04/1961	Three Little Fishes	Buzz Clifford	102	BB
10/04/1961	Love Or Money	The Blackwells	107	BB
10/04/1961	You Set My Heart To Music	Johnny Mathis	107	BB
10/04/1961	Pony Train	Titus Turner	115	BB
10/04/1961	Jenny (b-side)	Johnny Mathis	118	BB
15/04/1961	Sentimental Baby	Frank Sinatra	101	CB

15/04/1961	La Pachanga	Audrey Arno & The Hazy Osterwald Sextet	106	CB
15/04/1961	Continental With Me, Baby	The Vibrations	111	CB
15/04/1961	La Pachanga*	Hugo & Luigi With Their Children's Chorus	112	CB
15/04/1961	Do What You Want	Damita Jo Featuring The Mike Stewart Singers	114	CB
15/04/1961	Grapevine	Fabian	118	CB
15/04/1961	Take Me Tonight	Gene Pitney	123	CB
15/04/1961	Pony Train	Titus Turner	126	CB
15/04/1961	When You Dance (61 Version)	The Turbans	135	CB
17/04/1961	It's Been A Long, Long Time	Les Paul And Mary Ford	105	BB
17/04/1961	Lullaby Of The Bells	The Deltairs	114	BB
17/04/1961	When You Dance (new Version)	The Turbans	114	BB
22/04/1961	In My Heart	The Timetones	102	CB
22/04/1961	Opportunity	Freddy Cannon	105	CB
22/04/1961	Somebody Else's Boy	Connie Francis	109	CB
22/04/1961	The Junkernoo	The Vibrations	109	CB
22/04/1961	I Can't Do It By Myself	Anita Bryant	113	CB
22/04/1961	Here Comes The Night - Part I	Jimmy Norman	118	CB
22/04/1961	Theme From "HIPPODROME"	Jerry Murad's Harmonicats	119	CB
22/04/1961	Ballad Of The One Eyed Jacks	Johnny Burnette	126	CB
22/04/1961	Older And Wiser	Teresa Brewer	136	CB
22/04/1961	Swamp Meeting	Ernie Freeman	140	CB
24/04/1961	White Cliffs Of Dover	The Robins	108	BB
24/04/1961	The Junkernoo	The Vibrations	112	BB
24/04/1961	Opportunity	Freddy Cannon	114	BB
29/04/1961	You'd Better	Russell Byrd	107	CB
29/04/1961	Rimshot Pt. 1	The Roller Coasters	108	CB
29/04/1961	Willy Walk	Johnny Preston	111	CB
29/04/1961	Fountain Of Love	Barry Darvell	122	CB
29/04/1961	Good, Good Lovin'	ChuBBy Checker	129	CB
29/04/1961	Girl Machine	Johnny Walsh	131	CB

29/04/1961	Shy Away	Jerry Fuller	132	CB
29/04/1961	Abdul's Party	Larry Verne	135	CB
01/05/1961	It's Never Too Late	Brenda Lee	101	BB
01/05/1961	Sucu Sucu	Ping-Ping And The Al Verlane Orchestra	103	BB
01/05/1961	Sparkle And Shine	The Four Coquettes	107	BB
01/05/1961	Hey You, What Are You, Some Kind Of Nut?	Andy Cory	121	BB
06/05/1961	That's The Way With Love	Piero Soffici	104	CB
06/05/1961	That's The Way With Love (Viggio Nell' Infikito)	Don Costa & His Orchestra & Chorus	104	CB
06/05/1961	The Rebel - Johnny Yuma	Johnny Cash	109	CB
06/05/1961	Cha Cha Go Go (Chicago Cha Cha)	Danny & The Juniors	114	CB
06/05/1961	You're Movin' Me	Clyde Mcphatter	120	CB
06/05/1961	Happy Ending	Teddy Randazzo	133	CB
06/05/1961	Indian Giver	Annette With The Up Beats	135	CB
06/05/1961	My Darling	Ted Taylor	140	CB
08/05/1961	Unchained Melody	Gerry Granahan	109	BB
08/05/1961	He Needs Me	Gloria Lynne	111	BB
08/05/1961	Abdul's Party	Larry Verne	113	BB
08/05/1961	Baby Face	BoBBy Vee	119	BB
13/05/1961	Don't Be Afraid (To Fall In Love)	BoBBy Rydell	101	CB
13/05/1961	Milord	Teresa Brewer	105	CB
13/05/1961	Respectable	The Chants	107	CB
13/05/1961	Theme For A Dream	Cliff Richard & The Shadows	112	CB
13/05/1961	Here's My Confession	Wyatt (Earp) Mcpherson	121	CB
13/05/1961	Are You Sure	Aretha Franklin	134	CB
13/05/1961	Lil' Ole Me	Cornbread & Jerry	138	CB
13/05/1961	Oklahoma Hills	Hank Thompson & The Brazos Valley Boys	149	CB
13/05/1961	The Golden Chain	Tommy Edwards	150	CB
15/05/1961	Locked Up	Sonny Fulton	106	BB
15/05/1961	Every Beat Of My Heart	Henry Booth And The Midnighters	113	BB
15/05/1961	Exodus	Edith Piaf	116	BB

20/05/1961	Your Eyes	Brook Benton	115	CB
20/05/1961	A Cross Stands Alone	Jimmy Witter	117	CB
20/05/1961	Lonesome Whistle Blues	Freddy King	117	CB
20/05/1961	Great Shakin' Fever	Dorsey Burnette	132	CB
20/05/1961	What Will I Tell My Heart	The Harptones	145	CB
20/05/1961	They'll Never Take Her Love From Me	Johnny Horton	146	CB
22/05/1961	Bring Back Your Heart	The Del Vikings	101	BB
22/05/1961	Respectable	The Chants	101	BB
22/05/1961	The Honeydripper	The Clovers	110	BB
22/05/1961	Bacardi	Ralph Marterie	115	BB
27/05/1961	Our Parents Talked It Over	Kathy Young With The Innocents	101	CB
27/05/1961	I Left There Crying	Valerie Carr	106	CB
27/05/1961	(I've Got) Spring Fever	Little Willie John	111	CB
27/05/1961	Humorous	Kokomo	113	CB
27/05/1961	La Dolce Vita (The Sweet Life)	Ray Ellis & His Orchestra	113	CB
27/05/1961	La Dolce Vita (The Sweet Life)*	Harry Simeone Orchestra & Chorus	113	CB
27/05/1961	Bacardi	Ralph Marterie	123	CB
27/05/1961	Turn Around	Dodie Stevens	129	CB
27/05/1961	Goodnight Baby	The Imaginations	131	CB
27/05/1961	In Between Tears	Lenny Miles	131	CB
27/05/1961	In Between Tears*	Anna-King	131	CB
27/05/1961	I Just Cry	Fats Domino	132	CB
27/05/1961	Don't You Hear Me Calling - Baby	The Trend-Els	149	CB
29/05/1961	Monday To Sunday	Alan Dale	101	BB
29/05/1961	Book Of Love	BoBBy Bare	106	BB
29/05/1961	The Rebel-Johnny Yuma	Johnny Cash	108	BB
29/05/1961	Charlie Wasn't There	Barbara Evans	109	BB
03/06/1961	A Million Teardrops	Conway Twitty	106	CB
03/06/1961	Charlie Wasn't There	Barbara Evans	110	CB
03/06/1961	Wishbone	Donnie Brooks	128	CB

03/06/1961	Warpaint	Brooks Brothers	130	CB
03/06/1961	Cherokee	Jorgen Ingmann & His Guitar	140	CB
03/06/1961	They Call Me The Fool	Nick Noble	142	CB
05/06/1961	Life Is But A Dream	The Earls	107	BB
05/06/1961	Life Is But A Dream Sweetheart	The Classics	109	BB
05/06/1961	You Got To Show Me	Tony Lawrence	114	BB
10/06/1961	Sad Eyes (Don't You Cry)	The Echoes	102	CB
10/06/1961	Make Me Smile Again	Cathy Jean	111	CB
10/06/1961	Red Wing	Billy Vaughn & His Orchestra	112	CB
10/06/1961	The Presidential Press Conference (Parts 1 & 2) (Live)	The Sickniks	117	CB
10/06/1961	Dinky Doo	Eddie Bo	119	CB
10/06/1961	(Theme From Carnival) Love Makes The World Go 'ROUND	Jane Morgan	124	CB
10/06/1961	Look For My True Love	BoBBy Darin	131	CB
10/06/1961	Mary And Man-O	Lloyd Price & His Great Orchestra	136	CB
10/06/1961	Little Suzy	Clarence Henry	148	CB
12/06/1961	Solitaire	The Embers	103	BB
12/06/1961	The Matador	George Scott	104	BB
12/06/1961	Mary And Man-O	Lloyd Price And His Great Orchestra	110	BB
12/06/1961	Off To Work Again	Wilbert Harrison	114	BB
17/06/1961	Skin Tight, Pin Striped, Purple Pedal Pushers	Sheb Wooley	105	CB
17/06/1961	Lonely Life	Jackie Wilson	114	CB
17/06/1961	Dooley	The Olympics	115	CB
17/06/1961	Run, Run, Run	Ronny Douglas	115	CB
17/06/1961	You Thrill Me	Ray Peterson	115	CB
17/06/1961	Joanie	Frankie Calen	134	CB
17/06/1961	Follow That Girl	Vinnie Monte	144	CB
17/06/1961	Real Man	Ernie K-Doe	144	CB
17/06/1961	White Cliffs Of Dover	The Robins	146	CB
17/06/1961	You Came A Long Way From St. Louis	Merv Griffin With Sid Bass Orchestra	150	CB
19/06/1961	Old Smokie	Johnny And The Hurricanes	116	BB

24/06/1961	Boogie Woogie	B. Bumble & The Stingers	101	CB
24/06/1961	Teen Prayer	The Velveteens	101	CB
24/06/1961	The Float	Hank Ballard & The Midnighters	102	CB
24/06/1961	I'm Gonna Move To The Outskirts Of Town	Ray Charles	105	CB
24/06/1961	Old Smokie	Johnny & The Hurricanes	109	CB
24/06/1961	Tender Years	George Jones	110	CB
24/06/1961	Windy And Warm	Chet Atkins	132	CB
24/06/1961	Life Is But A Dream Sweetheart	The Classics	137	CB
24/06/1961	Near You	B. Bumble & The Stingers	139	CB
24/06/1961	Locked Up	Sonny Fulton	146	CB
24/06/1961	I Will Love You	Shelby Flint	147	CB
24/06/1961	Beware	The Innocents	148	CB
26/06/1961	The Presidential Press Conference (Part 1) [Live]	The Sickniks	105	BB
26/06/1961	The Presidential Press Conference (Part 2) [Live]	The Sickniks	105	BB
26/06/1961	Peace Of Mind	B.B. King	119	BB
01/07/1961	Summer Job	Marty Hill With Bill Ramal	106	CB
01/07/1961	Wooden Heart (Muss I Denn Zum Stadtele Hinaus)	Gus Backus	109	CB
01/07/1961	Down On My Knees	Walter Vaughn	119	CB
01/07/1961	Theme From The Motion Picture The Young Savages	Hugo Montenegro & His Orchestra	139	CB
01/07/1961	When A Girl Gives Her Heart (To A Boy)	Janice Ward	140	CB
01/07/1961	When A Girl Gives Her Heart To A Boy*	Billie Daye	141	CB
01/07/1961	Peg O' My Heart	Jerry Murad's Harmonicats	148	CB
01/07/1961	Make It Last	Nat King Cole	149	CB
03/07/1961	Voyage To The Bottom Of The Sea	Frankie Avalon	101	BB
03/07/1961	Wooden Heart (Muss I Denn Zum Stadtele Hinaus)	Gus Backus	102	BB
03/07/1961	Somebody Nobody Wants	Dion	103	BB
03/07/1961	Lonesome For You, Mama	Anita Bryant	108	BB
03/07/1961	Stranded In The Jungle (new Version)	The Vibrations	117	BB
08/07/1961	Mighty Good Lovin'	The Miracles	102	CB
08/07/1961	Mr. D. J.	Van Mccoy	105	CB

08/07/1961	How Can We Tell Him	Marv Johnson	112	CB
08/07/1961	The Guns Of Navarone*	Mitch Miller & The Gang	112	CB
08/07/1961	Voyage To The Bottom Of The Sea	Frankie Avalon	113	CB
08/07/1961	When I Go To Sleep At Night	The Tokens	117	CB
08/07/1961	Summertime Lies	Kitty Kallen	118	CB
08/07/1961	Broken Hearted	The Miracles	121	CB
08/07/1961	I Don't Need You No More	Maxine Brown	126	CB
08/07/1961	Tell Me What She Said	The Playmates Donny-Morey-Chic	131	CB
08/07/1961	Time	Jerry Jackson	138	CB
08/07/1961	John Brown's Baby	Jimmie Rodgers	141	CB
10/07/1961	Theme From "Come September"	Dick Jacobs And His Orchestra	104	BB
10/07/1961	Around The World	Buddy Greco	109	BB
10/07/1961	Mr. Johhny Q	The BoBBettes	120	BB
15/07/1961	Since Gary Went In The Navy	Marcy Joe	101	CB
15/07/1961	Here In My Heart	Al Martino	102	CB
15/07/1961	Summer Of '61	Frankie Avalon	118	CB
15/07/1961	This Little Boy Of Mine	Gloria Lynne	129	CB
15/07/1961	Heaven In Your Arms	Maxine Brown	132	CB
15/07/1961	Tennessee Waltz	Don Robertson	135	CB
17/07/1961	S.O.S. (I Love You)	Ronnie Hayden	108	BB
17/07/1961	I'm So Happy (Tra La La)	The Ducanes	109	BB
17/07/1961	St. Louis Blues	The Cousins	110	BB
17/07/1961	Theme From "Come September"	BoBBy Darin And His Orchestra	113	BB
22/07/1961	Girls	Johnny Burnette With The Johnny Mann Singers	112	CB
22/07/1961	Good Hearted Man	Fats Domino	121	CB
22/07/1961	Let The Sunshine In	Teddy Randazzo	131	CB
22/07/1961	Anyone But You	Ruth Brown	136	CB
22/07/1961	Around The World	Buddy Greco	146	CB
22/07/1961	Sermonette	Earl Grant	150	CB
24/07/1961	Tennessee Waltz	Don Robertson	117	BB

29/07/1961	I'm So Happy (Tra La La)	The Ducanes	111	CB
29/07/1961	Again	The Demensions	112	CB
29/07/1961	Big River, Big Man	Claude King	114	CB
29/07/1961	Now You Know	Little Willie John	116	CB
29/07/1961	Take My Love (I Want To Give It All To You)	Little Willie John	117	CB
29/07/1961	Again	The Concords	122	CB
29/07/1961	What Kind Of Girl (Do You Think I Am)	The Charmaines	126	CB
29/07/1961	Strange Desire	Jack Scott	129	CB
29/07/1961	Yo-Yo Girl	The Portraits	138	CB
29/07/1961	Glad To Be Back	The Chantels	146	CB
31/07/1961	Pretty, Pretty Girl (The New Beat)	The Time Tones	106	BB
31/07/1961	I've Got A Lot Of Things To Do	Johnny Burnette	109	BB
31/07/1961	Love And War (Ain't Much Difference In The Two)	Jerry Reed	117	BB
31/07/1961	Band Of Gold	The Roomates	119	BB
05/08/1961	A Far Far Better Thing	Della Reese	101	CB
05/08/1961	Little Miss Belong To No One	Teresa Brewer	111	CB
05/08/1961	Guess Who	Gladys Knight & The Pips	125	CB
05/08/1961	Gee Oh Gee	The Echoes	127	CB
05/08/1961	Skin Divin'	Eddie Rambeau	129	CB
05/08/1961	Hurtin' Inside	Lavern Baker	130	CB
05/08/1961	All I Have To Do Is Dream	The Everly Brothers	133	CB
05/08/1961	If	The Paragons	136	CB
05/08/1961	It Won't Happen With Me	Jerry Lee Lewis & His Pumping Piano	150	CB
07/08/1961	I'll Never Smile Again	The Wanderers	107	BB
07/08/1961	The Taste Of A Tear	Johnny & The Tokens	112	BB
12/08/1961	(You'll Have To Swing It) Mr. Paganini (Live)	Ella Fitzgerald	103	CB
12/08/1961	My Dream Come True	Jack Scott	120	CB
12/08/1961	Please Don't Talk To The Lifeguard	Andrea Carroll	123	CB
12/08/1961	That's My Desire	Pat Boone	126	CB
12/08/1961	So Close To Heaven	Ral Donner	128	CB

12/08/1961	Why Can't You	Clarence Henry	135	CB
12/08/1961	Private Eye	Bob Luman	142	CB
12/08/1961	Sugartime	Johnny Cash & The Tennessee Two	146	CB
12/08/1961	The Bells Are Ringing	The Van Dykes	148	CB
12/08/1961	Three Precious Words	The Edsels	148	CB
14/08/1961	(You'll Have To Swing It) Mr. Paganini [Live]	Ella Fitzgerald	103	BB
14/08/1961	A Far Far Better Thing	Della Reese	115	BB
14/08/1961	Somebody Cares	Zorro	118	BB
19/08/1961	Ole Slew-Foot	Johnny Horton	105	CB
19/08/1961	San-Ho-Zay	Freddy King	114	CB
19/08/1961	Romeo	Janie Grant	118	CB
19/08/1961	Nothing But Good	Hank Ballard & The Midnighters	119	CB
19/08/1961	Hully Gully Again	Little Caesar & The Romans	124	CB
19/08/1961	Baby, You're Right	James Brown & The Famous Flames	131	CB
19/08/1961	New Orleans Medley: I'm Walkin' / Blueberry Hill / Ain't That A Shame	The Drums Of Earl Palmer	132	CB
19/08/1961	Tight Sweater	The Marathons	136	CB
19/08/1961	All I Want Is A Chance	Dick Lee The Golden Boy	143	CB
19/08/1961	What Should I Do	Joe Tex	149	CB
21/08/1961	L-O-V-E	The Craftys	104	BB
21/08/1961	Blue Muu Muu	Annette With The Afterbeats Plus Four	107	BB
21/08/1961	Golden Teardrops	The Flamingos	108	BB
21/08/1961	Gee Oh Gee	The Echoes	112	BB
26/08/1961	Impossible	Gloria Lynne	105	CB
26/08/1961	A Little Dog Cried	Jimmie Rodgers	106	CB
26/08/1961	Drums	Kenny Chandler	124	CB
26/08/1961	I Got To Get Away From It All	Mitty Collier	139	CB
26/08/1961	First Love Never Dies	Jerry Fuller	141	CB
28/08/1961	That's Why	Curtis Knight	109	BB
28/08/1961	Crazy For You	Aquatones	119	BB
02/09/1961	Sleepless Nights	Tony Williams	112	CB

02/09/1961	Well-A, Well-A	Shirley & Lee	112	CB
02/09/1961	D.D.T. And The Boll Weevil	Lyn Earlington With Sherman Conrad & His Bourbon Street	117	CB
02/09/1961	Magic Is The Night	Kathy Young With The Innocents	120	CB
02/09/1961	I'm Mr. Luck	Jimmy Reed	121	CB
02/09/1961	How Soon (Will I Be Seeing You)	Bob Beckham	128	CB
02/09/1961	Hey, Look Me Over	Peggy Lee	129	CB
02/09/1961	It's Been A Long Long Time	Dotty Clark	132	CB
02/09/1961	Three Gassed Rats	The Handclappers	133	CB
02/09/1961	It's Unbearable	Dorothy Jones	140	CB
02/09/1961	Shake Shake Sherry	The Redwoods	146	CB
02/09/1961	Sorrow Tomorrow	BoBBy Darin	149	CB
04/09/1961	A Very True Story	Chris Kenner	103	BB
04/09/1961	You're The Reason	Hank Locklin	107	BB
04/09/1961	Ole Slew-Foot	Johnny Horton	110	BB
04/09/1961	Drums	Kenny Chandler	112	BB
04/09/1961	You Ain't Gonna Find	Cornell Blakely	116	BB
04/09/1961	You Broke My Heart	The Gleams	117	BB
09/09/1961	Packin' Up	Chris Kenner	104	CB
09/09/1961	Well, I Ask You	Eden Kane	104	CB
09/09/1961	She Put The Hurt On Me	Prince La La	105	CB
09/09/1961	I Talk To The Trees	Bud Dashiell & The Kinsmen	110	CB
09/09/1961	I Don't Like It Like That	The BoBBettes	111	CB
09/09/1961	Donald Where's Your Troosers?	Andy Stewart	114	CB
09/09/1961	In A Little Spanish Town	The Blue Diamonds	115	CB
09/09/1961	Dear Mr. D. J. Play It Again	Tina Robin	117	CB
09/09/1961	American Beauty Rose	Frank Sinatra	118	CB
09/09/1961	The Charleston Fish	Danny & The Juniors	123	CB
09/09/1961	Sincerely	The Tokens	130	CB
09/09/1961	It's A Sin	Slim & Ann	138	CB
09/09/1961	If	Roy Hamilton Orchestra & The Malcolm Dodds Singers	142	CB

09/09/1961	Vacation Time	Johnny Madara	149	CB
11/09/1961	Hey Little One	Bruce Bruno	103	BB
11/09/1961	Flying Blue Angels	Johnny George And The Pilots	108	BB
11/09/1961	Gin House Blues	Nina Simone	113	BB
16/09/1961	Honky Train	Bill Black's Combo	102	CB
16/09/1961	Well, I Ask Ya	Kay Starr	104	CB
16/09/1961	Autumn In Cheyenne	Al Caiola & His Orchestra	105	CB
16/09/1961	Pocketful Of Rainbows	Johnny Gatewood	119	CB
16/09/1961	Memories Of Those Oldies But Goodies	Little Caesar & The Romans	126	CB
16/09/1961	Late Date	The Parkays	127	CB
16/09/1961	Cozy Inn	Leon Mcauliff	135	CB
16/09/1961	Sad Movies (Make Me Cry)	The Lennon Sisters	147	CB
18/09/1961	Ev'rybody Pony	Teddy And The Continentals	101	BB
18/09/1961	Memories Of Those Oldies But Goodies	Little Caesar And The Romans	101	BB
18/09/1961	What Kind Of Girl (Do You Think I Am)	The Charmaines	117	BB
18/09/1961	Auf Wiederseh'n	Gus Backus	118	BB
18/09/1961	I Can't Forget	Marvin Rainwater	119	BB
18/09/1961	Sincerely	The Tokens	120	BB
23/09/1961	Let True Love Begin	Nat King Cole	102	CB
23/09/1961	Make Believe Wedding	The Castells	104	CB
23/09/1961	Married	Frankie Avalon	109	CB
23/09/1961	Satin Doll	Billy Maxted & His Manhattan Jazz Band	116	CB
23/09/1961	One Grain Of Sand	Eddy Arnold	117	CB
23/09/1961	A Very True Story	Chris Kenner	123	CB
23/09/1961	Somebody Else Is Taking My Place	Joni James	123	CB
23/09/1961	Sweet Sorrow	Conway Twitty	134	CB
23/09/1961	The Wedding (La Novia)	Anita Bryant	136	CB
23/09/1961	The Greenwood Tree	Connie Stevens	148	CB
25/09/1961	Mr. D.J.	Van Mccoy	104	BB
25/09/1961	Song Of The Nairobi Trio	The Fortune Tellers	114	BB

25/09/1961	Satin Doll	Billy Maxted And His Manhattan Jazz Band	117	BB
30/09/1961	Linda	Adam Wade	101	CB
30/09/1961	Broken Heart And A Pillow Filled With Tears	Patti Page	102	CB
30/09/1961	Rock-A-Bye Your Baby (With A Dixie Melody) (Live)*	Judy Garland	112	CB
30/09/1961	It Isn't Fair	Billy Eckstine	120	CB
30/09/1961	Faraway Star	The Chordettes	123	CB
30/09/1961	Auf Wiederseh'n	Gus Backus	125	CB
30/09/1961	Save The Last Dance For Me	Jerry Lee Lewis & His Pumping Piano	131	CB
30/09/1961	Night Train	Richard Hayman & His Orchestra	136	CB
30/09/1961	Shenandoah	The Deaxville Trio	137	CB
30/09/1961	My Love For You	Lawrence Welk, His Orchestra & Chorus	141	CB
30/09/1961	What Kind Of Girl Do You Think I Am	Erma Franklin	141	CB
02/10/1961	Aware Of Love	Jerry Butler	105	BB
02/10/1961	Dance With A Dolly (With A Hole In Her Stocking)	Damita Jo	105	BB
02/10/1961	Soft Rain	Ray Price	115	BB
02/10/1961	Well, I Ask You	Eden Kane	119	BB
07/10/1961	Blue Moon Of Kentucky	Dick Haiman (At The Organ) & The Dial Tones	106	CB
07/10/1961	The Closer You Are	The Magnificent Four	110	CB
07/10/1961	Wasn't The Summer Short?	Johnny Mathis	117	CB
07/10/1961	Aware Of Love	Jerry Butler	118	CB
07/10/1961	Dance With A Dolly (With A Hole In Her Stocking)	Damita Jo	123	CB
07/10/1961	Sombrero	Das Jochen Brauer - Sextett	132	CB
07/10/1961	Shout - Part 1	The Isley Brothers	138	CB
09/10/1961	Wanted, One Girl	Jan & Dean	104	BB
09/10/1961	Cappuccina	Nat King Cole	115	BB
09/10/1961	Lovers Never Say Goodbye	The Flamingos	117	BB
14/10/1961	I Apologize	Timi Yuro	116	CB
14/10/1961	Everybody Fish - Part Ii	The Harlequins	127	CB
14/10/1961	Mina Bird	The String-A-Longs	127	CB
14/10/1961	Settle Down	Dougie & The Dudes	139	CB

14/10/1961	Rip Van Winkle	Devotions	145	CB
16/10/1961	Sweet Sorrow	Conway Twitty	107	BB
16/10/1961	Lonesome	Jerry Wallace	110	BB
16/10/1961	Married	Frankie Avalon	112	BB
16/10/1961	Reach For The Stars	Shirley Bassey	120	BB
21/10/1961	I Wonder (If Your Love Will Ever Belong To Me)	The Pentagons	101	CB
21/10/1961	Somewhere Along The Way	Steve Lawrence	104	CB
21/10/1961	You'll Never Know	Shirley Bassey	110	CB
21/10/1961	Satan's Theme	The Rondels	116	CB
21/10/1961	Wanted, One Girl	Jan & Dean	130	CB
21/10/1961	Let's Pony Again	The Vibrations	133	CB
21/10/1961	Love Bound	The Universals	141	CB
21/10/1961	A Letter From Ann	The Videls	143	CB
23/10/1961	One Grain Of Sand	Eddy Arnold	107	BB
23/10/1961	Without Your Love	Wendy Hill	111	BB
23/10/1961	Be Careful How You Drive Young Joey	Jerry Keller	112	BB
23/10/1961	Berlin Top Ten	Dickie Goodman	116	BB
28/10/1961	A Certain Girl	Ernie K-Doe	103	CB
28/10/1961	My Last Cry	The Starlets	103	CB
28/10/1961	Let Them Love (And Be Loved)	The Dreamlovers	104	CB
28/10/1961	The Breaking Point	Chuck Jackson	108	CB
28/10/1961	After All We've Been Through	Maxine Brown	112	CB
28/10/1961	O Sole Mio	Robertino	118	CB
28/10/1961	In The Dark	Little Junior Parker	120	CB
28/10/1961	There You Go Again	Jeanette "Baby" Washington	133	CB
28/10/1961	Liar	The Regents	135	CB
28/10/1961	Rock Island Line	The Lonnie Donegan Skiffle Group	138	CB
28/10/1961	God Bless The Child	Eddie Harris	148	CB
30/10/1961	After All We've Been Through	Maxine Brown	102	BB
30/10/1961	Let Them Love (And Be Loved)	The Dreamlovers	102	BB

30/10/1961	Don't Walk Away From Me	Dee Clark	104	BB
30/10/1961	The Roach	Gene And Wendell	117	BB
04/11/1961	Shalom	Eddie Fisher	105	CB
04/11/1961	Little Lonely	Chad Allen	107	CB
04/11/1961	Losing Your Love	Jim Reeves	108	CB
04/11/1961	Tonight	Eddie Fisher	109	CB
04/11/1961	Theme From King Of Kings	Felix Slatkin	111	CB
04/11/1961	Theme From King Of Kings*	Vardi & The Medallion Strings	111	CB
04/11/1961	There's Our Song Again	The Chantels	115	CB
04/11/1961	They're Playing Our Song	Jamie Horton	118	CB
04/11/1961	Do The Bug With Me	Billy Bland	129	CB
04/11/1961	Just A Little Bit Sweet	Charlie Rich	129	CB
04/11/1961	Mexican Joe	David Carroll & His Orchestra	133	CB
04/11/1961	Give Myself A Party	Rosemary Clooney	143	CB
04/11/1961	You Don't Know	Helen Shapiro	147	CB
06/11/1961	Give Myself A Party	Rosemary Clooney	108	BB
06/11/1961	(If I'm Dreaming) Just Let Me Dream	Pat Boone	114	BB
06/11/1961	Lonely Sixteen	Janie Black	116	BB
06/11/1961	Feminine Touch	Dorsey Burnette	117	BB
11/11/1961	Greetings (This Is Uncle Sam)	The Valadiers	102	CB
11/11/1961	Prelude From King Of Kings*	Clebanoff & His Orchestra	111	CB
11/11/1961	The Roach	Gene & Wendell With The Sweethearts	111	CB
11/11/1961	I Won't Cry Anymore	The Embers	113	CB
11/11/1961	The Night I Cried	Brian Hyland	128	CB
11/11/1961	(If I'm Dreaming) Just Let Me Dream	Pat Boone	132	CB
13/11/1961	Trade Winds, Trade Winds	Aki Aleong	101	BB
13/11/1961	Fever	Pete Bennett & The Embers	105	BB
13/11/1961	Dreamin' About You	Annette And The Vonnair Sisters	106	BB
13/11/1961	Little Miss U.S.A.	Barry Mann	109	BB
13/11/1961	Just A Little Bit Sweet	Charlie Rich	111	BB

13/11/1961	Little Lonely	Chad Allen	112	BB
13/11/1961	My Buddy	Eddie Harris	114	BB
13/11/1961	God Bless The Child (b-side)	Eddie Harris	119	BB
18/11/1961	Milk And Honey	Eddie Fisher	104	CB
18/11/1961	Dreamin' About You	Annette & The Vonnair Sisters	108	CB
18/11/1961	Theme From "KING Of Kings"*	Ornadel & The Starlight Symphony Orchestra	111	CB
18/11/1961	Bad Blood	The Coasters	114	CB
18/11/1961	The Peppermint Twist	Danny Peppermint & The Jumping Jacks	115	CB
18/11/1961	My Life	Maxine Brown	122	CB
18/11/1961	Wild Party	Fabian With The Fabulous Four	128	CB
18/11/1961	Close Your Eyes	Rosemarie & Bo	142	CB
20/11/1961	Preview Of Paradise	Adam Wade	108	BB
20/11/1961	Standing In The Need Of Love	Clarence Henry	109	BB
20/11/1961	She Put The Hurt On Me	Prince La La	119	BB
20/11/1961	Theme From King Of Kings	Felix Slatkin	120	BB
25/11/1961	Don't Walk Away From Me	Dee Clark	107	CB
25/11/1961	(Ain't That) Just Like Me	The Coasters	109	CB
25/11/1961	Ev'rybody's Cryin'	Jimmie Beaumont	122	CB
25/11/1961	She Really Loves You	Timi Yuro	123	CB
25/11/1961	In The Same Old Way	Tommy Ridgley	128	CB
25/11/1961	Birmingham	Santo & Johnny	129	CB
25/11/1961	You're Telling Our Secrets	Dee Clark	136	CB
25/11/1961	Moving Day	Buzz Clifford	139	CB
25/11/1961	Love (I'm So Glad) I Found You	Spinners	142	CB
25/11/1961	Mexican Hat Twist	The Applejacks	145	CB
27/11/1961	Song For The Lonely (b-side)	The Platters	115	BB
27/11/1961	Tonight	Jay & The Americans	120	BB
02/12/1961	Room Full Of Tears	The Drifters	102	CB
02/12/1961	The Avenger	Duane Eddy & The Rebels	102	CB
02/12/1961	Walkin' Back To Happiness	Helen Shapiro	112	CB

02/12/1961	He's Old Enough To Know Better	The Crickets	121	CB
02/12/1961	Everybody's Twisting Down In Mexico	Billy Vaughn & His Orchestra	124	CB
02/12/1961	Song For The Lonely	The Platters	127	CB
02/12/1961	Image - Part I	Hank Levine & Orchestra	136	CB
02/12/1961	My Girl	Charles Mccullough & The Silks	140	CB
02/12/1961	The Basie Twist	Count Basie & His Orchestra	143	CB
02/12/1961	Scratch My Back (I Love It)	Ray Stevens	147	CB
02/12/1961	The Same Old Trouble	Don Gibson	150	CB
04/12/1961	The Bells At My Wedding	Paul Anka	104	BB
04/12/1961	Loveland (b-side)	Paul Anka	110	BB
04/12/1961	Sweethearts In Heaven	Chase Webster	116	BB
04/12/1961	A-One A-Two A-Cha Cha Cha	Lawrence Welk, His Orchestra And Chorus	117	BB
09/12/1961	Loveland	Paul Anka	101	CB
09/12/1961	Flying Blue Angels	George, Johnny & The Pilots	102	CB
09/12/1961	Can't Take The Heartbreaks	Mary Ann Fisher	106	CB
09/12/1961	Twistin' All Night Long	Danny & The Juniors With Freddy Cannon	106	CB
09/12/1961	I Hear You Knocking	Fats Domino	109	CB
09/12/1961	Peppermint Twist Time	The Twisters	115	CB
09/12/1961	You'll Come Back	Ronny Douglas	128	CB
09/12/1961	Nein Nein Fraulein	Cathy Carr	132	CB
09/12/1961	The Peppermint Twist	The Royaltones	139	CB
11/12/1961	The Things I Want To Hear (Pretty Words)	The Shirelles	107	BB
11/12/1961	You'll Never Know	The Platters	109	BB
11/12/1961	Everybody's Twisting Down In Mexico	Billy Vaughn And His Orchestra	119	BB
16/12/1961	A Sunday Kind Of Love	Jan & Dean	109	CB
16/12/1961	You Don't Have To Be A Tower Of Strength	Gloria Lynne	110	CB
16/12/1961	Jingle Bell Twist U.S.A.	The Happy Sound Of Johnny Mendell With Gill & His Premiers	115	CB
16/12/1961	Once Around The Block	The Four Preps	134	CB
16/12/1961	Sweet Water	The Stereos	134	CB
16/12/1961	The Waltz You Saved For Me	Ferlin Husky	140	CB

16/12/1961	And Then Came Love	Ed Townsend	148	CB
18/12/1961	Close Your Eyes	The Skyliners	105	BB
18/12/1961	He's Old Enough To Know Better	The Crickets	105	BB
18/12/1961	He's Not Just A Soldier	Little Richard "King Of The Gospel Singers"	113	BB
18/12/1961	And Then Came Love	Ed Townsend	114	BB
23/12/1961	Motorcycle	Tico & The Triumphs	103	CB
23/12/1961	Holler Hey	Jimmy Jones	119	CB
23/12/1961	Santa And The Touchables	Dickie Goodman	123	CB
23/12/1961	You Don't Have To Be A Baby To Cry	Joe Barry	123	CB
23/12/1961	One Degree North	The Mar-Keys	130	CB
25/12/1961	Jingle-Bell Rock	Chet Atkins	106	BB
25/12/1961	A Kiss For Christmas (O Tannenbaum)	Joe Dowell	110	BB
25/12/1961	Bye Bye Baby	Bob Conrad	113	BB
25/12/1961	Jingle Bell Imitations	ChuBBy Checker BoBBy Rydell	115	BB
25/12/1961	Lonesome Road	Don Shirley	116	BB
30/12/1961	Baby Don't Leave Me	Joe Henderson	102	CB
30/12/1961	Shimmy, Shimmy Walk, Part 1	The Megatons	104	CB
30/12/1961	A Kiss For Christmas (O Tannenbaum)	Joe Dowell	111	CB
30/12/1961	Portrait Of A Fool	Conway Twitty	113	CB
30/12/1961	The Things I Want To Hear (Pretty Words)	The Shirelles	115	CB
30/12/1961	Something You Got	Chris Kenner	124	CB
30/12/1961	Dear Gesu Bambino (Caro Gesu Bambino)	Christian Morandi	125	CB
30/12/1961	Bombay	Mike Clifford	140	CB
30/12/1961	Sittin' And Drinking	Christine Kittrell	144	CB
30/12/1961	Twistin' Bells	Santo & Johnny	150	CB
06/01/1962	The Avenger	Duane Eddy And The Rebels	101	BB
06/01/1962	Archie's Melody	The By Liners	106	CB
06/01/1962	Step Right Up (And Say You Love Me)	Nat King Cole	107	CB
06/01/1962	The Twist	Ernie Freeman	123	CB
06/01/1962	An Angel Cried	Hal Miller & The Rays	135	CB

06/01/1962	Midnight Special, Part 1	Jimmy Smith	144	CB
06/01/1962	Girls Are Sentimental	Van Mccoy	149	CB
13/01/1962	Happy Jose	Dave Appell And His Orchestra	104	BB
13/01/1962	Mommy And Daddy Were Twistin'	Susan Summers	106	CB
13/01/1962	Sometimes I'm Tempted	Marty RoBBins	109	BB
13/01/1962	Goodbye To Toyland	The Vonnair Sisters	115	BB
13/01/1962	Foxy	Mar-Keys	116	CB
20/01/1962	I Got A Funny Kind Of Feeling	Maxine Brown	104	CB
20/01/1962	Step Right Up (And Say You Love Me)	Nat "King" Cole	106	BB
20/01/1962	You Don't Miss Your Water	William Bell	108	CB
20/01/1962	A Little Bitty Tear	Wanda Jackson	112	CB
20/01/1962	Our Concerto	Steve Lawrence	116	CB
20/01/1962	Archie's Melody	The By Liners	117	BB
20/01/1962	Early Sunday	Mort Garson & His Orchestra	126	CB
20/01/1962	A Thousand Feet Below	Terry Tyler	127	CB
20/01/1962	Drown In My Own Tears	Don Shirley	127	CB
20/01/1962	The Thorn On The Rose	Joe Dowell	138	CB
20/01/1962	I've Heard That Song Before	Frank Sinatra	139	CB
20/01/1962	Ten Steps To Love	The Electras	140	CB
20/01/1962	Walking Cane	Billy Duke	142	CB
20/01/1962	Burnt Biscuits	The Triumphs	148	CB
20/01/1962	So Mean To Me	Little Milton	150	CB
27/01/1962	Do This Do That	Little Nat	102	CB
27/01/1962	Hello Again	Erma Franklin	102	CB
27/01/1962	Along Came Linda	Tommy Boyce	103	CB
27/01/1962	The DriBBle (Twist)	The Raging Storms	103	CB
27/01/1962	The Fools Hall Of Fame	Paul Anka	103	BB
27/01/1962	I Got A Funny Kind Of Feeling	Maxine Brown	104	BB
27/01/1962	Imagination	The Quotations	105	BB
27/01/1962	Mamie In The Afternoon	BoBBy Lewis	110	BB

27/01/1962	After You've Gone	Frankie Avalon	117	BB
27/01/1962	Grow Closer Together	The Impressions	117	CB
27/01/1962	Along Came Linda	Tommy Boyce	118	BB
27/01/1962	Mamie In The Afternoon	BoBBy Lewis	118	CB
27/01/1962	For All We Know	The Caslons	120	BB
27/01/1962	The Moon Was Yellow	Frank Sinatra	131	CB
27/01/1962	Brooklyn Bridge	BoBBy Bare	132	CB
27/01/1962	After You've Gone	Frankie Avalon	141	CB
27/01/1962	What'cha Gonna Say Tomorrow	Chuck Jackson	142	CB
03/02/1962	The Birth Of The Beat	Sandy Nelson	101	CB
03/02/1962	Our Concerto	Steve Lawrence	107	BB
03/02/1962	The Fools Hall Of Fame	Paul Anka	107	CB
03/02/1962	Echo In The Night	Bert Kaempfert And His Orchestra	108	BB
03/02/1962	It's Good To Have You Back With Me	Adam Wade	109	BB
03/02/1962	How Are Things In Lovers Lane (b-side)	Adam Wade	114	BB
03/02/1962	Walking Cane	Billy Duke	120	BB
03/02/1962	Let's Go	Floyd Cramer	123	CB
03/02/1962	Dance Party	The Tabs	128	CB
03/02/1962	Puppy Love	Little Jimmy Rivers & The Tops	128	CB
03/02/1962	Great Pretender	Kathy Young With The Innocents	141	CB
03/02/1962	One More Time	Danny Peppermint	148	CB
10/02/1962	Do You Know How To Twist	Hank Ballard	101	CB
10/02/1962	Love Theme From "EL Cid"	Billy Storm	104	CB
10/02/1962	Now Let's Popeye (Part Ii)	Eddie Bo	112	CB
10/02/1962	The Battle	Duane Eddy And The Rebels	114	BB
10/02/1962	The Tiger's Wide Awake (The Lion Sleeps Tonight)	The Romeos	117	CB
10/02/1962	(The Original) Nut Rocker*	Jack B. Nimble & The Quicks	125	CB
10/02/1962	How Low Is Low	Jamie Coe	128	CB
10/02/1962	Out Of Sight Out Of Mind	Rudy West & The Five Keys	130	CB
10/02/1962	The Actress	Roy Orbison	131	CB

10/02/1962	Sugar Babe	Buster Brown	139	CB
10/02/1962	The Snake	The Isley Brothers	140	CB
10/02/1962	Rough Lover	Aretha Franklin	141	CB
10/02/1962	Mr. Moto	The Belairs	150	CB
17/02/1962	Baby Don't Leave Me	Joe Henderson	106	BB
17/02/1962	I Want To Love You (So Much It Hurts Me)	Renee Roberts	109	CB
17/02/1962	I'm Asking Forgiveness	C.L. & The Pictures	109	CB
17/02/1962	Concerto For The X-15 "A Tribute To The X-15"	Elliott Evans	111	CB
17/02/1962	Midnight In Moscow	Jan Burgens & His New Orleans Syncopators	111	BB
17/02/1962	The White Rose Of Athens	Nana Mouskouri	114	CB
17/02/1962	Town Crier	Linda Scott	116	BB
17/02/1962	Baby It's Cold Outside	Ray Charles & Betty Carter	122	CB
17/02/1962	A Song For Young Love	The Lettermen	123	CB
17/02/1962	It Wasn't God Who Made Honky Tonk Angels	Kitty Kallen	137	CB
24/02/1962	Love Theme From "El Cid"	Billy Storm	105	BB
24/02/1962	Concerto For The X-15 "A Tribute To The X-15" "A Tribute To The X-	Elliott Evans	110	BB
24/02/1962	Shake Shake Sherry	The Edsels	113	CB
24/02/1962	Ida Jane	Fats Domino	118	CB
24/02/1962	Third Window From The Right	Dean Barlow	118	CB
24/02/1962	Step By Step, Little By Little	Anita Bryant	119	CB
24/02/1962	Tears Broke Out On Me	Eddy Arnold	127	CB
24/02/1962	Caldonia	The Rondels	137	CB
24/02/1962	Cool	Cal Tjader Quartet	148	CB
03/03/1962	It Wasn't God Who Made Honky Tonk Angels	Kitty Kallen	101	BB
03/03/1962	Tears Broke Out On Me	Eddy Arnold	102	BB
03/03/1962	Gee Baby	Ben & Bea	103	CB
03/03/1962	Step By Step, Little By Little	Anita Bryant	106	BB
03/03/1962	Summertime	Rick Nelson	111	CB
03/03/1962	Clown Shoes	Johnny Burnette	113	BB
03/03/1962	Help Me	Andy Williams	113	CB

Date	Title	Artist	Pos	Chart
03/03/1962	You Lied	Joanie Taylor & The Tabs	123	CB
03/03/1962	Mashed Potatoes (Part 1)	Steve Alaimo	124	CB
03/03/1962	Oh Johnny	Janie Grant With Hutch Davie Orch.	127	CB
03/03/1962	Isle Of Sirens	Jerry Butler	130	CB
03/03/1962	The Truth About Youth	Annette	132	CB
03/03/1962	Sugar Blues	Don Costa & His Orchestra	142	CB
03/03/1962	One Of The Guys	Vinnie Monte	143	CB
03/03/1962	Cry, Cry, Cry	Jack Scott	150	CB
10/03/1962	Just Another Fool	Curtis Lee	112	CB
10/03/1962	Ginny In The Mirror	Del Shannon	123	CB
10/03/1962	Sugartime Twist	The Mcguire Sisters	130	CB
10/03/1962	Guitar Boogie Shuffle Twist	The Virtues	134	CB
10/03/1962	To Know Him Is To Love Him	Nancy Sinatra	141	CB
10/03/1962	Paradise Cove	The Surfmen	143	CB
10/03/1962	Charlie's Shoes	Billy Walker	146	CB
17/03/1962	Here It Comes Again	The Chantels	101	CB
17/03/1962	Chapel By The Sea	Billy Vaughn & His Orchestra	107	CB
17/03/1962	Stardust	Frank Sinatra	108	CB
17/03/1962	One Love, One Heartache (O Sole Mio)	Billy Vaughn & His Orchestra	112	CB
17/03/1962	I Won't Be There	Del Shannon	113	BB
17/03/1962	All You Had To Do (Was Tell Me)	Chris Montez	114	CB
17/03/1962	Nut Rocker	Jack B. Nimble And The Quicks	115	BB
17/03/1962	Ginny In The Mirror (b-side)	Del Shannon	117	BB
17/03/1962	Here It Comes Again	The Chantels	118	BB
17/03/1962	Do The Surfer Stomp Part One	Bruce Johnston	121	CB
17/03/1962	Gonna Miss You Around Here	B.B. King	129	CB
17/03/1962	Street Of Palms (Via Margalene)	Ferrante & Teicher	133	CB
17/03/1962	Love Is A Swingin' Thing	The Shirelles	134	CB
17/03/1962	Hully Gully Callin' Time	Jive Five With Eugene Pitt	135	CB
17/03/1962	Paradise Cove*	Martin Denny	143	CB

17/03/1962	Crawl - Part 2	Willie Mitchell	144	CB
24/03/1962	Colinda	Rod Bernard	102	BB
24/03/1962	Cookin'	Al Casey Combo	105	CB
24/03/1962	Auf Wiedersehen Marlene	Bob Moore & His Orchestra & Chorus	108	CB
24/03/1962	Sugar Blues	Don Costa And His Orchestra	112	BB
24/03/1962	La Paloma Twist	ChuBBy Checker	114	CB
24/03/1962	A Losing Battle	Johnny Adams	122	CB
24/03/1962	The Joke	Reggie Hall	137	CB
31/03/1962	Twistin' Fever	The Marcels	103	BB
31/03/1962	Hully Gully Callin' Time	Jive Five With Eugene Pitt	105	BB
31/03/1962	Patricia - Twist	Perez Prado & His Orchestra	109	CB
31/03/1962	Shake The Hand Of A Fool	Johnny Hallyday With The Merry Melody Singers	110	CB
31/03/1962	The Right Thing To Say	Nat "King" Cole	110	BB
31/03/1962	The Town I Live In	Mckinley Mitchell	115	BB
31/03/1962	If You Want To	The Carousels	117	BB
31/03/1962	Gee Baby	Ben And Bea	119	BB
31/03/1962	Honky-Tonk Man	Johnny Horton	119	CB
31/03/1962	All Of This For Sally	Mark Dinning	129	CB
31/03/1962	The Wonderful World Of The Young	Andy Williams	139	CB
31/03/1962	You Are Like The Wind	Dee Clark	139	CB
31/03/1962	Bei Mir Bist Du Schoen	Frank Slay & His Orchestra	142	CB
31/03/1962	Eenie-Meenie-Minee-Mo	Lee Dorsey	149	CB
31/03/1962	It Has To Be	Sue Thompson	150	CB
07/04/1962	Buttons And Bows	Browns Featuring Jim Edward Brown	104	BB
07/04/1962	Hombre	The Belmonts With Pete Bennett Orch.	106	CB
07/04/1962	I'd Never Find Another You	Paul Anka	106	BB
07/04/1962	Sugartime Twist (new Version)	The Mcguire Sisters	107	BB
07/04/1962	All You Had To Do (Was Tell Me)	Chris Montez	108	BB
07/04/1962	Love Is A Swingin' Thing	The Shirelles	109	BB
07/04/1962	Just Another Fool	Curtis Lee	110	BB

07/04/1962	Spanish Harlem	Santo & Johnny	110	CB
07/04/1962	I Want To Love You (So Much It Hurts Me)	Renee Roberts	112	BB
07/04/1962	Pop-Eye Stroll	Mar-Keys	115	CB
07/04/1962	(Oooh Looka There) Ain't She Pretty	Billy Duke	117	CB
07/04/1962	Experiment In Terror	Henry Mancini & His Orchestra	119	CB
07/04/1962	Fun House	The Roosters	123	CB
07/04/1962	Just Plain Hurt	Chuck Reed	126	CB
07/04/1962	Need Your Love	The Metallics	136	CB
07/04/1962	One Mint Julep	Sarah Vaughan	143	CB
07/04/1962	I Know (I Love You)	Timi Yuro	147	CB
14/04/1962	Need Your Love	The Metallics	101	BB
14/04/1962	If You Want To	The Carousels	102	CB
14/04/1962	I've Been Good To You	The Miracles	103	BB
14/04/1962	Jane, Jane, Jane	The Kingston Trio	109	CB
14/04/1962	Lovesick Blues	Floyd Cramer	118	CB
14/04/1962	Swingin' Shepherd Blues Twist	Moe Koffman Quartette	130	CB
14/04/1962	I Found Love	Jackie Wilson & Linda Hopkins	136	CB
14/04/1962	Two Different Worlds	Robert Goulet	144	CB
14/04/1962	The Town I Live In	Mckinley Mitchell	145	CB
14/04/1962	Magic Circle	Buzz Clifford	147	CB
14/04/1962	Walkin'	Jerry Mcgee & The Cajuns	147	CB
21/04/1962	Spanish Harlem	Santo & Johnny	101	BB
21/04/1962	Walk On The Wild Side	Elmer Bernstein & Orchestra	102	BB
21/04/1962	Chapel Of Tears	Gene Mcdaniels	104	CB
21/04/1962	Trouble's Back In Town	The Wilburn Brothers	107	CB
21/04/1962	Such A Night	Dinah Washington	109	CB
21/04/1962	Drummin' Up A Storm	Sandy Nelson	110	CB
21/04/1962	Turkish Coffee	Tony Osborne With His Piano & Orchestra	119	CB
21/04/1962	To Make A Long Story Short	Eddie & The Starlites	120	CB
21/04/1962	(Hear My Song) Violetta	Ray Adams & Orchestra	127	CB

21/04/1962	My Name Is Mud	James O'gwynn	128	CB
21/04/1962	Funny	Gene Mcdaniels	134	CB
21/04/1962	I've Been Good To You	The Miracles	143	CB
21/04/1962	Jumpin' The Blues	Jimmy Smith	145	CB
28/04/1962	The Prince	Jackie Deshannon	108	BB
28/04/1962	Swingin' Shepherd Blues Twist (twist Version)	Moe Koffman Quartette	110	BB
28/04/1962	Walk On The Wild Side	Elmer Bernstein & Orchestra	112	CB
28/04/1962	Theme From Lolita	Orchestra Del Oro, Score By Don Costa	116	CB
28/04/1962	For The First Time In My Life	Adam Wade	118	BB
28/04/1962	For The First Time In My Life	Adam Wade	133	CB
28/04/1962	My Babe	Bill Black's Combo	137	CB
28/04/1962	Big Boat	The Tokens	144	CB
28/04/1962	My Little Angel	Johnnie Mae Matthews	148	CB
28/04/1962	Tarantella Twist	Hugo Montenegro & His Orchestra	149	CB
05/05/1962	After The Lights Go Down Low	George Maharis	104	BB
05/05/1962	Thanks To The Fool	Brook Benton	106	BB
05/05/1962	Teach Me To Twist	BoBBy Rydell ChuBBy Checker	109	BB
05/05/1962	Two Fools Are We	Don & Juan	118	CB
05/05/1962	(Hear My Song) Violetta	Ray Adams	119	BB
05/05/1962	Touch Me	Willie Nelson	124	CB
05/05/1962	Don't Take Away Your Love	Johnny Nash	129	CB
05/05/1962	The Lady Wants To Twist	Steve Lawrence	144	CB
12/05/1962	Na-Ne-No	Troy Shondell	103	CB
12/05/1962	Stranger On The Shore	The Drifters	103	CB
12/05/1962	Willing And Eager	Pat Boone	113	BB
12/05/1962	Gonna Git That Man	Connie Francis	117	CB
12/05/1962	Let's Stick Together	Wilbert Harrison	127	CB
12/05/1962	Troubles On My Mind	The Ikettes	132	CB
12/05/1962	Comfy 'N Cozy	Conway Twitty	133	CB
12/05/1962	I Can Mend Your Broken Heart	Don Gibson	135	CB

12/05/1962	Scotch And Soda (Live)	Henry Thome	141	CB
12/05/1962	Until Again My Love	Little Willie John	141	CB
12/05/1962	Arrivederci, Roma	Eddie Fisher	142	CB
12/05/1962	Valley Of Tears	Slim Whitman	148	CB
19/05/1962	Workout (Part 1)	Ricky Dee & The Embers	109	CB
19/05/1962	Arrivederci, Roma	Eddie Fisher	112	BB
19/05/1962	What Did Daddy Do	Shep & The Limelites	113	CB
19/05/1962	The Lady Wants To Twist	Steve Lawrence	120	BB
19/05/1962	Gloria	Vito & The Salutations	133	CB
19/05/1962	Wonderful Land	The Shadows	137	CB
19/05/1962	The Fool Of The Year	Johnny Burnette With The Johnny Mann Singers	147	CB
19/05/1962	Dream Myself A Sweetheart	Clarence Henry	149	CB
26/05/1962	Air Travel	Ray & Bob	101	CB
26/05/1962	Everybody Loves A Lover	The Angels	103	BB
26/05/1962	One O'clock Jump	Jimmy Smith	103	BB
26/05/1962	I Never Knew Your Name	Paul Anka	104	CB
26/05/1962	I Can Mend Your Broken Heart	Don Gibson	105	BB
26/05/1962	Gift Of Love	Jack Jones	108	CB
26/05/1962	Gee, It's Wonderful	BoBBy Rydell	109	BB
26/05/1962	Dancin' The Strand	Maureen Gray	110	CB
26/05/1962	Dream Myself A Sweetheart	Clarence Henry	112	BB
26/05/1962	Gee, It's Wonderful	BoBBy Rydell	112	CB
26/05/1962	I'm Hanging Up My Heart For You	Solomon Burke	112	CB
26/05/1962	Marianna	Johnny Mathis	113	CB
26/05/1962	The Story Of My Life	"Big" Al Downing	117	BB
26/05/1962	Love, Where Are You Now (Toselli Serenade)	Al Martino	119	BB
26/05/1962	Mama	Roy Orbison	119	CB
26/05/1962	In My Baby's Eyes	BoBBy Vee With The Johnny Mann Singers	121	CB
26/05/1962	Theme From The Brothers Grimm	Lawrence Welk & His Orchestra	130	CB
26/05/1962	He Got What He Wanted (But He Lost What He Had)	Little Richard	134	CB

26/05/1962	Candy Kisses	Tony Bennett	140	CB
02/06/1962	Baby Elephant Walk*	The Miniature Men	102	CB
02/06/1962	Work Out (Part 1)	Ricky Dee & The Embers	103	BB
02/06/1962	Please Mr. Columbus (Turn The Ship Around)	Lou Monte	104	CB
02/06/1962	Turn Around, Look At Me	The Lettermen	105	BB
02/06/1962	Na-Ne-No	Troy Shondell	107	BB
02/06/1962	Pretty Suzy Sunshine	Larry Finnegan	127	CB
02/06/1962	Instant Mashed	The Ventures	140	CB
02/06/1962	Red Top	Jerry Mccain	142	CB
09/06/1962	Instant Mashed	The Ventures	104	BB
09/06/1962	Cuore (Don't Suffer My Heart)	Tony Defranco	105	CB
09/06/1962	Please Mr. Columbus (Turn The Ship Around)	Lou Monte	109	BB
09/06/1962	If The Boy Only Knew	Sue Thompson	112	BB
09/06/1962	The Masquerade Is Over	The Five Satins	114	CB
09/06/1962	Potato Peeler	BoBBy Gregg & His Friends	121	CB
09/06/1962	Rome (Wasn't Built In A Day)	Johnnie Taylor	122	CB
09/06/1962	In The Jailhouse Now	Johnny Cash	131	CB
09/06/1962	If The Boy Only Knew	Sue Thompson	143	CB
16/06/1962	Baby Elephant Walk*	Carl Stevens	102	CB
16/06/1962	Everytime (I Think About You) - Part I	Joey Dee And The Starliters	105	BB
16/06/1962	Everybody Loves A Lover	The Angels	113	CB
16/06/1962	The Sound Of The Hammer	Vicki Tasso	118	BB
16/06/1962	A Heartache Named Johnny	Jaye P. Morgan	119	BB
16/06/1962	Our Favorite Melodies	Gary Criss	126	CB
16/06/1962	Dim Dark Corner	Leroy Van Dyke With The Merry Melody Singers	129	CB
16/06/1962	Ching - Ching And A Ding Ding Ding	Hayley Mills	137	CB
16/06/1962	Runaway Pony	Duane Eddy & The Rebels	141	CB
16/06/1962	Loveless Life	Ral Donner	142	CB
16/06/1962	A Little Heartache	Eddy Arnold	143	CB
16/06/1962	Too Late To Worry	Babs Tino	150	CB

23/06/1962	A Little Heartache	Eddy Arnold	103	BB
23/06/1962	Dardanella (Part 1)	Mr. Acker Bilk	105	BB
23/06/1962	Touch Me	Willie Nelson	109	BB
23/06/1962	Little Bitty Big John	Jimmy Dean	110	CB
23/06/1962	Rome (Wasn't Built In A Day)	Johnnie Taylor	112	BB
23/06/1962	I Miss You	The Dreamlovers	115	BB
23/06/1962	Mama, Here Comes The Bride	The Shirelles	115	CB
23/06/1962	Loveless Life	Ral Donner	117	BB
23/06/1962	America	The Arthur Lyman Group	140	CB
23/06/1962	Keep Your Hands In Your Pockets	The Playmates	147	CB
30/06/1962	Trouble's Back In Town	The Wilburn Brothers	101	BB
30/06/1962	Baby Elephant Walk*	Kai Winding & His Orchestra	102	CB
30/06/1962	Poor Little Puppet	Cathy Carroll	102	CB
30/06/1962	Down On The Beach	Ernie Maresca	103	CB
30/06/1962	Nothing New (Same Old Thing)	Fats Domino	104	CB
30/06/1962	You Should'a Treated Me Right	Ike & Tina Turner	105	CB
30/06/1962	Your Heart Belongs To Me	The Supremes	105	CB
30/06/1962	Mary Jane	Ernie Maresca	106	CB
30/06/1962	All Night Long	Sandy Nelson	108	CB
30/06/1962	Dance With Mr. Domino	Fats Domino	108	CB
30/06/1962	Rompin' And Stompin'	Sandy Nelson	108	CB
30/06/1962	Charlie's Shoes	Guy Mitchell	110	BB
30/06/1962	I Wish I Could Cry	Little Willie John	116	BB
30/06/1962	Little Young Lover	The Impressions	130	CB
30/06/1962	Don't Cry, Baby	Aretha Franklin	139	CB
30/06/1962	Charlie's Shoes	Guy Mitchell	143	CB
07/07/1962	A Taste Of Honey*	Eddie Cano	101	CB
07/07/1962	A Taste Of Honey*	Victor Feldman Quartet	101	CB
07/07/1962	Ching-Ching And A Ding Ding Ding	Hayley Mills	118	BB
07/07/1962	House Without Windows	Steve Lawrence	132	CB

07/07/1962	I Can't Forget	Patsy Cline	149	CB
14/07/1962	A Taste Of Honey*	Quincy Jones & His Orchestra	101	CB
14/07/1962	(A Girl Needs) To Love And Be Loved	Vic Dana	102	CB
14/07/1962	Mama, Here Comes The Bride	The Shirelles	104	BB
14/07/1962	This Is It	Jay & The Americans	109	BB
14/07/1962	They Knew About You	George Maharis	111	BB
14/07/1962	Come On Baby	Bruce Channel	113	CB
14/07/1962	Softly As I Leave You	Matt Monro	116	BB
14/07/1962	Don't Let Me Stand In Your Way	Frankie Avalon	117	CB
14/07/1962	I Misunderstood	Wanda Jackson	117	BB
14/07/1962	Sometimes I Wonder	The Drifters	118	CB
14/07/1962	Be Kind	Ronnie & The Hi-Lites	122	CB
14/07/1962	I'm Tossin' And Turnin' Again	BoBBy Lewis	122	CB
14/07/1962	The Boys Kept Hangin' Around	Dorsey Burnette	127	CB
14/07/1962	Soft Walkin'	Freddie Houston	134	CB
14/07/1962	Young At Heart	The Demensions	134	CB
14/07/1962	I'll Come Running Back To You	Roy Hamilton	135	CB
14/07/1962	Goody Goody	Frank Sinatra	136	CB
14/07/1962	Alice	The Four Preps	146	CB
21/07/1962	The Masquerade Is Over	The Five Satins	102	BB
21/07/1962	You're Stronger Than Me	Patsy Cline	107	BB
21/07/1962	Houdini	Walter Brennan	108	CB
21/07/1962	I'll Come Running Back To You	Roy Hamilton	110	BB
21/07/1962	Don't Let Me Stand In Your Way	Frankie Avalon	111	BB
21/07/1962	Don't Worry 'BOUT Me	Vincent Edwards	112	CB
21/07/1962	If You Think	Barbara George	114	BB
21/07/1962	Be Kind	Ronnie And The Hi-Lites	120	BB
21/07/1962	WoBBle Twist	King Curtis & Noble Knights	127	CB
21/07/1962	Callin' Doctor Casey	John D. Loudermilk	137	CB
21/07/1962	They Knew About You	George Maharis	137	CB

21/07/1962	Between The Window And The Phone	Wanda Jackson	141	CB
21/07/1962	Life's Just A Play	Dick & Deedee	142	CB
28/07/1962	Don't Break The Heart That Loves You	Bernie Leighton Piano & Orchestra	101	BB
28/07/1962	Lolita Ya Ya*	Sue Lyon	104	CB
28/07/1962	Three Fools	Patti Page With The Merry Melody Singers	110	CB
28/07/1962	Oh! What It Seemed To Be	The Castells	111	CB
28/07/1962	Don't Break The Heart That Loves You	Bernie Leighton Piano & Orchestra	115	CB
28/07/1962	The Biggest Sin Of All	Connie Francis	116	BB
28/07/1962	You'll Never Know	Jerry Wallace	117	CB
28/07/1962	Sally Was A Good Old Girl	Hank Cochran	128	CB
28/07/1962	The Cure	Smitty Williams	130	CB
04/08/1962	He Hit Me (And It Felt Like A Kiss)	The Crystals	107	CB
04/08/1962	I Want To Be Loved	Dinah Washington	109	CB
04/08/1962	Am I Blue	Dinah Washington	110	CB
04/08/1962	Poetry	Jack Jones	110	CB
04/08/1962	Summertime Guy	Eddie Rambeau	112	CB
04/08/1962	Tennessee Waltz	Damita Jo With The Merry Melody Singers	128	CB
04/08/1962	I'm Climbin' (The Wall)	Adam Wade	137	CB
04/08/1962	Come Back Into My Heart	The Volumes	139	CB
11/08/1962	Come Back Into My Heart	The Volumes	118	BB
11/08/1962	Who's Gonna Pick Up The Pieces	Chuck Jackson	119	BB
11/08/1962	WoBBle Twist	King Curtis And The Noble Knights	119	BB
11/08/1962	I've Got My Eyes On You (And I Like What I See)	Rick Nelson	130	CB
11/08/1962	At The Edge Of Tears	Tony Orlando	146	CB
11/08/1962	Welcome Stranger	Wade Flemons	149	CB
18/08/1962	Comin' Home Baby	Herbie Mann	101	BB
18/08/1962	Copy Cat	Gary (U.S.) Bonds	101	CB
18/08/1962	Lolita Ya Ya*	Nelson Riddle	104	CB
18/08/1962	I Wouldn't Know (What To Do)	Dinah Washington	112	CB
18/08/1962	I'm Gonna Change Everything	Jim Reeves	114	CB

18/08/1962	With The Touch Of Your Hand	Brook Benton	120	BB
18/08/1962	Mama (He Treats Your Daughter Mean)	Ruth Brown With The Milestone Singers	127	CB
18/08/1962	That's The Way It Is	Johnny Mathis	135	CB
18/08/1962	A Mile And A Quarter	Sonny James	137	CB
18/08/1962	Lida Rose	Ferrante & Teicher	144	CB
18/08/1962	Beating Like A Tom Tom	Ernie K-Doe	145	CB
18/08/1962	I Love Paris	Frank Sinatra	148	CB
25/08/1962	Let The Good Times Roll	The Velvets	102	BB
25/08/1962	Abigail	The Embers	104	CB
25/08/1962	409	The Beach Boys	105	CB
25/08/1962	I've Got My Eyes On You (And I Like What I See)	Rick Nelson	105	BB
25/08/1962	Right String But The Wrong Yo-Yo	Dr. Feelgood & The Interns	107	CB
25/08/1962	Send For Me (If You Need Some Lovin')	Barbara George	113	CB
25/08/1962	Handful Of Memories	Baby Washington	116	BB
25/08/1962	Abigail	The Embers	117	BB
25/08/1962	Forgive Me (For Giving You Such A Bad Time)	Babs Tino	117	BB
25/08/1962	I Wanna Thank Your Folks	Johnny Burnette	117	BB
25/08/1962	Elizabeth	Dave Ford & The Hollywood Flames	120	CB
25/08/1962	Waddle, Waddle	The Bracelets	128	CB
25/08/1962	Don't Ever Leave Me	Bob & Earl	133	CB
25/08/1962	Unchained Melody	Conway Twitty	138	CB
25/08/1962	Sweet Little Sixteen	Jerry Lee Lewis	147	CB
25/08/1962	Bonanza!	Johnny Cash	150	CB
01/09/1962	It's Love That Really Counts (In The Long Run)	The Shirelles	103	CB
01/09/1962	Richie	Gloria Dennis	105	CB
01/09/1962	Old Joe Clark	The Kingston Trio	113	BB
01/09/1962	The Old Master Painter	Browns Featuring Jim Edward Brown	118	BB
01/09/1962	(Let's Have A) Beach Party	Dave York & The Beachcombers	119	CB
01/09/1962	Bad Boy	The Donays	126	CB
01/09/1962	Try A Little Tenderness	Aretha Franklin	126	CB

01/09/1962	With The Touch Of Your Hand	Brook Benton	126	CB
01/09/1962	Comin' Home Baby	Herbie Mann	128	CB
01/09/1962	Live It Up	Sandy Nelson	128	CB
01/09/1962	Everybody Loves My Baby	Jimmy Smith	130	CB
01/09/1962	Gee Baby, What About You	Shep & The Limelites	138	CB
01/09/1962	Hey Baby I'm Dancin'	Barry Mann	146	CB
01/09/1962	Dance To The Locomotion	Teddy Randazzo & The Dazzlers	148	CB
08/09/1962	He's A Rebel*	Vikki Carr	102	CB
08/09/1962	Forever And A Day	Jackie Wilson	103	CB
08/09/1962	Chills	Tony Orlando	109	BB
08/09/1962	I Really Don't Want To Know	Solomon Burke	111	CB
08/09/1962	Tijuana Border (Wolverton Mountain)	El Clod	111	BB
08/09/1962	I Sat Back And Let It Happen	Leroy Van Dyke With The Merry Melody Singers	112	CB
08/09/1962	Hail To The Conquering Hero	James Darren	113	CB
08/09/1962	Wonderful One	The Shondells	119	CB
08/09/1962	Party Across The Hall	Yvonne Baker & The Sensations	127	CB
08/09/1962	Make It Be Me	The Flares	136	CB
08/09/1962	My Blue Heaven	The String-A-Longs	143	CB
15/09/1962	Live It Up	Sandy Nelson	101	BB
15/09/1962	Everybody Loves My Baby	Jimmy Smith	107	BB
15/09/1962	Maybe	Clyde Mcphatter	108	CB
15/09/1962	I Do Believe	Clyde Mcphatter	110	CB
15/09/1962	You Can't Lie To A Liar	Ketty Lester	111	CB
15/09/1962	D-O-D-G-E-R-S Song (Oh, Really? No, O'malley)	Danny Kaye	113	CB
15/09/1962	Waddle, Waddle	The Bracelets	113	BB
15/09/1962	Richie	Gloria Dennis	115	BB
15/09/1962	Ol' Man River	Johnny Nash	120	BB
15/09/1962	If It's Love (It's Alright)	Eddie Holland	129	CB
15/09/1962	Limbo Dance	The Champs	130	CB
15/09/1962	The Greatest Actor	Wanda Jackson	134	CB

15/09/1962	Tijuana Border (Wolverton Mountain)	El Clod	135	CB
15/09/1962	Something Precious	Skeeter Davis	136	CB
22/09/1962	Swing Low	Floyd Cramer	101	CB
22/09/1962	Susan	Tobin Matthews	104	CB
22/09/1962	Just For A Thrill	Aretha Franklin	111	BB
22/09/1962	My Heart Stood Still	Bernadette Carroll	111	CB
22/09/1962	How's My Ex Treating You	Jerry Lee Lewis	114	BB
22/09/1962	Tear For Tear	Gene "Duke Of Earl" Chandler	114	CB
22/09/1962	He's A Rebel	Vikki Carr	115	BB
22/09/1962	The Greatest Actor	Wanda Jackson	117	BB
22/09/1962	When My Little Girl Is Smiling	Jimmy Justice	119	CB
22/09/1962	How's My Ex Treating You	Jerry Lee Lewis	125	CB
22/09/1962	Way Over There	The Miracles	129	CB
22/09/1962	I Really Mean It	Trudy Pitts & Mr. Carney	135	CB
22/09/1962	Mashed Potatoes U.S.A.	James Brown & The Famous Flames	138	CB
22/09/1962	Father Knows Best	The Radiants	141	CB
29/09/1962	It's Love That Really Counts (In The Long Run)	The Shirelles	102	BB
29/09/1962	When The Boys Get Together	Joanie Sommers	104	CB
29/09/1962	What'll I Do	Johnny Tillotson	106	BB
29/09/1962	Poor Little Cupid	Joe Dowell With The Stephen Scott Singers	109	CB
29/09/1962	Swing Low	Floyd Cramer	110	BB
29/09/1962	Chills	Tony Orlando	111	CB
29/09/1962	Minstrel And Queen	The Impressions	113	CB
29/09/1962	Naked City Theme	Nelson Riddle	114	CB
29/09/1962	Stop The Clock	Fats Domino	118	CB
29/09/1962	Someday (When I'm Gone From You)	BoBBy Vee & The Crickets	129	CB
29/09/1962	Somewhere In This Town	Bruce Channel	132	CB
29/09/1962	You Know How	BoBBy Darin	135	CB
29/09/1962	If Your Mother Only Knew	Miracles	143	CB
06/10/1962	Why Can't He Be You	Patsy Cline	104	CB

06/10/1962	After Loving You (b-side)	Eddy Arnold	112	BB
06/10/1962	Piddle De Pat	Tommy Roe	118	CB
06/10/1962	Baby, That's All	Jackie Wilson	119	BB
06/10/1962	What Kind Of Fool Am I?	Vic Damone	131	BB
06/10/1962	Under Cover Of The Night	Dave Dudley	141	CB
13/10/1962	Bustin' Surfboards	The Tornadoes	102	BB
13/10/1962	Stop The Clock	Fats Domino	103	BB
13/10/1962	A True, True Love	BoBBy Darin	105	BB
13/10/1962	Maria	George Chakiris	110	BB
13/10/1962	Fiesta	Dave "Baby" Cortez	111	CB
13/10/1962	Right Now	Herbie Mann	111	BB
13/10/1962	Minstrel And Queen	The Impressions	113	BB
13/10/1962	25 Minutes To Go	The Brothers Four	114	CB
13/10/1962	I Found A New Love	The Blue Belles	114	CB
13/10/1962	Midnight Sun	The Five Whispers	115	BB
13/10/1962	Wonderful One	The Shondells	116	BB
13/10/1962	Somewhere In This Town	Bruce Channel	117	BB
13/10/1962	The Look Of Love	Frank Sinatra & His Orchestra	118	CB
13/10/1962	I Found A New Love	The Blue Belles	122	BB
13/10/1962	Please Remember Me	Dick Roman	126	CB
13/10/1962	Boy Trouble	The Rev-Lons	127	CB
13/10/1962	When My Little Girl Is Smiling	Jimmy Justice	127	BB
13/10/1962	Blueberry Hill	The Ramsey Lewis Trio	133	CB
13/10/1962	Sugar Lump	Kenny Williams	137	CB
13/10/1962	Echoes In The Night	The Castells	142	CB
20/10/1962	No One Can Make My Sunshine Smile	The Everly Brothers	102	CB
20/10/1962	I Dig This Station	Gary (U.S.) Bonds	108	CB
20/10/1962	Tear For Tear	Gene "Duke Of Earl" Chandler	114	BB
20/10/1962	The Music From The House Next Door	Toni Fisher	115	CB
20/10/1962	Four Walls	Kay Starr	119	CB

20/10/1962	Hello Out There	Carl Belew	120	BB
20/10/1962	Blue Flame	Billy Vaughn & His Orchestra	123	CB
20/10/1962	Losers Weepers (b-side)	Floyd Cramer	127	BB
20/10/1962	Naked City Theme	Nelson Riddle	130	BB
20/10/1962	Any Other Way	William Bell	131	BB
20/10/1962	Hercules	Frankie Vaughan	141	CB
20/10/1962	Big Blue Diamonds	Little Willie John	148	CB
27/10/1962	I Dig This Station	Gary (U.S.) Bonds	101	BB
27/10/1962	Magic Wand	Don & Juan	103	CB
27/10/1962	Why Can't He Be You	Patsy Cline	103	BB
27/10/1962	The Alley Cat Song	David Thorne	104	CB
27/10/1962	You Won't Forget Me	Jackie Deshannon	104	CB
27/10/1962	Blue Flame	Billy Vaughn And His Orchestra	107	BB
27/10/1962	Slightly Out Of Tune (Desafinado)	Julie London	110	BB
27/10/1962	Desafinado (Slightly Out Of Tune)	Pat Thomas	111	CB
27/10/1962	Desafinado (Slightly Out Of Tune)*	Ella Fitzgerald	111	CB
27/10/1962	Desafinado (Slightly Out Of Tune)*	Julie London	111	CB
27/10/1962	Bluebirds Over The Mountain	The Echoes With The Stephen Scott Singers	112	BB
27/10/1962	Where Do You Come From	Elvis Presley With The Jordanaires	128	CB
27/10/1962	A True, True Love	BoBBy Darin	133	CB
27/10/1962	Maria	George Chakiris	142	CB
27/10/1962	How Do You Fall Out Of Love	Burl Ives	143	CB
27/10/1962	Don't Stop The Wedding	Ann Cole	144	CB
27/10/1962	No More	The Uptones	148	CB
03/11/1962	Getting Ready For The Heartbreak	Chuck Jackson	101	CB
03/11/1962	The Look Of Love	Frank Sinatra And His Orchestra	101	BB
03/11/1962	Piddle De Pat	Tommy Roe	108	BB
03/11/1962	I'm Standing By	Ben E. King	111	BB
03/11/1962	Mind Over Matter (I'm Gonna Make You Mine)	Nolan Strong	112	BB
03/11/1962	Someone (b-side)	Billy Vaughn And His Orchestra	115	BB

03/11/1962	No One Can Make My Sunshine Smile	The Everly Brothers	117	BB
03/11/1962	The Best Man Cried	Clyde Mcphatter	118	BB
03/11/1962	Our Anniversary Of Love	Bob Braun	119	BB
03/11/1962	Day Train	Sandy Nelson	121	CB
03/11/1962	I'm Standing By	Ben E. King	123	CB
03/11/1962	Our Anniversary Of Love	Bob Braun	144	CB
03/11/1962	Cleo's Mood	Jr. Walker All Stars	145	CB
10/11/1962	This Land Is Your Land	The New Christy Minstrels	102	CB
10/11/1962	This Land Is Your Land*	Ketty Lester	102	CB
10/11/1962	Tomorrow Night	B.B. King	106	BB
10/11/1962	Little Girl	Dion	107	CB
10/11/1962	The Best Man Cried	Clyde Mcphatter	107	CB
10/11/1962	Volare	Ace Cannon & His Alto-Sax	107	BB
10/11/1962	Come To Me	Richard "Popcorn" Wylie	108	CB
10/11/1962	Sunrise Serenade	Willie Mitchell	111	CB
10/11/1962	Again	The Lettermen	120	BB
10/11/1962	Kiss Tomorrow Goodbye	Danny White	120	BB
10/11/1962	Hey, Good Lookin'	Connie Stevens	134	CB
10/11/1962	Theme From Northern Lights	Lister Shaw	134	CB
10/11/1962	Building Memories	Bob Beckham	140	CB
10/11/1962	To Whom It May Concern	BoBBy Bare	141	CB
10/11/1962	The Searching Is Over	Joe Henderson	149	CB
17/11/1962	Desafinado (Slightly Out Of Tune)	Ella Fitzgerald	102	BB
17/11/1962	Here I Am	Chip Taylor	113	BB
17/11/1962	Gotta Travel On	The Springfields	114	BB
17/11/1962	I Don't Believe I'll Fall In Love Today	BoBBy Bare	118	BB
17/11/1962	Under Your Spell Again	Lloyd Price	119	CB
17/11/1962	School Bells Are Ringing	Carole King	123	BB
17/11/1962	Under Your Spell Again	Lloyd Price	123	BB
17/11/1962	Black Cloud	Leroy Van Dyke With The Merry Melody Singers	125	CB

17/11/1962	(The Story Of) The In-Between Years	James Macarthur	132	CB
17/11/1962	I'm Gonna Get Him	Vicki Belmonte	137	CB
17/11/1962	Cold, Cold Heart	Dinah Washington	140	CB
17/11/1962	To Love	Ral Donner	140	CB
17/11/1962	Blues Stay Away From Me	Pat & Shirley Boone	142	CB
17/11/1962	Break Down And Cry	Fabian	144	CB
17/11/1962	The Submarine Race	The Visuals	147	CB
24/11/1962	My Man - He's A Loving Man	Betty Lavett	101	BB
24/11/1962	Here I Am	Chip Taylor	102	CB
24/11/1962	Hey, Good Lookin'	Connie Stevens	104	BB
24/11/1962	The Ballad Of Lover's Hill	Teresa Brewer With The Milestone Singers	118	CB
24/11/1962	Walkin' Through A Cemetery	Claudine Clark	122	CB
24/11/1962	I Feel Good All Over	The Fiestas	123	BB
24/11/1962	Happy Trumpeter	Bert Kaempfert & His Orchestra	128	CB
24/11/1962	Three Hearts In A Tangle	James Brown & The Famous Flames	128	CB
24/11/1962	The One Rose (That's Left In My Heart)	Bob Willow	129	CB
24/11/1962	Stupidity	The Van Dykes	133	CB
24/11/1962	The River Took My Baby	Dick & Deedee	138	CB
01/12/1962	Go Tiger, Go!	Guy Mitchell	101	BB
01/12/1962	Joey's Song	The Untouchable Sound Bill Black's Combo	101	CB
01/12/1962	Cast Your Fate To The Wind*	Martin Denny & His Orchestra	104	CB
01/12/1962	Big Noise From Winnetka Part I	Cozy Cole	105	CB
01/12/1962	Gonna Raise A Rukus Tonight	Jimmy Dean	105	CB
01/12/1962	Too Strong To Be Strung Along	The Marvelettes	106	CB
01/12/1962	Theme From Taras Bulba (The Wishing Star)	Jerry Butler	107	CB
01/12/1962	Theme From Taras Bulba (The Wishing Star)*	Ferrante & Teicher	107	CB
01/12/1962	Anonymous Phone Call	BoBBy Vee With The Johnny Mann Singers	108	CB
01/12/1962	The Longest Day	Mitch Miller With His Orchestra And Chorus	109	BB
01/12/1962	Paradise	The Temptations	122	BB
01/12/1962	Go Tiger, Go!	Guy Mitchell	123	CB

01/12/1962	Cast Your Fate To The Wind	Martin Denny	124	BB
01/12/1962	Does He Mean That Much To You?	Eddy Arnold	136	CB
01/12/1962	Watermelon Walk	The Five Counts	139	CB
01/12/1962	The Telephone Game	Claudine Clark	141	CB
08/12/1962	There'll Be No Teardrops Tonight	Adam Wade	104	BB
08/12/1962	Theme From Taras Bulba (The Wishing Star)*	Maxine Starr	107	CB
08/12/1962	The Cinnamon Cinder (It's A Very Nice Dance)	The Cinders	108	CB
08/12/1962	I've Got The World By The Tail	Claude King	111	BB
08/12/1962	Let Me Entertain You	Ray Anthony	113	CB
08/12/1962	Theme From Taras Bulba (The Wishing Star)	Ferrante & Teicher	116	BB
08/12/1962	Sailor Boy	Cathy Carr	120	CB
08/12/1962	Welcome Home	Frankie Avalon	129	BB
08/12/1962	Let Me Do It My Way	Jo Ann Campbell	131	CB
08/12/1962	Paradise	The Temptations	135	CB
08/12/1962	Welcome Home	Frankie Avalon	136	CB
08/12/1962	Angela Jones	John D. Loudermilk	137	CB
08/12/1962	Hands Across The Table	Fats Domino	141	CB
15/12/1962	Hush Heart	Baby Washington	102	BB
15/12/1962	Red Pepper I	Roosevelt Fountain & Pens Of Rhythm	103	CB
15/12/1962	Do You Hear What I Hear?	Harry Simeone Chorale	106	CB
15/12/1962	Mexican Joe	Pat Boone	112	CB
15/12/1962	My Coloring Book*	Barbra Streisand	112	CB
15/12/1962	Joey's Song	Bill Black's Combo	114	BB
15/12/1962	Somewhere	The Escorts	119	CB
15/12/1962	The (Bossa Nova) Bird	The Dells	123	CB
15/12/1962	Stardust Bossa Nova (b-side)	Ella Fitzgerald	129	BB
15/12/1962	Matilda	The String-A-Longs	133	BB
15/12/1962	Rainbow	Tommy Roe	143	CB
15/12/1962	Kentucky Means Paradise	The Green River Boys Featuring Glen Campbell	144	CB
15/12/1962	Matilda	The String-A-Longs	144	CB

15/12/1962	Book Of Songs	The Ly-Dells	146	CB
15/12/1962	How Do You Speak To An Angel	Etta James	146	CB
22/12/1962	Acapulco 1922	The Tijuana Brass Featuring Herb Alpert	102	CB
22/12/1962	Big Girls Don't Cry Limbo	David Carroll And His Orchestra	102	BB
22/12/1962	What Good Am I Without You?	Jackie Wilson	103	CB
22/12/1962	I've Got The World By The Tail	Claude King	105	CB
22/12/1962	Please Come Home For Christmas	Charles Brown	108	BB
22/12/1962	Baby's First Christmas	Connie Francis	113	BB
22/12/1962	Look At Me	Dobie Gray	114	CB
22/12/1962	You're Gonna Need Me	Barbara Lynn	114	CB
22/12/1962	Trouble In Mind	Aretha Franklin	124	CB
22/12/1962	These Golden Rings	Jive Five With Eugene Pitt	130	CB
22/12/1962	Never Let You Go	Five Discs	141	CB
22/12/1962	The Loneliest Girl In Town	Linda Scott	145	CB
29/12/1962	Miserlou	Dick Dale & The Del-Tones	102	CB
29/12/1962	Sailor Boy	Cathy Carr	103	BB
29/12/1962	Spanish Twist	The Roller Coasters	105	CB
29/12/1962	Let The Four Wings Blow	Sandy Nelson	107	BB
29/12/1962	Guilty	The Crests	108	CB
29/12/1962	Come To Me	Richard "Popcorn" Wylie	109	BB
29/12/1962	Kentucky Means Paradise	The Green River Boys Featuring Glen Campbell	114	BB
29/12/1962	Little White Lies	The Kenjolairs	116	BB
29/12/1962	Town Crier	Tommy Roe	121	CB
29/12/1962	Let The Four Winds Blow	Sandy Nelson	123	CB
29/12/1962	Hula Hula Dancin' Doll	Trade Martin	133	CB
29/12/1962	I Found A New Baby	BoBBy Darin	133	CB
29/12/1962	The Pickup	Conway Twitty	136	CB
05/01/1963	M.G. Blues	Jimmy Mcgriff	102	CB
05/01/1963	White Levis (Tennis Shoes - Surfin' Hat And Big Plaid Pendleton Shirt)	The Majorettes	103	CB
05/01/1963	How Do You Speak To An Angel	Etta James	109	BB

05/01/1963	Walk Right In	The Moments	110	CB
05/01/1963	That Certain Party	Bent Fabric And His Piano	117	BB
05/01/1963	What Good Am I Without You?	Jackie Wilson	121	BB
05/01/1963	Good Golly Miss Molly	Jerry Lee Lewis	140	CB
12/01/1963	Go Home Girl	Arthur Alexander	102	BB
12/01/1963	Mama-Oom-Mow-Mow (The Bird)	The Rivingtons	106	BB
12/01/1963	Mama Didn't Lie	The Fascinations	108	BB
12/01/1963	Nobody But Me	The Isley Brothers	109	CB
12/01/1963	Anonymous Phone Call	BoBBy Vee With The Johnny Mann Singers	110	BB
12/01/1963	Magic Star (Tel-Star)	Margie Singleton	110	CB
12/01/1963	Mama-Oom-Mow-Mow (The Bird)	The Rivingtons	111	CB
12/01/1963	Don't Take Her From Me	Kris Jensen	112	BB
12/01/1963	Comes Love	The Skyliners	119	CB
12/01/1963	Go Home Girl	Arthur Alexander	120	CB
12/01/1963	Kiss Tomorrow Goodbye	Danny White	123	CB
12/01/1963	Someone Somewhere	Junior Parker	136	CB
12/01/1963	Help Me Pick Up The Pieces	Joey Dee	148	CB
19/01/1963	The Same Old Hurt	Burl Ives	103	CB
19/01/1963	Zing! Went The Strings Of My Heart	The Furys	108	CB
19/01/1963	Telephone (Won't You Ring)	Shelley Fabares	109	BB
19/01/1963	Maybe You'll Be There	Billy And The Essentials	117	BB
19/01/1963	The Lone Teen Ranger	Jerry Landis	119	CB
19/01/1963	Tell Daddy	Ben E. King	122	BB
19/01/1963	Flapjacks - Part I	Googie Rene & His Combo	123	CB
19/01/1963	Fly Me To The Moon (In Other Words)	Mark Murphy	123	BB
19/01/1963	Any Other Way	Jackie Shane	124	BB
19/01/1963	Gonna Take A Chance	Tommy Roe	125	CB
19/01/1963	I Believe	Dick Stewart	126	CB
19/01/1963	Bonnie Do	Johnny Cooper	129	CB
19/01/1963	First Star	Frankie Love	140	CB

19/01/1963	Good Buddies	The Crawford Brothers (Johnny & BoBBy)	140	CB
19/01/1963	Baby, You're Driving Me Crazy	Joey Dee	143	CB
19/01/1963	Carrying That Load	Ray Charles	145	CB
19/01/1963	Don't Cry Donna	Tommy Roe	145	CB
26/01/1963	Half Time	The Routers	103	CB
26/01/1963	Nobody But Me	The Isley Brothers	106	BB
26/01/1963	Slop Time	The Sherrys	112	CB
26/01/1963	Only You (And You Alone)	Mr. Acker Bilk	114	CB
26/01/1963	Mr. Cool	The Champs	116	CB
26/01/1963	Four Letter Man	Freddy Cannon	117	CB
26/01/1963	Big Noise From Winnetka Part I	Cozy Cole	121	BB
26/01/1963	Magic Star (Tel-Star)	Margie Singleton	124	BB
26/01/1963	Anyone But Her	Joni James	126	CB
26/01/1963	Cool Water	The Blue Belles	127	BB
26/01/1963	Afraid	Jimmie Rodgers	143	CB
26/01/1963	Faded Love	Jackie Deshannon	144	CB
02/02/1963	Theme From Lawrence Of Arabia	Ferrante & Teicher	102	CB
02/02/1963	Is This Me?	Jim Reeves	103	BB
02/02/1963	The Bossa Nova Watusi Twist	Freddy King	103	BB
02/02/1963	Castaway	Hayley Mills	111	CB
02/02/1963	Mr. Cool	The Champs	111	BB
02/02/1963	Feelin' Sad	Ray Charles	113	BB
02/02/1963	I'm Sorry, Pillow	Lee Andrews	113	CB
02/02/1963	The Bird	The Dutones	117	CB
02/02/1963	Guilty	The Crests	123	BB
02/02/1963	Mama Didn't Lie	The Fasinations	125	CB
02/02/1963	Don't Wait Too Long	Erma Franklin	132	CB
02/02/1963	Denver	The New Christy Minstrels	137	CB
02/02/1963	Tell Daddy	Ben E. King	138	CB
09/02/1963	Shirley	Tony Orlando	109	CB

09/02/1963	Am I That Easy To Forget	Esther Phillips	112	BB
09/02/1963	I'm The One Who Loves You	The Impressions	116	CB
09/02/1963	Marlene	The Concords	117	CB
09/02/1963	Four Letter Man	Freddy Cannon	121	BB
16/02/1963	Pretty Boy Lonely	Patti Page	101	CB
16/02/1963	The Bird	The Dutones	101	BB
16/02/1963	Those Eyes	Fats Domino	105	CB
16/02/1963	Little Star	BoBBy Callender	112	CB
16/02/1963	Half Time	The Routers	115	BB
16/02/1963	Don't Let Me Cross Over	Adam Wade	117	BB
16/02/1963	Our Songs Of Love	The Love Notes	127	CB
16/02/1963	Comes Love	The Skyliners	128	BB
23/02/1963	Paradise	April Stevens & Nino Tempo	102	CB
23/02/1963	Don't Let Me Cross Over*	Adam Wade	105	CB
23/02/1963	The Brightest Smile In Town	Ray Charles & His Orchestra	108	CB
23/02/1963	Just A Simple Melody	Patti Page	109	CB
23/02/1963	Tore Up	Harmonica Fats	111	CB
23/02/1963	She'll Never Never Love You (Like I Do)	Teresa Brewer	113	CB
23/02/1963	Just A Simple Melody	Patti Page	114	BB
23/02/1963	Anything You Can Do	The Majors	117	BB
23/02/1963	Cool Water	The Blue Belles	119	CB
23/02/1963	Like Locomotion	The Tornadoes	119	BB
23/02/1963	L-O-V-E (Love)	The Emotions	119	CB
23/02/1963	Face In A Crowd	Jimmie Rodgers	129	BB
23/02/1963	Them Terrible Boots	The Orlons	130	CB
23/02/1963	Peanuts	The 4 Seasons	131	CB
23/02/1963	Shirley	Tony Orlando	133	BB
23/02/1963	I'll Release You	Ted Taylor	134	BB
23/02/1963	Gentleman Jim	Bert Kaempfert & His Orchestra	139	CB
23/02/1963	Teenage Wedding	Annette	144	CB

23/02/1963	Changing World	Dick Roman	146	CB
02/03/1963	Sax Fifth Avenue*	The Jack Cole Quintet	106	CB
02/03/1963	Seagrams	The Viceroys	108	CB
02/03/1963	I'm Not Jimmy	Ray Peterson	113	CB
02/03/1963	The Yellow Bandana	Faron Young With The Merry Melody Singers	114	BB
02/03/1963	Don't Fence Me In	George Maharis	121	CB
02/03/1963	Heartache Oh Heartache	The Lettermen	122	BB
02/03/1963	Baby Doll	Carlo	123	BB
02/03/1963	Hum Diddy Doo	Fats Domino	124	BB
02/03/1963	Denver	The New Christy Minstrels	127	BB
02/03/1963	Softly In The Night	The Cookies	127	CB
02/03/1963	Our Love Will Last	Arthur Prysock	128	BB
02/03/1963	Dear Waste Basket	BoBBy Bare	130	CB
02/03/1963	I'm A Soldier Boy	Dee Clark	133	CB
02/03/1963	Pretoria	The Highwaymen	138	CB
02/03/1963	Do Unto Others	Vernon Harrel	140	CB
02/03/1963	I Wanna Be Your Lover	Diane Emond	140	CB
02/03/1963	Matilda	The Ron-Dels	143	CB
02/03/1963	Diary Of Our Love	The Premeers	147	CB
09/03/1963	Teenager's Dad	Marty RoBBins	106	CB
09/03/1963	Days Of Wine And Roses	Pat Boone	117	BB
09/03/1963	Never	The Earls	119	BB
09/03/1963	Words	Solomon Burke	120	CB
09/03/1963	Waiting For Billy	Connie Francis	127	BB
09/03/1963	Laugh And The World Laughs With You	Jack Scott	130	CB
09/03/1963	Face In A Crowd	Jimmie Rodgers	136	CB
09/03/1963	(Let's Do) The Limbo	Chris Montez	142	CB
09/03/1963	Burning Desire	Wade Ray	145	CB
16/03/1963	The Fool	Jamie Coe	101	CB
16/03/1963	Hambone	Red Saunders & His Orchestra With Dolores Hawkins & The	103	CB

16/03/1963	The Rosy Dance	Johnny Thunder	104	CB
16/03/1963	Nancy's Minuet	The Everly Brothers	116	CB
16/03/1963	Words	Solomon Burke	121	BB
16/03/1963	She'll Never Never Love You (Like I Do)	Teresa Brewer	122	BB
16/03/1963	Shook Up Over You	Dee Clark	125	BB
16/03/1963	The Wayward Wind	Frank Ifield	125	CB
16/03/1963	There's No End	Ed Townsend	129	CB
16/03/1963	Hello Wall No. 2	Ben Colder	131	BB
16/03/1963	Face In A Crowd*	Dean Martin	136	CB
16/03/1963	Contract On Love	Little Stevie Wonder	137	CB
16/03/1963	I Got Burned	Ral Donner	139	CB
23/03/1963	Struttin' With Maria	Herb Alpert's Tijuana Brass	102	BB
23/03/1963	Prima Donna	Glen Campbell	103	BB
23/03/1963	Tore Up	Harmonica Fats	103	BB
23/03/1963	Peanuts [EP] (Peanuts/Never On Sunday/I Can't Give You Anything	The 4 Seasons	115	BB
23/03/1963	Turn Back	Jerry Jackson	115	CB
23/03/1963	Watermelon Man	Herbie Hancock	121	BB
23/03/1963	Tonight I Met An Angel	The Tokens	126	BB
23/03/1963	Work Out	Michael Clark	130	BB
23/03/1963	Any Way You Wanta	Harvey (Formerly Of The Moonglows)	131	BB
23/03/1963	Work Out	Michael Clark	132	CB
23/03/1963	My Little Girl	The Crickets	133	CB
23/03/1963	My Little Girl	The Crickets	134	BB
23/03/1963	Since I Met You Baby	Ace Cannon	134	CB
23/03/1963	Prima Donna	Glen Campbell	141	CB
23/03/1963	Here Comes The Hurt	Gayle Harris	142	CB
30/03/1963	Little Bird	The Pete Jolly Trio & Friends	102	CB
30/03/1963	The Wayward Wind	Frank Ifield	104	BB
30/03/1963	I Can Take A Hint	The Miracles	107	BB
30/03/1963	Nancy's Minuet	The Everly Brothers	107	BB

30/03/1963	Walkin' After Midnight	Patsy Cline	108	BB
30/03/1963	Skip To M'limbo	The Ventures	114	BB
30/03/1963	(So It Was...So It Is) So It Will Always Be (b-side)	The Everly Brothers	116	BB
30/03/1963	Skip To M' Limbo	The Ventures	120	CB
30/03/1963	Please Don't	Kitty Kallen	121	BB
30/03/1963	I Can Take A Hint	The Miracles	122	CB
30/03/1963	Play Those Oldies, Mr. Dee Jay	Anthony & The Sophomores	122	CB
30/03/1963	The Rosy Dance	Johnny Thunder	122	BB
30/03/1963	I Got Burned	Ral Donner	124	BB
30/03/1963	Baby Come Home To Me	Burl Ives	125	CB
30/03/1963	Paradise	April Stevens & Nino Tempo	126	BB
30/03/1963	Insult To Injury	Timi Yuro	127	CB
30/03/1963	Seagrams	The Viceroys	127	BB
30/03/1963	Face In A Crowd	Dean Martin	128	BB
30/03/1963	Half A Man	Willie Nelson	129	BB
30/03/1963	If You Want It (I've Got It)	"Little Esther" Phillips & "Big Al" Downing	129	BB
30/03/1963	She's New To You	Molly Bee	129	CB
30/03/1963	She's New To You	Molly Bee	130	BB
30/03/1963	Teardrop By Teardrop	Gene Pitney	130	BB
30/03/1963	What's Wrong Bill	Sue Thompson	135	BB
30/03/1963	Dance What You Wanna	Johnnie Taylor	140	CB
06/04/1963	You Should Have Been There	The Fleetwoods	107	CB
06/04/1963	Lonesome 7-7203	Hawkshaw Hawkins	108	BB
06/04/1963	Whatever You Want	Jerry Butler	114	CB
06/04/1963	Blue	Jack Reno	115	CB
06/04/1963	Crying In The Chapel	Little Richard	119	BB
06/04/1963	Since I Don't Have You [EP] (Since I Don't Have You/Alone/Why Do	The 4 Seasons	123	BB
06/04/1963	This Ole House	Jimmy Dean	126	CB
06/04/1963	This Ole House	Jimmy Dean	128	BB
06/04/1963	My Heart Can't Take It No More	The Supremes	129	BB

06/04/1963	Teenage Dream	The Ramadas	141	CB
06/04/1963	Where You Goin', Little Boy?	Zip & The Zippers	145	CB
13/04/1963	No Letter Today	Ray Charles And His Orchestra	105	BB
13/04/1963	One Among The Many	Ned Miller	111	CB
13/04/1963	Bill Bailey, Won't You Please Come Home (Live)	Ella Fitzgerald	113	CB
13/04/1963	Sandra	The Volumes	113	CB
13/04/1963	They Should Have Given You The Oscar	James Darren	114	CB
13/04/1963	You Should Have Been There	The Fleetwoods	114	BB
13/04/1963	He's So Heavenly	Brenda Lee	119	CB
13/04/1963	Arabia	The Delcos	123	CB
13/04/1963	Baby Come Home To Me	Burl Ives	131	BB
13/04/1963	Two Of Us	Robert Goulet	132	BB
13/04/1963	On The Trail	Roger Williams	140	CB
20/04/1963	Arabia	The Delcos	111	BB
20/04/1963	Back In Baby's Arms	Patsy Cline	113	CB
20/04/1963	Crazy Arms	Marion Worth	122	CB
20/04/1963	The Shampoo	Les Mccann	122	BB
20/04/1963	Everybody South Street	The Four-Evers	125	BB
20/04/1963	Hot Cakes! 1st Serving	Dave "Baby" Cortez	125	CB
20/04/1963	Cry On My Shoulder	Johnny Crawford	126	BB
20/04/1963	Rain	Jive Five	128	BB
20/04/1963	Cotton Fields (The Cotton Song)	Arthur Lyman Group	129	BB
20/04/1963	Since I Met You Baby	Ace Cannon	130	BB
20/04/1963	These Tears	Jan Bradley	133	CB
20/04/1963	Take All The Kisses	Ann-Margret	142	CB
20/04/1963	Mr. Fix-It	Jimmy Jones	143	CB
20/04/1963	Garbage Can	Les Cooper & The Soulrockers	144	CB
20/04/1963	On A Merry-Go-Round	Jerry Wallace	150	CB
27/04/1963	Bo Diddley	Buddy Holly	102	CB
27/04/1963	You Always Hurt The One You Love	Fats Domino	102	BB

27/04/1963	Love Will Find A Way	Sam Cooke	105	BB
27/04/1963	Since I Don't Have You	The 4 Seasons	106	CB
27/04/1963	Lonesome 7-7203	Hawkshaw Hawkins	110	CB
27/04/1963	Pearl Pearl Pearl	Lester Flatt, Earl Scruggs And The Foggy Mountain Boys	113	BB
27/04/1963	Bo Diddley	Buddy Holly	116	BB
27/04/1963	Portobello Sunset	Robert Mersey & His Orchestra	118	CB
27/04/1963	Tra La La	The Majors	118	CB
27/04/1963	Cu Cu Rru Cu Cu Paloma	Nancy Ames	120	CB
27/04/1963	R.P.M.	The Four Speeds	124	CB
27/04/1963	True Love Ways	Buddy Holly	124	CB
27/04/1963	Dear (Here Comes My Baby)	Toni Jones	125	CB
27/04/1963	Island Of Dreams	The Springfields	129	BB
27/04/1963	My Father's Voice	Judy Lynn	136	CB
27/04/1963	This Is All I Ask	Gordon Jenkins & His Orchestra	139	CB
27/04/1963	Crying In The Chapel	Little Richard	141	CB
27/04/1963	What A Dream	Gary (U.S.) Bonds	145	CB
04/05/1963	If You Don't Love Me	Junior Parker	101	BB
04/05/1963	I Know Better	The Flamingos	107	BB
04/05/1963	Little Bird	The Pete Jolly Trio And Friends	112	BB
04/05/1963	On The Trail	Roger Williams	113	BB
04/05/1963	Bo Diddley	Ronnie Hawkins	117	BB
04/05/1963	Pearl Pearl Pearl	Lester Flatt, Earl Scruggs & Foggy Mountain Boys	119	CB
04/05/1963	You Never Miss Your Water (Till The Well Runs Dry)	"Little Esther" Phillips & "Big Al" Downing	120	CB
04/05/1963	Bo Diddley	Ronnie Hawkins	121	CB
04/05/1963	Be Ever Wonderful	Ted Taylor And His Band	123	BB
04/05/1963	You'll Need Another Favor	Little Johnny Taylor	125	BB
04/05/1963	Soulville	Dinah Washington	126	CB
04/05/1963	Hard Head	Louis Jordan And His Tympany Five	128	BB
04/05/1963	(These Are) The Young Years	Floyd Cramer	129	BB
04/05/1963	Loved	Bill Pursell	130	CB

04/05/1963	Mess Around	Scotty Mckay	134	CB
04/05/1963	Cleopatra	Frankie Avalon	139	CB
04/05/1963	Trouble Blues	Fats Domino	144	CB
04/05/1963	Check Yourself	Gene Chandler	146	CB
11/05/1963	Saturday Night	The Sherrys	101	CB
11/05/1963	Tamoure'	Bill Justis	101	BB
11/05/1963	King Of The Surf Guitar	Dick Dale & The Del-Tones	110	CB
11/05/1963	Saturday Night	The Sherrys	116	BB
11/05/1963	Tamoure'	Bill Justis & Orchestra	116	CB
11/05/1963	All I Want To Do Is Run	The Elektras	125	CB
11/05/1963	Be Ever Wonderful	Ted Taylor & His Band	125	CB
11/05/1963	I Know Better	The Flamingos	126	CB
11/05/1963	No Bail In This Jail (Prisoner In Love)	The Ikettes	126	BB
11/05/1963	Let Go	Roy Hamilton	129	BB
11/05/1963	When I Fall In Love	Johnny Crawford	129	CB
11/05/1963	Dear Heart	Teddy Randazzo	131	CB
11/05/1963	If You Don't Love Me	Junior Parker	140	CB
11/05/1963	I'm Not Ready Yet	Marty RoBBins	140	CB
11/05/1963	Sometimes I Get Lonely	The Cotillions Feat. Gwen Richards	143	CB
11/05/1963	Nobody's Darlin' But Mine	WeBB Pierce	147	CB
18/05/1963	All I See Is Blue	Jack Scott	102	CB
18/05/1963	The Last Minute (Pt. I)	Jimmy Mcgriff	110	CB
18/05/1963	More (Theme From The Film "Mondo Cane")	Steve Lawrence	113	CB
18/05/1963	Bossa Nova Italiano	Lou Monte	115	CB
18/05/1963	Chariot (I Will Follow You)	Joe Sentieri (Ricordi Orchestra)	115	CB
18/05/1963	You're The Only One Can Hurt Me	Connie Francis	116	CB
18/05/1963	You'll Need Another Favor	Little Johnny Taylor	117	CB
18/05/1963	I Want A Love I Can See	The Temptations	124	CB
18/05/1963	Dear Teresa	Jerry Fuller	135	CB
18/05/1963	Pledge Of A Fool	The Barons	138	CB

25/05/1963	Sad, Sad Girl And Boy	The Impressions	104	CB
25/05/1963	It's Been Nice (Goodnight)	The Everly Brothers	114	CB
25/05/1963	Tears Of Joy	Chuck Jackson	116	CB
25/05/1963	I Know I Know	"Pookie" Hudson	117	CB
25/05/1963	Lovers	The Blendtones	118	BB
25/05/1963	Check Yourself	Gene Chandler	119	BB
25/05/1963	Loved	Bill Pursell	121	BB
25/05/1963	Charmaine	The Bachelors	123	CB
25/05/1963	Susie	Sue Thompson	127	CB
25/05/1963	Happy Cowboy	Billy Vaughn & His Orchestra	131	CB
25/05/1963	No Big Thing	The Royalettes	140	CB
25/05/1963	I Gotta Tell Her Now	The Duprees Featuring Joey Vann	141	CB
25/05/1963	Chittlins Con Carne, Part I	Kenny Burrell	144	CB
25/05/1963	True Confession	Sue Thompson	148	CB
01/06/1963	It's Been Nice (Goodnight)	The Everly Brothers	101	BB
01/06/1963	I Will Never Turn My Back On You	Chuck Jackson	110	BB
01/06/1963	More, Theme From "MONDO Cane"	Martin Denny	113	CB
01/06/1963	Will You Be My Baby	BoBBy Rydell	114	BB
01/06/1963	My Teenage Castle (Is Tumblin' Down)	Little Peggy March	121	CB
01/06/1963	Can't Go On Without You	Fats Domino	123	BB
01/06/1963	I'm Walkin'	Patti Page	127	BB
01/06/1963	Bossa Nova Italiano	Lou Monte	128	BB
01/06/1963	Underneath The Arches	Mr. Acker Bilk With The Leon Young String Chorale	129	CB
01/06/1963	Jailer, Bring Me Water	Johnny Thunder	132	CB
01/06/1963	No Signs Of Loneliness Here	Marty RoBBins	132	CB
01/06/1963	Just Walking In The Rain	Jerry Wallace	139	CB
01/06/1963	Tender	Diane Renay	143	CB
01/06/1963	Home In Your Heart	Solomon Burke	148	CB
08/06/1963	Kentucky	Bob Moore And His Orchestra	101	BB
08/06/1963	I'm The Boss	Burl Ives	110	CB

08/06/1963	King Of The Surf Guitar	Dick Dale And The Del-Tones	124	BB
08/06/1963	Distant Drums	Roy Orbison	130	CB
08/06/1963	Here's Where I Came In (Here's Where I Walk Out)	Aretha Franklin	150	CB
15/06/1963	Come Blow Your Horn	Frank Sinatra	108	BB
15/06/1963	Lovers	The Blendtones	108	CB
15/06/1963	My Best Friend	Orlons	112	CB
15/06/1963	More (Theme From "Mondo Cane")*	Della Reese	113	CB
15/06/1963	Yeh-Yeh!	Mongo Santamaria Orchestra	114	CB
15/06/1963	Get Him	The Exciters	115	CB
15/06/1963	The Peking Theme (So Little Time)	Andy Williams	115	BB
15/06/1963	My One And Only Love	Joe Harnell & His Orchestra	119	CB
15/06/1963	The Ninth Wave	The Ventures	122	BB
15/06/1963	Charmaine	The Four Preps	123	CB
15/06/1963	I Cried	Tammy Montgomery	123	CB
15/06/1963	We're Only Young Once	Bunny Paul	126	CB
15/06/1963	Hot Potato (Part 1)	The Rinkydinks	128	CB
15/06/1963	To Love Or Not To Love	Barbara Lynn	135	BB
15/06/1963	Manhattan Spiritual	Santo & Johnny	149	CB
22/06/1963	Little Dancing Doll	Shelby Flint	102	CB
22/06/1963	True Love	Richard Chamberlain	102	CB
22/06/1963	Love Is A Once In A Lifetime Thing	Dick & Deedee	103	BB
22/06/1963	A Long Vacation	Rick Nelson	107	CB
22/06/1963	River's Invitation	Percy Mayfield	109	CB
22/06/1963	Eyes	The Earls	111	CB
22/06/1963	More*	Danny Williams	113	CB
22/06/1963	More (Theme From The Film "Mondo Cane")	Steve Lawrence	117	BB
22/06/1963	Sands Of Gold	WeBB Pierce	117	CB
22/06/1963	Love Is A Once In A Lifetime Thing	Dick & Deedee	121	CB
22/06/1963	Guilty	Jim Reeves	122	CB
22/06/1963	Allentown Jail	The Lettermen	123	BB

22/06/1963	Goodbye My Lover Goodbye	Robert Mosley	123	CB
22/06/1963	Poor Boy	Jimmy Holiday	124	BB
22/06/1963	Here's Where I Came In (Here's Where I Walk Out) (b-side)	Aretha Franklin	125	BB
22/06/1963	All I Want To Do Is Run	The Elektras	126	BB
22/06/1963	Happy Cowboy	Billy Vaughn And His Orchestra	131	BB
22/06/1963	Soul City	Pervis Herder	131	CB
22/06/1963	How Do You Do It?	Gerry & The Pacemakers	132	CB
22/06/1963	Same Old Song	Joe South	133	CB
22/06/1963	Out Ridin'	Steve Rowland & The Ring Leaders	141	CB
22/06/1963	King Without A Queen	Dion	143	CB
22/06/1963	I Almost Lost My Mind	Jerry Butler	146	CB
29/06/1963	Breakwater	Lawrence Welk & His Orchestra	101	CB
29/06/1963	Where Can You Go (For A Broken Heart)	George Maharis	102	BB
29/06/1963	Baja	The Astronauts	105	CB
29/06/1963	Antony And Cleopatra Theme	Ferrante & Teicher	115	CB
29/06/1963	Charmaine	The Four Preps	116	BB
29/06/1963	Janie Is Her Name	Roger Williams	118	CB
29/06/1963	Sands Of Gold	WeBB Pierce	118	BB
29/06/1963	What A Fool I've Been	Carla Thomas	118	CB
29/06/1963	A Long Vacation	Rick Nelson	120	BB
29/06/1963	Anthony And Cleopatra Theme	Alex North	120	CB
29/06/1963	Mack The Knife	Erroll Garner	139	CB
29/06/1963	Somewhere In The Night (Naked City Theme)	Teri Thornton	139	CB
29/06/1963	The Ninth Wave	The Ventures	144	CB
06/07/1963	Cross Roads (Part 1)	Luther Randolph & Johnny Stiles	109	BB
06/07/1963	I'm The Boss	Burl Ives	111	BB
06/07/1963	Scarlet O'hara	BoBBy Gregg	112	BB
06/07/1963	Say It Isn't So	Aretha Franklin	113	BB
06/07/1963	If You Don't Come Back	The Drifters	116	CB
06/07/1963	In My Tenement	Jackie Shane	122	CB

06/07/1963	Eyes	The Earls	123	BB
06/07/1963	La Bamba (Part I) (Live)	Trini Lopez	123	CB
06/07/1963	Don't Let The Sun Catch You Crying	Steve Alaimo	126	CB
06/07/1963	Kiss And Run	Tommy Roe	137	CB
06/07/1963	Green Monkey	Garnell Cooper & The Kinfolks	139	CB
06/07/1963	Mr. Blah Blah	Ray Barretto & His Orchestra	147	CB
06/07/1963	Monsoon	The Chantay's	149	CB
13/07/1963	If You Don't Come Back	The Drifters	101	BB
13/07/1963	Cross Roads (Part 1)	Luther Randolph & Johnny Stiles	114	CB
13/07/1963	It Hurts To Be Sixteen*	Barbara Chandler	114	CB
13/07/1963	Make The Music Play	Dionne Warwick	114	CB
13/07/1963	You And I (Have A Right To Cry)	Lou Christie	119	CB
13/07/1963	Ain't It Funny What A Fool Will Do	George Jones	124	BB
13/07/1963	Darling, Darling, Darling	Ty Hunter	130	CB
13/07/1963	From Me To You	The Beatles	149	CB
20/07/1963	The Ice Cream Man	The Tornadoes	103	CB
20/07/1963	At The Shore	Johnny Caswell	106	CB
20/07/1963	You Get Ugly	The Contours	109	CB
20/07/1963	Old Cape Cod	Jerry Vale	114	CB
20/07/1963	Little Girl Bad	Joanie Sommers	125	CB
20/07/1963	Fraulein (new Version)	BoBBy Helms	127	BB
20/07/1963	That's What My Heart Needs	Otis Redding	133	CB
20/07/1963	Farewell My Love	The Temptations	137	CB
20/07/1963	Lover's Medley "The More I See You"/"When I Fall In Love"	Marcy Jo & Eddie Rambeau	142	CB
27/07/1963	Mala Femmina	Jimmy Roselli	101	CB
27/07/1963	What I Gotta Do (To Make You Jealous)	Little Eva	101	BB
27/07/1963	Little Dancing Doll	Shelby Flint	103	BB
27/07/1963	Treat Em' Tough	Jimmy Soul	108	BB
27/07/1963	How High The Moon	Floyd Cramer	109	CB
27/07/1963	Someone To Take Your Place	Joe Tex	113	CB

27/07/1963	It Hurts To Be Sixteen	Barbara Chandler	114	BB
27/07/1963	What Makes Little Girls Cry	The Victorians	120	BB
27/07/1963	A Doodlin' Song	Peggy Lee	135	CB
27/07/1963	Rats In My Room (Part I)	Joey & Danny With Ali Baba & 4 Thieves	141	CB
03/08/1963	The Happy Puppy	Bent Fabric And His Piano	102	BB
03/08/1963	From Me To You	The Beatles	116	BB
03/08/1963	Stop Pretending	The Clovers Featuring Buddy Bailey	116	CB
03/08/1963	My First Day Alone	The Cascades	121	CB
03/08/1963	When I'm Walking (Let Me Walk)	Fats Domino	126	CB
03/08/1963	Green Monkey	Garnell Cooper & The Kinfolks	132	BB
03/08/1963	I've Got A Right To Cry	Fats Domino	135	CB
03/08/1963	Ruler Of My Heart	Irma Thomas	141	CB
03/08/1963	A Million Years Or So	Eddy Arnold	144	CB
03/08/1963	Scarlet O'hara	Jet Harris & Tony Meehan	147	CB
10/08/1963	Gee What A Guy	Yvonne Carroll & The Roulettes	101	CB
10/08/1963	Dina	Dore Alpert	105	CB
10/08/1963	Mala Femmena	Connie Francis	114	BB
10/08/1963	When I'm Walking (Let Me Walk)	Fats Domino	114	BB
10/08/1963	A Slow Dance	Ronnie And The Hi-Lites	116	BB
10/08/1963	Old Cape Cod	Jerry Vale	118	BB
10/08/1963	Pretty Girls Everywhere	Arthur Alexander	118	BB
10/08/1963	A Slow Dance	Ronnie & The Hi-Lites	123	CB
10/08/1963	I've Got A Right To Cry (b-side)	Fats Domino	128	BB
10/08/1963	A Young Man's Fancy	Tommy Sands	129	CB
10/08/1963	True Blue Lou	Tony Bennett	132	CB
10/08/1963	What Happened To Janie	Johnny Crawford	132	CB
10/08/1963	Where Is Johnny Now?	The Sapphires	133	BB
10/08/1963	Mala Femmina	Jimmy Roselli	135	BB
10/08/1963	Maria Elena	Billy Mure	140	CB
10/08/1963	Roberta	Peppino Di Capri	148	CB

17/08/1963	Mala Femmena	Connie Francis	101	CB
17/08/1963	Sooner Or Later	Johnny Mathis	105	CB
17/08/1963	Faded Love	Patsy Cline	112	CB
17/08/1963	Scarlet O'hara	Claude King	114	CB
17/08/1963	A Little Like Lovin'	The Cascades	116	BB
17/08/1963	Flipped Over You	Paul & Paula	119	CB
17/08/1963	How High The Moon	Floyd Cramer	121	BB
17/08/1963	Don't Let The Sun Catch You Crying	Steve Alaimo	125	BB
17/08/1963	Look Again Theme From "Irma La Douce"	Roger Williams	127	CB
17/08/1963	Theme From Irma La Douce (LOOK Again)*	Adam Wade	127	CB
17/08/1963	A Little Like Lovin'	The Cascades	128	CB
17/08/1963	Lover's Medley "The More I See You"/"When I Fall In Love"	Marcy Jo	132	BB
17/08/1963	Stop Pretending	The Clovers Featuring Buddy Bailey	134	BB
17/08/1963	Dance, Everybody, Dance	The Dartells	145	CB
17/08/1963	Keep On Dancing	The Avantis	146	CB
17/08/1963	A-Ooga	The Routers	147	CB
17/08/1963	Nobody But Me	Dee Clark	148	CB
17/08/1963	There's Not A Minute	Rick Nelson	149	CB
24/08/1963	Lonely World	Dion	101	BB
24/08/1963	Undertow	Fabulous Continentals	102	CB
24/08/1963	My Laura	Harry Charles	107	BB
24/08/1963	Flipped Over You	Paul And Paula	108	BB
24/08/1963	Little Yellow Roses	Jackie Deshannon	108	CB
24/08/1963	She Never Looked Better	The Playmates	110	CB
24/08/1963	Talk Back Trembling Lips	Ernest Ashworth	110	CB
24/08/1963	Say There	The Wonders	112	CB
24/08/1963	I'm Not A Fool Anymore	T.K. Hulin	125	CB
24/08/1963	My Baby Loves To Dance	Chris Montez	129	BB
24/08/1963	If You Love Her	Barbara Lewis	131	BB
24/08/1963	Little Girl Bad	Joanie Sommers	132	BB

24/08/1963	Jungle Drums	Arthur Lyman Group	133	CB
24/08/1963	Not So Long Ago	Marty RoBBins	140	CB
24/08/1963	Little Queenie	BoBBy Rydell	142	CB
24/08/1963	From One To One	Clyde Mcphatter	143	CB
24/08/1963	Soul Waltzin'	Big Dee Irwin	146	CB
31/08/1963	I Call It Pretty Music, But The Old People Call It The Blues - Pt. I	Little Stevie Wonder	101	BB
31/08/1963	Sad Girl	Jay Wiggins	110	CB
31/08/1963	Perfidia	The Matadors (Tony, Vic & Manuel)	113	CB
31/08/1963	Gee What A Guy	Yvonne Caroll And The Roulettes	115	BB
31/08/1963	Dance The Froog	The Dovells	117	CB
31/08/1963	Windy And Warm	Boots Randolph & His Combo	117	CB
31/08/1963	I'm Coming Back To You	Julie London	118	BB
31/08/1963	Are You Sure	Betty Logan	120	CB
31/08/1963	The Sound Of Surf	Percy Faith & His Orchestra	122	CB
31/08/1963	I'm Coming Back To You	Julie London	123	CB
31/08/1963	Lonely World	Dion	136	CB
31/08/1963	Stay	Porgy & The Monarchs	136	CB
31/08/1963	My Laura	Harry Charles	143	CB
07/09/1963	Making Believe	Ray Charles With String Orchestra & Chorus	102	BB
07/09/1963	You Better Be A Good Girl Now	The Swans	103	CB
07/09/1963	Let's Fall In Love	Linda Scott	108	BB
07/09/1963	Can't He Take A Hint?	Kenni Woods	109	CB
07/09/1963	Halfway	Eddie Hodges	118	BB
07/09/1963	Blue Summer	The Royalettes	121	BB
07/09/1963	I Call It Pretty Music, But The Old People Call It The Blues - Pt. I	Little Stevie Wonder	125	CB
07/09/1963	There's Not A Minute	Rick Nelson	127	BB
07/09/1963	Are You Sure	Betty Logan	132	BB
07/09/1963	Down Yonder	Bill Mcelhiney & Orchestra Featuring Bob Johnson On Banjo	138	CB
07/09/1963	I Like Your Kind Of Love	Bob Luman & Sue Thompson	142	CB
07/09/1963	Halfway	Eddie Hodges	148	CB

07/09/1963	Cry, Cry, Cry	The Earls Featuring Larry Chance	150	CB
14/09/1963	Talk Back Trembling Lips	Ernest Ashworth	101	BB
14/09/1963	You Give Me Nothing To Go On	Ted Taylor	104	BB
14/09/1963	Down On Bending Knees	Johnny Copeland	105	BB
14/09/1963	Let's Fall In Love	Linda Scott	105	CB
14/09/1963	Cut You A-Loose	Ricky Allen	107	CB
14/09/1963	I'll Believe It When I See It	The Sierras	108	BB
14/09/1963	Little Yellow Roses	Jackie Deshannon	110	BB
14/09/1963	Nick Teen And Al K. Hall	Rolf Harris	120	CB
14/09/1963	Down Home	Rick Nelson	131	CB
14/09/1963	Where Did The Good Times Go	Dick & Deedee	137	CB
14/09/1963	You Gave My Number To Billy	Marcie Blane	143	CB
14/09/1963	Kissin'	The Earls Featuring Larry Chance	147	CB
21/09/1963	Cuando Calienta El Sol (When The Sun Is Hot)	Steve Allen & His Orchestra With The Copacabana Trio	103	CB
21/09/1963	Hootenanny Granny	Jim Lowe	103	BB
21/09/1963	I'm Your Part Time Love	Mitty Collier	104	CB
21/09/1963	The Day The Saw-Mill Closed Down	Dickey Lee	104	BB
21/09/1963	Michael - Pt. 1	Steve Alaimo	105	CB
21/09/1963	Cowboy Boots	Dave Dudley	106	CB
21/09/1963	Rev-Up	Manuel & The Renegades	108	CB
21/09/1963	Better To Give Than Receive	Joe Hinton	109	CB
21/09/1963	The Sound Of Surf	Percy Faith And His Orchestra	111	BB
21/09/1963	What'd I Say	Kenny Burrell And Jimmy Smith	113	BB
21/09/1963	Not So Long Ago	Marty RoBBins	115	BB
21/09/1963	Sad Girl	Jay Wiggins	116	BB
21/09/1963	Cotton Fields	The Angels	119	BB
21/09/1963	Mary-Mary	Jimmy Reed	119	BB
21/09/1963	P.S. I Love You	The Classics	120	BB
21/09/1963	Cut You A-Loose	Ricky Allen	126	BB
21/09/1963	From One To One	Clyde Mcphatter	127	BB

21/09/1963	Miracles	Pookie Hudson	127	CB
21/09/1963	Kick Out	Safaris	129	CB
21/09/1963	Hootenanny Granny	Jim Lowe	131	CB
21/09/1963	The Gorilla	The Ideals	134	CB
21/09/1963	Little Sally Walker	The Rivingtons	144	CB
28/09/1963	Blue Velvet	Lawrence Welk And His Orchestra	103	BB
28/09/1963	A Perfect Pair	Paul And Paula	105	BB
28/09/1963	Jenny Brown	The Smothers Brothers	105	CB
28/09/1963	Eefananny	The Ardells	109	BB
28/09/1963	Hymn To Freedom	Oscar Peterson Trio	109	BB
28/09/1963	Toys In The Attic	Jack Jones	115	CB
28/09/1963	What'd I Say?	Kenny Burrell & Jimmy Smith	122	CB
28/09/1963	A Perfect Pair	Paul & Paula	124	CB
28/09/1963	The Day The Saw-Mill Closed Down	Dickey Lee	124	CB
28/09/1963	Your Life Begins (At Sweet Sixteen)	The Majors	125	BB
28/09/1963	Detroit City No. 2	Ben Colder	130	CB
28/09/1963	Go 'WAY Christina	Jimmy Soul	136	CB
28/09/1963	Toys In The Attic	Dennis Regor & Paulette Sisters	137	CB
28/09/1963	Your Life Begins (At Sweet Sixtenn)	The Majors	139	CB
28/09/1963	P.S. I Love You	The Classics	141	CB
28/09/1963	Stella By Starlight	Arthur Prysock	145	CB
05/10/1963	Theme From "ANY Number Can Win"	Jimmy Smith	102	CB
05/10/1963	Fiesta (b-side)	Lawrence Welk And His Orchestra	106	BB
05/10/1963	Fiesta	Lawrence Welk & His Orchestra	111	CB
05/10/1963	Brown-Eyed Handsome Man	Buddy Holly	113	BB
05/10/1963	There He Goes	The Velvellettes	119	CB
05/10/1963	Four Strong Winds	Ian & Sylvia	122	CB
05/10/1963	Ninety Miles An Hour (Down A Dead End Street)	Hank Snow	124	BB
05/10/1963	Skylark	Aretha Franklin	124	CB
05/10/1963	Promise Me Anything	Annette	126	CB

05/10/1963	Theme From "A New Kind Of Love"	Frank Chacksfield & His Orchestra	126	CB
05/10/1963	There's No In Between	Joe Hinton	127	CB
05/10/1963	Application For Love	Roy Clark	137	CB
05/10/1963	Walkin' My Baby	Allen Wayne	144	CB
05/10/1963	Nobody	Patti Page	147	CB
12/10/1963	Please Write	The Tokens	108	BB
12/10/1963	A Story Untold	The Emotions	110	BB
12/10/1963	He's The One You Love	Inez Foxx	113	BB
12/10/1963	Toys In The Attic	Dennis Regor	115	BB
12/10/1963	Guitars, Guitars, Guitars	Al Casey With The K-C-Ettes	116	BB
12/10/1963	The Lonely One	Kai Winding	116	CB
12/10/1963	I Worry Bout You	Etta James	118	CB
12/10/1963	Love Isn't Just For The Young	Frank Sinatra	118	CB
12/10/1963	Kick Out	Safaris	120	BB
12/10/1963	It Comes And Goes	Burl Ives	124	BB
12/10/1963	The Gorilla	The Ideals	127	BB
12/10/1963	Undertow	Fabulous Continentals	128	BB
12/10/1963	Salt Water Taffy	Morty Jay & The Surferin' Cats	129	CB
12/10/1963	Ching-A-Ling Baby	The Rocky Fellers	150	CB
19/10/1963	Love Her	The Everly Brothers	104	CB
19/10/1963	It's A Mad, Mad, Mad, Mad World	The Shirelles	105	CB
19/10/1963	Tomorrow Is Another Day (b-side)	Doris Troy	118	BB
19/10/1963	Shy Boy	Lou Christie	119	BB
19/10/1963	It Comes And Goes	Burl Ives	121	CB
19/10/1963	Promise Me Anything	Annette	123	BB
19/10/1963	Down Home	Rick Nelson	126	BB
19/10/1963	Tomorrow Is Another Day	Doris Troy	127	CB
19/10/1963	Hey Lonely One	Baby Washington	131	CB
19/10/1963	Whatever Happened To Rosemarie	Connie Francis	132	CB
19/10/1963	Broken Hearted Fool	Inez Foxx	133	CB

19/10/1963	Shy Boy	Lou Christie	135	CB
19/10/1963	Eefin' Alvin	The Chipmunks (Alvin, Simon & Theodore) With David Seville	139	CB
19/10/1963	This Old Heart	The Monarchs	143	CB
19/10/1963	I Know He Needs Her	Sandy Stewart	145	CB
19/10/1963	Please Write	The Tokens	146	CB
26/10/1963	Love Isn't Just For The Young	Frank Sinatra	111	BB
26/10/1963	I Could Have Danced All Night	Ben E. King	112	CB
26/10/1963	Four Strong Winds	The Brothers Four	114	BB
26/10/1963	Love Her	The Everly Brothers	117	BB
26/10/1963	Hey Child	Johnny Thunder	118	BB
26/10/1963	Louie Louie	Paul Revere & The Raiders	118	CB
26/10/1963	Tobacco Road (Live)	Lou Rawls With The Onzy Matthews Band	121	CB
26/10/1963	I'll Be There	Tony Orlando	123	CB
26/10/1963	Washington Square	The Ames Brothers	129	BB
26/10/1963	Shiny Stockings	Ella Fitzgerald With The Count Basie Orchestra	130	CB
26/10/1963	I Love The Life I'm Living	Slim Harpo	134	CB
26/10/1963	I'm Crazy 'BOUT My Baby	Marvin Gaye	143	CB
26/10/1963	I Can't Say No	Myrna March	150	CB
02/11/1963	Never Love A Robin	BoBBy Vee	101	CB
02/11/1963	Swanee River	Ace Cannon	101	CB
02/11/1963	What'cha Gonna Do About It	Doris Troy	102	BB
02/11/1963	Louie, Louie	Paul Revere And The Raiders	103	BB
02/11/1963	Near To You	Wilbert Harrison	103	CB
02/11/1963	Stop Monkeyin' Aroun'	The Dovells	108	CB
02/11/1963	Rock Candy [Live]	Jack Mcduff	109	BB
02/11/1963	Blue Monday	James Davis	110	CB
02/11/1963	Lipstick Paint A Smile On Me	Demetriss Tapp	116	CB
02/11/1963	Senate Hearing	Dickie Goodman	116	BB
02/11/1963	Summer's Come And Gone	The Brandywine Singers	129	BB
02/11/1963	When The Boy's Happy (The Girl's Happy Too)	The Four Pennies	129	CB

02/11/1963	Found True Love	Billy Butler & The Four Enchanters	134	BB
02/11/1963	There's More Pretty Girls Than One	George Hamilton Iv	137	CB
02/11/1963	Going Through The Motions (Of Living)	Sonny James	140	CB
02/11/1963	Love, Love Go Away	BoBBy Rydell	144	CB
02/11/1963	Mountain Of Love	David Houston	147	CB
02/11/1963	Summer's Come And Gone	The Brandywine Singers	149	CB
02/11/1963	Chapel On A Hill	The Dynamics	150	CB
09/11/1963	We Shall Overcome (Live)	Joan Baez	101	CB
09/11/1963	Oh What A Night For Love	Roy Tyson	105	CB
09/11/1963	Hi Diddle Diddle	Inez Foxx	108	CB
09/11/1963	Stop Foolin'	Brook Benton & Damita Jo	108	BB
09/11/1963	See The Big Man Cry	Ed Bruce	109	BB
09/11/1963	Don't Envy Me	George Hamilton	110	CB
09/11/1963	Rumble	Jack Nitzsche	111	CB
09/11/1963	There's A Meetin' Here Tonite	Joe & Eddie	112	CB
09/11/1963	There's More Pretty Girls Than One	George Hamilton Iv	116	BB
09/11/1963	You're No Good	Dee Dee Warwick	117	BB
09/11/1963	Baby, Think It Over	The Martinels	119	CB
09/11/1963	What'cha Gonna Do About It	Doris Troy	120	CB
09/11/1963	Surfer Street	The Allisons	121	CB
09/11/1963	I'm Down To My Last Heartbreak	Wilson Pickett	123	CB
09/11/1963	Let Us Make Our Own Mistakes	Brian Hyland	123	BB
09/11/1963	I'll Be There	Tony Orlando	124	BB
09/11/1963	Big As I Can Dream	Kris Jensen	130	CB
09/11/1963	He Understands Me	Teresa Brewer	130	BB
09/11/1963	Four In The Floor	The Shut Downs	131	BB
09/11/1963	The Monkey Walk	The Flares	133	BB
09/11/1963	Keep An Eye On Her	The Jaynetts	135	CB
09/11/1963	Anyone Else	Gene Mcdaniels	143	CB
09/11/1963	He Understands Me	Teresa Brewer	145	CB

16/11/1963	Swanee River	Ace Cannon	103	BB
16/11/1963	Baby, You've Got It Made (b-side)	Brook Benton & Damita Jo	111	BB
16/11/1963	Lipstick Paint A Smile On Me	Demetriss Tapp	112	BB
16/11/1963	Near To You	Wilbert Harrison	118	BB
16/11/1963	Keep An Eye On Her	The Jaynetts	120	BB
16/11/1963	Let's Start The Party Again	Little Eva	123	BB
16/11/1963	Lonesome Traveler (Live)	Trini Lopez	135	CB
16/11/1963	Sweet Sue, Just You	Ray Conniff & Billy Butterfield & The Ray Conniff Sextet	136	CB
16/11/1963	Devil's Waitin' (On Bald Mountain)	The Glencoves	140	CB
16/11/1963	See The Big Man Cry	Ed Bruce	145	CB
23/11/1963	Hit The Road Jack	Jerry Lee Lewis	103	BB
23/11/1963	Shy Guy	Maurice Mcalister & The Radiants	104	BB
23/11/1963	Cold Cold Winter	The Pixies Three	106	CB
23/11/1963	Coming Back To You	Maxine Brown	108	CB
23/11/1963	The Feeling Is Gone	BoBBy Bland	111	CB
23/11/1963	Shy Guy	Maurice Mcalister & The Radiants	112	CB
23/11/1963	Where There's A Will	Lonnie Mack	112	CB
23/11/1963	Blue Monday	James Davis	113	BB
23/11/1963	Too Hurt To Cry, Too Much In Love To Say Goodbye	The Darnells	117	BB
23/11/1963	I Worry Bout You	Etta James	118	BB
23/11/1963	Mountain Of Love	David Houston	132	BB
23/11/1963	Baby, You've Got It Made	Brook Benton & Damita Jo	133	CB
23/11/1963	Natasha	Eric & The Serenaders	136	CB
23/11/1963	Heartaches	Kenny Ball & His Jazzmen	138	CB
23/11/1963	Time Is On My Side	Kai Winding With Vocal Group	143	CB
23/11/1963	Pen And Paper	Jerry Lee Lewis	145	CB
30/11/1963	Kidnapper	Jewell & The Rubies	107	CB
30/11/1963	Big Boss Man	Charlie Rich	108	BB
30/11/1963	Where There's A Will	Lonnie Mack	113	BB
30/11/1963	I Can't Give You Anything But Love	Fats Domino	114	BB

30/11/1963	Bless 'EM All	Jane Morgan	119	CB
30/11/1963	Forget About Me	Carolyn Crawford	119	CB
30/11/1963	Heartaches	Kenny Ball And His Jazzmen	119	BB
30/11/1963	Theme From "THE Cardinal"	Roger Williams	120	CB
30/11/1963	Whispering	The Bachelors	121	CB
30/11/1963	The Bowery	Mantovani	129	CB
30/11/1963	Crystal Fingers	Ferrante & Teicher	132	CB
30/11/1963	That Boy Is Messin' Up My Mind	The Orchids	133	CB
30/11/1963	Don't Envy Me	George Hamilton	134	BB
30/11/1963	I Had A Dream	Nathaniel Mayer & His Fabulous Twilights	146	CB
07/12/1963	Oh What A Night For Love	Roy Tyson	106	BB
07/12/1963	Did You Have A Happy Birthday?	Paul Anka	110	CB
07/12/1963	Baby, What's Wrong	Lonnie Mack	118	CB
07/12/1963	Why Do Kids Grow Up	Randy & The Rainbows	130	CB
14/12/1963	Do-Wah-Diddy	The Exciters	103	CB
14/12/1963	Holiday Hootenanny	Paul & Paula	105	CB
14/12/1963	The Little Drummer Boy	Johnny Mathis	108	CB
14/12/1963	For Your Sweet Love	The Cascades	121	CB
14/12/1963	Last Day In The Mines	Dave Dudley	125	BB
14/12/1963	Waitin' For The Evening Train	Anita Kerr Quartet	125	BB
14/12/1963	Crystal Fingers	Ferrante & Teicher	127	BB
14/12/1963	The Moment Of Truth	Tony Bennett	127	BB
14/12/1963	That's What I Want For Christmas	Nancy Wilson	128	CB
14/12/1963	The Man With The Cigar	Lew Courtney	135	CB
14/12/1963	Chicken Pot Pie	Ken Jones His Piano & Orchestra	137	CB
14/12/1963	Ol' Man Time	Ray Charles & His Orchestra	137	CB
14/12/1963	The Prisoner's Song	Vic Dana	143	CB
21/12/1963	Sneaky Sue	Patty Lace & The Petticoats	101	CB
21/12/1963	Billie Baby	Lloyd Price	102	CB
21/12/1963	I Can't Stop Singing	BoBBy Bland	106	BB

21/12/1963	Just A Lonely Man	Fats Domino	108	BB
21/12/1963	Theme From "The Cardinal"	Roger Williams	109	BB
21/12/1963	Red Don't Go With Blue	Jimmy Clanton	115	BB
21/12/1963	In The Summer Of His Years	Mahalia Jackson	116	BB
21/12/1963	Auf Wiedersehen	Jerry Wallace	121	CB
21/12/1963	Heartless Heart	Floyd Cramer	124	BB
21/12/1963	Mama Was A Cotton Picker	Jimmie Rodgers	131	BB
21/12/1963	Last Day In The Mines	Dave Dudley	138	CB
21/12/1963	Shape Up Or Ship Out	Leon Mcauliffe	142	CB
21/12/1963	Big Boss Man	Charlie Rich	146	CB
21/12/1963	Lost Little Boy	Rolf Harris	148	CB
21/12/1963	Snowman, Snowman, Sweet Potato Nose	The Jaynetts	149	CB
28/12/1963	In The Summer Of His Years	Millicent Martin	104	BB
28/12/1963	Sneaky Sue	Patty Lace And The Petticoats	104	BB
28/12/1963	Do The Slauson	Round Robin & The Parlays	105	CB
28/12/1963	Slipin' And Slidin'	Jim & Monica	108	CB
28/12/1963	I Gotta Move	Freddie Houston	111	CB
28/12/1963	Comin' In The Back Door	Wynton Kelly	112	CB
28/12/1963	Jingle Bell Rock	BoBBy Helms	118	CB
28/12/1963	I've Got To Change	James Brown & The Famous Flames	120	CB
28/12/1963	Judy Loves Me	Johnny Crawford	120	CB
28/12/1963	Queridita Mia (Little Darlin')	Keith Colley	122	BB
28/12/1963	The Wedge	Dick Dale	122	CB
28/12/1963	Lonely Lonely Lonely Me	Brenda Lee	125	CB
28/12/1963	He Was A Friend Of Mine	The Briarwood Singers	126	BB
28/12/1963	The Grasshopper (El Cigarron)	Amadeo & His Indian Harps	126	CB
28/12/1963	Hootenanny Saturday Night (Live)	The Brothers Four	127	CB
28/12/1963	Bless 'Em All	Jane Morgan	131	BB
28/12/1963	Jimmy Boy	Carol Shaw	132	BB
28/12/1963	I Wanna Be Free	Joe Tex	139	CB

04/01/1964	Baby What You Want Me To Do (Live)	Etta James	101	CB
04/01/1964	Soul Dance	Tommy Leonetti	105	BB
04/01/1964	Tribute	Anthony Newley	105	BB
04/01/1964	My Home Town	Steve Lawrence	106	BB
04/01/1964	I'll Search My Heart	Johnny Mathis	111	CB
04/01/1964	Snow Man	Diane Ray	112	CB
04/01/1964	Don't Cross Over (To My Side Of The Street)	Linda Brannon	115	BB
04/01/1964	Through The Eyes Of A Fool	Roy Clark	116	CB
04/01/1964	Chicken Pot Pie	Ken Jones His Piano & Orchestra	125	BB
04/01/1964	Beautiful Dreamer	Roy Orbison	144	CB
11/01/1964	Sinner Not A Saint	Trini Lopez	103	BB
11/01/1964	Big-Town Boy	Shirley Matthews And The Big Town Girls	104	BB
11/01/1964	How Much Can A Lonely Heart Stand	Skeeter Davis	104	CB
11/01/1964	Here's A Heart	The Diplomats	105	CB
11/01/1964	Promises (You Made Now Are Broken)	Ray Peterson	108	BB
11/01/1964	Don't Cross Over (To My Side Of The Street)	Linda Brannon	111	CB
11/01/1964	My Home Town	Steve Lawrence	113	CB
11/01/1964	Rock Candy (Live)	Jack Mcduff	134	CB
11/01/1964	Together	Jimmie Rodgers	136	CB
18/01/1964	The Greasy Spoon	Hank Marr	101	BB
18/01/1964	The Cow	Bill Robinson And The Quails	103	BB
18/01/1964	Stay With Me	Frank Sinatra	107	CB
18/01/1964	Peanuts [EP] (Peanuts/Never On Sunday/I Can't Give You Anything	The 4 Seasons	108	BB
18/01/1964	I Can't Wait Until I See My Baby	Justine Washington	111	CB
18/01/1964	A Room Without Windows (b-side)	Steve Lawrence	120	BB
18/01/1964	Scatter Shield	The Surfaris	120	CB
18/01/1964	The Cow	Bill Robinson & The Quails	126	CB
18/01/1964	Who Needs You	BoBBy Paris	128	BB
18/01/1964	Mind Your Own Business	Jimmy Dean	138	CB
18/01/1964	Red Don't Go With Blue	Jimmy Clanton	147	CB

18/01/1964	Bye Bye Baby	The Rocky Fellers	148	CB
25/01/1964	Welcome To My World	Jim Reeves	102	BB
25/01/1964	What Now My Love	Ben E. King	102	BB
25/01/1964	Main Theme From The Cardinal (Stay With Me)*	Nick Noble	107	CB
25/01/1964	Who's Been Sleeping In My Bed?	Linda Scott	110	CB
25/01/1964	(I'm Watching) Every Little Move You Make	Little Peggy March	112	CB
25/01/1964	Never Leave Me	The Stratfords	112	CB
25/01/1964	Go On And Have Yourself A Ball	The Mar. Vels	115	BB
25/01/1964	On And On	Jerry Vale	116	CB
25/01/1964	Why, Why, Won't You Believe Me	Shep And The Limelites	125	BB
25/01/1964	Through The Eyes Of A Fool	Roy Clark	128	BB
25/01/1964	Outside City Limits	The Cashelles	129	BB
25/01/1964	A Stranger On Earth	Dinah Washington	136	CB
25/01/1964	Promises (You Made Now Are Broken)	Ray Peterson	150	CB
01/02/1964	Willyam, Willyam	Dee Dee Sharp	102	CB
01/02/1964	The La-Dee-Da Song	The Village Stompers	103	CB
01/02/1964	The La-Dee-Da Song	The Village Stompers	104	BB
01/02/1964	Molly	Eddy Arnold & The Needmore Creek Singers	111	CB
01/02/1964	Welcome To My World	Jim Reeves	119	CB
01/02/1964	Oozi-Oozi-Ooh	The Charmettes	124	CB
01/02/1964	Custom Machine	Bruce & Terry	126	CB
01/02/1964	Roberta	Barry And The Tamerlanes	127	BB
01/02/1964	Gotta Find A Way	Theresa Lindsey	129	BB
01/02/1964	Stand Tall	The O'jays	131	BB
01/02/1964	Who Needs It	Gene Pitney	131	BB
01/02/1964	What Now My Love	Ben E. King	132	CB
08/02/1964	Please Don't Go Away	Johnny Tillotson	112	BB
08/02/1964	I'll Be There (To Bring You Love)	The Majors	113	BB
08/02/1964	All My Trials	Dick & Deedee	115	CB
08/02/1964	Out Of This World	Gino Washington & The Rochelles With The Atlantics	115	CB

08/02/1964	Tous Les Chemins (All The Roads)	Soeur Sourire (The Singing Nun)	115	BB
08/02/1964	Dark As A Dungeon	Johnny Cash	119	BB
08/02/1964	Strange Things Happening	Little Jr. Parker	119	CB
08/02/1964	You Can't Miss Nothing That You Never Had	Ike & Tina Turner	122	BB
08/02/1964	The Harem	Mr. Acker Bilk And His Paramount Jazz Bandmr. Acker Bilk And His	125	BB
08/02/1964	He Really Loves Me	DeBBie Rollins	136	CB
08/02/1964	Mo-Onions	Booker T. & The Mg's	137	CB
08/02/1964	Blue Moon	Ray Conniff & His Orchestra & Chorus	138	CB
08/02/1964	I Adore You	Patti Page	139	CB
08/02/1964	Convicted	The Dartells Featuring Doug & Corky	146	CB
15/02/1964	Think Nothing About It	Gene Chandler	101	CB
15/02/1964	I'm Leaving	Johnny Nash	103	CB
15/02/1964	I Am Woman	Barbra Streisand	108	CB
15/02/1964	He Walks Like A Man	Jody Miller	109	CB
15/02/1964	I'm Travelin' On	Jackie Wilson	121	CB
15/02/1964	Please Don't Go Away	Johnny Tillotson	122	CB
15/02/1964	On And On	Jerry Vale	123	BB
15/02/1964	Baby Come On Home	Hoagy Lands	124	BB
15/02/1964	Be My Girl	The Dovells	124	CB
15/02/1964	Competition Coupe	The Astronauts	124	BB
15/02/1964	Sweet Violets	Bob Braun	124	CB
15/02/1964	It Ain't No Use	Lou Johnson	126	CB
15/02/1964	Blue Train (Of The Heartbreak Line)	John D. Loudermilk	127	CB
15/02/1964	Beyond The Sea	The Reveres	144	CB
15/02/1964	Dark As A Dungeon	Johnny Cash	145	CB
15/02/1964	Go Now	Bessie Banks	146	CB
15/02/1964	Blue Skies (Moving In On Me)	Jack Scott	147	CB
22/02/1964	My Boyfriend Got A Beatle Haircut	Donna Lynn	101	CB
22/02/1964	There's A Meetin' Here Tonite	Joe & Eddie	101	BB
22/02/1964	Girl From Spanish Town	Marty RoBBins	106	BB

22/02/1964	Out Of Sight - Out Of Mind	Sunny & The Sunliners	113	CB
22/02/1964	Hitchhike Back To Georgia	Buddy Knox And The Rhythm Orchids	114	BB
22/02/1964	Curfew Lover	Anita Humes & The Essex	118	CB
22/02/1964	Five Little Fingers	Bill Anderson	118	BB
22/02/1964	The Boy With The Beatle Hair	The Swans	121	CB
22/02/1964	I'm Looking Over A Four Leaf Clover	Wayne Newton	123	BB
22/02/1964	Poorest Boy In Town	Paul Petersen	123	CB
22/02/1964	Never Leave Me	The Stratfords	124	BB
22/02/1964	Big Daddy	Sue Thompson	132	BB
22/02/1964	Sandy	Johnny Crawford	135	CB
22/02/1964	Henry's In (Part 1)	Sam Kimble Orchestra Featuring Henry, Taffy, Gail, Al & Leon	136	CB
22/02/1964	Permanently Lonely	Timi Yuro	136	CB
22/02/1964	Let Them Talk	Run-A-Rounds	150	CB
29/02/1964	Jailer, Bring Me Water (Live)	Trini Lopez	106	CB
29/02/1964	Think Nothing About It	Gene Chandler	107	BB
29/02/1964	Tic-Tac-Toe	Booker T. & The Mg's	109	BB
29/02/1964	A Heartbreak Ahead	The Murmaids	110	CB
29/02/1964	Stockholm	Lawrence Welk & His Orchestra	115	CB
29/02/1964	Blue Moon	Ray Conniff And His Orchestra And Chorus	119	BB
29/02/1964	Why Do Fools Fall In Love	The Beach Boys	120	BB
29/02/1964	I'm Travelin' On	Jackie Wilson	123	BB
29/02/1964	Last Night I Had The Strangest Dream	The Kingston Trio	124	BB
29/02/1964	Mary Jane	Del Shannon	124	CB
29/02/1964	Who's Going To Take Care Of Me	Justine Washington	125	BB
29/02/1964	Billy Old Buddy	Joey Powers	129	CB
29/02/1964	I Adore You	Patti Page	131	BB
29/02/1964	The Friendliest Thing	Eydie Gorme	133	BB
29/02/1964	Lonnie On The Move	Lonnie Mack	136	CB
29/02/1964	Hey, Big Boy	The Secrets	138	CB
29/02/1964	La Bomba	Les Brown & His Band Of Renown	150	CB

07/03/1964	The Waiting Game	Brenda Lee	101	BB
07/03/1964	You Can't Miss Nothing That You Never Had	Ike & Tina Turner	105	CB
07/03/1964	Sandy	Johnny Crawford	108	BB
07/03/1964	All You Had To Do (Was Tell Me)	Chris & Cathy	111	CB
07/03/1964	I'm The Hoochie Cooche Man	Dion Di Muci	113	BB
07/03/1964	Lazy Lady	Fats Domino	116	CB
07/03/1964	It Ain't No Use	Lou Johnson	117	BB
07/03/1964	Lonnie On The Move	Lonnie Mack	117	BB
07/03/1964	Midnight	David Rockingham Trio	119	BB
07/03/1964	Out Of This World	Gino Washington And The Rochelles With The Atlantics	120	BB
07/03/1964	Georgia On My Mind	Richard Chamberlain	123	CB
07/03/1964	I'm Just A Nobody (Part I)	BoBBy Byrd	128	CB
07/03/1964	Changing My Life For You	The Z-Debs	132	CB
14/03/1964	Congratulations	Rick Nelson	104	CB
14/03/1964	Your Cheatin' Heart	Fats Domino	112	BB
14/03/1964	Heartbreak Ahead	The Murmaids	116	BB
14/03/1964	Mondo Cane #2	Kai Winding & Orchestra	120	BB
14/03/1964	Someday You'll Want Me To Want You	Patsy Cline	123	BB
14/03/1964	Winter's Here	Robin Ward	123	BB
14/03/1964	Little Beatle Boy	The Angels	130	CB
14/03/1964	Here's To Our Love	Brian Hyland	131	CB
14/03/1964	Oh Boy	Jackie Deshannon	133	CB
14/03/1964	That's The Way Love Is	Del Shannon	133	BB
14/03/1964	Stella By Starlight	Richard Chamberlain	134	CB
14/03/1964	Naomi	Floyd Cramer	138	CB
14/03/1964	Please Little Angel	Doris Troy	145	CB
14/03/1964	Don't Blame Me	Frank Ifield	146	CB
21/03/1964	Stand By Me	Cassius Clay	102	BB
21/03/1964	Easy To Love (Hard To Get)	The Chiffons	105	BB
21/03/1964	Mexican Drummer Man	Herb Alpert's Tijuana Brass	111	CB

21/03/1964	I Am The Greatest [Live]	Cassius Clay	113	BB
21/03/1964	Easy To Love (So Hard To Get)	The Chiffons	118	CB
21/03/1964	Look Who's Talking (b-side)	Jim Reeves & Dottie West	121	BB
21/03/1964	Moonglow / Picnic Theme	Baja Marimba Band	121	BB
21/03/1964	I Don't Want To Set The World On Fire	Fats Domino	122	BB
21/03/1964	That's The Way Love Is	Del Shannon	122	CB
21/03/1964	Wonderland Of Love	The Tymes	124	BB
21/03/1964	Around The Corner	Ben E. King	125	BB
21/03/1964	Weejee Walk	The Rivingtons	125	CB
21/03/1964	Don't Blame Me	Frank Ifield	128	BB
21/03/1964	Here's To Our Love	Brian Hyland	129	BB
21/03/1964	Mondo Cane #2	Kai Winding	134	CB
28/03/1964	First Class Love	Little Johnny Taylor	102	CB
28/03/1964	Mr. John	Bill Spivery	108	CB
28/03/1964	I'll Find You	Valerie & Nick	110	CB
28/03/1964	Puppet On A String	Bob And Earl	111	BB
28/03/1964	We'll Never Break Up For Good	Paul & Paula	112	CB
28/03/1964	I Am Woman	Barbra Streisand	114	BB
28/03/1964	Grease Monkey [Live]	Brother Jack Mcduff	116	BB
28/03/1964	All My Loving	Jimmy Griffin	118	BB
28/03/1964	To The Aisle	Jimmy Velvet	118	BB
28/03/1964	I'm Leaving	Johnny Nash	120	BB
28/03/1964	Please Little Angel	Doris Troy	128	BB
28/03/1964	So Hard	Ted Taylor	130	CB
28/03/1964	The Beatles Souvenir Of Their Visit To America (EP)	The Beatles	130	CB
28/03/1964	The File	Bob Luman	139	CB
28/03/1964	Faith	Wallace Brothers (Ervin & Johnny)	141	CB
28/03/1964	I Got A Thing Going On	Sam & Dave	145	CB
28/03/1964	Bring Back The Beatles (To Me)	Bonnie Brooks	147	CB
04/04/1964	Somebody Stole My Dog	Rufus Thomas	104	CB

04/04/1964	We'll Never Break Up For Good	Paul And Paula	105	BB
04/04/1964	Vanishing Point	The Marketts	106	CB
04/04/1964	Oh Boy	Jackie Deshannon	112	BB
04/04/1964	Where Are You	The Duprees Featuring Joey Vann	114	BB
04/04/1964	Love Is No Excuse	Jim Reeves & Dottie West	115	BB
04/04/1964	Walk, Walk	The Freewheelers	117	CB
04/04/1964	Walk, Walk	The Freewheelers	119	BB
04/04/1964	Red Ryder	Murry Kellum	121	CB
04/04/1964	A Thousand Miles Away	Santo & Johnny	122	BB
04/04/1964	I'm Gonna Love That Guy (Like He's Never Been)	Linda Lloyd	122	BB
04/04/1964	Hello Walls	Little Esther	126	CB
04/04/1964	Some Things Are Better Left Unsaid	Ketty Lester	127	BB
04/04/1964	Permanently Lonely	Timi Yuro	130	BB
04/04/1964	That's What Mama Say	Walter Jackson	132	CB
04/04/1964	Baltimore	Sonny James	134	BB
04/04/1964	Some Things Are Better Left Unsaid	Ketty Lester	135	CB
04/04/1964	All My Loving	Jimmy Griffin	140	CB
04/04/1964	Look Who's Blue	Etta James	140	CB
04/04/1964	Moonglow/Picnic Theme	Baja Marimba Band	142	CB
04/04/1964	Draggin' Wagon	The Surfer Girls	150	CB
11/04/1964	If You Love Me (Like You Say) (b-side)	Little Johnny Taylor	101	BB
11/04/1964	Our Faded Love	The Royaltones	103	BB
11/04/1964	Louie - Go Home	Paul Revere & The Raiders	106	CB
11/04/1964	First Class Love	Little Johnny Taylor	107	BB
11/04/1964	Shout	Dion	108	BB
11/04/1964	Beatle Mania Blues	The Roaches	117	BB
11/04/1964	Rosemarie	Pat Boone	120	CB
11/04/1964	All You Had To Do (Was Tell Me)	Chris And Kathy (Chris Montez) (Kathy Young)	125	BB
11/04/1964	Blue Train (Of The Heartbreak Line)	John D. Loudermilk	132	BB
11/04/1964	A Thousand Miles Away	Santo & Johnny	135	CB

11/04/1964	Call Her Up	Jackie Wilson	135	CB
11/04/1964	Puppet On A String	Bob & Earl	141	CB
11/04/1964	The Big Build Up	Bert Kaempfert & His Orchestra	150	CB
18/04/1964	Yo Me Pregunto (I Ask Myself)	The Valrays	102	CB
18/04/1964	Little Tracy	Wynton Kelly	103	CB
18/04/1964	I Only Have Eyes For You	Cliff Richard	109	BB
18/04/1964	Call Her Up	Jackie Wilson	110	BB
18/04/1964	Shy One (Live)	Shirley Ellis	111	CB
18/04/1964	The Closest Thing To Heaven	Neil Sedaka	111	CB
18/04/1964	From Russia With Love*	Al Caiola	116	CB
18/04/1964	From Russia With Love*	Kenny Ball & His Jazzmen	116	CB
18/04/1964	Winkin', Blinkin' And Nod	The Simon Sisters	116	CB
18/04/1964	From Russia With Love	Al Caiola And His Orchestra	120	BB
18/04/1964	The Fall Of Love	Johnny Mathis	120	BB
18/04/1964	Fugitive	The Ventures	121	CB
18/04/1964	I'll Step Aside	Jimmy Clanton	121	CB
18/04/1964	I Only Have Eyes For You	Cliff Richard	127	CB
18/04/1964	I Wish I Knew What Dress To Wear	Ginny Arnell	130	BB
18/04/1964	Bluesette	Sarah Vaughan	131	BB
18/04/1964	I'm The One	Gerry & The Pacemakers	132	CB
18/04/1964	Walkin'	Al Hirt	134	CB
18/04/1964	Invisible Tears	Ned Miller	136	CB
18/04/1964	Guess Who	The Sunglows	145	CB
18/04/1964	Tell Me What Can I Do	Tony Orlando	147	CB
25/04/1964	Caldonia	James Brown & His Orchestra	104	CB
25/04/1964	If You Love Me, Really Love Me	Jackie Trent	106	BB
25/04/1964	Again	James Brown And The Famous Flames	107	BB
25/04/1964	The Closest Thing To Heaven	Neil Sedaka	107	BB
25/04/1964	Who's Afraid Of Virginia Woolf? (Part I)	Jimmy Smith	107	CB
25/04/1964	Bad News	The Trashmen	108	CB

25/04/1964	If You Love Me Really Love Me	Jackie Trent	112	CB
25/04/1964	The Fall Of Love	Johnny Mathis	114	CB
25/04/1964	Butch Babarian	Ray Stevens	117	CB
25/04/1964	I'll Find You	Valerie & Nick	117	BB
25/04/1964	Fugitive*	Jan Davis	121	CB
25/04/1964	In The Wee Wee Hours (Of The Night)	James Brown And The Famous Flames	125	BB
25/04/1964	Rosemarie	Pat Boone	129	BB
25/04/1964	Why	The Beatles With Tony Sheridan	129	CB
25/04/1964	Invisible Tears	Ned Miller	131	BB
25/04/1964	Burning Memories	Ray Price	132	CB
25/04/1964	If You Don't Look Around	The Kingston Trio	148	CB
25/04/1964	Again	James Brown & The Famous Flames	150	CB
02/05/1964	Big Party	Barbara & The Browns	103	CB
02/05/1964	Swing	The Tokens	105	BB
02/05/1964	Gypsy Woman Told Me	Eddie Powers	112	CB
02/05/1964	My Baby's Comin' Home	Paul Anka	113	BB
02/05/1964	Louie - Go Home	Paul Revere And The Raiders	118	BB
02/05/1964	Try To Find Another Man	The Righteous Brothers	119	BB
02/05/1964	She's A Bad Motorcycle	The Crestones	123	CB
02/05/1964	Tomorrow	Chris Crosby	124	BB
02/05/1964	I'm Watching My Watch	Johnny Tillotson	125	CB
02/05/1964	Fugitive	The Ventures	126	BB
02/05/1964	Suspicion	Elvis Presley With The Jordanaires	127	CB
02/05/1964	I've Had It	Lonnie Mack	128	BB
02/05/1964	Java Jones (Java)	Donna Lynn	129	BB
02/05/1964	Long Tall Shorty	Tommy Tucker	129	CB
02/05/1964	Ain't That Lovin' You Baby	The Everly Brothers	133	BB
02/05/1964	Draggin' Wagon	The Surfer Girls	134	BB
02/05/1964	I've Had It	Lonnie Mack	134	CB
02/05/1964	If You Love Me (Like You Say)	Little Johnny Taylor	138	CB

02/05/1964	Guitar Child	Duane Eddy	144	CB
09/05/1964	A World Without Love	BoBBy Rydell	103	CB
09/05/1964	Suspicion	Elvis Presley With The Jordanaires	103	BB
09/05/1964	Let's Have A Party	The Rivieras	104	CB
09/05/1964	Little Tracy	Wynton Kelly	113	BB
09/05/1964	Tequila	The Untouchable Sound Bill Black's Combo	113	CB
09/05/1964	My Baby Walks All Over Me	Johnny Sea	121	BB
09/05/1964	Soulville	Aretha Franklin	121	BB
09/05/1964	Yo Me Pregunto (I Ask Myself)	The Valrays	121	BB
09/05/1964	Nomad	Louis Armstrong And Dave Brubeck	122	BB
09/05/1964	Someday We're Gonna Love Again (b-side)	Barbara Lewis	124	BB
09/05/1964	Fugitive	Jan Davis	129	BB
09/05/1964	Help Me	The Diplomats	129	CB
09/05/1964	Shy One [Live]	Shirley Ellis	130	BB
09/05/1964	Sweeter Than Sugar	Ronnie Dove	141	CB
09/05/1964	Nomad	Louis Armstrong & Dave Brubeck	142	CB
09/05/1964	Gino Is A Coward	Gino Washington	145	CB
09/05/1964	Something You Got, Baby	Fats Domino	147	CB
16/05/1964	Gotta Get Away	Billy Butler & The Enchanters	101	BB
16/05/1964	It Will Stand	The Showmen	101	CB
16/05/1964	Trouble I've Had	Clarence Ashe	101	CB
16/05/1964	Security	Otis Redding	106	CB
16/05/1964	Precious Words	Wallace Brothers (Ervin And Johnny)	107	BB
16/05/1964	My Man	Walter Gates & His Orchestra	110	CB
16/05/1964	The Court Of King Caractacus (Live)	Rolf Harris	110	CB
16/05/1964	New York Town	The Dixiebelles	119	BB
16/05/1964	Have I Stayed Away Too Long	BoBBy Bare	122	CB
16/05/1964	Bad News	The Trashmen	124	BB
16/05/1964	Someday We're Gonna Love Again	Barbara Lewis	126	CB
16/05/1964	Ruby Red, Baby Blue	The Fleetwoods	134	BB

23/05/1964	Devil With The Blue Dress	Shorty Long	101	CB
23/05/1964	The Girl's Alright With Me	The Temptations	102	BB
23/05/1964	Big Boss Line	Jackie Wilson	104	CB
23/05/1964	Night Time Is The Right Time	Rufus & Carla	108	CB
23/05/1964	Blowin' In The Wind	Stan Getz	110	BB
23/05/1964	Help The Poor	B.B. King	111	CB
23/05/1964	Spend A Little Time	Barbara Lewis	119	BB
23/05/1964	If You Don't Look Around	The Kingston Trio	123	BB
23/05/1964	French Rivieria	WeBB Pierce	126	BB
23/05/1964	Look At Me	Jimmy Gilmer	133	BB
23/05/1964	Baby, Baby (I Still Love You)	The Cinderellas	134	BB
23/05/1964	She's A Bad Mototcycle	The Crestones	135	BB
23/05/1964	That's All That Matters	Ray Price	136	CB
23/05/1964	Gotta Get Away	Billy Butler & The Enchanters	139	CB
23/05/1964	Come Closer	Dee Clark	140	CB
23/05/1964	A Fool For A Fool	Ike & Tina Turner	142	CB
23/05/1964	New York Town	The Dixiebelles With Cornbread & Jerry	147	CB
30/05/1964	Let's Go Together	The Raindrops	109	BB
30/05/1964	Choose	Sammy Davis Jr.	112	BB
30/05/1964	I Understand Them (A Love Song To The Beatles)	The Patty Cakes	112	CB
30/05/1964	The Court Of King Caractacus [Live]	Rolf Harris	116	BB
30/05/1964	My Kind Of Town	Frank Sinatra	120	CB
30/05/1964	Run Little Girl	Donnie Elbert	122	CB
30/05/1964	Devil With The Blue Dress	Shorty Long	125	BB
30/05/1964	You Comb Her Hair	Joey Powers	128	CB
30/05/1964	You Take One Step (I'll Take Two)	Joe Henderson	128	BB
30/05/1964	Let's Go Together	The Raindrops	130	CB
30/05/1964	Things I Used To Do	Junior Parker	130	CB
30/05/1964	Soulville	Aretha Franklin	135	CB
30/05/1964	Star Dust	Peter Duchin His Piano With Orchestra & Chorus	143	CB

30/05/1964	Tell Me When	The Applejacks	146	CB
06/06/1964	My Dreams	Brenda Lee	112	CB
06/06/1964	Part Of Me	Johnny Adams	117	CB
06/06/1964	Bad Detective	The Coasters	118	CB
06/06/1964	Raunchy	Bill Black's Combo	118	BB
06/06/1964	Jamaica Ska	The Ska Kings	123	CB
06/06/1964	My Baby Walks All Over Me	Johnny Sea	128	CB
06/06/1964	Hello, Dolly! (Italian Style)	Lou Monte	130	CB
06/06/1964	Run Little Girl	Donnie Elbert	130	BB
06/06/1964	(They Call Her) La Bamba	The Crickets	131	CB
06/06/1964	Love Ain't Nothin'	Johnny Nash	133	CB
06/06/1964	Beachcomber	The Johnny Gibson Trio	134	CB
06/06/1964	How Long Darling (b-side) [Live]	James Brown And The Famous Flames	134	BB
06/06/1964	Tell Me When	The Applejacks	135	BB
06/06/1964	I Love You So	BoBBy Byrd	141	CB
06/06/1964	Shenandoah	The Goldebriars	142	CB
06/06/1964	Choose	Sammy Davis Jr.	146	CB
06/06/1964	Lavender Sax	Clifford Scott + 6 Stars	149	CB
13/06/1964	Long Lonely Nights	Four Seasons	102	BB
13/06/1964	Oh, Rock My Soul (Part I) (Live)	Peter, Paul & Mary	105	CB
13/06/1964	The Cowboy In The Continental Suit	Marty RoBBins	108	CB
13/06/1964	My Kind Of Town (Chicago Is)	Frank Sinatra	110	BB
13/06/1964	After It's Too Late	BoBBy Bland	111	BB
13/06/1964	A Thing Called Sadness	Chuck Howard	115	CB
13/06/1964	The Magic Of Our Summer Love	The Tymes	115	CB
13/06/1964	Beachcomber	The Johnny Gibson Trio	116	BB
13/06/1964	Just Once More	Rita Pavone	116	CB
13/06/1964	Thread Your Needle	Dean And Jean	123	BB
13/06/1964	Dance, Dance, Dance	Tommy Duncan	133	BB
13/06/1964	I Don't Want To Hear Anymore	Jerry Butler	142	CB

20/06/1964	Thread Your Needle	Dean & Jean	114	CB
20/06/1964	Rosie	ChuBBy Checker	116	BB
20/06/1964	Growin' Up Too Fast	Diane Renay	124	BB
20/06/1964	Taste Of Tears	Johnny Mathis	125	CB
20/06/1964	Ain't Love Good - Ain't Love Proud (Live)	Tony Clarke And You, His Audience	130	CB
20/06/1964	Hello Dolly (Italian Style)	Lou Monte	131	BB
20/06/1964	Don't Take Your Love From Me	Gloria Lynne	132	CB
20/06/1964	My Man	Walter Gates And His Orchestra	133	BB
20/06/1964	Juliet	The Four Pennies	140	CB
20/06/1964	The Dum-De-Dum Song (The Boy I Love)	Joanne Engel	144	CB
20/06/1964	So Long	James Brown & The Famous Flames	148	CB
27/06/1964	Bachelor Boy	Cliff Richard & The Shadows	103	CB
27/06/1964	The Cowboy In The Continental Suit	Marty RoBBins	103	BB
27/06/1964	Walkin'	Al Hirt	103	BB
27/06/1964	It's Summertime U.S.A.	The Pixies Three	106	CB
27/06/1964	Juliet	The Four Pennies	116	BB
27/06/1964	More (From The Film "Mondo Cane)	Danny Williams	117	CB
27/06/1964	Just Once More	Rita Pavone	123	BB
27/06/1964	Close Your Eyes	Arthur Prysock	124	BB
27/06/1964	Hello, Dolly!	Ella Fitzgerald	125	BB
27/06/1964	Time Is On My Side	Irma Thomas	129	CB
27/06/1964	So Long	James Brown And The Famous Flames	132	BB
27/06/1964	He's Coming Back To Me (b-side)	Theola Kilgore	133	BB
27/06/1964	Bee-Bom (b-side)	Sammy Davis Jr.	135	BB
27/06/1964	Tommy	Connie Francis	136	CB
27/06/1964	I'll Keep Trying	Theola Kilgore	139	CB
27/06/1964	Lefty Louie	David Rose & His Orchestra	142	CB
27/06/1964	I'm Gonna Cry	Wilson Pickett	143	CB
04/07/1964	If You See My Love	Lenny Welch	101	CB
04/07/1964	New Orleans	Bern Elliot & The Fenmen	101	CB

04/07/1964	I'm Sorry	Pete Drake & His Talking Steel Guitar	108	CB
04/07/1964	Lookin' For Boys	The Pin-Ups	108	CB
04/07/1964	Goofus	Brent Fabric & His Piano	109	CB
04/07/1964	More	Danny Williams	110	BB
04/07/1964	Nightingale Melody	Little Johnny Taylor	111	CB
04/07/1964	What Can A Man Do	Ben E. King	113	BB
04/07/1964	It's Summer Time U.S.A.	The Pixies Three	116	BB
04/07/1964	Only You	Wayne Newton	119	CB
04/07/1964	Johnny Loves Me	Florraine Darlin	121	BB
04/07/1964	Water Skiing	Duane Eddy	122	CB
04/07/1964	Happy I Long To Be	Betty Everett	126	BB
04/07/1964	Lucky Star	Rick Nelson	127	BB
04/07/1964	Johnny Loves Me	Florraine Darlin	128	CB
04/07/1964	Mary, Oh Mary	Fats Domino	131	CB
04/07/1964	Close Your Eyes	Arthur Prysock	134	CB
04/07/1964	I'd Rather Have You	Joe Tex	135	CB
04/07/1964	Annie Is Back	Little Richard	138	CB
11/07/1964	What Can A Man Do	Ben E. King	106	CB
11/07/1964	Hangin' On To My Baby	Tracey Dey	107	BB
11/07/1964	Bama Lama Bama Loo	Little Richard	109	CB
11/07/1964	Licorice Stick	Pete Fountain	115	BB
11/07/1964	A Casual Kiss	Leon Peels	120	CB
11/07/1964	Close Your Eyes	Jamie Coe & The Gigolo's	120	CB
11/07/1964	Oh What A Kiss	Johnny Rivers	120	BB
11/07/1964	Gino Is A Coward	Gino Washington	121	BB
11/07/1964	I'm Sorry	Pete Drake And His Talking Steel Guitar	122	BB
11/07/1964	I'm Gonna Cry (Cry Baby)	Wilson Pickett	124	BB
11/07/1964	Silver Dollar	Mike Minor	126	CB
11/07/1964	My Heart Skips A Beat	Buck Owens	130	CB
11/07/1964	Dance, Franny, Dance	Floyd Dakil Combo	142	CB

11/07/1964	Lucky Star	Rick Nelson	142	CB
11/07/1964	Pork Chop, Part I	Jimmy Smith	145	CB
18/07/1964	The Long Ships, Part 1	Charles Albertine	101	CB
18/07/1964	A Shot In The Dark	Henry Mancini & His Orchestra	102	CB
18/07/1964	More And More Of Your Amor	Nat King Cole	102	BB
18/07/1964	Summer Means Fun	Bruce & Terry	105	CB
18/07/1964	Nightingale Melody	Little Johnny Taylor	109	BB
18/07/1964	Me	Bill Anderson	121	CB
18/07/1964	The Seventh Dawn	Ferrante & Teicher	124	BB
18/07/1964	You'd Better Find Yourself Another Fool	Lavern Baker	128	BB
18/07/1964	Love Me Do	The Hollyridge Strings	134	BB
18/07/1964	Mickey Mouse	Denny Provisor	138	CB
18/07/1964	All My Loving	The Hollyridge Strings	144	CB
25/07/1964	Viva Las Vegas (EP)	Elvis Presley	102	CB
25/07/1964	I'll Keep Trying	Theola Kilgore	108	BB
25/07/1964	Never Ending	Elvis Presley With The Jordanaires	111	BB
25/07/1964	Fort Worth, Dallas Or Houston	George Hamilton Iv	116	CB
25/07/1964	More, More, More Love, Love, Love	Johnny Thunder	116	CB
25/07/1964	One Piece Topless Bathing Suit	The Rip Chords	119	CB
25/07/1964	A Spanish Boy	The Rubies	127	CB
25/07/1964	Mary, Oh Mary	Fats Domino	127	BB
25/07/1964	Theme From "A Summer Place"	The J's With Jamie	131	CB
25/07/1964	I Surrender Dear	Nino Tempo & April Stevens	132	CB
25/07/1964	Oh What A Kiss	Johnny Rivers	134	CB
25/07/1964	Shrimp Boats (Jamaican Ska)	Jerry Jackson	134	BB
25/07/1964	A Casual Kiss	Leon Peels	135	BB
25/07/1964	Ask Me Why	The Beatles	139	CB
25/07/1964	All The Colors Of The Rainbow (Turn To Blue)	Mike Clifford	143	CB
25/07/1964	Never Pick A Pretty Boy	Dee Dee Sharp	143	CB
01/08/1964	You're No Good	The Swinging Blue Jeans	101	CB

01/08/1964	I'll Always Love You	Brenda Holloway	102	CB
01/08/1964	And I Love Her	George Martin And His Orchestra	105	BB
01/08/1964	Let Me Get Close To You	Skeeter Davis	106	BB
01/08/1964	Down Where The Winds Blow (Chilly Winds)	The Serendipity Singers	112	BB
01/08/1964	Soul Dressing	Booker T. & The Mg's	112	CB
01/08/1964	Darling It's Wonderful	Dale & Grace	114	BB
01/08/1964	If I'm A Fool For Loving You	Jimmy Clanton	118	CB
01/08/1964	I Know	Billy J. Kramer With The Dakotas	122	CB
01/08/1964	Put Away Your Tear Drops	The Lettermen	125	CB
01/08/1964	Sole, Sole, Sole	Sarah Vaughan	132	CB
08/08/1964	Here I Go Again	The Hollies	107	BB
08/08/1964	You're Gonna Miss Me	B.B. King	107	BB
08/08/1964	A Million Drums	Jimmy Clanton	110	CB
08/08/1964	I'm Too Poor To Die	Louisiana Red	115	CB
08/08/1964	Theme From "A Summer Place"	The J's With Jamie	115	BB
08/08/1964	Silly Ol' Summertime	The New Christy Minstrels	116	CB
08/08/1964	Let Me Get Close To You	Skeeter Davis	117	CB
08/08/1964	Here I Go Again	The Hollies	118	CB
08/08/1964	Under Paris Skies	Andy Williams	121	BB
08/08/1964	Only You	Wayne Newton	122	BB
08/08/1964	That's How Strong My Love Is	O.V. Wright With The Keys	127	CB
08/08/1964	Never Pick A Pretty Boy	Dee Dee Sharp	131	BB
08/08/1964	Better Watch Out Boy	The Accents Featuring Sandi	133	BB
08/08/1964	New Fangled, Jingle Jangle, Swimming Suit From Paris	Frankie Avalon	133	CB
08/08/1964	He Was A Friend Of Mine	BoBBy Bare	134	BB
08/08/1964	Warm And Willing	John Gary	137	CB
08/08/1964	Imagination Is A Magic Dream	BoBBy Vinton	140	CB
08/08/1964	You Don't Love Me	Tommy Raye	141	CB
08/08/1964	What Kinda Love?	Jimmy Gilmer	148	CB
08/08/1964	Yours	Lucille Starr	149	CB

15/08/1964	Lonely Corner	Rick Nelson	105	CB
15/08/1964	Squeeze Her - Tease Her (But Love Her)	Jackie Wilson	108	CB
15/08/1964	Let Me Love You (b-side)	B.B. King	110	BB
15/08/1964	Follow The Rainbow	Terry Stafford	112	CB
15/08/1964	The Long Ships, Part 1	Charles Albertine	112	BB
15/08/1964	I've Got A Thing Going On	BoBBy Marchan	116	BB
15/08/1964	Something's Got A Hold Of Me [Live]	Don & Alleyne Cole	117	BB
15/08/1964	You Pulled A Fast One	The V.I.P.'S	117	BB
15/08/1964	I Just Don't Know What To Do With Myself	Tommy Hunt	119	BB
15/08/1964	New Girl	Accents	128	BB
15/08/1964	You Pulled A Fast One	The V.I.P.'S	130	CB
15/08/1964	Put Away Your Tear Drops	The Lettermen	132	BB
15/08/1964	He's Sure To Remember Me	Brenda Lee	135	BB
22/08/1964	Follow The Rainbow	Terry Stafford	101	BB
22/08/1964	Little Lonely Summer Girl	David Box	112	CB
22/08/1964	Give Me Back My Heart	Jackie Wilson	113	CB
22/08/1964	Heartbreak	Dee Clark	119	BB
22/08/1964	Maybe The Last Time	James Brown & His Orchestra	119	CB
22/08/1964	If	Timi Yuro	120	BB
22/08/1964	Can't Get Over (The Bossa Nova)	Eydie Gorme	122	CB
22/08/1964	Guitars And Bongos	Lou Christie	123	BB
22/08/1964	Brother Bill (The Last Clean Shirt)	Honeyman	130	CB
22/08/1964	Don't Let Her Know	Buck Owens	130	BB
22/08/1964	It's In Your Hands	Diane Renay	131	BB
22/08/1964	Get My Hands On Some Lovin'	Artistics	132	CB
22/08/1964	Ringo For President	The Young World Singers	132	BB
22/08/1964	Lovers Always Forgive	Gladys Knight & Pips	148	CB
29/08/1964	Loop De Loop	Soul Sisters	107	BB
29/08/1964	Ringo For President	The Young World Singers	107	CB
29/08/1964	It Hurts To Be In Love	Betty Everett	109	BB

29/08/1964	That's How Strong My Love Is	O.V. Wright With The Keys	109	BB
29/08/1964	Dern Ya	Ruby Wright	112	CB
29/08/1964	Lonely Corner	Rick Nelson	113	BB
29/08/1964	Mr. Sandman	The Fleetwoods	113	BB
29/08/1964	Softly As I Leave You*	Matt Monro	115	CB
29/08/1964	Thank You For Loving Me	Al Martino	118	BB
29/08/1964	Mr. Sandman	The Fleetwoods	119	CB
29/08/1964	Heartbreak	Dee Clark	122	CB
29/08/1964	La De Da I Love You	Inez & Charlie Foxx	124	BB
29/08/1964	What's So Sweet About Sweet Sixteen	Carole Quinn	124	CB
29/08/1964	Humbug	Pete Fountain	129	CB
29/08/1964	In The Name Of Love	Peggy Lee	132	BB
29/08/1964	What Kinda Love?	Jimmy Gilmer	133	BB
29/08/1964	La La (Hey Baby)	The Cobras	135	CB
29/08/1964	Prayer Meetin', Part I	Jimmy Smith	135	CB
29/08/1964	Devoted To You	Brian Hyland	140	CB
29/08/1964	Whistl'n	Roger Williams	140	CB
29/08/1964	Sa-Ba-Hoola	Lonnie Mack	147	CB
05/09/1964	Pocahontas	The Camelots	103	CB
05/09/1964	I Could Conquer The World	The Shevelles	104	BB
05/09/1964	I Could Conquer The World	The Shevelles	105	CB
05/09/1964	It's For You	Cilla Black	105	CB
05/09/1964	Rockin' Robin	The Rivieras	105	CB
05/09/1964	Gator Tails And Monkey Ribs	The Spats Featuring Dick Johnson	106	CB
05/09/1964	Little Queenie	The Untouchable Sound Bill Black's Combo	111	CB
05/09/1964	I Don't Know	Steve Alaimo	115	CB
05/09/1964	Trouble In Mind	Jimmy Ricks	115	BB
05/09/1964	(Say I Love You) Doo Bee Dum	The Four-Evers	125	CB
05/09/1964	Whole Lotta Shakin' Goin' On	Little Richard	126	BB
05/09/1964	Goodnight Irene (b-side)	Little Richard	128	BB

05/09/1964	Marta	Los Indios Tabajaras	133	CB
05/09/1964	Hugo	Linda Hall	143	CB
12/09/1964	She Knows Me Too Well	The Beach Boys	101	BB
12/09/1964	Baby Let Me Take You Home	The Animals	102	BB
12/09/1964	My Adorable One	Joe Simon	102	BB
12/09/1964	Dern Ya	Ruby Wright	103	BB
12/09/1964	I Don't Know	Steve Alaimo	103	BB
12/09/1964	Somebody New	Chuck Jackson	106	CB
12/09/1964	Ain't That Loving You Baby	Betty Everett & Jerry Butler	108	BB
12/09/1964	How's Your Sister	Steve Allen	111	BB
12/09/1964	Soon I'll Wed My Love	John Gary	111	CB
12/09/1964	La De Da I Love You	Inez & Charlie Foxx	113	CB
12/09/1964	Ooh La La	Nino Tempo & April Stevens	113	BB
12/09/1964	Fever	Alvin Robinson	115	CB
12/09/1964	I'm Too Poor To Die	Louisiana Red	117	BB
12/09/1964	(Say I Love You) Doo Bee Dum	The Four-Evers	119	BB
12/09/1964	Where Is She	BoBBy Vee, Vocal Background By The Eligibles	120	BB
12/09/1964	I Wanna Thank You	The Enchanters	121	CB
12/09/1964	Softly As I Leave You (shorter Version)	Matt Monro	121	BB
12/09/1964	(I'm Just) A Henpecked Guy	The Reflections	124	BB
12/09/1964	The Girl From Ipanema	Ernie Heckscher And His Orchestra	125	BB
12/09/1964	Car Hop	The Exports	128	CB
12/09/1964	Oh No!	Ray Peterson	128	BB
12/09/1964	Welcome, Welcome Home	Anita Bryant	130	BB
12/09/1964	Nice And Easy	Charlie Rich	131	BB
12/09/1964	The Invasion	Buchanan & Greenfield	134	CB
12/09/1964	In The Name Of Love	Peggy Lee	138	CB
12/09/1964	Let The Water Run Down	Ben E. King	144	CB
12/09/1964	Robot Walk	Pat & Lolly Vegas	149	CB
19/09/1964	Absent Minded Me	Barbra Streisand	105	CB

19/09/1964	Fever	Alvin Robinson	108	BB
19/09/1964	Get My Hands On Some Lovin'	The Artistics	118	BB
19/09/1964	Baby Let Me Take You Home	The Animals	123	CB
19/09/1964	Goin' Places	Orlons	125	CB
19/09/1964	Nancy's Theme	Earle Hagen	128	CB
19/09/1964	Sally Was A Good Old Girl	Fats Domino	128	CB
19/09/1964	That's When The Crying Begins	Kip Anderson	130	BB
19/09/1964	Guitars And Bongos	Lou Christie	131	CB
19/09/1964	I'd Rather Be Rich	Pearl Bailey	132	BB
19/09/1964	Sacrifice	Little Milton	138	CB
19/09/1964	A Whole Lotta Shakin' Goin' On	Little Richard	143	CB
26/09/1964	L-O-V-E	Nat King Cole	105	CB
26/09/1964	The End Of A Symphony - Part 1 [Live]	Allan Sherman Boston Pops Orchestra Arthur Fiedler,	113	BB
26/09/1964	To Wait For Love	Tony Orlando	119	CB
26/09/1964	Absent Minded Me	Barbra Streisand	123	BB
26/09/1964	His Lips Get In The Way	Bernadette Castro	123	BB
26/09/1964	Can't Live Without Her	Billy Butler & The Chanters	130	BB
26/09/1964	His Lips Get In The Way	Bernadette Castro	130	CB
26/09/1964	I Wanna Swim With Him	The Daisies	133	BB
26/09/1964	The Dog	Junior And The Classics	134	BB
26/09/1964	Sweet Words Of Love	The Underbeats	136	CB
26/09/1964	Annie Oakley	Premiers	141	CB
26/09/1964	One More Tear	The Raindrops	142	CB
03/10/1964	Oh! Marie	The Village Stompers	101	CB
03/10/1964	Once A Day	Connie Smith	101	BB
03/10/1964	Letter From Elaina	Casey Kasem	103	BB
03/10/1964	Wait For Me	Rita Pavone	104	BB
03/10/1964	Lost Without You	Teddy Randazzo	105	CB
03/10/1964	I Should Have Known Better	George Martin And His Orchestra	111	BB
03/10/1964	Apple Of My Eye	The Four Seasons	117	CB

03/10/1964	Letter From Elaina	Casey Kasem	120	CB
03/10/1964	The Invasion	Buchanan And Greenfield	120	BB
03/10/1964	I Won't Tell	Tracey Dey	121	CB
03/10/1964	A Hard's Day Night (b-side)	George Martin And His Orchestra	122	BB
03/10/1964	I Should Have Known Better	George Martin & His Orchestra	122	CB
03/10/1964	Without The One You Love	Arthur Prysock	126	BB
03/10/1964	Promise You'll Tell Her	The Swinging Blue Jeans	130	BB
03/10/1964	I'd Rather Be Rich	Robert Goulet	131	BB
03/10/1964	Oh! Marie	The Village Stompers	132	BB
03/10/1964	The Gypsy	Robert Davie	132	CB
03/10/1964	Over You	Paul Revere And The Raiders	133	BB
03/10/1964	Go Cat Go	Norma Jean	134	BB
03/10/1964	Goodbye Girl	Ritchie Dean	134	CB
03/10/1964	Everybody's Darlin', Plus Mine	Browns Featuring Jim Edward Brown	135	BB
10/10/1964	Gale Winds	Egyptian Combo	101	CB
10/10/1964	Don't Spread It Around	Barbara Lynn	102	CB
10/10/1964	Maybe Tonight	The Shirelles	102	CB
10/10/1964	She's All Right	Jackie Wilson	102	BB
10/10/1964	Yes I Do	Solomon Burke	103	CB
10/10/1964	Apple Of My Eye (new Version)	The Four Seasons	106	BB
10/10/1964	Thank You For Loving Me	The Sapphires	106	BB
10/10/1964	Maybe The Last Time	James Brown And His Orchestra	107	BB
10/10/1964	Watch Out	Jackie Wilson	115	CB
10/10/1964	That's All I Need To Know	BoBBy Wood	120	CB
10/10/1964	Every Minute Every Hour	Dean Martin	123	BB
10/10/1964	Thank You For Loving Me	The Sapphires	123	CB
10/10/1964	Lost Love	The Shirelles	125	BB
10/10/1964	After Laughter	Wendy Rene	134	BB
10/10/1964	I Can't Believe What You Say (For Seeing What You Do)	Ike & Tina Turner	134	CB
10/10/1964	Every Minute Every Hour	Dean Martin	140	CB

10/10/1964	Good	Dee Dee Sharp	142	CB
10/10/1964	I'm Making It Over	Anita Humes	142	CB
17/10/1964	Gale Winds	Egyptian Combo	103	BB
17/10/1964	Gotta Give Her Love	The Volumes	108	CB
17/10/1964	Heartbreak Hill	Fats Domino	112	CB
17/10/1964	She's All Right	Jackie Wilson	129	CB
17/10/1964	High Heel Sneakers (Live)	Jerry Lee Lewis	130	CB
17/10/1964	That's All I Need To Know	BoBBy Wood	130	BB
17/10/1964	Over You	Paul Revere & The Raiders	132	CB
17/10/1964	Spanish Guitars (b-side)	Jerry Wallace	132	BB
17/10/1964	Randy	Earl-Jean	147	CB
17/10/1964	After Laughter	Wendy Rene	150	CB
24/10/1964	Mumbles	Oscar Peterson Trio	101	BB
24/10/1964	Sometimes I Wish I Were A Boy	Lesley Gore	102	CB
24/10/1964	Kentucky Bluebird (Send A Message To Martha)	Lou Johnson	104	BB
24/10/1964	Don't Shut Me Out	Sammy Davis Jr.	106	BB
24/10/1964	The Lumberjack	Hal Willis	106	CB
24/10/1964	Hide Away	King Curtis	112	BB
24/10/1964	This Little Girl Of Mine	The Righteous Brothers	114	BB
24/10/1964	Empty Arms	Ace Cannon	115	CB
24/10/1964	Gotta Give Her Love	The Volumes	117	BB
24/10/1964	I Just Don't Understand	Tommy Adderley With Max Merritt & His Meteors	118	CB
24/10/1964	Empty Arms	Ace Cannon	120	BB
24/10/1964	Move It Baby	Simon Scott	128	BB
24/10/1964	When You Walk In The Room	Jackie Deshannon	131	CB
24/10/1964	Spanish Guitars	Jerry Wallace	137	CB
24/10/1964	Go, BoBBy Soxer	Chuck Berry	147	CB
31/10/1964	I Hope He Breaks Your Heart	Neil Sedaka	104	BB
31/10/1964	Mumbles	Oscar Peterson Trio	105	CB
31/10/1964	Sloop Dance	The Vibrations	109	BB

31/10/1964	A Thousand Cups Of Happiness	Joe Hinton	111	BB
31/10/1964	I Hope He Breaks Your Heart	Neil Sedaka	112	CB
31/10/1964	Pushin' A Good Thing Too Far	Barbara Lewis	113	BB
31/10/1964	Even The Bad Times Are Good	Jerry Wallace	114	BB
31/10/1964	Same Old Reason	The Serendipity Singers	114	CB
31/10/1964	Stop Takin' Me For Granted	Mary Wells	116	CB
31/10/1964	Hurtin' Inside	Barbara & Brenda	120	CB
31/10/1964	The Lumberjack	Hal Willis	120	BB
31/10/1964	I Love You (I Just Love You)	Lloyd Price	123	BB
31/10/1964	Kentucky Bluebird (Send A Message To Martha)	Lou Johnson	126	CB
31/10/1964	We Have Something More (Than A Summer Love)	Connie Francis	128	BB
31/10/1964	Hide Away	King Curtis	133	CB
31/10/1964	Mira Mira	The Latin Quarters	137	CB
31/10/1964	Move It Baby	Simon Scott	138	CB
31/10/1964	All My Loving	The Chipmunks	139	CB
07/11/1964	I Don't Know You Anymore	BoBBy Goldsboro	105	BB
07/11/1964	Julie Knows	Randy Sparks	111	CB
07/11/1964	Silly Little Girl	The Tams	112	CB
07/11/1964	He's Just A Playboy	The Drifters	115	BB
07/11/1964	Either Way I Lose	Gladys Knight & The Pips	119	BB
07/11/1964	What Am I Gonna Do With You	Skeeter Davis	123	BB
07/11/1964	Up In The Air	Marty RoBBins	127	CB
07/11/1964	Find Another Love	The Tams	129	BB
07/11/1964	Lost Without You	Teddy Randazzo	130	BB
07/11/1964	Never Trust A Woman	B.B. King	132	CB
07/11/1964	Rap City	The Ventures	132	CB
07/11/1964	All My Loving	The Chipmunks	134	BB
07/11/1964	I Don't Know You Anymore	BoBBy Goldsboro	136	CB
07/11/1964	Pushin' A Good Thiing Too Far	Barbara Lewis	140	CB
07/11/1964	Moody River	Johnny Rivers	148	CB

14/11/1964	Don't It Make You Feel Good	The Overlanders	101	CB
14/11/1964	One Of These Days	Marty RoBBins	105	BB
14/11/1964	Shake A Lady	Ray Bryant	108	BB
14/11/1964	Tell Her Johnny Said Goodbye	Jerry Jackson	109	CB
14/11/1964	Don't Shut Me Out	Sammy Davis Jr.	118	CB
14/11/1964	Chittlins	Gus Jenkins	119	CB
14/11/1964	Topkapi	Jimmy Mcgriff	133	BB
14/11/1964	The Big Jerk - Pt. I	Clyde And The Blue Jays	134	BB
14/11/1964	(That's The Way Our Love Goes) One Step Forward, Two Steps	Brian Hyland	137	CB
14/11/1964	Hope You Understand	The Kingston Trio	146	CB
21/11/1964	Big Brother	Dickey Lee	101	BB
21/11/1964	My Ramblin' Boy	The Kingston Trio	101	CB
21/11/1964	I'm The Lover Man	Little Jerry Williams	102	BB
21/11/1964	And Satisfy	Nancy Wilson	106	BB
21/11/1964	Talk To Me Baby	Barry Mann	106	CB
21/11/1964	Either Way I Lose	Gladys Knight & The Pips	120	CB
21/11/1964	Long, Long Winter	The Impressions	122	CB
21/11/1964	The Good Life	Mr. Acker Bilk With The Leon Young String Chorale	134	CB
21/11/1964	Rap City	The Ventures	135	BB
21/11/1964	Runaround	Ann Marie	140	CB
21/11/1964	Everybody Wants To Fall In Love	The Valentinos	142	CB
28/11/1964	Watch Out, Sally!	Diane Renay	101	BB
28/11/1964	I'm The Lover Man	Little Jerry Williams	107	CB
28/11/1964	Kiss And Run	BoBBy Skel	108	CB
28/11/1964	Wooden Heart	Elvis Presley	111	CB
28/11/1964	Chittlins	Gus Jenkins	113	BB
28/11/1964	I Want You To Have Everything	Lee Rogers	114	BB
28/11/1964	And Satisfy	Nancy Wilson	117	CB
28/11/1964	I Just Can't Say Goodbye	BoBBy Rydell	119	CB
28/11/1964	I Don't Wanna Love You	Cliff Richard	120	CB

28/11/1964	Don't Bring Me Down	The Pretty Things	121	CB
28/11/1964	Nevertheless	Billy Butler & The Chanters	127	CB
28/11/1964	The Monster Swim	BoBBy Pickett And The Rolling Bones	135	BB
28/11/1964	Blue Christmas	Elvis Presley	143	CB
28/11/1964	Hey Now Baby	The Horizons	147	CB
05/12/1964	Google Eye	The Nashville Teens	102	CB
05/12/1964	Nevertheless	Billy Butler & The Chanters	102	BB
05/12/1964	Hey Little One	J. Frank Wilson & The Cavaliers	103	CB
05/12/1964	Take This Hurt Off Me	Don Covay	107	CB
05/12/1964	Wooden Heart	Elvis Presley	107	BB
05/12/1964	Tiger In The Tank	The Chariots	110	CB
05/12/1964	Little Star	Randy & The Rainbows	114	CB
05/12/1964	Tell Her Johnny Said Goodbye	Jerry Jackson	114	BB
05/12/1964	Mustang 2 + 2 (Big Mule)	The Casuals	117	BB
05/12/1964	Together	P. J. Proby	117	BB
05/12/1964	Please, Please Make It Easy	Brook Benton	119	BB
05/12/1964	El Pussy Cat	Mongo Santamaria	123	CB
05/12/1964	Strung Out	James Crawford	124	CB
05/12/1964	Haste Makes Waste	Jackie Ross	126	BB
05/12/1964	If I Knew Then	The Ray Conniff Singers	126	BB
05/12/1964	Julie Knows	Randy Sparks	126	BB
05/12/1964	Don't Let Me Be Misunderstood	Nina Simone	131	BB
05/12/1964	Have You Ever Been Lonely	Clarence "Frogman" Henry	135	BB
12/12/1964	Danny Boy	Patti Labelle & Her Bluebells	103	CB
12/12/1964	Party Girl	Tommy Roe	104	CB
12/12/1964	Rome Will Never Leave You	Richard Chamberlain	109	CB
12/12/1964	Google Eye	The Nashville Teens	117	BB
12/12/1964	Gotta Get A'goin'	The New Christy Minstrels	118	CB
12/12/1964	Send Her To Me	Johnny Thunder	121	BB
12/12/1964	Love, Love (That's All I Want From You)	Strange Loves	122	CB

12/12/1964	Mellow Fellow	Etta James	127	CB
12/12/1964	Tokyo Melody	Sheridan Hollenbeck Orchestra & Chorus	128	CB
12/12/1964	Tokyo Melody*	Helmut Zacharias	128	CB
12/12/1964	Frenchy	Vic Dana	129	CB
12/12/1964	Hawaii Tattoo	Martin Denny	132	BB
12/12/1964	Send Me No Flowers	Doris Day	135	BB
12/12/1964	Low Grades And High Fever	Linda Laine With The Sinners	141	CB
12/12/1964	I'd Do It Again	BoBBy Wood	142	CB
19/12/1964	It's Better To Have It	Barbara Lynn	105	CB
19/12/1964	Across The Street (It's A Million Miles Away)	Ray Peterson	106	BB
19/12/1964	The Man With All The Toys	The Beach Boys	116	CB
19/12/1964	If I Knew Then	The Ray Conniff Singers	118	CB
19/12/1964	Love Is Strange	Betty Everett & Jerry Butler	118	CB
19/12/1964	Love, Love (That's All I Want From You)	Strange Loves	122	BB
19/12/1964	The Little Drummer Boy	Harry Simeone Chorale	123	CB
19/12/1964	Anema E Core (With All My Heart And Soul)	Jimmy Roselli	125	CB
19/12/1964	The Other Ringo (A Tribute To Ringo Starr)	Larry Finnegan	130	BB
19/12/1964	Those Lonely, Lonely Nights	Vernon & Jewell	130	CB
19/12/1964	Little Star	Randy And The Rainbows	133	BB
26/12/1964	I'll Come Running	Lulu	105	BB
26/12/1964	Maybe	The Shangri-Las	107	CB
26/12/1964	Guess Who?	Dusty Springfield	109	BB
26/12/1964	Little Brown Jug	The Serendipity Singers	114	CB
26/12/1964	The Richest Man Alive	Mel Carter	116	CB
26/12/1964	Can't Be Still	Booker T. & The Mg's	119	CB
26/12/1964	Amen	Lloyd Price	124	BB
26/12/1964	I Won't Forget You	Jim Reeves	132	CB
26/12/1964	O' Bambino (One Cold And Blessed Winter)	Harry Simeone Chorale	136	CB
26/12/1964	Christmas Celebration	B.B. King	140	CB
26/12/1964	Haste Makes Waste	Jackie Ross	142	CB

26/12/1964	Silver Bells	Al Martino	145	CB
26/12/1964	White Cliffs Of Dover	Sir Raleigh & The Cupons	145	CB
26/12/1964	Take What I Have	Nancy Wilson	150	CB
02/01/1965	Have Mercy Baby	James Brown & The Famous Flames	102	CB
02/01/1965	Finders Keepers, Losers Weepers	Nella Dodds	104	CB
02/01/1965	Percolatin'	Willie Mitchell	104	CB
02/01/1965	A Little Bit Of Soap	Garnet Mimms & The Enchanters	108	CB
02/01/1965	Gotta Get A Goin'	The New Christy Minstrels	111	BB
02/01/1965	Long Green	The Kingsmen	112	CB
02/01/1965	Don't Answer The Door (Part 1)	Jimmy Johnson & His Band Featuring Hank Alexander	113	CB
02/01/1965	I Will Wait For You	Steve Lawrence	113	CB
02/01/1965	Baby What's Wrong	Johnnie Mae Matthews	114	CB
02/01/1965	The Race Is On	George Jones	114	CB
02/01/1965	Strain On My Heart	Roscoe Shelton	119	CB
02/01/1965	Pearly Shells (Popo O Ewa)	Billy Vaughn And His Orchestra	120	BB
02/01/1965	ShaBBy Little Hut	The Reflections	121	BB
02/01/1965	Ringo Beat	Ella Fitzgerald	127	BB
02/01/1965	Tanya	King Curtis	130	BB
02/01/1965	Popping Popcorn	Dave "Baby" Cortez	132	BB
02/01/1965	The Sidewinder, Part 1	Lee Morgan	132	CB
02/01/1965	A Tribute To Ringo Starr The Other Ringo	Larry Finnegan	149	CB
09/01/1965	Bewitched	Steve Lawrence	103	BB
09/01/1965	O' Bambino (One Cold And Blessed Winter)	Harry Simeone Chorale	105	BB
09/01/1965	I Want You To Be My Boy	The Exciters	106	CB
09/01/1965	Terry	Twinkle	106	CB
09/01/1965	Leroy	Norma Tracey & The Cinderella Kids	108	CB
09/01/1965	I Will Wait For You (b-side)	Steve Lawrence	113	BB
09/01/1965	Baby Don't Go	Sonny & Cher	117	CB
09/01/1965	This Diamond Ring	Sammy Ambrose	117	BB
09/01/1965	Fall Away	Eddie Albert	119	BB

09/01/1965	Little Brown Jug	The Serendipity Singers	124	BB
09/01/1965	Dial That Telephone Part I	Effie Smith	127	CB
09/01/1965	Live It Up (b-side)	Dusty Springfield	128	BB
09/01/1965	Long Tall Sally	The Kinks	129	BB
09/01/1965	Black Night	BoBBy Bland	131	CB
09/01/1965	Oh, How You Hurt Me	The O'jays	133	CB
09/01/1965	The Wild Side Of Life	Tommy Quickly	137	CB
16/01/1965	I'm Going Home	The Kingston Trio	104	BB
16/01/1965	I'll Come Running	Lulu	111	CB
16/01/1965	Everyday	The Rogues	112	CB
16/01/1965	Do-Do Do Bah-Ah	Bert Keyes	114	CB
16/01/1965	Then And Only Then	Connie Smith	116	BB
16/01/1965	Fall Away	Eddie Albert	124	CB
16/01/1965	What A Shame	The Rolling Stones	125	CB
16/01/1965	Talkin' To Your Picture	Tony Martin	133	BB
16/01/1965	Never On Sunday	The 4 Seasons	146	CB
16/01/1965	(Main Theme) The Addams Family	Vic Mizzy & His Orchestra	147	CB
16/01/1965	Don't Wait Too Long	Bettye Swann	149	CB
23/01/1965	Everyday	The Rogues	101	BB
23/01/1965	Six Boys	J. Frank Wilson And The Cavaliers	101	BB
23/01/1965	Little Miss Raggedy Ann	Aretha Franklin	103	CB
23/01/1965	The Richest Man Alive	Mel Carter	104	BB
23/01/1965	Terry	Twinkle	110	BB
23/01/1965	Comin' On Too Strong	Wayne Newton	114	CB
23/01/1965	I Wonder	The Butterflys	117	BB
23/01/1965	(I Hear You) Call My Name	Burl Ives	118	CB
23/01/1965	Hey-O-Daddy-O	The Newbeats	118	BB
23/01/1965	Crying In The Chapel	Adam Wade	121	CB
23/01/1965	My Gal Sal	Burl Ives	122	BB
23/01/1965	Something's Got A Hold On Me	Sunny & The Sunliners	128	BB

23/01/1965	Poor-Unfortunate-Me (I Ain't Got Nobody)	J.J. Barnes	129	CB
23/01/1965	I Want A Little Girl	Joe Hinton	135	CB
23/01/1965	A New Leaf	Jimmy Reed	136	CB
23/01/1965	Watusi '64	Jay Bentley & The Jet Set	141	CB
23/01/1965	Cinnamon Cindy	Jimmy Gilmer	143	CB
23/01/1965	I Know Why	Springers	143	CB
23/01/1965	The Phillie	The M-M & The Peanuts	144	CB
23/01/1965	I Want To Get Married	The Delicates	148	CB
30/01/1965	Cross My Heart	BoBBy Vee	101	CB
30/01/1965	My Gal Sal	Burl Ives	105	CB
30/01/1965	Leroy	Norma Tracey And The Cinderella Kids	107	BB
30/01/1965	My Babe	The Righteous Brothers	107	CB
30/01/1965	Fly Me To The Moon	Lavern Baker	109	CB
30/01/1965	Strain On My Heart	Roscoe Shelton	109	BB
30/01/1965	Sweet, Sweet Baby	Dion Di Muci	109	CB
30/01/1965	I Want To Get Married	The Delicates	120	BB
30/01/1965	Run My Heart	Baby Washington	121	BB
30/01/1965	What A Shame	The Rolling Stones	124	BB
30/01/1965	Get Out (And Let Me Cry)	Harold Melvin And The Blue Notes	125	BB
30/01/1965	I Love You Baby	Dottie And Ray	126	BB
30/01/1965	Jambalaya (On The Bayou)	Buddy Greco	127	CB
30/01/1965	Cross The Brazos At Waco	Billy Walker	128	BB
30/01/1965	Watusi '64	Jay Bentley And The Jet Set	128	BB
30/01/1965	Do-Do Do Bah-Ah	Bert Keyes	132	BB
30/01/1965	Goldfinger*	The Oxford 12	134	CB
30/01/1965	Lonely Man	Freddie Scott	136	CB
30/01/1965	Keep On Keeping On	The Vibrations	137	CB
30/01/1965	Patch It Up	Linda Scott	138	CB
06/02/1965	Can't You Just See Me	Aretha Franklin	101	CB
06/02/1965	My Babe	The Righteous Brothers	101	BB

06/02/1965	The Boy Next Door	The Standells	102	BB
06/02/1965	We Can't Believe You're Gone	BoBBy Harris	107	BB
06/02/1965	Diana	BoBBy Rydell	110	CB
06/02/1965	You're My Girl	The Everly Brothers	110	BB
06/02/1965	Teardrops From My Eyes	Ray Charles And His Orchestra	112	BB
06/02/1965	Come On Home	Bill Black's Combo	124	BB
06/02/1965	The Worst Thing In My Life	B.B. King	128	CB
06/02/1965	Come On Down Baby Baby	The Orlons	129	CB
06/02/1965	I Ain't Comin' Back	The Orlons	129	BB
06/02/1965	I Want A Little Girl	Joe Hinton	132	BB
06/02/1965	The Hullabaloo	BoBBy Gregg And His Friends	133	BB
06/02/1965	Run My Heart	Baby Washington	135	CB
06/02/1965	The Crying Man	Lee Lamont	142	CB
13/02/1965	Come Home Baby	Wilson Pickett	103	CB
13/02/1965	Camel Walk	The Iketts	107	BB
13/02/1965	We Are In Love	BoBBy Byrd	107	CB
13/02/1965	Whipped Cream*	The Stokes	113	CB
13/02/1965	Hello, Dolly!	BoBBy Darin	114	CB
13/02/1965	Bring Your Love To Me	The Righteous Brothers	116	CB
13/02/1965	Fannie Mae	The Righteous Brothers	117	BB
13/02/1965	Keep On Keeping On	The Vibrations	118	BB
13/02/1965	Fannie Mae	The Righteous Brothers	119	CB
13/02/1965	Don't Answer The Door (Part 1)	Jimmy Johnson And His Band Featuring Hank Alexander	128	BB
13/02/1965	Time Waits For No One	Eddie & Ernie	133	CB
13/02/1965	Come On Home	Bill Black's Combo	134	CB
13/02/1965	Patch It Up	Linda Scott	135	BB
13/02/1965	You're My Girl	The Everly Brothers	136	CB
13/02/1965	Just Say I Love Her	Jimmy Roselli	140	CB
13/02/1965	I'll Step Aside	Wallace Brothers	146	CB
20/02/1965	Everybody Let's Dance	Gene Chandler	106	CB

20/02/1965	Did You Ever	The Hullaballoos	107	CB
20/02/1965	You're The Cream Of The Crop	Lee Rogers	110	CB
20/02/1965	A Dear John Letter	Skeeter Davis & BoBBy Bare	111	CB
20/02/1965	Danny Boy	Jackie Wilson	113	CB
20/02/1965	You Can Have Him	Timi Yuro	118	CB
20/02/1965	The Last Girl	The Isley Brothers	119	CB
20/02/1965	Cool Water	Dale & Grace	123	CB
20/02/1965	How Do You Quit (Someone You Love)	Carla Thomas	126	CB
20/02/1965	I've Been Trying	The Impressions	133	BB
20/02/1965	Nevertheless (I'm In Love With You)	Ruby & The Romantics	133	CB
20/02/1965	The Telephone Song	Stan Getz/Astrud Gilberto	134	CB
20/02/1965	Camel Walk	The Iketts	135	CB
20/02/1965	If I Ruled The World	Sammy Davis Jr.	135	BB
20/02/1965	The Greatest Story Ever Told	Ferrante & Teicher	143	CB
27/02/1965	The Greatest Story Ever Told	Ferrante & Teicher	101	BB
27/02/1965	Find My Way Back Home	The Nashville Teens	107	CB
27/02/1965	Tell Her I'm Not Home	Ike & Tina Turner	108	BB
27/02/1965	Begin To Love (Cominciamo Ad Amarci)	Robert Goulet	110	BB
27/02/1965	It Hurts Me	BoBBy Sherman	110	CB
27/02/1965	Freeway Flyer	Jan & Dean	114	CB
27/02/1965	We Were Lovers	Darin D. Anna	115	CB
27/02/1965	Let Her Love Me	Otis Leavill	116	BB
27/02/1965	We Are In Love	BoBBy Byrd	120	BB
27/02/1965	You'll Be Gone	Elvis Presley With The Jordanaires	124	CB
27/02/1965	Times Are Gettin' Hard	BoBBy Bare	126	CB
27/02/1965	Baby, Hold Me Close	Jerry Lee Lewis	129	BB
27/02/1965	Walk	The Fenways	129	CB
27/02/1965	Somewhere	The Brothers Four	131	BB
27/02/1965	For Mama	Matt Monro	135	BB
27/02/1965	You're Breakin' My Heart	The Chartbusters	135	CB

27/02/1965	Big Chief - Part 2	Professor Longhair	144	CB
27/02/1965	I'll Be Seeing You	Dean Martin	148	CB
06/03/1965	Goldfinger (Part 1)	Jimmy Smith	105	BB
06/03/1965	Why Don't You Let Yourself Go	Mary Wells	106	CB
06/03/1965	Why Don't You Let Yourself Go	Mary Wells	107	BB
06/03/1965	The Special Years	Brook Benton	109	CB
06/03/1965	You Don't Miss A Good Thing (Until It's Gone)	Irma Thomas	109	BB
06/03/1965	Who Can I Turn To	Dionne Warwick	110	CB
06/03/1965	You Don't Miss A Good Thing (Until It's Gone)	Irma Thomas	116	CB
06/03/1965	It Hurts Me	BoBBy Sherman	118	BB
06/03/1965	You'll Be Gone	Elvis Presley With The Jordanaires	121	BB
06/03/1965	Little Latin Lupe Lu	The Chancellors	122	CB
06/03/1965	Let The People Talk	Neil Sedaka	124	CB
06/03/1965	Why Don't You Do It Right	Fats Domino	128	CB
06/03/1965	Heart Full Of Love	The Invincibles	132	CB
06/03/1965	Tell Her I'm Not Home	Ike & Tina Turner	135	CB
06/03/1965	Sylvie Sleepin'	The Tokens	138	CB
06/03/1965	Don't Mess Around	The Gestures	141	CB
06/03/1965	Love Me, Love Me	Tommy Roe & The Oremans	142	CB
06/03/1965	Chop-Chop	Sandy Nelson	143	CB
13/03/1965	Baby, Please Don't Go	Them	102	BB
13/03/1965	Let The People Talk	Neil Sedaka	107	BB
13/03/1965	Simon Says	The Isley Brothers	107	CB
13/03/1965	A Dear John Letter	Skeeter Davis & BoBBy Bare	114	BB
13/03/1965	Do I Hear A Waltz?	Eydie Gorme	116	CB
13/03/1965	With All My Heart	Al Martino	122	BB
13/03/1965	Stop And Get A Hold Of Myself	Gladys Knight & The Pips	123	BB
13/03/1965	Do It With All Your Heart	Dee Dee Warwick	124	BB
13/03/1965	Is It Love?	Cilla Black	133	BB
13/03/1965	Reach For A Star	Sandy Nelson	133	BB

20/03/1965	Banana Juice	The Mar-Keys	102	CB
20/03/1965	Carmen	Bruce & Terry	111	CB
20/03/1965	That'll Be The Day	The Everly Brothers	111	BB
20/03/1965	Treat Him Tender, Maureen (Now That Ringo Belongs To You)	Angie & The Chicklettes	112	CB
20/03/1965	Without A Song	Earl Grant	113	CB
20/03/1965	Why Don't They Understand	Tony Conigliaro	121	CB
20/03/1965	Stop And Get A Hold Of Myself	Gladys Knight & The Pips	125	CB
20/03/1965	Come On Now	The Kinks	129	CB
20/03/1965	The Special Years	Brook Benton	129	BB
20/03/1965	T.C.B.	Dee Clark	130	CB
20/03/1965	Mickey's East Coast Jerk	The Larks	132	BB
20/03/1965	(Gary, Please Don't Sell) My Diamond Ring	Wendy Hill	134	BB
20/03/1965	It Was Nice	Jimmy Hughes	148	CB
27/03/1965	Silver Dollar	Damita Jo	104	CB
27/03/1965	Carmen	Bruce And Terry	107	BB
27/03/1965	Devil's Hideaway	James Brown At The Organ & His Orchestra	107	CB
27/03/1965	Girl With A Little Tin Heart	The Lettermen	112	CB
27/03/1965	It Was I	The Fantastic Baggys	115	CB
27/03/1965	Think Summer	Susan Wayne	118	CB
27/03/1965	My Heart Keeps Following You	The Serendipity Singers	122	CB
27/03/1965	Tomorrow Night	Damita Jo	124	BB
27/03/1965	Simon Says	The Isley Brothers	131	BB
27/03/1965	Silver Spoon	Hank Marr	134	BB
27/03/1965	Play With Fire	The Rolling Stones	137	CB
03/04/1965	Ain't No Telling	BoBBy Bland	102	CB
03/04/1965	Since I Don't Have You	The Four Seasons	105	BB
03/04/1965	Eyes Of Mine (Occi Mici)	Rita Pavone	113	CB
03/04/1965	Mexican Pearls	Don Randi	113	BB
03/04/1965	I'll Keep Holding On (Just To Your Love)	Sonny James	116	BB
03/04/1965	I Apologize	P.J. Proby	117	CB

03/04/1965	Who Are You	Stacey Cane	119	CB
03/04/1965	Banana Juice	Mar-Keys	121	BB
03/04/1965	Lucky To Be Loved (By You)	Emanuel Lasky	130	CB
03/04/1965	Don't Wait Too Long	Bettye Swann	131	BB
03/04/1965	Land Of A Thousand Dances "The Na Na Song" [Live]	Round Robin	135	BB
03/04/1965	Evening Time	Elena	138	CB
10/04/1965	If You Wish	Peter & Gordon	101	CB
10/04/1965	The Record	H.B. Barnum	105	CB
10/04/1965	The Record (Baby, I Love You)	Ben E. King	105	CB
10/04/1965	Since I Don't Have You	The Four Seasons	110	CB
10/04/1965	She's Lost You	The Zephyrs	112	CB
10/04/1965	(Somebody) Ease My Troublin' Mind	Sam Cooke	115	BB
10/04/1965	Chim Chim Cheree	Burl Ives	120	BB
10/04/1965	Do I Hear A Waltz?	Eydie Gorme	122	BB
10/04/1965	One Step Ahead	Aretha Franklin	122	CB
10/04/1965	Cry Me A River	Marie Knight	124	BB
10/04/1965	Funny How Love Can Be	The Ivy League	124	CB
10/04/1965	Thanks Mr. Florist	The Four Lads	126	CB
10/04/1965	(Somebody) Ease My Troublin' Mind	Sam Cooke	127	CB
10/04/1965	The Square	Dick Whittinghill	129	CB
10/04/1965	T.C.B. (Take Care Off Business)	Dee Clark	132	BB
10/04/1965	I'll Keep Holding On (Just To Your Love)	Sonny James	133	CB
10/04/1965	Girl With A Little Tin Heart	The Lettermen	135	BB
10/04/1965	Three Kids	Jonathan, David & Elbert	135	CB
10/04/1965	Last Exit To Brooklyn	Scott Bedford Four	136	CB
17/04/1965	In The Meantime	Georgie Fame & The Blue Flames	103	CB
17/04/1965	Over The Rainbow	Billy Thorpe & The Aztecs	107	CB
17/04/1965	She's Lost You	The Zephyrs	109	BB
17/04/1965	Tomorrow Is Another Day	Steve Alaimo	109	CB
17/04/1965	Poor Boy	The Royalettes Featuring Sheila Ross	113	BB

17/04/1965	Tomorrow Never Comes	Glen Campbell	118	BB
17/04/1965	P's And Q's	Nella Dodds	123	CB
17/04/1965	I Can't Help It (If I'm Still In Love With You)	Skeeter Davis	126	BB
17/04/1965	Losin' My Touch	Peggy March	127	CB
17/04/1965	I'm Thinking	Dave Clark Five	128	BB
17/04/1965	I'll Never Fall In Love Again	BoBBy Freeman	131	BB
17/04/1965	Come On, Let's Go	The Rogues	140	CB
17/04/1965	Gabrielle	Jimmy Bing	142	CB
17/04/1965	That's The Way	The Honeycombs	143	CB
17/04/1965	Sea Cruise	Ace Cannon	144	CB
17/04/1965	Why Do I Cry	The Remains	144	CB
24/04/1965	Magic Trumpet (Trompeta Magica)	Comparsa Universitaria De La Laguna	102	CB
24/04/1965	Let Me Down Easy	Betty Lavette	103	BB
24/04/1965	He Ain't No Angel	The Ad Libs	104	CB
24/04/1965	I'll Cry Alone	Gale Garnett	108	BB
24/04/1965	Devil's Hideaway	James Brown At The Organ And His Orchestra	114	BB
24/04/1965	To Be Or Not To Be	Otis Leavill	115	CB
24/04/1965	Searchin' For My Baby	The Manhattans	116	CB
24/04/1965	To Have And To Hold	The Distant Cousins	123	CB
24/04/1965	It Was Easier To Hurt Her	Garnet Mimms	124	BB
24/04/1965	In The Night	Freddy Cannon	125	CB
24/04/1965	My Baby	The Freeman Brothers	127	CB
24/04/1965	Who Knows (b-side)	Gladys Knight & The Pips	129	BB
24/04/1965	I Can't Remember	Connie Smith	130	BB
24/04/1965	Please, Stop The Wedding	Lou Johnson	131	CB
24/04/1965	Venice Blue (Que C'est Triste Venise)	BoBBy Darin	133	BB
24/04/1965	Sea Cruise	Ace Cannon	135	BB
24/04/1965	Stop Th' Music	Sue Thompson	135	CB
24/04/1965	I'll Cry Alone	Gale Garnett	144	CB
01/05/1965	Without You (I Cannot Live)	Matt Monro	101	BB

01/05/1965	Crying Won't Help You Now	Clyde Mcphatter	104	CB
01/05/1965	Jerk It	The Gypsies	106	CB
01/05/1965	Tiger-A-Go-Go	Buzz And Bucky	107	BB
01/05/1965	Yes It Is	The Beatles	107	CB
01/05/1965	Darling Come Talk To Me	Joe Hinton	111	CB
01/05/1965	Mustang Sally	Sir Mack Rice	111	CB
01/05/1965	Snake In The Grass	Paul Martin	116	CB
01/05/1965	Crying Won't Help You Now	Clyde Mcphatter	117	BB
01/05/1965	Without A Song (Part 1)	Ray Charles With Orchestra & Chorus	117	CB
01/05/1965	Learning The Game	The Hullaballoos	121	BB
01/05/1965	Chilly Wind	The Seekers	122	BB
01/05/1965	Honey, I Need	The Pretty Things	123	CB
01/05/1965	Somebody's Got To Pay	Little Johnny Taylor	125	CB
01/05/1965	Hey Baby	The Hi-Lites	128	BB
01/05/1965	The Girl From Greenwich Village	The Trade Winds	129	BB
01/05/1965	Over The Rainbow	Billy Thorpe And The Aztecs	130	BB
01/05/1965	In The Night	Freddy Cannon	132	BB
01/05/1965	Our Crazy Affair	Jack Laforge, His Piano & Orchestra	137	CB
01/05/1965	I'm Gonna Cry Till My Tears Run Dry	Irma Thomas	138	CB
08/05/1965	It Hurts Me Too	Elmore James	105	CB
08/05/1965	Magic Trumpet (Trompeta Magica)	Comparsa Universitaria De La Laguna	107	BB
08/05/1965	Jerk It	The Gypsies	111	BB
08/05/1965	Stop Th' Music	Sue Thompson	115	BB
08/05/1965	Gotta Travel On	Damita Jo	119	BB
08/05/1965	You've Lost That Lovin' Feelin'	Lincoln Mayorga	120	CB
08/05/1965	You Gave Me Somebody To Love	The Dreamlovers	121	BB
08/05/1965	Welcome, Welcome	Nancy Wilson	125	BB
08/05/1965	To Be Or Not To Be	Otis Leavill	128	BB
08/05/1965	Last Exit To Brooklyn	Scott Bedford Four	129	BB
08/05/1965	Welcome, Welcome	Nancy Wilson	129	CB

08/05/1965	Brother, Can You Spare A Dime?	The Village Stompers	137	CB
08/05/1965	I Want Your Love	The Pussycats	138	CB
15/05/1965	(I Want) No One But You	Buck Owens	101	CB
15/05/1965	RiBBon Of Darkness	Marty RoBBins	103	BB
15/05/1965	Hold On Baby	Sam Hawkins	104	CB
15/05/1965	The Price Of Love	The Everly Brothers	104	BB
15/05/1965	(He's Gonna Be) Fine, Fine, Fine	The Ikettes	106	CB
15/05/1965	Mustang Sally	Sir Mack Rice	108	BB
15/05/1965	Without A Song-Part 1	Ray Charles With Orchestra & Chorus	112	BB
15/05/1965	One Step Ahead	Aretha Franklin	119	BB
15/05/1965	Good Bye, So Long	Ike & Tina Turner	120	CB
15/05/1965	My Man (Sweetest Man In The World)	Johnnie Mae Matthews	121	CB
15/05/1965	Se Piangi, Se Ridi	The New Christy Minstrels	123	CB
15/05/1965	Dust Got In Daddy's Eyes	BoBBy Bland	125	BB
15/05/1965	I'm Gonna Cry Till My Tears Run Dry	Irma Thomas	130	BB
15/05/1965	Sometimes	Paul Revere And The Raiders	131	BB
15/05/1965	Queen Of The Senior Prom	Vaughn Monroe	132	BB
15/05/1965	The Ballad Of Cat Ballou	Nat King Cole & StuBBy Kaye	136	CB
15/05/1965	In Paradise	The Showmen	138	CB
15/05/1965	Some Things Just Stick In Your Mind	Dick & Deedee	141	CB
15/05/1965	Chilly Wind	The Seekers	143	CB
15/05/1965	Laurie Don't Worry	Frankie Fanelli	144	CB
15/05/1965	Sneakin' Up On You	Peggy Lee	145	CB
15/05/1965	It Ain't Necessarily So (From "Porgy And Bess")	Doc Severinsen & His Orchestra	149	CB
22/05/1965	The Real Thing	Tina Britt	103	BB
22/05/1965	Three O'clock In The Morning	Lou Rawls	103	CB
22/05/1965	It Hurts Me Too	Elmore James	106	BB
22/05/1965	Darling Take Me Back (I'm Sorry)*	Ray Pollard	114	CB
22/05/1965	No One Can Live Forever	Sammy Davis Jr.	117	BB
22/05/1965	The Real Thing	Tina Britt	117	CB

22/05/1965	I'll Still Love You	Jeff Barry	120	CB
22/05/1965	Let There Be Drums '66 [Live]	Sandy Nelson	120	BB
22/05/1965	Chim Chim Cheree	Dick Van Dyke With The Jack Halloran Singers	123	BB
22/05/1965	Senorita From Detroit	Jack Nitzsche	123	CB
22/05/1965	When It's All Over	Jay & The Americans	129	BB
22/05/1965	Stay In My Corner	The Dells	131	CB
22/05/1965	The Girl From Greenwich Village	The Trade Winds	131	CB
22/05/1965	No, Not Much	Vincent Edwards	134	CB
22/05/1965	Searchin' For My Baby	The Manhattans	135	BB
22/05/1965	Say It Softly	BoBBy Whiteside	137	CB
22/05/1965	Just Dance On By	Eydie Gorme	140	CB
29/05/1965	In Hollywood	Dobie Gray	103	CB
29/05/1965	Your Baby Doesn't Love You Anymore	Ruby & The Romantics	103	CB
29/05/1965	Don't Jump	Fontella Bass & BoBBy Mcclure	110	CB
29/05/1965	No One Can Live Forever	Sammy Davis Jr.	115	CB
29/05/1965	Mae	Herb Alpert & The Tijuana Brass	116	BB
29/05/1965	The Price Of Love	The Everly Brothers	118	CB
29/05/1965	The Little Bird	The Nashville Teens	119	CB
29/05/1965	Cast Your Fate To The Wind	Steve Alaimo	120	CB
29/05/1965	Let Me Love You	George Goodman & His Headliners	121	CB
29/05/1965	Geeto Tiger	The Tigers	122	CB
29/05/1965	It's Alright	BoBBy Bare	122	BB
29/05/1965	(He's Gonna Be) Fine, Fine, Fine	The Ikettes	125	BB
29/05/1965	Gotta Travel On	Pete Fountain	129	CB
29/05/1965	End Up Crying	The Vibrations	130	BB
29/05/1965	Mae	Pete Fountain	130	CB
29/05/1965	Soupy	Maggie Thrett	130	CB
29/05/1965	Let Me Cry On Your Shoulder	Georgia GiBBs	132	BB
29/05/1965	Rindercella [Live]	Archie Campbell	132	BB
29/05/1965	You Turned My Bitter Into Sweet	Mary Love	133	BB

29/05/1965	La Raspa	Henry Mancini & His Orchestra	134	CB
29/05/1965	Bimbo	Darin D. Anna	136	CB
05/06/1965	Are You Sincere	Trini Lopez	106	CB
05/06/1965	Good Bye, So Long	Ike & Tina Turner	107	BB
05/06/1965	No, Not Much	Vincent Edwards	108	BB
05/06/1965	Gonna Be Ready	Betty Everett	117	BB
05/06/1965	Geeto Tiger	The Tigers	119	BB
05/06/1965	Just Dance On By	Eydie Gorme	124	BB
05/06/1965	Last Night I Made A Little Girl Cry	Steve Lawrence	126	BB
05/06/1965	Swing Me	Nino Tempo & April Stevens	127	BB
05/06/1965	Wait Johnny For Me	Bernadette Peters	127	CB
05/06/1965	She's Gone Again	Ben E. King	128	BB
05/06/1965	Four Times Faster	Fish 'N' Chips	129	CB
05/06/1965	You Gave Me Somebody To Love	The Dreamlovers	133	CB
05/06/1965	You Better Make Up Your Mind	Brooks O'dell	134	CB
05/06/1965	RiBBon Of Darkness	Marty RoBBins	139	CB
05/06/1965	Que Sera, Sera	Earl Royce & The Olympics	141	CB
05/06/1965	A Thrill A Moment	Kim Weston	143	CB
12/06/1965	Take The Time	Johnny Mathis	104	BB
12/06/1965	I'm Learnin'	Mary Wells	106	CB
12/06/1965	Where Can I Go	Steve Lawrence	106	CB
12/06/1965	Sunrise, Sunset	Eddie Fisher	119	CB
12/06/1965	Stay In My Corner	The Dells	122	BB
12/06/1965	The Little Bird	The Nashville Teens	123	BB
12/06/1965	Born To Be With You	The Capitol Showband	126	BB
12/06/1965	Travellin' On	Jack Jones	132	BB
12/06/1965	A Summer Thought	Reparata With Hash Brown & His Orchestra	144	CB
19/06/1965	I Put A Spell On You	Nina Simone	107	CB
19/06/1965	In The Hall Of The Mountain King	Sounds, Incorporated	107	CB
19/06/1965	Please Do Something	Don Covay & The Goodtimers	109	CB

19/06/1965	Anyway Anyhow Anywhere	The Who	112	CB
19/06/1965	The First Thing Ev'ry Morning (And The Last Thing Ev'ry Night)	Jimmy Dean	112	CB
19/06/1965	Yellow Haired Woman	Frankie Randall	114	CB
19/06/1965	Sunrise, Sunset	Eddie Fisher	119	BB
19/06/1965	Come Out Dancin'	Rick Nelson	131	CB
19/06/1965	Nau Ninny Nau	Cannibal & The Headhunters	132	CB
19/06/1965	Hold On Baby	Sam Hawkins	133	BB
19/06/1965	Because I Love Her	The Human Beings	136	CB
26/06/1965	Your Baby Doesn't Love You Anymore	Ruby And The Romantics	108	BB
26/06/1965	The Outside World	The Drifters	112	CB
26/06/1965	The Loneliest Boy In The World	Paul Anka	113	CB
26/06/1965	I'm A Fool To Care	George And Gene George Jones & Gene Pitney	115	BB
26/06/1965	I'm A Hurting Inside	Shep & The Limelites	119	CB
26/06/1965	I Put A Spell On You	Nina Simone	120	BB
26/06/1965	Remember When I Loved Her	The Zombies	122	CB
26/06/1965	My Little Red Book	Manfred Mann	124	BB
26/06/1965	I Found A Daisy (In The City)	Barry Darvell	128	CB
26/06/1965	Alimony	Tommy Tucker	129	CB
26/06/1965	Gonna Make Him My Baby	April Young	129	CB
26/06/1965	Mae	Pete Fountain	129	BB
26/06/1965	But I Do	The Jewels	130	BB
26/06/1965	Nau Ninny Nau	Cannibal And The Headhunters	133	BB
26/06/1965	The Word Game	Benny Spellman	137	CB
26/06/1965	Depend On Yourself	Joe & Eddie	149	CB
03/07/1965	Gee The Moon Is Shining Bright	The Dixie Cups	102	BB
03/07/1965	Poor Boy	Tony Clarke	102	CB
03/07/1965	Boss Love	Lee Rogers	106	CB
03/07/1965	March (You'll Be Sorry)	The Shirelles	108	BB
03/07/1965	Follow Me	The Drifters	111	CB
03/07/1965	Frankfurter Sandwiches	The Streamliners With Joanne	117	BB

03/07/1965	You've Never Been In Love Like This Before	Unit Four Plus Two	117	CB
03/07/1965	I Can't Stand To See You Cry	Jerry Butler	120	CB
03/07/1965	In The Middle Of Nowhere	Dusty Springfield	123	CB
03/07/1965	The Streets Of Laredo	Johnny Cash	124	BB
03/07/1965	So Much In Love With You	Ian & The Zodiacs	125	CB
03/07/1965	Gee The Moon Is Shining Bright	The Dixie Cups	126	CB
03/07/1965	Come Out Dancin'	Rick Nelson	130	BB
03/07/1965	Side Show	BoBBy Rydell	131	CB
03/07/1965	(Love Is Like A) Ramblin' Rose	Ted Taylor	132	BB
03/07/1965	My Little Red Book	Manfred Mann	132	CB
03/07/1965	My Little Red Book (All I Do Is Talk About You)*	Burt Bacharach & His Orchestra Featuring Tony Middleton	132	CB
03/07/1965	I'm The One That Love Forgot	The Manhattans	133	CB
03/07/1965	New Orleans [Live]	The Chartbusters	134	BB
03/07/1965	March (You'll Be Sorry)	The Shirelles	140	CB
10/07/1965	Whittier Blvd.	Thee Midniters	102	CB
10/07/1965	99 Plus 1	J. Gardner	104	CB
10/07/1965	If I Had My Life To Live Over	Lloyd Price	107	BB
10/07/1965	Happy Feet Time	The Monclairs	108	BB
10/07/1965	In The Middle Of Nowhere	Dusty Springfield	108	BB
10/07/1965	Tiger Woman	Claude King	110	BB
10/07/1965	Hallelujah	The Invitations	111	BB
10/07/1965	My Name Is Mud	Eddie Rambeau	116	CB
10/07/1965	You Can't Grow Peaches On A Cherry Tree	Browns Featuring Jim Edward Brown	120	BB
10/07/1965	I Can't Stand To See You Cry	Jerry Butler	122	BB
10/07/1965	Why Don't You Believe Me	Vic Damone	127	BB
10/07/1965	Tiger Woman	Claude King	129	CB
10/07/1965	Mae	Herb Alpert & The Tijuana Brass	130	CB
10/07/1965	The Legend Of Shenandoah	James Stewart	133	BB
10/07/1965	You Can't Grow Peaches On A Cherry Tree	The Browns Featuring Jim Edward Brown	134	CB
17/07/1965	Alimony	Tommy Tucker	103	BB

17/07/1965	It Happened Just That Way	Roger Miller	105	BB
17/07/1965	The Tracker	Sir Douglas Quintet	110	CB
17/07/1965	Moonglow & Theme From Picnic	Esther Phillips	111	CB
17/07/1965	Louie Louie	The Kingsmen	112	CB
17/07/1965	My Name Is Mud	Eddie Rambeau	112	BB
17/07/1965	The End Of The World	Herman's Hermits	113	CB
17/07/1965	(No, No) I'm Losing You	Aretha Franklin	114	BB
17/07/1965	That Goes To Show You	Garnet Mimms	115	BB
17/07/1965	Do The "45"	Sharpees	117	BB
17/07/1965	The Sweetheart Tree	Henry Mancini, His Orchestra & Chorus	117	BB
17/07/1965	Southern Country Boy	The Carter Brothers	123	CB
17/07/1965	Those Magnificent Men In Their Flying Machines	The Village Stompers	130	BB
17/07/1965	Southern Country Boy	The Carter Brothers	133	BB
17/07/1965	Let The Water Run Down	P.J. Proby	134	CB
17/07/1965	Salt Water Guitar	Burl Ives	138	CB
17/07/1965	My Prayer	Shelley Fabares	144	CB
17/07/1965	The Legend Of Shenandoah	James Stewart	144	CB
17/07/1965	Those Magnificent Men In Their Flying Machines	The Village Stompers	146	CB
24/07/1965	I'll Feel A Whole Lot Better	The Byrds	103	BB
24/07/1965	The Tracker	Sir Douglas Quintet	105	BB
24/07/1965	You've Got To Earn It	The Temptations	109	CB
24/07/1965	Moonglow & Theme From Picnic	Esther Phillips	115	BB
24/07/1965	That Goes To Show You	Garnet Mimms	119	CB
24/07/1965	Arkansas (Part 1)	Jimmy Mccracklin	132	BB
24/07/1965	Un-Wind The Twine	Alvin Cash & The Crawlers	134	BB
24/07/1965	I'm The One That Love Forgot (b-side)	The Manhattans	135	BB
24/07/1965	Tansy	Pee Wee Spitelera	142	CB
24/07/1965	Take Me For A Little While	Jackie Ross	147	CB
31/07/1965	I'll Feel A Whole Lot Better	The Byrds	104	CB
31/07/1965	Out In The Sun (Hey-O)	The Beach-Nuts	106	BB

31/07/1965	I Left My Heart In San Francisco	Fats Domino	111	CB
31/07/1965	I Don't Want To Live (Without Your Love)	BoBBi Martin	115	BB
31/07/1965	The Turnaround, Part I	Hank Mobley	118	CB
31/07/1965	Only You (Can Break My Heart)	Buck Owens	120	BB
31/07/1965	You've Got To Earn It	The Temptations	123	BB
31/07/1965	If I Had My Life To Live Over	Lloyd Price	126	CB
31/07/1965	So Much In Love With You	Ian & The Zodiacs	131	BB
31/07/1965	Let's Have A Beach Party	The Pleasures	136	CB
31/07/1965	I Don't Want To Live (Without Your Love)	BoBBi Martin	138	CB
31/07/1965	Joyride	Randy & The Rainbows	138	CB
31/07/1965	A Little Bit Of Happiness	The New Christy Minstrels	147	CB
07/08/1965	I'm Down	The Beatles	101	BB
07/08/1965	I'm Alive	The Hollies	103	BB
07/08/1965	Good Times	Gene Chandler	106	CB
07/08/1965	Truck Drivin' Son-Of-A-Gun	Dave Dudley	106	CB
07/08/1965	I Don't Believe "Call On Me"	The Guilloteens	108	CB
07/08/1965	Sweetheart Tree	Johnny Mathis	108	BB
07/08/1965	Do The "45"	Sharpees	119	CB
07/08/1965	Truck Drivin' Son-Of-A-Gun	Dave Dudley	125	BB
07/08/1965	I'm Down	The Beatles	126	CB
07/08/1965	Storm Warning	The Volcanos	126	CB
07/08/1965	Let Her Dance	BoBBy Fuller Four	133	BB
07/08/1965	I Don't Need	Ike & Tina Turner	134	BB
07/08/1965	I'm Letting You Go	Eddy Arnold	135	BB
07/08/1965	People Say	John & Paul	135	CB
07/08/1965	I Told You So	Shirley Ellis	149	CB
14/08/1965	99 Plus 1	J. Gardner	102	BB
14/08/1965	Take Me For A Little While	Evie Sands	114	BB
14/08/1965	It's The Only Way To Fly	Jewel Akens	120	BB
14/08/1965	Great Goo-Ga-Moo-Ga	Tom & Jerrio	123	BB

14/08/1965	I'll Stop At Nothing	Sandie Shaw	123	BB
14/08/1965	My Ship Is Comin' In	Jimmy Radcliffe	128	CB
14/08/1965	Whole Lot Of Woman	Radiants	129	CB
14/08/1965	Great Goo-Ga-Moo-Ga	Tom & Jerrio	130	CB
14/08/1965	I Can't Begin To Tell You	Buddy Greco	132	BB
14/08/1965	Hey Little Girl	Z.Z. Hill	134	BB
14/08/1965	Spootin'	Bill Black's Combo	135	BB
14/08/1965	Where Does Love Go	Charles Boyer	148	CB
21/08/1965	Summer Wind	Roger Williams & The Harry Simeone Chorale	109	BB
21/08/1965	You're The Reason	Gerry And The Pacemakers	117	BB
21/08/1965	Move It On Over	Del Shannon	121	CB
21/08/1965	Love Is Strange	The Everly Brothers	128	BB
21/08/1965	The Silence (Il Silenzio)	Al Hirt	129	CB
21/08/1965	It's The Only Way To Fly	Jewel Akens	136	CB
21/08/1965	Bumming Around	Dean Martin	141	CB
28/08/1965	Got To Find A Way	Harold Burrage	103	CB
28/08/1965	Millions Of Roses	Steve Lawrence	106	BB
28/08/1965	(I've Got A Feeling) You're Gonna Be Sorry	Billy Butler	109	CB
28/08/1965	(It's A) Long Lonely Highway	Elvis Presley With The Jordanaires	112	BB
28/08/1965	Behind The Tear	Sonny James	113	BB
28/08/1965	Let Her Dance	BoBBy Fuller Four	113	CB
28/08/1965	Life	Joe Leahy	118	CB
28/08/1965	Millions Of Roses	Steve Lawrence	118	CB
28/08/1965	The Sons Of Katie Elder	Johnny Cash	119	BB
28/08/1965	Sun Glasses	Skeeter Davis	120	BB
28/08/1965	The Girl In The Black Bikini	The In Crowd	121	CB
28/08/1965	Sun Glasses	Skeeter Davis	123	CB
28/08/1965	Take Me For A Little While	Evie Sands	124	CB
28/08/1965	Without My Sweet Baby	Little Milton	126	CB
28/08/1965	Move It On Over	Del Shannon	128	BB

28/08/1965	Half As Much	Them	130	CB
28/08/1965	Fool's Paradise	BoBBy Wood	132	CB
28/08/1965	The Sweetheart Tree	The King Family	147	CB
04/09/1965	When Somebody Loves You	Frank Sinatra	102	BB
04/09/1965	(I've Got A Feeling) You're Gonna Be Sorry	Billy Butler	103	BB
04/09/1965	When Somebody Loves You	Frank Sinatra	104	CB
04/09/1965	Drums A-Go-Go	The Hollywood Persuaders	109	BB
04/09/1965	Whenever You're Ready	The Zombies	110	BB
04/09/1965	September In The Rain	Chad & Jeremy	112	CB
04/09/1965	Whenever You're Ready	The Zombies	114	CB
04/09/1965	As I Sit Here	The Whispers	116	CB
04/09/1965	Whole Lot Of Woman	The Radiants	116	BB
04/09/1965	Livin' In A House Full Of Love	David Houston	117	BB
04/09/1965	Hey Ho What You Do To Me	Chad Allan & The Expressions (The Guess Who)	125	BB
04/09/1965	Whittier Blvd.	Thee Midniters	127	BB
04/09/1965	The Bells Of St. Mary	The Tokens	149	CB
11/09/1965	Close Your Eyes	The 3° Degrees	105	CB
11/09/1965	Run Like The Devil	BoBBy Vee	106	CB
11/09/1965	Happy, Happy Birthday Baby	Dolly Parton	122	CB
11/09/1965	The Twelfth Of Never	Cliff Richard	129	CB
11/09/1965	I'm Not A Plaything	Marv Johnson	133	CB
11/09/1965	The Way Of The D.J.	Ray Hildebrand	135	CB
11/09/1965	Can't Help Falling In Love	Donald Height	139	CB
18/09/1965	Here Come The Tears	Gene Chandler	102	BB
18/09/1965	I Still Love You	The Vejtables	109	CB
18/09/1965	Let's Do It Over	Joe Simon	111	CB
18/09/1965	Steal Away	Billy Joe Royal	111	CB
18/09/1965	Yes, Mr. Peters	Roy Drusky & Priscilla Mitchell	122	CB
18/09/1965	Drums A Go-Go	Sandy Nelson	124	BB
18/09/1965	My Love, Forgive Me (Amore, Scusami)	The Ray Charles Singers	124	BB

18/09/1965	Little Sally Tease	Don & The Goodtimes	128	CB
18/09/1965	Blowin' In The Wind	Steve Alaimo	139	CB
25/09/1965	Come Back To Me, My Love	Robert Goulet	107	CB
25/09/1965	The Cincinnati Kid	Ray Charles	115	BB
25/09/1965	You Can Cry On My Shoulder	Brenda Holloway	116	BB
25/09/1965	Send A Letter To Me	Freddie & The Dreamers	120	CB
25/09/1965	You Can Cry On My Shoulder	Brenda Holloway	123	CB
25/09/1965	Love And Kisses	Rick Nelson	124	CB
25/09/1965	Run Like The Devil	BoBBy Vee	124	BB
25/09/1965	Got To Find A Way	Harold Burrage	128	BB
25/09/1965	My Heart Belongs To You	The Shirelles	133	CB
25/09/1965	Only A Fool Breaks His Own Heart	Arthur Prysock	140	CB
02/10/1965	Let Me Know When It's Over	Esther Phillips	102	CB
02/10/1965	Happy, Happy Birthday Baby	Dolly Parton	108	BB
02/10/1965	The Cincinnati Kid	Ray Charles	109	CB
02/10/1965	Come Back To Me, My Love	Robert Goulet	118	BB
02/10/1965	The Funny Thing About It	Nancy Ames	119	BB
02/10/1965	I'll Keep On Trying	Walter Jackson	120	BB
02/10/1965	Tweetie Pie	Dave "Baby" Cortez	122	CB
02/10/1965	Hark	Unit Four Plus Two	123	CB
02/10/1965	Send A Letter To Me	Freddie And The Dreamers	123	BB
02/10/1965	Shotgun Wedding	Roy "C"	125	CB
02/10/1965	The Funny Thing About It	Nancy Ames	125	CB
02/10/1965	And That Reminds Me	Della Reese	126	CB
02/10/1965	Close Your Eyes	The 3° Degrees	126	BB
02/10/1965	Tweetie Pie	Dave "Baby" Cortez	135	BB
02/10/1965	Teardrops 'TILL Dawn	Timi Yuro	146	CB
09/10/1965	For Your Love	The Righteous Brothers	103	BB
09/10/1965	Mr. Jones (A Ballad Of A Thin Man)	The Grass Roots	104	CB
09/10/1965	Don't You Know Why	The Searchers	105	CB

09/10/1965	Sea Cruise	Herman's Hermits	108	CB
09/10/1965	Open Up Your Heart	Arthur Prysock	109	CB
09/10/1965	For Your Love	The Righteous Brothers	111	CB
09/10/1965	Can You Hear Me	Lee Dorsey	114	CB
09/10/1965	Stay Together Young Lovers	Ben Aiken	115	CB
09/10/1965	I Feel Strange	The Wonderettes	117	CB
09/10/1965	We Didn't Ask To Be Brought Here	BoBBy Darin	117	BB
09/10/1965	Don't Fool With Fu Manchu	The Rockin' Ramrods	119	CB
09/10/1965	Can You Please Crawl Out Your Window?	The Vacels	120	CB
09/10/1965	Work, Work, Work	Lee Dorsey	121	BB
09/10/1965	Only A Fool Breaks His Own Heart	Arthur Prysock	125	BB
09/10/1965	Hark	Unit Four Plus Two	131	BB
09/10/1965	Big Mistake	Timi Yuro	135	CB
09/10/1965	The Sun Ain't Gonna Shine (Anymore)	Frankie Valli	141	CB
16/10/1965	Ev'rybody Has The Right To Be Wrong! (At Least Once)	Frank Sinatra	101	CB
16/10/1965	Ii Silenzio	Nini Rosso	101	BB
16/10/1965	See My Friends	The Kinks	102	CB
16/10/1965	Here Come The Tears	Gene Chandler	106	CB
16/10/1965	Never Had It So Good	Ronnie Milsap	106	BB
16/10/1965	Sea Cruise	The Hondells	110	CB
16/10/1965	See My Friends	The Kinks	111	BB
16/10/1965	A Bench In The Park	The Jive Five Featuring Eugene Pitt	112	CB
16/10/1965	The Times They Are A-Changing	Peter Antell	112	CB
16/10/1965	Deep In Your Heart	Jerry Vale	118	BB
16/10/1965	On A Clear Day You Can See Forever (b-side)	Robert Goulet	119	BB
16/10/1965	Twilight Time	Billy J. Kramer With The Dakotas	119	CB
16/10/1965	Trouble With A Woman	Kip & Ken	123	CB
16/10/1965	I Need You So	Chuck Jackson & Maxine Brown	125	CB
16/10/1965	My Heart Belongs To You	The Shirelles	125	BB
16/10/1965	Sea Cruise	The Hondells	131	BB

16/10/1965	Don't Throw The Roses Away	John Gary	132	BB
16/10/1965	Feelin' Fruggy	Al Hirt	135	CB
16/10/1965	Side By Side	Jane Morgan	141	CB
16/10/1965	Drums A-Go-Go	The Hollywood Persuaders	143	CB
16/10/1965	Right Now And Not Later	The Shangri-Las	150	CB
23/10/1965	Boys	The Beatles	102	BB
23/10/1965	Upon A Painted Ocean	Barry Mcguire	103	CB
23/10/1965	The Letter	Sonny & Cher	104	CB
23/10/1965	The True Picture	Jack Jones	109	CB
23/10/1965	Heartbeat Part 1	Gloria Jones	112	CB
23/10/1965	Two Is A Couple	Ike & Tina Turner	113	CB
23/10/1965	Stay Together Young Lovers	Ben Aiken	121	BB
23/10/1965	Should I	Chad & Jeremy	128	BB
23/10/1965	Love Minus Zero	Eddie Hodges	130	CB
23/10/1965	The True Picture	Jack Jones	134	BB
23/10/1965	Heide	Horst Jankowski, His Orchestra & Chorus	135	CB
23/10/1965	Your Daddy Wants His Baby Back	Derek Martin	135	CB
23/10/1965	Love Ain't What It Used To Be	The Diplomats	137	CB
23/10/1965	Fizz	Ian Whitcomb	138	CB
30/10/1965	A Bench In The Park	The Jive Five Featuring Eugene Pitt	106	BB
30/10/1965	Let Me Show You Where It's At	Freddy Cannon	115	CB
30/10/1965	Upon A Painted Ocean	Barry Mcguire	117	BB
30/10/1965	Mr. Jones (A Ballad Of A Thin Man)	The Grass Roots	121	BB
30/10/1965	You Got What It Takes	Barbara Mason	126	CB
30/10/1965	The Sun Ain't Gonna Shine (Anymore)	Frankie Valli	128	BB
30/10/1965	Let Me Know When It's Over	Esther Phillips	129	BB
30/10/1965	(You Got) The Gamma Goochee (Live)	Gamma Goochee Himself	131	CB
30/10/1965	A World Without Sunshine	George Maharis	133	CB
30/10/1965	I Know Your Heart Has Been Broken	Roscoe Shelton	135	BB
30/10/1965	Believe In Me	Jerry Butler	136	CB

30/10/1965	Every Good-Bye Ain't Gone	G.L. Crockett	140	CB
30/10/1965	Gotta Get A Hold Of Myself	Dee Dee Warwick	141	CB
06/11/1965	Autumn Leaves - 1965	Roger Williams	110	CB
06/11/1965	Just Out Of Reach	The Zombies	113	BB
06/11/1965	My Place	The Crystals	117	CB
06/11/1965	Everything Is Gonna Be Alright	Willie Mitchell	126	BB
06/11/1965	Happy To Be With You	Johnny Cash	127	CB
06/11/1965	Let Me Show You Where It's All	Freddy Cannon	127	BB
06/11/1965	The Train	Eddie Rambeau	129	BB
06/11/1965	Everybody Has The Right To Be Wrong! (At Least Once)	Frank Sinatra	131	BB
06/11/1965	Love Minus Zero	Eddie Hodges	134	BB
06/11/1965	The Times They Are A-Changing	Pete Antell	135	BB
06/11/1965	You're The Reason I'm In Love	Dean Martin	136	CB
06/11/1965	Gee (But I'd Give The World)	Anthony & The Sophomores	138	CB
06/11/1965	Myra (Shake Up The Party)	The Seekers	138	CB
06/11/1965	Blueberry Hill	The San Remo Golden Strings	139	CB
13/11/1965	Goodbye Babe	The Castaways	101	BB
13/11/1965	Everybody Loves A Good Time	Major Lance	102	CB
13/11/1965	Everybody Loves A Good Time	Major Lance	109	BB
13/11/1965	Just Out Of Reach	The Zombies	110	CB
13/11/1965	Wooden Heart	Elvis Presley	110	BB
13/11/1965	The Three Bells (The Jimmy Brown Song)	The Tokens	112	CB
13/11/1965	A Boy And A Girl	Sounds Orchestral	113	CB
13/11/1965	I Know It's All Right	Sam Hawkins	117	BB
13/11/1965	Take A Look	Irma Thomas	118	BB
13/11/1965	Magic Town	Jody Miller	120	CB
13/11/1965	Mama's Got A Bag Of Her Own	Anna King	120	CB
13/11/1965	The Three Bells (The Jimmy Brown Song)	The Tokens	120	BB
13/11/1965	I Know It's All Right	Sam Hawkins	125	CB
13/11/1965	Heartbeat Part 1	Gloria Jones	128	BB

13/11/1965	Poor Boy	O.V. Wright	129	CB
13/11/1965	It Wasn't Me	Chuck Berry	138	CB
13/11/1965	If You Don't (Love Me, Tell Me So)	Barbara Mason	141	CB
20/11/1965	What The New Breed Say	The Barbarians	102	BB
20/11/1965	The Carnival Is Over	The Seekers	105	BB
20/11/1965	Halloween Mary	P.F. Sloan	110	CB
20/11/1965	Everything Is Gonna Be Alright	Willie Mitchell	117	CB
20/11/1965	Look At Me	The Three Dimensions (with The Thing)	121	CB
20/11/1965	No Time For Pity	Baby Washington	125	CB
20/11/1965	Cast Your Fate To The Wind	We Five	133	CB
20/11/1965	As Long As There Is L-O-V-E Love	Jimmy Ruffin	137	CB
20/11/1965	You're Absolutely Right	The Apollas	138	CB
20/11/1965	Too Careless With My Love	Dee Edwards	139	CB
20/11/1965	Hole In The Wall	George Stone	145	CB
27/11/1965	The New Breed	Jimmy Holiday	115	BB
27/11/1965	What's Come Over This World?	Billy Carr	116	BB
27/11/1965	The Last Thing On My Mind	The Vejtables	117	BB
27/11/1965	Rising Sun	The Deep Six	122	BB
27/11/1965	No Time For Pity	Baby Washington	125	BB
27/11/1965	Should I Give My Love Tonight	The Wooden Nickels	128	CB
27/11/1965	Plastic	The Serendipity Singers	129	CB
27/11/1965	These Kind Of Blues (Pt. 1)	Junior Parker	133	CB
27/11/1965	That Darn Cat	Buddy Greco	136	CB
27/11/1965	Walk Hand In Hand	Gerry & The Pacemakers	137	CB
04/12/1965	Baby, You're My Everything	Little Jerry Williams	102	CB
04/12/1965	A Boy And A Girl	Sounds Orchestral	104	BB
04/12/1965	Good Things Come To Those Who Wait	Chuck Jackson	105	BB
04/12/1965	You're Gonna' Love My Baby	Barbara Mcnair	106	CB
04/12/1965	This Precious Time	Barry Mcguire	108	CB
04/12/1965	Grab This Thing (Pt 1)	Mar-Keys	111	BB

04/12/1965	Look At Me Girl	The Three Dimensions (with The Thing)	113	BB
04/12/1965	Private John Q	Glen Campbell	114	BB
04/12/1965	Plastic	The Serendipity Singers	118	BB
04/12/1965	Magic Town	Jody Miller	125	BB
04/12/1965	Take A Heart	The Sorrows	129	BB
04/12/1965	We Gotta Sing	The Drifters	130	CB
04/12/1965	Love Is Strange	Salvatore Bono & Cher Lapiere Aka Caeser & Cleo	131	BB
04/12/1965	Love Is Strange	Salvatore Bono & Cher Lapiere Aka Caeser & Cleo	132	CB
04/12/1965	The Man In The Glass	The Underdogs	133	CB
04/12/1965	Take A Heart	The Sorrows	134	CB
04/12/1965	Our Love Is Slipping Away	The Ivy League	139	CB
04/12/1965	Outcast	Eddie & Ernie	148	CB
11/12/1965	Walk Hand In Hand	Gerry And The Pacemakers	103	BB
11/12/1965	Good Things Come To Those Who Wait	Chuck Jackson	109	CB
11/12/1965	I Can't Go On	Charlie Rich	109	CB
11/12/1965	Parchment Farm (Blues)	The Kingston Trio	114	CB
11/12/1965	The Little Black Egg	The Nightcrawlers	120	CB
11/12/1965	Chills And Fever	Paul Kelly	123	BB
11/12/1965	Looking Back	Nat "King" Cole	123	BB
11/12/1965	Rising Sun	The Deep Six	124	CB
11/12/1965	Chills & Fever	Tom Jones	125	BB
11/12/1965	I Can't Go On	Charlie Rich	132	BB
11/12/1965	Bo Diddley	The Juveniles	140	CB
11/12/1965	Friends And Lovers Forever	Nancy Ames	140	CB
11/12/1965	Thunderball	Jimmy Sedlar & His Orchestra	144	CB
18/12/1965	Santa Looked A Lot Like Daddy	Buck Owens	101	CB
18/12/1965	Your People	Little Milton	106	BB
18/12/1965	Tears (For Souvenirs)	Ken Dodd	107	BB
18/12/1965	Good Hard Rock	Ian Whitcomb	108	CB
18/12/1965	Tears (For Souvenirs)	Ken Dodds	108	CB

18/12/1965	You Made Me Love You	Aretha Franklin	109	BB
18/12/1965	I Can Tell	Reparata & The Delrons	110	CB
18/12/1965	This Heart Of Mine	The Artistics	115	BB
18/12/1965	How Can You Tell	Sandie Shaw	122	CB
18/12/1965	I Feel Like I'm Falling In Love	Jimmy Beaumont	123	BB
18/12/1965	Nina-Kocka-Nina	The Dinks	125	CB
18/12/1965	Party People	Ray Stevens	130	BB
18/12/1965	The Little Black Egg	The Nightcrawlers	135	BB
18/12/1965	Turn It On Girl	Tony & Tyrone	147	CB
18/12/1965	You Lost And I Won	The Ideals	148	CB
25/12/1965	My Heart Belongs To You	Wilson Pickett	109	BB
25/12/1965	Careless	BoBBy Vinton	111	BB
25/12/1965	This Heart Of Mine	The Artistics	113	CB
25/12/1965	Moment To Moment	Frank Sinatra	115	BB
25/12/1965	Skokiaan	Bob Moore & His Orchestra	117	CB
25/12/1965	I Want You	Tony & Terri	119	CB
25/12/1965	Meet Me At The Altar	Perry Como	120	CB
25/12/1965	(You Got) The Gamma Goochee	The Kingsmen	122	BB
25/12/1965	Some Sunday Morning	Wayne Newton	123	BB
25/12/1965	Harlem Shuffle	Wayne Cochran	127	BB
25/12/1965	Party People	Ray Stevens	130	CB
25/12/1965	How Can You Tell	Sandie Shaw	131	BB
25/12/1965	Hot Barbecue	Brother Jack Mcduff	133	CB
25/12/1965	I'm Gonna Love You Tomorrow	Dey & Knight	134	CB
25/12/1965	Tears Come Tumbling	Teardrops	136	CB
25/12/1965	What Kinda Deal Is This	Bill Carlisle	140	CB
01/01/1966	Fly Me To The Moon	Sam & Bill	103	CB
01/01/1966	A Beginning From An End	Jan & Dean	109	BB
01/01/1966	A Beginning From An End	Jan & Dean	110	CB
01/01/1966	Big Bright Eyes	Danny Hutton	112	CB

01/01/1966	Get Back	Roy Head	112	CB
01/01/1966	As Long As There Is L-O-V-E Love	Jimmy Ruffin	120	BB
01/01/1966	Once A Day	Timi Yuro	123	CB
01/01/1966	Please Don't Hurt Me (I've Never Been In Love Before)	Jackie Wilson & Lavern Baker	128	BB
08/01/1966	Brown Paper Sack	The Gentrys	101	BB
08/01/1966	Big Bright Eyes	Danny Hutton	102	BB
08/01/1966	Sweet September	The Lettermen	114	BB
08/01/1966	Brown Paper Sack	The Gentrys	115	CB
08/01/1966	Once A Day	Timi Yuro	118	BB
08/01/1966	Michelle	The Spokesmen	124	CB
08/01/1966	Lara's Theme	The Mgm Singing Strings	127	CB
08/01/1966	Getting Through To Me	Annabelle Fox	136	CB
15/01/1966	There Won't Be Any Snow (Christmas In The Jungle)	Derik Roberts	105	BB
15/01/1966	Wait A Minute	Tim Tam & The Turn-Ons	105	CB
15/01/1966	Michelle	The Spokesmen	106	BB
15/01/1966	The Keys To My Soul	The Silkie	111	CB
15/01/1966	Baby, You're My Everything	Little Jerry Williams	122	BB
15/01/1966	Friends And Lovers Forever	Nancy Ames	123	BB
15/01/1966	You Ain't Tuff	The Uniques	127	CB
15/01/1966	Play A Simple Melody	Horst Jankowski, Piano & Orchestra	139	CB
15/01/1966	Can't Chance A Break Up	Ike & Tina Turner	142	CB
22/01/1966	I Dig You Baby	Lorraine Ellison	103	BB
22/01/1966	The Arena	Al (He's The King) Hirt, Trumpet	115	CB
22/01/1966	A Most Unusual Boy	Patti Austin	116	CB
22/01/1966	(Never More) Lonely For You	The Ikettes	122	BB
22/01/1966	Cherry Pie	Charles Christy & The Crystals	124	CB
22/01/1966	The Keys To My Soul	The Silkie	124	BB
22/01/1966	Where Did She Go	Steff	124	BB
22/01/1966	Little Boy Sad	The Gants	125	CB
22/01/1966	Angels (Watching Over Me)	Medical Missionaries Of Mary Choral Group	131	CB

22/01/1966	Crazy Heart Of Mine	Robert Goulet	133	CB
22/01/1966	Booze In The Bottle	Carter Brothers	139	CB
22/01/1966	Spanish Harlem	King Curtis	139	CB
29/01/1966	Easy Going Fellow	Roscoe Shelton	102	BB
29/01/1966	Funny (Not Much)	Walter Jackson	103	BB
29/01/1966	Hello Enemy	Johnny Tillotson	104	CB
29/01/1966	Comfort Me	Carla Thomas	112	CB
29/01/1966	Made In Paris	Trini Lopez	113	CB
29/01/1966	Is It Me?	Barbara Mason	116	CB
29/01/1966	One Of Those Songs	The Ray Charles Singers	123	CB
29/01/1966	Moment To Moment	Henry Mancini, His Orchestra & Chorus	126	CB
29/01/1966	Only The Young	Steve Lawrence	128	CB
05/02/1966	You Bring Me Down	The Royalettes	101	CB
05/02/1966	Don't Forget About Me	Barbara Lewis	103	CB
05/02/1966	If You Can't Bite, Don't Growl	Tommy Collins	105	BB
05/02/1966	Made In Paris	Trini Lopez	113	BB
05/02/1966	Flowers On The Wall	Chet Baker & The Mariachi Brass	115	BB
05/02/1966	You Bring Me Down	The Royalettes	116	BB
05/02/1966	Angels (Watching Over Me)	Medical Missionaries Of Mary Choral Group	117	BB
05/02/1966	Don't Take It Out On Me	BoBBi Martin	119	BB
05/02/1966	Nashville, Tennessee	Barry Young	120	CB
05/02/1966	The Weekend	Jack Jones	123	BB
05/02/1966	Hello Enemy	Johnny Tillotson	128	BB
05/02/1966	Flowers On The Wall	Chet Baker & The Mariachi Brass	129	CB
05/02/1966	Since You Have Gone From Me	Barry Young	130	BB
05/02/1966	Teenage Failure	Chad & Jeremy	131	BB
05/02/1966	Ever See A Diver Kiss His Wife While The BuBBles Bounce About	Shirley Ellis	135	BB
05/02/1966	Song From "THE Oscar"	Tony Bennett	135	CB
05/02/1966	A Thousand Miles Away	Wayne Anthony	136	CB
05/02/1966	Let The Rest Of The World Go By	Sunny Gale	139	CB

05/02/1966	I Wish I Didn't Love You So	Mel Carter	143	CB
05/02/1966	Feel It	Sam Cooke	144	CB
05/02/1966	Private Wilson White	Marty RoBBins	145	CB
12/02/1966	S.O.S. (Heart In Distress)	Christine Cooper	101	BB
12/02/1966	When The Ship Hits The Sand	"Little" Jimmy Dickens	103	BB
12/02/1966	I'm Satisfied	Chuck Jackson & Maxine Brown	112	BB
12/02/1966	Temptation Walk (People Don't Look No More)	The Entertainers Iv	113	CB
12/02/1966	The Week-End	Steve Lawrence	117	CB
12/02/1966	You'll Be Needin' Me	The Lettermen	118	CB
12/02/1966	Bye Bye Blues	Andy Williams	123	CB
12/02/1966	For Your Precious Love (1966 Version)	Jerry Butler	126	CB
12/02/1966	The Fat Man Part 1	T-K-O's	126	CB
12/02/1966	The Arena	Al (He's The King) Hirt, Trumpet	129	BB
12/02/1966	I Can't Stop Loving You	Earl Grant	135	CB
12/02/1966	Feeling Good	Joe Sherman & The Arena Brass	140	CB
12/02/1966	Lost Someone (Live)	James Brown & The Famous Flames	144	CB
19/02/1966	I've Been A Long Time Leavin' (But I'll Be A Long Time Gone)	Roger Miller	103	BB
19/02/1966	My Darling Hildegarde	The Statler Brothers	105	CB
19/02/1966	3 Days 1 Hour 30 Minutes	Jackie Wilson	106	CB
19/02/1966	Batman And Robin	The Spotlights	111	BB
19/02/1966	Five Card Stud	Lorne Greene	112	BB
19/02/1966	Mr. Moon	The Coachmen	114	BB
19/02/1966	Communication	David Mccallum	117	BB
19/02/1966	I'll Drown In My Tears	Earl Grant	117	CB
19/02/1966	Peeping And Hiding	Lloyd Price	119	CB
19/02/1966	Night Train	The Viscounts	122	BB
19/02/1966	Bye Bye Blues	Andy Williams	127	BB
19/02/1966	The Week-End	Steve Lawrence	131	BB
19/02/1966	One Of Those Songs	The Ray Charles Singers	134	BB
19/02/1966	One Of Those Songs	Jimmy Durante	135	BB

19/02/1966	Tighten Up Your Tie, Button Up Your Jacket (Make It For The Door)	Aretha Franklin	141	CB
19/02/1966	Over The Rainbow	Patti Labelle & The Bluebelles	142	CB
19/02/1966	Georgianna	The Princetons	148	CB
26/02/1966	Funny (How Time Slips Away)	Ace Cannon	102	BB
26/02/1966	It's A Good Time	Billy Joe Royal	104	BB
26/02/1966	Song From "The Oscar"	Tony Bennett	104	BB
26/02/1966	My Darling Hildegarde	The Statler Brothers	110	BB
26/02/1966	Funny (How Time Slips Away)	Ace Cannon	114	CB
26/02/1966	Chain Reaction	The Spellbinders	117	CB
26/02/1966	A Public Execution	Mouse	121	BB
26/02/1966	After The Laughter	Wayne Newton	123	CB
26/02/1966	It's A Good Time	Billy Joe Royal	124	CB
26/02/1966	Together 'Til The End Of Time	Brenda Holloway	125	BB
26/02/1966	Custody	Patti Page	126	BB
26/02/1966	Happiness Is All I Need	Z.Z. Hill	126	CB
26/02/1966	Till You Come Back To Me	Patti Page	127	CB
26/02/1966	That's Part Of The Game	The Daytrippers	129	BB
26/02/1966	Till You Come Back To Me (b-side)	Patti Page	130	BB
26/02/1966	A Girl I Used To Know	BoBBy Vee	133	BB
26/02/1966	Please Don't Hurt Me	Chuck Jackson & Maxine Brown	138	CB
26/02/1966	From A Distance	P.F. Sloan	142	CB
05/03/1966	Desiree	The Charts	105	CB
05/03/1966	Your P-E-R-S-O-N-A-L-L-T-Y	Jackie Lee	111	BB
05/03/1966	Do Something For Yourself	BoBBy Powell	117	CB
05/03/1966	Only A Girl Like You	Brook Benton	122	BB
05/03/1966	Help Me - Part I (Get The Feeling)	Ray Sharpe With The King Curtis Orchestra	126	CB
05/03/1966	Sharing You	Carl Henderson	126	BB
05/03/1966	That's When The Tears Start (b-side)	The Blossoms	128	BB
05/03/1966	That's My Life (My Love And My Home)	Freddie Lennon	133	CB
12/03/1966	Watching The Late Late Show	Don Covay & The Goodtimers	101	BB

12/03/1966	Only A Girl Like You	Brook Benton	102	CB
12/03/1966	Rags To Riches	Lenny Welch	102	BB
12/03/1966	Too Little Time	Brenda Lee	102	CB
12/03/1966	Too Young	Tommy Vann And The Echoes	103	BB
12/03/1966	My Prayer	Johnny Thunder	106	BB
12/03/1966	Giddyup Go	Wink Martindale	114	BB
12/03/1966	Hawg Jaw	Charlie Rich	125	BB
12/03/1966	Time And Time Again (b-side)	Brenda Lee	126	BB
12/03/1966	A Public Execution	Mouse	127	CB
12/03/1966	One Of Us Must Know (Sooner Or Later)	Bob Dylan	135	CB
12/03/1966	Don't Make Me Over	The Swinging Blue Jeans	138	CB
19/03/1966	He Wore The Green Beret	Lesley Miller	101	BB
19/03/1966	Second-Hand Man [Live]	The Back Porch Majority	104	BB
19/03/1966	Don't Push Me	Hedgehoppers Anonymous	110	BB
19/03/1966	Call My Name	Them	111	CB
19/03/1966	Nessuno Mi Puo' Giudcare	Gene Pitney	115	BB
19/03/1966	You Let A Love Burn Out	We Five	115	CB
19/03/1966	Don't Make Me Over	The Swinging Blue Jeans	116	BB
19/03/1966	Here's To My Jenny	Mike Douglas	116	CB
19/03/1966	Chain Reaction	The Spellbinders	118	BB
19/03/1966	He Wore The Green Beret	Nancy Ames	118	CB
19/03/1966	It's A Funny Situation	Dee Dee Sharp	126	BB
19/03/1966	That's When The Tears Start	The Blossoms	127	CB
19/03/1966	He Wore The Green Beret	Lesley Miller	129	CB
19/03/1966	In The Same Old Way	BoBBy Bare	131	BB
19/03/1966	Watching The Late Late Show	Don Covay & The Goodtimers	140	CB
26/03/1966	May My Heart Be Cast Into Stone	The Toys	102	CB
26/03/1966	Don't Push Me	Hedgehoppers Anonymous	113	CB
26/03/1966	Funny (Not Much)	Walter Jackson	115	CB
26/03/1966	Somebody To Love Me	Ronny & The Daytonas	115	CB

26/03/1966	Somebody To Love Me	Ronny And The Daytonas	115	BB
26/03/1966	Mucho Soul	The Romeos	119	CB
26/03/1966	One Of Us Must Know (Sooner Or Later)	Bob Dylan	119	BB
26/03/1966	Too Little Time	Brenda Lee	123	BB
26/03/1966	Canadian Sunset	The Vibrations	128	CB
26/03/1966	Daddy's Baby	Ted Taylor	129	BB
26/03/1966	Mirror, Mirror	Pinkerton's 'Assort'. Colors	130	CB
26/03/1966	Desiree (new Version)	The Charts	132	BB
26/03/1966	I Met Him On A Sunday - '66	The Shirelles	139	CB
02/04/1966	Good Good Lovin'	The Blossoms	101	BB
02/04/1966	Pin The Tail On The Donkey	Paul Peek	108	CB
02/04/1966	From A Distance	P.F. Sloan	109	BB
02/04/1966	The Snapper	Johnny Lytle	114	CB
02/04/1966	You Better Come Home	The Exciters	123	CB
02/04/1966	Viet Nam Blues	Dave Dudley	127	BB
02/04/1966	I'm A Good Guy	The C.O.D.'s	128	BB
02/04/1966	Goin' Wild	The Jive Five Featuring Eugene Pitt	129	CB
02/04/1966	I Feel A Sin Coming On	Solomon Burke	131	CB
02/04/1966	Why? (Am I Treated So Bad)	The Staples Singers	131	CB
02/04/1966	From Nashville With Love	Chet Atkins	132	BB
02/04/1966	Book Of Love	The Underbeats	137	CB
02/04/1966	What Did I Have That I Don't Have?	Eydie Gorme	138	CB
09/04/1966	Cinnamint Shuffle (Mexican Shuffle)	The Johnny Mann Singers	102	CB
09/04/1966	Gonna Be Strong	The Intruders	108	CB
09/04/1966	Too Young	Tommy Vann & The Echoes	111	CB
09/04/1966	I Had A Dream	Johnnie Taylor	115	CB
09/04/1966	Night Time Girl	Modern Folk Quintet	122	BB
09/04/1966	Louie Louie	Travis Wammack	128	BB
09/04/1966	When She Touches Me "Nothing Else Matters"	Rodge Martin	131	BB
09/04/1966	Doing The Philly Dog	Lou Lawton	133	BB

09/04/1966	Mame	Al (He's The King) Hirt, Trumpet	136	CB
16/04/1966	I'm Satisfied	Otis Clay	105	BB
16/04/1966	Let's Go Steady Again	Sam Cooke	110	CB
16/04/1966	The Cruel War	Chad & Jill Stuart	110	BB
16/04/1966	I Lie Awake	The New Colony Six	111	BB
16/04/1966	Take Me Back To New Orleans	Gary (U.S.) Bonds	117	CB
16/04/1966	Young Man, Old Man	The Stokes	122	CB
16/04/1966	Better Man Than I	Terry Knight And The Pack	125	BB
16/04/1966	I Fall To You	Bob Morrison	138	CB
16/04/1966	I've Got A Secret	The Sharpees	141	CB
16/04/1966	Some Day, One Day	The Seekers	143	CB
23/04/1966	I Lie Awake	The New Colony Six	103	CB
23/04/1966	Don't Stop Now	Eddie Holman	104	BB
23/04/1966	Don't Stop Now	Eddie Holman	104	CB
23/04/1966	I Can't Rest	Fontella Bass	108	CB
23/04/1966	I'm So Lonesome I Could Cry	Hank Williams	109	BB
23/04/1966	Speak Her Name	David & Jonathan	109	BB
23/04/1966	Do The Temptation Walk	Jackie Lee	113	BB
23/04/1966	Doing The Philly Dog	Lou Lawton	118	CB
23/04/1966	Don't You Know	Keith Everett	119	CB
23/04/1966	Do Something For Yourself	BoBBy Powell	120	BB
23/04/1966	That's My Story	Paul Simon & Arthur Garfunkel	123	BB
23/04/1966	Think Twice Before You Speak	Al King	123	CB
23/04/1966	Cinnamint Shuffle (Mexican Shuffle)	Johnny Mann Singers	126	BB
23/04/1966	Diddy Wah Diddy	The Remains	129	BB
23/04/1966	My Young Misery	Darrow Fletcher	129	CB
23/04/1966	Once Upon A Time (This World Was Mine)	Teddy & The Pandas	130	CB
23/04/1966	It Ain't Necessary	Mamie Galore	132	BB
23/04/1966	Pick Me Up On Your Way Down	Hank Thompson	134	BB
23/04/1966	Speak Her Name	David & Jonathan	138	CB

23/04/1966	It Ain't Necessary	Mamie Galore	142	CB
23/04/1966	Laura Lee	Wayne Newton	144	CB
30/04/1966	I Love You Drops	Don Cherry	112	BB
30/04/1966	You're Ready Now	Frankie Valli	112	BB
30/04/1966	The Exodus Song	The Duprees	118	CB
30/04/1966	You Couldn't Get My Love Back (If You Tried)	Leroy Van Dyke	120	BB
30/04/1966	Second-Hand Man (Live)	The Back Porch Majority	125	CB
30/04/1966	She Needs Company	Manfred Mann	125	CB
30/04/1966	Confusion	Lee Dorsey	130	CB
30/04/1966	Cheryl's Goin' Home	The Cascades	131	BB
30/04/1966	Boys Are Made To Love	Karen Small	133	CB
30/04/1966	Once Upon A Time (This World Was Mine)	Teddy And The Pandas	134	BB
30/04/1966	You're A Drag	The Runarounds	141	CB
30/04/1966	What Should I Do	Sue Thompson	148	CB
07/05/1966	New Breed (Part 1) (The Boo-Ga-Loo)	James Brown	102	BB
07/05/1966	Crying My Heart Out	The Newbeats	103	CB
07/05/1966	The Last Thing On My Mind	The Womenfolk	105	BB
07/05/1966	Love Me With All Your Heart (Cuando Calienta El Sol)	Jim Nabors	111	CB
07/05/1966	Silver Spoon	The Toys	111	BB
07/05/1966	Silver Spoon	The Toys	111	CB
07/05/1966	Why Am I Lonely	Billy Stewart	113	CB
07/05/1966	Bouquet Of Roses	Dean Martin	116	CB
07/05/1966	Take Me Back To New Orleans	Gary (U.S.) Bonds	121	BB
07/05/1966	Function At The Junction	Shorty Long	123	CB
07/05/1966	Strangers In The Night	Bert Kaempfert And His Orchestra	124	BB
07/05/1966	Shy Girl	Johnny & The Expressions	126	CB
07/05/1966	You Don't Love Me	Gary Walker	131	CB
07/05/1966	I've Got A Secret	Sharpees	133	BB
07/05/1966	Quarter To Three	Sir Douglas Quintet	133	CB
07/05/1966	Do The Temptation Walk	Jackie Lee	139	CB

07/05/1966	Cheryl's Goin' Home	The Cascades	142	CB
07/05/1966	All In My Mind	Chuck Jackson	143	CB
07/05/1966	The Greatest Show On Earth	Freddy Cannon	150	CB
14/05/1966	Somewhere	Johnny Nash	118	CB
14/05/1966	A Street That Rhymes At Six A.M.	Norma Tanega	120	CB
14/05/1966	Stranger With A Black Dove	Peter And Gordon	130	BB
14/05/1966	Diddy Wah Diddy	Captain Beefheart & His Magic Band	131	CB
14/05/1966	Sugar Sugar	The Mad Lads	132	CB
14/05/1966	Don't Touch Me	Wilma Burgess	149	CB
21/05/1966	River Deep - Mountain High	Ike & Tina Turner	105	CB
21/05/1966	She Rides With Me	The G.T.O.'s	105	CB
21/05/1966	Wigglin' And Gigglin'	Roy Head	110	BB
21/05/1966	Truly Yours	The Spinners	111	BB
21/05/1966	I'll Go Crazy	The Buckinghams	112	BB
21/05/1966	Somewhere	Johnny Nash	120	BB
21/05/1966	If I Could Start My Life Again	The New Christy Minstrels	121	CB
21/05/1966	Get Your Lie The Way You Want It	Bonnie Guitar	125	CB
21/05/1966	I'm Nobody's Baby Now	Reparata & The Delrons	128	CB
21/05/1966	A Street That Rhymes At Six A.M.	Norma Tanega	129	BB
21/05/1966	Quarter To Three	Sir Douglas Quintet	129	BB
21/05/1966	I'll Go Crazy	The Buckinghams	132	CB
21/05/1966	Funny How Love Can Be	Danny Hutton	133	CB
21/05/1966	What's A Nice Kid Like You Doing In A Place Like This?	Scat Man Crothers	134	BB
21/05/1966	I Feel Good	The Sheep	136	CB
28/05/1966	Greatest Moments In A Girl's Life	The Tokens	102	BB
28/05/1966	I Put A Spell On You	Alan Price Set	105	CB
28/05/1966	He's Ready	The Poppies	106	BB
28/05/1966	Dedicated To The Greatest	Johnny Copeland	108	CB
28/05/1966	Off And Running	Lesley Gore	108	BB
28/05/1966	Stagecoach To Cheyenne	Wayne Newton	113	BB

28/05/1966	Everyday I Have To Cry	The Gentrys	115	CB
28/05/1966	There Stands The Door	We Five	116	BB
28/05/1966	Love Me	Billy Stewart	119	CB
28/05/1966	Funny How Love Can Be	Danny Hutton	120	BB
28/05/1966	Greatest Moments In A Girl's Life	The Tokens	123	CB
28/05/1966	Too Much Good Lovin' (No Good For Me)	Brook Benton	126	BB
28/05/1966	Goodbye Little Girl	Junior Parker	128	BB
28/05/1966	You Don't Love Me	Gary Walker	129	BB
28/05/1966	I Feel Good	The Sheep	130	BB
28/05/1966	You've Got Me High	The New Order	130	CB
28/05/1966	It's A Different World	Connie Francis	134	BB
28/05/1966	Girl I Got News For You	The Birdwatchers	139	CB
28/05/1966	Counting	The Deep Six	147	CB
28/05/1966	It's A Big Mistake	The Royalettes	150	CB
04/06/1966	Look Before You Leap	Dave Clark Five	101	BB
04/06/1966	Cheryl Ann	Tim Tam & The Turn-Ons	102	CB
04/06/1966	How Can I Tell Her It's Over	Andy Williams	109	CB
04/06/1966	Underwater	The T-Bones	110	CB
04/06/1966	Wigglin' And Gigglin'	Roy Head	115	CB
04/06/1966	I'll Be Gone	Pozo-Seco Singers	120	CB
04/06/1966	We're Acting Like Lovers	The Spellbinders	130	BB
04/06/1966	It's A Different World	Connie Francis	142	CB
04/06/1966	Stagecoach To Cheyenne	Wayne Newton	148	CB
11/06/1966	He Will Break Your Heart	The Righteous Brothers	101	CB
11/06/1966	Race With The Wind	The RoBBs	101	CB
11/06/1966	That New Girl	The Manhattans	101	CB
11/06/1966	Race With The Wind	The RoBBs	103	BB
11/06/1966	How Can I Tell Her It's Over	Andy Williams	109	BB
11/06/1966	High On Love	The Knickerbockers	112	CB
11/06/1966	Up In The Streets Of Harlem	The Drifters	115	CB

11/06/1966	It's You Alone	The Wailers	118	BB
11/06/1966	Come Back	The Turtles	119	CB
11/06/1966	Blue Star	The Ventures	120	BB
11/06/1966	Boys Are Made To Love	Karen Small	123	BB
11/06/1966	Hey, Good Lookin'	Bill Black's Combo	124	BB
11/06/1966	Five Miles From Home (Soon I'll See Mary)	Pat Boone	127	BB
11/06/1966	Coo Coo Roo Coo Coo Paloma	Perry Como	128	BB
18/06/1966	I Call Your Name	The Buckinghams	102	CB
18/06/1966	You Just Can't Quit	Rick Nelson	108	BB
18/06/1966	We Gotta Go	The Shy Guys	118	CB
18/06/1966	It's A Man's-Woman's World - Part I	Irma Thomas	119	BB
18/06/1966	If He Walked Into My Life	Eydie Gorme	120	BB
18/06/1966	It's You Alone	The Wailers	120	CB
18/06/1966	Yours	Baja Marimba Band	122	CB
18/06/1966	Johnny B. Goode	The Mudd Family	126	CB
18/06/1966	Pretty Flamingo	Tommy Vann & The Echoes	130	CB
18/06/1966	Day Of Decision	Buddy Starcher	131	BB
18/06/1966	Investigate	Major Lance	132	BB
18/06/1966	1-2-3	Jane Morgan	135	BB
25/06/1966	Go Go Train	Jackie Paine	103	CB
25/06/1966	On The Good Ship Lollipop	The Wonder Who?	107	CB
25/06/1966	I've Got To Go On Without You	The Van Dykes	109	BB
25/06/1966	Sock It To 'Em J.B. - Part I	Rex Garvin (and The Mighty Cravers)	110	BB
25/06/1966	I Just Let It Take Me	Bob Lind	116	CB
25/06/1966	Hand Jive	The Strangeloves	117	CB
25/06/1966	Beg, Borrow And Steal	The Rare Breed	118	CB
25/06/1966	You Can't Love Them All	The Drifters	127	BB
25/06/1966	Trumpet Pickin'	Al (He's The King) Hirt, Trumpet	129	CB
25/06/1966	Honey And Wine	Back Porch Majority	133	CB
25/06/1966	"FATS" Shake 'M Up - Pt. 1	Claude "Fats" Greene Orch.	141	CB

02/07/1966	Dirty Work Going On	Little Joe Blue	102	CB
02/07/1966	Because Of You	Rome & Paris (Bob Feldman & Jerry Goldstein)	104	BB
02/07/1966	Uptight (Everything's Alright)	Nancy Wilson	104	CB
02/07/1966	I'm A Practical Guy	Lee Rogers	106	CB
02/07/1966	Just A Little Bit Of You	Dallas Frazier	108	BB
02/07/1966	Come What May	Elvis Presley With The Jordanaires	109	BB
02/07/1966	Pass The Hatchet (Part I)	Roger & The Gypsies	115	CB
02/07/1966	Just A Little Bit Of You	Dallas Frazier	119	CB
02/07/1966	Standing In The Shadows	Hank Williams Jr.	120	CB
02/07/1966	Baby I Love You	Jimmy Holiday	122	CB
02/07/1966	Farmer John	Tidal Waves	123	BB
02/07/1966	Let It Be Me (Je T'appartiens)	Arthur Prysock	124	BB
02/07/1966	The Streets Of Baltimore	BoBBy Bare	124	BB
02/07/1966	It's A Sin To Tell A Lie	BoBBi Martin	125	CB
02/07/1966	Pretty Flamingo	Tommy Vann And The Echoes	125	BB
02/07/1966	Johnny Willow	Frankie Laine	133	CB
02/07/1966	Call Me	Eddie Bishop	134	CB
02/07/1966	The Magic Touch	BoBBy Fuller Four	138	CB
02/07/1966	Love Drops	Barry Allen	140	CB
02/07/1966	Baby, It's Over	Bob & Earl	142	CB
09/07/1966	A Letter From A Soldier (Dear Mama)	Connie Francis	105	BB
09/07/1966	Who Do You Think You Are	The Shindogs	106	CB
09/07/1966	Come On Home	Wayne Fontana	117	BB
09/07/1966	This Is My House (But Nobody Calls)	The Moody Blues	119	BB
09/07/1966	Daddy	PeBBles & Bamm Bamm Of The Flintstones	122	CB
09/07/1966	Sittin' On A Fence	Twice As Much	122	BB
09/07/1966	Ain't That Peculiar	Ramsey Lewis	129	BB
16/07/1966	Look At Me Girl	The Playboys Of Edinburg	108	BB
16/07/1966	The Laughing Song	Freddy Cannon	111	BB
16/07/1966	The Magic Touch	BoBBy Fuller Four	117	BB

16/07/1966	Most Of All	The Cowsills	118	BB
16/07/1966	A Letter From A Soldier (Dear Mama)	Connie Francis	119	CB
16/07/1966	So Young (And So Innocent)	The Poets	121	CB
16/07/1966	I Just Let It Take Me	Bob Lind	123	BB
16/07/1966	Take Your Love	BoBBy Goldsboro	123	CB
16/07/1966	It's Been Such A Long Way Home	Garnet Mimms	125	BB
16/07/1966	Just Walk In My Shoes	Gladys Knight & The Pips	129	BB
16/07/1966	Don't Take Yourself Too Seriously	The Sunrays	130	CB
16/07/1966	With A Child's Heart	Stevie Wonder	131	BB
16/07/1966	Good Times	The Five Americans	135	CB
16/07/1966	We Can Make It	Ruby & The Romantics	136	CB
16/07/1966	Lara's Theme (From Dr. Zhivago)	The Brass Ring	138	CB
16/07/1966	Heartburn	Johnny Maestro With The Crests	140	CB
23/07/1966	When You Wake Up	Cash Mc Call	102	BB
23/07/1966	Love (Oh, How Sweet It Is)	Jerry Butler	103	BB
23/07/1966	Takin' All I Can Get	Mitch Ryder & Detroit Wheels	110	CB
23/07/1966	Take Your Love	BoBBy Goldsboro	114	BB
23/07/1966	Shake Your Hips	Slim Harpo	116	BB
23/07/1966	Sweet Dreams (Of You)	Mighty Sam	117	CB
23/07/1966	Most Of All	The Cowsills	119	CB
23/07/1966	It'll Take A Little Time	Jerry Vale	120	BB
23/07/1966	Poor Dog (Who Can't Wag His Own Tail)	Little Richard	121	BB
23/07/1966	Lara's Theme (from Dr. Zhivago)	The Brass Ring	126	BB
23/07/1966	Pretend	The Tymes	127	CB
23/07/1966	I'm A Good Woman	Barbara Lynn	129	BB
23/07/1966	In My Neighborhood	The Jive Five	134	CB
23/07/1966	After I'm Number One	Don Cherry	139	CB
23/07/1966	The Laughing Song	Freddy Cannon	149	CB
30/07/1966	We Can Work It Out	Maxine Brown	109	CB
30/07/1966	Angelica	Barry Mann	111	BB

30/07/1966	Dirty Work Going On	Little Joe Blue	111	BB
30/07/1966	This Is My House (But Nobody Calls)	The Moody Blues	112	CB
30/07/1966	Summer Kisses	Floyd & Jerry With The Counterpoints	116	CB
30/07/1966	(I Lost My Love In The) Big City	The Daniels	120	CB
30/07/1966	These Chains Of Love (Are Breaking Me Down)	Chuck Jackson	127	CB
30/07/1966	Put Yourself In My Place	Buddy Greco	132	CB
30/07/1966	Too Many People	The Leaves	136	CB
30/07/1966	(Baby) You Don't Have To Tell Me	The Walker Bros.	141	CB
06/08/1966	You Better Take It Easy Baby	Little Anthony & The Imperials	111	CB
06/08/1966	El Pito (I'll Never Go Back To Georgia)	Joe Cuba Sextet	115	BB
06/08/1966	Sock It To 'EM J.B. - Part I	Rex Garvin (& The Mighty Cravers)	117	CB
06/08/1966	Who-Dun-It?	Monk Higgins	117	BB
06/08/1966	I Want A Girl	The Mad Lads	119	CB
06/08/1966	We Can Make It	Ruby And The Romantics	120	BB
06/08/1966	Love (Oh, How Sweet It Is)	Jerry Butler	123	CB
06/08/1966	My Heart Reminds Me - Part 1	Vikki Carr	127	CB
06/08/1966	Without A Song (Part 1)	James Cleveland And The Cleveland Singers	129	BB
06/08/1966	Put It Back (Where You Found It)	Sue Thompson	131	BB
06/08/1966	Born To Be With You	The Silkie	133	BB
06/08/1966	Cadillac	The New Colony Six	140	CB
06/08/1966	Poor Dog (Who Can't Wag His Own Tail)	Little Richard	150	CB
13/08/1966	Jug Band Music	The Mugwumps	102	CB
13/08/1966	Chapel In The Fields	The Knickerbockers	106	BB
13/08/1966	The Kids Are Alright	The Who	106	BB
13/08/1966	No Greater Love	The Holidays	107	CB
13/08/1966	A Change On The Way	Terry Knight And The Pack	111	BB
13/08/1966	Man Loves Two	Little Milton	115	CB
13/08/1966	Devri	The Platters	117	CB
13/08/1966	Kissin' My Life Away	The Hondells	118	BB
13/08/1966	Man Loves Two	Little Milton	127	BB

13/08/1966	The Best Of Luck To You	Earl Gaines	128	CB
13/08/1966	Come On Sunshine	Gil & Johnny	130	CB
13/08/1966	Two In The Morning	Spooner's Crowd	141	CB
13/08/1966	May I	The Zodiacs	150	CB
20/08/1966	Just Like A Woman	Manfred Mann	101	BB
20/08/1966	We Can't Go On This Way	Teddy And The Pandas	103	BB
20/08/1966	Kissin' My Life Away	The Hondells	109	CB
20/08/1966	Nowadays Clancy Can't Even Sing	The Buffalo Springfield	110	BB
20/08/1966	Come On Sunshine	Gil & Johnny	112	BB
20/08/1966	I Was Born A Loser	BoBBy Lee	114	CB
20/08/1966	I Worship The Ground You Walk On	Jimmy Hughes	115	CB
20/08/1966	You Better Take It Easy Baby	Little Anthony And The Imperials	125	BB
20/08/1966	Lovers Of The World Unite	David & Jonathan	138	CB
20/08/1966	You Got Your Head On Backwards	The Sonics	140	CB
27/08/1966	She Ain't Lovin' You	The Distant Cousins	102	BB
27/08/1966	Impressions	The Jones Boys	104	CB
27/08/1966	Keep Looking	Solomon Burke	109	BB
27/08/1966	The Clown	Gene Summers	112	CB
27/08/1966	We'll Meet Again	The Turtles	116	CB
27/08/1966	A Woman Of The World	The Gentrys	119	CB
27/08/1966	The Joker	Sergio Mendes & Brasil '66	120	CB
27/08/1966	It's The Beat	Major Lance	128	BB
27/08/1966	Deep Inside	The Jagged Edge	129	BB
27/08/1966	I Keep Changing My Mind	Just Us	131	CB
27/08/1966	The Best Of Luck To You	Earl Gains	133	BB
27/08/1966	Batman To The Rescue	Lavern Baker	135	BB
27/08/1966	Counting	Marianne Faithfull	138	CB
27/08/1966	Gonna Fix You Good (Every Time You're Bad)	Little Anthony & The Imperials	141	CB
03/09/1966	Impressions	The Jones Boys	101	BB
03/09/1966	Sticky, Sticky	BoBBy Harris	101	BB

03/09/1966	Land Of A Thousand Dances	Cannibal And The Headhunters	106	BB
03/09/1966	Boa Constrictor	Johnny Cash	107	BB
03/09/1966	San Francisco Woman	Bob Lind	107	CB
03/09/1966	A Woman Of The World	The Gentrys	112	BB
03/09/1966	Green Hornet Theme	The Ventures	116	BB
03/09/1966	Green Hornet Theme	Al (He's The King) Hirt, Trumpet	121	CB
03/09/1966	Safe And Sound	Fontella Bass	124	CB
03/09/1966	I'm Gonna Love You Anyway	The Birdwatchers	125	BB
03/09/1966	Jug Band Music	The Mugwumps	127	BB
03/09/1966	I've Been Wrong	The Buckinghams	129	CB
03/09/1966	After You There Can Be Nothing	Walter Jackson	130	BB
03/09/1966	If You Got The Loving (I Got The Time)	Sam & Dave	131	CB
03/09/1966	Oh, Lonesome Me	BoBBi Martin	134	BB
03/09/1966	What A Party	Tom Jones	140	CB
03/09/1966	(Say It Isn't So) Say You'd Never Go	The Fascinations	142	CB
03/09/1966	Nowadays Clancy Can't Even Sing	The Buffalo Springfield	142	CB
10/09/1966	He'll Be Back	The Players	107	BB
10/09/1966	Dommage, Dommage (Too Bad, Too Bad)	Paul Vance	108	CB
10/09/1966	Devri	The Platters	111	BB
10/09/1966	It's The Beat	Major Lance	111	CB
10/09/1966	A Change Is Gonna Come	Brother Jack Mcduff	112	CB
10/09/1966	A Time For Love	Tony Bennett	113	CB
10/09/1966	(In The) Cold Light Of Day	Gene Pitney	115	BB
10/09/1966	My Baby	Garnet Mimms	119	CB
10/09/1966	What A Party	Tom Jones	120	BB
10/09/1966	So Nice (Summer Samba)	Connie Francis	121	CB
10/09/1966	Green Hornet Theme	Al (He's The King) Hirt, Trumpet	126	BB
10/09/1966	Boa Constrictor	Johnny Cash	128	CB
10/09/1966	Under My Thumb	Del Shannon	128	BB
10/09/1966	Hold On! I'm A Comin'	Billy Larkin And The Delegates	130	BB

10/09/1966	Green Hornet Theme	The Ventures	131	CB
10/09/1966	Sunday, The Day Before Monday	Tommy Boyce	132	BB
10/09/1966	The Other Side Of This Life	Peter, Paul & Mary	134	CB
10/09/1966	San Francisco Woman	Bob Lind	135	BB
10/09/1966	The Ballad Of The Green Hornet	Lee Merril & The Golden Horns	136	CB
10/09/1966	After You There Can Be Nothing	Walter Jackson	138	CB
10/09/1966	Alfie	Cilla Black	139	CB
10/09/1966	It's Only Love	Jeannie Seely	143	CB
10/09/1966	What Makes A Man Feel Good	Joe Simon	148	CB
17/09/1966	Pollyanna	The Classics	106	BB
17/09/1966	Love Is A Wonderful Thing	The Isley Brothers	110	BB
17/09/1966	Roller Coaster	The Ides Of March	112	CB
17/09/1966	I Struck It Rich	Len Barry	114	CB
17/09/1966	Treat Me Like A Lady	Lesley Gore	115	BB
17/09/1966	If My Car Could Only Talk	Lou Christie	118	BB
17/09/1966	A Time For Love	Tony Bennett	119	BB
17/09/1966	Shake Sherry	Harvey Russell & The Rogues	123	CB
17/09/1966	Gloria's Dream (Round And Around)	The Belfast Gipsies	124	BB
17/09/1966	Out Of Time	Chris Farlowe	125	CB
17/09/1966	The Scratch	Robert Parker	128	BB
17/09/1966	I Remember You	Slim Whitman	134	BB
17/09/1966	I Cover The Waterfront	Jimmy Mcgriff	135	BB
17/09/1966	Tarzan (Tarzan's Dance)	The Marketts	139	CB
17/09/1966	Hi-Lili, Hi-Lo	Alan Price Set	143	CB
24/09/1966	What Now My Love	"Groove" Holmes	102	CB
24/09/1966	Dommage, Dommage (Too Bad, Too Bad)	Jerry Vale	113	CB
24/09/1966	Rosanna	The Capreez	115	BB
24/09/1966	Heart	2 Of Clubs	117	CB
24/09/1966	Every Day And Every Night	The Trolls	119	CB
24/09/1966	Fannie Mae	Mighty Sam	120	BB

24/09/1966	Gloria's Dream (Round And Around)	The Belfast Gipsies	120	CB
24/09/1966	Here, There And Everywhere	The Fourmost	120	BB
24/09/1966	Shake Sherry	Harvey Russell & The Rogues	131	BB
24/09/1966	The Scratch	Robert Parker	132	CB
24/09/1966	My Way Of Life	Sonny Curtis	134	CB
24/09/1966	It Was A Very Good Year	Della Reese With The BoBBy Bryant Quintet	136	CB
24/09/1966	To Make A Big Man Cry	Roy Head	139	CB
24/09/1966	You Can't Take Love	Cash Mccall	141	CB
01/10/1966	These Things Will Keep Me Loving You	The Velvelettes	102	BB
01/10/1966	Love's Gone Bad	Chris Clark	105	BB
01/10/1966	Pipeline	Chantay's	106	BB
01/10/1966	Shake Your Tambourine	BoBBy Marchan	106	CB
01/10/1966	Stand In For Love	The O'jays	109	CB
01/10/1966	I Can't Do Without You	Deon Jackson	111	BB
01/10/1966	Almost Persuaded	Patti Page	116	CB
01/10/1966	Secret Love	Richard "Groove" Holmes	119	CB
01/10/1966	When Summer's Gone	The Royalettes	124	CB
01/10/1966	Love's Gone Bad	Chris Clark	125	CB
01/10/1966	Lookin' For Love	Ray Conniff & The Singers	126	CB
01/10/1966	My Baby	Garnet Mimms	132	BB
08/10/1966	You Are She	Chad & Jeremy	103	CB
08/10/1966	You Left The Water Running	Barbara Lynn	110	BB
08/10/1966	Patch My Heart	The Mad Lads	111	CB
08/10/1966	Almost Persuaded	Patti Page	113	BB
08/10/1966	The Willy	The Willies	113	BB
08/10/1966	One More Time	Clefs Of Lavender Hill	114	BB
08/10/1966	Shades Of Blue	The Shirelles	122	BB
08/10/1966	Hurting	Gary Stites	123	BB
08/10/1966	Heart	2 Of Clubs	125	BB
08/10/1966	Run And Hide	The Uniques	126	BB

08/10/1966	Stop, Look And Listen	The Chiffons	133	CB
08/10/1966	My Way Of Life	Sonny Curtis	134	BB
08/10/1966	Hurting	Gary Stites	140	CB
15/10/1966	Meditation (Meditacao)	Claudine Longet	107	CB
15/10/1966	East Side Story	Bob Seger & The Last Heard	111	CB
15/10/1966	Chanson D'amour	The Lettermen	117	CB
15/10/1966	And I Love Her	The Vibrations	118	BB
15/10/1966	The White Cliffs Of Dover	The Righteous Brothers	118	BB
15/10/1966	Kimberly	Tim Tam & The Turn-Ons	120	CB
15/10/1966	She's My Girl	The Coastliners	121	BB
15/10/1966	Fifi The Flea	The Sidekicks	125	CB
15/10/1966	Got To Get You Into My Life	The Hands Of Time	127	CB
15/10/1966	Mercy	Willie Mitchell	127	BB
15/10/1966	One Day Nearer Home	Ssgt. Barry Sadler - U.S Army Special Forces	132	CB
15/10/1966	Four Women	Nina Simone	138	CB
15/10/1966	Philly Dog	Herbie Mann	144	CB
15/10/1966	Help Me (Get Myself Back Together Again)	The Spellbinders	146	CB
15/10/1966	Think It Over	Tommy Mclain	147	CB
22/10/1966	Standing On Guard	The Falcons	101	CB
22/10/1966	Wedding Bell Blues	Laura Nyro	103	BB
22/10/1966	Distant Drums	Vic Dana	114	BB
22/10/1966	Happy Feet	Robert Parker	115	CB
22/10/1966	Can You Blame Me	Jimmy Norman	121	CB
22/10/1966	Clock	Eddie Rambeau	122	BB
22/10/1966	(We Wear) Lavender Bleu	Finders Keepers	123	BB
22/10/1966	The Portuguese Washerwomen	Baja Marimba Band	126	BB
22/10/1966	Somebody's Got To Love You	Don Covay & The Goodtimers	127	BB
22/10/1966	There's Nothing Else On My Mind	Barry Mcguire	129	CB
22/10/1966	Love Is A Bird	The Knickerbockers	133	BB
22/10/1966	Dusty	Floyd & Jerry	145	CB

22/10/1966	Synthetic Man	The Chosen Few	148	CB
29/10/1966	Am I A Loser (from The Start)	Eddie Holman	101	BB
29/10/1966	Windows And Doors	Jackie Deshannon	108	BB
29/10/1966	Winchester Cathedral	The New Happiness	109	CB
29/10/1966	Theme From The Wild Angels	Davie Allan & The Arrows	112	CB
29/10/1966	Winchester Cathedral	The New Happiness	112	BB
29/10/1966	Another Tear Falls	The Walker Bros.	114	CB
29/10/1966	Sweet Thang	Nat Stuckey	114	CB
29/10/1966	Fifi The Flea	The Sidekicks	115	BB
29/10/1966	Cabaret	Marilyn Maye	116	CB
29/10/1966	Wild Thing	The Ventures	116	BB
29/10/1966	Urge For Going	Tom Rush	118	CB
29/10/1966	Society's Child (Baby I've Been Thinking)	Janis Ian	120	CB
29/10/1966	Turn On Your Lovelight	Dean Parrish	120	CB
29/10/1966	Penetration	The Ventures	121	CB
29/10/1966	Done Got Over	BoBBy Powell (with Jackie Johnson)	127	CB
29/10/1966	If I Need Someone	The Kingsmen	128	CB
29/10/1966	Cabaret	Mike Douglas	129	BB
29/10/1966	Music	The Festivals	130	BB
29/10/1966	She Digs My Love	Sir Douglas Quintet	132	BB
29/10/1966	Woman How Do You Make Me Love You Like I Do	Solomon Burke	133	CB
29/10/1966	Shades Of Blue	The Shirelles	139	CB
29/10/1966	Love Is A Bird	The Knickerbockers	140	CB
29/10/1966	The Hard Life	The Goodtimes	145	CB
29/10/1966	I Can Hear Music	The Ronettes Featuring Veronica	146	CB
29/10/1966	If I Had A Hammer	Willie Hightower	146	CB
05/11/1966	It's Not The Same	Anthony & The Imperials	101	CB
05/11/1966	Show Biz	The Surfaris	102	CB
05/11/1966	For Emily, Whenever I May Find Her	Simon & Garfunkel	105	CB
05/11/1966	Standing On Guard	The Falcons	107	BB

05/11/1966	Chanson D'amour	The Lettermen	112	BB
05/11/1966	Long Haired Music	The Guise (and Their Mod Sound)	123	BB
05/11/1966	Good Lovin'	The Gilberto Sextet	131	CB
05/11/1966	Tiny BuBBles	Billy Vaughn And His Orchestra	131	BB
05/11/1966	"LOVE Theme" From Is Paris Burning	Doc Severinsen & His Orchestra	139	CB
05/11/1966	It's-A-Happening	The Magic Mushrooms	141	CB
05/11/1966	Married	Don Cherry	145	CB
12/11/1966	Never Let Me Go	The Van Dykes	105	CB
12/11/1966	And I Love Her	The Vibrations	114	CB
12/11/1966	Games That Lovers Play	Mantovani And His Orchestra	122	BB
12/11/1966	Out Of Time	Chris Farlowe	122	BB
12/11/1966	How Much Pressure (Do You Think I Can Stand)	Roscoe Robinson	125	BB
12/11/1966	Goin' Too Far	The Fifth Order	127	CB
12/11/1966	Turn The World Around The Other Way	Timi Yuro	129	CB
12/11/1966	Booker-Loo	Booker T. & The Mg's	131	CB
12/11/1966	I Can't Make It Alone	P. J. Proby	131	BB
12/11/1966	Cabaret	Mike Douglas	133	CB
12/11/1966	Pipeline	The Chantay's	134	CB
12/11/1966	The First Time	We Five	136	CB
12/11/1966	Windows And Doors	Jackie Deshannon	147	CB
19/11/1966	I Don't Need No Doctor	Ray Charles & His Orchestra	102	CB
19/11/1966	Don't Pass Me By	Big Maybelle	111	CB
19/11/1966	Cry Like A Baby	Aretha Franklin	113	BB
19/11/1966	Hymn No. 5	The Mighty Hannibal	115	BB
19/11/1966	Magic In The Air	Cher	119	CB
19/11/1966	Buzzzzzz	Jimmy Gordon	121	BB
19/11/1966	Forget About Me	Prince Harold	123	CB
19/11/1966	Hard To Get Thing Called Love	Tony Bruno	124	CB
19/11/1966	I Bet'cha (Couldn't Love Me)	The Manhattans	128	BB
19/11/1966	Someone	The Contrails (Vocal By Dick & Jack)	130	CB

19/11/1966	That Lucky Old Sun	Cash Mccall	130	CB
19/11/1966	I'll Think Of Summer	Ronny And The Daytonas	133	BB
19/11/1966	How Much Pressure (Do You Think I Can Stand)	Roscoe Robinson	136	CB
19/11/1966	Don't Cry (Una Casa La Cima Al Mondo)	The Ray Charles Singers	141	CB
19/11/1966	Let's Get Lost On A Country Road	The Kit-Kats	144	CB
26/11/1966	Since I Don't Have You	Lou Christie	101	CB
26/11/1966	Where Did Robinson Crusoe Go With Friday On Saturday Night?	Ian Whitcomb And His Seaside Syncopators	101	BB
26/11/1966	Your Ever Changin' Mind	Crispian St. Peters	106	BB
26/11/1966	Long Haired Music	The Guise (& Their Mod Sound)	110	CB
26/11/1966	Taking Inventory	Danny White	113	CB
26/11/1966	Devil With An Angel's Smile	The Intruders	117	CB
26/11/1966	Love Me, Please Love Me	Jimmie Rodgers	118	CB
26/11/1966	Where Did Robinson Crusoe Go With Friday On Saturday Night?	Ian Whitcomb & His Seaside Syncopators	118	CB
26/11/1966	Let's Get Lost On A Country Road	The Kit-Kats	119	BB
26/11/1966	The Bears	The Fastest Group Alive	121	CB
26/11/1966	(We're Gonna) Bring The Country To The City	Tony Mason	125	BB
26/11/1966	Blue Snow Night	The Gurus	126	CB
26/11/1966	Born Free	Matt Monro	126	BB
26/11/1966	Plain Jane	B.J. Thomas	126	CB
26/11/1966	Reverbaration (Doubt)	The Thirteenth Floor Elevators	129	BB
26/11/1966	My Baby's Gone	Donald Height	132	CB
26/11/1966	The Bears	The Fastest Group Alive	133	BB
26/11/1966	Honky Tonk Ii 66 Style	Tommy Wills (Man With A Horn)	145	CB
26/11/1966	Buzzzzzz	Jimmy Gordon	146	CB
03/12/1966	Back In The Same Old Bag Again	BoBBy Bland	102	BB
03/12/1966	Since I Don't Have You	Lou Christie	102	BB
03/12/1966	Sweet Little Baby Boy (Part 1)	James Brown & The Famous Flames	104	CB
03/12/1966	Our Day Will Come	James Brown At The Organ	105	CB
03/12/1966	Your Ever Changin' Mind	Crispian St. Peters	116	CB
03/12/1966	My Boyfriend's Back	The Chiffons	117	BB

03/12/1966	Poor Girl In Trouble	Barbara Mason	129	CB
03/12/1966	In A Dusty Old Room	Noel Harrison	130	CB
03/12/1966	My Boyfriend's Back	The Chiffons	133	CB
03/12/1966	My Yesterday Love	The Newbeats	135	CB
10/12/1966	I Love My Dog	Cat Stevens	106	CB
10/12/1966	Sunshine Superman	Willie Bobo	107	BB
10/12/1966	I'll Make It Easy (If You'll Come On Home)	The Incredibles	108	BB
10/12/1966	Here Comes My Baby	Perry Como With Anita Kerr Quartet	109	CB
10/12/1966	Yo-Yo	Billy Joe Royal	111	CB
10/12/1966	Soul Superman	The Hesitations	112	CB
10/12/1966	Forget About Me	Prince Harold	114	BB
10/12/1966	Hard Lovin' Loser	Judy Collins	114	CB
10/12/1966	Yo-Yo	Billy Joe Royal	117	BB
10/12/1966	Cheganca	Walter Wanderley	120	CB
10/12/1966	Peace Of Mind	Count Five	125	BB
10/12/1966	I Don't Need Anything	Maxine Brown	129	BB
10/12/1966	I'm Glad I Waited	The Players	130	BB
10/12/1966	Let Love Come Between Us	The RuBBer Band	130	CB
10/12/1966	Where Could I Go? (But To Her)	David Houston	133	BB
10/12/1966	We Can Make It If We Try	Neil Sedaka	135	CB
10/12/1966	Baby Won't You Let Me Tell You How I Lost My Mind	The Spike Drivers	141	CB
17/12/1966	Slow Hot Wind	Sergio Mendes & Brasil '66	112	CB
17/12/1966	What Is Soul?	Ben E. King	113	CB
17/12/1966	Fortune Teller	The Hardtimes	117	CB
17/12/1966	I Love My Dog	Cat Stevens	118	BB
17/12/1966	Mama (When My Dollies Have Babies)	Cher	124	BB
17/12/1966	Plain Jane	B.J. Thomas	129	BB
17/12/1966	The Children Of St. Monica	Don Grady With The Windupwatchband	131	CB
17/12/1966	The More I See You	"Groove" Holmes	131	BB
17/12/1966	Your Ever Changin' Mind	Trini Lopez	131	CB

17/12/1966	Come By Here	Inez Foxx With Charlie Foxx	138	CB
17/12/1966	Soul Sister	Four Gents	139	CB
17/12/1966	It's Been A Change	The Staple Singers	143	CB
17/12/1966	As Time Goes By	Ace Cannon	150	CB
24/12/1966	That's The Tune	The Vogues	103	CB
24/12/1966	Theme From "The Wild Angels"	The Ventures	110	BB
24/12/1966	Hurry Sundown	Peter, Paul & Mary	116	CB
24/12/1966	I'm Gonna Sit Right Down And Write Myself A Letter	The Palm Beach Band Boys	117	BB
24/12/1966	A Good Love	Lorraine Ellison	121	CB
24/12/1966	I've Lost My Heart Again	Jerry Vale	123	CB
24/12/1966	My Baby Likes To Boogaloo	Don Gardner	126	BB
24/12/1966	Grown Up Games	Vic Dana	127	CB
24/12/1966	I Can't Please You	Jimmy Robins	131	BB
24/12/1966	Born Free	Matt Monro	132	CB
24/12/1966	Catch Me In The Meadow	The Trade Winds	132	BB
24/12/1966	That's Life	Big Maybelle	134	CB
24/12/1966	Little White Lies	The Motley Blues Band Featuring: Bob Eberly Jr.	140	CB
24/12/1966	Why Do You Want To Hurt The One That Loves You	The Marvellos	141	CB
24/12/1966	The Sweet Sounds Of Summer	The Shangri-Las	143	CB
24/12/1966	(A Touch Of) Baby	The Tymes	148	CB
31/12/1966	Smashed! Blocked!	John's Children	102	BB
31/12/1966	At The Party	Hector Rivera	104	BB
31/12/1966	Ooh Baby	Bo Diddley	104	CB
31/12/1966	Day Tripper	Ramsey Lewis	106	CB
31/12/1966	Bend It	Dave Dee, Dozy, Beaky, Mick And Tich	110	BB
31/12/1966	I'm Your Bread Maker, Baby	Slim Harpo	116	BB
31/12/1966	What Makes It Happen	Tony Bennett	119	CB
31/12/1966	Midnight Hour	Kit & The Outlaws	123	CB
31/12/1966	Back In The Same Old Bag Again	BoBBy Bland	127	CB
31/12/1966	I'm Gonna Make You Mine	The Shadows Of Knight	129	CB

31/12/1966	Catch Me In The Meadow	The Trade Winds	130	CB
31/12/1966	A Good Love	Lorraine Ellison	131	BB
31/12/1966	The Children Of St. Monica	Don Grady With The Windupwatchband	132	BB
31/12/1966	Soul Sister	Four Gents	133	BB
31/12/1966	Ain't No Soul (In These Old Shoes)	Major Lance	134	CB
31/12/1966	A Loser's Cathedral (b-side)	David Houston	135	BB
31/12/1966	Nasty	Richard & The Young Lions	136	CB
31/12/1966	You Don't Have To Say You Love Me	Arthur Prysock	141	CB
31/12/1966	The Habit Of Lovin' You Baby	Nino Tempo & April Stevens	149	CB
07/01/1967	Dominique	Tony Sandler & Ralph Young	110	CB
07/01/1967	There Goes My Everything	Don Cherry	113	BB
07/01/1967	I'm Gonna Sit Right Down And Write Myself A Letter	The Palm Beach Band Boys	114	CB
07/01/1967	Nature Boy	Joe Harnell & His Orchestra	117	CB
07/01/1967	Music To Watch Girls By	Al (He's The King) Hirt, Trumpet	119	BB
07/01/1967	We Can Make It If We Try	Neil Sedaka	121	BB
07/01/1967	Hurry Sundown	Peter, Paul & Mary	123	BB
07/01/1967	The Sweet Sounds Of Summer	The Shangri-Las	123	BB
07/01/1967	Here Comes My Baby	Perry Como	124	BB
07/01/1967	I've Lost My Heart Again	Jerry Vale	132	BB
07/01/1967	What Would I Be	Val Doonican	142	CB
14/01/1967	Grits 'N Corn Bread	Soul Runners	103	BB
14/01/1967	Feel So Bad	Little Milton	104	CB
14/01/1967	Tip Toe	Robert Parker	105	CB
14/01/1967	Waitin' On You	B.B. King & His Orchestra	109	CB
14/01/1967	Just Let It Happen	The Arbors	111	CB
14/01/1967	Waitin' On You	B.B. King And His Orchestra	112	BB
14/01/1967	Our Winter Love	The Lettermen	120	CB
14/01/1967	Two Ways To Skin (A Cat)	Jimmy Reed	125	BB
14/01/1967	Snow Queen	Roger Nichols Trio	126	CB
14/01/1967	Nothing To Lose	The Classics Iv	142	CB

14/01/1967	Lucky Lindy	Stutz Bearcat & The Vanity Fair	150	CB
21/01/1967	Cabaret	King Richard's Fleugel Knights	112	CB
21/01/1967	I Won't Come In While He's There	Jim Reeves	112	BB
21/01/1967	Kick Me Charlie	Tommy Roe	113	CB
21/01/1967	That's Life	O.C. Smith	127	BB
21/01/1967	Gimme Some Lovin'	The Jordan Bros.	129	BB
21/01/1967	Theme From "THE Wild Angels"	The Ventures	129	CB
21/01/1967	I Won't Come In While He's There	Jim Reeves	131	CB
21/01/1967	Midnight Hour	Kit And The Outlaws	131	BB
21/01/1967	That's How Strong My Love Is	Mattie Moultrie	132	BB
21/01/1967	You'll Be Needing Me Baby	Nino Tempo & April Stevens	133	BB
21/01/1967	Ballad Of Walter Wart (Brrriggett)	The Thorndike Pickledish Choir	136	CB
21/01/1967	There Goes My Everything	Jack Greene	136	CB
21/01/1967	I Was Only Playing Games	Unit Four Plus Two	141	CB
21/01/1967	I'll Make It Easy (If You Come On Home)	The Incredibles	143	CB
21/01/1967	Green Plant	The Tokens	145	CB
28/01/1967	She's Looking Good	Rodger Collins	101	BB
28/01/1967	Fools Fall In Love	Elvis Presley With The Jordanaires	102	BB
28/01/1967	Sweet Maria	The Billy Vaughn Singers	105	BB
28/01/1967	Love's Gone Bad	The Underdogs	107	CB
28/01/1967	Mr. Farmer	The Seeds	109	CB
28/01/1967	Don't Go Home (My Little Darlin')	The Shirelles	110	BB
28/01/1967	Humphrey Stomp	Earl Harrison	110	CB
28/01/1967	I'm A Boy	The Who	110	CB
28/01/1967	Life Is Groovy	United States Double Quartet: The Tokens The Kirby Stone Four	110	BB
28/01/1967	Black Olives	The Bad Boys	111	CB
28/01/1967	Looking Glass	The Association	113	BB
28/01/1967	Bittersweet	The RoBBs	117	CB
28/01/1967	Softly, As I Leave You	Eydie Gorme	117	BB
28/01/1967	What Will My Mary Say	Jay Black	119	CB

28/01/1967	Something On Your Mind	King Curtis	120	CB
28/01/1967	You Don't Have To Say You Love Me	Arthur Prysock	120	BB
28/01/1967	Kiss Tomorrow Goodbye (Capri C'est Fini)	Jane Morgan	121	BB
28/01/1967	Kiss Tomorrow Goodbye	Lainie Kazan	123	BB
28/01/1967	Stood Up	Floyd Cramer	128	CB
28/01/1967	Snow Queen	Roger Nichols Trio	129	BB
28/01/1967	(Don't It Make You) Feel Kind Of Bad	The Radiants	139	CB
04/02/1967	The Biggest Man	Tommy Hunt	102	CB
04/02/1967	My Best Friend	Jefferson Airplane	103	BB
04/02/1967	Rain Rain Go Away	Lee Dorsey	105	BB
04/02/1967	Marryin' Kind Of Love	The Critters	106	CB
04/02/1967	Just Let It Happen	The Arbors	113	BB
04/02/1967	Kind Of Hush	Gary & The Hornets	114	CB
04/02/1967	Another Page	Connie Francis	121	BB
04/02/1967	Love's Gone Bad	The Underdogs	122	BB
04/02/1967	Rain Rain Go Away	Lee Dorsey	126	CB
04/02/1967	The Cry Of The Wild Goose	Baja Marimba Band	130	CB
04/02/1967	Ballad Of Walter Wart (Brrriggett)	The Thorndike Pickledish Choir	131	BB
04/02/1967	If I Were A Rich Man	Herschel Bernardi	134	CB
04/02/1967	Echoes From The Thunder	Paul Hampton	139	CB
04/02/1967	Cabaret	Ray Conniff	140	CB
04/02/1967	Misty	Willie Mitchell	143	CB
11/02/1967	Just Like A Man	Margaret Whiting	104	CB
11/02/1967	Along Came Jones	The Righteous Brothers	108	BB
11/02/1967	Fools Fall In Love	Elvis Presley With The Jordanaires	113	CB
11/02/1967	Since I Lost You Girl	The Monitors	117	BB
11/02/1967	Cabaret	Ray Conniff	118	BB
11/02/1967	This Precious Time (b-side)	Terry Knight And The Pack	120	BB
11/02/1967	Along Came Jones	The Righteous Brothers	121	CB
11/02/1967	Kiss Tomorrow Goodbye (Capri C'est Fini)	Jane Morgan	125	CB

11/02/1967	Kind Of Hush	Gary & The Hornets	127	BB
11/02/1967	She	Del Shannon	131	BB
11/02/1967	The Loser	Peter Courtney	131	CB
11/02/1967	Three Hundred And Sixty Five Days	Donald Height	131	CB
11/02/1967	Shingaling '67	Don Covay	133	BB
11/02/1967	Lying And Trying	The Shillings	136	CB
11/02/1967	Life Is Groovy	United States Double Quartet: The Tokens The Kirby Stone Four	137	CB
11/02/1967	It Was A Very Good Year	The Three Sounds	138	CB
11/02/1967	Come On Down (From The Top Of That Hill)	Jackie Deshannon	147	CB
18/02/1967	Just Be Sincere	Jackie Wilson	103	CB
18/02/1967	Marryin' Kind Of Love	The Critters	111	BB
18/02/1967	The Cry Of The Wild Goose	Baja Marimba Band	113	BB
18/02/1967	Where Does The Good Times Go	Buck Owens And The Buckaroos	114	BB
18/02/1967	I Want To Talk About You	Ray Charles	119	CB
18/02/1967	Come On Down (From The Top Of That Hill)	Jackie Deshannon	121	BB
18/02/1967	Come Spy With Me	Smokey Robinson & The Miracles	121	CB
18/02/1967	The Biggest Man	Tommy Hunt	124	BB
18/02/1967	Greatest Love	Willie West	134	CB
18/02/1967	When I Stop Lovin' You	George Jackson	135	CB
18/02/1967	If I Had A Hammer (The Hammer Song)	Lorraine Ellison	144	CB
25/02/1967	It's A Happening Thing	The Peanut Butter Conspiracy	102	CB
25/02/1967	Stormy Weather	The Magnificent Men	105	CB
25/02/1967	Yellow Balloon	Jan & Dean	116	CB
25/02/1967	All Strung Out Over You	The Chambers Brothers	120	CB
25/02/1967	Here, There And Everywhere	Claudine Longet	126	CB
25/02/1967	If You're Thinkin' What I'm Thinkin'	Dino, Desi & Billy	128	BB
25/02/1967	Stormy Weather	The Magnificent Men	133	BB
04/03/1967	So Good	Roy Orbison	103	CB
04/03/1967	I'll Give You Time (To Think It Over)	The Outsiders Featuring Sonny Geraci	110	CB
04/03/1967	As Time Goes By	Mel Carter	111	BB

04/03/1967	If You're Thinkin' What I'm Thinkin'	Dino, Desi & Billy	117	CB
04/03/1967	I'll Give You Time (To Think It Over)	The Outsiders Featuring Sonny Geraci	118	BB
04/03/1967	Ice Melts In The Sun	Gary Lewis And The Playboys	121	BB
04/03/1967	The Loser	Peter Courtney	121	BB
04/03/1967	Don't Tie Me Down	Anthony And The Imperials	123	BB
04/03/1967	Here, There And Everywhere	Claudine Longet	126	BB
04/03/1967	It Must Be Love	The Intruders	127	CB
04/03/1967	Just Like A Man	Margaret Whiting	132	BB
04/03/1967	Riot On Sunset Strip	The Standells	134	CB
04/03/1967	It's Got To Be A Miracle (This Thing Called Love)	Marvin Gaye & Kim Weston	144	CB
11/03/1967	Break Out The Wine	The Spike Drivers	102	CB
11/03/1967	Excuse Me Dear Martha	Pozo-Seco Singers	102	BB
11/03/1967	Break On Through (To The Other Side)	The Doors	104	CB
11/03/1967	Animal Crackers (In Cellophane Boxes)	Gene Pitney	106	BB
11/03/1967	Something Inside Me	Ray Charles, Ray Charles Orchestra	112	BB
11/03/1967	Matthew And Son	Cat Stevens	115	BB
11/03/1967	Excuse Me Dear Martha	Pozo-Seco Singers	122	CB
11/03/1967	Is This What I Get For Loving You?	Marianne Faithfull	125	BB
11/03/1967	Animal Crackers (In Cellophane Boxes)	Gene Pitney	129	CB
11/03/1967	Touch Me, Kiss Me, Hold Me	The Inspirations	130	CB
11/03/1967	If I Only Had A Song To Sing	Wayne Newton	132	CB
11/03/1967	Chantilly Lace	Shorty Long	135	CB
11/03/1967	Fraulein	Vic Dana	138	CB
11/03/1967	Hang On To Me	John Gary	145	CB
18/03/1967	Summer Wine	Nancy Sinatra With Lee Hazlewood	105	CB
18/03/1967	Yellow Balloon	Jan & Dean	111	BB
18/03/1967	Persecution Smith	Bob Seger & The Last Heard	118	CB
18/03/1967	Everything Turned Blue	Billy Joe Royal	121	CB
18/03/1967	What's That Got To Do With Me	Jim & Jean	123	BB
18/03/1967	Tightrope	Inez & Charlie Foxx	124	CB

18/03/1967	After The Ball	Bob Crewe	126	BB
18/03/1967	Time Waits For No One	The Knack	130	CB
18/03/1967	You Make Me Feel So Good	The Gentrys	130	BB
18/03/1967	Since I Fell For You	Lenny Welch	134	BB
18/03/1967	Give It To Me	The Troggs	135	CB
25/03/1967	Go Go Radio Moscow	Nikita The K And The Friends Of Ed Labunski	105	BB
25/03/1967	Tears, Tears, Tears	Ben E. King	105	CB
25/03/1967	One Monkey Don't Stop No Show	Terry Knight & The Pack	116	CB
25/03/1967	(Hey You) Set My Soul On Fire	Mary Wells	120	CB
25/03/1967	Mr. Unreliable	The Cryan' Shames	127	BB
25/03/1967	Popcorn, Double Feature	The Searchers	127	CB
25/03/1967	The Right To Cry	Lenny Welch	128	BB
25/03/1967	So Good	Roy Orbison	132	BB
25/03/1967	Riot On Sunset Strip	The Standells	133	BB
25/03/1967	After The Ball	Bob Crewe	136	CB
01/04/1967	Goodbye To All You Women	BoBBy Goldsboro	103	CB
01/04/1967	Mr. Unreliable	The Cryan' Shames	106	CB
01/04/1967	Space Rock - Part 2	The Baskerville Hounds	110	CB
01/04/1967	She's Got The Time (She's Got The Changes)	The Poor	111	CB
01/04/1967	All I Need Is Your Love	The Manhattans	112	CB
01/04/1967	Time Alone Will Tell (Non Pensare A Me)	Connie Francis	114	CB
01/04/1967	Everybody Needs Help	Jimmy Holiday	116	BB
01/04/1967	(Hey You) Set My Soul On Fire	Mary Wells	122	BB
01/04/1967	Here Comes The Tears	Darrell Banks	124	BB
01/04/1967	I Don't Think You Know Me	The American Breed	124	CB
01/04/1967	Always Something There To Remind Me	Patti Labelle & The Blue Belles	125	BB
01/04/1967	Later For Tomorrow	Ernie K-Doe	141	CB
08/04/1967	Merry-Go-Round	The Youngbloods	101	CB
08/04/1967	Goodbye To All You Women	BoBBy Goldsboro	102	BB
08/04/1967	My Old Flame	Nino Tempo & April Stevens	104	CB

08/04/1967	The Beat Goes On	Lawrence Welk And His Orchestra	104	BB
08/04/1967	Shake	The British Walkers	106	BB
08/04/1967	You're Gonna Be Mine	The New Colony Six	108	BB
08/04/1967	I Want To Go Back There Again	Chris Clark	113	CB
08/04/1967	I Want To Go Back There Again	Chris Clark	114	BB
08/04/1967	California On My Mind	The Coastliners	115	BB
08/04/1967	In The Midnight Hour	The Wanted	118	BB
08/04/1967	Get It While You Can	Howard Tate	119	CB
08/04/1967	Break On Through (To The Other Side)	The Doors	126	BB
08/04/1967	Take Me	Brenda Lee	126	BB
08/04/1967	Love, Don't Let Me Down	BoBBy Bloom	130	CB
08/04/1967	She's Got The Time (She's Got The Changes)	The Poor	133	BB
08/04/1967	Get It While You Can	Howard Tate	134	BB
08/04/1967	One (Two Hearts Are One)	Dick Lee	135	CB
08/04/1967	Hijack	Jackie Hairston	144	CB
08/04/1967	Until The Real Thing Comes Along	Lenny Welch	146	CB
08/04/1967	The World Will Smile Again	Ray Conniff	148	CB
15/04/1967	My Old Flame	Nino Tempo & April Stevens	101	BB
15/04/1967	I'll Make Him Love Me	Barbara Lewis	103	CB
15/04/1967	Sweet Misery	Jimmy Dean	116	CB
15/04/1967	Make A Little Love	Lowell Fulsom	119	CB
15/04/1967	Later For Tomorrow	Ernie K-Doe	122	BB
15/04/1967	Groovin' Out (On Your Good, Good Lovin')	The Uniques	133	CB
15/04/1967	Rough Dried Woman Part 1	Big Mac	133	CB
15/04/1967	Edelweiss	Vince Hill	134	CB
22/04/1967	Unchanging Love	Carla Thomas	102	CB
22/04/1967	The Flower Children	Marcia Strassman	105	BB
22/04/1967	Midnight Hour	Michael & The Messengers	116	BB
22/04/1967	Edelweiss	Vince Hill	119	BB
22/04/1967	Everybody Needs Help	Jimmy Holiday	119	CB

22/04/1967	Since I Don't Have You	James Darren	123	BB
22/04/1967	Story Of My Life	The Unrelated Segments	124	CB
22/04/1967	Time Alone Will Tell (Non Pensare A Me)	Jerry Vale	126	BB
22/04/1967	Born To Be By Your Side (b-side)	Brenda Lee	134	BB
22/04/1967	Sweet Maria	Steve Lawrence	137	CB
22/04/1967	I Love Everything About You	BoBBy HeBB	140	CB
22/04/1967	Midnite Hour	Billy Lee Riley	145	CB
22/04/1967	Midnight Hour	The Messengers	148	CB
29/04/1967	Ivy, Ivy	The Left Banke	106	CB
29/04/1967	I Found A Rainbow	The Swingin' Medallions	107	BB
29/04/1967	Jump Back	King Curtis	111	CB
29/04/1967	You Don't Know Like I Know	Steve Alaimo	116	CB
29/04/1967	The Moving Finger Writes	Len Barry	124	BB
29/04/1967	Patty Cake	The Capitols	125	BB
29/04/1967	Everybody Loves My Baby	King Richard's Fluegel Knights	131	CB
29/04/1967	Gotta Leave Us Alone	The Outsiders	131	CB
29/04/1967	Down Home Girl	The Coasters	133	CB
29/04/1967	Patty Cake	The Capitols	144	CB
29/04/1967	Miniskirts In Moscow Or...	The Bob Crewe Generation	147	CB
06/05/1967	Function At The Junction	Ramsey Lewis	108	CB
06/05/1967	Georgy Girl	Baja Marimba Band	110	CB
06/05/1967	I Stand Accused	Inez & Charlie Foxx	117	CB
06/05/1967	All That's Left Is The Lemon Tree	Don Ho	118	CB
06/05/1967	Ivy, Ivy	The Left Banke	119	BB
06/05/1967	Gotta Leave Us Alone	The Outsiders	121	BB
06/05/1967	Rapid Transit	The RoBBs	123	BB
06/05/1967	Miniskirts In Moscow Or...	The Bob Crewe Generation	129	BB
06/05/1967	Pick Me	The Vibrations	133	CB
13/05/1967	Glass	The Sandpipers	104	CB
13/05/1967	Somebody Ought To Write A Book About It	Ray Charles	105	BB

13/05/1967	Love, Love, Love, Love, Love	Terry Knight & The Pack	107	CB
13/05/1967	Double Yellow Line	The Music Machine	111	BB
13/05/1967	I Believed It All	Pozo-Seco Singers	112	CB
13/05/1967	Hi-Ho Silver Lining	Jeff Beck	119	CB
13/05/1967	Creators Of Rain	Smokey And His Sister	121	BB
13/05/1967	Round, Round	Jonathan King	122	BB
13/05/1967	Here I Am Baby	Barbara Mcnair	125	BB
13/05/1967	Rapid Transit	The RoBBs	125	CB
13/05/1967	Everybody Loves My Baby	King Richard's Fluegel Knights	126	BB
13/05/1967	I Don't Want You Cuttin' Off Your Hair	B.B. King	126	CB
13/05/1967	Round, Round	Jonathan King	126	CB
13/05/1967	Someone Else's Arms	Rick Coyne	129	CB
13/05/1967	These Are Not My People	Billy Joe Royal	134	CB
13/05/1967	I Can't Get No Satisfaction	Jimmy Mcgriff	141	CB
13/05/1967	All I Want Is You	Pic & Bill	147	CB
20/05/1967	Love Song	The Artistics	111	BB
20/05/1967	Glass	The Sandpipers	112	BB
20/05/1967	Hi-Ho Silver Lining	Jeff Beck	123	BB
20/05/1967	Guess I Must Be Dreamin'	Delaney Bramlett	126	CB
20/05/1967	I Can't Get No Satisfaction	Jimmy Mcgriff	130	BB
20/05/1967	Now I Know	Eddie Fisher	135	CB
20/05/1967	The Three Bells (The Jimmy Brown Song)	Jane Morgan	139	CB
27/05/1967	More, More, More Of Your Love	Bob Brady & The Con Chords	102	CB
27/05/1967	All The Time	Jack Greene	103	BB
27/05/1967	Out Of Nowhere	Frank Ifield	103	CB
27/05/1967	Finchley Central	The New Vaudeville Band (featuring Tristam Vii)	106	CB
27/05/1967	Hello, Hello	Claudine Longet	113	CB
27/05/1967	Love, Love, Love, Love, Love	Terry Knight And The Pack	117	BB
27/05/1967	Ain't Nothin' But A House Party	The Show Stoppers	118	BB
27/05/1967	Up To Now	Trini Lopez	123	BB

27/05/1967	Stay Together Young Lovers	Brenda & The Tabulations	126	CB
27/05/1967	Baby It's You	Gary & The Hornets	138	CB
27/05/1967	Sugar, Let's Shing-A-Ling	Shirley Ellis	138	CB
27/05/1967	Sing Me A Rainbow	Sons Of Champlin	139	CB
03/06/1967	Finchley Central	The New Vaudeville Band (featuring Tristam Vii)	102	BB
03/06/1967	The Jokers	Peter & Gordon	104	CB
03/06/1967	February Sunshine	Giant Sunflower	106	BB
03/06/1967	Up-Up And Away	Johnny Mann Singers	111	CB
03/06/1967	These Are Not My People	Billy Joe Royal	113	BB
03/06/1967	Tonight Carmen	Marty RoBBins	114	BB
03/06/1967	California Sunshine Girl	The Shackelfords	115	BB
03/06/1967	Keep Smiling At Trouble (Trouble's A BuBBle)	Tony Bennett	121	CB
03/06/1967	Sing Me A Rainbow	Sons Of Champlin	124	BB
03/06/1967	I Stand Accused	Inez & Charlie Foxx	127	BB
03/06/1967	Life Turned Her That Way	Mel Tillis	128	BB
03/06/1967	Puppet On A String	Al Hirt	129	BB
03/06/1967	Now I Know	Eddie Fisher	131	BB
03/06/1967	Ruthless	Statler Brothers	131	CB
03/06/1967	Little By Little And Bit By Bit	The Ray Charles Singers	135	BB
03/06/1967	All I Do Is Think About You	The Innocence	140	CB
10/06/1967	All's Quiet On West 23rd	The Jet Stream	101	BB
10/06/1967	Don't Worry Baby	The Wanted	105	CB
10/06/1967	Creators Of Rain	Smokey & His Sister	106	CB
10/06/1967	Let It Happen	James Carr	106	BB
10/06/1967	No More Running Around	The Lamp Of Childhood	116	BB
10/06/1967	The Greatest Love (b-side)	Billy Joe Royal	117	BB
10/06/1967	Work With Me Annie	P. J. Proby	119	BB
10/06/1967	You Got Me Runnin'	The Impressions	120	CB
10/06/1967	You Only Live Twice	The Bob Crewe Generation	124	CB
10/06/1967	Baby, I Love You	Howard Tate	127	CB

10/06/1967	When The Good Sun Shines	Elmo & Almo	136	CB
10/06/1967	40 Days - 40 Nights	Don Covay & The Goodtimers	137	CB
10/06/1967	For All We Know	The Spinners	137	CB
10/06/1967	Here I Am Baby	Barbara Mcnair	144	CB
17/06/1967	39-21-46	The Showmen	101	BB
17/06/1967	More, More, More Of Your Love	Bob Brady & The Con Chords	104	BB
17/06/1967	Devil's Angels	Davie Allen & The Arrows	110	CB
17/06/1967	Katherine	Ben E. King	113	CB
17/06/1967	All's Quiet On West 23rd	The Jet Stream	115	CB
17/06/1967	How Long Has It Been	The Casinos	121	BB
17/06/1967	The Greatest Love	Billy Joe Royal	125	CB
17/06/1967	Losin' Boy	Eddy Giles	127	BB
17/06/1967	So Sharp	Dyke And The Blazers	130	BB
17/06/1967	They're Here	Boots Walker	140	CB
24/06/1967	Good Feelin' Time	The Yellow Balloon	101	BB
24/06/1967	Not So Sweet Martha Lorraine	Country Joe & The Fish	103	CB
24/06/1967	Dr. Do-Good	The Electric Prunes	105	CB
24/06/1967	Slippin' And Slidin'	Willie Mitchell	109	CB
24/06/1967	Deep In The Heart Of Harlem	Walter Jackson	110	BB
24/06/1967	Keep On Running	Telstars	112	CB
24/06/1967	She May Call You Up Tonight	The Left Banke	120	BB
24/06/1967	Just One Look	The Soul Twins	123	BB
24/06/1967	She's Leaving Home	David & Jonathan	123	BB
24/06/1967	Sweet Sweet Lovin'	Paul Kelly	126	BB
24/06/1967	A Woman Will Do Wrong	Helene Smith	128	BB
24/06/1967	So Sharp	Dyke & The Blazers	135	CB
24/06/1967	Ain't Nothin' But A House Party	The Show Stoppers	136	CB
24/06/1967	Lizbeth Peach	Terry Knight	137	CB
01/07/1967	City Of Windows	Stephen Monahan	101	BB
01/07/1967	You Don't Miss Your Water	King Curtis	105	BB

01/07/1967	Theme From Endless Summer	The Ventures	106	BB
01/07/1967	Try It	The Standells	111	CB
01/07/1967	Dog (Part I)	Jimmy Mccracklin	112	BB
01/07/1967	I'll Never Need More Than This	Ike & Tina Turner	114	BB
01/07/1967	The Boat That I Row	Lulu	115	BB
01/07/1967	The Bramble Bush	Trini Lopez	117	CB
01/07/1967	She May Call You Up Tonight	The Left Banke	118	CB
01/07/1967	Morning Glory Days	The Pleasure Fair	121	CB
01/07/1967	Love Is	BoBBy Goldsboro	122	CB
01/07/1967	You Make Me Feel Like Someone	The Babies	123	CB
01/07/1967	39-21-46	The Showmen	126	CB
01/07/1967	Dr. Do-Good	The Electric Prunes	128	BB
01/07/1967	I Can't See Nobody	The Bee Gees	128	BB
01/07/1967	Out Of Nowhere	Frank Ifield	132	BB
01/07/1967	You Ain't Ready	Lou Courtney	141	CB
01/07/1967	And I Don't Want Your Love	The Keepers Of The Light	145	CB
08/07/1967	Lovin' Sound	Ian And Sylvia	101	BB
08/07/1967	I'm All Ears	Los Bravos	107	CB
08/07/1967	It's Such A Pretty World Today	Andy Russell	119	BB
08/07/1967	Don't Lose Your Good Thing	Jimmy Hughes	121	BB
08/07/1967	You Make Me Feel Like Someone	Babies	122	BB
08/07/1967	It Ain't Happened	The Springfield Rifle	123	CB
08/07/1967	Agnes English	John Fred & His Playboy Band	126	CB
08/07/1967	Self Exprression (The Kids On The Street Will Never Give In)	Lou Christie	127	CB
08/07/1967	My Elusive Dreams	Curly Putman	134	BB
08/07/1967	I'd Rather Go To Jail	Mitch Ryder	140	CB
08/07/1967	Night Owl	The Flying Machine	143	CB
15/07/1967	Last Minute Miracle	The Shirelles	104	CB
15/07/1967	Timeless Love	Ed Ames	109	CB
15/07/1967	Heart And Soul	The Incredibles	116	CB

15/07/1967	Four Walls (Three Windows And Two Doors)	J.J. Jackson	123	BB
15/07/1967	Happy And Me	Don & The Goodtimes	125	CB
15/07/1967	Hey Grandma	Moby Grape	127	BB
15/07/1967	I'm Just Waiting (Anticipating For Her To Show Up)	The New Colony Six	128	CB
15/07/1967	Rollin' And Tumblin'	Canned Heat	139	CB
15/07/1967	Darling Be Home Soon	BoBBy Darin	140	CB
15/07/1967	My Elusive Dreams	Curly Putman	149	CB
22/07/1967	Hold On	The Mauds	105	CB
22/07/1967	That's The Way Love Is	The Isley Brothers	105	CB
22/07/1967	Theme From Endless Summer	The Ventures	111	CB
22/07/1967	When We're Made As One	The Manhattans	119	CB
22/07/1967	A Woman Will Do Wrong	Helene Smith	126	CB
22/07/1967	I'm Just Waitin' (Anticipatin' For Her To Show Up)	The New Colony Six	128	BB
22/07/1967	Romeo & Juliet	Michael & The Messengers	129	BB
22/07/1967	Morning Glory Days	The Pleasure Fair	134	BB
22/07/1967	Heartaches-Heartaches	O.V. Wright	136	CB
22/07/1967	The Boat That I Row	Lulu	138	CB
29/07/1967	Drums	Jon & Robin	102	CB
29/07/1967	Let The Four Winds Blow	Jerry Jaye	107	BB
29/07/1967	Hold On	The Mauds	114	BB
29/07/1967	Rollin' And Tumblin'	Canned Heat	115	BB
29/07/1967	As Long As I Live (I Live For You)	Fantastic Four	116	CB
29/07/1967	I Can't Go On Living Baby Without You	Nino Tempo & April Stevens	118	CB
29/07/1967	Heart And Soul	The Incredibles	122	BB
29/07/1967	Let The Four Winds Blow	Jerry Jaye	122	CB
29/07/1967	Sunny Goodge Street	Tom Northcott	123	BB
29/07/1967	Agnes English	John Fred & His Playboy Band	125	BB
29/07/1967	Crying Like A Baby	The Jive Five Featuring Eugene Pitt	127	BB
29/07/1967	Into Something Fine	The Raelets	130	CB
29/07/1967	I Wanna Help Hurry My Brothers Home	Jimmy Holiday	132	BB

29/07/1967	Foolin' Around	Chris Montez	135	BB
29/07/1967	Piece Of Silk	The Marvellos	137	CB
05/08/1967	Get The Message	Brian Hyland	109	CB
05/08/1967	Look In Your Eyes	Scott Mac Kenzie	111	BB
05/08/1967	What Does It Take (To Keep A Man Like You Satisfied)	Skeeter Davis	115	CB
05/08/1967	I'll See You In The Summertime	The Outsiders Featuring Sonny Geraci	117	CB
05/08/1967	Romeo And Juliet	Michael & The Messengers	121	CB
05/08/1967	I've Been Good To You	The Temptations	124	BB
05/08/1967	That's The Way Love Is	The Isley Brothers	125	BB
05/08/1967	Would You Believe	The Tempests	127	BB
05/08/1967	Put Your Trust In Me (Depend On Me)	Joe Simon	129	BB
05/08/1967	Good Day Sunshine	Claudine Longet	131	CB
05/08/1967	Summer Day Reflection Song	Donovan	135	BB
05/08/1967	Let It Be Me	The Sweet Inspirations	136	CB
05/08/1967	Gina	Lou Christie	139	CB
05/08/1967	Truly Right	Nitty Gritty Dirt Band	141	CB
05/08/1967	The Great Banana Hoax	The Electric Prunes	142	CB
12/08/1967	Sally Sayin' Somethin'	Billy Harner	103	CB
12/08/1967	Try, Try, Try	Jim Valley	106	BB
12/08/1967	Don't Forget About Me	The American Breed	107	BB
12/08/1967	Stout-Hearted Men	Barbra Streisand	108	CB
12/08/1967	My Heart Cries For You	Connie Francis	118	BB
12/08/1967	The Touch Of You	Five Stairsteps	118	CB
12/08/1967	Respect	Jimmy Smith	119	CB
12/08/1967	He Will Break Your Heart	Freddie Scott	120	BB
12/08/1967	Be Not Too Hard	Joan Baez	126	CB
12/08/1967	Tip On In (Part 1)	Slim Harpo	127	BB
12/08/1967	Look In Your Eyes	Scott Mac Kenzie	130	CB
12/08/1967	Where Love Is	Brenda Lee	134	BB
12/08/1967	I Wanna Be There	Blues Magoos	135	CB

19/08/1967	Sally Sayin' Somethin'	Billy Harner	118	BB
19/08/1967	With You Girl	The Arbors	125	CB
19/08/1967	Hi-Heel Sneakers	Jimmy Hughes	130	CB
19/08/1967	(We'll Meet In The) "Yellow Forest"	Jay & The Americans	131	BB
19/08/1967	No One Here To Play With	The Choir	134	CB
19/08/1967	Ain't It The Truth	The Drifters	135	CB
26/08/1967	Wednesday	The Royal Guardsmen	101	CB
26/08/1967	Sugar Man	Keith	104	CB
26/08/1967	Substitute	The Who	105	CB
26/08/1967	Lovers Of The World Unite	The Vogues	109	CB
26/08/1967	Do Something To Me	? And The Mysterians	110	BB
26/08/1967	On The Other Side	The Seekers	115	BB
26/08/1967	Under The Street Lamp	The Exits	116	BB
26/08/1967	Laura What's He Got That I Ain't Got	Leon Ashley	120	BB
26/08/1967	What Does It Take (To Keep A Man Like You Satisfied)	Skeeter Davis	121	BB
26/08/1967	You Can't Do That	Nilsson	122	BB
26/08/1967	Johnny B. Goode	The Coronados	128	CB
26/08/1967	I Wanna Be There	Blues Magoos	133	BB
26/08/1967	Someday Morning	The Wildweeds	141	CB
26/08/1967	Come Home, Baby	Terry Knight	144	CB
02/09/1967	She Knows	BoBBy Darin	120	CB
02/09/1967	Staight Shooter	The Mamas And The Papas	130	BB
02/09/1967	Take Me Back	The Flock	131	CB
02/09/1967	That's How It Is (When You're In Love)	Otis Clay	131	BB
02/09/1967	That's How Strong My Love Is	The Sweet Inspirations	131	CB
09/09/1967	Heavy Music (Part I)	Bob Seger & The Last Heard	103	BB
09/09/1967	I'll Release You	Joann Bon & The Coquettes	105	BB
09/09/1967	She Knows	BoBBy Darin	105	BB
09/09/1967	Heart Be Still	Lorraine Ellison	106	CB
09/09/1967	Would You Believe	The Tempests	107	CB

09/09/1967	Blindman	Big Brother And The Holding Company	110	BB
09/09/1967	I'm A Fool For You	James Carr	112	CB
09/09/1967	Runaway [Live]	Del Shannon	112	BB
09/09/1967	Requiem For The Masses	The Association	113	CB
09/09/1967	Soulsation	The Capreez	115	CB
09/09/1967	Bye, Bye Baby	Big Brother And The Holding Company	118	BB
09/09/1967	Do Something To Me	? & The Mysterians	123	CB
09/09/1967	That's How Strong My Love Is	The Sweet Inspirations	123	BB
09/09/1967	Soulsation	The Capreez	125	BB
09/09/1967	Love Is A Doggone Good Thing	Eddie Floyd	132	CB
16/09/1967	Kitty Doyle	Dino, Desi & Billy	108	BB
16/09/1967	(I Love You Babe But) Give Me My Freedom	The Glories	124	BB
16/09/1967	New Orleans	Steve Alaimo	126	BB
16/09/1967	See Emily Play	The Pink Floyd	134	BB
16/09/1967	Masters Of War	Barry Mcguire	137	CB
16/09/1967	Just Another Face	The Blades Of Grass	140	CB
23/09/1967	Runaway (Live)	Del Shannon	105	CB
23/09/1967	A Visit To A Sad Planet	Leonard Nimoy	114	CB
23/09/1967	Two Heads	Jefferson Airplane	114	CB
23/09/1967	Banned In Boston	Sam The Sham	116	CB
23/09/1967	Banned In Boston	Sam The Sham	117	BB
23/09/1967	Seven Days Too Long	Chuck Wood	119	BB
23/09/1967	A Visit To A Sad Planet	Leonard Nimoy	121	BB
23/09/1967	Turn Around And Take A Look	The Lemon Pipers	121	CB
23/09/1967	Blindman	Big Brother & The Holding Company	122	CB
23/09/1967	Lover's Roulette	Mel Torme	122	CB
23/09/1967	See Emily Play	The Pink Floyd	125	CB
23/09/1967	The Frog	Sergio Mendes & Brasil '66	126	BB
23/09/1967	Just Holding On	P. J. Proby	130	BB
23/09/1967	Ooh Baby, You Turn Me On	Willie Mitchell	131	CB

23/09/1967	Tears Of Joy	Vicki Anderson	131	BB
23/09/1967	Falling Off The Edge Of The World (Seeing You With Him)	The Easybeats	138	CB
23/09/1967	Something's Gotten Hold Of My Heart	Gene Pitney	138	CB
23/09/1967	Waterloo Sunset	The Kinks	141	CB
30/09/1967	Sea Of Love	The Kit-Kats	102	CB
30/09/1967	All The Time	Jimmy Roselli	107	CB
30/09/1967	February Sunshine	Giant Sunflower	110	CB
30/09/1967	It's All In The Game	Jackie Deshannon	110	BB
30/09/1967	Sometimes She's A Little Girl	Tommy Boyce & BoBBy Hart	110	BB
30/09/1967	Small Talk	Claudine Longet	118	CB
30/09/1967	Two Heads	Jefferson Airplane	124	BB
30/09/1967	Been So Nice	The Righteous Brothers	128	BB
30/09/1967	The Frog	Sergio Mendes & Brasil '66	133	CB
07/10/1967	As Long As You're Here	Zalman Yanovsky (Zally)	101	BB
07/10/1967	Walkin' Proud	Pete Klint Quintet	103	CB
07/10/1967	Open For Business As Usual	Jack Jones	104	CB
07/10/1967	From Head To Toe	Chris Clark	108	CB
07/10/1967	Reflections Of Charles Brown	Rubert's People	111	BB
07/10/1967	Splash 1	The Clique	113	BB
07/10/1967	Take Me Along	The Ray Charles Singers	113	CB
07/10/1967	Believe In Me Baby - Part I	Jesse James	116	CB
07/10/1967	I'm A Drifter	Lowell Fulsom	118	BB
07/10/1967	A Hunk Of Funk	Gene Dozier And The Brotherhood	121	BB
07/10/1967	Mystery Of Tallahatchie Bridge	Roger White	123	BB
07/10/1967	I'm Gonna Keep What I've Got	Slim Harpo	124	CB
07/10/1967	Really, Really Love You	Ronnie Walker	128	BB
07/10/1967	Melancholy Mood	Tommy Roe	129	CB
07/10/1967	Sea Of Love	The Kit-Kats	130	BB
07/10/1967	Something's Gotten Hold Of My Heart	Gene Pitney	130	BB
07/10/1967	Turn Around And Take A Look	The Lemon Pipers	132	BB

07/10/1967	I Can't Happen Without You	The Power Plant	134	BB
07/10/1967	A Strange Song	Harry Belafonte	137	CB
07/10/1967	Mystery Of Tallahatchie Bridge	Roger White	140	CB
07/10/1967	Honey And Wine	Glenn Yarbrough	142	CB
14/10/1967	We Gotta Go Home	The Music Explosion	103	BB
14/10/1967	What's So Good About Good-Bye	The Giant Sunflower	104	CB
14/10/1967	Little Girl	The Critters	105	CB
14/10/1967	When The Good Apples Fall	The Seekers	106	CB
14/10/1967	More Than A Miracle	Roger Williams	108	BB
14/10/1967	What Are We Gonna Do	Just Us	113	CB
14/10/1967	I Got A Feeling	Barbara Randolph	116	BB
14/10/1967	What's So Good About Good-Bye	Giant Sunflower	116	BB
14/10/1967	Boppa Do Down Down	The Third Rail	119	CB
14/10/1967	You Can Lead Your Woman To The Altar	Oscar Toney Jr.	120	BB
14/10/1967	Hole In My Shoe	Traffic	122	CB
14/10/1967	Desireé	The Left Banke	127	CB
14/10/1967	Window Shopping	The Messengers	132	BB
14/10/1967	Giving Up Your Love Is Like (Giving Up The World)	The Twentie Grans	140	CB
21/10/1967	The Ballad Of Waterhole #3 (Code Of The West)	Roger Miller	102	BB
21/10/1967	I Almost Called Your Name	Margaret Whiting	108	BB
21/10/1967	Excerpt From "A Teenage Opera" (Grocer Jack)	Keith West	109	BB
21/10/1967	Little Girl	The Critters	113	BB
21/10/1967	Baby It's Wonderful	Chris Bartley	118	CB
21/10/1967	Don't Mess With My Money	Jesse Gee	122	CB
21/10/1967	Richard & Me	Gene & Tommy	122	BB
21/10/1967	My Ship Is Comin' In	Walter Jackson	124	BB
21/10/1967	Bo Diddley Bach	The Kingsmen	128	BB
21/10/1967	Be My Love	Mel Carter	132	BB
21/10/1967	Window Shopping	The Messengers	135	CB
21/10/1967	Be My Love	Mel Carter	138	CB

28/10/1967	Love Of The Common People	Wayne Newton	106	BB
28/10/1967	Sand	Nancy Sinatra & Lee Hazlewood	107	BB
28/10/1967	Birds Of Britain	The Bob Crewe Generation	109	CB
28/10/1967	I Want Action	Ruby Winters	109	BB
28/10/1967	California My Way	The Committee	110	BB
28/10/1967	It Takes People Like You (To Make People Like Me)	Buck Owens And The Buckaroos	114	BB
28/10/1967	We Gotta Go Home	The Music Explosion	114	CB
28/10/1967	She	Roy Orbison	119	BB
28/10/1967	Love Of The Common People	Everly Brothers	127	CB
28/10/1967	I Want Action	Ruby Winters	128	CB
28/10/1967	Open For Business As Usual	Jack Jones	130	BB
28/10/1967	A Hunk Of Funk	Gene Dozier & The Brotherhood	132	CB
28/10/1967	(It Will Have To Do) Until The Real Thing Comes Along	Ernie K. Doe	133	CB
28/10/1967	Hey Girl	The Mamas And The Papas	134	BB
28/10/1967	Bo Diddley Bach	The Kingsmen	139	CB
28/10/1967	Where You Gonna Go?	The Unrelated Segments	141	CB
04/11/1967	Lapland	The Baltimore And Ohio Marching Band	101	CB
04/11/1967	For A Few Dollars More	Hugo Montenegro, His Orchestra And Chorus	102	BB
04/11/1967	Oh! What A Fool I've Been	The Sweet Inspirations	104	CB
04/11/1967	Where's The Melody?	Brenda Lee	105	BB
04/11/1967	Ro Ro Rosey	Van Morrison	107	BB
04/11/1967	I Want Some More	Jon & Robin And The In Crowd	108	BB
04/11/1967	I Want Some More	Jon & Robin & The In Crowd	111	CB
04/11/1967	Love Of The Common People	The Everly Brothers	114	BB
04/11/1967	Ro Ro Rosey	Van Morrison	115	CB
04/11/1967	Wish You Were Here With Me	The Fawns	118	CB
04/11/1967	Hey Mama (What'cha Got Good For Daddy)	Flaming Embers	119	CB
04/11/1967	I Want My Baby Back	Edwin Starr	120	BB
04/11/1967	Just Loving You	Anita Harris	120	BB
04/11/1967	Stop Light	The Five Americans	123	CB

04/11/1967	You Can Have Him	The Cake	124	CB
04/11/1967	Baby It's Wonderful	Chris Bartley	125	BB
04/11/1967	For A Few Dollars More	Hugo Montenegro, His Orchestra & Chorus	130	CB
04/11/1967	Magic In The Air	Group Therapy	132	CB
04/11/1967	(You'll) Go To Hell	Nina Simone	133	BB
04/11/1967	Rain	The Four Larks	140	CB
04/11/1967	I'm So Proud	Keith	147	CB
04/11/1967	The World Of Broken Hearts	The Amen Corner	149	CB
11/11/1967	Just Loving You	Anita Harris	106	CB
11/11/1967	Kites Are Fun	The Free Design	119	CB
11/11/1967	Where's The Melody?	Brenda Lee	128	CB
11/11/1967	Stop Light	The Five Americans	132	BB
11/11/1967	I'm So Proud	Keith	135	BB
11/11/1967	Apologize	Brian Hyland	139	CB
18/11/1967	Live For Life	Carmen Mcrae & Herbie Mann	101	BB
18/11/1967	Tony Rome	Nancy Sinatra	101	CB
18/11/1967	Freedom Bird	The Lewis & Clarke Expedition	104	CB
18/11/1967	Goin' Down	The Monkees	104	BB
18/11/1967	For What It's Worth	King Curtis & The Kingpins	107	CB
18/11/1967	Face The Autumn	The Family	113	CB
18/11/1967	Holly	Andy Williams	113	BB
18/11/1967	Uptown	The Chambers Brothers	126	BB
25/11/1967	Ooh Baby	Deon Jackson	101	CB
25/11/1967	Finders Keepers	Al Kent	104	CB
25/11/1967	Jo Jo's Place	BoBBy Goldsboro	111	BB
25/11/1967	You've Got Me Hummin'	The Hassles	112	BB
25/11/1967	I Wish I Knew How It Would Feel To Be Free	Nina Simone	118	CB
25/11/1967	She	Roy Orbison	118	CB
25/11/1967	When The Lights Go On Again (All Over The World)	Kay Starr With The California Dreamers	120	CB
25/11/1967	I Found A Reason	The First Edition	121	CB

25/11/1967	Treat Her Groovy	The New Colony Six	125	CB
25/11/1967	I Want To Be Loved	Lorraine Ellison	137	CB
02/12/1967	Do Unto Others	Paul Revere And The Raiders Featuring Mark Lindsey	102	BB
02/12/1967	This Thing Called Love	The Webs	102	BB
02/12/1967	Detroit City	Solomon Burke	104	BB
02/12/1967	Mellow Moonlight	Leon Haywood	105	CB
02/12/1967	The Soul Of J.B.	James Brown & The Famous Flames	125	CB
02/12/1967	Hey Boy! (The Girl's In Love With You)	The Eighth Day	130	CB
02/12/1967	Too Old To Go 'WAY Little Girl	The Shame	131	CB
02/12/1967	That Lucky Old Sun (Just Rolls Around Heaven All Day)	Bill Medley (Of The Righteous Brothers)	132	CB
02/12/1967	Never Too Much Love	The Bards	134	CB
02/12/1967	Heartbreaker	B.B. King	136	CB
02/12/1967	Don't Lose Your Groove	Lavell Hardy	139	CB
09/12/1967	Hey Joyce	Lou Courtney	105	CB
09/12/1967	Shout	Lulu	108	CB
09/12/1967	Insanity Comes Quietly To The Structured Mind	Janis Ian	109	BB
09/12/1967	Yakety Yak	Sam The Sham	111	CB
09/12/1967	Turn Of The Century	The Cyrkle	112	BB
09/12/1967	Little Bit Of Lovin'	The Outsiders	117	BB
09/12/1967	Do Unto Others	Paul Revere & The Raiders Featuring Mark Lindsey	118	CB
09/12/1967	How Beautiful Our Love Is	The Platters	120	CB
09/12/1967	Please Believe Me	Jimmy Roselli	125	CB
09/12/1967	Psychedelic Soul	Chylds	129	CB
09/12/1967	Old Toy Trains	Roger Miller	133	CB
09/12/1967	Keep Your Cool	Terry & The Chain Reaction	140	CB
09/12/1967	South End Incident (I'm Afraid)	The Beacon Street Union	142	CB
16/12/1967	7:30 Guided Tour	The Five Americans	103	CB
16/12/1967	Big Daddy	Boots Randolph	107	CB
16/12/1967	Yakety Yak	Sam The Sham	110	BB
16/12/1967	Come See About Me	Mitch Ryder And The Detroit Wheels	113	BB

16/12/1967	Good Good Lovin'	The Blossoms	115	BB
16/12/1967	I Feel Free	Cream	116	BB
16/12/1967	Letter From A Teenage Son	Brandon Wade	120	BB
16/12/1967	Magic Colors	Lesley Gore	125	CB
16/12/1967	Oh How Much I Love You (Dio Come Ti Amo)	Jack Jones	129	CB
16/12/1967	What A Strange Town (The People Had No Faces)	Jimmie Rodgers	141	CB
16/12/1967	Son Of Ice Bag (Live)	Hugh Masekela	146	CB
23/12/1967	Love Lots Of Lovin'	Lee Dorsey & Betty Harris	110	BB
23/12/1967	Living In A World Of Make Believe	Good & Plenty	111	BB
23/12/1967	Kites Are Fun	The Free Design	114	BB
23/12/1967	Pledge Of Love (b-side)	BoBBy Goldsboro	118	BB
30/12/1967	Big Daddy	Boots Randolph	105	BB
30/12/1967	I Wish I Had Time	The Last Word	105	BB
30/12/1967	Deep In The Night	The Candymen	107	CB
30/12/1967	I Wish I Had Time	The Last Words	108	CB
30/12/1967	Living In A World Of Make Believe	Good & Plenty	116	CB
30/12/1967	Camelot	King Richard's Fluegel Knights	124	CB
30/12/1967	I Can't Shake This Feeling	The Carmel	126	CB
06/01/1968	Blessed Are The Lonely	Robert Knight	101	CB
06/01/1968	Do What You Gotta Do	Al Wilson	102	BB
06/01/1968	Break My Mind	BoBBy Wood	110	BB
06/01/1968	Still Burning In My Heart	The Drifters	111	BB
06/01/1968	Another Time	Sagittarius	114	CB
06/01/1968	October Country	The October Country	122	CB
13/01/1968	Birds Of A Feather	Joe South	106	BB
13/01/1968	Camelot	King Richard's Fluegel Knights	107	BB
13/01/1968	It's A Gas	The Hombres	113	BB
13/01/1968	Trespassin'	The Ohio Players	117	CB
13/01/1968	A House Built On Sand	Leslie Uggams	121	CB
13/01/1968	That's All Right	Brenda Lee	123	CB

13/01/1968	To Be My Girl	John Roberts	133	CB
13/01/1968	Why Girl	The Precisions	146	CB
20/01/1968	Jezebel	The Rumbles, Ltd.	106	CB
20/01/1968	Dear Delilah	Grapefruit	107	CB
20/01/1968	Sunshine Help Me	Spooky Tooth	126	CB
20/01/1968	Quicksand	The Youngbloods	131	CB
20/01/1968	I Need A Woman Of My Own	Tommy Hunt	134	CB
20/01/1968	Come Ride, Come Ride	The Merry-Go-Round	138	CB
27/01/1968	No One Knows	Every Mother's Son	101	CB
27/01/1968	Say A Little Prayer	Sergio Mendes	106	BB
27/01/1968	Red, Green, Yellow And Blue	Dickey Lee	107	BB
27/01/1968	What Can You Do When You Ain't Got Nobody	Soul Brothers Six	107	BB
27/01/1968	Red, Green, Yellow And Blue	Dickey Lee	108	CB
27/01/1968	Green Green Grass Of Home	Skitch Henderson His Piano And His Orchestra	110	BB
27/01/1968	Love Is Blue (L'Amour Est Bleu)	Manny Kellem, His & Voices	111	CB
27/01/1968	Get Together	Jimmy Mccracklin	114	BB
27/01/1968	A World Of Our Own	Sonny James, The Southern Gentleman	118	BB
27/01/1968	That's All Right	Brenda Lee	118	BB
27/01/1968	Angel Of The Morning	Danny Michaels	145	CB
03/02/1968	You Haven't Seen My Love	The Ones	107	CB
03/02/1968	Pledge Of Love	BoBBy Goldsboro	109	CB
03/02/1968	Who Am I	Country Joe And The Fish	114	BB
03/02/1968	Mr. Soul Satisfaction	Timmy Willis	120	BB
03/02/1968	Here I Am	The Righteous Brothers	121	BB
03/02/1968	I Love How You Love Me	Claudine Longet	122	CB
03/02/1968	Ode To Otis Redding	Mark Johnson	122	BB
03/02/1968	The Goose (That Laid The Golden Egg)	The Parliaments	123	CB
03/02/1968	Captain Of Your Ship	Reparata And The Delrons	127	BB
10/02/1968	I Cannot Stop You	The Cherry Slush	103	CB
10/02/1968	Nights In White Satin (short Version)	The Moody Blues	103	BB

10/02/1968	Captain Of Your Ship	Reparata & The Delrons	111	CB
10/02/1968	My Ancestors	Lou Rawls	113	CB
10/02/1968	Dottie I Like It	Tommy Roe	114	BB
10/02/1968	Life Is But A Moment (Canta Ragazzina)	Eydie Gorme	115	BB
10/02/1968	You Haven't Seen My Love	The Ones	117	BB
10/02/1968	What You Want (Baby I Want You)	The Music Explosion	119	BB
10/02/1968	If The Whole World Stopped Lovin'	Val Doonican	125	CB
10/02/1968	What You Want (Baby I Want You)	The Music Explosion	126	CB
10/02/1968	Mr. Soul Satisfaction	Timmy Willis	132	CB
10/02/1968	All The Time	Wayne Newton	134	CB
10/02/1968	Who Am I	Country Joe & The Fish	147	CB
17/02/1968	Something I'll Remember	Sandy Posey	102	BB
17/02/1968	Circus	Sonny & Cher	106	CB
17/02/1968	Sally Was A Good Old Girl	Trini Lopez	106	CB
17/02/1968	Darling Stay With Me	Lenny Welch	112	BB
17/02/1968	My Ancestors	Lou Rawls	113	BB
17/02/1968	Hang Up City	The Berkeley Kites	115	CB
17/02/1968	1941	Tom Northcott	117	CB
17/02/1968	Mama Said	The Next Five	134	CB
17/02/1968	It's Love Now	Lou Courtney	147	CB
24/02/1968	In The Heat Of The Night	Dick Hyman & "The Group"	105	CB
24/02/1968	Funky North Philly	Bill Cosby	109	CB
24/02/1968	Love Is Blue (L'Amour Est Bleu)	Claudine Longet	110	CB
24/02/1968	You Say	The Esquires	113	CB
24/02/1968	It Keeps Right On A Hurtin'	Margaret Whiting	115	BB
24/02/1968	Outside Of A Small Circle Of Friends	Phil Ochs	118	BB
24/02/1968	I Cannot Stop You	The Cherry Slush	119	BB
24/02/1968	O Surdato 'NNAMMURATO (Soldiers Sweetheart)	Jimmy Roselli	122	CB
24/02/1968	We Got A Thing Going On	Ben E. King & Dee Dee Sharp	122	CB
24/02/1968	A Melody For You	The Grass Roots	123	BB

24/02/1968	Bear Mash	Ramsey Lewis	123	BB
24/02/1968	The Radio Song	The Parade	127	BB
24/02/1968	Animal Girl	The Standells	133	CB
24/02/1968	Cry On My Shoulder	Phil Flowers	136	CB
24/02/1968	Think Before You Walk Away	The Platters	137	CB
02/03/1968	Baby Please Don't Go	The Amboy Dukes	106	BB
02/03/1968	Flights Of Fantasy	The Ventures	110	CB
02/03/1968	Baby What I Mean	Spiral Starecase	111	BB
02/03/1968	A Melody For You	The Grass Roots	120	CB
02/03/1968	Atlanta Georgia Stray	Sonny Curtis	120	BB
02/03/1968	In The Morning	The Mighty Marvelows	124	CB
02/03/1968	We Got A Thing Going On	Ben E. King & Dee Dee Sharp	127	BB
02/03/1968	If The Whole World Stopped Lovin'	Val Doonican	128	BB
02/03/1968	Every Step I Take (Every Move I Make)	The Hassles	133	CB
09/03/1968	(Sittin' On) The Dock Of The Bay	King Curtis & The Kingpins	101	CB
09/03/1968	In The Heat Of The Night	Dick Hyman And "The Group"	106	BB
09/03/1968	Chain Of Fools (Part 1)	Jimmy Smith	107	CB
09/03/1968	By The Time I Get To Phoenix	The Magnificent Men	109	CB
09/03/1968	Up From The Skies	The Jimi Hendrix Experience	109	CB
09/03/1968	Can't Find The Time	Orpheus	111	BB
09/03/1968	Me About You	Jackie Deshannon	119	BB
09/03/1968	Instant Heartbreak (Just Add Tears)	The Precisions	121	CB
09/03/1968	Atlanta Georgia Stray	Sonny Curtis	123	CB
09/03/1968	You Say	The Esquires	126	BB
09/03/1968	I Hate To See Me Go (b-side)	Margaret Whiting	127	BB
09/03/1968	Cotton Candy Sandman (Sandman's Coming)	Harpers Bizarre	131	CB
09/03/1968	Big Bird	Eddie Floyd	132	BB
16/03/1968	You've Got To Change Your Mind	BoBBy Byrd & James Brown	102	BB
16/03/1968	If My World Falls Through	The Rose Garden Featuring Diane Derose	104	CB
16/03/1968	Come Live With Me	Tony Scotti	105	CB

16/03/1968	Our Corner Of The Night	Barbra Streisand	107	BB
16/03/1968	It's Time To Say Goodbye	The Third Rail	113	BB
16/03/1968	Me About You	Jackie Deshannon	113	CB
16/03/1968	No Other Love	Jay & The Americans	114	BB
16/03/1968	Brown Sugar	The Watts 103rd Street Rhythm Band	118	CB
16/03/1968	A Fool Of Fools	Tony Bennett	119	BB
16/03/1968	Do Drop Inn	The Fifth Estate	122	BB
16/03/1968	Mean Man	Betty Harris	123	CB
16/03/1968	Small Talk	Lesley Gore	124	BB
16/03/1968	Come Live With Me	Tony Scotti	126	BB
16/03/1968	Love Is Kind, Love Is Wine	The Seekers	135	BB
16/03/1968	I Don't Want To Love You	Barry Lee Show	142	CB
23/03/1968	I've Come A Long Way	Wilson Pickett	101	BB
23/03/1968	Come Down	Honey Ltd.	104	CB
23/03/1968	Honey	Bob Shane	104	BB
23/03/1968	Party People	Solomon Burke	112	BB
23/03/1968	Black On White	The North Atlantic Invasion Force	114	CB
23/03/1968	Ways	The Candymen	114	CB
23/03/1968	Do Drop Inn	The Fifth Estate	115	CB
23/03/1968	A Woman With The Blues	The Lamp Sisters	116	CB
23/03/1968	What Is Love	Miriam Makeba	116	CB
23/03/1968	I'll Be Yours (Nel Sol)	Wayne Thomas	117	CB
23/03/1968	Denver	Steve Alaimo	118	BB
23/03/1968	African Boo-Ga-Loo	Jackie Lee	121	BB
23/03/1968	What Is Love	Miriam Makeba	123	BB
23/03/1968	Lovey Dovey Kinda Lovin'	Brenton Wood	127	CB
23/03/1968	The Gypsies, The Jugglers And The Clowns	Jack Jones	134	CB
23/03/1968	With A Little Help From My Friends	Sergio Mendes & Brasil '66	137	CB
30/03/1968	Come To Me Softly	Jimmy James & The Vagabonds	103	CB
30/03/1968	Wind Song	Wes Montgomery	103	BB

30/03/1968	In The Morning	The Mighty Marvelows	105	BB
30/03/1968	The Legend Of Xanadu	Dave Dee, Dozy, Beaky, Mick & Tich	113	CB
30/03/1968	The Last Goodbye	Dick Miles	114	BB
30/03/1968	I Truly, Truly Believe	The Temptations	116	BB
30/03/1968	So Fine	Ike & Tina And The Ikettes	117	BB
30/03/1968	No Other Love	Jay & The Americans	119	CB
30/03/1968	Days Of Pearly Spencer	David Mcwilliams	122	CB
30/03/1968	Illusion	Bob Brady & The Con Chords	125	CB
30/03/1968	I Guess That Don't Make Me A Loser	Brothers Of Soul	126	CB
30/03/1968	Check Yourself	DeBBie Taylor	127	CB
06/04/1968	Look At What I Almost Missed	The Parliaments	101	CB
06/04/1968	Why Say Goodbye (A Comme Amour)	Connie Francis	103	CB
06/04/1968	A Stop Along The Way	Timothy Carr	107	CB
06/04/1968	If You Loved Me (Soul Coaxing-Ame Caline)	Peggy March	107	CB
06/04/1968	Billy Sunshine	Evie Sands	115	CB
06/04/1968	Every Man Oughta Have A Woman	William Bell	115	BB
06/04/1968	She Wears My Ring	Solomon King	117	BB
06/04/1968	I Found You	Frankie Laine	118	BB
06/04/1968	I Don't Know	The Violinaires	121	BB
06/04/1968	If You Didn't Hear Me The First Time (I'll Say It Again)	The SandpeBBles	122	BB
06/04/1968	The Bonnie And Clyde	The New Vaudeville Band	122	BB
06/04/1968	The Power Of Love	Robert Knight	147	CB
13/04/1968	Look At What I Almost Missed	The Parliaments	104	BB
13/04/1968	I Got A Sure Thing	Ollie & The Nightingales	105	CB
13/04/1968	Mood Indigo	Brenda Lee & Pete Fountain	112	CB
13/04/1968	Feelings	The Grassroots	118	CB
13/04/1968	What A Day	The Contrasts Featuring Bob Morrison	120	BB
13/04/1968	Take Me In Your Arms (Rock Me A Little While)	The Isley Brothers	121	BB
13/04/1968	Call On You	Chuck Trois & The Amazing Maze	123	CB
13/04/1968	The Legend Of Xanadu	Dave Dee, Dozy, Beaky, Mick And Tich	123	BB

13/04/1968	The House That Jack Built	Thelma Jones	132	BB
13/04/1968	Get-E-Up (The Horse)	The Preparations	134	BB
13/04/1968	No Where To Run No Where To Hide	Witches & The Warlock	138	CB
13/04/1968	The Life Of The Party	Louis Armstrong	146	CB
20/04/1968	Fat Albert (Hey, Hey, Hey)	The Fat Albert Orchestra & Chorus	103	CB
20/04/1968	Love Machine	The Roosters	106	BB
20/04/1968	We Call On Him	Elvis Presley With The Jordanaires	106	BB
20/04/1968	By The Time I Get To Phoenix	Ace Cannon	110	BB
20/04/1968	A Stop Along The Way	Timothy Carr	112	BB
20/04/1968	I Am The Man For You Baby	Edwin Starr	112	BB
20/04/1968	Yesterday I Heard The Rain (Esta Tarde Vi Llover)	Tony Bennett	114	CB
20/04/1968	Don't Hurt Me No More	Al Greene	117	CB
20/04/1968	Old Macdonald Had A Boogaloo Farm	Sam The Sham & The Pharaohs	124	CB
20/04/1968	Holy Man	Scott Mckenzie	126	BB
20/04/1968	Don't Hurt Me No More	Al Greene	127	BB
20/04/1968	Mamam	Arthur Prysock	127	CB
27/04/1968	Faithfully	Margaret Whiting	103	CB
27/04/1968	Oh, I'll Never Be The Same	Young Hearts	109	BB
27/04/1968	With Pen In Hand	Johnny Darrell	112	CB
27/04/1968	The Singer Sang His Song	The Bee Gees	116	BB
27/04/1968	You'll Never Walk Alone	Elvis Presley With The Jordanaires	116	CB
27/04/1968	Don't Take Your Love From Me	Ben E. King	117	BB
27/04/1968	Slick	Herb Alpert & The Tijuana Brass	119	BB
27/04/1968	Fat Albert (Hey, Hey, Hey)	The Fat Albert Orchestra And Chorus	120	BB
27/04/1968	As Long As I Got You	Laura Lee	123	BB
27/04/1968	We Can Fly/Up-Up And Away	Al Hirt	129	BB
27/04/1968	Yesterday I Heard The Rain	Tony Bennett	130	BB
27/04/1968	After Tea	The Spencer Davis Group	131	CB
27/04/1968	Why Can't I Stop	The Esquires	131	CB
27/04/1968	Why Say Goodbye (A Comme Amour)	Connie Francis	132	BB

27/04/1968	Billy Sunshine	Evie Sands	133	BB
27/04/1968	Mamam	Arthur Prysock	134	BB
04/05/1968	Only Me	The First Edition	102	CB
04/05/1968	Finders Keepers	Salt Water Taffy	104	CB
04/05/1968	The Prodigal	The Hombres	110	CB
04/05/1968	Elevator	Grapefruit	113	BB
04/05/1968	Lazy Sunday	Small Faces	114	BB
04/05/1968	Lazy Sunday	Small Faces	119	CB
04/05/1968	Alone Again Or	Love	123	BB
04/05/1968	All I Took Was Love	The Uniques	128	CB
04/05/1968	Chain Around The Flowers	The Lewis & Clarke Expedition	131	BB
04/05/1968	Sugar (Don't Take Away My Candy)	The Jive Five Featuring Eugene Pitt	131	CB
11/05/1968	You're Good For Me	Lou Rawls	103	BB
11/05/1968	Finders Keepers	Salt Water Taffy	105	BB
11/05/1968	Shhhhhhhh (For A Little While)	James Brown & The Famous Flames	108	CB
11/05/1968	Looking Back	Spencer Davis Group	113	BB
11/05/1968	Follow Me	Jack Jones	117	BB
11/05/1968	Elevator	Grapefruit	118	CB
11/05/1968	Randy	The Happenings	118	BB
11/05/1968	Can I Carry Your Balloon	The Swampseeds	124	BB
11/05/1968	Do I Love You?	The Magic Ring	125	CB
11/05/1968	I Can't Go Back To Denver	The Gentrys	132	BB
11/05/1968	Only Me	The First Edition	133	BB
11/05/1968	Oh What It Seemed To Be	Jimmy Roselli	134	CB
11/05/1968	I've Got To Hold On	The Ohio Players	137	CB
18/05/1968	Un-Mundo	The Buffalo Springfield	105	BB
18/05/1968	Ruby Baby & Peaches On A Cherry Tree	Mitch Ryder	106	BB
18/05/1968	Open Up Your Soul	Erma Franklin	107	BB
18/05/1968	La La La (He Gives Me Love)	Raymond Lefevre And His Orchestra	110	BB
18/05/1968	It's My Time	The Everly Brothers	112	BB

18/05/1968	Let's Get Together	The Sunshine Company	112	BB
18/05/1968	A Dime A Dozen	Carla Thomas	114	BB
18/05/1968	Listen, Listen!	The Merry-Go-Round	114	CB
18/05/1968	Please Stay	Dave Clark Five	115	BB
18/05/1968	Faithfully	Margaret Whiting	117	BB
18/05/1968	He Don't Really Love You	The Delfonics	117	CB
18/05/1968	Happy With You	Kenny O'dell	118	BB
18/05/1968	We Played Games	John Fred & His Playboy Band	122	CB
18/05/1968	Backwards And Forwards	December's Children	123	BB
18/05/1968	Mechanical World	Spirit	123	BB
18/05/1968	Goodnight Sweet Josephine	The Yardbirds	127	BB
18/05/1968	A Stone Good Lover	Jo Armstead	128	CB
18/05/1968	It Can't Be Too Late	SmuBBs	129	CB
18/05/1968	I Apologize Baby	P. J. Proby	135	BB
25/05/1968	Helule Helule	The Tremeloes	110	CB
25/05/1968	Now I Taste The Tears	The Smiths	110	CB
25/05/1968	Sock It To Me Sunshine	The Curtain Calls	116	BB
25/05/1968	With Pen In Hand	Johnny Darrell	126	BB
25/05/1968	Let It Be Me	Nino Tempo & April Stevens	127	BB
25/05/1968	A Stone Good Lover	Jo Armstead	129	BB
25/05/1968	We Played Games	John Fred & His Playboy Band	130	BB
25/05/1968	Hangin' From Your Lovin' Tree	The In Crowd	131	BB
25/05/1968	I Got To Have Ya	The Trolls	135	CB
01/06/1968	All The Grey Haired Men	The Lettermen	116	CB
01/06/1968	Sugar (Don't Take Away My Candy)	Jive Five Featuring Eugene Pitt	119	BB
01/06/1968	Helule Helule	The Tremeloes	122	BB
01/06/1968	Valley Of The Dolls	King Curtis & The Kingpins	125	CB
01/06/1968	Ruby Baby & Peaches On A Cherry Tree	Mitch Ryder	130	CB
01/06/1968	Both Sides Now	Harpers Bizarre	133	CB
01/06/1968	Days Of Pearly Spencer	David Mcwilliams	134	BB

08/06/1968	Mister Sandman	Bert Kaempfert & His Orchestra	101	CB
08/06/1968	Don't Break My Pretty Balloon	Vikki Carr	103	CB
08/06/1968	Rose (A Ring To The Name Of Rose)	Tony Scotti	104	CB
08/06/1968	When Do We Go	Billy Vera & Judy Clay	107	BB
08/06/1968	All The Grey Haired Men	The Lettermen	109	BB
08/06/1968	I'm Gonna Change	The Montanas	118	CB
08/06/1968	He Gives Me Love (La La La)	Lesley Gore	119	BB
08/06/1968	Sometimes You Just Can't Win	Mouse And The Traps	125	BB
08/06/1968	White Horses	Claudine Longet	127	CB
08/06/1968	Remembering	Wayne Newton	128	CB
08/06/1968	The Battle Hymn Of The Republic - '68	The Bob Crewe Generation Choir	132	CB
15/06/1968	Shhhhhhhh (For A Little While)	James Brown And The Famous Flames	104	BB
15/06/1968	Yours Until Tomorrow	Vivian Reed	113	BB
15/06/1968	Don't Break My Pretty Balloon	Vikki Carr	114	BB
15/06/1968	Save It	Solomon Burke	114	CB
15/06/1968	I've Got To Have You	Fantastic Four	115	CB
15/06/1968	Any Old Time (You're Lonely And Sad)	The Foundations	117	CB
15/06/1968	Rock Around The Clock	Bill Haley And His Comets	118	BB
15/06/1968	Rock Around The Clock	Freddie Cannon	118	CB
15/06/1968	The Lights Of Night	Mitch Ryder	122	BB
15/06/1968	Both Sides Now	Harpers Bizarre	123	BB
15/06/1968	Quando M'innamore	The Sandpipers	124	BB
15/06/1968	Here Come The Judge (Part 1)	Finky Fuzz	126	CB
15/06/1968	Sock It To Me, Baby	Bill Minin As Senator BoBBy	128	BB
15/06/1968	I Got To Have Ya	The Trolls	129	BB
15/06/1968	Twenty Years Ago (In Speedy's Kitchen)	T.C. Atlantic	130	CB
15/06/1968	Happy Man	Perry Como	134	BB
22/06/1968	Saturday's Father	The 4 Seasons Featuring The "sound" Of Frankie Valli	103	BB
22/06/1968	Boy	Lulu	105	CB
22/06/1968	Yes Sir, That's My Baby	Julius Wechter & The Baja Marimba Band	109	BB

22/06/1968	Little Green Apples	Patti Page	110	CB
22/06/1968	Venus	Johnny Mathis	111	BB
22/06/1968	I'm Dreaming	The Wildweeds	112	CB
22/06/1968	Funny Man	Ray Stevens	121	CB
22/06/1968	Rock Around The Clock	Freddie Cannon	121	BB
22/06/1968	Sinbad The Sailor	The Tidal Wave	142	CB
22/06/1968	Move In A Little Closer	The Victorians	147	CB
29/06/1968	Classical Gas	Midnight String Quartet	107	CB
29/06/1968	Boy	Lulu	108	BB
29/06/1968	Take Me Back	Frankie Laine	111	CB
29/06/1968	Lullaby From "ROSEMARY'S Baby" Part 1	Mia Farrow	114	CB
29/06/1968	Sheila Ann	BoBBy Skel	117	CB
29/06/1968	Cry Baby Cry	Van & Titus	128	CB
29/06/1968	You've Had Better Times	Peter & Gordon	128	CB
29/06/1968	Dino's Song	Quicksilver Messenger Service	133	CB
29/06/1968	Kid Games And Nursery Rhymes	Shirley & Alfred	134	CB
29/06/1968	Child Of The Moon	The Rolling Stones	138	CB
29/06/1968	La La La (He Gives Me Love)	Raymond Lefevre & His Orchestra	139	CB
06/07/1968	Snoopy For President	The Royal Guardsmen	107	CB
06/07/1968	This Wheel's On Fire	Julie Driscoll, Brian Auger & Trinity	108	CB
06/07/1968	Understanding	Ray Charles	108	CB
06/07/1968	You Got Style	Jon & Robin	110	BB
06/07/1968	Sealed With A Kiss	The Toys	112	BB
06/07/1968	Who Will Answer	The Hesitations	112	BB
06/07/1968	Who Will Answer	The Hesitations	113	CB
06/07/1968	On A Beautiful Day	The Sunshine Company	114	CB
06/07/1968	Take Me Back	Frankie Laine	115	BB
06/07/1968	What A Wonderful World	Louis Armstrong	116	BB
06/07/1968	Yes Sir	The Music Explosion	120	BB
06/07/1968	You Can Cry If You Want To	The Troggs	120	BB

06/07/1968	Walk On	Roy Orbison	121	BB
06/07/1968	The Odd Couple	Neal Hefti, His Orchestra & Chorus	132	CB
06/07/1968	I'll Be Your Baby Tonight	Burl Ives	133	BB
06/07/1968	Walking In Different Circles	The Peppermint Rainbow	136	CB
13/07/1968	Georgia On My Mind	Wes Montgomery	104	CB
13/07/1968	My Name Is Jack	Manfred Mann	104	BB
13/07/1968	Sandcastles	The 31st Of February	105	CB
13/07/1968	Hold On	The Radiants	106	CB
13/07/1968	This Wheel's On Fire	Julie Driscoll, Brian Auger & The Trinity	106	BB
13/07/1968	4 5 6 (Now I'm Alone)	Len Barry	122	CB
13/07/1968	Down In Tennessee	Kasenetz-Katz Singing Orchestral Circus	124	BB
13/07/1968	Main Street Mission	O.C. Smith	124	CB
13/07/1968	Lonely Lonely Man Am I	Jimmy Ruffin	126	CB
13/07/1968	Hushabye Mountain	Tony Bennett	130	CB
13/07/1968	Stop! (Don't Worry About It)	Lonette	141	CB
20/07/1968	Soul Meeting	The Soul Clan	101	CB
20/07/1968	Sunday Morning 6 O'clock	The Camel Drivers	106	CB
20/07/1968	Funny Man	Ray Stevens	122	BB
20/07/1968	The Mighty Quinn	Joe Harnell	122	CB
20/07/1968	People Make The World	Roosevelt Grier	129	CB
20/07/1968	Zabadak	Horst Jankowski	133	CB
20/07/1968	What A Wonderful World	Louis Armstrong	134	CB
27/07/1968	There Was A Time	The Dapps Featuring Alfred Ellis	103	BB
27/07/1968	Main Street Mission	O.C. Smith	105	BB
27/07/1968	On A Beautiful Day	The Sunshine Company	106	BB
27/07/1968	Mister Nico	Four Jacks And A Jill	108	CB
27/07/1968	You're Tuff Enough	Junior Wells	120	CB
27/07/1968	I Heard It Thru The Grapevine	King Curtis & The Kingpins	123	CB
27/07/1968	River Deep, Mountain High	Leslie Uggams	127	CB
27/07/1968	Everybody's Goin' To The Love-In	Bob Brady & The Con Chords	135	CB

03/08/1968	The Windmills Of Your Mind	Noel Harrison	103	CB
03/08/1968	Open My Eyes	Nazz	104	CB
03/08/1968	All My Love's Laughter	Ed Ames	106	CB
03/08/1968	Lullaby From "Rosemary's Baby" Part 1	Mia Farrow	111	BB
03/08/1968	Life Turned Her That Way	James Carr	112	BB
03/08/1968	Breakin' Down The Walls Of Heartache	The Bandwagon	115	BB
03/08/1968	Rain And Tears	Aphrodites Child	118	CB
10/08/1968	Sunshine Girl	Herman's Hermits	101	BB
10/08/1968	San Francisco (Wear Some Flowers In Your Hair)	Paul Mauriat And His Orchestra	103	BB
10/08/1968	That Old Time Feelin'	Dean Martin	104	BB
10/08/1968	April Again (b-side)	Dean Martin	105	BB
10/08/1968	Break My Mind	Sammy Davis Jr.	106	BB
10/08/1968	Do You Wanna Dance	Love Society	108	BB
10/08/1968	Everybody's Talkin'	Nilsson	113	BB
10/08/1968	Singles Game	Jay & The Techniques	116	BB
10/08/1968	Soul Clappin'	The Buena Vistas	116	CB
10/08/1968	Storybook Children	Billy Joe Royal	117	BB
10/08/1968	Me And You	Brenton Wood	121	BB
10/08/1968	All My Love's Laughter	Ed Ames	122	BB
10/08/1968	The Woman I Love	B.B. King	123	CB
10/08/1968	People Make The World	Roosevelt Grier	126	BB
10/08/1968	Get Ready-Uptight	Little Eva Harris	128	CB
17/08/1968	Mary Elizabeth	The Osmond Brothers	103	CB
17/08/1968	Storybook Children	Billy Joe Royal	108	CB
17/08/1968	Gentle On My Mind	Boots Randolph	113	CB
17/08/1968	Hard To Get A Thing Called Love	The Platters	117	CB
24/08/1968	Do You Wanna Dance	Love Society	106	CB
24/08/1968	Unchained Melody	The Sweet Inspirations	109	CB
24/08/1968	(As I Went Down To) Jerusalem	The Hello People	123	BB
24/08/1968	I'm Lonely For You	Bettye Swann	123	CB

24/08/1968	Hard To Get A Thing Called Love	The Platters	125	BB
24/08/1968	Me And You	Brenton Wood	125	CB
24/08/1968	You Gotta Have A Thing Of Your Own	Sonny & Cher	126	CB
24/08/1968	The Muffin Man	World Of Oz	128	CB
24/08/1968	You Want To Change Me	BoBBy HeBB	129	CB
24/08/1968	Do The Best You Can	The Hollies	133	CB
24/08/1968	This Guy's In Love With You	Tony Mottola	142	CB
31/08/1968	Love Heals	Colours	106	BB
31/08/1968	Don't Let Him Take Your Love From Me	Jimmy Ruffin	113	BB
31/08/1968	Harper Valley, P.T.A.	BoBBi Martin	114	BB
31/08/1968	The Sun Ain't Gonna Shine Anymore	Fuzzy Bunnies	115	BB
31/08/1968	You've Had Better Times	Peter And Gordon	118	BB
31/08/1968	Fill My Soul	The Pop Explosion	120	CB
31/08/1968	D.W. Washburn/L. David Sloane (A Good Man Is Hard To Find)	The Hutch Davie Calliope Band	137	CB
07/09/1968	L.A. Break Down (And Take Me In)	Larry Marks	102	CB
07/09/1968	Special Care	The Buffalo Springfield	107	BB
07/09/1968	Apple Cider	People	111	BB
07/09/1968	Don't Bogart Me	Fraternity Of Man	113	CB
07/09/1968	Soul Clappin	The Buena Vistas	126	BB
07/09/1968	That's In The Past	Brenda & The Tabulations	128	CB
14/09/1968	The Choice	The O'jays	103	CB
14/09/1968	Birmingham	The Movers	104	CB
14/09/1968	5 Card Stud	Dean Martin	107	BB
14/09/1968	Laugh At The World	The Tams	108	CB
14/09/1968	Hello, Hello	Tiny Tim	109	CB
14/09/1968	I Couldn't Spell !!*@!	Sam The Sham	111	CB
14/09/1968	(Till I) Run With You	The Lovin' Spoonful Featuring Joe Butler	113	CB
14/09/1968	You've Lost That Lovin' Feeling/(You're My) Soul And	Vivian Reed	115	BB
14/09/1968	Birmingham	The Movers	116	BB
14/09/1968	Sunshine Among Us	Eternity's Children	117	BB

14/09/1968	You've Lost That Lovin' Feeling/(You're My) Soul And	Vivian Reed	117	CB
14/09/1968	I'm Gonna Make You Love Me	Aesops Fables	123	BB
14/09/1968	Make Your Own Kind Of Music	The Will-O-Bees	126	CB
14/09/1968	Do You Know The Way To San Jose	Julius Wechter & The Baja Marimba Band	129	CB
14/09/1968	He's My Man	Patti La Belle & The Bluebelles	143	CB
21/09/1968	(I Can Feel Your Love) Slipping Away	Barbara Mason	101	CB
21/09/1968	Gentle On My Mind	Glen Campbell	103	CB
21/09/1968	Battle Of New Orleans	Harpers Bizarre	111	CB
21/09/1968	Open My Eyes	Nazz	112	BB
21/09/1968	What's Easy For Two Is Hard For One	The Marvelettes	114	BB
21/09/1968	Harper Valley P.T.A.	King Curtis & The Kingpins	118	CB
21/09/1968	Mom (Can I Talk To You?)	Jan Rhodes	118	CB
21/09/1968	One Of The Nicer Things	Jimmy WeBB	118	CB
21/09/1968	Mission Impossible Theme/Norwegian Wood	Alan Copeland	120	BB
21/09/1968	Hello, Hello	Tiny Tim	122	BB
21/09/1968	Land Of Love	Moon People	123	CB
21/09/1968	Like A Rolling Stone	Flatt & Scruggs	125	BB
21/09/1968	(Till I) Run With You	The Lovin' Spoonful Featuring Joe Butler	128	BB
21/09/1968	Per-So-Nal-Ly	BoBBy Paris	129	BB
21/09/1968	Lovin' Is Livin'	The Five Americans	131	CB
21/09/1968	Don't Bogart Me	Fraternity Of Man	133	BB
21/09/1968	Do Me So La So So	Hugh Masekela	141	CB
28/09/1968	Funky Bull Pt. I	Dyke And The Blazers	102	BB
28/09/1968	Hole In My Pocket	Barry Goldberg Reunion	103	BB
28/09/1968	Isn't It Lonely Together	Robert Knight	112	CB
28/09/1968	You Got It	Etta James	113	BB
28/09/1968	Light My Fire	The Doors	114	CB
28/09/1968	Eeny Meeny	The Show Stoppers	116	CB
28/09/1968	Sour Milk Sea	Jackie Lomax	117	BB
28/09/1968	Trouble Maker	The Tams	118	BB

28/09/1968	I've Been Loving You Too Long	Billy Vera	121	BB
28/09/1968	I Close My Eyes And Count To Ten	Dusty Springfield	122	BB
28/09/1968	So Nice	Mad Lads	122	CB
28/09/1968	Can't Get You Out Of My Mind	Margaret Whiting	124	BB
28/09/1968	I Get The Blues When It Rains	Ray Anthony	124	BB
28/09/1968	Please Forgive Me	Frankie Laine	124	CB
28/09/1968	I Can See A Light	The Good Earth	133	CB
28/09/1968	Can't Get You Out Of My Mind	Margaret Whiting	139	CB
28/09/1968	The Boy With The Green Eyes	The Angels	140	CB
05/10/1968	How Lucky (Can One Man Be)	The Uniques	105	CB
05/10/1968	You're So Young	Shane Martin	107	CB
05/10/1968	Don't Leave Me	Robert John	108	BB
05/10/1968	Getting To Know You	Sajid Khan	114	CB
05/10/1968	Greenburg, Glickstein, Charles, David Smith & Jones	The Cryan' Shames	115	BB
05/10/1968	A Little Bit For Sandy	Paul Petersen	117	CB
05/10/1968	I Couldn't Spell !!'@!	Sam The Sham	120	BB
05/10/1968	Lord Of The Manor	The Everly Brothers	121	CB
05/10/1968	Cadillac Jack	Andre Williams	124	CB
05/10/1968	Wake Up To Me Gentle	Al Martino	125	CB
05/10/1968	L.A. Break Down (And Take Me In)	Larry Marks	129	BB
05/10/1968	You Got What I Need	Z.Z. Hill	129	BB
05/10/1968	Standing On The Outside	Brenda Jo Harris	131	BB
05/10/1968	Look Into My Teardrops	Crispian St. Peters	133	BB
05/10/1968	What Kind Of Lady	Dee Dee Sharp	149	CB
12/10/1968	46 Drums-1 Guitar	Little Carl Carlton 14 Year Old Sensation	105	BB
12/10/1968	As We Go Along	The Monkees	106	BB
12/10/1968	Getting To Know You	Sajid Khan	108	BB
12/10/1968	Mohair Sam	Slim Harpo	113	CB
12/10/1968	You Talk Sunshine, I Breathe Fire	The Amboy Dukes	114	BB
12/10/1968	How Lucky (Can One Man Be)	The Uniques	115	BB

12/10/1968	Are My Thoughts With You	The First Edition	119	BB
12/10/1968	Do Your Own Thing	Brook Benton	128	CB
12/10/1968	The Most Beautiful Thing In My Life	Herman's Hermits	131	BB
12/10/1968	Paper Castle	Rotary Connection	132	BB
12/10/1968	Don't Leave Me	Robert John	134	CB
12/10/1968	I'm So Happy Now	Company Front	139	CB
12/10/1968	You Got What I Need	Z.Z. Hill	145	CB
19/10/1968	Where Do I Go	Carla Thomas	103	CB
19/10/1968	Heartache	Roy Orbison	104	BB
19/10/1968	Both Sides Now	The Johnstons	106	CB
19/10/1968	Way Over There	Edwin Starr	107	CB
19/10/1968	You're All Around Me	Percy Sledge	109	BB
19/10/1968	Hitchcock Railway	José Feliciano	110	CB
19/10/1968	Crazy Rhythm	The Happenings	111	CB
19/10/1968	Willie Jean	The Sunshine Company	111	BB
19/10/1968	Love City (Postcards To Duluth)	Peter, Paul & Mary	113	BB
19/10/1968	Wake Up To Me Gentle	Al Martino	120	BB
19/10/1968	You Could Never Love Him (Like I Love Him)	Barbara Mcnair	120	CB
19/10/1968	My Groovy Baby	Tom Dooley & His Lovelights	130	CB
19/10/1968	Can I Get A Witness	Barbara Randolph	135	CB
26/10/1968	Do What You Gotta Do	Nina Simone	101	CB
26/10/1968	Today	Jimmie Rodgers	104	BB
26/10/1968	(Funky) Four Corners	Jerry O	109	CB
26/10/1968	Feelin' Alright?	Traffic	109	CB
26/10/1968	Crazy Rhythm	The Happenings	114	BB
26/10/1968	I Can Give You Love	The Diplomats	117	BB
26/10/1968	A Man, A Horse, And A Gun	Henry Mancini, His Orchestra & Chorus	120	CB
26/10/1968	It Was Fun While It Lasted	Jimmy George	121	CB
26/10/1968	Run To Me	The Montanas	121	BB
26/10/1968	Feelin' Alright?	Traffic	123	BB

26/10/1968	The Eagle Laughs At You (b-side)	Jackie Lomax	125	BB
26/10/1968	My Little Lady	The Tremeloes	127	BB
26/10/1968	Paralyzed	The Legendary Stardust Cowboy	127	CB
26/10/1968	Listen To The Music	The Second Time	128	CB
26/10/1968	Paul's Midnight Ride	The Delights Orchestra	128	BB
26/10/1968	Our Town	Susann Farrar	146	CB
02/11/1968	Main Street	Gary Lewis And The Playboys	101	BB
02/11/1968	The Great Escape	Ray Stevens	114	BB
02/11/1968	The Continuing Story Of Harper Valley P.T.A.	Dee Mullins	117	CB
02/11/1968	Never My Love	The SandpeBBles	121	CB
02/11/1968	Crown Of Creation	Jefferson Airplane	122	CB
02/11/1968	Only For Lovers	Roger Williams	123	CB
02/11/1968	Where Did You Come From	The Buckinghams	125	CB
02/11/1968	Dang Me	Sam Hutchins	127	CB
02/11/1968	Don't Make The Good Girls Go Bad	Della Humphrey	135	CB
02/11/1968	Make A Noise Like Love	Gene & DeBBe	137	CB
02/11/1968	Without Him	Lulu	141	CB
09/11/1968	Hard To Handle	Patti Drew	101	CB
09/11/1968	He's Bad Bad Bad	Betty Wright	103	BB
09/11/1968	The Path Of Love	John Cowsill	111	CB
09/11/1968	Release Me	Johnny Adams	112	CB
09/11/1968	Stand By Your Man	Patti Page	121	BB
09/11/1968	We're All Going To The Same Place	Tommy Boyce & BoBBy Hart	124	CB
09/11/1968	Both Sides Now	The Johnstons	128	BB
09/11/1968	Listen To Me	The Hollies	129	BB
09/11/1968	Hey Mister	Four Jacks And A Jill	130	BB
09/11/1968	The Path Of Love	John Cowsill	132	BB
09/11/1968	We Belong Together	The Webs	133	CB
09/11/1968	Those Were The Days	The Larry Page Orchestra	139	CB
09/11/1968	Pain	Nova's Nine	145	CB

16/11/1968	Sock It To 'Em Judge	Pigmeat Markham	103	BB
16/11/1968	The Split	Lou Rawls	104	CB
16/11/1968	Aladdin	Rotary Connection	113	BB
16/11/1968	Goodnight My Love	The Duprees	113	BB
16/11/1968	We Got A Good Thing Goin'	Jimmy Holiday	113	CB
16/11/1968	Take My Overwhelming Love (And Cram It Up Your Heart)	The Hombres	115	CB
16/11/1968	The Hobo	The Good Rats	116	CB
16/11/1968	Where Did You Come From	The Buckinghams	117	BB
16/11/1968	Way Over There	Edwin Starr	119	BB
16/11/1968	We're All Going To The Same Place	Tommy Boyce & BoBBy Hart	123	BB
16/11/1968	I'm A Fool	The Peanut Butter Conspiracy	125	BB
16/11/1968	Make A Noise Like Love	Gene & DeBBe	127	BB
16/11/1968	Turn Out The Fire	The Soul Survivors	132	CB
23/11/1968	What Time Did You Say It Is In Salt Lake City?	Fever Tree	105	CB
23/11/1968	Coo Coo	Big Brother & The Holding Company	107	CB
23/11/1968	Keep The Faith	The American Breed	107	CB
23/11/1968	I'm Gonna Use What I Got (To Get What I Need)	Jimmy Holiday	110	CB
23/11/1968	Stand By Me	Quicksilver Messenger Service	110	BB
23/11/1968	The Continuing Story Of Harper Valley P.T.A.	Dee Mullins	111	BB
23/11/1968	Honey Do	The Strangeloves	120	BB
23/11/1968	I'm A Fool	The Peanut Butter Conspiracy	121	CB
23/11/1968	The Split	Lou Rawls	123	BB
23/11/1968	Yummy, Yummy, Yummy	Julie London	125	BB
30/11/1968	Please Send Me Someone To Love	B.B. King	102	BB
30/11/1968	Please Send Me Someone To Love	B.B. King	102	CB
30/11/1968	Nightmare	The Crazy World Of Arthur Brown	107	BB
30/11/1968	What The World Needs Now Is Love	Cilla Black	107	CB
30/11/1968	Hayride	The Saturday Morning Cartoon Show	110	CB
30/11/1968	Edge Of Reality	Elvis Presley	112	BB
30/11/1968	Get On Your Knees	Los Canarios	122	CB

30/11/1968	King Croesus	World Of Oz	126	BB
30/11/1968	What The World Needs Now Is Love	The Sweet Inspirations	128	BB
30/11/1968	Little Sister	Dick Dodd	136	CB
30/11/1968	Long Black Veil	Jerry Jaye	149	CB
07/12/1968	Saturday Night At The World	Mason Williams	101	CB
07/12/1968	L.A. Break Down (And Take Me In)	Jack Jones	106	BB
07/12/1968	Ain't Got No; I Got Life	Nina Simone	107	CB
07/12/1968	Fifty Two Per Cent	Max Frost & The Troopers	113	CB
07/12/1968	The Dance At St. Francis	The Barracuda	113	BB
07/12/1968	The Candy Kid (From The Mission On The Bowery)	The Cowsills	118	BB
07/12/1968	Only For Lovers	Roger Williams	119	BB
07/12/1968	Why Are We Sleeping?	The Soft Machine	124	CB
07/12/1968	Til I Can't Take It Anymore	Ben E. King	135	CB
07/12/1968	I'm A Tiger	Lulu	141	CB
14/12/1968	Take Five	Willie Mitchell	101	CB
14/12/1968	By The Time I Get To Phoenix/I Say A Little Prayer (Medley)	Dee Irwin & Mamie Galore	114	BB
14/12/1968	In A Long White Room	Nancy Wilson	117	BB
14/12/1968	Sock It To Me Part I	The Deacons	121	BB
14/12/1968	Fifty Two Per Cent	Max Frost And The Troopers	123	BB
14/12/1968	Born To Be With You	Sonny James	127	CB
14/12/1968	The Candy Kid (From The Mission On The Bowery)	The Cowsills	128	CB
14/12/1968	Fly With Me!	Avant Garde	130	BB
14/12/1968	Let Me Get Through To You, Baby	Ginny Tiu & The Few	136	CB
21/12/1968	Sweets For My Sweet	Central Park West	104	CB
21/12/1968	The Meditation	Tnt Band	106	CB
21/12/1968	Fox On The Run	Manfred Mann	108	CB
21/12/1968	So True	The Sweethearts Of Soul: Peaches & Herb	108	CB
21/12/1968	I Put A Spell On You (b-side)	The Crazy World Of Arthur Brown	111	BB
21/12/1968	I Who Have Nothing	Linda Jones	116	BB
21/12/1968	The Worm	Jimmy Mcgriff	119	CB

21/12/1968	Let's Go All The Way	Troy Shondell	121	CB
21/12/1968	Heart - Teaser	Flavor	123	CB
21/12/1968	Til I Can't Take It Anymore	Ben E. King	134	BB
28/12/1968	My Baby Specializes	William Bell & Judy Clay	104	BB
28/12/1968	My Man (68 Version)	Barbra Streisand	107	CB
28/12/1968	My Song	Aretha Franklin	108	CB
28/12/1968	Stoney End	Peggy Lipton	121	BB
28/12/1968	Soul Brother, Soul Sister	The Capitols	126	CB
28/12/1968	Untie Me	James & BoBBy Purify	128	CB
28/12/1968	Love Won't Wear Off (As The Years Wear On)	J.R. Bailey	133	CB
04/01/1969	I'm In Love With You	Kasenetz-Katz Super Circus	105	BB
04/01/1969	Ring Your Bell	Mitch Ryder And The Spirit Feel	125	BB
04/01/1969	So True	The Sweethearts Of Soul Peaches & Herb	126	BB
04/01/1969	Play It Cool	Freddy King	127	BB
04/01/1969	Let's Go All The Way	Troy Shondell	129	BB
04/01/1969	The Hive	Richard Harris	130	CB
04/01/1969	Where Have All The Flowers Gone?	Wes Montgomery	132	CB
04/01/1969	The Tra La La Song (One Banana, Two Banana)	The Banana Splits	133	CB
04/01/1969	Julie	Billy Vera	135	CB
04/01/1969	Some People Sleep	The Tokens	146	CB
11/01/1969	When I Stop Dreaming	Ray Charles	112	BB
11/01/1969	Step Inside Love	Madeline Bell	121	CB
18/01/1969	A Broken Man	The Malibu's	102	CB
18/01/1969	Light My Fire	Rhetta Hughes	102	BB
18/01/1969	She Touched Me	Herb Alpert & The Tijuana Brass	108	CB
18/01/1969	Sleep In The Grass	Ann-Margret Lee Hazlewood	109	CB
18/01/1969	Direct Me	Otis Redding	111	CB
18/01/1969	Don't Be Afraid (Do As I Say)	Frankie Karl & The Dreams	119	CB
18/01/1969	Good Vibrations	Hugo Montenegro, His Orchestra & Chorus	125	CB
25/01/1969	My Special Prayer	Percy Sledge	102	CB

25/01/1969	Red Red Wine	Jimmy James & The Vagabonds	105	CB
25/01/1969	Sleep In The Grass	Ann-Margret Lee Hazlewood	113	BB
25/01/1969	Dream	Sajid Khan	114	CB
25/01/1969	Carlie	BoBBy Russell	115	BB
25/01/1969	Nobody	Three Dog Night	116	BB
25/01/1969	I'm Just An Average Guy	The Masqueraders	117	CB
25/01/1969	The Meditation	Tnt Band	117	BB
25/01/1969	Where Have All The Flowers Gone?	Wes Montgomery	119	BB
25/01/1969	Carlie	BoBBy Russell	120	CB
25/01/1969	A Broken Man	The Malibu's	121	BB
25/01/1969	She's Almost You	Billy Harner	121	BB
25/01/1969	Classical Gas/Scarborough Fair	The Alan Copeland Singers	123	BB
25/01/1969	My Heart Cries For You	Jimmy Roselli	123	CB
25/01/1969	Flyin' High	Julius Wechter & The Baja Marimba Band	125	BB
25/01/1969	Willie Jean	The Sunshine Company	126	CB
25/01/1969	Come Live With Me	Shadow Mann	129	CB
25/01/1969	Love In Them There Hills	Maxine Brown	130	CB
25/01/1969	Stoney End	Peggy Lipton	136	CB
25/01/1969	Don't Make Promises (You Can't Keep)	Z.Z. Hill	141	CB
01/02/1969	Dream	The Mills Brothers	111	CB
01/02/1969	Apple Cider	Five By Five	112	CB
01/02/1969	Don't Waste My Time	B.B. King	113	BB
01/02/1969	Red Balloon	Cook E. Jarr	113	CB
01/02/1969	She's Not There	The Road	114	BB
01/02/1969	Memories Are Made Of This	Gene & DeBBe	116	CB
01/02/1969	Dream	Sajid Khan	119	BB
01/02/1969	Here Comes The Rain	Leapy Lee	128	CB
01/02/1969	Up Tight Good Woman	Solomon Burke	140	CB
08/02/1969	I've Got To Have Your Love	Eddie Floyd	102	BB
08/02/1969	Give Her A Transplant	The Intruders	104	BB

08/02/1969	November Snow	Rejoice!	105	CB
08/02/1969	Who's Gonna Mow Your Grass	Buck Owens And The Buckaroos	106	BB
08/02/1969	She's Almost You	Billy Harner	109	CB
08/02/1969	Chitty Chitty Bang Bang	The New Christy Minstrels	114	BB
08/02/1969	If	Al Hirt	116	BB
08/02/1969	Woman, You Made Me	BoBBy Dixon	128	CB
08/02/1969	Chitty Chitty Bang Bang	The New Christy Minstrels	129	CB
08/02/1969	Games People Play	Boots Randolph	131	CB
15/02/1969	Baby Make Me Feel So Good	Five Stairsteps & Cubie	101	BB
15/02/1969	Good Vibrations	Hugo Montenegro, His Orchestra And Chorus	112	BB
15/02/1969	Lily The Pink	The Irish Rovers	113	BB
15/02/1969	Memories Are Made Of This	Gene & DeBBe	114	BB
15/02/1969	Kaw-Liga [Live]	Charley Pride	120	BB
15/02/1969	Too Late To Worry, Too Blue To Cry	Esther Phillips	121	BB
15/02/1969	Too Late To Worry, Too Blue To Cry	Esther Phillips	121	CB
15/02/1969	I Really Love You	The Ambassadors	123	BB
15/02/1969	I'd Do It All Again	Eloise Laws	127	CB
15/02/1969	Red Red Wine	Jimmy James & The Vagabonds	127	BB
15/02/1969	I Wouldn't Change The Man He Is	Blinky	128	BB
15/02/1969	I Saw The Light	The Nashville Brass Featuring Danny Davis	129	BB
15/02/1969	Race With The Devil	The Gun	129	CB
15/02/1969	Lovey Dovey	Johnny Nash	130	BB
15/02/1969	Lady Samantha	Elton John	139	CB
22/02/1969	As The Years Go Passing By	Albert King	102	CB
22/02/1969	Gentle On My Mind	Dean Martin	103	BB
22/02/1969	Mescalito	Shango	103	CB
22/02/1969	My Deceiving Heart	The Impressions	104	BB
22/02/1969	This Is A Love Song	Bill Medley	110	CB
22/02/1969	This Is A Love Song	Bill Medley	112	BB
22/02/1969	Up Tight Good Woman	Solomon Burke	116	BB

22/02/1969	A Man Without A Dream	The Monkees	127	CB
22/02/1969	Changing, Changing	Ed Ames	130	BB
22/02/1969	Coal Man	Mack Rice	135	BB
22/02/1969	Gonna Have A Good Time (Good Times)	The Easybeats	144	CB
22/02/1969	I Don't Know How (To Say I Love You) Don't Walk Away	The Superlatives	147	CB
01/03/1969	First Train To California	Cryan' Shames	103	CB
01/03/1969	Feelings	The Cherry People	106	CB
01/03/1969	Lilly's Back	Verrill Keene	109	CB
01/03/1969	What's Wrong With My World	Ronnie Dove	111	CB
01/03/1969	Changing, Changing	Ed Ames	112	CB
01/03/1969	Medicated Goo	Traffic	118	CB
01/03/1969	Sabre Dance	Love Sculpture	118	CB
01/03/1969	Something's Happening	Herman's Hermits	123	CB
01/03/1969	I Have Dreamed	The Lettermen	129	BB
01/03/1969	Is There Anything Better Than Making Love?	The Fantastic Johnny C	129	CB
01/03/1969	Something's Happening	Herman's Hermits	130	BB
01/03/1969	What's Wrong With My World	Ronnie Dove	131	BB
01/03/1969	Virginia Girl	Michael Rabon And The Five Americans	133	BB
01/03/1969	You Are My Destiny	Vic Dana	133	CB
01/03/1969	Snowball	American Machine	141	CB
08/03/1969	I Didn't Know What Time It Was	Ray Charles	105	BB
08/03/1969	Look Homeward Angel	The Velvet Crest	110	CB
08/03/1969	Las Cosas	Rene & Rene	113	CB
08/03/1969	Love Theme From "LA Strada"	Roger Williams	122	CB
08/03/1969	Hey Jude	Paul Mauriat & His Orchestra	124	CB
08/03/1969	November Snow	Rejoice!	126	BB
08/03/1969	As The Years Go Passing By	Albert King	132	BB
08/03/1969	Apple Cider	Five By Five	133	BB
08/03/1969	You'd Better Go	Nancy Wilson	137	CB
15/03/1969	L.U.V. (Let Us Vote)	Tommy Boyce & BoBBy Hart	111	BB

15/03/1969	Virginia Girl	Michael Rabon & The Five Americans	111	CB
15/03/1969	You'd Better Go	Nancy Wilson	111	BB
15/03/1969	Are You Ready	The Chambers Brothers	113	BB
15/03/1969	Are You Ready	The Chambers Brothers	119	CB
15/03/1969	Hey Jude	Paul Mauriat And His Orchestra	119	BB
15/03/1969	I Left My Heart In San Francisco	BoBBy Womack	119	BB
15/03/1969	The Conspiracy Of Homer Jones	Dallas Frazier	120	BB
15/03/1969	Las Costas	Rene & Rene	128	BB
15/03/1969	Don't You Know A True Love	The O'jays	130	CB
15/03/1969	A Change Is Gonna Come	Brenton Wood	131	BB
15/03/1969	The Jimtown Road	The Mills Brothers	131	CB
15/03/1969	Did You See Her Eyes	The Illusion	133	CB
15/03/1969	Feelings	The Cherry People	134	BB
22/03/1969	Something's On Her Mind	The 4 Seasons Featuring Frankie Valli	101	CB
22/03/1969	Tracks Of My Tears	Aretha Franklin	102	CB
22/03/1969	Albatross	Fleetwood Mac	104	BB
22/03/1969	I Left My Heart In San Francisco	BoBBy Womack	104	CB
22/03/1969	Lily The Pink	The Irish Rovers	104	CB
22/03/1969	I Still Love You	Jackie Wilson	105	BB
22/03/1969	Tell Me Why	Frijid Pink	109	CB
22/03/1969	Tricia Tell Your Daddy	Andy Kim	110	BB
22/03/1969	Look What We Have Joined Together	The Sugar Blues	113	CB
22/03/1969	Games People Play	King Curtis & The Kingpins	116	BB
22/03/1969	Come A Little Bit Closer	Trini Lopez	121	BB
22/03/1969	Emmaretta	Deep Purple	128	BB
22/03/1969	Is There Anything Better Than Making Love?	The Fantastic Johnny C	130	BB
22/03/1969	Without Him	Cilla Black	134	CB
22/03/1969	Tunesmith	The Bards	135	CB
22/03/1969	I Stand Accused	Al Wilson	142	CB
22/03/1969	Games People Play	King Curtis & The Kingpins	144	CB

28/03/1969	Carolina In My Mind	James Taylor	128	CB
29/03/1969	Home To You	Earth Opera	106	CB
29/03/1969	Then She's A Lover	BoBBy Russell	115	CB
29/03/1969	Sing A Simple Song	Sly & Family Stone	123	CB
29/03/1969	Please Don't Go	Eddy Arnold	129	BB
29/03/1969	Yesterday I Heard The Rain (Esta Tarde Vi Llover)	Nino Tempo & April Stevens	136	CB
29/03/1969	A Long Ways From Home	Hugh Masekela	140	CB
29/03/1969	Do What You Wanna	Ramsey Lewis	148	CB
05/04/1969	California Girl (And The Tennessee Square)	Tompall & Glaser Brothers	101	CB
05/04/1969	You Are The Circus	C & The Shells	101	CB
05/04/1969	Castschok (Life Is A Dance)	Alexadrow Karazov	104	CB
05/04/1969	New Babe (Since I Found You)	Invictus	105	CB
05/04/1969	Turn Around And Love You	Rita Coolidge	107	CB
05/04/1969	You Came, You Saw, You Conquered!	The Ronettes (Featuring The Voice Of Veronica)	108	BB
05/04/1969	Soul Pride (Part 1)	James Brown Plays & Directs	117	BB
05/04/1969	Always Keep Me In Your Heart	The Four Aces	120	CB
05/04/1969	I'm Alive	Johnny Thunder	122	BB
05/04/1969	Rhythm Of Life	Sammy Davis Jr. And Ensemble	124	BB
05/04/1969	After The Smoke Is Gone	Steve Alaimo & Betty Wright	126	CB
05/04/1969	Sha-La Love	The Uniques	140	CB
12/04/1969	Baby Driver	Simon & Garfunkel	101	BB
12/04/1969	Just A Little Bit	Little Milton	102	CB
12/04/1969	I Stand Accused	Al Wilson	106	BB
12/04/1969	A Long Ways From Home	Hugh Masekela	107	BB
12/04/1969	Are You Lonely For Me Baby	Chuck Jackson	107	BB
12/04/1969	I Was A Boy (When You Needed A Man)	Billy Shields	109	BB
12/04/1969	I Feel Like I'm Falling In Love Again	The Fantastic Four	111	BB
12/04/1969	Mother Where's Your Daughter	The Royal Guardsmen	112	BB
12/04/1969	Hurting Each Other	Ruby And The Romantics	113	BB
12/04/1969	Run On	Arthur Conley	115	BB

12/04/1969	We Can't Go On This Way	The Unchained Mynds	115	BB
12/04/1969	Carolina In My Mind	James Taylor	118	BB
12/04/1969	Denver	Ronnie Milsap	118	CB
12/04/1969	Walk Away	Ann Peebles	120	CB
12/04/1969	Hurting Each Other	Ruby & The Romantics	122	CB
12/04/1969	Foot Pattin', Part Ii (b-side)	King Curtis & The Kingpins	123	BB
12/04/1969	Every Little Bit Hurts	Peggy Scott	126	BB
12/04/1969	It's A Miracle	Willie Hightower	130	BB
12/04/1969	Sing A Simple Song	The Noble Knights	132	BB
19/04/1969	Are You Lonely For Me	Chuck Jackson	108	CB
19/04/1969	Crying In The Rain	The Sweet Inspirations	112	BB
19/04/1969	Crying In The Rain	The Sweet Inspirations	113	CB
19/04/1969	Devil Or Angel	Tony Scotti	116	CB
19/04/1969	Runaway Child, Running Wild	Earl Van Dyke	124	CB
19/04/1969	Just A Little Closer	Archie Bell & The Drells	128	BB
19/04/1969	Little Green Apples	Gene Chandler & Barbara Acklin	130	CB
19/04/1969	Please Don't Go	Eddy Arnold	130	CB
19/04/1969	Rhythm Of Life	Sammy Davis Jr. & Ensemble	131	CB
26/04/1969	How Great Thou Art	Elvis Presley With The Jordanaires And The Imperials Quartet	101	BB
26/04/1969	When Somethiing Is Wrong With My Baby	Otis & Carla	101	CB
26/04/1969	Scotch And Soda (Live)	The Kingston Trio	104	CB
26/04/1969	I Don't Want To Hear It Anymore	Dusty Springfield	105	BB
26/04/1969	Love Is Strange	Buddy Holly	105	BB
26/04/1969	Change Your Mind	Jay & The Techniques	106	CB
26/04/1969	Change Your Mind	Jay & The Techniques	107	BB
26/04/1969	When Something Is Wrong With My Baby	Otis And Carla	109	BB
26/04/1969	Young People	Willie Mitchell	112	CB
26/04/1969	Baby Driver	Simon & Garfunkel	114	CB
26/04/1969	Under Branches	The Association	117	BB
26/04/1969	Go Away Little Girl/Young Girl	The Tokens	118	BB

26/04/1969	Me & Mr. Hohner	BoBBy Darin	119	CB
26/04/1969	Real True Lovin'	Steve & Eydie	119	BB
26/04/1969	Oh, Deed I Do	Elyse Weinberg	120	CB
26/04/1969	O-Wow	Panic Buttons	123	CB
26/04/1969	Just A Dream	Ruby Winters	129	CB
26/04/1969	It's Getting Better	Freddie Gelfand	130	CB
26/04/1969	Two Different Worlds	The Duprees	133	CB
03/05/1969	Ivory	Bob Seger System	101	CB
03/05/1969	Hunky Funky	The American Breed	107	BB
03/05/1969	The Bible Salesman	Billy Vera	110	CB
03/05/1969	Runaway Child, Running Wild	Earl Van Dyke	114	BB
03/05/1969	Devil Or Angel	Tony Scotti	117	BB
03/05/1969	Rose Garden	Dobie Gray	119	BB
03/05/1969	Castschok (Life Is A Dance)	Alexadrow Karazov	120	BB
03/05/1969	Darkness, Darkness	The Youngbloods	121	CB
03/05/1969	The Windmills Of Your Mind	Jimmie Rodgers	123	BB
03/05/1969	My Prayer	BoBBy Hatfield	124	CB
03/05/1969	Scotch And Soda [Live]	The Kingston Trio	124	BB
03/05/1969	Big Black Bird (Spirit Of Our Love)	Jack Blanchard & Misty Morgan	127	CB
03/05/1969	Rollin' And Tumblin'	Johnny Winter	129	BB
03/05/1969	Mama Soul	The Soul Survivors	131	CB
03/05/1969	Red Clay County Line	Peggy Lipton	134	CB
03/05/1969	I Struck It Rich	Billy Harner	143	CB
10/05/1969	Plastic Fantastic Lover (Live)	Jefferson Airplane	104	CB
10/05/1969	Go Away Little Girl/Young Girl	The Tokens	107	CB
10/05/1969	Leanin' On You	Joe South	108	CB
10/05/1969	Goodnight Baby	The King Tones	114	CB
10/05/1969	Mama Soul	The Soul Survivors	115	BB
10/05/1969	Whippoorwill	Don Cherry	119	CB
10/05/1969	Denver	Ronnie Milsap	123	BB

10/05/1969	Me & Mr. Hohner	BoBBy Darin	123	BB
10/05/1969	Darkness, Darkness	The Youngbloods	124	BB
10/05/1969	Hunky Funky	The American Breed	125	CB
10/05/1969	Easy To Be Hard	Jennifer	128	BB
10/05/1969	Here We Go Again	Nancy Sinatra	128	CB
10/05/1969	Ah, Ha, Ha, Do Your Thing	The Hit Parade	131	BB
10/05/1969	We Try Harder	Kim Weston Johnny Nash	135	BB
17/05/1969	It Didn't Even Bring Me Down	Sir Douglas Quintet	101	CB
17/05/1969	Leanin' On You	Joe South	104	BB
17/05/1969	Bring Me Sunshine	Brenda Lee	107	CB
17/05/1969	It Didn't Even Bring Me Down	Sir Douglas Quintet	108	BB
17/05/1969	Imagine The Swan	The Zombies	109	BB
17/05/1969	Some Kind-A Wonderful	Thee Prophets	111	BB
17/05/1969	The Bible Salesman	Billy Vera	112	BB
17/05/1969	To Think You've Chosen Me	Don Cherry	112	CB
17/05/1969	Green Door	The Jerms	115	CB
17/05/1969	Mama Lion	Shango	118	CB
17/05/1969	Once Again She's All Alone	The First Edition	126	BB
17/05/1969	Ragamuffin Man	Manfred Mann	126	CB
17/05/1969	Everyday Livin' Days	Merrilee Rush	127	CB
24/05/1969	Instant Groove	King Curtis & The Kingpins	101	CB
24/05/1969	Some Velvet Morning	Vanilla Fudge	103	BB
24/05/1969	Paradise (Is Half As Nice)	Dave Clark Five	104	CB
24/05/1969	Cajun Baby	Hank Williams Jr.	107	BB
24/05/1969	For His Namesake	The Amboy Dukes	108	CB
24/05/1969	Just A Melody	Young-Holt Unlimited	110	CB
24/05/1969	Follow The Leader	Major Lance	111	CB
24/05/1969	Johnny B. Goode [Live]	Buck Owens And The Buckaroos	114	BB
24/05/1969	Some Kind-A Wonderful	Thee Prophets	114	CB
24/05/1969	Bit By Bit	The Merging Traffic	115	CB

24/05/1969	Everyday Livin' Days	Merrilee Rush	130	BB
31/05/1969	Oo Wee Baby I Love You	Roscoe Robinson	105	CB
31/05/1969	Stomp	Nrbq	106	CB
31/05/1969	That's Not Love	Dee Dee Warwick	106	BB
31/05/1969	Manhattan Spiritual	Sandy Nelson	108	CB
31/05/1969	It's In Your Power	Joe Odom	109	BB
31/05/1969	Do Unto Others	Sandy Salisbury	110	CB
31/05/1969	Happy Together	Hugo Montenegro, His Orchestra And Chorus	112	BB
31/05/1969	I Can't Let Go	Mojo	112	CB
31/05/1969	Touch 'Em With Love	BoBBie Gentry	113	BB
31/05/1969	I Have But One Life To Live	Sammy Davis Jr.	119	BB
31/05/1969	Ob-La-Di, Ob-La-Da	Paul Desmond	120	CB
31/05/1969	I'll Never Fall In Love Again	Johnny Mathis	122	CB
31/05/1969	I'll Share My World With You	George Jones	124	BB
31/05/1969	Touch 'EM With Love	BoBBie Gentry	125	CB
31/05/1969	The Angels Listened In	Percy Sledge	126	BB
31/05/1969	Instant Groove	King Curtis & The Kingpins	127	BB
31/05/1969	If I Had A Reason	The BuBBle Puppy	128	BB
31/05/1969	Green Door	The Jerms	129	BB
31/05/1969	Don't Let The Sun Catch You Cryin'	Trini Lopez	133	BB
31/05/1969	Plastic Fantastic Lover [Live]	Jefferson Airplane	133	BB
31/05/1969	It's Not Fair	Dee Dee Warwick	148	CB
07/06/1969	Spring	John Tipton	118	BB
07/06/1969	Manhattan Spiritual	Sandy Nelson	119	BB
07/06/1969	Tears On My Pillow	Johnny Tillotson With The Jimmy Bowen Orchestra & Chorus	119	BB
07/06/1969	Crossroads Of The Stepping Stones	The Elephants Memory	120	BB
07/06/1969	Young People	Willie Mitchell	120	BB
07/06/1969	Break My Mind	Pawnee Drive	130	CB
07/06/1969	Lay Lady Lay	The Byrds	132	BB
14/06/1969	Lollipop (I Like You)	The Intruders	101	BB

14/06/1969	I'll Never Fall In Love Again	Burt Bacharach	105	CB
14/06/1969	Hippy Dippy Funky Monkey Double BuBBle Sitar Man	The HuBBels	112	CB
14/06/1969	Take Your Love (And Shove It)	Kane's Cousins	116	BB
14/06/1969	But For Love	Eddy Arnold	117	CB
14/06/1969	That's The Price You Have To Pay	Brenda & The Tabulations	125	CB
14/06/1969	Capt. Groovy And His BuBBlegum Army	Capt. Groovy And His BuBBlegum Army	128	BB
14/06/1969	I Wanna Spend My Whole Life Loving You	Ken Stella	133	CB
14/06/1969	Oh Happy Day	Billy Mitchell Group	134	CB
14/06/1969	Merry Go Round Of Love	Roberta Quinlan	140	CB
14/06/1969	I Have But One Life To Live	Sammy Davis Jr.	141	CB
21/06/1969	Wake Up	Chambers Brothers	101	CB
21/06/1969	Here I Go Again	Country Joe & The Fish	103	CB
21/06/1969	Angel Of The Morning	Bettye Swann	109	BB
21/06/1969	My Sentimental Friend	Herman's Hermits	109	CB
21/06/1969	The Rib	Jeannie C. Riley	111	CB
21/06/1969	The Hunter	Ike & Tina Turner	114	CB
21/06/1969	If I Had A Reason	The BuBBle Puppy	119	CB
21/06/1969	New Day	Jackie Lomax	120	CB
21/06/1969	Big Bruce	Steve Greenberg	122	CB
21/06/1969	These Are The Things That Make Me Know You're Gone	Howard Tate	123	CB
21/06/1969	Delia's Gone	Waylon Jennings	124	CB
21/06/1969	But For Love	Eddy Arnold	125	BB
21/06/1969	Follow The Leader	Major Lance	125	BB
21/06/1969	Comin' Back To Me	Del Shannon	127	BB
21/06/1969	If This Was The Last Song	Thelma Houston	129	CB
28/06/1969	Sunshine, Red Wine	Crazy Elephant	104	BB
28/06/1969	Saint Paul	Terry Knight	114	BB
28/06/1969	Oh Happy Day	Billy Mitchell Group	115	BB
28/06/1969	Stomp	Nrbq	122	BB
28/06/1969	Thou Shall Not Steal	The Newbeats	128	BB

28/06/1969	Different Shades	Koffie & James	130	CB
28/06/1969	Capt. Groovy And His BuBBlegum Army	Capt. Groovy & His BuBBlegum Army	131	CB
28/06/1969	Today Has Been Cancelled	Billy Meshel	144	CB
05/07/1969	Frozen Orange Juice	Peter Sarstedt	103	CB
05/07/1969	A Famous Myth	The Groop	110	CB
05/07/1969	The Rib	Jeannie C. Riley	111	BB
05/07/1969	Love's Sweet Sensation	William Bell, Mavis Staples	113	CB
05/07/1969	Statue Of A Fool	Jack Greene	116	CB
05/07/1969	Cover Girl	The Gross National Product	119	CB
05/07/1969	Those Lazy, Hazy, Crazy Days Of Summer	Tony Scotti	119	CB
05/07/1969	Me And BoBBy Mcgee	Roger Miller	122	BB
05/07/1969	Crossroads Of The Stepping Stones	The Elephants Memory	124	CB
05/07/1969	Delia's Gone	Waylon Jennings	124	BB
05/07/1969	I Need Love	Rhinoceros	132	CB
05/07/1969	Oh! Sweet Love	Gideon	134	CB
12/07/1969	Yes, I Will	The Association	101	CB
12/07/1969	Things Got To Get Better	Marva Whitney	103	CB
12/07/1969	Ring Of Bright Water	Dee Dee Warwick	105	CB
12/07/1969	Here I Go Again	Country Joe And The Fish	106	BB
12/07/1969	I Need You Woman	William Bell, Carla Thomas	106	BB
12/07/1969	Never, Never Let You Go	Eddie Floyd Mavis Staples	107	BB
12/07/1969	Frozen Orange Juice	Peter Sarstedt	116	BB
12/07/1969	Toshisumasu	The Unifics	117	CB
12/07/1969	Me And BoBBy Mcgee	Roger Miller	118	CB
12/07/1969	The Love That A Woman Should Give To A Man	Patti Drew	119	BB
12/07/1969	My Dark Hour	Steve Miller Band	126	BB
12/07/1969	That Lucky Old Man	Solomon Burke	129	BB
12/07/1969	Rainy Jane	Neil Sedaka	131	CB
12/07/1969	Birds Of A Feather	Joe South	140	CB
19/07/1969	Better Homes And Gardens	BoBBy Russell	110	CB

19/07/1969	Ring Of Bright Water	Dee Dee Warwick	113	BB
19/07/1969	A Time For Us	Astrud Gilberto	114	CB
19/07/1969	Hands Of The Clock	Life	120	BB
19/07/1969	Yes, I Will	The Association	120	BB
19/07/1969	Everybody's Got A Hang Up	BoBBy Freeman	122	BB
19/07/1969	You Never Know Who Your Friends Are	Al Kooper	135	CB
26/07/1969	Let Me Be The Man My Daddy Was	Chi-Lites	107	CB
26/07/1969	Live And Learn	Andy Williams	111	CB
26/07/1969	South Carolina	The Flirtations	111	BB
26/07/1969	Theme From "A Summer Place" (vocal Version)	Percy Faith, His Orchestra & Chorus	111	BB
26/07/1969	The Smallest Astronaut (A Race To The Moon With The Red Baron)	Barry Winslow	113	CB
26/07/1969	These Are Not My People	Freddy Weller	113	BB
26/07/1969	A Gift Of Song	Mason Williams	118	BB
26/07/1969	Age (Where I Started Again)	Horatio	119	BB
26/07/1969	I Don't Want To Walk Without You	Julius Wechter & The Baja Marimba Band	121	BB
26/07/1969	Memphis Train	Buddy Miles Express	123	CB
26/07/1969	Silly People	The Litter	124	CB
26/07/1969	Sunny Sunny Feeling	The Toy Factory	128	CB
26/07/1969	Got It Together	Nancy Wilson	131	CB
26/07/1969	La Jeanne	King Curtis	133	CB
26/07/1969	Happy	William Bell	141	CB
02/08/1969	She's A Woman	José Feliciano	101	CB
02/08/1969	Free Me	Otis Redding	103	BB
02/08/1969	Saved By The Bell	Robin GiBB	103	CB
02/08/1969	She's A Woman	José Feliciano	103	BB
02/08/1969	Kind Woman	Percy Sledge	104	CB
02/08/1969	South Carolina	The Flirtations	104	CB
02/08/1969	Toys Are Made For Children	The Uniques	105	BB
02/08/1969	Hallelujah (I Am The Preacher)	Deep Purple	108	BB
02/08/1969	Straight Ahead	Young-Holt Unlimited	110	BB

02/08/1969	Light Of Love	The Cherry People	113	CB
02/08/1969	Got It Together	Nancy Wilson	114	BB
02/08/1969	Just Keep On Loving Me	Johnnie Taylor, Carla Thomas	115	BB
02/08/1969	Age (Where I Started Again)	Horatio	121	CB
02/08/1969	Hallelujah (I Am The Preacher)	Deep Purple	123	CB
02/08/1969	Lost And Found	The Peoples Choice	130	CB
09/08/1969	Ain't It Like Him	Edwin Hawkins Singers	101	BB
09/08/1969	Who Do You Love	Quicksilver Messenger Service	102	CB
09/08/1969	No One Is Going To Hurt You	The Neon Philharmonic	107	CB
09/08/1969	The Real Thing (Part I)	Russell Morris	107	BB
09/08/1969	Ob-La-Di, Ob-La-Da	Herb Alpert & The Tijuana Brass	109	CB
09/08/1969	Did She Mention My Name	Irish Rovers	115	CB
09/08/1969	Kind Woman	Percy Sledge	116	BB
09/08/1969	Live And Learn	Andy Williams	119	BB
09/08/1969	Son Of A Preacher Man	The Carnival	119	CB
09/08/1969	Midnight Cowboy	The Bar-Kays	120	CB
09/08/1969	No One Is Going To Hurt You	The Neon Philharmonic	120	BB
09/08/1969	Time To Make A Turn	Crow	123	BB
09/08/1969	All The Waiting Is Not In Vain	Tyrone Davis	125	BB
09/08/1969	I Want You So Bad	B.B. King	127	BB
09/08/1969	Room At The Top	The American Breed	127	CB
09/08/1969	La Jeanne	King Curtis	128	BB
09/08/1969	Happy	William Bell	129	BB
09/08/1969	Love And Peace	Johnny Nash	132	BB
09/08/1969	Journey To The Moon Part I	Genesis	148	CB
16/08/1969	(You're Love Has Lifted Me) Higher And Higher (b-side)	Otis Redding	110	BB
16/08/1969	Noah	The Bob Seger System	114	CB
16/08/1969	Ob-La-Di, Ob-La-Da	Herb Alpert & The Tijuana Brass	118	BB
16/08/1969	It's True I'm Gonna Miss You	Carolyn Franklin	119	BB
16/08/1969	Poor Moon	Canned Heat	119	BB

16/08/1969	I Don't Know How (To Fall Out Of Love)	The Persians	120	CB
16/08/1969	It's Gonna Rain	BoBBy Womack	121	CB
16/08/1969	Pain	The Mystics	121	CB
16/08/1969	Space Oddity	David Bowie	124	BB
16/08/1969	Shadows Of The Night (Quentin's Theme)	Robert Cobert Orchestra	125	BB
16/08/1969	The Real Thing (Part I)	Russell Morris	125	CB
16/08/1969	Aquarius (b-side)	Dick Hyman	126	BB
16/08/1969	Ain't It Like Him	Edwin Hawkins Singers	145	CB
23/08/1969	Noah	The Bob Seger System	103	BB
23/08/1969	Things Got To Get Better (Get Together)	Marva Whitney	110	BB
23/08/1969	Need Love	Vanilla Fudge	111	BB
23/08/1969	Living In The U.S.A.	Wilmer & The Dukes	114	BB
23/08/1969	Pain	The Mystics	116	BB
23/08/1969	Billy, I've Got To Go To Town	Geraldine Stevens	117	BB
23/08/1969	Farewell Love Scene	Juliet: Olivia Hussey, Romeo: Leonard Whiting, Nurse: Pat	117	CB
23/08/1969	I've Fallen In Love	Carla Thomas	117	BB
23/08/1969	Jive	Bob Darin	122	CB
23/08/1969	Marjorine	Herb Alpert & The Tijuana Brass	129	CB
23/08/1969	I'm Gonna Make It Up To You	BoBBy Vee	132	CB
23/08/1969	Son-Of-A-Preacherman	The Gayletts	138	CB
30/08/1969	(Your Love Has Lifted Me) Higher And Higher	Otis Redding	116	CB
30/08/1969	It's Too Late	Ted Taylor	118	BB
30/08/1969	Penny Arcade	Roy Orbison	134	CB
30/08/1969	Born On The Bayou	The Short-Kuts	141	CB
06/09/1969	One Woman	Steve Alaimo	101	BB
06/09/1969	Heighty Hi	Lee Michaels	106	BB
06/09/1969	I Love You	Eddie Holman	106	CB
06/09/1969	Green Onions	Dick Hyman	109	BB
06/09/1969	It's Too Late	Ted Taylor	111	CB
06/09/1969	Jive	Bob Darin	111	BB

06/09/1969	My Woman's Good To Me	George Benson	113	BB
06/09/1969	Happy Together	Hugo Montenegro, His Orchestra & Chorus	117	CB
06/09/1969	If The Creek Don't Rise	Liz Anderson	120	CB
06/09/1969	Hummin'	The Majic Ship	127	CB
06/09/1969	One Woman	Steve Alaimo	132	CB
06/09/1969	Time To Get It Together	Up 'N Adam	135	CB
06/09/1969	Loddy	Tax	137	CB
06/09/1969	The Twelfth Of Never	The Chi-Lites	137	CB
13/09/1969	The Best Part Of A Love Affair	The Emotions	101	BB
13/09/1969	We Can Make It	Ray Charles	101	BB
13/09/1969	Taking My Love (And Leaving Me)	Martha Reeves & The Vandellas	102	BB
13/09/1969	September Song	Roy Clark	103	BB
13/09/1969	Harlan County	Jim Ford	106	BB
13/09/1969	Helpless	Jackie Wilson	108	BB
13/09/1969	Born On The Bayou	The Short-Kuts	109	BB
13/09/1969	San Francisco Is A Lonely Town	Joe Simon	109	CB
13/09/1969	Living In The Past	Jethro Tull	111	CB
13/09/1969	Dreams Of Milk And Honey	Leslie West	114	CB
13/09/1969	Back In L.A.	The Peanut Butter Conspiracy	116	CB
13/09/1969	Gimme Some More	Crazy Elephant	116	BB
13/09/1969	Maybe	Betty Everett	116	BB
13/09/1969	Sign On For The Good Times	Merrilee Rush	119	CB
13/09/1969	Hey Jude	Captain Milk (Edwin HuBBard)	120	CB
13/09/1969	For What It's Worth	Cher	125	BB
13/09/1969	It's A Beautiful Day (For Lovin')	The Buckinghams	126	BB
13/09/1969	You Fool	Eddy Arnold	127	CB
13/09/1969	Be's That-A-Way Sometime	Scientists Of Soul	128	CB
13/09/1969	My Woman's Good To Me	George Benson	131	CB
13/09/1969	The Lights Of Night	Deni Lynn	132	CB
13/09/1969	Penny Arcade	Roy Orbison	133	BB

13/09/1969	Footprints On The Moon	The Johnny Harris Orchestra	134	CB
13/09/1969	Dealin' (Groovin' With The Feelin')	The Flamingos	142	CB
20/09/1969	Love And Let Love	The Hardy Boys	103	CB
20/09/1969	Long Red	Leslie West	108	CB
20/09/1969	How Are You? - Part One	Jake Holmes	109	CB
20/09/1969	Mommy And Daddy	The Monkees	109	BB
20/09/1969	White Bird	It's A Beautiful Day	110	CB
20/09/1969	All God's Children Got Soul	Dorothy Morrison	118	CB
20/09/1969	These Are The Things That Make Me Know You Are Gone	Howard Tate	120	BB
20/09/1969	The Twelfth Of Never	The Chi-Lites	122	BB
20/09/1969	Never In Public	Candi Staton	124	BB
20/09/1969	In A Moment Of Madness	The Flower Pot Men	129	CB
20/09/1969	Gimme Some More	Crazy Elephant	135	CB
27/09/1969	Get Ready	Ella Fitzgerald	106	CB
27/09/1969	It's A Beautiful Day (For Lovin')	The Buckinghams	110	CB
27/09/1969	(I'd Kill) For The Love Of A Lady	Jay & The Americans	113	CB
27/09/1969	Can You Dance To It?	Cat Mother And The All Night Newsboys	115	BB
27/09/1969	Things Go Better With Love	Jeannie C. Riley	117	CB
27/09/1969	Dark Eyed Woman	Spirit	118	BB
27/09/1969	Dismal Day	Bread	120	CB
27/09/1969	She's Too Good To Me	The Five Americans	137	CB
04/10/1969	Love And Let Love	The Hardy Boys	101	BB
04/10/1969	I Guess The Lord Must Be In New York City	Sagittarius (featuring Gary Usher)	111	CB
04/10/1969	Things Go Better With Love	Jeannie C. Riley	111	BB
04/10/1969	In The Land Of Make Believe	Dusty Springfield	113	BB
04/10/1969	Stone Free	The Jimi Hendrix Experience	113	CB
04/10/1969	Don't Shut Me Out	Underground Sunshine	114	CB
04/10/1969	It Ain't Sanitary	Joe Tex	117	BB
04/10/1969	White Bird	It's A Beautiful Day	118	BB
04/10/1969	Always David	Ruby Winters	121	BB

04/10/1969	Where	The Moments	121	CB
04/10/1969	It's A Funky Thing - Right On (pt. 1)	Herbie Mann	122	CB
04/10/1969	Sign On For The Good Times	Merrilee Rush	125	BB
04/10/1969	Get Ready	Ella Fitzgerald	126	BB
04/10/1969	Miss Pitiful	Etta James	131	CB
04/10/1969	Feelin' Bad	Spooky Tooth	132	BB
04/10/1969	Dong-Dong-Diki-Di-Ki-Dong	Kasenetz-Katz "Super Cirkus"	142	CB
11/10/1969	Today I Sing The Blues	Aretha Franklin	101	BB
11/10/1969	Don't Shut Me Out	Underground Sunshine	102	BB
11/10/1969	Poor Man	Little Milton	103	BB
11/10/1969	Like A Rolling Stone	Phil Flowers & The Flower Shop	104	BB
11/10/1969	Mr. Turnkey	Zagar & Evans	106	BB
11/10/1969	I Who Have Nothing	Dee Dee Warwick	107	CB
11/10/1969	Dreamin' Till Then	Joe Jeffrey	108	BB
11/10/1969	How Does It Feel	The Illusion	108	CB
11/10/1969	See That Girl	The Vogues	108	CB
11/10/1969	Comment (b-side)	Charles Wright And The Watts 103rd Street Rhythm Band	109	BB
11/10/1969	How Does It Feel	The Illusion	110	BB
11/10/1969	Comment	Charles Wright & The Watts 103rd Street Rhythm Band	113	CB
11/10/1969	Baby You Come Rollin' 'CROSS My Mind	John Beland	115	CB
11/10/1969	Midnight Cowboy	John Barry And His Orchestra	116	BB
11/10/1969	I Can't Help But Deceive You Little Girl	Iron Butterfly	118	BB
11/10/1969	Mary Don't Take Me On No Bad Trip	Fugi	130	CB
18/10/1969	It Ain't Sanitary	Joe Tex	101	CB
18/10/1969	Mommy And Daddy	The Monkees	101	CB
18/10/1969	Some Of Shelly's Blues	Nitty Gritty Dirt Band	106	BB
18/10/1969	Some Of Shelly's Blues	The Nitty Gritty Dirt Band	106	CB
18/10/1969	River Deep-Mountain High	Ike & Tina Turner	112	BB
18/10/1969	Horoscope	Young-Holt Unlimited	116	CB
18/10/1969	Love, Love, Love	The Tams	116	CB

18/10/1969	I Know	Ike & Tina Turner	126	BB
18/10/1969	River Deep - Mountain High	Ike & Tina Turner	129	CB
18/10/1969	Stone Free	The Jimi Hendrix Experience	130	BB
18/10/1969	We Got Latin Soul	Mongo Santamaria	132	BB
18/10/1969	Amen	Ace Cannon & His Alto Sax	139	CB
25/10/1969	Honey Come Back	Chuck Jackson	107	CB
25/10/1969	One Cup Of Happiness (And One Peace Of Mind)	Dean Martin	107	BB
25/10/1969	A Place In The Sun	Monk Montgomery	109	CB
25/10/1969	My Idea	Crème Caramel	109	CB
25/10/1969	Dry Spell	The Meters	114	CB
25/10/1969	Unbelievable	Vivian Reed	126	CB
25/10/1969	My Idea	Crème Caramel	128	BB
25/10/1969	Movin'	The RoBBs	131	BB
25/10/1969	I Guess The Lord Must Be In New York City	Sagittarius (featuring Gary Usher)	135	BB
25/10/1969	I've Got My Finger On Your Trigger	Slim Harpo	138	CB
01/11/1969	Curly	Jimmy Clanton	106	CB
01/11/1969	When I'm In Your Arms	The Dells	108	BB
01/11/1969	A Brand New Me	Jerry Butler	109	BB
01/11/1969	A Woman's Way	Andy Williams	109	BB
01/11/1969	Lady Jane	The Plastic Cow Goes Mooooooog	113	BB
01/11/1969	Horoscope	Young-Holt Unlimited	115	BB
01/11/1969	My Babe	Willie Mitchell	125	CB
01/11/1969	Everybody's Talkin' At Me Theme From "Midnight Cowboy"	Spanky & Our Gang	126	CB
01/11/1969	15 Going On 20	Five By Five	136	CB
08/11/1969	Tonight	Mc 5	101	CB
08/11/1969	Free	The Pearly Gate	102	CB
08/11/1969	Beautiful People	Melanie	104	CB
08/11/1969	Okie From Muskogee	Merle Haggard & Strangers	105	CB
08/11/1969	Baby You Come Rollin' 'Cross My Mind	John Beland	110	BB
08/11/1969	Sunlight	The Youngbloods	114	BB

08/11/1969	My Babe	Willie Mitchell	115	BB
08/11/1969	Memories Of A Broken Promise (b-side)	Motherlode	116	BB
08/11/1969	I'm Gonna Tear You A New Heart	Clarence Reid	120	BB
08/11/1969	Any Way That You Want Me	Walter Jackson	121	CB
08/11/1969	Must Be Your Thing	Charles Wright & The Watts 103rd Street Rhythm Band	126	CB
08/11/1969	Blowin' In The Wind	Edwin Hawkins Singers	129	CB
08/11/1969	Lady Jane	The Plastic Cow Goes Moooooog	133	CB
15/11/1969	Don't You Ever Get Tired (Of Hurting Me)	Bettye Swann	102	BB
15/11/1969	Jesamine	Shannon	104	CB
15/11/1969	(When Johnny Comes Marching Home Again) I Can't See You No	Joe Tex	105	BB
15/11/1969	Too Many Cooks (Spoil The Soup)	100 Proof Aged In Soul	108	CB
15/11/1969	Blowin' In The Wind	Edwin Hawkins Singers	109	BB
15/11/1969	I Gotta Have You	Horatio	111	CB
15/11/1969	Golden Slumbers/Carry That Weight	Trash	112	BB
15/11/1969	(One Of These Days) Sunday's Gonna' Come On Tuesday	The New Establishment	120	CB
15/11/1969	Jumpin' Jack Flash	Thelma Houston	123	CB
15/11/1969	Love Fever	Leer Brothers	129	CB
15/11/1969	Camel Back	A.B. Skhy	135	CB
15/11/1969	The Greatest Love	The Winstons	135	CB
15/11/1969	Since December	Eddy Arnold	150	CB
22/11/1969	Bless Your Heart	The Isley Brothers	101	CB
22/11/1969	Cowboy Convention	Ohio Express	101	BB
22/11/1969	Me And You	O.C. Smith	103	BB
22/11/1969	Must Be Your Thing	Charles Wright And The Watts 103rd Street Rhythm Band	103	BB
22/11/1969	You Are My Life	Herb Alpert & The Tijuana Brass	109	BB
22/11/1969	Bad Conditions	Lloyd Price	118	CB
22/11/1969	When We Get Married	1910 Fruitgum Co.	118	BB
22/11/1969	Wichita Lineman	Sergio Mendes & Brasil '66	121	CB
22/11/1969	Hey Girl	Panhandle	122	BB
22/11/1969	Wendegahl The Warlock	The Rugbys	122	CB

22/11/1969	Papa Joe's Thing	Papa Joe's Music Box	126	CB
22/11/1969	Something Is Wrong	Gary Lewis & The Playboys	126	CB
22/11/1969	Let's Get Back To Rock And Roll	The Playboys Of Edinburg	130	CB
29/11/1969	The Ballad Of Paul	The Mystery Tour	104	BB
29/11/1969	Been A Long Time	Betty Everett	105	CB
29/11/1969	Hey Hey Woman	Joe Jeffrey	111	CB
29/11/1969	What Does It Take (To Win Your Love)	Motherlode	111	BB
29/11/1969	The Jet Song (When The Weekend's Over)	The Groop	112	BB
29/11/1969	Morning Dew (Walk Me Out In The)	Sound Foundation	118	BB
29/11/1969	Jealous Feeling	Dick Jensen	120	CB
29/11/1969	Cow Pie	The Masked Marauders	123	BB
29/11/1969	Right Or Left At Oak Street	Roy Clark	123	BB
29/11/1969	Cow Pie	The Masked Marauders	125	CB
29/11/1969	Wasn't Born To Follow	The Byrds	125	CB
29/11/1969	Hurry Change (If You're Coming)	Tennison Stephens	135	CB
06/12/1969	Free	The Pearly Gate	104	BB
06/12/1969	Bless Your Heart	The Isley Brothers	105	BB
06/12/1969	Morning Dew	Damnation Of Adam Blessing	109	CB
06/12/1969	What A Beautiful Feeling	The California Earthquake	113	CB
06/12/1969	I Fall To Pieces	Diana Trask	114	BB
06/12/1969	Have A Little Talk With Myself	Ray Stevens	115	CB
06/12/1969	Maybe	The Chantels	116	BB
06/12/1969	(Gotta Find) A Brand New Lover (Part 1)	The Sweet Inspirations	128	CB
06/12/1969	It's Only Make Believe	Roy Hamilton	132	CB
06/12/1969	You're The Best Thing Since Candy	The O'jays	137	CB
13/12/1969	(I'm So) Afraid Of Losing You Again	Charley Pride	102	CB
13/12/1969	Farewell Is A Lonely Sound	Jimmy Ruffin	104	BB
13/12/1969	Whistle For Happiness	Peggy Lee	104	CB
13/12/1969	Theme Music For The Film "2001 A Space Odyssey" (Also Sprach	Berlin Philharmonic	110	CB
13/12/1969	Alice's Restaurant Massacree	Garry Sherman And His Orchestra	112	BB

13/12/1969	Trouble Maker	Lee Hazlewood	116	BB
13/12/1969	Have A Little Talk With Myself	Ray Stevens	123	BB
13/12/1969	Funk No. 48	The James Gang	126	BB
13/12/1969	Ready To Ride	Southwind	127	BB
20/12/1969	Alice's Rock & Roll Restaurant	Arlo Guthrie	102	CB
20/12/1969	At The Crossroads	Sir Douglas Quintet	104	BB
20/12/1969	Claudie Mae	Ray Charles	108	CB
20/12/1969	Don't Think That I'm A Violent Guy	Garland Green	108	CB
20/12/1969	Take Her Back	Gemini	108	CB
20/12/1969	Amen (1970)	The Impressions	110	BB
20/12/1969	Anyway That You Want Me	Walter Jackson	111	BB
20/12/1969	Claudie Mae	Ray Charles	111	BB
20/12/1969	She Lets Her Hair Down (Early In The Morning)	Don Young	112	CB
20/12/1969	(Gotta Find) A Brand New Lover- Part 1	The Sweet Inspirations	117	BB
20/12/1969	The Marvelous Toy	Peter, Paul & Mary	120	CB
20/12/1969	Hello Sunshine	Rev. Maceo Woods And The Christian Tabernacle Baptist	121	BB
20/12/1969	Hey Girl	Panhandle	122	CB
20/12/1969	My Baby Loves Me	David T. Walker	128	BB
20/12/1969	What A Beautiful Feeling	The California Earthquake	133	BB
27/12/1969	She Let Her Hair Down (Early In The Morning)	Don Young	104	BB
27/12/1969	A Sign For Love	John & Anne Ryder	105	CB
27/12/1969	The Last Time	The Buchanan Brothers	106	BB
27/12/1969	Hey Hey Woman	Joe Jeffrey	109	BB
27/12/1969	To Love You	Country Stone	112	CB
27/12/1969	Don't Think That I'm A Violent Guy	Garland Green	113	BB
27/12/1969	I'll Hold Out My Hand	Wind	114	CB
27/12/1969	Proud Woman	Johnny Adams	129	CB
27/12/1969	It's Gonna Take A Lot To Bring Me Back	The Manhattans	137	CB
27/12/1969	My Cloud	Joe Bataan	137	CB
03/01/1970	Say Goodbye To Daddy	Richard Spencer & The Winstons	107	BB

03/01/1970	Wabash Cannon Ball	Danny Davis & The Nashville Brass	107	CB
03/01/1970	Freight Train	Duane Eddy	110	BB
03/01/1970	A World Without Music	Archie Bell & The Drells	111	CB
03/01/1970	Remember Then	Sha Na Na	114	CB
03/01/1970	Crazy Annie	Evie Sands	116	BB
03/01/1970	Tie Me To Your Apron Strings Again	Michael Parks	117	BB
03/01/1970	Proud Woman	Johnny Adams	121	BB
03/01/1970	The Unhooked Generation	Freda Payne	127	CB
03/01/1970	Compared To What (b-side)	Della Reese	128	BB
03/01/1970	Lovely Way She Loves	The Moments	132	CB
03/01/1970	Russian Roulette	Cy Coleman	138	CB
10/01/1970	Room To Move [Live]	John Mayall	102	BB
10/01/1970	To Love You	Country Stone	103	BB
10/01/1970	A Thing Called Love	Ed Ames	115	CB
10/01/1970	Games People Play	Della Reese	118	CB
10/01/1970	He Made A Woman Out Of Me	Betty Lavette	118	CB
10/01/1970	Games People Play	Della Reese	121	BB
10/01/1970	You Are My Sunshine	Dyke And The Blazers	121	BB
10/01/1970	Angel On My Shoulder	Merrilee Rush	122	BB
10/01/1970	Stay Awhile	Jerry Vale	127	CB
10/01/1970	Tightrope	Ten Wheel Drive With Genya Ravan	136	CB
10/01/1970	Country Girl	Jeannie C. Riley	150	CB
17/01/1970	Johnny B. Goode	Johnny Winter	103	CB
17/01/1970	My Cherie Amour	The Ramsey Lewis Trio	107	CB
17/01/1970	Never Goin' Back To Georgia	Blues Magoos	113	CB
17/01/1970	Answer Me, My Love	The Happenings	115	BB
17/01/1970	Feelin' Groovy	Southwest F.O.B.	115	BB
17/01/1970	Take Her Back	Gemini	119	BB
17/01/1970	Ice Cream Man (The Gimme Game)	Don Covay & Jefferson Lemon Blues Band	124	CB
24/01/1970	Back To Dreamin' Again	Pat Shannon	103	BB

24/01/1970	Church St. Soul Revival	The Exiles	104	BB
24/01/1970	The Maltese Melody	Herb Alpert & The Tijuana Brass	110	CB
24/01/1970	Never Goin' Back To Georgia	Blues Magoos	113	BB
24/01/1970	God Only Knows	The Vogues	114	CB
24/01/1970	Love Is For The Two Of Us	Rene & Rene	120	CB
24/01/1970	Lovely Way She Loves	The Moments	120	BB
24/01/1970	Hikky Burr - Part One	Bill Cosby With The Bunions Bradford Band	124	BB
24/01/1970	I'll Be With You	The Saints	128	CB
24/01/1970	Wherever She Leadeth Me (b-side)	The Impressions	128	BB
24/01/1970	There You Go	Frummox	129	CB
24/01/1970	Wabash Cannon Ball	Danny Davis And The Nashville Brass	131	BB
31/01/1970	Church St. Soul Revival	The Exiles	101	CB
31/01/1970	God Only Knows	The Vogues	101	BB
31/01/1970	In And Out Of Love	BoBBy Vee	105	CB
31/01/1970	Love Story	Peggy Lee	105	BB
31/01/1970	The Maltese Melody	Herb Alpert & The Tijuana Brass	108	BB
31/01/1970	Here I Go Again	Archie Bell & The Drells	112	BB
31/01/1970	Crazy Annie	Evie Sands	123	CB
31/01/1970	Rock And Roll Music (Live)	The Frost	123	CB
31/01/1970	Mr. Bus Driver	Neal Dover	128	CB
07/02/1970	Lu	Peggy Lipton	102	BB
07/02/1970	Try (Just A Little Bit Harder)	Janis Joplin	103	BB
07/02/1970	Try (Just A Little Bit Harder)	Janis Joplin	103	CB
07/02/1970	24 Hours Of Sadness	The Chi-Lites	105	CB
07/02/1970	Country Girl	Jeannie C. Riley	106	BB
07/02/1970	This Empty Place	The Tangeers	107	CB
07/02/1970	Two Little Boys	Rolf Harris	108	CB
07/02/1970	You Say It	Al Green	108	CB
07/02/1970	I'll See Him Through	Tammy Wynette	113	CB
07/02/1970	Little Things Mean A Lot	Bettye Swann	114	BB

07/02/1970	Dig The Way I Feel	Mary Wells	115	BB
14/02/1970	You've Made Me So Very Happy	Lou Rawls	102	CB
14/02/1970	Time	Edwin Starr	112	CB
14/02/1970	Love Story	Peggy Lee	113	CB
14/02/1970	Don't Get Close	Little Anthony And The Imperials	116	BB
14/02/1970	Jesus Is Just Alright	The Byrds	121	CB
14/02/1970	Maybe So Maybe No	New Holidays	133	CB
14/02/1970	Arkansas State Prison	BoBBy Womack	135	CB
14/02/1970	Love, Peace And Happiness	The Chambers Brothers	135	CB
14/02/1970	Love Equals Love	Ohio Express	138	CB
21/02/1970	Gonna Give Her All The Love I've Got	Marvin Gaye	103	CB
21/02/1970	Diane	The Golden Gate	104	CB
21/02/1970	Rock And Roll Music [Live]	The Frost	105	BB
21/02/1970	Norwegian Wood	Sergio Mendes & Brasil '66	107	BB
21/02/1970	Free As The Wind	The Brooklyn Bridge	109	BB
21/02/1970	Moody	O.C. Smith	114	BB
21/02/1970	You	Andy Kim	115	CB
21/02/1970	Rosianna	The Buchanan Brothers	119	CB
21/02/1970	Tighten Up Your Own Thing	Etta James	119	CB
21/02/1970	Oh What A Time	Maurice & Mac	124	CB
21/02/1970	Music To My Heart	The Obsession	130	CB
28/02/1970	Tender (Was The Love We Knew)	The Intruders	101	CB
28/02/1970	Just About The Same	The Association	106	BB
28/02/1970	Wan-Tu-Wah-Zuree	George Tindley	106	CB
28/02/1970	In And Out Of Love	BoBBy Vee	111	BB
28/02/1970	Peter And The Wolf	The Charles Randolph Grean Sounde	114	CB
28/02/1970	I'll Be Your Baby Tonight	Ray Stevens	117	CB
28/02/1970	Night Owl	The Bad Habits	121	CB
28/02/1970	(Call Me) Number One	Tremeloes	124	CB
28/02/1970	Norwegian Wood	Sergio Mendes & Brazil '66	125	CB

28/02/1970	Kool It (Here Comes The Fuzz)	Kool & The Gang	134	CB
07/03/1970	I'll Be Your Baby Tonight	Ray Stevens	112	BB
07/03/1970	To Live The Past	Percy Mayfield	113	CB
07/03/1970	Laura (What's He Got That I Ain't Got)	The Newbeats	115	BB
07/03/1970	Theme From "Z" (Life Goes On)	Henry Mancini And His Orchestra	115	BB
07/03/1970	Baby-Baby Don't Stop Now	Sam & Dave	117	BB
07/03/1970	Time	Edwin Starr	117	BB
07/03/1970	Chains Of Love	Ronnie Dove	118	CB
07/03/1970	Come On Down	Dean Martin	121	CB
07/03/1970	Rhymes And Reasons	The Irish Rovers	130	CB
14/03/1970	Does Anybody Know What Time It Is	Copper N' Brass	103	BB
14/03/1970	Diane	The Golden Gate	105	BB
14/03/1970	Peter And The Wolf	The Charles Randolph Green Sounde	108	BB
14/03/1970	I Would Be In Love (Anyway)	Frank Sinatra	118	CB
14/03/1970	24 Hours Of Sadness	The Chi-Lites	119	BB
14/03/1970	Laugh, Funny Funny	Everyday Hudson	141	CB
21/03/1970	Hang On Sloopy	The Lettermen	101	CB
21/03/1970	Does Anybody Know What Time It Is	Copper N' Brass	102	CB
21/03/1970	Slow Down	Crow	103	BB
21/03/1970	Help One Man Today	Zager & Evans	104	CB
21/03/1970	Holly Go Softly	Cornerstone	104	BB
21/03/1970	Tippicaw Calley	Lenny Damon & The Bah Humbug Band	107	BB
21/03/1970	All That I've Got (I'm Gonna Give It To You)	Billy Preston	108	BB
21/03/1970	But You Know I Love You	Evie Sands	110	BB
21/03/1970	Wichita Lineman	José Feliciano	111	CB
21/03/1970	Me Without You	Billy Joe Royal	112	CB
21/03/1970	Two Little Boys	Rolf Harris	119	BB
21/03/1970	There Goes My Baby/Be My Baby	The Shirelles	121	CB
28/03/1970	(What A) Groovey Feeling	Johnny Nash	102	BB
28/03/1970	Check Yourself	I.A.P. Co. (The Italian Asphalt & Pavement Company)	103	CB

28/03/1970	Mr. Monday	The Original Caste	108	CB
28/03/1970	Theme From "Z" ("Life Goes On" To Yelasto Pedi)	Henry Mancini & His Orchestra	112	CB
28/03/1970	Rain Dance	The Electric Indian	115	CB
28/03/1970	Tender (Was The Love We Knew)	The Intruders	119	BB
28/03/1970	I'm A Good Woman	Cold Blood	125	BB
28/03/1970	Too Many Rivers To Cross	Percy Sledge	125	CB
28/03/1970	But You Know I Love You	Evie Sands	130	CB
28/03/1970	Tippicaw Calley	Lenny Damon & The Bah Humbug Band	132	CB
28/03/1970	Keep A Knockin'/Get Back/Etc.	Blizzard	137	CB
04/04/1970	All In My Mind	Pure Love & Pleasure	104	BB
04/04/1970	Demonstration	Otis Redding	105	BB
04/04/1970	Will You Love Me Tomorrow?	Linda Ronstadt	111	BB
04/04/1970	High Sheriff Of Calhoun Parrish	Tony Joe White	112	BB
04/04/1970	What I'm Saying Is True	Steam	117	CB
04/04/1970	Jimmy Newman	Tom Paxton	120	CB
04/04/1970	Mama Said	Little Eva	120	CB
04/04/1970	He - I Believe	Cissy Houston	134	CB
11/04/1970	Goodbye Jo	Cashman, Pistilli & West	105	BB
11/04/1970	Guide Me Well	Carla Thomas	107	CB
11/04/1970	Since I Don't Have You	Eddie Holman	107	CB
11/04/1970	Take Me With You	The Honey Cone	108	BB
11/04/1970	My Baby Loves Lovin'	Joe Jeffrey	115	BB
11/04/1970	All In My Mind	Pure Love & Pleasure	117	CB
11/04/1970	Uhh	Dyke And The Blazers	118	BB
11/04/1970	Sympathy	Rare Bird	121	BB
11/04/1970	The Onion Song	Marvin Gaye & Tammi Terrell	122	CB
11/04/1970	Teasin'	King Curtis With Delaney Bramlett, Eric Clapton & Friends	128	BB
18/04/1970	Goodbye Jo	Cashman, Pistilli & West	104	CB
18/04/1970	God Bless	Arthur Conley	107	BB
18/04/1970	Maybe	Janis Joplin	110	BB

18/04/1970	To Be Loved/Glory Of Love	Lenny Welch	110	BB
18/04/1970	Last Of The Wine	The RoBBs	112	CB
18/04/1970	Bitter Green	Ronnie Hawkins	118	BB
18/04/1970	Heighdy-Ho Princess	The Neon Philharmonic	121	CB
18/04/1970	Greatest Love	Judy Clay	122	BB
18/04/1970	Theme From The Molly Maguires	Henry Mancini & His Orchestra	123	CB
18/04/1970	Love's Gonna Tear Your Playhouse Down Part I	Chuck Brooks	126	CB
18/04/1970	Timothy	Buoys	128	CB
18/04/1970	(What A) Groovey Feeling	Johnny Nash	131	CB
18/04/1970	There Ain't No Umbopo	Crazy Elephant	135	CB
25/04/1970	Boogie Woogie Country Girl	Southwind	107	CB
25/04/1970	Don't Let The Music Slip Away	Archie Bell & The Drells	113	CB
25/04/1970	If He Can, You Can	The Isley Brothers	113	BB
25/04/1970	So Young (Love Theme From "Zabriskie Point")	Roy Orbison	114	CB
25/04/1970	Mr. Monday	The Original Caste	119	BB
25/04/1970	One Part Love - Two Parts Pain	Sam & Dave With The Dixie Flyers	123	BB
25/04/1970	Street Singer	Merle Haggard And The Strangers	124	BB
25/04/1970	My Love	Sonny James, The Southern Gentleman	125	BB
25/04/1970	3 Minutes 2 - Hey Girl	George Kerr	130	CB
25/04/1970	I Treasure Thee	Ross Bagdasarian	136	CB
25/04/1970	Tobacco Road	Jamul	137	CB
25/04/1970	Love The Way You Love	O.V. Wright	139	CB
02/05/1970	Hey, That's No Way To Say Goodbye	The Vogues	101	BB
02/05/1970	Boogie Woogie Country Girl	Southwind	105	BB
02/05/1970	Anna	Boots Randolph	108	CB
02/05/1970	Thank You Girl	Street People	112	CB
02/05/1970	Last Of The Wine	The RoBBs	114	BB
02/05/1970	Hey, That's No Way To Say Goodbye	The Vogues	118	CB
02/05/1970	It Takes A Little Longer	Sonny Charles	119	CB
02/05/1970	So Young (Love Theme From "Zabriskie Point")	Roy Orbison	122	BB

02/05/1970	Lovin' La La	Linus & The Little People	123	CB
02/05/1970	I'll Be There	Cissy Houston	124	CB
02/05/1970	And Don't Be Late	Grinder's Switch Featuring Garland Jeffreys	128	CB
02/05/1970	I'd Love Making Love To You	Jimmy Huff	130	CB
02/05/1970	If You Let Me Make Love To You Then Why Can't I Touch You?	Jive Fyve	134	CB
09/05/1970	Feeling Bad	Mel And Tim	106	BB
09/05/1970	If He Can, You Can	The Isley Brothers	110	CB
09/05/1970	Tomorrow Today Will Be Yesterday	The Happenings	111	CB
09/05/1970	Gone Movin' On	Raiders Vocal By: Mark Lindsay	120	BB
09/05/1970	3 Minutes 2 - Hey Girl	George Kerr	124	BB
09/05/1970	I Got A Problem	Jesse Anderson	127	CB
09/05/1970	Mystery Of Love	The Leer Bros. Band	133	CB
16/05/1970	Cottonfields	The Beach Boys	101	CB
16/05/1970	You Keep Me Hangin' On/Hurt So Bad	Jackie Deshannon	101	CB
16/05/1970	I Shall Be Released	Rick Nelson And The Stone Canyon Band	102	BB
16/05/1970	Cottonfields	The Beach Boys	103	BB
16/05/1970	I Wanna Be A Free Girl	Dusty Springfield	105	BB
16/05/1970	Mr. Balloon Man	Ray Hildebrand	106	CB
16/05/1970	Magical Connection	John Sebastian	109	CB
16/05/1970	Anna	Boots Randolph	111	BB
16/05/1970	Just A Little Bit More	The Intrigues	111	CB
16/05/1970	Time And Place	Lee Moses	122	CB
16/05/1970	Feeling Bad	Mel & Tim	129	CB
23/05/1970	I'm A Man	The Yellow Payges	102	BB
23/05/1970	On The Brighter Side Of A Blue World	Fantastic Four	102	CB
23/05/1970	People And Me	The New Colony Six	103	CB
23/05/1970	It's Just A Game, Love	Peaches & Herb	110	BB
23/05/1970	I Shall Be Released	Freddie Scott	112	CB
23/05/1970	Please Take Me Back	The Masqueraders	114	CB
23/05/1970	People And Me	The New Colony Six	116	BB

23/05/1970	For The Love Of A Woman	Dean Martin	122	CB
23/05/1970	Hanging On The Edge Of Sadness	The Flying Machine	135	CB
23/05/1970	Raindrops Keep Fallin' On My Head	Barbara Mason	112a	BB
30/05/1970	Free The People	Delaney & Bonnie & Friends	101	CB
30/05/1970	Let's Do It (Do It Together)	The Chambers Brothers	103	BB
30/05/1970	What Do You Say To A Naked Lady	Errol Sober	106	BB
30/05/1970	Walk A Mile In My Shoes	Willie Hightower	107	BB
30/05/1970	Feet Start Walking	Doris Duke	109	BB
30/05/1970	Love For Living	The Glass Bottle	109	BB
30/05/1970	I Got Love	Melba Moore	111	BB
30/05/1970	Mama's Baby-Daddy's Maybe	Swamp Dogg	113	BB
30/05/1970	Everybody Saw You	Ruby Andrews	118	BB
30/05/1970	Watch What Happens	Lena Horne	119	BB
30/05/1970	Lift Ev'ry Voice And Sing	Kim Weston	120	BB
30/05/1970	What Do You Say To A Naked Lady	Errol Sober	130	CB
30/05/1970	If You Knew Him Like I Do	Barbara Mason	112b	BB
06/06/1970	Down By The River	Brooklyn Bridge	103	CB
06/06/1970	Can't See You When I Want To	David Porter	105	BB
06/06/1970	Forget It, I Got It	Ambergris	107	CB
06/06/1970	Guide Me Well	Carla Thomas	107	BB
06/06/1970	Birds Of All Nations	George Mccannon Iii	111	BB
06/06/1970	Let's Get A Little Sentimental	The Montanas	113	CB
06/06/1970	Go Away	1910 Fruitgum Co.	117	CB
06/06/1970	Never Goin' Home	Owen B.	119	CB
06/06/1970	Mail Call Time	Mel & Tim	120	CB
06/06/1970	California Rock'n Roll	Crowfoot	133	CB
13/06/1970	Eve Of Destruction	The Turtles	105	CB
13/06/1970	If You Knew Him Like I Do	Barbara Mason	107	CB
13/06/1970	Jesus, Take A Hold	Merle Haggard And The Strangers	107	BB
13/06/1970	I Wish I Had A Mommy Like You	Patti Page	114	BB

13/06/1970	On The Sunny Side Of The Street	Frankie Laine	120	CB
13/06/1970	I Never Picked Cotton	Roy Clark	122	BB
13/06/1970	Do I Love You?	Jay & The Americans	123	CB
13/06/1970	What's Now Is Now	Frank Sinatra	123	BB
13/06/1970	Let Somebody Love Me	Chuck Jackson	133	CB
20/06/1970	I'll Be There	Eddie Holman	101	CB
20/06/1970	I.O.I.O.	The Bee Gees	102	CB
20/06/1970	The Thrill Is Gone	Aretha Franklin With The Dixie Flyers	103	CB
20/06/1970	The Lights Of Tucson	Jim Campbell	106	CB
20/06/1970	Circles In The Sand	Frankie Valli	108	CB
20/06/1970	Wash, Mama, Wash	Dr. John The Night Tripper	108	BB
20/06/1970	Wear Your Love Like Heaven	Peggy Lipton	108	BB
20/06/1970	Roll Away The Stone	Leon Russell	109	BB
20/06/1970	Handsome Johnny	Richie Havens	115	BB
20/06/1970	I'll Be There	Eddie Holman	115	BB
20/06/1970	Let's Make Each Other Happy	The Illusion	118	CB
20/06/1970	World Of Darkness	Little Anthony And The Imperials	121	BB
20/06/1970	Walking In The Sand	Al Martino	123	BB
20/06/1970	Watch What Happens	Lena Horne	124	CB
20/06/1970	I'll Be There	Cissy Houston	125	BB
20/06/1970	Wherefore And Why	Johnny Mathis	126	CB
20/06/1970	A Street Called Hope	Gene Pitney	132	CB
27/06/1970	Love Is There	Bridge	104	CB
27/06/1970	Passport To The Future	Jean Jacques Perrey	106	BB
27/06/1970	Wear Your Love Like Heaven	Peggy Lipton	129	CB
27/06/1970	Exuma, The Obeah Man	Exuma	130	CB
27/06/1970	Susie-Q	José Feliciano	137	CB
27/06/1970	Take Me For A Little While	Evie Sands	138	CB
04/07/1970	Runaway People	Dyke & The Blazers	101	CB
04/07/1970	Two Little Rooms	Janet Lawson	109	CB

04/07/1970	Eleanor Rigby	El Chicano	115	BB
04/07/1970	After The Feeling Is Gone	Lulu With The Dixie Flyers	117	BB
04/07/1970	Let Me Love You One More Time (Un Poquito Mas)	Jerry Ross Symposium	117	CB
04/07/1970	I Gotta Get Away (From My Own Self)	Ray Godfrey	120	CB
04/07/1970	If Johnny Comes Marching Home	Goliath	122	CB
04/07/1970	For The Love Of A Woman	Dean Martin	123	BB
04/07/1970	Drivin' Home	Jerry Smith	125	BB
04/07/1970	Mexico	Jefferson Airplane	102a	BB
04/07/1970	Have You Seen The Saucers (b-side)	Jefferson Airplane	102b	BB
11/07/1970	I Heard The Voice Of Jesus	Turley Richards	106	CB
11/07/1970	Some Things A Man's Gotta Do	Shango	107	BB
11/07/1970	Mill Valley	Miss Abrams & The Strawberry Point School Third Grade Class	109	CB
11/07/1970	Crazy Love	The Happenings	113	CB
11/07/1970	Down To The Valley	Nilsson	114	CB
11/07/1970	Nothing Can Touch Me (Don't Worry Baby, It's Alright)	The Original Caste	114	BB
11/07/1970	Higher & Higher	Canada Goose	121	CB
11/07/1970	Wonder Could I Live There Anymore	Charley Pride	122	CB
11/07/1970	Let Me Love You One More Time (Un Poquito Mas)	Jerry Ross Symposium	123	BB
11/07/1970	Two Little Rooms	Janet Lawson	124	BB
11/07/1970	One Way Ticket To Nowhere	Syl Johnson	125	BB
11/07/1970	Captain BoBBy Stout	The Jerry Hahn Brotherhood	135	CB
18/07/1970	Vibrations (Made Us Fall In Love)	Eric & The Vikings	104	CB
18/07/1970	Let's Do It (Do It Together)	The Chambers Brothers	108	CB
18/07/1970	I'll Paint You A Song	Mac Davis	110	BB
18/07/1970	My Girl	Eddie Floyd	116	BB
18/07/1970	Smoke Signals	The Vibrations	116	CB
18/07/1970	It's All Over Now	Rod Stewart	126	BB
18/07/1970	Can't You See What You're Doing To Me	Albert King	127	BB
18/07/1970	God Knows I Loved Her	Dennis Yost & The Classics Iv	128	BB
18/07/1970	Sorry Suzanne	The Glass Bottle	130	CB

18/07/1970	Dear Ike (Remember I'm John's Girl)	The Sister And Brothers	131	BB
25/07/1970	Come On Down	Savage Grace Vocal: Al & Ron	104	BB
25/07/1970	Set Me Free	Esther Phillips With The Dixie Flyers	118	BB
25/07/1970	Please Baby Please	Realistic's	119	CB
25/07/1970	Runaway People	Dyke And The Blazers	119	BB
25/07/1970	That's When The World Really Began	Mel Wynn Trend	127	CB
25/07/1970	He'll Never Love You	The Gentrys	129	CB
25/07/1970	One More Time Billy Brown	Burl Ives	134	CB
25/07/1970	Here Comes Summer	The Dave Clark Five	135	CB
01/08/1970	She Works In A Woman's Way	Edison Lighthouse	105	CB
01/08/1970	It's Gonna Change	BoBBy Goldsboro	108	BB
01/08/1970	Sally (Was A Gentle Woman)	Michael Parks	109	CB
01/08/1970	My Woman, My Woman, My Wife	Dean Martin	110	BB
01/08/1970	Now Is The Time	Sisters Love	111	CB
01/08/1970	Set Me Free	Esther Phillips With The Dixie Flyers	111	CB
01/08/1970	We Can Make It Baby	The Originals	112	CB
01/08/1970	I Will Survive	Arrival	114	CB
01/08/1970	He'll Never Love You	The Gentrys	116	BB
01/08/1970	I'll Paint You A Song	Mac Davis	125	CB
01/08/1970	My Baby Specializes	Bad Habits	137	CB
08/08/1970	Yakety Yak	The Pipkins	101	CB
08/08/1970	Let Me Bring You Up	Ron Dante	102	BB
08/08/1970	A Song That Never Comes	Mama Cass Elliot	104	CB
08/08/1970	Better Times	Rhinoceros	109	BB
08/08/1970	Wipe Out	The Surfaris	110	BB
08/08/1970	Let Me Bring You Up	Ron Dante	118	CB
08/08/1970	Sweet Gingerbread Man	The Mike Curb Congregation	126	CB
08/08/1970	Too Much Foolin' Around	The Tams	133	CB
15/08/1970	Comin' Back To Me (Ooh Baby)	Smith	101	BB
15/08/1970	Sing Out The Love (In My Heart)	Arkade	101	CB

15/08/1970	What A Bummer	The Jaggerz	102	CB
15/08/1970	Simple Song Of Freedom	Spirit Of Us	106	BB
15/08/1970	The Circle Game	Buffy Sainte-Marie	109	BB
15/08/1970	The Circle Game	Buffy Sainte-Marie	112	CB
15/08/1970	Border Song (Holy Moses)	Dorothy Morrison	114	BB
15/08/1970	Wait For Summer	Jack Wild	115	BB
15/08/1970	The Bigger You Love (The Harder You Fall)	Sisters Love	123	CB
15/08/1970	Better Times	Rhinoceros	127	CB
15/08/1970	Dear Ike (Remember I'm John's Girl)	The Sister & Brothers	142	CB
22/08/1970	Have You Had Any Lately?	Sylvia Robinson	102	BB
22/08/1970	I Like Your Style	The Originals	108	CB
22/08/1970	I Won't Cry	Johnny Adams	109	CB
22/08/1970	Apart Of Me	Country Funk	117	CB
22/08/1970	Years May Come, Years May Go	The Irish Rovers	119	CB
29/08/1970	For What It's Worth	Sergio Mendes & Brasil '66	101	BB
29/08/1970	Pure Love	Betty Wright	104	CB
29/08/1970	Un Rayo De Sol	Los Diablos	110	CB
29/08/1970	Seeing Is Believin'	The Mad Lads	115	CB
29/08/1970	All I Want To Be Is Your Woman	Carolyn Franklin	117	CB
29/08/1970	Don't Nobody Want To Get Married (Part Ii)	Jesse James	117	BB
29/08/1970	South	Roger Miller	119	CB
29/08/1970	Lost	Dusty Springfield	123	CB
29/08/1970	Heart Association	The Emotions	126	CB
29/08/1970	And You Do	Charade	128	CB
05/09/1970	Roly Poly	Stamford Bridge	101	CB
05/09/1970	Every Night	Billy Joe Royal	103	CB
05/09/1970	I Wanna Love You	George Baker Selection	103	BB
05/09/1970	I Wanna Love You	George Baker Selection	105	CB
05/09/1970	Changes	The Outsiders (featuring Sonny Geraci)	107	BB
05/09/1970	Lonely Soldier	William Bell	107	CB

05/09/1970	Revolution In My Soul	The Reivers	112	BB
05/09/1970	When Will It End	The Honey Cone	113	CB
05/09/1970	Here I Stand	Crossroads	115	BB
05/09/1970	Gimme Some (Part I)	General Crook	119	CB
05/09/1970	Two Little Rooms	Trella Hart	120	BB
05/09/1970	Half As Much	Sonny Charles	121	CB
05/09/1970	Pieces Of Dreams	Johnny Mathis	129	CB
12/09/1970	Wait For Summer	Jack Wild	101	CB
12/09/1970	Father Come On Home	Pacific Gas & Electric	102	CB
12/09/1970	Money Music	The Boys In The Band Featuring Herman Griffin	104	CB
12/09/1970	I'll Never Get Enough	The RoBBs	106	BB
12/09/1970	For Yasgur's Farm	Mountain	107	BB
12/09/1970	All I Want To Be Is Your Woman	Carolyn Franklin	108	BB
12/09/1970	Alone Again Or	Love	111	CB
12/09/1970	All These Things	The Uniques	112	BB
12/09/1970	Baby Don't Take Your Love	Faith, Hope & Charity	113	CB
12/09/1970	Rainmaker	The Moods	113	BB
12/09/1970	And You Do	Charade	116	BB
12/09/1970	Knock Knock Who's There	Liv Maessen	118	CB
12/09/1970	Roxanna (Thank You For Getting Me High)	Wild Butter	118	CB
19/09/1970	Money Music	The Boys In The Band Featuring Herman Griffin	103	BB
19/09/1970	Loving You Is A Natural Thing	Ronnie Milsap	104	CB
19/09/1970	The Song Is Love	Petula Clark	106	CB
19/09/1970	Why Don't They Understand	BoBBy Vinton	109	BB
19/09/1970	You're Gonna Make It	The Festivals	114	BB
19/09/1970	Days Of Icy Fingers	Country Store	117	CB
19/09/1970	When Will It End	The Honey Cone	117	BB
19/09/1970	Ain't That Tellin' You People	The Original Caste	120	CB
19/09/1970	Shady Lady	Gene Pitney	139	CB
26/09/1970	Mellow Dreaming	Young-Holt Unlimited	106	BB

26/09/1970	Every Night	Billy Joe Royal	113	BB
26/09/1970	My God And I	BoBBy Goldsboro	116	CB
26/09/1970	It's Me I'm Running From	The Source	120	CB
26/09/1970	Reverend Lee	Roberta Flack	125	CB
26/09/1970	Wild World	Jimmy Cliff	132	CB
26/09/1970	Fool	Blue Cheer	136	CB
26/09/1970	Man Without A Dream	Mauds	138	CB
03/10/1970	Laugh	The Neighborhood	104	BB
03/10/1970	The Best Years Of My Life	Eddie Floyd	105	CB
03/10/1970	From Atlanta To Goodbye	The Manhattans	107	CB
03/10/1970	Too Many People	Cold Blood	107	BB
03/10/1970	Jolie Girl	Marty RoBBins	115	CB
03/10/1970	Half As Much	Sonny Charles	116	BB
03/10/1970	Ain't That Tellin' You People	The Original Caste	117	BB
03/10/1970	Why Does A Man Do What He Has To Do	Joe South	118	BB
03/10/1970	Mellow Dreaming	Young-Holt Unlimited	121	CB
03/10/1970	Melody	The Ides Of March	121	CB
03/10/1970	Melody	The Ides Of March	122	BB
03/10/1970	Watch Out Girl	O'kaysions	130	CB
10/10/1970	Dreams	Buddy Miles	101	CB
10/10/1970	Country Road	Merry Clayton	103	BB
10/10/1970	Lucy	CraBBy Appleton	103	CB
10/10/1970	One Light Two Lights	The Satisfactions	107	CB
10/10/1970	We All Sung Together	Grin	108	BB
10/10/1970	Measure The Valleys	Keith Textor Singers	112	BB
17/10/1970	Cathy Called	Eddie Holman	102	CB
17/10/1970	Hey, Girl	The Lettermen	111	CB
17/10/1970	Stop! I Don't Wanna' Hear It Anymore	Melanie	112	BB
17/10/1970	The Best Years Of My Life	Eddie Floyd	118	BB
17/10/1970	This World	The Sweet Inspirations	119	CB

17/10/1970	I Did It	Barbara Acklin	121	BB
17/10/1970	Willpower	Jackie Moore	129	CB
17/10/1970	I Can't Be Myself	Merle Haggard And The Strangers	106a	BB
24/10/1970	Spirit In The Sky	Dorothy Morrison	101	CB
24/10/1970	Valley To Pray	Arlo Guthrie	102	BB
24/10/1970	The Good Times Are Coming	Mamas Cass Elliot	104	BB
24/10/1970	Endlessly	Sonny James, The Southern Gentleman	108	BB
24/10/1970	Jolie Girl	Marty RoBBins	108	BB
24/10/1970	Young Man (Blues) (Live)	The Who	109	CB
24/10/1970	I Believe In Music	Mac Davis	117	BB
24/10/1970	They Call It Rock & Roll Music	Delaney & Bonnie & Friends	119	BB
24/10/1970	Something In The Air	Thunderclap Newman	120	BB
24/10/1970	The Good Times Are Coming	Mamas Cass Elliot	121	CB
24/10/1970	Poquito Soul	One G Plus Three	122	BB
24/10/1970	Sidewalks Of Chicago (b-side)	Merle Haggard And The Strangers	106b	BB
31/10/1970	Detroit City	Dean Martin	101	BB
31/10/1970	Me About You	The Turtles	101	CB
31/10/1970	I Loved You Like I Love My Very Life	Carla Thomas	104	CB
31/10/1970	The Man, The Wife And The Little Baby Daughter	Phil Flowers	108	CB
31/10/1970	Run, Woman, Run	Tammy Wynette	114	CB
31/10/1970	A Woman's Way	Rozetta Johnson	119	CB
31/10/1970	This World	The Sweet Inspirations	123	BB
07/11/1970	From The Very Start	The Children	103	CB
07/11/1970	Hey, Girl	The Lettermen	104	BB
07/11/1970	From The Very Start	The Children	105	BB
07/11/1970	Me About You	The Turtles	105	BB
07/11/1970	Workin' Together	Ike & Tina Turner	105	BB
07/11/1970	Special Memory	Jerry Butler	109	BB
07/11/1970	To The Other Man	Luther Ingram	110	BB
07/11/1970	True Love Is Greater Than Friendship	Al Martino	110	CB

07/11/1970	From Atlanta To Goodbye	The Manhattans	113	BB
07/11/1970	Lucy	CraBBy Appleton	114	BB
07/11/1970	We All Sung Together	Grin	114	CB
07/11/1970	Steve Miller's Midnight Tango	Steve Miller Band	117	BB
07/11/1970	Evil Ways	Johnny Mathis	118	CB
07/11/1970	Stealing Moments From Another Woman's Life	The Glass House	121	BB
07/11/1970	Ten Pound Note	Steel River	121	CB
14/11/1970	Lead Me On	Gwen Mccrae	102	BB
14/11/1970	Mama Mama	James Anderson	106	BB
14/11/1970	For A Friend	The Bugaloos	107	CB
14/11/1970	Ten Pound Note	Steel River	109	BB
14/11/1970	Brush A Little Sunshine	Tommy Roe	117	BB
14/11/1970	Lead Me On	Gwen Mccrae	120	CB
14/11/1970	Hey, Mr. Holy Man	Kiss Inc.	122	CB
14/11/1970	Right On Be Free	The Voices Of East Harlem	123	CB
14/11/1970	The Young Hearts Get Lonely Too	The New Young Hearts	123	BB
21/11/1970	Life Is That Way	José Feliciano	101	CB
21/11/1970	Back To The River	Damnation Of Adam Blessing	102	BB
21/11/1970	Johnny B. Badde	Mungo Jerry	103	CB
21/11/1970	You Can Get It If You Really Want	Desmond Dekker & The Aces	103	BB
21/11/1970	Montego Bay	The Bar-Kays	108	CB
21/11/1970	Goddess Of Love	The Gentrys	119	BB
21/11/1970	Goddess Of Love	The Gentrys	121	CB
21/11/1970	Wait A Minute	The Lost Generation	127	BB
28/11/1970	Brush A Little Sunshine	Tommy Roe	102	CB
28/11/1970	Think About Your Children	Mary Hopkin	104	CB
28/11/1970	Indian Lady	Lou Christie	106	BB
28/11/1970	Scratch My Back	Tony Joe White	111	CB
28/11/1970	Gasoline Alley Bred	Hollies	113	CB
28/11/1970	No Such Animal Part I	Jimi Hendrix	115	CB

28/11/1970	Strawberry Fields/Something	Pozo Seco	115	BB
28/11/1970	Scratch My Back	Tony Joe White	117	BB
28/11/1970	Until It's Time For You To Go	Buffy Sainte-Marie	122	CB
05/12/1970	Lady Day	Frank Sinatra	104	CB
05/12/1970	The Shape I'm In	The Band	104	CB
05/12/1970	The Wonders You Perform	Tammy Wynette	104	BB
05/12/1970	Hang In There, Baby	Robin Mcnamara	105	CB
05/12/1970	Can't You	Paul Davis	106	CB
05/12/1970	I Wouldn't Live In New York City (If They Gave Me The Whole Dang	Buck Owens And The Buckaroos	110	BB
05/12/1970	Somebody's Changin' My Sweet Baby's Mind	Little Milton Campbell	110	CB
05/12/1970	There's A Love For Everyone	The Whispers	110	CB
05/12/1970	I'm Alright	Lynn Anderson	112	BB
05/12/1970	Changes - Part Ii	King Curtis & The Kingpins	116	CB
05/12/1970	Down To The Wire	Yellow Hand	120	BB
05/12/1970	Don't Let The Good Life Pass You By	Mamas Cass Elliot	124	CB
12/12/1970	When There's No Love Left	The New Seekers	101	CB
12/12/1970	Hey America	James Brown	105	BB
12/12/1970	The Man, The Wife, & The Little Baby Daughter	Phil Flowers	106	BB
12/12/1970	Airport Song	Magna Carta	111	BB
12/12/1970	Don't Let The Sun Catch You Crying	Gerry And The Pacemakers	112	BB
19/12/1970	Now That I Have Found You	Larry Santos	103	CB
19/12/1970	Funky	The Chambers Brothers	106	BB
19/12/1970	I Was A Boy When You Needed A Man	Michael Allen	109	CB
19/12/1970	Don't Let The Good Life Pass You By	Mamas Cass Elliot	110	BB
19/12/1970	Can't You	Paul Davis	118	BB
19/12/1970	Chestnut Mare	The Byrds	121	BB
19/12/1970	A Rose By Any Other Name (Is Still A Rose)	Ronnie Milsap	125	BB
19/12/1970	For A Friend	The Bugaloos	128	BB
26/12/1970	Never Marry A Railroad Man	The Shocking Blue	102	BB
26/12/1970	Together We Two	The Archies	113	CB

26/12/1970	Right On	The Rascals	116	CB
26/12/1970	There's A Love For Everyone	The Whispers	116	BB
26/12/1970	Hey America	James Brown	126	CB
02/01/1971	Must Be Love Coming Down	Major Lance	103	CB
02/01/1971	Coal Miner's Daughter	Loretta Lynn	107	CB
02/01/1971	Mama	Heintje	112	BB
02/01/1971	Now That I Have Found You	Larry Santos	114	BB
02/01/1971	Bein' Green	Frank Sinatra	115	CB
02/01/1971	Georgia Sunshine	Dean Martin	117	CB
02/01/1971	Revival (Love Is Everywhere)	The Allman Brothers Band	119	CB
02/01/1971	Right On	The Rascals	119	BB
02/01/1971	The Shape I'm In	The Band	121	BB
09/01/1971	We Can Make The World (A Whole Lot Brighter)	Gravy	107	CB
09/01/1971	Joshua	Dolly Parton	108	BB
09/01/1971	Something To Make You Happy	Mason & Cass	110	CB
09/01/1971	A Good Year For The Roses	George Jones	112	BB
09/01/1971	Padre	Marty RoBBins	113	BB
09/01/1971	Love Vibrations	David T. Walker	117	BB
09/01/1971	Love Vibrations	David T. Walker	118	CB
09/01/1971	Together We Two	The Archies	122	BB
16/01/1971	Because It's Time	Mckendree Spring	105	BB
16/01/1971	Rainin' In My Heart	Hank Williams, Jr. With The Mike Curb Congregation	108	BB
16/01/1971	Who's Gonna Take The Weight (Part One)	Kool & The Gang	113	BB
23/01/1971	Now I'm A Woman	Nancy Wilson	101	CB
23/01/1971	Super Highway	Ballin' Jack	102	CB
23/01/1971	Little Miss Goodie Two Shoes	Tommy Roe	104	BB
23/01/1971	Medley From "SUPERSTAR" (A Rock Opera)	The Assembled Multitude	106	CB
23/01/1971	Nothing Rhymed	Gilbert O'sullivan	106	CB
23/01/1971	Are You My Woman? (Tell Me So)	The Chi-Lites	108	CB
23/01/1971	Help For My Waiting	The Dorians	112	CB

23/01/1971	Theme From "LOVE Story"	Peter Nero	112	CB
23/01/1971	Keep The Candle Burning	Raintree	115	CB
23/01/1971	Georgia Sunshine	Dean Martin	118	BB
23/01/1971	When I'm Dead And Gone	Bob Summers	118	BB
23/01/1971	Must Be Love Coming Down	Major Lance	119	BB
23/01/1971	A Child No One Wanted	Brenda & The Tabulations	120	BB
23/01/1971	What'll I Do	The New Birth	120	CB
23/01/1971	Brand New Day	Rufus	121	CB
23/01/1971	Guess Who	Slim Whitman	121	BB
23/01/1971	Come Sundown	BoBBy Bare	122	BB
23/01/1971	I've Been Loving You Too Long (Live)	Otis Redding	122	CB
23/01/1971	Beside You	The New York Rock Ensemble	123	BB
30/01/1971	Wooly Bully	Canned Heat	101	CB
30/01/1971	Because It's Time	Mckendree Spring	108	CB
30/01/1971	When I'm Dead And Gone	Bob Summers	113	CB
30/01/1971	She's Comin' Back	Alfie Khan	118	CB
30/01/1971	The Sheriff Of Boone County	Kenny Price	119	BB
30/01/1971	All Kinds Of People	Burt Bacharach	120	CB
06/02/1971	Carolina Day	Livingston Taylor	104	CB
06/02/1971	I've Been Loving You Too Long [Live]	Otis Redding	110	BB
06/02/1971	Drownin' On Dry Land	Junior Parker	114	BB
06/02/1971	All Kinds Of People	Burt Bacharach	116	BB
06/02/1971	Baby Jump	Mungo Jerry	116	CB
06/02/1971	What Good Is I Love You	Dusty Springfield	116	CB
06/02/1971	I'll Be Home	Vikki Carr	117	CB
06/02/1971	Little Miss Goody Two Shoes	Tommy Roe	130	CB
13/02/1971	Stop The World And Let Me Off	The Flaming Ember	101	BB
13/02/1971	Get Your Lie Straight	Bill Coday	105	BB
13/02/1971	(Where Do I Begin) Love Story	Tony Bennett	114	BB
13/02/1971	Cold Night In Georgia	Dee Dee Warwick	118	CB

13/02/1971	Too Many Lovers	Shack	118	BB
13/02/1971	Waitin' On You	Dave Mason	122	CB
20/02/1971	Don't Stop Loving Me	David Ruffin	103	CB
20/02/1971	Pencil Marks On The Wall	Herschel Bernardi	105	CB
20/02/1971	London Bridge	Alive 'N Kickin'	107	CB
20/02/1971	I Can't Help It	The Moments	108	BB
20/02/1971	Carry Your Own Load	Jr. Walker & The All Stars	117	BB
20/02/1971	Shake Your Big Hips	Israel "Popper Stopper" Tolbert	120	CB
27/02/1971	Who Do You Love	Tom Rush	105	BB
27/02/1971	Pencil Marks On The Wall	Herschel Bernardi	107	BB
27/02/1971	Life	Rick Nelson And The Stone Canyon Band	109	BB
27/02/1971	Watching Can Waste Up The Time	Crow	110	CB
06/03/1971	Come Into My Life (Lass Das Weinen Sein)	Al Martino	104	CB
06/03/1971	Wooly Bully	Canned Heat	105	BB
06/03/1971	Gettin' In Over My Head	Badge	110	CB
06/03/1971	Life	Rick Nelson & The Stone Canyon Band	110	CB
06/03/1971	Skyscrapter Commando	Elephant's Memory	110	CB
06/03/1971	I Believe In Music	Marian Love	111	BB
06/03/1971	Don't Stop Loving Me	David Ruffin	112	BB
06/03/1971	Nothing Rhymed	Gilbert O'sullivan	114	BB
06/03/1971	A Stranger In My Place	Anne Murray	115	CB
06/03/1971	When You Took Your Love From Me	O.V. Wright	118	BB
06/03/1971	A Stranger In My Place	Anne Murray	122	BB
06/03/1971	No Love At All	BoBBi Martin	123	BB
06/03/1971	Anytime Sunshine	Crazy Paving	126	CB
13/03/1971	Anytime Sunshine	Crazy Paving	103	BB
13/03/1971	Chirpy Chirpy, Cheep Cheep	Lally Stott	110	CB
13/03/1971	Save My Love For A Rainy Day	The Undisputed Truth	111	CB
13/03/1971	Hey, Does Somebody Care	God's Children	112	BB
13/03/1971	The Arms Of A Fool	Mel Tillis And The Statesiders	114	BB

13/03/1971	Girls In The City	The Esquires	120	BB
13/03/1971	The Promised Land	Freddy Weller	125	BB
13/03/1971	When Love Is Near	The Original Caste	128	CB
20/03/1971	(Do The) Hot Pants	Mr. Jim & The Rhythm Machine	102	CB
20/03/1971	We Sure Can Love Each Other	Tammy Wynette	103	BB
20/03/1971	On My Side	The Cowsills	109	CB
20/03/1971	Nature's Way	Spirit	111	BB
20/03/1971	I'd Rather Love You	Charley Pride	113	CB
20/03/1971	My Heart Is Yours	Wilbert Harrison	116	CB
20/03/1971	Get Your Lie Straight	Bill Coday	117	CB
20/03/1971	Bridge Over Troubled Water	Buck Owens And The Buckaroos	119	BB
20/03/1971	Getting' In Over My Head	Badge	119	BB
20/03/1971	Go On Fool	Marion Black	124	BB
20/03/1971	Signs	BoBBy Vee	125	CB
20/03/1971	You Wants To Play	Oscar Weathers	125	BB
20/03/1971	Do Right Woman - Do Right Man	Barbara Mandrell	128	BB
27/03/1971	Shake A Hand	José Feliciano	106	CB
27/03/1971	I Play Dirty	Little Milton	109	CB
27/03/1971	I Can't Stop	The Osmond Brothers	119	CB
27/03/1971	I've Been There	O.C. Smith	120	CB
27/03/1971	The Highway Song	Free	129	CB
03/04/1971	I'll Make You My Baby	BoBBy Vinton	101	BB
03/04/1971	Live Till You Die	Emitt Rhodes	103	CB
03/04/1971	Lonely Feelin'	War Featuring Lonnie Jordan	107	BB
03/04/1971	On My Side	The Cowsills	108	BB
03/04/1971	If I Could	Gordon Lightfoot	111	BB
03/04/1971	Warpath	Isley Brothers	111	BB
03/04/1971	Knock Three Times	Billy "Crash" Craddock	113	BB
03/04/1971	Early Mornin' Rain	Oliver	118	CB
03/04/1971	I'll Make You My Baby	BoBBy Vinton	122	CB

03/04/1971	We Sure Can Love Each Other	Tammy Wynette	125	CB
03/04/1971	Tomorrow Night In Baltimore	Roger Miller	128	CB
10/04/1971	Light As A Feather	Redbone	105	CB
10/04/1971	Home Cookin'	Eric Burdon And War	108	BB
10/04/1971	Married To A Memory	Judy Lynn	109	CB
10/04/1971	The Troublemaker	Della Reese	110	CB
10/04/1971	If I Could	Gordon Lightfoot	112	CB
10/04/1971	Driving Wheel	Al Green	115	BB
10/04/1971	I Need You Baby	Jesse James	118	CB
10/04/1971	Home Cookin'	Eric Burdon & War	119	CB
10/04/1971	Heaven Help Us All	Brook Benton With The Dixie Flyers	120	CB
17/04/1971	Sweet Mary	Argent	102	BB
17/04/1971	To Lay Down Beside You	Joe Simon	102	CB
17/04/1971	How Much More Can She Stand	Conway Twitty	105	BB
17/04/1971	California Blues	Redwing	108	BB
17/04/1971	Plain And Simple Girl	Garland Green	109	BB
17/04/1971	Always Remember	Bill Anderson	111	BB
17/04/1971	It's Time For Love	Dennis Yost & The Classics Iv	111	CB
17/04/1971	Help Me Make It Through The Night	Percy Sledge	115	CB
17/04/1971	A Child Is Coming	Paul Kantner - Jefferson Starship	121	CB
17/04/1971	Pistol Legged Mama	Tommy Roe	124	BB
17/04/1971	Crazy Love	Rita Coolidge	129	CB
24/04/1971	Let The Sun Shine In	Magic Lanterns	103	BB
24/04/1971	Married To A Memory	Judy Lynn	104	BB
24/04/1971	Baby Blue	Blizzard	106	BB
24/04/1971	Sailin'	Jo Mama	107	CB
24/04/1971	Mr. And Mrs. Untrue	Candi Staton	109	BB
24/04/1971	The Battle Hymn Of Lt. Calley	John Deer	114	BB
24/04/1971	Baby Show It	The Festivals	116	BB
24/04/1971	Creeping Away	Swamp Dogg	117	CB

24/04/1971	Teddy Bear	Reggie Garner	117	BB
24/04/1971	To Lay Down Beside You	Joe Simon	117	BB
24/04/1971	Brother	The New Christy Minstrels	124	CB
01/05/1971	Jumpin' Jack Flash (Live)	Johnny Winter	101	CB
01/05/1971	Do What You Gotta Do	Roberta Flack	106	CB
01/05/1971	Stop Your Cryin'	Chocolate Syrup	107	CB
01/05/1971	Ain't Nothing Gonna Change Me	Betty Everett	113	BB
01/05/1971	Get High On Jesus	The U.S. Apple Corps	120	CB
01/05/1971	She's A Little Bit Country	Dean Martin	121	CB
01/05/1971	My Little One	The Marmalade	123	BB
01/05/1971	Early Mornin' Rain	Oliver	124	BB
08/05/1971	My Little One	The Marmalade	125	CB
15/05/1971	Love Song	The Vogues	101	CB
15/05/1971	We're All Goin' Home	BoBBy Bloom	105	CB
15/05/1971	Sunshine	The Flaming Ember	108	CB
15/05/1971	Hanging On (To) A Memory	Chairmen Of The Board	110	BB
15/05/1971	Only One Song	Sha Na Na	110	BB
15/05/1971	Then You Walk In	Sammi Smith	118	BB
15/05/1971	Someday, Someway (You're Gonna Love Me)	The Center Stage	122	CB
22/05/1971	Hanging On (To) A Memory	Chairmen Of The Board	102	CB
22/05/1971	When My Love Hand Comes Down	David & Jimmy Ruffin	104	CB
22/05/1971	California Earthquake	Norman Greenbaum	105	CB
22/05/1971	Awaiting On You All	Silver Hawk	108	BB
22/05/1971	Matthew And Son	Cat Stevens	109	CB
22/05/1971	Touching Home	Jerry Lee Lewis	110	BB
22/05/1971	Something Old, Something New	The Fantastics	111	CB
22/05/1971	Do What You Gotta Do	Roberta Flack	117	BB
22/05/1971	Sunshine	The Flaming Ember	117	BB
22/05/1971	I Only Want To Say (Gethsemane)	José Feliciano	119	CB
22/05/1971	Then You Walk In	Sammi Smith	120	CB

29/05/1971	Something Old, Something New	The Fantastics	102	BB
29/05/1971	Let Me Live	Charley Pride	104	BB
29/05/1971	The Preacher (Part 2)/More Than I Can Stand	BoBBy Womack	111	BB
29/05/1971	That's How It Feels	The Moments	118	CB
29/05/1971	It's A Sad Thing	Ollie Nightingale	121	BB
29/05/1971	I Only Want To Say (Gethsemane)	José Feliciano	122	BB
29/05/1971	Ten And Two (Take This Woman Off The Corner)	Gene & Jerry	123	CB
05/06/1971	And When She Smiles	The Wildweeds	101	CB
05/06/1971	It Won't Hurt To Try It	Tony Scotti	106	CB
05/06/1971	Are You Lonely?	Sisters Love	108	BB
05/06/1971	Call Me Up In Dreamland	Van Morrison	112	CB
05/06/1971	Money (That's What I Want)	The Mob	112	CB
05/06/1971	That's How It Feels	The Moments	115	BB
05/06/1971	Summertime	Herb Alpert & The Tijuana Brass	117	CB
05/06/1971	The Summer Knows (Theme From "Summer Of '42")	Roger Williams	118	CB
05/06/1971	Got To Get Enough (Of Your Sweet Love Stuff)	Roy "C"	120	CB
05/06/1971	(The World Is A Bit Under The Weather) Doodle-Oop	The Meters	124	CB
05/06/1971	Come Down In Time	Eugene Pitt & The Jyve Fyve	126	CB
12/06/1971	I've Got A Right To Cry	Hank Williams Jr.	102	BB
12/06/1971	Ruby (Are You Mad)	Buck Owens And The Buckaroos	106	BB
12/06/1971	Summertime	Herb Alpert & The Tijuana Brass	114	BB
12/06/1971	It Won't Hurt To Try It	Tony Scotti	118	BB
12/06/1971	Love Song	The Vogues	118	BB
12/06/1971	Sunlight	The Youngbloods	123	BB
19/06/1971	When My Little Girl Is Smiling	Steve Alaimo	101	CB
19/06/1971	In These Changing Times	Four Tops	102	CB
19/06/1971	I Want To Take You Higher [Live]	Kool & The Gang	105	BB
19/06/1971	Near You	Boz Scaggs	108	CB
19/06/1971	Bad Feet	Joe Tex	124	CB
19/06/1971	Singing In Viet Nam Talking Blues	Johnny Cash	124	BB

19/06/1971	Apple Bend	Johnny Tillotson	127	BB
26/06/1971	Jack In The Box	Clodagh Rodgers	116	CB
26/06/1971	You're A Lady	Gene Chandler	116	BB
26/06/1971	I Know You Got Soul	BoBBy Byrd	117	BB
26/06/1971	Touch Me Jesus	The Glass House	118	CB
26/06/1971	Just One Time	Connie Smith	119	BB
26/06/1971	So Long, Marianne	Brian Hyland	120	BB
26/06/1971	Driveway	100 Proof (Aged In Soul)	121	BB
26/06/1971	I'm Sorry	BoBBy Bland	121	CB
26/06/1971	Gwen (Congratulations)	Tommy Overstreet	123	BB
26/06/1971	Where Would I Be (Without You)	Edgar Winter's White Trash Featuring Jerry La Croix	128	BB
03/07/1971	Breezin'	Gabor Szabo/BoBBy Womack	103	CB
03/07/1971	Poor Little Pearl	Billy Joe Royal	103	CB
03/07/1971	Take My Hand	Kenny Rogers & The First Edition	103	CB
03/07/1971	Make It With You	Ralfi Pagan	104	CB
03/07/1971	Pray For Me	The Intruders	105	BB
03/07/1971	That Other Woman Got My Man And Gone	Margie Joseph	109	CB
03/07/1971	Step Into My World (Part 2)	The Magic Touch	114	BB
03/07/1971	Something In Your Blood	Crow	115	CB
03/07/1971	Charley's Picture	Porter Wagoner	116	BB
03/07/1971	The Chair	Marty RoBBins	121	BB
03/07/1971	The City	Mark-Almond	122	CB
03/07/1971	Ten And Two (Take This Woman Off The Corner)	Gene & Jerry	126	BB
03/07/1971	Reap What I've Sowed	Climax Blues Band	128	CB
10/07/1971	Poor Little Pearl	Billy Joe Royal	111	BB
10/07/1971	1-2-3-4	Lucky Peterson Blues Band	112	CB
10/07/1971	And When She Smiles	The Wildweeds	113	BB
10/07/1971	I Want To Take You Higher (Live)	Kool & The Gang	115	CB
17/07/1971	Indian Lake	Freddy Weller	108	BB
17/07/1971	Take My Hand	Mel Tillis And Sherry Bryce With The Statesiders	110	BB

17/07/1971	Nobody	The Doobie Brothers	122	BB
24/07/1971	Mare, Take Me Home	Matthews' Southern Comfort	101	CB
24/07/1971	Make It With You	Ralfi Pagan	104	BB
24/07/1971	Southbound Train	Steel River	106	BB
24/07/1971	Chicken Heads	BoBBy Rush	107	CB
24/07/1971	Here I Go Again	The Raeletts Featuring Estella Yarbrough	113	CB
24/07/1971	I Know You Got Soul	BoBBy Byrd	123	CB
24/07/1971	Hey! Love	The Delfonics	124	CB
24/07/1971	Are You Goin' My Way?	Free 'N' Easy	130	CB
31/07/1971	Here I Go Again	The Raeletts Featuring Estella Yarbrough	101	BB
31/07/1971	Orleans	David Crosby	101	CB
31/07/1971	California On My Mind	Morning Mist	102	CB
31/07/1971	Candy Apple Red	R. Dean Taylor	104	BB
31/07/1971	Good Lovin' (Makes It Right)	Tammy Wynette	111	BB
31/07/1971	I Can Make It Better	Castle Creek	112	CB
31/07/1971	I Wonder What She'll Think About Me Leaving	Conway Twitty	112	BB
31/07/1971	Tie-Dye Princess	The Ides Of March	113	BB
31/07/1971	Someday We'll Look Back	Merle Haggard And The Strangers	119	BB
31/07/1971	I've Been Loving You Too Long	Ike & Tina Turner	120	BB
31/07/1971	Are You Lonely?	Sisters Love	121	CB
07/08/1971	Amanda	Dionne Warwicke	101	CB
07/08/1971	It Takes All Kinds Of People	Stoney & Meatloaf	108	CB
07/08/1971	Love Me	The Impressions	111	CB
07/08/1971	Girl, I've Got News For You	Cherokee	116	BB
07/08/1971	I've Been Loving You Too Long	Ike & Tina Turner	121	CB
07/08/1971	Chotto Matte Kudasai (Never Say Goodbye)	The Sandpipers	125	CB
07/08/1971	God's Children	The Kinks	127	CB
14/08/1971	Got To Have Your Lovin'	King Floyd	101	BB
14/08/1971	If This Is Our Last Time	Brenda Lee	106	CB
14/08/1971	Breakdown	Parliament	107	BB

14/08/1971	Funky L.A.	Paul Humphrey & His Cool Aid Chemists	109	BB
14/08/1971	I Love The Way You Love	Betty Wright	109	BB
14/08/1971	Sweet Gingerbread Man	Mike Curb Congregation	115	BB
21/08/1971	1-2-3-4	Lucky Peterson Blues Band	102	BB
21/08/1971	Gotta' Get Over The Hump	Simtec & Wylie	104	CB
21/08/1971	A Song For You	Jaye P. Morgan	105	BB
21/08/1971	The Right Combination	Porter Wagoner And Dolly Parton	106	BB
21/08/1971	A Long Time, A Long Way To Go	Runt-Todd Rundgren	113	CB
28/08/1971	Lord Have Mercy On My Soul	Black Oak Arkansas	105	CB
28/08/1971	(Holy Moses!) Everything's Coming Up Roses	Jack Wild	107	BB
28/08/1971	A Song For You	Jaye P. Morgan	108	CB
28/08/1971	Zoo De Zoo Zong	Twiggy & Friends	110	CB
28/08/1971	Summer Side Of Life	Gordon Lightfoot	116	CB
28/08/1971	The Song Is Love	Mary Travers	118	CB
04/09/1971	Goodbye Media Man Part I	Tom Fogerty	103	BB
04/09/1971	Keep Me	Originals	103	CB
04/09/1971	New Jersey	England Dan & John Ford Coley	103	BB
04/09/1971	Blue Monday	Dave Edmunds	104	BB
04/09/1971	Hey Willy	The Hollies	110	BB
04/09/1971	Take You Where The Music's Playing	Dallas	114	CB
11/09/1971	Gotta' Get Over The Hump	Simtec & Wylie	101	BB
11/09/1971	Bend Me, Shape Me	Storm	105	BB
11/09/1971	Smackwater Jack	Carole King	112	CB
18/09/1971	Day By Day (Godspell Medley)	Holly Sherwood	104	BB
18/09/1971	Monkey Spanner	Dave & Ansell Collins	109	CB
25/09/1971	I'm An Easy Rider	My Friends	102	CB
25/09/1971	Solo	Billie Sans	102	CB
25/09/1971	A Nickel And A Nail	O.V. Wright	103	BB
25/09/1971	I Can't Give Back The Love I Feel For You	Vikki Carr	103	CB
25/09/1971	A Hard Rain's A Gonna Fall	Leon Russell	105	BB

25/09/1971	Girl, I've Got News For You	Cherokee	111	CB
25/09/1971	Keep It In The Family	The Road Home	113	CB
25/09/1971	Slipped, Tripped And Fell In Love	Ann Peebles	113	BB
25/09/1971	Thank You For The Love	The Bad Habits	116	CB
25/09/1971	Friends Of Mine	Mcguinness Flint	117	CB
25/09/1971	Keep It In The Family	The Road Home	120	BB
02/10/1971	Fallin', Lady	Punch	110	BB
02/10/1971	Saunders' Ferry Line	Sammi Smith	111	CB
02/10/1971	Monkey Tamarind	The Beginning Of The End	113	CB
09/10/1971	Give The Baby Anything The Baby Wants	Joe Tex	102	BB
09/10/1971	Try On My Love For Size	Chairmen Of The Board	103	BB
09/10/1971	Used To Be	Just Us	103	BB
09/10/1971	Funky RuBBer Band	Popcorn Wylie	105	CB
09/10/1971	Changes (Part I)	King Curtis	109	CB
09/10/1971	Glory, Glory	The Byrds	110	BB
16/10/1971	Tonight	The New Seekers	107	CB
16/10/1971	For All We Know	Shirley Bassey	108	CB
16/10/1971	Please Mrs. Henry	Manfred Mann	108	CB
23/10/1971	Everybody Wants To Go To Heaven	Albert King	103	BB
23/10/1971	Papa Was A Good Man	Johnny Cash And The Evangel Temple Choir	104	BB
23/10/1971	I Really Love You	Davy Jones	107	BB
23/10/1971	Chokin' Kind	Z.Z. Hill	108	BB
23/10/1971	Funky RuBBer Band	Popcorn Wylie	109	BB
30/10/1971	Look What We've Done To Love	The Glass House	101	BB
30/10/1971	Turn Your Radio On	Ray Stevens	102	CB
30/10/1971	Monday Man	Mike Curb Congregation	105	CB
30/10/1971	Mammy Blue	James Darren	107	BB
30/10/1971	Please Mrs. Henry	Manfred Mann	108	BB
30/10/1971	Serenade	The Shocking Blue	110	BB
30/10/1971	Down By The River	Joey Gregorash	113	BB

30/10/1971	Only The Children Know	Jeanie Greene	114	BB
30/10/1971	Tell Me Why	Matthews' Southern Comfort	114	CB
30/10/1971	Fireball	Deep Purple	120	CB
06/11/1971	Don't Turn Around	Black Ivory	104	CB
06/11/1971	People, Let's Stop The War	Grand Funk Railroad	105	CB
06/11/1971	Tomorrow	BoBBi Martin	112	CB
06/11/1971	Roses And Thorns	Jeannie C. Riley	115	CB
13/11/1971	A Child Of God (It's Hard To Believe)	Millie Jackson	102	BB
13/11/1971	I'm Yours (Use Me Anyway You Wanna)	Ike & Tina Turner	104	BB
13/11/1971	To You With Love	The Moments	106	CB
13/11/1971	A Child Of God (It's Hard To Believe)	Millie Jackson	107	CB
13/11/1971	Danny Is A Mirror To Me	BoBBy Goldsboro	107	BB
13/11/1971	Look What We've Done To Love	The Glass House	107	CB
13/11/1971	Marblehead Messenger	Seatrain	108	BB
13/11/1971	Just For Me And You	Poco	110	BB
20/11/1971	Can I	Eddie Kendricks	101	BB
20/11/1971	The Love You Left Behind	Syl Johnson	108	CB
20/11/1971	Lost Son	Frijid Pink	113	CB
20/11/1971	Danny Is A Mirror To Me	BoBBy Goldsboro	119	CB
20/11/1971	Help Me Make It Through The Night	O.C. Smith	120	CB
27/11/1971	Don't Pull Your Love	Sam & Dave	102	BB
27/11/1971	How Can I Pretend	The Continental 4	105	CB
27/11/1971	Movin' On (Part 2)	Buckwheat	105	CB
27/11/1971	Treat Me Like A Good Piece Of Candy	Dusk	106	BB
27/11/1971	Hope	Mason Proffit	108	BB
27/11/1971	Hope	Mason Proffit	110	CB
27/11/1971	I Used To Be A King	Graham Nash	111	BB
04/12/1971	Really Wanted You	Emitt Rhodes	108	CB
04/12/1971	Long Time To Be Alone	The New Colony Six	112	CB
04/12/1971	The Love Of My Man	Dionne Warwicke	117	CB

11/12/1971	Scratch My Back (And Mumble In My Ear)	Clarence Carter	101	BB
11/12/1971	The Rangers Waltz	The Moms And Dads	101	BB
11/12/1971	Sanctuary	Dion	103	BB
11/12/1971	Men Are Getting Scarce	Chairmen Of The Board	104	BB
11/12/1971	Can't Help But Love You	The Whispers	105	CB
11/12/1971	Space Captain	Barbra Streisand, Backed By Fanny	107	CB
11/12/1971	The Love Of My Man	Dionne Warwicke	107	BB
11/12/1971	To You With Love	The Moments	107	BB
11/12/1971	Bless The Beasts And Children	Carpenters	113	CB
11/12/1971	Rock Love	Steve Miller Band	118	CB
11/12/1971	To Know You Is To Love You	The Bells	119	CB
18/12/1971	The Pilgrim: Chapter 33	Kris Kristofferson	101	CB
18/12/1971	I'd Do It All Again	Vikki Carr	102	CB
18/12/1971	Let One Hurt Do	L.J. Reynolds & Chocolate Syrup	104	BB
18/12/1971	When I Meet Them	Seals & Crofts	104	BB
18/12/1971	Space Captain	Barbra Streisand, Backed By Fanny	105	BB
18/12/1971	(We've Got To) Pull Together	The Nite-Liters	110	CB
18/12/1971	Hey Ruby (Shut Your Mouth)	Ruby & The Party Gang	117	CB
25/12/1971	Love And Liberty	Laura Lee	101	CB
25/12/1971	Hey Ruby (Shut Your Mouth)	Ruby And The Party Gang	105	BB
25/12/1971	Sensuous Woman	The Mystic Moods Orchestra	106	BB
25/12/1971	I'm Leaving This Time	The Main Ingredient	108	CB
25/12/1971	Joy	The Ventures	109	BB
25/12/1971	When I Meet Them	Seals & Crofts	112	CB
01/01/1972	Rock 'N' Roll	Detroit Featuring Mitch Ryder	107	BB
01/01/1972	Water, Paper & Clay	Mary Hopkin	113	BB
08/01/1972	Oklahoma Sunday Morning	Glen Campbell	102	CB
08/01/1972	Music From Across The Way	James Last	103	CB
08/01/1972	Oklahoma Sunday Morning	Glen Campbell	104	BB
08/01/1972	Rock & Roll Stew...Part 1	Traffic	105	CB

08/01/1972	I Can't Do It For You	Trade Martin	106	BB
08/01/1972	Why Didn't I Think Of That	Brenda & The Tabulations	107	BB
08/01/1972	Roll Over Beethoven	Mountain	111	CB
08/01/1972	Bedtime Story	Tammy Wynette	114	CB
08/01/1972	Tryin' To Stay 'Live	The Asylum Choir (lead Vocal: Leon Russell)	115	BB
15/01/1972	The Road We Didn't Take	Freda Payne	101	CB
15/01/1972	Bound	Ponderosa Twins + One	102	BB
15/01/1972	When You Get Right Down To It	Barry Mann	105	BB
15/01/1972	You Really Got A Hold On Me	Gayle Mccormick	109	CB
15/01/1972	A Mother's Prayer	Joe Tex	113	CB
15/01/1972	When You Get Right Down To It	Barry Mann	114	CB
15/01/1972	See What You Done, Done (Hymn #9)	Delia Gartrell	120	CB
22/01/1972	See What You've Done, Done (Hymn #9)	Delia Gartrell	101	BB
22/01/1972	I Love You - Stop	The Stairsteps	110	CB
22/01/1972	Music From Across The Way	Andy Williams	111	CB
22/01/1972	A Heartache, A Shadow, A Lifetime (I'll Be Home)	Dave Mason	117	CB
29/01/1972	Cotton Jenny	Anne Murray	102	CB
29/01/1972	A Thing Called Love	Johnny Cash And The Evangel Temple Choir	103	BB
29/01/1972	You Got Me Walking	Jackie Wilson	112	CB
29/01/1972	20th Century Man	The Kinks	113	CB
29/01/1972	What's Yesterday	Dean Martin	115	CB
29/01/1972	I Can't Do It For You	Trade Martin	119	CB
05/02/1972	Get Out Of Bed	Livingston Taylor	101	CB
05/02/1972	Tokoloshe Man	John Kongos	106	CB
05/02/1972	City Of New Orleans	Steve Goodman	113	BB
05/02/1972	A Breath Taking Guy	The Marvelettes	118	CB
05/02/1972	It's Gonna Take A Miracle	Laura Nyro	120	CB
05/02/1972	Theme From Nicholas And Alexandra	Henry Mancini, His Orchestra & Chorus	121	CB
12/02/1972	It's Gonna Take A Miracle	Laura Nyro	103	BB
12/02/1972	Step Out	The Mamas & The Papas	103	CB

12/02/1972	His Song Shall Be Sung	Lou Rawls	105	BB
12/02/1972	20th Century Man	The Kinks	106	BB
12/02/1972	Your Love	The Persians	108	BB
12/02/1972	I Love You - Stop	The Stairsteps	115	BB
12/02/1972	I Think About Lovin' You	Earth, Wind & Fire	115	CB
12/02/1972	That's Alright (I Don't Mind It)	Alzo	116	BB
12/02/1972	You And Me Together Forever	Freddie North	116	BB
12/02/1972	Your Love	The Persians	120	CB
12/02/1972	A Poem For My Little Lady	BoBBy Goldsboro	130	CB
19/02/1972	In And Out Of My Life	Martha Reeves & The Vandellas	102	BB
19/02/1972	Brian's Song	Peter Nero	105	BB
19/02/1972	A Man Who Sings	Richard Landis	106	CB
19/02/1972	Tokoloshe Man	John Kongos	111	BB
19/02/1972	Can't Help But Love You	The Whispers	114	BB
19/02/1972	Sophisticated Lady	R.E.O. Speedwagon	115	CB
19/02/1972	We Got To Have Peace	Curtis Mayfield	115	BB
19/02/1972	Will The Circle Be Unbroken	Joan Baez	115	CB
19/02/1972	A Thing Called Love	Johnny Cash & The Evangel Temple Choir	120	CB
19/02/1972	Down From Dover	Nancy Sinatra And Lee Hazlewood	120	BB
26/02/1972	Breaking Up Somebody's Home	Ann Peebles	101	BB
26/02/1972	Everybody's Reaching Out For Someone	Pat Daisy	101	CB
26/02/1972	Rock Me On The Water	Linda Ronstadt	101	CB
26/02/1972	A Man Who Sings	Richard Landis	102	BB
26/02/1972	Brian's Song	Peter Nero	105	CB
26/02/1972	Da Doo Ron Ron (When He Walked Me Home)	Ian Matthews	105	CB
26/02/1972	Good Friends?	The Poppy Family Vocal: Susan Jacks	105	BB
26/02/1972	Love The Life You Live (Part Ii)	Kool & The Gang	107	BB
26/02/1972	Missing You	Luther Ingram	108	BB
26/02/1972	Stoney Ground	The Foundations	113	BB
26/02/1972	Time To Change	The Brady Bunch	116	CB

26/02/1972	Yum Yum Yum (I Want Some)	Eddie Floyd	122	BB
04/03/1972	I'm Someone Who Cares	The Originals	113	BB
04/03/1972	Sally Sunshine	The Mills Brothers	118	CB
04/03/1972	Sophisticated Lady	Reo Speedwagon	122	BB
11/03/1972	Monday Morning Choo-Choo	Stampeders	103	CB
11/03/1972	Everybody's Reaching Out For Someone	Pat Daisy	112	BB
11/03/1972	Frisco Bay	Navajo	116	CB
11/03/1972	Love Brought You Here	Pat Johnson	116	CB
11/03/1972	It's Four In The Morning	Faron Young	119	CB
11/03/1972	Ironside (Theme From "IRONSIDE" - Nbc-Tv)*	Quincy Jones	120	CB
11/03/1972	Sea Trip	Homar Jackson	122	CB
11/03/1972	Love The Life You Live (Part I)	Kool & The Gang	126	CB
18/03/1972	Poppa Joe	The Sweet	105	CB
18/03/1972	Leavin' It's Over	Hudson	110	BB
18/03/1972	One Good Woman	Hamilton, Joe Frank & Reynolds	110	CB
18/03/1972	One Good Woman	Hamilton, Joe Frank & Reynolds	113	BB
18/03/1972	Inner City Blues	Grover Washington, Jr.	120	BB
18/03/1972	(Is This The Way To) Amarillo	Tony Christie	126	CB
18/03/1972	Train Of Glory	Johnathan Edwards	101a	BB
18/03/1972	Everybody Knows Her (b-side)	Johnathan Edwards	106b	BB
25/03/1972	Rockin' With The King	Canned Heat	102	CB
25/03/1972	Little Ghetto Boy (Live)	Donny Hathaway	104	CB
25/03/1972	Open Up Your Heart	Rainbow	105	CB
25/03/1972	Darling Baby	Jackie Moore	106	BB
25/03/1972	Eve	Jim Capaldi	111	CB
25/03/1972	My Honey And Me	The Emotions	113	BB
25/03/1972	(Is This The Way To) Amarillo	Tony Christie	121	BB
01/04/1972	Hot Thang	Eddy Senay	101	CB
01/04/1972	I'm Gettin' Tired Baby	Betty Wright	108	CB
01/04/1972	When You Got Trouble	Redbone	111	BB

01/04/1972	Sing A Song	David Clayton Thomas	112	BB
01/04/1972	Manhattan Kansas	Glen Campbell	114	BB
01/04/1972	Love Theme From The Godfather	Roger Williams	116	BB
01/04/1972	The Bus	Billy Preston	117	CB
01/04/1972	(Straight To Your Heart) Like A Cannonball	Van Morrison	119	BB
01/04/1972	Don't Ever Take Away My Freedom	Peter Yarrow	120	CB
01/04/1972	Angel Of Mercy	Albert King	128	CB
08/04/1972	Hot Thang	Eddy Senay	104	BB
08/04/1972	School Teacher	Kenny Rogers & The First Edition	104	CB
08/04/1972	Doing My Own Thing (Part 1)	Johnnie Taylor (The Soul Philosopher)	109	BB
08/04/1972	Little Ghetto Boy [Live]	Donny Hathaway	109	BB
08/04/1972	Love Theme From "THE Godfather"	Ferrante & Teicher	110	CB
08/04/1972	You And I	Black Ivory	111	BB
08/04/1972	Take Up The Hammer Of Hope	Mike Curb Congregation	114	CB
08/04/1972	Love Theme From The Godfather	Roger Williams	115	CB
08/04/1972	I'm Gettin' Tired Baby (b-side)	Betty Wright	121	BB
08/04/1972	My Hang-Up Is You	Freddie Hart	121	CB
15/04/1972	Mother Of Mine	Little Jimmy Osmond	101	BB
15/04/1972	Let Me Run Into Your Lonely Heart	Eddie Kendricks	103	CB
15/04/1972	Mother Of Mine	Little Jimmy Osmond	107	CB
15/04/1972	California Wine	BoBBy Goldsboro	108	BB
15/04/1972	We'll Make It - I Know We Will	Lobo	108	CB
15/04/1972	Someone, Sometime	The New Colony Six	109	BB
15/04/1972	Open Up Your Heart	Rainbow	114	BB
15/04/1972	The Albatross	Lobo	128	CB
22/04/1972	He Will Break Your Heart	Johnny Williams	104	BB
22/04/1972	If You Love Me The Way You Say You Love Me	Betty Wright	104	BB
22/04/1972	Do You Remember These	The Statler Brothers	105	BB
22/04/1972	Feel The Need	Damon Shawn	105	BB
22/04/1972	Little Dog Heaven	June Jackson	105	CB

22/04/1972	Keep On Truckin'	Hot Tuna	108	CB
22/04/1972	Love Theme From "THE Godfather"	Hugo Montenegro	108	CB
22/04/1972	California Wine	BoBBy Goldsboro	113	CB
22/04/1972	This Love's For Real	The Impressions	119	CB
22/04/1972	This I Find Is Beautiful	Storm	121	CB
22/04/1972	Home Is Where The Hatred Is	Esther Phillips	122	BB
22/04/1972	I Think Somebody Loves Me	James Darren	122	CB
29/04/1972	Feel The Need	Damon Shawn	103	CB
29/04/1972	Hold On To Freedom	Lee Michaels	104	CB
29/04/1972	The Lonesomest Lonesome	Ray Price	109	BB
29/04/1972	Free Your Mind	The Politicians	110	BB
29/04/1972	Before The Honeymoon	Little Milton	117	CB
29/04/1972	To Be Free	Dave Mason	121	BB
06/05/1972	I Can't Quit Your Love	Four Tops	108	CB
06/05/1972	Raindrops Keep Falling On My Head	Dionne Warwicke	108	CB
06/05/1972	Where There's A Will There's A Way	Delaney & Bonnie	110	CB
06/05/1972	Free Your Mind	The Politicians	115	CB
06/05/1972	House On Holly Road	David Idema	116	CB
13/05/1972	Feel Good	Ike & Tina Turner	101	CB
13/05/1972	If You Got A Love You Better (Hold On To It)	BoBBy Byrd	103	CB
13/05/1972	Darling Be Home Soon	The Association	104	BB
13/05/1972	Sweeter Than Sweetness	Freddie North	107	CB
13/05/1972	Mighty Mighty And Roly Poly	Mal	108	BB
13/05/1972	Kum Ba Yah	The Hillside Singers	112	CB
13/05/1972	Thundermama	Thundermama	117	CB
13/05/1972	Do You Remember These	The Statler Brothers	120	CB
13/05/1972	The Masterpiece	Charles Randolph Grean Sounde	124	CB
20/05/1972	I Can't Quit Your Love	Four Tops	102	BB
20/05/1972	I Can Feel It	Chase	105	BB
20/05/1972	I Thank You	Donny Hathaway & June Conquest	105	CB

20/05/1972	Life Is What You Make It (Part 1)	Buddy Miles	107	CB
20/05/1972	It's So Easy (To Be Bad)	Ranji	109	BB
20/05/1972	I Can Feel You	Addrisi Brothers	110	BB
20/05/1972	Body And Soul (That's The Way It's Got To Be)	Soul Generation	114	CB
20/05/1972	The Livin' I'm Doin' (Ain't Worth The Lovin' I'm Getting')	Mike Kennedy	115	CB
20/05/1972	Song For Paula	BoBBy Whitlock	121	CB
27/05/1972	Wild Eyes	Stampeders	101	CB
27/05/1972	Poor Little Fool	Frank Mills	106	BB
27/05/1972	Some Day I'll Be A Farmer	Melanie	106	BB
27/05/1972	Love, Love, Love	J.R. Bailey	107	CB
27/05/1972	Looking For My Lady	The James Gang	108	BB
27/05/1972	Weave Me The Sunshine [Live]	Peter Yarrow	110	BB
27/05/1972	(Lost Her Love) On Our Last Date	Conway Twitty	112	BB
27/05/1972	I Only Meant To Wet My Feet	The Whispers	112	CB
27/05/1972	A Million To One	The Manhattans	114	BB
27/05/1972	That's The Way It's Got To Be (Body And Soul)	Soul Generation	115	BB
27/05/1972	Mighty Mighty And Roly Poly	Mal	124	CB
27/05/1972	I Can Feel It	Chase	129	CB
03/06/1972	I Don't Need No Doctor	New Riders Of The Purple Sage	104	CB
03/06/1972	Down To The Bone	Cold Blood	108	CB
03/06/1972	I Found A Love	Etta James	108	BB
03/06/1972	Mother Earth	Tom Rush	111	BB
03/06/1972	Little Bit Of Love	Free	119	BB
03/06/1972	Beyond The River Jordan	Potliquor	132	CB
10/06/1972	Is There Anyone Home	Jimmy Druiett	102	CB
10/06/1972	Why Do Fools Fall In Love	Ponderosa Twins	102	BB
10/06/1972	Gotta Be Funky	Monk Higgins & The Specialties	105	BB
10/06/1972	Looking For My Lady	The James Gang	108	CB
10/06/1972	We'll Always Be Friends	The Brady Bunch	117	CB
10/06/1972	Earth Omen	Frijid Pink	123	CB

17/06/1972	Is It You Girl	Betty Wright	101	BB
17/06/1972	Tear It On Down	Martha Reeves & The Vandellas	103	BB
17/06/1972	Metal Guru	T. Rex	106	CB
17/06/1972	Little Bit O' Soul	Bullet	107	BB
17/06/1972	We're Almost Home	Solomon Burke	110	CB
17/06/1972	Listen To A Country Song	Lynn Anderson	111	CB
17/06/1972	Love Trap	Rufus Thomas	114	BB
17/06/1972	Second Chance	Z.Z. Hill	117	CB
24/06/1972	Café	Malo	102	CB
24/06/1972	See You In September	Mike Curb Congregation	108	BB
24/06/1972	Little Bit Of Love	Free	116	CB
01/07/1972	Breaking Up Is Hard To Do	Heaven Bound With Tony Scotti	101	BB
01/07/1972	Hot Fun In The Summertime	David T. Walker	104	BB
01/07/1972	Bad Side Of The Moon	April Wine	106	BB
01/07/1972	Listen To A Country Song	Lynn Anderson	107	BB
01/07/1972	One A.M.	The Dillards	111	BB
01/07/1972	Say What I Feel	B.W. Stevenson	114	BB
01/07/1972	Get Up And Dance	The Doors	115	CB
01/07/1972	There's A Party Goin' On	Jody Miller	115	BB
01/07/1972	Baby, I'm For Real	Esther Phillips	118	CB
01/07/1972	Mother Earth	Tom Rush	120	CB
08/07/1972	Breaking Up Is Hard To Do	Heaven Bound With Tony Scotti	101	CB
08/07/1972	Café	Malo	101	BB
08/07/1972	He's An Indian Cowboy In The Rodeo	Buffy Sainte-Marie	104	CB
08/07/1972	Is It You Girl	Betty Wright	104	CB
08/07/1972	Circus	Mike Quatro Jam Band	108	BB
08/07/1972	Marcella	The Beach Boys	116	CB
08/07/1972	April Fools	Aretha Franklin	117	CB
08/07/1972	Who Has The Answers?	Andy Kim	118	CB
15/07/1972	Walk On By	The Dells	102	CB

15/07/1972	Funky Music Sho Nuff Turns Me On	The Temptations	105	CB
15/07/1972	Say What I Feel	B.W. Stevenson	109	CB
15/07/1972	Marcella	The Beach Boys	110	BB
22/07/1972	Slipping Into Darkness	Ramsey Lewis	101	BB
22/07/1972	Couldn't I Just Tell You	Todd Rundgren	104	CB
22/07/1972	Delta Dawn	Tanya Tucker	107	CB
22/07/1972	Big Hurt	Vikki Carr	108	BB
22/07/1972	Steppin'	Melanie	108	CB
22/07/1972	Jesahel	The English Congregation	109	BB
22/07/1972	Touching Me	The Ovations	111	CB
22/07/1972	I'm Up And I'm Leaving	Manfred Mann's Earth Band	112	BB
22/07/1972	It's Gonna Take A Little Bit Longer	Charley Pride	113	CB
22/07/1972	I.O.I.O.	Butch Patrick	114	CB
22/07/1972	Good Feeling To Know	Poco	119	CB
22/07/1972	There's A Party Goin' On	Jody Miller	120	CB
22/07/1972	What Are Heavy?	The Cy Coleman Co-Op	122	CB
22/07/1972	I'm Living A Lie	Barbara Jean English	125	CB
29/07/1972	Southbound Train	Graham Nash & David Crosby	101	CB
29/07/1972	Rock And Roll Crazies	Stephen Stills & Manassas	111	CB
29/07/1972	If You Can't Be My Woman	Boones Farm	114	CB
29/07/1972	Somebody's On Your Case	Ann Peebles	119	CB
29/07/1972	Lonely Weekends	Jerry Lee Lewis	129	CB
05/08/1972	It's Gonna Take A Little Bit Longer	Charley Pride	102	BB
05/08/1972	Macarthur Park	Andy Williams	102	BB
05/08/1972	Make It Easy On Yourself	Johnny Mathis	103	BB
05/08/1972	Groove Thang	Jr. Walker & All Stars	104	CB
05/08/1972	Macarthur Park	Andy Williams	114	CB
12/08/1972	Luther The Anthropoid (Ape Man)	Jimmy Castor Bunch	105	BB
12/08/1972	The Big Parade	Michael Allen	111	CB
12/08/1972	Who Has The Answers?	Andy Kim	111	BB

12/08/1972	Luther The Anthropoid (Ape Man)	Jimmy Castor Bunch	113	CB
12/08/1972	Is It Really True Boy - Is It Really Me	Love Unlimited	122	CB
19/08/1972	Is It Really True Boy-Is It Really Me	Love Unlimited	101	BB
19/08/1972	Best Thing	Styx	102	CB
19/08/1972	Don't Take My Kindness For Weakness	The Soul Children	102	BB
19/08/1972	Melissa	The Allman Brothers Band	103	CB
19/08/1972	Git It All	Mandrill	104	CB
19/08/1972	Touching Me	The Ovations	104	BB
19/08/1972	It's Too Late	Bill Deal & The Rhondels	108	BB
19/08/1972	Rita	Arthur Conley	108	CB
19/08/1972	Then Again Maybe	Gary Lewis	110	CB
26/08/1972	Happiness Train	Sugar Bears	102	CB
26/08/1972	Don't Ask Me Why	Alzo	106	CB
26/08/1972	I'm Your Puppet	Dionne Warwicke	113	BB
26/08/1972	Somebody's On Your Case	Ann Peebles	117	BB
26/08/1972	Come And Get This Ring	Tyrone Davis	119	BB
02/09/1972	Come Back Charleston Blue	Donny Hathaway With Margie Joseph	102	BB
02/09/1972	(Win, Place Or Show) She's A Winner	The Intruders	104	CB
02/09/1972	River	Universal Jones	115	BB
02/09/1972	(If You're Gonna) Break Another Heart	Cass Elliot	120	CB
09/09/1972	Oney	Johnny Cash	101	BB
09/09/1972	When The Snow Is On The Roses	Sonny James	103	BB
09/09/1972	I Ain't Never Seen A White Man	Wolfman Jack	106	CB
09/09/1972	Who Is The Leader Of The People	Edwin Starr	120	CB
09/09/1972	Bounce In Your Buggy	Sha Na Na	124	CB
16/09/1972	Mean Little Woman, Rosalie	Tommy Roe	102	CB
16/09/1972	Trouble	Frederick Knight	102	BB
16/09/1972	Dinah Flo	Boz Scaggs	106	CB
16/09/1972	Fool's Paradise	The Sylvers	109	CB
16/09/1972	River	Universal Jones	115	CB

16/09/1972	I'll Always Have You There	Doug GiBBs	116	CB
23/09/1972	Sincerely	The Moonglows	101	CB
23/09/1972	Itch And Scratch (Part I)	Rufus Thomas	103	BB
23/09/1972	I Ain't Never Seen A White Man	Wolfman Jack	106	BB
23/09/1972	Sea Side Shuffle	Terry Dactyl & The Dinosaurs	113	CB
23/09/1972	When The Snow Is On The Roses	Sonny James	113	CB
23/09/1972	I Just Want To Be There	The Independents	114	CB
23/09/1972	Lonely Boy	Donny Osmond	114	CB
23/09/1972	There's Gonna Be A Showdown	The Rance Allen Group	117	CB
30/09/1972	Stop Doggin' Me	Johnnie Taylor	101	BB
30/09/1972	Hard Life, Hard Times (Prisoners)	John Denver	103	BB
30/09/1972	Hey Little Girl	Buckwheat	108	CB
30/09/1972	Good Times	Kool & The Gang	116	CB
07/10/1972	Anyway The Wind Blows	The Grass Roots	101	CB
07/10/1972	Innocent Til Proven Guilty	The Honey Cone	101	BB
07/10/1972	So Far Away	The Crusaders	102	CB
07/10/1972	If You Got The Time	Brook Benton	104	BB
07/10/1972	Long John Silver	Jefferson Airplane	104	BB
07/10/1972	Hard Life, Hard Times (Prisoners)	John Denver	105	CB
07/10/1972	Dance, Dance, Dance	The New Seekers	106	CB
07/10/1972	Anyway The Wind Blows	The Grass Roots	107	BB
07/10/1972	Sixty Minute Man	The Trammps	108	BB
07/10/1972	The Slider	T. Rex	112	CB
07/10/1972	(But I Could) Reach The Wisdom Of Soloman	Mancini & Fox	115	CB
07/10/1972	Brown Girl	Exuma	119	CB
07/10/1972	I Know	Wright's Wonderwheel	119	CB
14/10/1972	Sixty Minute Man	The Trammps	107	CB
14/10/1972	You Made Me (A Brand New World)	We The People	108	CB
14/10/1972	Supersonic Rocket Ship	The Kinks	111	BB
14/10/1972	It's A Tall Order For A Short Guy	Jonathan King	116	CB

14/10/1972	Had Enough	The James Gang	123	CB
21/10/1972	One Life To Live	The Manhattans	102	BB
21/10/1972	There Are Too Many Saviours On My Cross	Richard Harris	102	CB
21/10/1972	If You Had A Change In Mind	Tyrone Davis	107	BB
21/10/1972	Paradise	Jackie Deshannon	110	BB
21/10/1972	Bang!	Washrag	112	BB
21/10/1972	Sing A Song/Make Your Own Kind Of Music (Live)	Barbra Streisand	120	CB
28/10/1972	There Are Too Many Saviors On My Cross	Richard Harris	107	BB
28/10/1972	Endlessly	Mavis Staples	109	BB
28/10/1972	I Just Want To Be There	The Independents	113	BB
28/10/1972	Margie, Who's Watching The Baby	R.B. Greaves	115	BB
04/11/1972	Tragedy	Argent	106	BB
04/11/1972	Walk On In	Lou Rawls	106	BB
04/11/1972	Had Enough	The James Gang	111	BB
04/11/1972	Wonder Girl	Sparks	112	BB
04/11/1972	Mississippi Lady	Griffin	114	BB
04/11/1972	People Need Love	Björn & Benny (with Svenska Flicka)	114	CB
04/11/1972	Redwood Tree	Van Morrison	119	CB
11/11/1972	Peace In The Valley Of Love	Persuaders	104	BB
11/11/1972	Moment Of Truth	Shepstone & DiBBens	107	CB
11/11/1972	Latin Bugaloo	Malo	109	CB
11/11/1972	Feel The Need In Me	Detroit Emeralds	110	BB
11/11/1972	Fool Me	Lynn Anderson	112	CB
11/11/1972	So Far Away	The Crusaders	114	BB
18/11/1972	Fool Me	Lynn Anderson	101	BB
18/11/1972	Hey Mister	Ray Charles	101	CB
18/11/1972	Don't Misunderstand	O.C. Smith	102	BB
18/11/1972	One Way Out	The Allman Brothers Band	103	CB
18/11/1972	Bitter With The Sweet	Carole King	105	CB
18/11/1972	Girl You're Alright	The Undisputed Truth	107	BB

18/11/1972	Walk On In	Lou Rawls	116	CB
18/11/1972	All Together	The Rowan Brothers	124	CB
18/11/1972	Round & Round	Edgar Winter Group	126	CB
25/11/1972	Angel Of The Morning	Chip Taylor	102	CB
25/11/1972	Wild Honey Part I	The State Dept.	104	CB
25/11/1972	I Just Want To Make Love To You	Foghat	107	CB
25/11/1972	(I Got) So Much Trouble In My Mind Pt. 1	Joe Quarterman & Free Soul	109	CB
25/11/1972	Lo And Behold!	Marjoe	109	BB
25/11/1972	America (The Lady Of The Harbor)	The Dillards	112	CB
25/11/1972	Melanie Makes Me Smile	Terry Williams	112	BB
25/11/1972	There You Are (I See You)	Chocolate Chips	127	CB
02/12/1972	Africa	Thundermug	102	CB
02/12/1972	That Same Old Obsession (b-side)	Gordon Lightfoot	102	BB
02/12/1972	Latin Bugaloo	Malo	103	BB
02/12/1972	Because Of You (The Sun Don't Set)	Kracker	104	BB
02/12/1972	Because Of You (The Sun Don't Set)	Kracker	104	CB
02/12/1972	America	Simon & Garfunkel	105	CB
02/12/1972	Lady, Play Your Symphony	Kenny Rogers And The First Edition	105	BB
02/12/1972	Lady, Play Your Symphony	Kenny Rogers & The First Edition	110	CB
02/12/1972	All Together	The Rowan Brothers	112	BB
02/12/1972	Tuffer Than Tuff	Ace Cannon	127	CB
09/12/1972	I've Never Found A Man (To Love Me Like You Do)	Esther Phillips	106	BB
09/12/1972	That Same Old Obsession	Gordon Lightfoot	108	CB
09/12/1972	Living Together, Growing Together	Tony Bennett With The Mike Curb Congregation	111	BB
09/12/1972	Love Story	Nino Tempo & April Stevens	113	BB
16/12/1972	Tequila	Hot Butter	103	CB
16/12/1972	Africa	Thundermug	110	BB
16/12/1972	Somebody Loves You	The Whispers	111	CB
23/12/1972	Crumbs Off The Table	Laura Lee	107	BB
23/12/1972	(I Don't Want To) Hang Up My Rock And Roll Shoes	The Band	113	BB

23/12/1972	Hey Mister	Ray Charles	115	BB
30/12/1972	Cho Choo Mama	Ten Years After	101	CB
30/12/1972	Come Go With Me ('72 Version)	The Del Vikings	101	CB
30/12/1972	Don't Misunderstand	O.C. Smith	102	CB
30/12/1972	The Road	Danny O'keefe	102	BB
30/12/1972	I Can't Move No Mountains	Blood, Sweat & Tears	103	BB
30/12/1972	Do You Believe	Melanie	108	CB
30/12/1972	Heaven Help Us All	Beverly Bremers	110	BB
30/12/1972	From Toys To Boys	The Emotions	116	CB
30/12/1972	Grand Central Shuttle	Johnny Griffith, Inc.	116	CB
06/01/1973	I'm Gonna Love You Too	Terry Jacks	102	CB
06/01/1973	Trying To Live My Life Without You	Otis Clay	102	BB
06/01/1973	You Can't Get There From Here	Casey Kelly	110	BB
06/01/1973	Loving You Is Just An Old Habit	Jim Weatherly	116	BB
06/01/1973	I Won't Let That Chump Break Your Heart	Carl Carlton	119	CB
13/01/1973	Better Place To Be	Harry Chapin	101	CB
13/01/1973	Gypsy	Van Morrison	101	BB
13/01/1973	(I've Been A Winner, I've Been A Loser) I've Been In Love	Smith Connection	104	CB
13/01/1973	The Truth Shall Make You Free (St. John 8:32)	King Hannibal	105	BB
13/01/1973	Go Like Elijah	Chi Coltrane	107	BB
13/01/1973	Robot Man	Jay & The Techniques	112	CB
13/01/1973	'TIL I Get It Right	Tammy Wynette	113	CB
13/01/1973	Do You Believe	Melanie	115	BB
13/01/1973	(I Don't Want To) Hang Up My Rock And Roll Shoes	The Band	117	CB
20/01/1973	Heaven Is My Woman's Love	Tommy Overstreet	102	BB
20/01/1973	Slippin' Away	Jean Shepard	105	CB
20/01/1973	Tequila	Hot Butter	105	BB
20/01/1973	'Til I Get It Right	Tammy Wynette	106	BB
20/01/1973	From Toys To Boys	The Emotions	112	BB
20/01/1973	Back In Your Arms	Clarence Carter	117	CB

20/01/1973	Marietta Station	Gladstone	117	CB
20/01/1973	The Road	Danny O'keefe	120	CB
27/01/1973	Think It Over	The Delfonics	101	BB
27/01/1973	Every Saturday Night	Ray Charles	103	CB
27/01/1973	I Think You Need Love	Dionne Warwicke	103	CB
27/01/1973	You Girl	Lighthouse	107	CB
27/01/1973	Salty Tears	Mara Lynn Brown	108	CB
27/01/1973	Stop And Start It All Again	Jonathan Edwards	110	CB
27/01/1973	Come Go With Me (new Version)	The Del Vikings	112	BB
27/01/1973	(The Best Part Of) Breakin' Up	The Seashells	115	BB
27/01/1973	I'm Gonna Love You Too	Terry Jacks	116	BB
27/01/1973	We're Gonna Have A Good Time	Rare Earth	118	CB
27/01/1973	You Are What I Am	Gordon Lightfoot	126	CB
03/02/1973	Sarah Cynthia Sylvia Stout (Would Not Take The Garbage Out)	Shel Silverstein	107	BB
03/02/1973	I'm Gonna Tear Your Playhouse Down	Ann Peebles	111	BB
03/02/1973	Back Up	The Manhattans	112	CB
03/02/1973	Better Place To Be	Harry Chapin	118	BB
03/02/1973	I'm Gonna Tear Your Playhouse Down	Ann Peebles	118	CB
03/02/1973	I'm Sorry	Barbara Jean English	120	CB
03/02/1973	Crazy Legs	Donald Austin	121	BB
03/02/1973	Heaven Is My Woman's Love	Tommy Overstreet	123	CB
03/02/1973	Stella's Candy Store	The Sweet Marie	123	BB
10/02/1973	Dreamland	Danny Bonaduce	106	CB
10/02/1973	Gimme That Beat (Part 1)	Jr. Walker & The All Stars	109	CB
10/02/1973	Darling	Stories	111	BB
10/02/1973	Gillian Frank	Jerry Hudson	117	BB
10/02/1973	Salty Tears	Mara Lynn Brown	118	BB
10/02/1973	Drowning On Dry Land	O.V. Wright	119	CB
10/02/1973	Caroline This Time	Climax Featuring Sonny Geraci	123	CB
17/02/1973	Why Do Fools Fall In Love	Summer Wine	103	BB

17/02/1973	Brand New Kind Of Love	BoBBy Goldsboro	104	CB
17/02/1973	Mom	Earth, Wind & Fire	104	BB
17/02/1973	I Don't Have To Tell You	Richard Harris	106	BB
17/02/1973	I Don't Have To Tell You	Richard Harris	108	CB
17/02/1973	A Shoulder To Cry On	Charley Pride	112	CB
17/02/1973	Stop And Start It All Again	Johnathan Edwards	112	BB
17/02/1973	You Girl	Lighthouse	114	BB
17/02/1973	Gypsy	Abraham's Children	119	BB
17/02/1973	Until It's Time For You To Go	The New Birth	120	CB
17/02/1973	Blackbird	Billy Preston	122	CB
17/02/1973	Sha La Boom Boom	BoBBy Bloom	123	BB
24/02/1973	Gimme That Beat (Part 1)	Jr. Walker & The All Stars	101	BB
24/02/1973	You Are What I Am	Gordon Lightfoot	101	BB
24/02/1973	Mom	Earth, Wind & Fire	102	CB
24/02/1973	Back Up	The Manhattans	107	BB
24/02/1973	We'll Make Love	Al Anderson	108	CB
24/02/1973	Eyesight To The Blind	Richie Havens	111	BB
24/02/1973	Sharon	David Bromberg	117	BB
24/02/1973	Don't Go To Mexico	B.W. Stevenson	118	CB
24/02/1973	Right Here Is Where You Belong	Jerry Washington	120	BB
03/03/1973	Eyesight To The Blind	Richie Havens	101	CB
03/03/1973	Wishing Well	Free	101	CB
03/03/1973	Heaven Help The Child	Mickey Newbury	103	BB
03/03/1973	Woman Stealer	Joe Tex	103	BB
03/03/1973	Crazy	Joey Heatherton	104	CB
03/03/1973	Keep Me In Mind	Lynn Anderson	104	BB
03/03/1973	Rainbow Man	Looking Glass	104	BB
03/03/1973	Can I	Vee Allen	107	BB
03/03/1973	I May Not Be What You Want	Mel And Tim	113	BB
03/03/1973	Time Is Love	Black Ivory	114	CB

03/03/1973	(Is Anybody Going To) San Antone	Doug Sahm And Band	115	BB
03/03/1973	Brand New Kind Of Love	BoBBy Goldsboro	116	BB
10/03/1973	A Shoulder To Cry On	Charley Pride	101	BB
10/03/1973	It Ain't Always What You Do (It's Who You Let See You Do It)	The Soul Children	105	BB
10/03/1973	I Won't Last A Day Without You	Paul Williams	106	BB
10/03/1973	Are You Really Happy Together	Bulldog	112	BB
10/03/1973	Wishing Well	Free	112	BB
10/03/1973	Don't Take Away The Music	Posse	115	CB
10/03/1973	Midnite Train To Georgia	Cissy Houston	115	CB
10/03/1973	She Lets Her Hair Down	Pastors	119	CB
10/03/1973	Too Many Mondays	Mary Travers	122	BB
17/03/1973	So In Love With You	Leroy Hutson	101	CB
17/03/1973	Where Have All The Flowers Gone	Earth, Wind & Fire	103	CB
17/03/1973	Why Does Love Got To Be So Bad	Derek & The Dominos	106	CB
17/03/1973	Put On Your Shoes And Walk	Clarence Carter	112	BB
17/03/1973	Sunshine Lover	Daniel Boone	112	CB
17/03/1973	Loose Booty	Funkadelic	118	BB
17/03/1973	Stacy Brown Got Two	Shel Silverstein	118	CB
24/03/1973	We'll Make Love	Al Anderson	101	BB
24/03/1973	The Last Tango In Paris	Doc Severinsen	106	BB
24/03/1973	Love Music	Lloyd Price	108	CB
24/03/1973	Mama I Got A Brand New Thing (Don't Say No)	The Undisputed Truth	109	BB
24/03/1973	Carol	Roy Head	111	CB
24/03/1973	You Can Have Her	Waylon Jennings	114	BB
24/03/1973	Oh My Lady	Stampeders	115	BB
24/03/1973	Who Gets Your Love	Dusty Springfield	121	BB
24/03/1973	Hey Lawdy Lawdy	The Wackers	124	BB
31/03/1973	Friends Or Lovers	Act 1	101	BB
31/03/1973	Black Coffee	Humble Pie	107	CB
31/03/1973	While We're Still Young	Wayne Newton	107	BB

31/03/1973	The Dutchman	Steve Goodman	110	CB
31/03/1973	Last Tango In Paris	Willie Mitchell	111	CB
31/03/1973	Mama I Got A Brand New Thing (Don't Say No)	The Undisputed Truth	112	CB
31/03/1973	The Last Tango In Paris	Doc Severinsen	118	CB
31/03/1973	Why Does Love Got To Be So Sad	Derek & The Dominos	120	BB
31/03/1973	Orange Blossom Special	Charlie Mccoy	124	CB
07/04/1973	Zip A Dee Doo Dah	Christopher Cloud	102	CB
07/04/1973	Black Coffee	Humble Pie	113	BB
07/04/1973	Oh My Lady	Stampeders	117	CB
14/04/1973	"Ma"	Rare Earth	108	BB
14/04/1973	I Can Understand It-Part I	Valentinos	109	BB
14/04/1973	Early In The Morning	BoBBy Sherman	113	BB
14/04/1973	Love Music	Sergio Mendes & Brasil '77	113	BB
14/04/1973	Let's Stay Together	Margie Joseph	116	CB
14/04/1973	"MA"	Rare Earth	121	CB
21/04/1973	Orange Blossom Special	Charlie Mccoy	101	BB
21/04/1973	They Say The Girl's Crazy	The Invitations	101	CB
21/04/1973	They're Coming To Take Me Away, Ha-Haaa!	Napoleon Xiv	101	CB
21/04/1973	Yes, I'm Ready (73 Version)	Barbara Mason	101	CB
21/04/1973	Love Music	Lloyd Price	102	BB
21/04/1973	International Playboy	Wilson Pickett	103	CB
21/04/1973	Mama Feelgood	Lyn Collins (The Female Preacher)	103	CB
21/04/1973	Rolling Down A Mountainside	Isaac Hayes	104	BB
21/04/1973	Rolling Down A Mountainside	Isaac Hayes	105	CB
21/04/1973	Percolator	Hot Butter	106	BB
21/04/1973	Man Of The World	Robin Trower	109	BB
21/04/1973	Breakaway	Millie Jackson	110	BB
21/04/1973	Slip N' Slide	Rufus	110	BB
21/04/1973	Part Of The Union	Strawbs	111	BB
21/04/1973	Beware Of The Stranger	Hypnotics	115	BB

21/04/1973	God Gave Rock And Roll To You	Argent	117	CB
21/04/1973	Hymn	James Taylor	118	CB
21/04/1973	On The Road	Michael Johnson	118	BB
28/04/1973	Whiskey, Whiskey	Rita Coolidge	106	BB
28/04/1973	By The Devil I Was Tempted	Blue Mink	111	CB
28/04/1973	Mama's Little Girl	Dusty Springfield	113	CB
28/04/1973	God Gave Rock And Roll To You	Argent	114	BB
28/04/1973	Rock And Roll Lullaby	Barbara Lewis	115	CB
28/04/1973	She Showed Me	Sailcat	115	BB
05/05/1973	(I'd Be) A Legend In My Time	Sammy Davis Jr.	104	CB
05/05/1973	Beautiful City	Godspell	105	CB
05/05/1973	If That's The Way You Want It	Diamond Head	106	BB
05/05/1973	Full Circle	The Byrds	109	BB
05/05/1973	(I'd Be) A Legend In My Time	Sammy Davis Jr.	116	BB
05/05/1973	You Don't Know What Love Is	Susan Jacks And The Poppy Family	116	BB
05/05/1973	Well Hello	Yellowstone & Voice	117	BB
05/05/1973	Sincerely Yours (The Next One's On You)	Sleepy Hollow	122	CB
05/05/1973	No Return	Megan Mcdonough	124	CB
12/05/1973	Blues Band, Opus 50, Part I	Siegel-Schwall Band And San Francisco Symphony Orchestra,	105	BB
12/05/1973	Rest In Peace	Gallery Featuring Jim Gold	110	CB
12/05/1973	Am I Blue	Cher	111	BB
12/05/1973	Yesterday And You	Holly Sherwood	114	CB
19/05/1973	International Playboy	Wilson Pickett	104	BB
19/05/1973	This Feeling Of Loneliness	Cliff Nobles	108	CB
19/05/1973	Power To All Our Friends	Cliff Richard	109	BB
19/05/1973	Get Down To It	Humble Pie	112	CB
19/05/1973	Parrty - Part I	Maceo & The Macks	114	CB
19/05/1973	Hurt	BoBBy Vinton	117	CB
19/05/1973	Yesterday And You	Holly Sherwood	117	BB
19/05/1973	Mama's Little Girl	Dusty Springfield	118	BB

19/05/1973	A Thousand Miles Away	The Temprees	119	CB
26/05/1973	You Can Call Me Rover	The Main Ingredient	101	BB
26/05/1973	Bad, Bold And Beautiful, Girl	The Persuaders	105	BB
26/05/1973	Jesus Was A Crossmaker	The Hollies	105	CB
26/05/1973	Kids Say The Darndest Things	Tammy Wynette	108	CB
26/05/1973	Wasn't It Nice In New York City	Tommy Leonetti	112	CB
26/05/1973	Wild About My Lovin'	Adrian Smith	114	BB
26/05/1973	Last Tango In Paris	Ferrante & Teicher	115	CB
26/05/1973	Power To All Our Friends	Cliff Richard	119	CB
26/05/1973	Shangri-La	Al Capps	119	BB
26/05/1973	Take Me Home, Country Roads	Olivia Newton-John	119	BB
26/05/1973	Maybe I Know	Ellie Greenwich	122	BB
02/06/1973	The Last Thing On My Mind	Austin Roberts	101	CB
02/06/1973	Blue Canadian Rocky Dream	Lou Christie	102	CB
02/06/1973	Forever	Baby Washington & Don Gardner	105	CB
02/06/1973	Moonshine (Friend Of Mine)	John Kay	105	BB
02/06/1973	One Of The Survivors	The Kinks	108	BB
02/06/1973	Something's Burning	Candi Staton	108	CB
02/06/1973	Anello (Where Are You)	Shawn Phillips	112	BB
02/06/1973	Maybe I Know	Ellie Greenwich	115	CB
02/06/1973	Grand Hotel	Procol Harum	120	CB
02/06/1973	The Last Thing On My Mind	Austin Roberts	120	BB
09/06/1973	Gypsy Davy	Arlo Guthrie	105	BB
09/06/1973	Hurt	BoBBy Vinton	106	BB
09/06/1973	Lovin' Naturally	Sandalwood	110	CB
09/06/1973	Silver Train	Johnny Winter	112	CB
09/06/1973	Ain't Nothing You Can Do	Z.Z. Hill	114	BB
09/06/1973	Satellite Of Love	Lou Reed	119	BB
09/06/1973	Secret Gardens	Judy Collins	122	BB
09/06/1973	Don't Burn Me	Paul Kelly	125	CB

09/06/1973	Yes, I'm Ready (new Version)	Barbara Mason	125	BB
16/06/1973	Gypsy Davy	Arlo Guthrie	101	CB
16/06/1973	They Say The Girl's Crazy	The Invitations	110	BB
16/06/1973	Grand Hotel	Procol Harum	117	BB
16/06/1973	Satellite Of Love	Lou Reed	118	CB
16/06/1973	Roller Coaster	Mark James	125	CB
23/06/1973	Watergate Blues	Tom T. Hall	101	BB
23/06/1973	Lovin' Naturally	Sandalwood	111	BB
23/06/1973	No Easy Road	Wishbone Ash	112	CB
23/06/1973	Tell It Like It Is - Part 2	Oscar Weathers	115	CB
23/06/1973	Son Of Checkers (The Watergate Case)	Don Imus	122	CB
30/06/1973	Bra	Cymande	102	BB
30/06/1973	Should I Tie A Yellow RiBBon Round The Ole Oak Tree? "The	Connie Francis	104	BB
30/06/1973	Old Betsy Goes Boing, Boing, Boing	The Hummers	105	CB
30/06/1973	Ooh-La-La	Faces	106	CB
30/06/1973	Nitty Gritty	Sir Douglas Quintet	113	CB
30/06/1973	Wouldn't I Be Someone	The Bee Gees	115	BB
30/06/1973	Cosmic Cowboy - Part 1	Nitty Gritty Dirt Band	123	BB
07/07/1973	Don't Fight The Feelings Of Love	Charley Pride	101	BB
07/07/1973	Lovin' On Borrowed Time	William Bell	101	BB
07/07/1973	Rock And Roll Heaven	Climax Featuring Sonny Geraci	102	CB
07/07/1973	Seeds	Melanie	102	CB
07/07/1973	Music, Music, Music	Teresa Brewer	112	CB
07/07/1973	Next Door Neighbor's Kid	Jud Strunk	117	CB
07/07/1973	Forever	Baby Washington & Don Gardner	119	BB
07/07/1973	Street Dance	The Fatback Band	121	CB
07/07/1973	Put It Where You Want It	Nino & April	122	BB
07/07/1973	Part Of You	Arthur, Hurley & Gottlieb	125	CB
14/07/1973	You're Gettin' A Little Too Smart	Detroit Emeralds	101	BB
14/07/1973	Loneliness (Will Bring Us Together Again)	Brown Sugar	107	BB

14/07/1973	Music, Music, Music	Teresa Brewer	109	BB
14/07/1973	I Only Get This Feeling	Chuck Jackson	117	BB
14/07/1973	Maybe Baby	Gallery Featuring Jim Gold	118	BB
14/07/1973	How Long Can I Keep It Up Part I	Lyn Collins (The Female Preacher)	119	CB
14/07/1973	Maybe Baby	Gallery Featuring Jim Gold	125	CB
14/07/1973	Songs	B.J. Thomas	126	CB
14/07/1973	It Takes Both Of Us	Act I	128	CB
21/07/1973	Let Me Be Your Eyes	Timmy Thomas	107	BB
21/07/1973	Let The Good Times Roll/Feel So Fine	Slade	107	CB
21/07/1973	Sometimes I Don't Know What To Feel	Todd Rundgren	111	CB
21/07/1973	Medley: Searchin'/So Fine	Johnny Rivers	113	BB
21/07/1973	Lonely Days, Lonely Nights	Don Downing	121	CB
28/07/1973	Hands	DeBBie Dawn	102	CB
28/07/1973	Tell It Like It Is-Part 1	Oscar Weathers	113	BB
04/08/1973	Alfie	The Delfonics	105	CB
04/08/1973	Loneliness (Will Bring Us Together Again)	Brown Sugar	109	CB
04/08/1973	Reggae My Way	ChuBBy Checker	112	CB
04/08/1973	Naughty Girl	Guy Shannon	115	CB
04/08/1973	Wouldn't I Be Someone	The Bee Gees	122	CB
11/08/1973	Summer In The City	Quincy Jones	102	BB
11/08/1973	Birdman-Part One (Title No. 1 Again)	Rare Bird	104	CB
11/08/1973	No Headstone On My Grave	Jerry Lee Lewis	104	BB
11/08/1973	That's How I Feel	The Crusaders	105	CB
11/08/1973	Can't Help Falling In Love	Soft Tones	120	CB
11/08/1973	I Need You/Isn't Life Strange/Without You	The Pastors	125	CB
18/08/1973	Yes, We Finally Made It	Love Unlimited	101	BB
18/08/1973	Open Up Your Heart	Roger Miller	105	BB
18/08/1973	He	Today's People	109	CB
25/08/1973	Easy Evil	John Kay	102	BB
25/08/1973	Old Betsy Goes Boing, Boing, Boing	The Hummers	104	BB

25/08/1973	Grapefruit - Juicy Fruit	Jimmy Buffett	106	CB
25/08/1973	Boogie Man	Catfish Hodge	109	CB
25/08/1973	Let's Spend The Night Together	David Bowie	109	BB
25/08/1973	Since I Don't Have You	Lenny Welch	111	CB
25/08/1973	Can't You See	The Marshall Tucker Band	114	CB
25/08/1973	Glory Hallelujah	David Huff	125	CB
01/09/1973	Think	James Brown	101	CB
01/09/1973	Kiss It And Make It Better	Mac Davis	105	BB
01/09/1973	I'll Have To Go Away	Skylark	106	BB
01/09/1973	Dueling Tubas	Martin Mull & Orchestra	107	CB
01/09/1973	Sparkling In The Sand	Tower Of Power	107	BB
01/09/1973	Can't You See	The Marshall Tucker Band	108	BB
01/09/1973	It's A Small Small World	The Mike Curb Congregation	108	BB
01/09/1973	Bondi Junction	Peter Foldy	113	BB
01/09/1973	Let The Good Times Roll/Feel So Fine	Slade	114	BB
01/09/1973	Walking On Back	Edward Bear	115	BB
01/09/1973	Haldeman, Ehrlichman, Mitchell And Dean	The Creep	116	BB
01/09/1973	Welcome Home	Peters And Lee	119	BB
01/09/1973	One Word	Austin Roberts	121	CB
01/09/1973	Birdman - Part One (Title No. 1 Again)	Rare Bird	122	BB
08/09/1973	Love Is The Foundation	Loretta Lynn	102	BB
08/09/1973	Cosmic Slop	Funkadelic	104	CB
08/09/1973	Freewheelin'	The Fabulous Rhinestones	105	CB
08/09/1973	Kid Stuff	Barbara Fairchild	106	CB
08/09/1973	I Can Hear Music	Larry Lurex	115	BB
15/09/1973	Shiddle-Ee-Dee	Clint Holmes	101	CB
15/09/1973	She Brings Sunshine	Kyle	102	CB
15/09/1973	Shiddle-Ee-Dee	Clint Holmes	106	BB
15/09/1973	Shady Lady	Shepstone & DiBBens	111	BB
15/09/1973	Love Me For What I Am	Lobo	114	CB

15/09/1973	The Purple People Eater	Dickie Goodman	119	BB
15/09/1973	Slag Solution	Hot Butter	123	CB
22/09/1973	I Can't Believe That It's All Over	Skeeter Davis	101	BB
22/09/1973	For Ol' Times Sake	Elvis Presley	104	CB
22/09/1973	Dangwa	Manu Dibango	115	CB
22/09/1973	Southside Shuffle	The J. Geils Band	115	CB
22/09/1973	Press On	David T. Walker	118	CB
22/09/1973	Girl Blue	The Main Ingredient	119	BB
29/09/1973	Ooh What A Feeling	Johnny Nash	103	BB
29/09/1973	A Passion Play (Edit #10)	Jethro Tull	105	BB
29/09/1973	Kiss It And Make It Better	Mac Davis	105	CB
29/09/1973	Pour Me A Little More Wine	Wayne Newton	107	CB
29/09/1973	Hum Along And Dance	Rare Earth	110	BB
29/09/1973	Girl Blue	The Main Ingredient	111	CB
29/09/1973	Trash	New York Dolls	111	CB
29/09/1973	Razamanaz	Nazareth	115	CB
29/09/1973	Me And My Mummy	BoBBy (Boris) Pickett	118	CB
06/10/1973	Tossin' And Turnin'	Bunny Sigler	101	CB
06/10/1973	Cosmic Slop	Funkadelic	102	BB
06/10/1973	Love Don't Care (Where It Grows)	Perry Como	102	CB
06/10/1973	I Just Can't Stop Loving You	Cornelius Brothers & Sister Rose	104	BB
06/10/1973	Dancing On The Moon	Judi Pulver	118	BB
13/10/1973	All The Way Down	Etta James	101	BB
13/10/1973	Lifestream	Rick Nelson & The Stone Canyon Band	105	CB
13/10/1973	Love Don't Care (Where It Grows)	Perry Como	106	BB
13/10/1973	Back In The Hills	The Blue Ridge Rangers	107	BB
13/10/1973	Wig-Wam Bam	The Sweet	114	CB
13/10/1973	You Can't Hide Love	Creative Source	114	BB
20/10/1973	I'm Through Trying To Prove My Love To You	BoBBy Womack	101	BB
20/10/1973	You Oughta' Be Here With Me	Annette Snell	102	BB

20/10/1973	Let There Be Drums	The Incredible Bongo Band	107	BB
20/10/1973	Take The Highway	The Marshall Tucker Band	108	CB
20/10/1973	Together (Body And Soulin')	The Mission	108	BB
20/10/1973	Dangwa	Manu Dibango	109	BB
20/10/1973	Angel Spread Your Wings	Danny O'keefe	110	BB
20/10/1973	Wherefore And Why	Glen Campbell	110	CB
20/10/1973	Together (Body And Soulin')	The Mission	111	CB
20/10/1973	Wherefore And Why	Glen Campbell	111	BB
20/10/1973	Take Life A Little Easier	Rodney Allen Rippy	112	BB
20/10/1973	Mango Meat	Mandrill	125	CB
27/10/1973	Reason To Feel	Scuffy Shew	103	CB
03/11/1973	Ships In The Night	Vicki Lawrence	106	CB
03/11/1973	In The Rain	Arthur Prysock	110	BB
03/11/1973	If You Don't Get It The First Time, Back Up And Try It Again, Party	Fred Wesley & The J.B.'s	114	CB
03/11/1973	My Girl	Wolfman Jack	118	CB
03/11/1973	The Best Years Of My Life	General Crook	118	CB
03/11/1973	Njia (Nija) Walk (Street Walk)	The Fatback Band	122	CB
10/11/1973	Sally From Syracuse	Stu Nunnery	101	BB
10/11/1973	Good Old Song	Dobie Gray	104	CB
10/11/1973	Walking In The Georgia Rain	Sonny Geraci & Climax	107	CB
10/11/1973	Reason To Feel	Scuffy Shew	112	BB
17/11/1973	Both Ends Against The Middle	Jackie Moore	102	BB
17/11/1973	What Can I Tell You	Timmy Thomas	102	BB
17/11/1973	If You Don't Get It The First Time, Back Up And Try It Again, Party	Fred Wesley & The J.B.'s	104	BB
17/11/1973	Mango Meat	Mandrill	107	BB
17/11/1973	Miracle Maker (Sweet Soul Shaker)	The Hues Corporation	112	CB
24/11/1973	I'm The Midnight Special	Clarence Carter	101	BB
24/11/1973	Biff, The Friendly Purple Bear	Dick Feller	105	CB
24/11/1973	Sing About Love	Lynn Anderson	110	CB
24/11/1973	Sunshine Lady	Willie Hutch	117	CB

24/11/1973	Louie - Part I	Lou Zerato	121	CB
01/12/1973	Good Old Song	Dobie Gray	103	BB
01/12/1973	The House Of The Rising Sun	Jody Miller	120	CB
01/12/1973	Somewhere Over The Rainbow	Livingston Taylor	124	CB
08/12/1973	Down Drinking At The Bar	Loudon Wainwright Iii	101	CB
08/12/1973	Soft Soul Boogie Woogie	Wilson Pickett	103	BB
08/12/1973	Inspiration	Paul Williams	108	BB
08/12/1973	The Best Years Of My Life	General Crook	108	BB
08/12/1973	The Way You Do The Things You Do	The Newbeats	116	CB
15/12/1973	What Is Hip?	Tower Of Power	103	CB
15/12/1973	Hello Stranger	Fire & Rain	104	CB
15/12/1973	Soft Soul Boogie Woogie	Wilson Pickett	105	CB
15/12/1973	Wild In The Streets	Garland Jeffreys	106	CB
15/12/1973	What Can I Tell Her	Timmy Thomas	107	CB
15/12/1973	California Saga (On My Way To Sunny Californ-I-A)	The Beach Boys	110	CB
15/12/1973	Love For You	Sonoma	112	BB
15/12/1973	Soul Power 74 (Part I)	Maceo & The Macks	119	CB
22/12/1973	Rainbow Song	America	102	CB
22/12/1973	Time Fades Away [Live]	Neil Young	108	BB
22/12/1973	Give Me Just Another Day	The Miracles	111	BB
29/12/1973	Biff, The Friendly Purple Bear	Dick Feller	101	BB
29/12/1973	Lay Lady Lay	Brook Benton	107	CB
29/12/1973	Time Fades Away (Live)	Neil Young	111	CB
29/12/1973	I Think I'm Gonna Like It	Barnaby Bye	113	CB
05/01/1974	Wish That You Were Mine	The Manhattans	106	CB
05/01/1974	I Told You So	The Delfonics	107	CB
05/01/1974	Keep Yourself Alive	Queen	112	CB
05/01/1974	Remember	Andy Williams & Noelle	117	CB
12/01/1974	Another Lonely Song	Tammy Wynette	104	CB
19/01/1974	Marlena	BoBBy Goldsboro	101	CB

19/01/1974	It Wouldn't Have Made Any Difference	Tom Middleton	103	CB
19/01/1974	The First Time We Met	The Independents	103	BB
19/01/1974	Deeper And Deeper	Bo Donaldson & The Heywoods	107	CB
19/01/1974	You're Too Good To Be True	Creative Source	108	BB
19/01/1974	Soul Power 74 (Part I)	Maceo And The Macks	109	BB
26/01/1974	Stormy Monday	Latimore	102	BB
26/01/1974	Free As The Wind	Engelbert Humperdinck	103	CB
26/01/1974	Same Old Feeling	Edward Bear	108	CB
26/01/1974	Wild In The Streets	Garland Jeffreys	115	BB
26/01/1974	If It Were Left Up To Me	Sly & The Family Stone	118	CB
02/02/1974	Ridin' The Storm Out	Reo Speedwagon	102	CB
02/02/1974	Boobs A Lot	The Holy Modal Rounders	103	BB
02/02/1974	I Will	Ruby Winters	110	CB
02/02/1974	Love Song	Mandrill	111	CB
02/02/1974	Don't Nobody Live Here (By The Name Of Fool)	Denise Lasalle	116	CB
09/02/1974	Apple Of My Eye	Badfinger	102	BB
09/02/1974	Bicycle Morning	Billie Sans	103	BB
09/02/1974	You Will Be My Music	Frank Sinatra	107	CB
09/02/1974	SaBBath, Bloody SaBBath	Black SaBBath	108	CB
09/02/1974	Big Time Lover	Cornelius Brothers & Sister Rose	109	CB
09/02/1974	Ain't It Hell Up In Harlem	Edwin Starr	112	CB
09/02/1974	Fool's Paradise	Don Mclean	112	CB
09/02/1974	Beyond Tomorrow (Love Theme From "Serpico")	Perry Como	118	CB
16/02/1974	I Got To Try It One Time	Millie Jackson	101	CB
16/02/1974	I Told You So	The Delfonics	101	BB
16/02/1974	When I Look In Your Eyes	Santana	102	BB
16/02/1974	Did You No Wrong	J. Geils Band	104	BB
16/02/1974	Fool's Paradise	Don Mclean	107	BB
16/02/1974	Singin' In The Rain	Sammy Davis Jr.	110	CB
16/02/1974	The Americans (A Canadian's Opinion)	Tex Ritter	111	CB

16/02/1974	Gumbo Jones	Charlie Allen & Pacific Gas & Electric	113	CB
16/02/1974	Windfall	Rick Nelson & The Stone Canyon Band	116	CB
16/02/1974	Follow The Spirit	Daniel Moore	120	CB
02/03/1974	Us And Them	Pink Floyd	101	BB
02/03/1974	My Fellow Americans	Chris Glendon	102	CB
02/03/1974	A European (Speaks Up For The U.S.)	Guido Sarducci	103	CB
02/03/1974	Rock Me On The Water	Eugene Wallace	103	CB
02/03/1974	Stone County	Johnny Winter	106	CB
02/03/1974	I'm Falling In Love (I Feel Good All Over)	Fantastic Four	109	CB
02/03/1974	Lovin' The Easy Way	Dobie Gray	110	CB
02/03/1974	Saxophones	Jimmy Buffett	110	CB
09/03/1974	She's My Lady (She's All I Need)	Don Reed	107	CB
09/03/1974	Willie Pass The Water	Ripple	108	BB
09/03/1974	Colour My World	Arthur Prysock	117	CB
16/03/1974	Ma-Ma-Ma Belle	Electric Light Orchestra	102	CB
16/03/1974	Saxophones	Jimmy Buffett	105	BB
16/03/1974	Let's Go, Let's Go, Let's Go	The Chambers Brothers	106	BB
16/03/1974	Madelaine	Stu Nunnery	107	BB
16/03/1974	Your Funny Moods	Skip Mchoney And The Casuals	113	BB
16/03/1974	Changes	David Bowie	119	CB
23/03/1974	Nice To Be Around	Maureen Mcgovern	101	BB
23/03/1974	Bad, Bad Leroy Brown	Frank Sinatra	106	CB
23/03/1974	Ain't It Hell Up In Harlem	Edwin Starr	110	BB
23/03/1974	Ecstacy	Raspberries	116	CB
23/03/1974	Love Me Tender	Mick Ronson	117	CB
23/03/1974	Sweet Jane (Live)	Lou Reed	118	CB
30/03/1974	I Wouldn't Give You Up	Ecstasy, Passion & Pain	102	BB
30/03/1974	Streakin'	The Streakers	103	CB
30/03/1974	Sweet Stuff	Sylvia	103	BB
30/03/1974	Headline Hustler	10 C.C.	105	CB

30/03/1974	I Wouldn't Give You Up	Ecstasy, Passion & Pain	105	CB
30/03/1974	Chicago, Damn	BoBBi Humphrey	108	CB
30/03/1974	Let's Go, Let's Go, Let's Go	The Chambers Brothers	116	CB
06/04/1974	Do It Again (Live)	Deodato/Airto	105	CB
06/04/1974	Steam Heat	Pointer Sisters	108	BB
06/04/1974	Sweet Rhode Island Red	Ike & Tina Turner	109	CB
06/04/1974	Look For The Light	B.W. Stevenson	111	CB
06/04/1974	Superstreaker	Flesh Gordon & The Nude Hollywood Argyles	118	CB
13/04/1974	You Make It So Hard (To Say No)	Boz Scaggs	104	CB
13/04/1974	Same Old Song And Dance	Aerosmith	106	CB
13/04/1974	Theme Of Foxy Brown	Willie Hutch	110	CB
20/04/1974	Traveling Boy	Garfunkel	102	BB
20/04/1974	Don't Mess Up A Good Thing	Greg Allman	106	BB
20/04/1974	Nothin' To Lose	Kiss	106	CB
20/04/1974	Main Theme From "THE Young And The Restless"	The Ventures	118	CB
27/04/1974	Love That Really Counts	Natural Four	102	CB
27/04/1974	Boney Moroney	Johnny Winter	103	CB
27/04/1974	Davy	Shirley Bassey	104	CB
27/04/1974	Prisoner Of Love	The Vogues	107	CB
27/04/1974	That's The Way It Will Stay	Tomorrow's Promise	112	CB
04/05/1974	(You Keep Me) Hangin' On	Ann Peebles	102	BB
04/05/1974	We Can Make It Last Forever	Ronnie Dyson	102	CB
04/05/1974	(You Keep Me) Hanging On	Ann Peebles	104	CB
04/05/1974	Chicago, Damn	BoBBi Humphrey	106	BB
04/05/1974	New York City Girl	Rob Hegel	106	CB
04/05/1974	Sweet Rhode Island Red	Ike & Tina Turner	106	BB
04/05/1974	O Heaven (How You've Changed To Me)	Melissa Manchester	112	CB
11/05/1974	Wonderful	Isaac Hayes	101	CB
11/05/1974	I Fell In Love With You Sometime	Gary & Dave	117	CB
11/05/1974	Strut Your Stuff	Tom Scott & The L.A. Express	117	CB

11/05/1974	I Only Have Eyes For You	Mel Carter	119	CB
11/05/1974	Be That Way	Jimmy Gray Hall	120	CB
18/05/1974	There Will Never Be Any Peace (Until God Is Seated At The	The Chi-Lites	101	CB
18/05/1974	Something	Johnny Rodriguez	102	CB
18/05/1974	I Believe	The Ebonys	104	CB
18/05/1974	I Only Have Eyes For You	Mel Carter	104	BB
18/05/1974	Dime Senor	Mocedades	107	CB
18/05/1974	Something There Is About You	Bob Dylan	107	BB
18/05/1974	Blue Monday	Frankie Ford	118	CB
18/05/1974	Behind Closed Doors	Little Milton	120	CB
25/05/1974	Standing In The Rain	The James Gang	101	BB
25/05/1974	Sadie Take A Lover	Sam Neely	103	BB
25/05/1974	Sadie Take A Lover	Sam Neely	103	CB
01/06/1974	Lean It All On Me	Diana Trask	101	BB
01/06/1974	Honey Bee	Gloria Gaynor	103	BB
01/06/1974	Burn	Deep Purple	105	BB
01/06/1974	Rock 'N' Roll Streaker	Elephants Memory	110	CB
01/06/1974	You'll Never Know	Denny Doherty	114	CB
01/06/1974	Do It Over	Olympic Runners	115	CB
01/06/1974	Sweet Child	Johnny Mathis	117	CB
01/06/1974	Goodbye Maria	Clint Holmes	122	CB
08/06/1974	Stranded In The Jungle	New York Dolls	105	CB
08/06/1974	Six Days On The Road	Johnny Rivers	110	CB
08/06/1974	Burn	Deep Purple	115	CB
08/06/1974	Lying To Myself	Delfonics	118	CB
15/06/1974	Six Days On The Road	Johnny Rivers	106	BB
15/06/1974	Love Train (Part One)	Bunny Sigler	111	CB
22/06/1974	The Man You Are In Me	Janis Ian	105	CB
22/06/1974	The Best Time Of My Life	Joe Simon	106	CB
22/06/1974	Wovoka	Redbone	113	CB

22/06/1974	(I Think You Better) Think About Forgetting Me	Ronn Price	120	CB
22/06/1974	Arise And Shine (Let's Get It On)	The Independents	121	CB
22/06/1974	Where Do We Go From Here	Trammps	122	CB
29/06/1974	Take Your Pleasure Where You Find It	Wilson Pickett	106	CB
29/06/1974	Flight 309 To Tennessee	Vicki Britton	110	CB
29/06/1974	Forever Young	Joan Baez	117	CB
06/07/1974	Wovoka	Redbone	101	BB
06/07/1974	Dance Party Music	Carl James & Jackie Irvin	105	CB
06/07/1974	Watermelon Man	Herbie Hancock	105	CB
06/07/1974	Caddo Queen	Maggie Bell	110	CB
06/07/1974	Main Line	Ashford & Simpson	111	CB
13/07/1974	Tell Me That I'm Wrong	Blood, Sweat & Tears	101	CB
13/07/1974	Light Shine	Jesse Colin Young	102	CB
13/07/1974	One Man Band	Leo Sayer	103	BB
13/07/1974	The Wall Street Shuffle	10 C.C.	103	BB
13/07/1974	The Man You Are In Me	Janis Ian	104	BB
13/07/1974	Super Cool	Kiki Dee	108	BB
13/07/1974	What Goes Up (Must Come Down)	Tyrone Davis	110	CB
20/07/1974	You Turned My World Around	Frank Sinatra	104	CB
20/07/1974	Desperado	Linda Ronstadt	105	CB
20/07/1974	Anytime...Babe	David Clayton-Thomas	107	CB
20/07/1974	Do It Over	Olympic Runners	107	BB
20/07/1974	Colorado	Linda Ronstadt	108	BB
20/07/1974	Come On Say It	Henry Gross	109	BB
20/07/1974	Warmin' Up The Band	Don Everly	110	BB
20/07/1974	Put The Music Where Your Mouth Is	Olympic Runners	111	CB
20/07/1974	Raindrops	Barbara Acklin	112	CB
20/07/1974	Save The Sunlight	Herb Alpert & The T.J.B. Featuring Lani Hall	113	CB
27/07/1974	Summertime In The City	The Manhattans	103	CB
27/07/1974	Game Called Love	The Originals	105	CB

27/07/1974	Jump Back	Tom Scott & The L.A. Express	110	CB
03/08/1974	Song For Anna (Chanson D' Anna)	Ohta-San	104	BB
03/08/1974	Many Rivers To Cross	Nilsson	109	BB
03/08/1974	Shang-A-Lang	Tinker's Moon	114	CB
03/08/1974	Let's Make Love (At Home Sometime)	The Escorts	116	CB
03/08/1974	Funky Music Sho Nuff Turns Me On	Yvonne Fair	117	CB
03/08/1974	You	Bill Withers	118	CB
03/08/1974	1-2-3	The Chambers Brothers	121	CB
03/08/1974	I Need It Just As Bad As You	Laura Lee	121	CB
10/08/1974	Free	Fresh Start	104	BB
10/08/1974	Little Bit Of Understanding	B.W. Stevenson	108	CB
17/08/1974	Jesse James (Is An Outlaw, Honey)	Rick Cunha	102	CB
17/08/1974	Leaving Whipporwhill	Leon Russell	104	CB
17/08/1974	Lover's Cross	Melanie	109	BB
17/08/1974	If I Ever Lose This Heaven	Quincy Jones	110	CB
17/08/1974	Summer Love (b-side)	The Blackbyrds	101b	BB
24/08/1974	Put The Music Where Your Mouth Is	Olympic Runners	103	BB
24/08/1974	I Overlooked An Orchid	Mickey Gilley	104	CB
24/08/1974	Dancing In The Street	The Dovells	105	BB
24/08/1974	Summer Girl	Craig Ruhnke	107	BB
24/08/1974	Sugar Lump	Leon Haywood	108	BB
24/08/1974	Rock N' Roll A-B-C's	Freddy Cannon	121	CB
31/08/1974	Suzie Girl	Redbone	108	BB
31/08/1974	A Woman's Place	Gilbert O'sullivan	109	CB
31/08/1974	Hello Summertime	BoBBy Goldsboro	112	CB
31/08/1974	Kissin' In The Back Row Of The Movies	The Drifters	114	CB
07/09/1974	America	David Essex	101	BB
07/09/1974	Standing On The Verge Of Getting It On	Funkadelic	105	CB
07/09/1974	America	David Essex	106	CB
07/09/1974	I Wash My Hands Of The Whole Damn Deal, Part I	The New Birth	106	CB

07/09/1974	Psycho	Jack Kittel	114	CB
14/09/1974	Meet Me On The Corner Down At Joe's Café	Peter Noone	101	BB
14/09/1974	Love Is Like A Butterfly	Dolly Parton	102	CB
14/09/1974	The Ballad Of Evel Knievel	John Culliton Mahoney	105	BB
14/09/1974	Little Gold Band	The Gentrys	110	CB
14/09/1974	You've Been Doing Wrong For So Long	Thelma Houston	118	CB
14/09/1974	Love Makes It Right	The Soul Children	120	CB
21/09/1974	In My Little Corner Of The World	Marie Osmond	102	BB
21/09/1974	Nothing You Can Do	Average White Band	102	CB
21/09/1974	Watch Out For Lucy	Dobie Gray	107	BB
21/09/1974	U.S. Blues	Grateful Dead	109	CB
21/09/1974	Forever And Ever (Baby I'm Gonna Be Yours)	Keith Hampshire	113	CB
21/09/1974	Don't Let Me Down	Hollies	114	CB
21/09/1974	Delta Dirt	Larry Gatlin	118	CB
21/09/1974	Dancin' To The Music	Rockin' Horse	120	CB
21/09/1974	Laughter In The Rain	Lea Roberts	125	CB
28/09/1974	Walking In The Wind	Traffic	101	CB
28/09/1974	You Call Me Back	Clyde Brown	101	CB
28/09/1974	Write Me A Letter	Defranco Family Featuring Tony Defranco	104	BB
28/09/1974	Love Is Like A Butterfly	Dolly Parton	105	BB
28/09/1974	Voo-Doo Magic	The Rhodes Kids	105	CB
28/09/1974	She's Gone	Lou Rawls	115	CB
05/10/1974	Look Away	Ozark Mountain Daredevils	101	BB
05/10/1974	Pencil Thin Mustache	Jimmy Buffett	101	BB
05/10/1974	Time	Mighty Clouds Of Joy	102	BB
05/10/1974	Worn Out Broken Heart	Sam Dees	103	CB
05/10/1974	Let Go	Brian Cadd	112	CB
05/10/1974	I Did What I Did For Maria	Errol Sober	113	CB
05/10/1974	City Of Brotherly Love	Soul Survivors	116	CB
05/10/1974	Rock 'N Roll With Me	Donovan	116	CB

05/10/1974	Write Me A Letter	Defranco Family Featuring Tony Defranco	120	CB
12/10/1974	I Did What I Did For Maria	Errol Sober	108	BB
12/10/1974	Subterranean Homesick Blues	Nilsson	108	CB
12/10/1974	Pencil Thin Mustache	Jimmy Buffett	119	CB
19/10/1974	The Ballad Of Lucy Jordan	Dr. Hook & The Medicine Show	102	CB
19/10/1974	Train Kept A Rollin'	Aerosmith	108	CB
19/10/1974	Hey Ya'll	Black Oak Arkansas	120	CB
19/10/1974	Touch Too Much	Arrows	123	CB
26/10/1974	Please Mr. Postman	The Pat Boone Family	101	CB
26/10/1974	Evergreen	Booker T	103	CB
26/10/1974	I Keep On Lovin' You	Z.Z. Hill	104	BB
26/10/1974	Names, Tags, Numbers & Labels	Albert Hammond	107	CB
26/10/1974	Time	Mighty Clouds Of Joy	107	CB
26/10/1974	Falling Out Of Love	Buster Brown	111	CB
26/10/1974	Ladies Love Outlaws	Tom Rush	117	CB
26/10/1974	First Time Ever I Saw Your Face	The Clams	124	CB
02/11/1974	Carousel Man	Cher	104	CB
02/11/1974	Laughter In The Rain	Lea Roberts	109	BB
02/11/1974	One More Time	Redbone	110	CB
02/11/1974	Roses Are Red My Love	Wednesday	116	CB
02/11/1974	Sally Can't Dance	Lou Reed	118	CB
09/11/1974	Sally Can't Dance	Lou Reed	103	BB
09/11/1974	When Mabel Comes In The Room	Michael Allen	104	CB
09/11/1974	You Can't Go Halfway	Johnny Nash	105	BB
09/11/1974	Is It In	Eddie Harris	107	BB
09/11/1974	I Need Time	Bloodstone	108	BB
09/11/1974	I Don't Know How To Say Goodbye	Andy & David Williams	114	CB
09/11/1974	Palm Grease	Herbie Hancock	115	CB
09/11/1974	Bring Back The Love Of Yesterday	The Dells	123	CB
16/11/1974	Lady Lay	Wayne Newton	101	BB

16/11/1974	Trusting Heart	The Trammps	101	BB
16/11/1974	Charade	Bee Gees	102	CB
16/11/1974	U.S. Of A	Donna Fargo	102	CB
16/11/1974	Charade	Bee Gees	103	BB
16/11/1974	Careful Man	John Edwards	109	BB
16/11/1974	RuBBer Bands And Bits Of String	Telly Savalas	113	CB
16/11/1974	Feel Like Making Love	Bob James	115	CB
23/11/1974	Mississippi Cotton Picking Delta Town	Charley Pride	105	CB
23/11/1974	The Credit Card Song	Dick Feller	105	BB
23/11/1974	Lil' Red Ridin' Hood	The Undisputed Truth	106	BB
23/11/1974	California My Way	The Main Ingredient	108	CB
23/11/1974	Four Or Five Times	Peter Dean	108	CB
23/11/1974	We Got Love	Buddy Miles	108	BB
23/11/1974	Roller Coaster Weekend	Joe Vitale	116	CB
07/12/1974	Guilty	First Choice	103	BB
07/12/1974	Gonna Make You A Star	David Essex	105	BB
07/12/1974	Just Leave Me Alone	Don Potter	109	CB
07/12/1974	La La Love You	Don Mclean	111	CB
14/12/1974	Get Into The Wind	Steppenwolf	111	CB
14/12/1974	Heroes Are Hard To Find	Fleetwood Mac	122	CB
21/12/1974	Baby Blues	Love Unlimited Orchestra	102	BB
21/12/1974	Mine For Me	Rod Stewart	106	CB
21/12/1974	I Know (You Don't Want Me No More)	Newbeats	113	CB
21/12/1974	Boogie Joe, The Grinder	Quincy Jones	114	CB
28/12/1974	Sunshine (Part Ii) (Live)	The O'jays	101	CB
28/12/1974	Pledging My Love	Tom Jones	106	CB
28/12/1974	Bring It On Home To Me	Dave Mason	119	CB
28/12/1974	Generation	Buffy Sainte-Marie	119	CB
04/01/1975	Do Your Thing	James And BoBBy Purify	101	BB
04/01/1975	Since I Found My Baby	Cornelius Brothers & Sister Rose	105	CB

04/01/1975	Words (Are Impossible)	Margie Joseph	115	CB
11/01/1975	Grab It	Olympic Runners	103	BB
11/01/1975	Guilty	First Choice	103	CB
11/01/1975	Love Don't You Go Through No Changes On Me	Sister Sledge	103	CB
11/01/1975	Coochie Coochie Coo	Hudson Brothers	104	CB
11/01/1975	Love Is What You Make It	New York City	104	BB
11/01/1975	Alaska Bloodline	Don Kirshner Introducing Joe & Bing	105	CB
18/01/1975	Super Duper Love - Part 1 (Are You Diggin' On Me)	Sugar Billy	102	CB
18/01/1975	Chico And The Man (Main Theme)	José Feliciano	104	CB
18/01/1975	Wolfman Jack	Todd Rundgren (featuring Wolfman Jack)	105	BB
18/01/1975	I Hear Those Church Bells Ringing/Chapel Of Love	Shirley	106	CB
18/01/1975	Get It Up For Love	Johnny Rivers	111	CB
25/01/1975	Where Have They Gone	Jimmy Beaumont & The Skyliners	103	CB
25/01/1975	Coochie Coochie Coo	Hudson Brothers	108	BB
25/01/1975	Raised On Rock	Johnny Winter	108	BB
01/02/1975	Changes (Messin' With My Mind)	Vernon Burch	101	BB
01/02/1975	Disco-Tekin	Reunion	101	BB
01/02/1975	Raised On Rock	Johnny Winter	107	CB
01/02/1975	Lover Please	Kris Kristofferson & Rita Coolidge	113	CB
08/02/1975	All Our Dreams Are Coming True	Gene Page	104	BB
08/02/1975	Snookeroo	Ringo Starr	105	CB
08/02/1975	Nashville	Hoyt Axton	106	BB
08/02/1975	Walking Slow	Jackson Browne	114	CB
08/02/1975	Tonight Is The Night	Betty Wright	119	CB
08/02/1975	Paper Money	Montrose	122	CB
15/02/1975	Stomp And Buck Dance	The Crusaders	102	BB
15/02/1975	Smokey Factory Blues	Steppenwolf	105	CB
15/02/1975	You're Not A Bad Ghost, Just An Old Song	Melanie	116	CB
15/02/1975	Believe Half Of What You See (And None Of What You Hear)	Leon Haywood	120	CB
22/02/1975	Caroline	Jefferson Starship	101	CB

22/02/1975	Hey Girl, Come And Get It	The Stylistics	101	CB
22/02/1975	Givin' It All Up	The J. Geils Band	106	BB
22/02/1975	Runaway	The Rhodes Kids	107	BB
01/03/1975	Uproar	Anne Murray	101	CB
01/03/1975	Only So Much Oil In The Ground	Tower Of Power	102	BB
01/03/1975	Powerful People	Gino Vannelli	102	CB
01/03/1975	Smokin' Room	Carl Carlton	104	CB
01/03/1975	No Love In The Room	The 5th Dimension	105	BB
08/03/1975	Toby	The Chi-Lites	104	CB
08/03/1975	Changes (Messin' With My Mind)	Vernon Burch	119	CB
08/03/1975	Dancin' (On A Saturday Night)	Bond	119	CB
15/03/1975	This Ol' Cowboy	The Marshall Tucker Band	101	CB
15/03/1975	Speed Trap	Hoyt Axton	105	BB
15/03/1975	Runaway	The Rhodes Kids	119	CB
22/03/1975	Kojak Columbo	Nilsson	104	CB
22/03/1975	Smokey Factory Blues	Steppenwolf	108	BB
29/03/1975	It Do Feel Good	Donna Fargo	101	CB
29/03/1975	The Bottle (La Botella)	Bataan	102	BB
29/03/1975	The Essence Of Joan (Ain't It Funny How Love Can Own You)	Andy Kim	103	CB
29/03/1975	Your Mama Won't Like Me	Suzi Quatro	103	CB
29/03/1975	You Make It So Hard (To Say No)	Boz Scaggs	108	CB
29/03/1975	2 + 2	The Jaggerz	118	CB
29/03/1975	The Old Schoolyard	Linda Lewis	124	CB
05/04/1975	A Pirate Looks At Forty	Jimmy Buffett	101	BB
05/04/1975	Leave It Alone	Dynamic Superiors	102	BB
05/04/1975	Save Me	Silver Bird	103	BB
05/04/1975	The Next Best Thing	Carl Graves	103	BB
05/04/1975	Got To Get You Back In My Life	New York City	105	BB
05/04/1975	Blue Eyed Soul (PT. I)	Carl Douglas Band	110	CB
12/04/1975	Leave My World	Johnny Bristol	104	BB

12/04/1975	Hold On (Just A Little Bit Longer)	Anthony And The Imperials	106	BB
12/04/1975	You Make It So Hard (To Say No)	Boz Scaggs	107	BB
12/04/1975	Pick Up The Pieces One By One	A.A.B.B.	108	BB
12/04/1975	Shoot 'EM Up	Joe Vitale	109	CB
12/04/1975	Good Vibrations	The Troggs	111	CB
12/04/1975	The Hands Of Time (Brian's Song)	Atlantic & Pacific Featuring Peter Gormann	113	CB
12/04/1975	Willing To Learn	Tower Of Power	117	CB
19/04/1975	All Right Now	Lea Roberts	101	CB
19/04/1975	They Don't Make 'EM Like That Anymore	Reunion	101	CB
19/04/1975	Good Vibrations	The Troggs	102	BB
19/04/1975	You Can't Get Off With Your Shoes On	Barefoot Jerry	102	CB
26/04/1975	Crystal World	Crystal Grass	102	BB
26/04/1975	Gringo En Mexico	Maria Muldaur	103	CB
26/04/1975	Astral Man	Nektar	111	CB
26/04/1975	Achoo	Sparks	112	CB
26/04/1975	When The Party's Over	Janis Ian	112	CB
26/04/1975	Just Like Romeo And Juliet	Fallen Angels	116	CB
03/05/1975	All Cried Out	Lamont Dozier	101	BB
03/05/1975	Just Like Romeo And Juliet	Fallen Angels	106	BB
10/05/1975	Gemini	The Miracles	101	BB
10/05/1975	Survivors	John Stewart	108	CB
10/05/1975	Rock And Roll Till I Die	Diamond Reo	115	CB
17/05/1975	Coney Island	Herb Alpert & The T.J.B.	101	CB
17/05/1975	Classified	C.W. Mccall	102	CB
17/05/1975	It Ain't No Fun	Shirley Brown	103	CB
17/05/1975	Take It From Me	Dionne Warwicke	110	CB
17/05/1975	Come On Down (Get Your Head Out Of The Clouds)	Greg Perry	124	CB
24/05/1975	Sex Machine (Part I)	James Brown	102	CB
24/05/1975	Beautiful Loser	Bob Seger	103	BB
24/05/1975	Isn't It A Shame	Randy Edelman	109	BB

31/05/1975	Another Night	The Hollies	101	CB
31/05/1975	I Ain't All Bad	Charley Pride	101	BB
31/05/1975	Honey Baby (Be Mine)	Innervision	106	BB
31/05/1975	Take Good Care Of Her	The Rhodes Kids	107	CB
31/05/1975	You Can't Get Off With Your Shoes On	Barefoot Jerry	109	BB
31/05/1975	Run Tell The People	Daniel Boone	117	CB
31/05/1975	It's All Up To You	Jim Capaldi	118	CB
07/06/1975	Bye Bye Baby	Bay City Rollers	104	CB
07/06/1975	Christina	Terry Jacks	106	BB
07/06/1975	Your Love (Is The Only Love)	Paul Revere & The Raiders	123	CB
14/06/1975	One Man Band	Leo Sayer	101	CB
14/06/1975	Too Late To Worry, Too Blue To Cry	Ronnie Milsap	101	BB
14/06/1975	Paradise	Ted Neeley	102	BB
14/06/1975	Think Twice	Donald Byrd	104	BB
14/06/1975	Walk On By	Gloria Gaynor	104	CB
14/06/1975	Mary Anne	Fallenrock	111	CB
14/06/1975	I Betcha Didn't Know That	Frederick Knight	113	CB
21/06/1975	Stars In My Eyes	Sugarloaf/Jerry Corbetta	104	CB
21/06/1975	My Honky Tonk Ways	Kenny O'dell	105	BB
21/06/1975	Supership	George "Bad" Benson	105	BB
21/06/1975	It's All Up To You	Jim Capaldi	110	BB
21/06/1975	Isn't It Always Love	Karen Alexander	112	CB
21/06/1975	Cry Cry Cry	Shirley (And Company)	123	CB
28/06/1975	Classified	C.W. Mccall	101	BB
28/06/1975	Superman Superman	Les Variations	103	CB
28/06/1975	Yolanda	BoBBy Bland	104	BB
28/06/1975	Paradise	Ted Neeley	112	CB
28/06/1975	Island Woman	Pablo Cruise	115	CB
05/07/1975	It's All Over Now	BoBBy Womack & Bill Withers	101	CB
05/07/1975	Our Last Song Together	BoBBy Sherman	103	CB

05/07/1975	Life And Death In G&A	Love Childs Afro Cuban Blues Band	105	CB
05/07/1975	Songbird	Jesse Colin Young	115	CB
05/07/1975	Gimme Some Lovin'	John Livigni	120	CB
12/07/1975	(Baby) Don't Let It Mess Your Mind	Donny Gerrard	104	BB
12/07/1975	Hi-Jack	Barrabas	104	BB
12/07/1975	Love Do Me Right	Rockin' Horse	104	BB
12/07/1975	I Feel A Song (In My Heart)	Bob James	105	BB
12/07/1975	Love Being Your Fool	Charlie Whitehead	106	BB
12/07/1975	El Bimbo	Herb Alpert & The T.J.B.	110	CB
12/07/1975	Barbara Ann	The Beach Boys	111	CB
12/07/1975	The Entertainer (If They Could Only See Me Now)	J.R. Bailey	119	CB
19/07/1975	Hot Summer Girls	Flash Cadillac & The Continental Kids	101	CB
19/07/1975	Hot Summer Girls	Flash Cadillac And The Continental Kids	102	BB
19/07/1975	Love For Sale	James Last	106	BB
19/07/1975	What An Animal	Fludd	118	CB
26/07/1975	Barbara Ann	The Beach Boys	101	BB
26/07/1975	Can't Live This Way	Barnaby Bye	101	CB
26/07/1975	Island Woman	Pablo Cruise	104	BB
26/07/1975	Naked As The Day I Was Born	Stanley Turrentine	105	BB
26/07/1975	It's In His Kiss	Linda Lewis	107	BB
26/07/1975	Please Tell Him That I Said Hello	DeBBie Campbell	112	CB
26/07/1975	Drag It Over Here	Olympic Runners	117	CB
26/07/1975	High Above My Head	Ray Thomas	117	CB
26/07/1975	If You Think You Know How To Love Me	Smokey	125	CB
02/08/1975	Back Door Man	Black Oak Arkansas	101	CB
02/08/1975	Door Number Three	Jimmy Buffett	102	BB
02/08/1975	Rock And Roll Music	Humble Pie	105	BB
02/08/1975	Door Number Three	Jimmy Buffett	109	CB
09/08/1975	Get It Up For Love	David Cassidy	108	CB
09/08/1975	I Created A Monster	Z.Z. Hill	109	BB

16/08/1975	I Can Understand It	Kokomo	101	BB
16/08/1975	Rosanne	The Guess Who	103	CB
16/08/1975	Wouldn't It Be Nice	The Beach Boys	103	BB
16/08/1975	Work Hard Labor	Diamond Reo	108	BB
16/08/1975	Drag It Over Here	Olympic Runners	109	BB
16/08/1975	Waymore's Blues	Waylon Jennings	110	BB
16/08/1975	For Your Love	Christopher Paul & Shawn	115	CB
16/08/1975	The Serenade That We Played	Diane Gilland	116	CB
16/08/1975	(Call Me Your) Anything Man	BoBBy Moore	118	CB
23/08/1975	Minstrel In The Gallery	Jethro Tull	102	CB
23/08/1975	The Seeker	Dolly Parton	105	BB
23/08/1975	Giddyap Girl (Ride Your Horsey Home)	The Bareback Rockers	111	CB
23/08/1975	Morning	Michael Kenny	112	CB
30/08/1975	When You're Young And In Love	The Choice Four	103	CB
30/08/1975	Rosanne	The Guess Who	105	BB
30/08/1975	Control Tower	Magic Disco Machine	106	BB
30/08/1975	Ooola La	Betty Wright	106	CB
30/08/1975	Knockin' On Heaven's Door	Eric Clapton	109	CB
30/08/1975	Summer Days	Lou Christie	120	CB
06/09/1975	When You're Young And In Love	Ralph Carter	107	CB
06/09/1975	Gimme Some (Part One)	Jimmy "Bo" Horn	112	CB
06/09/1975	Time Will Tell	Flash Cadillac & The Continental Kids	113	CB
13/09/1975	Messin' With My Mind	Labelle	101	CB
13/09/1975	(If You Want It) Do It Yourself	Gloria Gaynor	103	CB
13/09/1975	Love Me Now	Gino Vannelli	103	CB
13/09/1975	Ice Cream Sodas And Lollipops And A Red Hot Spinning Top	Paul Delicato	106	CB
13/09/1975	Right From The Shark's Jaws (The Jaws Interview)	Byron Mcnaughton & His All News Orchestra	106	BB
13/09/1975	Love Don't Come No Stronger (Than Yours And Mine)	Jeff Perry	108	BB
20/09/1975	Bad Sneakers	Steely Dan	103	BB
20/09/1975	I Just Can't Make It (Without You)	Philly Devotions	106	BB

20/09/1975	I Don't Love You But I Think I Like You	Gilbert O'sullivan	107	CB
20/09/1975	Don't It Make You Wanna Dance?	Rusty Wier	119	CB
20/09/1975	I'm Ready To Love You Now	Sarah Johns	122	CB
20/09/1975	Peace In The Family	The Johnson Family	124	CB
27/09/1975	That's How Long I'll Be Loving You	Bunny Sigler	102	BB
27/09/1975	Super "Jaws"	Seven Seas	104	BB
27/09/1975	Thin Ice	Ozark Mountain Daredevils	109	CB
27/09/1975	Oh Baby	Wayne Miran & Rush Release	110	CB
27/09/1975	Stuck In A Hole	Caravan	110	BB
27/09/1975	As I Look Into The Fire	Heartsfield	113	CB
27/09/1975	No Rollin' Boogie	Eric Quincy Tate	114	CB
27/09/1975	Lookout	Sons Of Champlin	116	CB
04/10/1975	I'm Down	The Hollies	104	BB
04/10/1975	You Got A Lock On Me	Jerry Reed	104	BB
04/10/1975	Ii Est Toujours Temps Pour Partir (Never Can Say Goodbye)	Napoli & Glasson	106	BB
04/10/1975	Magic In My Life	The 5th Dimension	107	CB
04/10/1975	Be True To Your School	Papa Doo Run Run	116	CB
11/10/1975	I'm Still Gonna Need You	The Osmonds	102	CB
11/10/1975	Lookout	Sons Of Champlin	103	BB
11/10/1975	Oh Baby	Wayne Miran And Rush Release	104	BB
11/10/1975	Barbados	Typically Tropical	108	BB
11/10/1975	Just Out Of Reach	Perry Como	110	CB
11/10/1975	Something Lacking In Me	Nigel Olsson	111	CB
18/10/1975	Hold On To Love	Peter Skellern	106	BB
18/10/1975	Southern Lady	Timi Yuro	108	BB
18/10/1975	Stuck In A Hole	Caravan	112	CB
25/10/1975	Love Don't Come No Stronger (Than Yours And Mine)	Jeff Perry	103	CB
25/10/1975	Do You Wonder	Shawn Phillips	106	BB
25/10/1975	Can't Smile Without You	David Martin	114	CB
25/10/1975	Can I Change My Mind	Johnny Rivers	120	CB

25/10/1975	Rolling Stone	David Essex	120	CB
01/11/1975	Moonlighting	Leo Sayer	102	CB
01/11/1975	Put Another Log On The Fire (Male Chauvinist National Anthem)	Tompall	103	BB
01/11/1975	You Were So Warm	Dwight Twilley Band	103	BB
01/11/1975	Using The Power	Climax Blues Band	104	CB
01/11/1975	I Got A Song	Sugarloaf/Jerry Corbetta	110	BB
01/11/1975	I Only Have Love	Syl Johnson	118	CB
08/11/1975	Louisiana Lou And Three Card Monty John	The Allman Brothers Band	101	CB
08/11/1975	(I'm Going By) The Stars In Your Eyes	Ron Banks & The Dramatics	102	CB
08/11/1975	When The Band Was Singin' "Shaking All Over"	The Guess Who	102	BB
08/11/1975	Give Me Your Heart	Bloodstone	103	CB
08/11/1975	Let's Do The Latin Hustle	Eddie Drennon & B.B.S. Unlimited	104	CB
08/11/1975	It Makes You Happy (But It Ain't Gonna Last Too Long)	Rare Earth	106	BB
08/11/1975	The Promised Land	Michael Dinner	111	CB
15/11/1975	They All Ask'd For You	The Meters	101	CB
15/11/1975	Building Fires	Flying Burrito Brothers	108	CB
15/11/1975	Using The Power	Climax Blues Band	110	BB
15/11/1975	It's Time For Love	The Chi-Lites	120	CB
22/11/1975	Breakfast For Two	Country Joe Mcdonald	103	CB
22/11/1975	You Set My Heart On Fire	Tina Charles	104	BB
22/11/1975	Loving Arms	Millie Jackson	110	CB
22/11/1975	Crazy	Atlanta Rhythm Section	111	CB
22/11/1975	I'll Take A Tango	Cilla Black	114	CB
29/11/1975	Birmingham Blues	The Charlie Daniels Band	101	BB
29/11/1975	Next Time	Dan Fogelberg	116	CB
29/11/1975	Alone Too Long	Daryl Hall & John Oates	123	CB
06/12/1975	This Is What You Mean To Me	Engelbert Humperdinck	102	BB
06/12/1975	The Zip	Mfsb	115	CB
06/12/1975	Have A Cigar	Pink Floyd	119	CB
13/12/1975	Through The Eyes Of Little Children	Larry Jon Wilson	119	CB

20/12/1975	A Fool In Love	The Frankie Miller Band	101	CB
20/12/1975	We Got To Get Our Thing Together	The Dells	104	BB
20/12/1975	Can't Take My Eyes Off You	Gerri Granger	108	BB
20/12/1975	Get It While The Gettin' Is Good	Leo & Libra With The Mystic Moods	109	BB
27/12/1975	I Had A Love	Ben E. King	104	CB
27/12/1975	Beyond The Milky Way	Iron Butterfly	108	BB
27/12/1975	Children Of The Rain	Austin Roberts	114	CB
27/12/1975	The Little Drummer Boy	Moonlion	116	CB
03/01/1976	Get Outside	Robert Palmer	105	BB
03/01/1976	Mama Coco	Gino Vannelli	105	CB
03/01/1976	Longhaired Redneck	David Allan Coe	117	CB
10/01/1976	Call My Name	Little Richard	106	BB
10/01/1976	Walk Right In	Yvonne Elliman	107	CB
10/01/1976	Where There's A Will, There's A Way	BoBBy Womack	107	CB
10/01/1976	Walk Right In	Yvonne Elliman	109	BB
17/01/1976	Just Your Fool	Leon Haywood	102	CB
17/01/1976	Strong Enough To Be Gentle	Black Oak Arkansas	102	CB
17/01/1976	Baby I'm Sorry	The Blues Busters	105	BB
17/01/1976	Give Me An Inch Girl	Robert Palmer	106	BB
17/01/1976	Mama You're All Right With Me	Four Tops	107	BB
17/01/1976	Fools Rush In	Joey Porrello	108	BB
17/01/1976	Shame On The World	The Main Ingredient	110	CB
24/01/1976	You're Fooling You	The Dramatics	101	CB
24/01/1976	Dolannes Melodie	Jean-Claude Borelly And His Orchestra	106	BB
24/01/1976	A Girl Like You	Nigel Olsson	107	BB
24/01/1976	Last Day Of December	Chilliwack	109	BB
24/01/1976	We're On The Right Track	South Shore Commission	115	CB
24/01/1976	Disco Sax	Houston Person	116	CB
31/01/1976	Just Your Fool	Leon Haywood	102	BB
31/01/1976	Shake Me, Wake Me (When It's Over)	Barbra Streisand	104	CB

31/01/1976	Tonight's The Night	S.S.O.	104	CB
31/01/1976	Chloe	Cy Coleman	107	CB
07/02/1976	(Call Me) The Traveling Man	The Masqueraders	101	BB
07/02/1976	Motels And Memories	T.G. Sheppard	102	BB
07/02/1976	Loving Power	Impressions	103	BB
07/02/1976	The Power Of Love	The Dells	106	BB
14/02/1976	The Happiness Of Having You	Charley Pride	103	CB
14/02/1976	Lovin' As You Wanna Be	Pete Wingfield	108	BB
14/02/1976	Abyssinia Jones	Edwin Starr	113	CB
14/02/1976	The Ashville Union Rescue Mission	Brian Gari	116	CB
21/02/1976	Broken Lady	Larry Gatlin With Family & Friends	101	CB
21/02/1976	I'm So Lonesome I Could Cry	Terry Bradshaw	101	CB
21/02/1976	Love Lifted Me	Kenny Rogers	101	CB
21/02/1976	If Love Must Go	Dobie Gray	102	CB
21/02/1976	Below The Surface	Dan Fogelberg	115	CB
28/02/1976	Take The Money And Run	David Crosby/Graham Nash	103	CB
28/02/1976	Searchin' For A Rainbow	The Marshall Tucker Band	104	BB
28/02/1976	Titles	Barclay James Harvest	113	CB
06/03/1976	Hustle On Up (Do The Bump)	Hidden Strength	105	CB
06/03/1976	Merry-Go-Round Pt. I	Monday After	106	BB
06/03/1976	Spinning The Wheel (With The Girl You Love)	Hudson Brothers	109	CB
06/03/1976	From Us To You	Stairsteps	110	CB
06/03/1976	Sway (Disco Version)	BoBBy Rydell	115	CB
13/03/1976	From Us To You	Stairsteps	102	BB
13/03/1976	Wow	(The Disco Sound Of) Andre Gagnon	102	CB
13/03/1976	Dance, Dance, Dance	Charlie Calello	104	BB
13/03/1976	Hustle On Up (Do The Bump)	Hidden Strength	105	BB
13/03/1976	How Can I Be A Witness	R.B. Hudmon	107	CB
13/03/1976	Holding On	The Road Apples	110	BB
20/03/1976	Strangers In The Night	Bette Midler	101	CB

20/03/1976	Born To Get Down (Born To Mess Around)	Muscle Shoals Horns	105	BB
20/03/1976	Holding On	The Road Apples	106	CB
20/03/1976	Titles	Barclay James Harvest	107	BB
20/03/1976	Cara Mia	Paul Delicato	108	BB
20/03/1976	Colorado Call	Shad O'shea & The 18 Wheelers	110	BB
20/03/1976	It's Been A Long Long Time	Stuff 'N' Ramjett	116	CB
27/03/1976	Love And Understanding (Come Together)	Kool & The Gang	101	CB
27/03/1976	Spanish Hustle	The Fatback Band	101	BB
27/03/1976	More	Carol Williams	102	BB
27/03/1976	Too Young To Feel This Old	Mckendree Spring	110	BB
27/03/1976	Cara Mia	Paul Delicato	112	CB
27/03/1976	You're My One Weakness Girl	Street People	116	CB
27/03/1976	Too Young To Feel This Old	Mckendree Spring	118	CB
27/03/1976	She's A Disco Queen	Oliver Sain	103a	BB
27/03/1976	Party Hearty (b-side)	Oliver Sain	103b	BB
03/04/1976	(Everybody's Goin') Hollywood	Marc Allen Trujillo	102	CB
03/04/1976	Sleep Walkin'	Golden Earring	109	BB
03/04/1976	Today I Started Loving You Again	BoBBy Bland	111	CB
10/04/1976	America The Beautiful	Ray Charles	102	CB
10/04/1976	Today I Started Loving You Again	BoBBy Bland	103	BB
10/04/1976	Do What You Feel	The Atlanta Disco Band	104	BB
10/04/1976	Concrete And Clay	Randy Edelman	108	BB
10/04/1976	Night And Day	John Davis And The Monster Orchestra	109	BB
10/04/1976	Moonlight Serenade	BoBBy Vinton	113	CB
10/04/1976	Peacemaker	Loggins & Messina	113	CB
10/04/1976	The Love I Never Had	Tavares	119	CB
17/04/1976	I Gotta Get Drunk [Live]	Willie Nelson	101	BB
17/04/1976	You Got The Magic	John Fogerty	101	CB
17/04/1976	Grateful	Blue Magic	104	BB
17/04/1976	Forever Lovers	Mac Davis	106	CB

17/04/1976	Love Really Hurts Without You	Alex Brown	107	CB
17/04/1976	Great Balls Of Fire	Black Oak Arkansas	113	CB
24/04/1976	Married, But Not To Each Other	Denise Lasalle	101	CB
24/04/1976	Town Cryer	Scott Key	101	CB
24/04/1976	Sunshine Day	Osibisa	108	BB
24/04/1976	Mississippi Lady	Jim Croce	110	BB
01/05/1976	Yes, I'm Ready	Tom Sullivan	103	BB
01/05/1976	Hey, What's That Dance You're Doing	The Choice Four	107	BB
01/05/1976	Fallen Angel	Rogue	108	BB
01/05/1976	California Strut	Walter Murphy & The Big Apple Band	116	CB
08/05/1976	Baretta's Theme ("Keep Your Eye On The Sparrow")	Sammy Davis Jr.	101	BB
08/05/1976	I Love To Love	Al Downing	107	BB
08/05/1976	It's Cool	The Tymes	107	CB
08/05/1976	Midnight Groove	Love Unlimited Orchestra	108	BB
08/05/1976	Yes, I'm Ready	Tom Sullivan	111	CB
08/05/1976	Baretta's Theme	Sammy Davis Jr.	114	CB
15/05/1976	Open	Smokey Robinson	102	CB
15/05/1976	This Is It	Melba Moore	102	CB
15/05/1976	(What A) Wonderful World	Johnny Nash	103	BB
15/05/1976	Let It Shine	Al Green	107	CB
15/05/1976	Theme From One Flew Over The Cuckoo's Nest	Jack Nitzsche Orchestra	109	BB
15/05/1976	You Know The Feelin'	Steve Wightman	110	BB
15/05/1976	Tubular Bells	The Champs' Boys Orchestra	115	CB
22/05/1976	Lady Of The Lake	Starcastle	101	BB
22/05/1976	You Are So Beautiful	Ray Stevens	101	BB
22/05/1976	Let It Shine	Santana	102	CB
22/05/1976	It's Better Than Walkin' Out	Marlena Shaw	103	BB
22/05/1976	Save Your Kisses For Me	BoBBy Vinton	105	CB
22/05/1976	Smoke Gets In Your Eyes	Penny Mclean	108	BB
29/05/1976	It's Good For The Soul - Pt. I	Luther Vandross	102	BB

29/05/1976	Breaker - Breaker	Outlaws	107	CB
05/06/1976	Do You Wanna Do A Thing	Bloodstone	101	BB
05/06/1976	Tvc 15	David Bowie	101	CB
05/06/1976	A Butterfly For Bucky	BoBBy Goldsboro	102	CB
05/06/1976	Walk Away [Live]	Joe Walsh	105	BB
05/06/1976	Song From M*A*S*H	The New Marketts	106	CB
05/06/1976	Born To Be With You	Dion	108	BB
12/06/1976	That'll Be The Day	Pure Prairie League	106	BB
12/06/1976	The Flag	Charlie Van Dyke	106	CB
12/06/1976	A Time For Celebration	Faith, Hope & Charity With The Choice Four	107	BB
12/06/1976	Hello, Operator	Gerard	109	BB
12/06/1976	It Must Be Love	Tony Joe White	119	CB
19/06/1976	It Ain't The Real Thing	BoBBy Bland	101	CB
19/06/1976	Strokin' (Pt. Ii)	Leon Haywood	101	BB
19/06/1976	Wichita Jail	The Charlie Daniels Band	101	CB
19/06/1976	Married, But Not To Each Other	Denise Lasalle	102	BB
19/06/1976	Up The Creek (Without A Paddle)	The Temptations	102	CB
19/06/1976	I'll Get Over You	Crystal Gayle	109	CB
19/06/1976	Lie To Me	Bill Labounty	109	BB
26/06/1976	A Butterfly For Bucky	BoBBy Goldsboro	101	BB
26/06/1976	Hear The Words, Feel The Feeling	Margie Joseph	111	CB
03/07/1976	Solitary Man	T.G. Sheppard	101	CB
03/07/1976	Sidewalk Surfin' (76 Version)	Jan & Dean	119	CB
04/07/1976	Universal Sound	Kool & The Gang	101	BB
04/07/1976	Tell Me Why	Stairsteps	106	BB
04/07/1976	Town Cryer	Scott Key	110	BB
10/07/1976	Kid Charlemagne	Steely Dan	101	CB
10/07/1976	It Must Be Love	Tony Joe White	108	BB
10/07/1976	You To Me Are Everything, Part I	Revelation	110	CB
10/07/1976	Get It While It's Hot	Eddie Kendricks	112	CB

17/07/1976	Light Up The World With Sunshine	Hamilton, Joe Frank & Dennison	101	CB
17/07/1976	You To Me Are Everything	Broadway	104	CB
17/07/1976	Devil With A Blue Dress	Pratt & Mcclain	105	CB
17/07/1976	Don't Let Me Be Wrong	The Dodgers	107	CB
17/07/1976	Stranger	Johnny Duncan	111	CB
24/07/1976	Let The Good Times Roll [Live]	BoBBy Bland & B.B. King	101	BB
24/07/1976	Slow Motion	The Dells	102	BB
24/07/1976	Cherry Bomb	The Runaways	103	CB
24/07/1976	Sidewalk Surfin' (new Version)	Jan & Dean	107	BB
24/07/1976	Lady Of Spain	Ray Stevens	108	BB
24/07/1976	Another Night	Camel	109	BB
31/07/1976	Struttin' My Stuff	Elvin Bishop	101	CB
31/07/1976	We Both Need Each Other	Norman Connors	101	BB
31/07/1976	Rescue Me	Melissa Manchester	108	CB
31/07/1976	Better Than Average	Brian Gari	116	CB
31/07/1976	Lazy Ways	10cc	104a	BB
31/07/1976	Life Is A Minestrone (b-side)	10cc	104b	BB
07/08/1976	Kill That Roach	Miami	102	BB
07/08/1976	I Don't Want To Go Home	Southside Johnny & The Asbury Jukes	105	BB
07/08/1976	Cherry Bomb	The Runaways	106	BB
14/08/1976	Disco-Fied	Rhythm Heritage	101	BB
14/08/1976	I Need It	Johnny "Guitar" Watson	101	BB
14/08/1976	Give A Broken Heart A Break	Impact	102	BB
14/08/1976	L.O.D. (Love On Delivery)	Billy Ocean	102	CB
14/08/1976	Sing Your Own Song	Mark Lindsay	103	CB
14/08/1976	L.O.D. (Love On Delivery)	Billy Ocean	106	BB
14/08/1976	Yellow Van	Ronnie & The Dirt Riders	111	CB
21/08/1976	The More I See You	Peter Allen	101	CB
21/08/1976	Dead Flowers	New Riders Of The Purple Sage	105	BB
21/08/1976	Nitty Gritty Rock And Roll	Coyote Mccloud	109	CB

21/08/1976	Take Me Away	Roger Mcguinn	110	BB
28/08/1976	Bring It On Home To Me	Mickey Gilley	101	BB
28/08/1976	I Need It	Johnny Guitar Watson	101	CB
28/08/1976	Juicy Fruit (Disco Freak) Pt. I	Isaac Hayes	102	BB
28/08/1976	The More I See You	Peter Allen	108	BB
04/09/1976	Fire	Mother's Finest	108	CB
04/09/1976	Wanna Make Love (Come Flic My Bic)	Sun	109	CB
04/09/1976	Grasshopper	Spin	110	CB
11/09/1976	Energy To Burn	B.T. Express	101	CB
11/09/1976	Come Get To This	Joe Simon	102	BB
11/09/1976	If I Ever Do Wrong	Betty Wright	102	CB
11/09/1976	Cowboy Song	Thin Lizzy	105	CB
18/09/1976	Staying Power	Barbi Benton	104	CB
18/09/1976	Sweet Lady From Georgia	Brotherhood Of Man	104	CB
18/09/1976	Find 'EM, Fool 'EM & Forget 'EM	Dobie Gray	106	CB
18/09/1976	If You Can't Beat 'Em, Join 'Em	Mark Radice	110	BB
25/09/1976	(I'm A) Stand By My Woman Man	Ronnie Milsap	101	CB
25/09/1976	One Night	Roy Head	101	CB
25/09/1976	Little Joe	Red Sovine	102	BB
25/09/1976	Imagination's Sake	Sons Of Champlin	107	BB
25/09/1976	I Wanna Spend My Whole Life With You	Street People	109	BB
25/09/1976	Born To Love	American Tears	118	CB
02/10/1976	Just Can't Be That Way (Ruth's Song)	Weapons Of Peace	102	CB
02/10/1976	Doin' It	Herbie Hancock	104	BB
02/10/1976	Staying Power	Barbi Benton	108	BB
09/10/1976	Daydream Believer	The Monkees	101	CB
09/10/1976	Spotlight	David Crosby/Graham Nash	109	BB
09/10/1976	I Want You (Part I)	Gato Barbieri	110	BB
09/10/1976	Let Me Down Easy	American Flyer	114	CB
09/10/1976	Skateboardin'	Sneakers & Lace	115	CB

16/10/1976	Get You Somebody New	Labelle	102	BB
16/10/1976	The Streets Will Love You To Death - Part I	Leon Haywood	107	BB
16/10/1976	Stand Up And Shout	Gary Toms	109	BB
16/10/1976	Star Child (Mothership Connection)	Parliament	110	CB
16/10/1976	Here's Some Love	Tanya Tucker	116	CB
23/10/1976	You And Me	Tammy Wynette	101	BB
23/10/1976	Undisco Kidd	Funkadelic	102	BB
23/10/1976	You're The One	Blood, Sweat & Tears	106	CB
23/10/1976	Salty Tears	Thelma Jones	107	CB
23/10/1976	Comin'	Chocolate Milk	112	CB
23/10/1976	Dropkick Me, Jesus	BoBBy Bare	114	CB
30/10/1976	Living Together (In Sin)	The Whispers	101	BB
30/10/1976	Duke Of Earl	Bergen White	102	CB
30/10/1976	She Never Knew Me	Don Williams	103	BB
30/10/1976	Dancin' Mama	El Chicano	108	BB
30/10/1976	Things	Anne Murray	113	CB
06/11/1976	Make It Up To Me In Love	Odia Coates & Paul Anka	101	CB
06/11/1976	Ride A Wild Horse	The Sex-O-Lettes	105	BB
06/11/1976	One Last Memory	Impact	107	BB
06/11/1976	It's So Easy/Listen To Me	Denny Laine	108	BB
06/11/1976	Long, Long Time	Larry Santos	109	CB
13/11/1976	Superman Lover	Johnny "Guitar" Watson	101	BB
13/11/1976	Someday (I Didn't Want To Have To Be The One)	Henry Gross	104	CB
20/11/1976	Green Grass And High Tides	Outlaws	101	CB
20/11/1976	Heart On My Sleeve	Bryan Ferry	102	CB
20/11/1976	Midnight Soul Patrol	Quincy Jones	104	BB
20/11/1976	Ninety-Nine And A Half	The Trammps	105	BB
27/11/1976	Every Now And Then	Mac Davis	104	CB
27/11/1976	You're The One	Blood, Sweat & Tears	106	BB
04/12/1976	Far East Mississippi	Ohio Players	101	CB

04/12/1976	I'm Not In Love	Richie Havens	102	BB
04/12/1976	Sherry	The Keane Brothers	103	CB
04/12/1976	Gettin' It In The Street	David Cassidy	105	BB
04/12/1976	Ooh Cha	Soul Train Gang	107	BB
04/12/1976	Don't Fight The Hands (That Need You)	Hamilton, Joe Frank & Dennison	108	CB
11/12/1976	Can't Let A Woman	Ambrosia	102	BB
11/12/1976	Dancing In The Aisles (Takes Me Higher)	Silver Convention	102	BB
11/12/1976	With You	Moments	102	CB
11/12/1976	Who Are You	The Temptations	103	CB
11/12/1976	You Gotta Believe	Pointer Sisters	103	BB
11/12/1976	(We Don't Want Your Money) We Want Mine	Crack The Sky	108	BB
11/12/1976	Long, Long Time	Larry Santos	109	BB
18/12/1976	Feelings	Walter Jackson	101	CB
18/12/1976	King Kong (Your Song)	BoBBy Pickett & Peter Ferrara	101	CB
18/12/1976	Round The World With The RuBBer Duck	C.W. Mccall	101	BB
18/12/1976	Midnight On The Bay	The Stills-Young Band	105	BB
18/12/1976	King Kong (Your Song)	BoBBy Pickett And Peter Ferrara	107	BB
25/12/1976	Be My Girl	Michael Henderson	101	BB
25/12/1976	PhychotiCBumpschool	Bootsy's RuBBer Band	104	BB
25/12/1976	Are You Ready For The Country	Waylon Jennings	106	CB
01/01/1977	Summer Snow	Blue Magic	101	CB
01/01/1977	ROUND The World With The RuBBer Duck	C.W. Mccall	105	CB
15/01/1977	A Love Of Your Own	Awb	101	BB
15/01/1977	Sweet Dreams (Live)	Emmylou Harris	101	CB
15/01/1977	Betcha By Golly Wow	Norman Connors Featuring Phyllis Hyman	102	BB
15/01/1977	Be My Girl	Michael Henderson	103	CB
15/01/1977	Free And Single	The Brothers Johnson	103	BB
15/01/1977	Rita May	Bob Dylan	110a	BB
15/01/1977	Stuck Inside Of Mobile With The Memphis Blues Again [Live]	Bob Dylan	110b	BB
22/01/1977	Ha Cha Cha (Funktion)	Brass Construction	102	CB

22/01/1977	Isn't It A Shame	Labelle	104	CB
22/01/1977	Should I Stay/I Won't Let You Go	Vicki Sue Robinson With The New York Community Choir	104	BB
22/01/1977	The Shuffle	Van Mccoy	105	BB
22/01/1977	Love Is Still Blue	Paul Mauriat And His Orchestra	109	BB
29/01/1977	Bless The Beasts And Children	Barry Devorzon & Perry Botkin Jr.	102	CB
29/01/1977	Don't Make Me Wait Too Long	Barry White	105	BB
29/01/1977	Ashes And Sand	Johnny Rivers	107	CB
05/02/1977	Midnight Love Affair	Carol Douglas	102	BB
05/02/1977	Spy For Brotherhood	The Miracles Featuring Billy Griffin	104	BB
05/02/1977	Bodyheat (Part 1)	James Brown	110	CB
19/02/1977	Dancing Queen	Carol Douglas	110	BB
26/02/1977	I Tried To Tell Myself	Al Green	101	BB
26/02/1977	Fiesta	Gato Barbieri	104	BB
26/02/1977	My Love Is Free	Double Exposure	104	BB
26/02/1977	Get Up And Dance	The Memphis Horns	108	BB
05/03/1977	Dr. Funkenstein	Parliament	102	BB
05/03/1977	Rigor Mortis	Cameo	103	BB
05/03/1977	Every Little Teardrop	Gallagher & Lyle	106	BB
05/03/1977	The Way You Make Me Feel	Melba Moore	108	BB
12/03/1977	Space Age	Jimmy Castor Bunch	101	BB
12/03/1977	You Turned Me On To Love	Johnny Bristol	106	BB
12/03/1977	Heartbeat	The Runaways	110	BB
19/03/1977	Let The Children Play	Santana	102	BB
19/03/1977	Life Is Music	The Ritchie Family	102	BB
19/03/1977	Me And The Elephants	BoBBy Goldsboro	104	BB
19/03/1977	Disco Boy	Frank Zappa	105	BB
19/03/1977	Never Have To Say Goodbye Again	Deardorff & Joseph	109	BB
26/03/1977	To One In Paradise	Alan Parsons Project	108	BB
02/04/1977	Disco Reggae (Tony's Groove) Part 1	Kalyan	102	BB
02/04/1977	Ooh Child	Valerie Carter	103	BB

02/04/1977	(Let Me Get) Sweet On You (b-side)	Graham Parker And The Rumour	107b	BB
09/04/1977	Tattoo Man	Denise Mccann	106	BB
09/04/1977	We're Still Together	Peaches & Herb	107	BB
16/04/1977	Only Love Can Break A Heart	Dionne Warwick	109	BB
23/04/1977	Blessed Is The Woman (With A Man Like Mine)	Shirley Brown	102	BB
23/04/1977	Isn't She Lovely	David Parton	105	BB
23/04/1977	Painting My Love Song	Henry Gross	110	BB
30/04/1977	All The Kids On The Street	The Hollywood Stars	102	CB
30/04/1977	Rhapsody In Blue	Walter Murphy	102	BB
30/04/1977	A Little Love And Understanding	Parker Mcgee	103	CB
30/04/1977	Twenty-Four Hours A Day	Barbara Pennington	107	BB
30/04/1977	Easily	Frankie Valli	108	BB
07/05/1977	Body Vibes	Ohio Players	101	CB
07/05/1977	Super Band	Kool & The Gang	101	BB
14/05/1977	I Can't Get Over You	The Dramatics	101	BB
14/05/1977	Hats Off To Mama	Philippe' Wynn	102	CB
14/05/1977	Only Love Can Break A Heart	BoBBy Vinton	105	CB
14/05/1977	Some Broken Hearts Never Mend	Don Williams	108	BB
14/05/1977	Crystal Ball	Styx	109	BB
21/05/1977	Loving You-Losing You	Phyllis Hyman	103	BB
21/05/1977	I Like Your Style	Tony Wilson	107	CB
21/05/1977	Freddie	Charlene	108	CB
21/05/1977	On And On	Kenny Rankin	110	BB
28/05/1977	Can I Stay	Andy Adams & Egg Cream	109	CB
04/06/1977	This Will Be A Night To Remember	Eddie Holman	102	CB
04/06/1977	Enjoy And Get It On	Zz Top	105	BB
04/06/1977	Picking Up The Pieces Of My Life	Mac Davis	105	CB
04/06/1977	Everything Must Change	George Benson	106	BB
11/06/1977	Light Of A Clear Blue Morning	Dolly Parton	101	CB
11/06/1977	After You Love Me, Why Do You Leave Me	Harold Melvin & The Blue Notes, Featuring Sharon Page	102	BB

11/06/1977	I Love A Mellow Groove	Jimmy Castor Bunch	108	BB
18/06/1977	Take Me Tonight	Tom Jones	101	BB
18/06/1977	Telegram	Silver Convention	103	BB
18/06/1977	Do It For Me	Jennifer	110	BB
25/06/1977	Making Believe	Emmylou Harris	101	CB
25/06/1977	Take Me Tonight	Tom Jones	101	CB
25/06/1977	Your Love Is Rated X	Johnnie Taylor	101	CB
25/06/1977	Let Me Love You Once Before You Go	Dusty Springfield	105	CB
25/06/1977	Short Shorts	The Salsoul Orchestra	106	BB
25/06/1977	Smokey Mountain Log Cabin Jones	The Winters Brothers Band	106	CB
25/06/1977	I Don't Know Why (I Just Do)	Marty RoBBins	108	BB
02/07/1977	If You See Me Getting Smaller I'm Leaving	Jimmy WeBB	103	CB
02/07/1977	I Feel Like I've Been Livin' (On The Dark Side Of The Moon)	The Trampps	105	BB
02/07/1977	Higher & Higher	Jesse Colin Young	109	BB
02/07/1977	What A Sound	Henry Gross	110	BB
09/07/1977	Can't Stay Away	Bootsy's RuBBer Band	104	BB
09/07/1977	Party - Pt. 1	Silk	107	BB
09/07/1977	Magic Of The Music	Stallion	108	BB
09/07/1977	Let Me Love You Once Before You Go	Dusty Springfield	110	BB
16/07/1977	Funky Music	Ju-Par Universal Orchestra	101	BB
16/07/1977	Theme From Star Wars	David Matthews	102	BB
16/07/1977	I Get Lifted	Latimore	104	BB
16/07/1977	Sweet Summertime	Q	108	BB
16/07/1977	You'll Never Rock Alone	Tata Vega	108	BB
23/07/1977	Theme From Star Wars	David Matthews	103	CB
23/07/1977	Getaway	The Salsoul Orchestra	106	CB
23/07/1977	Sunshine	The Undisputed Truth	109	BB
23/07/1977	Who Was It Stole Your Heart Away	Barbara Dickson	110	BB
30/07/1977	I'll Be Leaving Alone	Charley Pride	101	CB
30/07/1977	Rollin' With The Flow	Charlie Rich	101	BB

30/07/1977	This I Swear	Tyrone Davis	102	BB
30/07/1977	Love And Happiness	Al Green	104	BB
30/07/1977	We Never Danced To A Love Song	The Manhattans	104	CB
30/07/1977	Love's Been Known	Big Wha-Koo	107	CB
30/07/1977	Getaway	The Salsoul Orchestra	105a	BB
30/07/1977	Magic Bird Of Fire (b-side)	The Salsoul Orchestra	105b	BB
06/08/1977	Vitamin U	Smokey Robinson	101	BB
06/08/1977	Exodus	Bob Marley & The Wailers	103	CB
06/08/1977	I Can't Help It	Michael Henderson	103	BB
13/08/1977	Exodus	Bob Marley And The Wailers	103	BB
13/08/1977	That's What Friends Are For	Deniece Williams	103	BB
13/08/1977	Theme From "New York, New York"	Liza Minnelli	104	BB
13/08/1977	A Song In The Night	Johnny Duncan	105	BB
13/08/1977	Oh Let Me Know It (pt. 1)	Special Delivery	105	CB
13/08/1977	Work On Me	O'jays	106	CB
13/08/1977	I Don't Wanna Go	The Moments	108	CB
13/08/1977	Lady Of Magic	Maze Featuring Frankie Beverly	108	BB
20/08/1977	Too Hot To Handle	Ufo	106	BB
20/08/1977	Oh Let Me Know It (pt. 1)	Special Delivery	107	BB
20/08/1977	Disco Calypso	Beckett	108	BB
20/08/1977	Kentucky Mornin'	Al Martino	110	CB
27/08/1977	Turn This Mutha Out (Part 1)	Idris Muhammad	102	BB
27/08/1977	Alone At Last	Neil Sedaka	104	BB
03/09/1977	Nights On Broadway	Candi Staton	102	BB
03/09/1977	(Feel So Good) Slow Dancing	John Travolta	106	BB
03/09/1977	Main Title (From The 20th Century-Fox Film "Star Wars")	Maynard Ferguson	107	BB
10/09/1977	The Whole Town's Laughing At Me	Teddy Pendergrass	102	BB
10/09/1977	(I've Been Lookin' For) A New Way To Say I Love You	Driver	109	BB
10/09/1977	You've Got Me Dangling On A String	Donny Osmond	109	BB
17/09/1977	Love Is So Good When You're Stealing It	Z.Z. Hill	102	BB

17/09/1977	East Bound And Down	Jerry Reed	103	BB
17/09/1977	Funk Funk	Cameo	104	BB
17/09/1977	Shoo Doo Fu Fu Ooh! [Live]	Lenny Williams	105	BB
17/09/1977	We Do It	Carol Douglas	108	BB
17/09/1977	I'm Just A Country Boy	Don Williams	110	BB
24/09/1977	Bad Boy	Mac Mcanally	104	CB
24/09/1977	My Own Way To Rock	Burton Cummings	105	CB
24/09/1977	Pipeline	Bruce Johnston	109	BB
01/10/1977	Just For Your Love	The Memphis Horns	101	BB
01/10/1977	My Eyes Get Blurry	Kenny Nolan	102	CB
01/10/1977	Just Let Me Hold You For A Night	David Ruffin	108	BB
08/10/1977	Heaven On Earth (So Fine)	Spinners	105	CB
08/10/1977	Shoo Doo Fu Fu Ooh! (Live)	Lenny Williams	105	CB
08/10/1977	It Ain't Love	Tom Powers	106	CB
08/10/1977	East Bound And Down	Jerry Reed	107	CB
15/10/1977	San Francisco (You've Got Me)	Village People	102	BB
15/10/1977	Come Softly To Me	Brenton Wood	107	CB
22/10/1977	Can't Wait	Piper	105	CB
29/10/1977	From Here To Eternity	Giorgio	109	BB
29/10/1977	Radio Loves You	P.R. Battle	110	CB
05/11/1977	You Don't Have To Say You Love Me	The Floaters	102	CB
12/11/1977	Crying In My Sleep	Art Garfunkel	101	CB
12/11/1977	Just For Your Love	The Memphis Horns	103	CB
12/11/1977	Strengthen My Love	Tim Moore	109	CB
19/11/1977	Kiss Me (The Way I Like It)	George Mccrae	110	BB
26/11/1977	Soldier Of Fortune	Alan O'day	103	CB
03/12/1977	Bop Gun (Endangered Species)	Parliament	102	BB
03/12/1977	Send It	Ashford & Simpson	104	CB
10/12/1977	Choosing You	Lenny Williams	101	CB
10/12/1977	Baby Blue	Chilliwack	110	BB

17/12/1977	On Fire	T-Connection	103	BB
24/12/1977	Don't Change	Daryl Hall & John Oates	103	CB
24/12/1977	The Night The Lights Went Out	The Trammps	104	BB
31/12/1977	Shout It Out Loud (Live)	Kiss	101	CB
07/01/1978	Good Luck Charm (Part I)	Ohio Players	101	BB
07/01/1978	Soft And Easy	The Blackbyrds	102	BB
07/01/1978	Show Some Emotion	Joan Armatrading	110	BB
14/01/1978	Soft And Easy	The Blackbyrds	102	CB
14/01/1978	With Pen In Hand	Dorothy Moore	103	CB
14/01/1978	Runnin' For Your Lovin'	The Brothers Johnson	107	BB
14/01/1978	Choosing You	Lenny Williams	108	BB
14/01/1978	La Vie En Rose	Grace Jones	109	BB
21/01/1978	With Pen In Hand	Dorothy Moore	101	BB
21/01/1978	Somebody's Gotta Win, Somebody's Gotta Lose	The Controllers	102	BB
21/01/1978	Out Of The Ghetto	Isaac Hayes	107	BB
28/01/1978	Dance A Little Bit Closer	Charo With The Salsoul Orchestra	104	BB
28/01/1978	Touch And Gone	Gary Wright	104	CB
28/01/1978	Shouting Out Love	The Emotions	105	CB
04/02/1978	Headliner	Fandango	110	BB
11/02/1978	Playing Your Game, Baby	Barry White	101	BB
11/02/1978	Let's Have Some Fun	The Bar-Kays	102	BB
11/02/1978	L-O-V-E-U	Brass Construction	104	BB
11/02/1978	Starlight	Cory Wells	105	CB
18/02/1978	Easy Come, Easy Go	Spinners	104	CB
25/02/1978	Two Hot For Love	Thp Orchestra	103	BB
25/02/1978	Night Fever	Carol Douglas	106	BB
25/02/1978	The House Of The Rising Sun	Santa Esmeralda	106	CB
25/02/1978	The Party Song	Slave	110	BB
04/03/1978	Am I Losing You	The Manhattans	101	BB
04/03/1978	Wishing On A Star	Rose Royce	101	BB

04/03/1978	To Daddy	Emmylou Harris	102	BB
11/03/1978	Don't Break The Heart That Loves You	Margo Smith	104	BB
18/03/1978	Every Time Two Fools Collide	Kenny Rogers & Dottie West	101	BB
18/03/1978	All The Way Lover	Millie Jackson	102	BB
18/03/1978	Fallin'	Ronnie Mcdowell	102	CB
18/03/1978	The Passenger	Allan Clarke	110	CB
25/03/1978	Turn Up The Music	Sammy Hagar	101	CB
25/03/1978	Get On Up (Disco)	Tyrone Davis	102	BB
25/03/1978	Number One	Eloise Laws	106	CB
25/03/1978	Watching The Detectives	Elvis Costello	108	BB
01/04/1978	Flying With Broken Wings (Without You)	Angel	102	CB
01/04/1978	Confunkshunizeya	Con Funk Shun	103	BB
01/04/1978	Walk Right Back	Anne Murray	103	BB
01/04/1978	If You Can Touch Her At All	Willie Nelson	104	BB
08/04/1978	Let's Put Our Love Back Together	Micky Denne/Ken Gold	105	CB
08/04/1978	I'll Be Waiting	Santana	107	CB
15/04/1978	I Love Her, She Loves Me	Nrbq	105	CB
22/04/1978	Keep On Dancing	Johnnie Taylor	101	BB
22/04/1978	Supernatural Feeling	The Blackbyrds	102	BB
22/04/1978	Trust In Me	Vicki Sue Robinson	110	BB
29/04/1978	Get It Up	Aerosmith	102	CB
29/04/1978	Slick Superchick	Kool & The Gang	102	BB
29/04/1978	I Feel Good	Al Green	103	BB
29/04/1978	A Lover's Question	Jacky Ward	106	BB
06/05/1978	I Love New York	Metropolis	105	BB
06/05/1978	Rainy Day	Nigel Olsson	105	CB
06/05/1978	It's Serious	Cameo	106	CB
06/05/1978	Ocean Of Thoughts And Dreams	The Dramatics	106	BB
13/05/1978	(You're Such A) Fabulous Dancer	Wha-Koo	101	BB
13/05/1978	Almighty Fire (Woman Of The Future)	Aretha Franklin	103	BB

20/05/1978	(You're Such A) Fabulous Dancer	Wha-Koo	101	CB
20/05/1978	Lipstick Traces (On A Cigarette)	Ringo Starr	102	CB
20/05/1978	Softly, As I Leave You [Live]	Elvis Presley	109	BB
20/05/1978	You're The Best	The Paley Brothers	109	BB
27/05/1978	Dukey Stick (Part One)	George Duke	110	CB
03/06/1978	(Let's Go) All The Way	The Whispers	101	BB
03/06/1978	Anytime	Journey	101	CB
03/06/1978	Someone To Lay Down Beside Me	Karla Bonoff	101	CB
10/06/1978	Annie Mae	Natalie Cole	102	CB
10/06/1978	Reaching For The Sky	Peabo Bryson	102	BB
10/06/1978	Girl Callin'	Chocolate Milk	103	BB
10/06/1978	Almighty Fire (Woman Of The Future)	Aretha Franklin	104	CB
17/06/1978	This Magic Moment	Richie Furay	101	BB
17/06/1978	Midtown American Main Street Gang	Dion	102	CB
17/06/1978	Manhattan Skyline	David Shire	105	CB
17/06/1978	God Knows	DeBBy Boone	107	CB
17/06/1978	Reelin'	Garland Jeffreys And Phoebe Snow	107	BB
24/06/1978	Take It Off The Top	Dixie Dregs	102	BB
24/06/1978	Drifting Away (I've Been Drifting Away)	Uproar	105	BB
01/07/1978	Stand By Me	Pousette-Dart Band	103	CB
01/07/1978	From Now On	BoBBy Arvon	104	BB
01/07/1978	Save Me	Tanya Tucker	105	BB
08/07/1978	I Just Want To Be With You	The Floaters	103	BB
08/07/1978	If You're Ready (Here It Comes)	Enchantment	104	CB
08/07/1978	Flying Over America	Fresh Aire	108	BB
22/07/1978	I'll Be True To You	Oak Ridge Boys	102	BB
22/07/1978	Tonight	Barbara Mandrell	103	BB
22/07/1978	Dance Little Dreamer	Bionic Boogie	105	BB
22/07/1978	Big City Sidewalk	C.J. & Co.	106	BB
22/07/1978	Lovin' You Is Gonna See Me Thru	Tower Of Power	106	BB

22/07/1978	So It Goes	Nick Lowe	109	BB
22/07/1978	The Other Side (So When I See You Again)	Fotomaker	110	BB
29/07/1978	Stop Your Weeping	The Dramatics	101	CB
29/07/1978	Stay The Night	Jane Olivor	102	CB
29/07/1978	1 2 3 Kind Of Love	Wild Cherry	104	CB
29/07/1978	Discomania (Part I)	Café Créme	105	BB
29/07/1978	One More Night With You	The Sutherland Brothers	105	CB
29/07/1978	Beauty School Dropout	Frankie Avalon	110	CB
05/08/1978	Talk To Me	Freddy Fender	103	BB
05/08/1978	Bigfoot	Rick Dees And His Cast Of Idiots	110	BB
12/08/1978	Honey I'm Rich	Raydio	102	BB
12/08/1978	Never Make A Move Too Soon	B.B. King	102	BB
12/08/1978	Smile	The Emotions	102	BB
12/08/1978	Moonlight Serenade	Tuxedo Junction	103	BB
19/08/1978	I Wanna Live Again	Carillo	101	BB
19/08/1978	It's The Falling In Love	Carole Bayer Sager	102	CB
19/08/1978	If I Sing You A Love Song	Bonnie Tyler	103	BB
19/08/1978	There's No Surf In Cleveland	Euclid Beach Band	103	CB
19/08/1978	You Got Me Running	Lenny Williams	104	BB
19/08/1978	Takin' It Easy	Seals & Crofts	105	CB
19/08/1978	If The World Ran Out Of Love Tonight	England Dan & John Ford Coley	106	CB
19/08/1978	Honey I'm Rich	Raydio	107	CB
26/08/1978	(Let Me Be Your) Teddy Bear	Elvis Presley With The Jordanaires	105	BB
26/08/1978	Blue Love	Rufus Featuring Chaka Khan	105	BB
26/08/1978	If My Friends Could See Me Now	Linda Clifford	109	CB
26/08/1978	Saturday	Norma Jean	110	CB
09/09/1978	I Like Girls	Fatback	101	BB
09/09/1978	Saturday	Norma Jean Wright	103	BB
09/09/1978	Super Woman	The Dells	108	BB
09/09/1978	What Goes Up	Alan Parsons Project	Np6	CB

09/09/1978	Rock 'N' Roll Damnation	Ac/Dc	Np8	CB
16/09/1978	Let's Start The Dance	Hamilton Bohannon	101	BB
23/09/1978	Funk-O-Nots	Ohio Players	105	BB
07/10/1978	Cryin' Again	Oak Ridge Boys	107	BB
14/10/1978	Think It Over	Cissy Houston	106	BB
21/10/1978	Ride-O-Rocket	The Brothers Johnson	104	BB
21/10/1978	Into The Night	Toby Beau	Np5	CB
28/10/1978	Substitute	Gloria Gaynor	107	BB
28/10/1978	Into The Night	Toby Beau	108	BB
04/11/1978	Down South Jukin'	Lynyrd Skynyrd	103	BB
04/11/1978	Remember	Greg Kihn Band	105	BB
04/11/1978	Single Again/What Time Does The Balloon Go Up	Odyssey	107	BB
04/11/1978	Wuthering Heights	Kate Bush	108	BB
04/11/1978	(You Got To Walk And) Don't Look Back	Peter Tosh	Np4	CB
11/11/1978	Children Of Sanchez	Chuck Mangione	104	BB
11/11/1978	Over And Over	Joe Walsh	106	BB
11/11/1978	Well All Right	Santana	Np4	CB
18/11/1978	Sleeping Single In A Double Bed	Barbara Mandrell	102	BB
18/11/1978	Haven't Stopped Dancing Yet	Gonzalez	106	BB
18/11/1978	Take It On Up	Pockets	106	BB
25/11/1978	Midnight Girl	Lenny Williams	102	BB
25/11/1978	You Fooled Me	Grey And Hanks	104	BB
25/11/1978	The Wedding Song (There Is Love)	Mary Macgregor	Np4	CB
02/12/1978	Take A Ride On A Riverboat	Louisiana's Le Roux	109	BB
02/12/1978	You Love The Thunder	Jackson Browne	109	BB
09/12/1978	Long Stroke	Adc Band	101	BB
09/12/1978	Newsy Neighbors	Double Exposure	107	BB
09/12/1978	Don't You Let Me Down	Peter Criss	Np4	CB
09/12/1978	Mañana	Jimmy Buffett	Np4	CB
23/12/1978	Disco To Go	The Brides Of Funkenstein	101	BB

23/12/1978	Bad Brakes	Cat Stevens	Np6	CB
23/12/1978	California Man	Cheap Trick	Np6	CB
23/12/1978	Haven't Stopped Dancing Yet (78 Mix)	Gonzalez	Np6	CB
30/12/1978	Moment By Moment	Yvonne Elliman	Np7	CB
06/01/1979	I Might As Well Forget About Loving You	Kinsman Dazz	104	BB
06/01/1979	Only You	Teddy Pendergrass	106	BB
13/01/1979	Ain't We Funkin' Now	The Brothers Johnson	102	BB
13/01/1979	I'll Be Waiting	Robert Johnson	106	BB
13/01/1979	Trick Of The Light	The Who	107	BB
13/01/1979	Turn To Stone	Joe Walsh	109	BB
13/01/1979	My Love (Burning Love)	Robin Trower	110	BB
20/01/1979	Tulsa Time	Don Williams	106	BB
20/01/1979	We Both Deserve Each Other's Love	L.T.D.	107	BB
27/01/1979	Star Cruiser	Gregg Diamond	102	BB
27/01/1979	I'm So Into You	Peabo Bryson	109	BB
27/01/1979	The Man With The Child In His Eyes	Kate Bush	Np5	CB
27/01/1979	Fancy Dancer	Frankie Valli	Np6	CB
03/02/1979	Just The Way You Are	Barry White	102	BB
03/02/1979	Just Freak	Slave	110	BB
10/02/1979	Living In A Dream	Sea Level	101	BB
17/02/1979	A Funky Space Reincarnation (Part I)	Marvin Gaye	106	BB
17/02/1979	Keep It Together (Declaration Of Love)	Rufus	109	BB
17/02/1979	Keep The Change	Kayak	Np5	CB
24/02/1979	My Guns Are Loaded	Bonnie Tyler	107	BB
24/02/1979	Body Heat	Alicia Bridges	Np6	CB
03/03/1979	Dancing In The Streets	Boney M.	103	BB
03/03/1979	Darlin'	Frankie Miller	103	BB
03/03/1979	Last Night I Wrote A Letter	Starz	104	BB
03/03/1979	Downhill Stuff	John Denver	106	BB
03/03/1979	Lipstick Traces (On A Cigarette)	Amazing Rhythm Aces	Np6	CB

10/03/1979	High On Your Love Suite	Rick James	Np6	CB
10/03/1979	Accidents Will Happen	Elvis Costello	Np7	CB
17/03/1979	Keep Your Body Workin	Kleeer	101	BB
24/03/1979	Stand By	Natalie Cole	108	BB
24/03/1979	In A Little While (I'll Be On My Way)	Art Garfunkel	Np6	CB
31/03/1979	Nightime Fantasy	Vicki Sue Robinson	102	BB
31/03/1979	Anyway You Want It	Enchantment	109	BB
31/03/1979	Boogie Motion	Beautiful Bend	110	BB
07/04/1979	Lover Goodbye	Tanya Tucker	103	BB
07/04/1979	Lipstick Traces (On A Cigarette)	Amazing Rhythm Aces	104	BB
07/04/1979	Song For Guy	Elton John	110	BB
14/04/1979	Accidents Will Happen	Elvis Costello	101	BB
14/04/1979	Shine	Bar-Kays	102	BB
14/04/1979	What's Your Sign Girl?	Mr. Danny Pearson	106	BB
21/04/1979	What's On Your Mind	John Denver	107	BB
21/04/1979	All I Ever Need Is You	Kenny Rogers & Dottie West	Np4	CB
28/04/1979	Good, Good Feelin'	War	101	BB
28/04/1979	It's All The Way Live (Part 1)	Lakeside	102	BB
28/04/1979	Pick Me Up, I'll Dance	Melba Moore	103	BB
05/05/1979	Rockin' My Life Away	Jerry Lee Lewis	101	BB
12/05/1979	Double Cross	First Choice	104	BB
12/05/1979	This Time I'll Be Sweeter	Angela Bofill	104	BB
12/05/1979	Go For It	Billy Preston & Syreeta	108	BB
12/05/1979	Dreams I'll Never See	Molly Hatchet	Np6	CB
12/05/1979	For Your Love	Chilly	Np6	CB
12/05/1979	You Never Know What You've Got	Bell & James	Np6	CB
19/05/1979	All I Ever Need Is You	Kenny Rogers & Dottie West	102	BB
19/05/1979	For Your Love	Chilly	108	BB
19/05/1979	Alison	Linda Ronstadt	Np7	CB
26/05/1979	Can't Say Goodbye	BoBBy Caldwell	103	BB

26/05/1979	Let's Fly Away	Voyage	105	BB
02/06/1979	Shake	The Gap Band	101	BB
02/06/1979	You Never Know What You've Got	Bell & James	103	BB
02/06/1979	When The Daylight Comes	Ian Hunter	108	BB
09/06/1979	Baby Fat	Robert Byrne	101	BB
09/06/1979	Love Is For The Best In Us	James Walsh Gypsy Band	103	BB
09/06/1979	Music Box	Evelyn "Champagne" King	Np5	CB
16/06/1979	Shoulda Gone Dancin'	High Inergy	101	BB
16/06/1979	Ready "N" Steady	D.A.	102	BB
16/06/1979	Dreams I'll Never See	Molly Hatchet	106	BB
23/06/1979	Anybody Wanna Party?	Gloria Gaynor	105	BB
23/06/1979	Sorry	Natalie Cole	109	BB
30/06/1979	Easy Way Out	Roy Orbison	109	BB
07/07/1979	Fill My Life With Love	Saint Tropez	102	BB
07/07/1979	Surrender To Me	Mcguinn, Clark & Hillman	104	BB
07/07/1979	Can't Take It With You	The Allman Brothers Band	105	BB
07/07/1979	If Heaven Could Find Me	Ambrosia	107	BB
07/07/1979	It Was Only The Radio	Boatz	107	BB
07/07/1979	Simply Jessie (From The Movie "Sooner Or Later")	Rex Smith	Np4	CB
14/07/1979	I Want Johnny's Job	Ray Sawyer	Np4	CB
14/07/1979	Maureen	Eddie Money	Np4	CB
28/07/1979	I Want You Back (Alive)	Graham Parker	103	BB
28/07/1979	D.J.	David Bowie	106	BB
28/07/1979	I Need You Now	Tata Vega	107	BB
04/08/1979	I'm A Sucker For Your Love	Teena Marie	102	BB
11/08/1979	Nobody	Doucette	108	BB
18/08/1979	Dr. Rock	Captain Sky	105	BB
25/08/1979	You Can Do It	Al Hudson & The Partners	101	BB
25/08/1979	Give A Little	Nicolette Larson	104	BB
25/08/1979	Love Is On The Way	The Sweet Inspirations	104	BB

25/08/1979	Only Game In Town	America	107	BB
15/09/1979	After The First One	Yonah	102	BB
15/09/1979	Legend	Poco	103	BB
15/09/1979	Family Tradition	Hank Williams Jr.	104	BB
15/09/1979	Better Not Look Down	B.B. King	110	BB
29/09/1979	Is It Love You're After	Rose Royce	105	BB
29/09/1979	Don't You Want My Love	DeBBie Jacobs	106	BB
06/10/1979	You Get Me Hot	Jimmy "Bo" Horne	101	BB
06/10/1979	What's Right	David Werner	104	BB
06/10/1979	Emptiness	Sad Café	108	BB
20/10/1979	More Than One Way To Love A Woman	Raydio	103	BB
20/10/1979	Sooner Or Later	Rex Smith	109	BB
20/10/1979	No More Lonely Nights	Blue Steel	110	BB
27/10/1979	Sing A Happy Song	The O'jays	102	BB
27/10/1979	I Found Love	Deniece Williams	105	BB
03/11/1979	Only Time	Robert John	102	BB
03/11/1979	Body Language	Spinners	103	BB
03/11/1979	Remember Who You Are	Sly And The Family Stone	104	BB
03/11/1979	Blind Faith	Pointer Sisters	107	BB
03/11/1979	Bright Side Of The Road	Van Morrison	110	BB
10/11/1979	How High	The Salsoul Orchestra Featuring Cognac	105	BB
10/11/1979	This Is Hot	Pamala Stanley	108	BB
17/11/1979	It's Different For Girls	Joe Jackson	101	BB
17/11/1979	You Can Get Over	Stephanie Mills	101	BB
17/11/1979	Jealous	Robert Palmer	106	BB
24/11/1979	Who Do You Love	Pointer Sisters	106	BB
24/11/1979	Switch Board Susan	Nick Lowe	107	BB
01/12/1979	Do It In A Heartbeat	Carlene Carter	108	BB
08/12/1979	Total Control	The Motels	109	BB
08/12/1979	Under My Thumb	Hounds	110	BB

15/12/1979	When You Walk In The Room	Karla Bonoff	101	BB
15/12/1979	Back Up Against The Wall	Atlanta Rhythm Section	103	BB
15/12/1979	New Lines On Love	Sniff 'N' The Tears	108	BB
22/12/1979	Stay With Me Till Dawn	Judie Tzuke	101	BB
22/12/1979	Gimme Some Time	Natalie Cole & Peabo Bryson	102	BB
05/01/1980	Draw The Line	Oak	108	BB
12/01/1980	My Feet Keep Dancing	Chic	101	BB
12/01/1980	Say Hello	April Wine	104	BB
12/01/1980	Automobile	Hansie	109	BB
19/01/1980	Do You Want To Dance	Jim Messina	110	BB
26/01/1980	Got To Be Real	Head East	103	BB
02/02/1980	The Very First Time	Michael Johnson	101	BB
02/02/1980	You Know How To Love Me	Phyllis Hyman	101	BB
02/02/1980	Bodyshine	Instant Funk	103	BB
02/02/1980	Steppin' (Out)	The Gap Band	103	BB
02/02/1980	Touch Too Much	Ac/Dc	106	BB
09/02/1980	Ravel's Bolero	Henry Mancini And His Orchestra	101	BB
09/02/1980	White Rhythm And Blues	J.D. Souther	105	BB
09/02/1980	You Won't Be There	Alan Parsons Project	105	BB
16/02/1980	The Walk	The Inmates	107	BB
16/02/1980	You Got It (Release It)	Pearl Harbor & The Explosions	108	BB
01/03/1980	Shriner's Convention	Ray Stevens	101	BB
01/03/1980	Years	Barbara Mandrell	102	BB
01/03/1980	Won't Give It Up	Sue Saad And The Next	107	BB
08/03/1980	Any Love	Rufus And Chaka	102	BB
08/03/1980	Is This The Best (Bop-Doo-Wah)	L.A. Boppers	103	BB
08/03/1980	Relight My Fire	Dan Hartman	104	BB
08/03/1980	All Night Long	Rainbow	110	BB
15/03/1980	Love Is Good News	Ava Cherry	107	BB
15/03/1980	This Is My Country, Thank You Canada	Shelley Looney	109	BB

22/03/1980	Who Said The World Was Fair	Daryl Hall & John Oates	110	BB
29/03/1980	I Don't Believe You Want To Get Up And Dance (Opps, Up Side Your	The Gap Band	102	BB
29/03/1980	Street Life	Herb Alpert	104	BB
29/03/1980	Seasons	Grace Slick	I102	CB
05/04/1980	Don't Let Go Of Me	Jane Olivor	108	BB
05/04/1980	Goin' On	The Beach Boys	I101	CB
19/04/1980	Reach Your Peak	Sister Sledge	101	BB
19/04/1980	A Little Night Dancin'	John Cougar	105	BB
19/04/1980	I Only Want To Be With You	The Tourists	I101	CB
19/04/1980	You Gave Me Love	Crown Heights Affair	I102	CB
26/04/1980	You Gave Me Love	Crown Heights Affair	102	BB
03/05/1980	Got To Be Enough	Con Funk Shun	101	BB
03/05/1980	Overnight Sensation	Jerry Knight	103	BB
03/05/1980	Dallas	Floyd Cramer	104	BB
03/05/1980	Give Me Some Emotion	Webster Lewis	107	BB
10/05/1980	High	Skyy	102	BB
17/05/1980	Clouds	Chaka Khan	103	BB
17/05/1980	Hangin' Out	Kool & The Gang	103	BB
17/05/1980	Let The Music Do The Talking	Joe Perry Project	110	BB
24/05/1980	I Don't Wanna Get Drafted	Frank Zappa	103	BB
24/05/1980	Entre Nous	Rush	110	BB
24/05/1980	(Odin) Spirit Of The Water	John Stewart	I103	CB
31/05/1980	You Got Me	Tommy James	101	BB
31/05/1980	Taking Somebody With Me When I Fall	Larry Gatlin And The Gatlin Brothers	108	BB
31/05/1980	Romance (Give Me A Chance)	Johnny Rivers	I103	CB
07/06/1980	Don't Fight It	Red Rider	103	BB
07/06/1980	Good To Have Love Back	Felix Cavaliere	105	BB
07/06/1980	It's All Over	Willie Nile	106	BB
07/06/1980	Spellbound	Rachel Sweet	107	BB
07/06/1980	Shotgun Rider	Joe Sun	I102	CB

14/06/1980	Does She Have A Friend?	Gene Chandler	101	BB
14/06/1980	Sitting In The Park	Gq	101	BB
14/06/1980	Rebel Girl	Survivor	103	BB
14/06/1980	Bebe Le Strange	Heart	109	BB
14/06/1980	Marseilles	Angel City	109	BB
21/06/1980	All The Way	Brick	106	BB
28/06/1980	Are 'Friends' Electric?	Gary Numan & Tubeway Army	105	BB
28/06/1980	Don't Tell Me, Tell Her	Odyssey	105	BB
05/07/1980	Never Givin' Up	Al Jarreau	102	BB
05/07/1980	The Pyramid Song	J.C. Cunningham	104	BB
05/07/1980	Rock Brigade	Def Leppard	106	BB
05/07/1980	We Gotta' Get Out Of Here	Ian Hunter	108	BB
05/07/1980	I'm Happy Just To Dance With You	Anne Murray	I101	CB
12/07/1980	Crackers	Barbara Mandrell	105	BB
12/07/1980	Boney Moronie	Cheeks	110	BB
19/07/1980	Clyde	Waylon	103	BB
19/07/1980	(I Like) The Way You Play	Glass Moon	108	BB
26/07/1980	This Time (I'm Giving All I've Got)	France Joli	103	BB
26/07/1980	Dreams	Grace Slick	104	BB
26/07/1980	Percolator	Spyro Gyra	105	BB
26/07/1980	Your Precious Love	Stephen Bishop & Yvonne Elliman	105	BB
26/07/1980	You're Good For Me	Exile	105	BB
26/07/1980	Give It To You	Rcr	108	BB
02/08/1980	Turn On Your Light	In Transit	107	BB
02/08/1980	Hold Tight	Jimmy Spheeris	110	BB
02/08/1980	Everything Is Alright	Spider	I101	CB
02/08/1980	Day Tripper	Cheap Trick	I102	CB
09/08/1980	You May Be Right	The Chipmunks	101	BB
09/08/1980	Cowboys And Clowns	Ronnie Milsap	103	BB
09/08/1980	When Love Is Gone	Photoglo	106	BB

09/08/1980	Lola (Live)	The Kinks	l103	CB
16/08/1980	Doc	Earl Klugh	105	BB
16/08/1980	Only His Name	Holly Penfield	105	BB
16/08/1980	How Glad I Am	Joyce CoBB	107	BB
16/08/1980	Tommy, Judy & Me	Rob Hegel	109	BB
16/08/1980	Waterfalls	Paul Mccartney	l103	CB
23/08/1980	It's All In The Game	Isaac Hayes	107	BB
23/08/1980	Treasure	The Brothers Johnson	l102	CB
23/08/1980	Searching	Change, Lead Vocal By Luther Vandross	l103	CB
30/08/1980	Waterfalls	Paul Mccartney	106	BB
30/08/1980	Starlight	Ray Kennedy	109	BB
30/08/1980	Hold Tight	Jimmy Spheeris	l101	CB
06/09/1980	The Rest Of The Night	Clif Newton	101	BB
06/09/1980	Givin' It All	Player	105	BB
06/09/1980	Letting Go	Neil Sedaka	107	BB
13/09/1980	Longshot	Henry Paul Band	103	BB
13/09/1980	Even The Score	Toronto	104	BB
13/09/1980	The Traveller	Chris De Burgh	106	BB
20/09/1980	Heart Of Mine	Oak Ridge Boys	105	BB
20/09/1980	I'm The Lucky One	Tim Weisberg	106	BB
20/09/1980	Falling For You	Sammy Johns	l102	CB
20/09/1980	If This Is Love	Melissa Manchester	l103	CB
27/09/1980	I Die: You Die	Gary Numan	102	BB
27/09/1980	Don't Make Me Wait Too Long	Roberta Flack	104	BB
27/09/1980	Let Me Be Your Fantasy	Le Roux	105	BB
27/09/1980	Mama Sez	Love Affair	109	BB
27/09/1980	Case Of You	Frank Stallone	l103	CB
04/10/1980	Oh Yeah (On The Radio)	Roxy Music	102	BB
04/10/1980	Why Do Fools Fall In Love [Live]	Joni Mitchell	102	BB
04/10/1980	Ooh Child	Lenny Williams	109	BB

11/10/1980	I Ain't Much	Atlanta Rhythm Section	101	BB
11/10/1980	Falling For You	Sammy Johns	103	BB
11/10/1980	Baby Don't Give Up	The Bay Brothers	108	BB
11/10/1980	Love Theme From Shogun (Mariko's Theme)	Meco	l101	CB
11/10/1980	When We Get Married	Larry Graham	l102	CB
18/10/1980	If This Is Love	Melissa Manchester	102	BB
18/10/1980	Take Me Down	Exile	102	BB
18/10/1980	For You, For Love	Average White Band	106	BB
18/10/1980	Badlands	The Dirt Band	107	BB
25/10/1980	Ashes To Ashes	David Bowie	101	BB
25/10/1980	Uptown	Prince	101	BB
25/10/1980	Dreams	Barry Goudreau	103	BB
25/10/1980	Into The Lens (I Am A Camera)	Yes	104	BB
25/10/1980	Rumours Of Glory	Bruce Cockburn	104	BB
25/10/1980	634-5789	Johnny Van Zant Band	105	BB
01/11/1980	Bomb Iran	Vince Vance & The Valiants	101	BB
01/11/1980	Hometown Girls	Benny Mardones	103	BB
01/11/1980	Beatin' The Odds	Molly Hatchet	107	BB
01/11/1980	Fallin' In Love (Bein' Friends)	Rocky Burnette	109	BB
01/11/1980	In The Midnight Hour	Roxy Music	l103	CB
08/11/1980	In The Midnight Hour	Roxy Music	106	BB
08/11/1980	Somebody Wants You	Aussie Band	109	BB
08/11/1980	Blues Power (Live)	Eric Clapton & His Band	l103	CB
15/11/1980	That's All That Matters	Mickey Gilley	101	BB
15/11/1980	If You Feel The Funk	Latoya Jackson	103	BB
15/11/1980	Runaway	Sailor	103	BB
15/11/1980	No Big Deal	Ambrosia	105	BB
22/11/1980	One In A Million	Johnny Lee	102	BB
22/11/1980	Gangsters Of The Groove	Heatwave	110	BB
29/11/1980	Do Me Right	Dynasty	103	BB

29/11/1980	People Who Died	Jim Carroll Band	103	BB
29/11/1980	Looking For Clues	Robert Palmer	105	BB
29/11/1980	Kid Stuff	Twennynine Featuring Lenny White	106	BB
29/11/1980	I Don't Remember	Peter Gabriel	107	BB
06/12/1980	Love To Ride	Keith Sykes	108	BB
13/12/1980	Take Me As I Am	Carly Simon	102	BB
13/12/1980	I'll Never Find Another (Find Another Like You)	The Manhattans	109	BB
13/12/1980	Set The Night On Fire	Oak	l101	CB
13/12/1980	Toccata	Sky	l103	CB
20/12/1980	Silver Eagle	Atlanta Rhythm Section	101	BB
20/12/1980	Freedom Of Choice	Devo	103	BB
20/12/1980	This Is Not The First Time	Captain & Tennille	106	BB
20/12/1980	Lovers For The Night	BoBBy Hart	110	BB
27/12/1980	I Yam What I Yam	Robin Williams (Popeye)	104	BB
27/12/1980	Turn Out The Lamplight	George Benson	109	BB
27/12/1980	It's Gonna Hurt	Jimmie Mack	l103	CB
10/01/1981	Here Is My Love	Tommy Dee	107	BB
17/01/1981	Some Are Born	Jon Anderson	109	BB
24/01/1981	Look Up	Patrice Rushen	102	BB
24/01/1981	Hold On, Hold Out	Jackson Browne	103	BB
24/01/1981	Generals And Majors	Xtc	104	BB
24/01/1981	Waiting For A Friend	Roger Daltrey	104	BB
31/01/1981	Outside	Ambrosia	102	BB
31/01/1981	Love Gone Bad	Moon Martin	105	BB
31/01/1981	Two Lonely Nights	Nielsen/Pearson	110	BB
31/01/1981	Cow Patti	Jim Stafford	l103	CB
07/02/1981	Cow Patti	Jim Stafford	102	BB
07/02/1981	Once In A Lifetime	Talking Heads	103	BB
07/02/1981	Generals And Majors	Xtc	l102	CB
07/02/1981	Let's Pick It Up (Where We Left Off)	Chris Montan	l103	CB

14/02/1981	Blackjack	Rupert Holmes	103	BB
14/02/1981	Ain't No Love In The Heart Of The City [Live]	Whitesnake	109	BB
21/02/1981	Eugene	Crazy Joe And The Variable Speed Band	105	BB
21/02/1981	Where Did The Time Go?	Pointer Sisters	I101	CB
28/02/1981	Let's Pick It Up (Where We Left Off)	Chris Montan	106	BB
28/02/1981	Ooo-Eee	Nicolette Larson	110	BB
07/03/1981	Hooked On Music	Mac Davis	102	BB
07/03/1981	Goodbye Elenore	Toto	107	BB
07/03/1981	Going Back To Miami [Live]	Blues Brothers	108	BB
14/03/1981	Foolish Child	Ali Thomson	105	BB
14/03/1981	Second Choice	Any Trouble	108	BB
14/03/1981	Come To My Arms	Graf	110	BB
14/03/1981	Hooked On Music	Mac Davis	I102	CB
21/03/1981	Praise	Marvin Gaye	101	BB
21/03/1981	Another One Rides The Bus	"Weird Al" Yankovic	104	BB
21/03/1981	For You	Manfred Mann's Earth Band	106	BB
21/03/1981	Don't Let Me Know	The Kings	109	BB
21/03/1981	One More Try	Melanie	110	BB
21/03/1981	If I Was A Dancer (Dance Pt. 2)	The Rolling Stones	I101	CB
21/03/1981	To Love Again	Diana Ross	I103	CB
28/03/1981	Time Heals	Todd Rundgren	107	BB
28/03/1981	Let Me Love You Goodbye	BoBBy Vinton	108	BB
04/04/1981	Invitation To Love	Dazz Band	109	BB
11/04/1981	When Love Calls	Atlantic Starr	101	BB
11/04/1981	You're Too Late	Fantasy	104	BB
11/04/1981	Let Me Stay With You Tonight	Point Blank	107	BB
11/04/1981	Send A Little Love My Way (Like Always)	Stephen Bishop	108	BB
11/04/1981	Dddddddance	Rox	109	BB
11/04/1981	Sheila	Greg Kihn	I103	CB
18/04/1981	I Can't Stop Loving You	Outlaws	102	BB

18/04/1981	Darlin'	Tom Jones	103	BB
18/04/1981	I Surrender	Rainbow	105	BB
25/04/1981	You're The Reason God Made Oklahoma	David Frizzell & Shelly West	I101	CB
02/05/1981	Sheila	Greg Kihn	102	BB
02/05/1981	Old Flame	Alabama	103	BB
02/05/1981	Cool Down	Life	106	BB
09/05/1981	Magic Man	Robert Winters & Fall	101	BB
09/05/1981	Is This A Disco Or A Honky Tonk?	Susan Hart	109	BB
16/05/1981	I Can Make It Better	The Whispers	105	BB
16/05/1981	Let Her Dance	Phil Seymour	110	BB
23/05/1981	Call It What You Want	Bill Summers And Summers Heat	103	BB
23/05/1981	Only Heaven Knows	The Roulettes	I103	CB
30/05/1981	Try It Out	Gino Soccio	103	BB
30/05/1981	Gotta Get Away	Randy Meisner	104	BB
30/05/1981	This Time I Believe	The Marshall Tucker Band	106	BB
30/05/1981	Let's Get Crazy	Roger Taylor	I103	CB
06/06/1981	Pull Up To The Bumper	Grace Jones	101	BB
06/06/1981	Pocket Calculator	Kraftwerk	102	BB
06/06/1981	Only Heaven Knows	The Roulettes	105	BB
06/06/1981	Pocket Calculator	Kraftwerk	I101	CB
13/06/1981	Love Is A Crazy Feeling	Joe Chemay Band	105	BB
13/06/1981	I Don't Have To Crawl	Emmylou Harris	106	BB
13/06/1981	You Stopped Loving Me	Roberta Flack	108	BB
20/06/1981	Night (Feel Like Getting Down)	Billy Ocean	103	BB
27/06/1981	One Step Ahead	Split Enz	104	BB
27/06/1981	Shall We Dance?	Bram Tchaikovsky	109	BB
04/07/1981	Freaky Dancin'	Cameo	102	BB
04/07/1981	Crazy Train	Ozzy Osbourne	106	BB
04/07/1981	Ddt	New England	I103	CB
11/07/1981	Sweet Home Alabama (Live)	Charlie Daniels Band	I101	CB

11/07/1981	Crazy Train	Ozzy Osbourne	I103	CB
18/07/1981	Lay Back In The Arms Of Someone	Savoy Brown	107	BB
18/07/1981	Sweet Home Alabama [Live]	Charlie Daniels Band	110	BB
18/07/1981	You're Mine Tonight	Pure Prairie League	I102	CB
25/07/1981	Summer '81 Medley	The Cantina Band (featuring Lou Christie)	I101	CB
25/07/1981	Feels Like I'm In Love	Kelly Marie	I103	CB
01/08/1981	So This Is Love?	Van Halen	110	BB
01/08/1981	Magic Man	Herb Alpert	I102	CB
01/08/1981	La-Di-Da	Sad Café	I103	CB
08/08/1981	Night Train	Steve Winwood	104	BB
08/08/1981	A Woman's Got The Power	The A's	106	BB
08/08/1981	The Rapper (Live)	Donnie Iris	I101	CB
08/08/1981	Marty Feldman Eyes	Bruce "Baby Man" Baum W/Little Roger & The Goosebumps	I103	CB
15/08/1981	Live Now-Pay Later	Foghat	102	BB
15/08/1981	Memphis	Fred Knoblock	102	BB
15/08/1981	Teardrops	George Harrison	102	BB
15/08/1981	All Girls Want It	Jody Moreing	103	BB
15/08/1981	Searchin'	Billy Preston & Syreeta	106	BB
15/08/1981	What In The World's Come Over You	Tom Jones	109	BB
15/08/1981	All Girls Want It	Jody Moreing	I102	CB
22/08/1981	Heaven	Carl Wilson	107	BB
22/08/1981	What's He Got?	The Producers	108	BB
22/08/1981	Dancin' The Night Away	Voggue	109	BB
22/08/1981	Mama Lied	Phil Gentili	110	BB
22/08/1981	More To Love	Jim Photoglo	I103	CB
29/08/1981	Story Of A Life	Harry Chapin	105	BB
29/08/1981	Stay The Night	Jim Messina With Pauline Wilson	110	BB
05/09/1981	I Can't Live Without Your Love	Teddy Pendergrass	103	BB
05/09/1981	Blue Moon	Meco	I101	CB
05/09/1981	The House Of The Rising Sun	Dolly Parton	I102	CB

12/09/1981	I'm Gonna Love Her For Both Of Us	Meat Loaf	I102	CB
19/09/1981	The Closer You Get	Rita Coolidge	103	BB
19/09/1981	Blue Moon	Meco	106	BB
19/09/1981	New Romeo	Tim Goodman	107	BB
19/09/1981	Searchin'	Santana	I101	CB
26/09/1981	Mony Mony	Billy Idol	107	BB
26/09/1981	Searchin'	Blackfoot	108	BB
26/09/1981	All I Need	Dan Hartman	110	BB
03/10/1981	Heart And Soul	Exile	102	BB
03/10/1981	Fancy Free	Oak Ridge Boys	104	BB
03/10/1981	The Girl Most Likely	Greg Kihn	104	BB
10/10/1981	It's Over	Teddy Baker	101	BB
10/10/1981	Talk To Ya Later	The Tubes	101	BB
10/10/1981	Stars On The Water	Rodney Crowell	105	BB
17/10/1981	Stranded In The Moonlight	Jet	105	BB
17/10/1981	Louie Louie	The Pretenders	110	BB
17/10/1981	All Roads Lead To You	Steve Wariner	I103	CB
24/10/1981	Night Fades Away	Nils Lofgren	109	BB
31/10/1981	She Don't Let Nobody (But Me)	Curtis Mayfield	103	BB
31/10/1981	Save Your Love	Jefferson Starship	104	BB
31/10/1981	Heartbeat	Gary Wright	107	BB
31/10/1981	You Go Your Way (I'll Go Mine)	Spinners	110	BB
07/11/1981	Too Late The Hero	John Entwistle	101	BB
07/11/1981	Loved By The One You Love	Rupert Holmes	103	BB
07/11/1981	Summer Strut	Spyro Gyra	108	BB
07/11/1981	Midnight Confession	Karla Devito	109	BB
07/11/1981	Fool Me Again	Nicolette Larson	I103	CB
14/11/1981	Beautiful World	Devo	102	BB
14/11/1981	All Roads Lead To You	Steve Wariner	107	BB
21/11/1981	Sandy Beaches	Delbert Mcclinton	101	BB

21/11/1981	Fool Me Again	Nicolette Larson	105	BB
21/11/1981	You're My Bestest Friend	Mac Davis	106	BB
28/11/1981	Oh, What A Night	The Temptations	104	BB
28/11/1981	Two To Do	Bob Welch	107	BB
28/11/1981	Stuck In The Middle	Grand Funk Railroad	I101	CB
05/12/1981	Kickin' Back	L.T.D.	102	BB
05/12/1981	Looker	Sue Saad	I102	CB
05/12/1981	Some Guys Have All The Luck	Nikki Wills	I103	CB
12/12/1981	Hit And Run	Bar-Kays	101	BB
12/12/1981	Numbers	Kraftwerk	103	BB
12/12/1981	Looker	Sue Saad	104	BB
12/12/1981	Stuck In The Middle	Grand Funk Railroad	108	BB
12/12/1981	Tube Snake Boogie	Zz Top	I102	CB
12/12/1981	Kickin' Back	L.T.D.	I103	CB
19/12/1981	Hurt	Carly Simon	106	BB
19/12/1981	Some Guys Have All The Luck	Nikki Wills	109	BB
26/12/1981	Tube Snake Boogie	Zz Top	103	BB
09/01/1982	Love Connection (Raise The Window Down)	Spinners	107	BB
16/01/1982	Spies In The Night	The Manhattan Transfer	103	BB
16/01/1982	Wait For Me	Slave	103	BB
16/01/1982	Goin' Back To China	Diesel	105	BB
16/01/1982	Don't You Know That?	Luther Vandross	107	BB
16/01/1982	My Old Piano	Diana Ross	109	BB
16/01/1982	Destroyer	The Kinks	I103	CB
23/01/1982	Fool For Your Love	Charlie	I103	CB
30/01/1982	Rain Is Falling	Elo	101	BB
30/01/1982	Ghetto Life	Rick James	102	BB
30/01/1982	Let's Work	Prince	104	BB
30/01/1982	Stage Fright	Chic	105	BB
30/01/1982	Natural Love	Petula Clark	I102	CB

06/02/1982	Right In The Middle (Of Falling In Love)	Bettye Lavette	103	BB
06/02/1982	Tattoo	Novo Combo	103	BB
06/02/1982	Sad Girl	Gq	I103	CB
13/02/1982	I Want To Hold Your Hand	Lakeside	102	BB
13/02/1982	Say Goodbye	Triumph	102	BB
13/02/1982	In The Raw	The Whispers	103	BB
13/02/1982	Nobody's Business	Maxus	I101	CB
20/02/1982	Glad To Know You	Chas Jankel	102	BB
20/02/1982	Blue Moon With Heartache	Rosanne Cash	104	BB
20/02/1982	Tonight I'm Gonna Love You All Over	The Four Tops	I102	CB
20/02/1982	I'll Miss You	Stella Parton	I103	CB
27/02/1982	The Longer You Wait	Gino Vannelli	I102	CB
27/02/1982	Make It Last	Chris Christian	I103	CB
06/03/1982	If You Think You're Lonely Now	BoBBy Womack	101	BB
06/03/1982	Brown Eyed Girl	Henry Paul Band	105	BB
06/03/1982	As	Jean-Luc Ponty	108	BB
13/03/1982	Keep This Heart In Mind	Bonnie Raitt	104	BB
13/03/1982	Nobody's Business	Maxus	109	BB
20/03/1982	Mountain Music	Alabama	101	BB
20/03/1982	It Was I	Lindsey Buckingham	110	BB
27/03/1982	Try Jah Love	Third World	101	BB
27/03/1982	Jamaica	BoBBy Caldwell	105	BB
27/03/1982	Somebody To Love	Dwight Twilley	106	BB
03/04/1982	Come To Me	Jennifer Warnes	107	BB
03/04/1982	Can't Get You Out Of My Mind	Dan Seals	110	BB
10/04/1982	Jamming	Grover Washington Jr.	102	BB
10/04/1982	Who's Foolin' Who	Lulu	106	BB
10/04/1982	Sea Of Heartbreak	Poco	109	BB
17/04/1982	You Sure Fooled Me	The John Hall Band	109	BB
17/04/1982	Crank It Up	The Dregs	110	BB

24/04/1982	Just Be Yourself	Cameo	101	BB
24/04/1982	Work That Sucker To Death	Xavier	104	BB
24/04/1982	Through Being Cool	Devo	107	BB
01/05/1982	Take A Lickin' And Keep On Kickin'	William "Bootsy" Collins	103	BB
01/05/1982	Let Her Go	Point Blank	109	BB
08/05/1982	I Just Want To Satisfy	The O'jays	101	BB
15/05/1982	Wordy Rappinghood	Tom Tom Club	105	BB
22/05/1982	Something About That Woman	Lakeside	110	BB
29/05/1982	Don't Stop When You're Hot	Larry Graham	102	BB
29/05/1982	Do The Donkey Kong	Buckner & Garcia	103	BB
29/05/1982	Harder Than Diamond	ChuBBy Checker	104	BB
05/06/1982	Six Months In A Leaky Boat	Split Enz	104	BB
05/06/1982	Slow Down	Lacy J. Dalton	106	BB
05/06/1982	Me And The Boys	Bonnie Raitt	109	BB
05/06/1982	One Hello	Randy Crawford	110	BB
12/06/1982	Big Band Medley	Meco	101	BB
12/06/1982	Too Late	Junior	102	BB
12/06/1982	Fallen On Hard Times	Jethro Tull	108	BB
19/06/1982	Song On The Radio	The Pinups	110	BB
26/06/1982	President Rap's [Live]	Rich Little	105	BB
26/06/1982	Never Gonna Look Back	Bill Labounty	110	BB
03/07/1982	Just An Illusion	Imagination	102	BB
03/07/1982	It's Alright	Gino Soccio	108	BB
10/07/1982	Black Coffee In Bed	Squeeze	103	BB
10/07/1982	Take A Chance With Me	Roxy Music	104	BB
17/07/1982	Dance Floor (Part I)	Zapp	101	BB
17/07/1982	Theme From E.T. (The Extra-Terrestrial)	John Williams	103	BB
17/07/1982	Ragin' Cajun	Charlie Daniels Band	109	BB
24/07/1982	Which Man Are You	Tommy Tutone	101	BB
24/07/1982	I Can Make You Feel Good	Shalamar	102	BB

24/07/1982	Instant Love	Cheryl Lynn	105	BB
24/07/1982	It Ain't Easy Comin' Down	Charlene	109	BB
31/07/1982	Don't Throw It All Away	Stacy Lattisaw	101	BB
31/07/1982	Last Night	Stephanie Mills	101	BB
31/07/1982	Waiting By The Hotline	Deniece Williams	103	BB
31/07/1982	Love Leads To Madness	Nazareth	105	BB
31/07/1982	Yes It's You Lady	Smokey Robinson	107	BB
31/07/1982	Sooner Or Later	Larry Graham	110	BB
07/08/1982	Inside Out	Odyssey	104	BB
07/08/1982	Face Dances Part Two	Pete Townshend	105	BB
28/08/1982	Favourite Shirts (Boy Meets Girl)	Haircut One Hundred	101	BB
28/08/1982	Li'l Suzy	Ozone	109	BB
11/09/1982	Nobody But Me	George Thorogood & The Destroyers	106	BB
18/09/1982	What!	Soft Cell	101	BB
18/09/1982	Hot Spot	Midnight Star	108	BB
18/09/1982	Rock 'N' Roll Party In The Streets	Axe	109	BB
18/09/1982	One Of A Kind	Orleans	110	BB
25/09/1982	So Fine	Howard Johnson	105	BB
25/09/1982	That's The Way That It Is	Uriah Heep	106	BB
25/09/1982	If Love Takes You Away	Stephen Bishop	108	BB
02/10/1982	Nasty Girl	Vanity 6	101	BB
02/10/1982	Baby, Oh No	Bow Wow Wow	103	BB
02/10/1982	She's Just A Groupie	BoBBy Nunn	104	BB
09/10/1982	Ghost Town	Poco	108	BB
16/10/1982	If This World Were Mine	Cheryl Lynn (with Luther Vandross)	101	BB
23/10/1982	Baby I Need Your Loving	Carl Carlton	103	BB
23/10/1982	It's Our Own Affair	Ray Parker Jr.	106	BB
23/10/1982	There She Goes Again	Marshall Crenshaw	110	BB
30/10/1982	Your Precious Love	Al Jarreau And Randy Crawford	102	BB
30/10/1982	Pack Jam (Look Out For The Ovc)	The Jonzun Crew	108	BB

06/11/1982	Doo Wa Ditty (Blow That Thing)	Zapp	103	BB
06/11/1982	Love's Comin' At Ya	Melba Moore	104	BB
06/11/1982	Peek • A • Boo!	Devo	106	BB
13/11/1982	Nipple To The Bottle	Grace Jones	103	BB
13/11/1982	He Was Really Sayin' Somethin'	Bananarama	108	BB
27/11/1982	White Wedding	Billy Idol	108	BB
11/12/1982	Jump	Loverboy	101	BB
18/12/1982	The Walk	The Time	104	BB
25/12/1982	The Best Is Yet To Come	Grover Washington Jr. With Patti Labelle	104	BB
25/12/1982	Everybody	Madonna	107	BB
25/12/1982	Hey There Lonely Boy	Stacy Lattisaw	108	BB
08/01/1983	Talk To Me	Mickey Gilley	106	BB
15/01/1983	Heartbeats	Yarbrough & Peoples	101	BB
15/01/1983	That's Good	Devo	104	BB
15/01/1983	Subdivisions	Rush	105	BB
15/01/1983	Back In My Arms Again	Cynthia Manley	109	BB
22/01/1983	I Love It Loud	Kiss	102	BB
29/01/1983	Imagine [Live]	Randy Crawford	108	BB
29/01/1983	My Time To Fly	Tané Cain	108	BB
05/02/1983	Kelly's Eyes	André Cymone	107	BB
12/02/1983	Everything's Beautiful (In It's Own Way)	Dolly Parton Willie Nelson	102	BB
12/02/1983	Baby Gets High	Peter Brown	104	BB
12/02/1983	One Of Us	ABBa	107	BB
19/02/1983	Life Is Something Special	New York Citi Peech Boys	108	BB
26/02/1983	Last Night A D.J. Saved My Life	Indeep	101	BB
05/03/1983	Atomic Dog	George Clinton	101	BB
12/03/1983	I've Made Love To You A Thousand Times	Smokey Robinson	101	BB
12/03/1983	Red Skies	The Fixx	101	BB
12/03/1983	Secret Information	Chilliwack	110	BB
19/03/1983	You Are The One	Phil Garland	109	BB

26/03/1983	I Just Gotta Have You (Lover Turn Me On)	Kashif	103	BB
26/03/1983	Dancing In Heaven (Orbital Be-Bop)	Q-Feel	110	BB
02/04/1983	Don't Run (Come Back To Me)	Kc & The Sunshine Band (with Teri Desario)	103	BB
02/04/1983	Images Of Heaven	Peter Godwin	105	BB
09/04/1983	I Confess	English Beat	104	BB
09/04/1983	What Does It Take (To Win Your Love)	Garland Jeffreys	107	BB
09/04/1983	Let's Go To Bed	The Cure	109	BB
16/04/1983	Twisting By The Pool	Dire Straits	105	BB
16/04/1983	I Love L.A.	Randy Newman	110	BB
30/04/1983	Amor	Julio Iglesias	105	BB
07/05/1983	Just Another Saturday Night	Alex Call	101	BB
07/05/1983	Na Na Hey Hey Kiss Him Goodbye	Bananarama	101	BB
07/05/1983	Do It For Love	Marty Balin	102	BB
07/05/1983	Here We'll Stay	Frida & Phil Collins	102	BB
14/05/1983	Body Talk	Kix	104	BB
14/05/1983	Touch The Sky	Smokey Robinson	110	BB
21/05/1983	Save It For Later	English Beat	106	BB
28/05/1983	Always Gonna' Love You	Gary Moore	103	BB
04/06/1983	Candy Man	Mary Jane Girls	101	BB
04/06/1983	More Than This	Roxy Music	102	BB
04/06/1983	Lifeline	Spandau Ballet	108	BB
04/06/1983	Anytime You Want Me	Amy Holland	110	BB
11/06/1983	Watch Your Step	Carlos Santana	107	BB
18/06/1983	Between The Sheets	The Isley Brothers	101	BB
18/06/1983	Whenever You're On My Mind	Marshall Crenshaw	103	BB
18/06/1983	Threw It Away	Joe Cocker	104	BB
18/06/1983	Change Reaction	Robert Hazard	106	BB
25/06/1983	Do What You Feel	Deniece Williams	102	BB
02/07/1983	Two Hearts Beat As One	U2	101	BB
02/07/1983	Nights Are Forever	Jennifer Warnes	105	BB

02/07/1983	Don't Be So Serious	Starpoint	107	BB
09/07/1983	We Live So Fast	Heaven 17	102	BB
16/07/1983	All The Love In The World	Dionne Warwick	101	BB
16/07/1983	I Love You	Yello	103	BB
16/07/1983	Scatterlings Of Africa	Juluka	106	BB
16/07/1983	Loverboy	Shor Patrol	108	BB
23/07/1983	Falling In Love With You	Gary Moore	110	BB
30/07/1983	Teenage Idol	Blackfoot	103	BB
06/08/1983	Message Is You	Gary Myrick	103	BB
06/08/1983	Back In My Arms Again	High Inergy	105	BB
06/08/1983	I Love Rocky Road	"Weird Al" Yankovic	106	BB
06/08/1983	The Star Sisters Melody	Stars On 45 Proudly Presents The Star Sisters	107	BB
06/08/1983	Who Says Girls Can't Rock & Roll	Rebecca Hall	109	BB
13/08/1983	All Night Long	Mary Jane Girls	101	BB
20/08/1983	I Can Make You Dance (Part I)	Zapp	102	BB
20/08/1983	I Wanted To Tell Her	Ministry	106	BB
20/08/1983	At 15	Kagny & The Dirty Rats	110	BB
27/08/1983	If I Only Had A Brain	The Coconuts	108	BB
27/08/1983	Heat In The Street	Axe	109	BB
27/08/1983	Lonely But Only For You	Sissy Spacek	110	BB
10/09/1983	Party Train	The Gap Band	101	BB
10/09/1983	Dancing With Myself	Billy Idol With Gen X	102	BB
10/09/1983	Tell Me What You Want	Zebra	107	BB
17/09/1983	The Man With The 4-Way Hips	Tom Tom Club	106	BB
24/09/1983	I.O.U.	Freeez	104	BB
24/09/1983	Information	Dave Edmunds	106	BB
01/10/1983	Will You, Won't You	Pablo Cruise	107	BB
01/10/1983	This Time	The Whispers	110	BB
08/10/1983	Take It To The Limit	Wille Nelson & Waylon Jennings	102	BB
08/10/1983	So Many Men, So Little Time	Miquel Brown	107	BB

22/10/1983	Party Animal	James Ingram	101	BB
22/10/1983	Never Say Never Again	Lani Hall	103	BB
22/10/1983	Juliet	Robin GiBB	104	BB
22/10/1983	Don't Count The Rainy Days	Michael Murphey	106	BB
29/10/1983	Boys	Mary Jane Girls	102	BB
05/11/1983	Runaway Love	Firefall	103	BB
05/11/1983	Trash It Up	Southside Johnny & The Jukes	108	BB
05/11/1983	Rock It Out	Pia Zadora	110	BB
12/11/1983	U Bring The Freak Out	Rick James	101	BB
12/11/1983	Smile	Was (Not Was)	106	BB
12/11/1983	Heartbreaker (Part I)	Zapp	107	BB
19/11/1983	Make Believe It's Your First Time	Carpenters	101	BB
19/11/1983	White Lines (Don't Don't Do It)	Grandmaster & Melle Mel	101	BB
19/11/1983	Stranger	Elo	105	BB
26/11/1983	Cut Loose	Paul Rodgers	102	BB
03/12/1983	Don't Play Another Love Song	Smokey Robinson	103	BB
03/12/1983	Hero (Wind Beneath My Wings)	Gladys Knight & The Pips	104	BB
03/12/1983	Always Be Mine	Aldo Nova	107	BB
10/12/1983	Bad Girls	Don Felder	104	BB
17/12/1983	I Am What I Am	Gloria Gaynor	102	BB
24/12/1983	Just Let Me Wait	Jennifer Holliday	103	BB
07/01/1984	Show Her	Ronnie Milsap	103	BB
14/01/1984	I'll Let You Slide	Luther Vandross	102	BB
21/01/1984	Rush, Rush	DeBBie Harry	105	BB
21/01/1984	Knocked Down, Made Small (Treated Like A RuBBer Ball)	Was (Not Was)	109	BB
21/01/1984	Popcorn Love	New Edition	101a	BB
21/01/1984	Jealous Girl (b-side)	New Edition	101b	BB
28/01/1984	You Can Count On Me	Shalamar	101	BB
28/01/1984	Touch	Earth, Wind & Fire	103	BB
28/01/1984	Pop Goes My Love	Freeez	104	BB

11/02/1984	One Million Kisses	Rufus And Chaka Khan	102	BB
11/02/1984	Melody	Boy's Brigade	104	BB
11/02/1984	Lost Without Your Love	Jacqui Brookes	105	BB
11/02/1984	The Love Cats	The Cure	107	BB
11/02/1984	Bark At The Moon	Ozzy Osbourne	109	BB
18/02/1984	I Never Stopped Loving You	Survivor	104	BB
18/02/1984	Jealousy	Mary Jane Girls	106	BB
18/02/1984	Fo-Fi-Fo	Pieces Of A Dream	107	BB
25/02/1984	Trommeltanz (Din Daa Daa)	George Kranz	110	BB
03/03/1984	Oogity Boogity	Jon St. James	105	BB
03/03/1984	Tied Up In Love	Ted Nugent	107	BB
10/03/1984	So Tired	Ozzy Osbourne	104	BB
10/03/1984	That's Not The Way (It's S'posed To Be)	Anne Murray	106	BB
17/03/1984	You Just Can't Walk Away	The Dells	107	BB
17/03/1984	Livin' For Your Love	Melba Moore	108	BB
24/03/1984	Love Cares	Endgames	105	BB
31/03/1984	Love Won't Let Me Wait	Johnny Mathis (with Deniece Williams)	106	BB
07/04/1984	Beat Box	The Art Of Noise	101	BB
07/04/1984	All Night Passion	Alisha	103	BB
07/04/1984	Don't Let Your Love Grow Cold	Con Funk Shun	103	BB
07/04/1984	Bop Girl	Pat Wilson	104	BB
07/04/1984	Lollipop Luv	Bryan Loren	105	BB
14/04/1984	Right Or Wrong	Spinners	104	BB
14/04/1984	Saddest Victory	Sandy Stewart	105	BB
14/04/1984	Sixty Eight Guns	The Alarm	106	BB
21/04/1984	Shake Down	Evelyn "Champagne" King	107	BB
28/04/1984	Mystery	The Manhattan Transfer	102	BB
28/04/1984	They Only Come Out At Night	Peter Brown	102	BB
28/04/1984	Street Dance	Break Machine	105	BB
05/05/1984	If You're Not Here (By My Side)	Menudo	102	BB

05/05/1984	Just A Dream	Nena	102	BB
05/05/1984	Are You Ready	Kc	104	BB
12/05/1984	Voices	Russ Ballard	110	BB
19/05/1984	And I Don't Love You	Smokey Robinson	106	BB
26/05/1984	Baby It's You	Stacy Lattisaw & Johnny Gill	102	BB
02/06/1984	Mega-Mix (Includes: Rockit, Autodrive, Future Shock, Tfs,	Herbie Hancock	105	BB
02/06/1984	5:01 A.M. (The Pros And Cons Of Hitch Hiking)	Roger Waters	110	BB
09/06/1984	Lovelite	O'bryan	101	BB
09/06/1984	Reunited	Greg Kihn Band	101	BB
09/06/1984	Borrowed Time	John Lennon	108	BB
16/06/1984	Coming Out Of Hiding	Pamala Stanley	106	BB
23/06/1984	The Mask	Roger Glover	102	BB
30/06/1984	Cold Kid	Glassmoon	103	BB
30/06/1984	Straight Ahead	Kool & The Gang	103	BB
07/07/1984	Dancing With Tears In My Eyes	Ultravox	108	BB
07/07/1984	My Male Curiosity	Kid Creole & The Coconuts	110	BB
14/07/1984	Somebody's Eyes	Karla Bonoff	109	BB
21/07/1984	You Keep Me Coming Back	The Brothers Johnson	102	BB
21/07/1984	Go Ahead And Rain	J.D. Souther	104	BB
21/07/1984	The Deceiver	The Alarm	104	BB
21/07/1984	Body Electric	Rush	105	BB
28/07/1984	Fine, Fine Line	Andy Fraser	101	BB
28/07/1984	Outrageous	Lakeside	101	BB
28/07/1984	With All My Might	Sparks	104	BB
04/08/1984	Rescue Me	Duke Jupiter	101	BB
04/08/1984	Two Silhouettes	Russ Ballard	106	BB
04/08/1984	Rock	Greg Kihn Band	107	BB
04/08/1984	Baby Don't Break Your Baby's Heart	Kashif	108	BB
04/08/1984	Half A Boy And Half A Man	Nick Lowe	110	BB
11/08/1984	New Romeo	Southside Johnny & The Jukes	103	BB

18/08/1984	Close (To The Edit)	The Art Of Noise	102	BB
18/08/1984	Your Love's Got A Hold On Me	Lillo Thomas	102	BB
18/08/1984	Ice Cream Castles	The Time	106	BB
18/08/1984	Beat Street Strut	Juicy	107	BB
25/08/1984	Young Hearts	Commuter	101	BB
25/08/1984	Pearl In The Shell	Howard Jones	108	BB
01/09/1984	Rock You	Helix	101	BB
08/09/1984	Don't Stand Another Chance	Janet Jackson	101	BB
08/09/1984	Eat Your Heart Out	Xavion	103	BB
08/09/1984	Dance Baby	Alfonso Ribeiro	104	BB
15/09/1984	If We Ever Get Back	Frank Stallone	105	BB
15/09/1984	I'll Keep Holding On	Jim Capaldi	106	BB
22/09/1984	Everytime I See Your Picture	Luba	105	BB
29/09/1984	Use It Or Lose It	Michael Furlong	103	BB
29/09/1984	One Heart For Sale	The Stompers	110	BB
06/10/1984	You Get The Best From Me (say, Say, Say)	Alicia Myers	105	BB
06/10/1984	I Can't Find	Smokey Robinson	109	BB
13/10/1984	So Fine	Marc Anthony Thompson	101	BB
13/10/1984	Nobody Loves Me Like You Do	Anne Murray (with Dave Loggins)	103	BB
20/10/1984	In The Air Tonight	Phil Collins	102	BB
20/10/1984	Moonlight Lady	Julio Iglesias	102	BB
20/10/1984	Special Girl	America	106	BB
27/10/1984	Playin' It Cool	Timothy B. Schmit	101	BB
27/10/1984	Slippery People	The Staple Singers	109	BB
10/11/1984	No One's Gonna Love You	The S.O.S. Band	102	BB
10/11/1984	Off And On Love	Champaign	104	BB
17/11/1984	C.O.D. (I'll Deliver)	Mtume	104	BB
17/11/1984	I Promise (I Do Love You)	Dreamboy	106	BB
24/11/1984	Slow Dancing	Lindsey Buckingham	106	BB
01/12/1984	Get Nekked	Rick Dees	104	BB

01/12/1984	Just For The Night	Evelyn "Champagne" King	107	BB
08/12/1984	Hang On To Your Love	Sade	102	BB
08/12/1984	Contagious	The Whispers	105	BB
15/12/1984	Tears	Force M.D.'s	102	BB
15/12/1984	I Love You Love	Joan Jett And The Blackhearts	105	BB
22/12/1984	Skylark	Linda Ronstadt	101	BB
22/12/1984	Jail House Rap	Fat Boys	105	BB
05/01/1985	The Price	Twisted Sister	107	BB
12/01/1985	Beep A Freak	The Gap Band	103	BB
12/01/1985	Mechanical Emotion	Vanity	107	BB
19/01/1985	Request Line	Rock Master Scott And The Dynamic Three	103	BB
26/01/1985	Freaks Come Out At Night	Whodini	104	BB
26/01/1985	Hearts On Fire	Sam Harris	108	BB
02/02/1985	Outta The World	Ashford & Simpson	102	BB
02/02/1985	The Men All Pause	Klymaxx	105	BB
09/02/1985	Love In Moderation	Gwen Guthrie	110	BB
16/02/1985	(No Matter How High I Get) I'll Still Be Lookin' Up To You	Wilton Felder Featuring BoBBy Womack And Introducing Alltrina	102	BB
16/02/1985	My Time	Gladys Knight & The Pips	102	BB
16/02/1985	Just Got Lucky	Dokken	105	BB
23/02/1985	I Want To Know What Love Is	The New Jersey Mass Choir Featuring Donnie Harper And	101	BB
23/02/1985	Tonight	Ready For The World	103	BB
23/02/1985	Gimme, Gimme, Gimme	Narada Michael Walden (with Patti Austin)	106	BB
23/02/1985	He's A Cobra	Rockwell	108	BB
02/03/1985	Premonition	Jack Wagner	101	BB
09/03/1985	Bad Habits	Jenny Burton	101	BB
09/03/1985	Roxanne's Revenge	Roxanne Shanté	109	BB
16/03/1985	Can You Feel It	Fat Boys	101	BB
16/03/1985	Never You Done That	General Public	105	BB
16/03/1985	Believe In The Beat	Carol Lynn Townes	109	BB
23/03/1985	Love & Happiness	David Sanborn	103	BB

23/03/1985	My Girl Loves Me	Shalamar	106	BB
23/03/1985	Some Kinda Lover	The Whispers	106	BB
23/03/1985	King Of Rock	Run-D.M.C.	108	BB
23/03/1985	Heartbeat	Dazz Band	110	BB
30/03/1985	Innocent	Alexander O'neal	101	BB
30/03/1985	Tore Down A La Rimbaud	Van Morrison	101	BB
30/03/1985	Blowing Up Detroit	John Palumbo	109	BB
06/04/1985	I Just Wanna Hang Around You	George Benson	102	BB
06/04/1985	Step By Step	Jeff Lorber Featuring Audrey Wheeler	105	BB
13/04/1985	BackstaBBin'	Eddie-"D"	103	BB
13/04/1985	Read My Lips	Melba Moore	104	BB
13/04/1985	The Riddle	Nik Kershaw	107	BB
20/04/1985	Reggae Rock N Roll	B.E. Taylor Group	102	BB
27/04/1985	Feel So Real	Steve Arrington	104	BB
04/05/1985	Electric Lady	Con Funk Shun	102	BB
11/05/1985	Sanctified Lady	Marvin Gaye	101	BB
11/05/1985	Into The Night	B.B. King	107	BB
11/05/1985	Fire In The Twilight	Wang Chung	110	BB
18/05/1985	Thinking About Your Love	Skipworth & Turner	104	BB
18/05/1985	Gentle (Calling Your Name)	Frederick	108	BB
18/05/1985	Zie Zie Won't Dance	Peter Brown	108	BB
25/05/1985	I'm The One Who Loves You	Santana	102	BB
25/05/1985	Oh Yeah!	Bill Withers	106	BB
01/06/1985	Can You Help Me	Jesse Johnson's Revue	110	BB
08/06/1985	Material Thangz	The Deele	101	BB
08/06/1985	Babies	Ashford & Simpson	102	BB
08/06/1985	You've Got To Believe In Love	Van Zant	102	BB
08/06/1985	You Talk Too Much	Run-D.M.C.	107	BB
08/06/1985	Boy's Won't (Leave The Girls Alone)	Greg Kihn	110	BB
15/06/1985	Double Oh-Oh	George Clinton	101	BB

15/06/1985	Too Many Games	Maze Featuring Frankie Beverly	103	BB
15/06/1985	Itchin' For A Scratch	Force M.D.'s	105	BB
15/06/1985	One Bad Apple	Nolan Thomas	105	BB
15/06/1985	Call Me Mr. 'Telephone' (Answering Service)	Cheyne	106	BB
15/06/1985	Slave To Love	Bryan Ferry	109	BB
22/06/1985	Road To Nowhere	Talking Heads	105	BB
29/06/1985	It's Over Now	Luther Vandross	101	BB
29/06/1985	Save Your Love (For #1)	René & Angela	101	BB
29/06/1985	When You Love Me Like This	Melba Moore	106	BB
29/06/1985	Midnight Mission	Textones	109	BB
06/07/1985	Padlock	Gwen Guthrie	102	BB
13/07/1985	The Fire Still Burns	Russ Ballard	105	BB
20/07/1985	Tight Connection To My Heart (Has Anybody Seen My Love)	Bob Dylan	103	BB
20/07/1985	Swing Low	R.J.'S Latest Arrival	107	BB
20/07/1985	Cool, Calm, Collected	Atlantic Starr	110	BB
27/07/1985	Please Be Good To Me	Menudo	104	BB
27/07/1985	Glow	Rick James	106	BB
27/07/1985	I Freak For You	Carol Lynn Townes	106	BB
27/07/1985	The Perfect Kiss	New Order	109	BB
03/08/1985	Sister Fate	Shelia E.	102	BB
03/08/1985	My Secret (Didja Gitit Yet?)	New Edition	103	BB
03/08/1985	Well-A-Wiggy	The Weather Girls	107	BB
03/08/1985	Too Loud	Robert Plant	108	BB
10/08/1985	The Pleasure Seekers	The System	108	BB
10/08/1985	History	Mai Tai	109	BB
17/08/1985	A Fly Girl	The Boogie Boys	102	BB
17/08/1985	Stronger Together	Shannon	103	BB
17/08/1985	Can't Get There From Here	R.E.M.	110	BB

? & The Mysterians	Do Something To Me	09/09/1967	123	CB
? And The Mysterians	Do Something To Me	26/08/1967	110	BB
10 C.C.	Headline Hustler	30/03/1974	105	CB
10 C.C.	The Wall Street Shuffle	13/07/1974	103	BB
100 Proof (Aged In Soul)	Driveway	26/06/1971	121	BB
100 Proof Aged In Soul	Too Many Cooks (Spoil The Soup)	15/11/1969	108	CB
100 Strings & Joni (James)	You Belong To Me	09/04/1960	114	CB
100 Strings And Joni (James)	You Belong To Me	28/03/1960	101	BB
10cc	Lazy Ways	31/07/1976	104a	BB
10cc	Life Is A Minestrone (b-side)	31/07/1976	104b	BB
1910 Fruitgum Co.	When We Get Married	22/11/1969	118	BB
1910 Fruitgum Co.	Go Away	06/06/1970	117	CB
2 Of Clubs	Heart	24/09/1966	117	CB
2 Of Clubs	Heart	08/10/1966	125	BB
A.A.B.B.	Pick Up The Pieces One By One	12/04/1975	108	BB
A.B. Skhy	Camel Back	15/11/1969	135	CB
Aaron Neville	Over You	15/08/1960	111	BB
Aaron Neville	Over You	17/09/1960	112	CB
ABBa	One Of Us	12/02/1983	107	BB
Abraham's Children	Gypsy	17/02/1973	119	BB
Ac/Dc	Rock 'N' Roll Damnation	09/09/1978	Np8	CB
Ac/Dc	Touch Too Much	02/02/1980	106	BB
Accents	New Girl	15/08/1964	128	BB
Ace Cannon	Since I Met You Baby	23/03/1963	134	CB
Ace Cannon	Since I Met You Baby	20/04/1963	130	BB
Ace Cannon	Swanee River	02/11/1963	101	CB
Ace Cannon	Swanee River	16/11/1963	103	BB
Ace Cannon	Empty Arms	24/10/1964	115	CB
Ace Cannon	Empty Arms	24/10/1964	120	BB
Ace Cannon	Sea Cruise	17/04/1965	144	CB

Ace Cannon	Sea Cruise	24/04/1965	135	BB
Ace Cannon	Funny (How Time Slips Away)	26/02/1966	102	BB
Ace Cannon	Funny (How Time Slips Away)	26/02/1966	114	CB
Ace Cannon	As Time Goes By	17/12/1966	150	CB
Ace Cannon	By The Time I Get To Phoenix	20/04/1968	110	BB
Ace Cannon	Tuffer Than Tuff	02/12/1972	127	CB
Ace Cannon & His Alto Sax	Amen	18/10/1969	139	CB
Ace Cannon & His Alto-Sax	Volare	10/11/1962	107	BB
Act 1	Friends Or Lovers	31/03/1973	101	BB
Act I	It Takes Both Of Us	14/07/1973	128	CB
Adam Wade	Speaking Of Her	03/09/1960	108	CB
Adam Wade	Linda	30/09/1961	101	CB
Adam Wade	Preview Of Paradise	20/11/1961	108	BB
Adam Wade	It's Good To Have You Back With Me	03/02/1962	109	BB
Adam Wade	How Are Things In Lovers Lane (b-side)	03/02/1962	114	BB
Adam Wade	For The First Time In My Life	28/04/1962	118	BB
Adam Wade	For The First Time In My Life	28/04/1962	133	CB
Adam Wade	I'm Climbin' (The Wall)	04/08/1962	137	CB
Adam Wade	There'll Be No Teardrops Tonight	08/12/1962	104	BB
Adam Wade	Don't Let Me Cross Over	16/02/1963	117	BB
Adam Wade	Don't Let Me Cross Over*	23/02/1963	105	CB
Adam Wade	Theme From Irma La Douce (LOOK Again)*	17/08/1963	127	CB
Adam Wade	Crying In The Chapel	23/01/1965	121	CB
Adc Band	Long Stroke	09/12/1978	101	BB
Addrisi Brothers	I Can Feel You	20/05/1972	110	BB
Adrian Smith	Wild About My Lovin'	26/05/1973	114	BB
Aerosmith	Same Old Song And Dance	13/04/1974	106	CB
Aerosmith	Train Kept A Rollin'	19/10/1974	108	CB
Aerosmith	Get It Up	29/04/1978	102	CB
Aesops Fables	I'm Gonna Make You Love Me	14/09/1968	123	BB

Aki Aleong	Trade Winds, Trade Winds	13/11/1961	101	BB
Al (He's The King) Hirt, Trumpet	The Arena	22/01/1966	115	CB
Al (He's The King) Hirt, Trumpet	The Arena	12/02/1966	129	BB
Al (He's The King) Hirt, Trumpet	Mame	09/04/1966	136	CB
Al (He's The King) Hirt, Trumpet	Trumpet Pickin'	25/06/1966	129	CB
Al (He's The King) Hirt, Trumpet	Green Hornet Theme	03/09/1966	121	CB
Al (He's The King) Hirt, Trumpet	Green Hornet Theme	10/09/1966	126	BB
Al (He's The King) Hirt, Trumpet	Music To Watch Girls By	07/01/1967	119	BB
Al Anderson	We'll Make Love	24/02/1973	108	CB
Al Anderson	We'll Make Love	24/03/1973	101	BB
Al Caiola	From Russia With Love*	18/04/1964	116	CB
Al Caiola & His Orchestra	Autumn In Cheyenne	16/09/1961	105	CB
Al Caiola And His Orchestra	From Russia With Love	18/04/1964	120	BB
Al Capps	Shangri-La	26/05/1973	119	BB
Al Casey Combo	Cookin'	24/03/1962	105	CB
Al Casey With The K-C-Ettes	Guitars, Guitars, Guitars	12/10/1963	116	BB
Al Downing	I Love To Love	08/05/1976	107	BB
Al Green	You Say It	07/02/1970	108	CB
Al Green	Driving Wheel	10/04/1971	115	BB
Al Green	Let It Shine	15/05/1976	107	CB
Al Green	I Tried To Tell Myself	26/02/1977	101	BB
Al Green	Love And Happiness	30/07/1977	104	BB
Al Green	I Feel Good	29/04/1978	103	BB
Al Greene	Don't Hurt Me No More	20/04/1968	117	CB
Al Greene	Don't Hurt Me No More	20/04/1968	127	BB
Al Hirt	Walkin'	18/04/1964	134	CB
Al Hirt	Walkin'	27/06/1964	103	BB
Al Hirt	The Silence (Il Silenzio)	21/08/1965	129	CB
Al Hirt	Feelin' Fruggy	16/10/1965	135	CB
Al Hirt	Puppet On A String	03/06/1967	129	BB

Al Hirt	We Can Fly/Up-Up And Away	27/04/1968	129	BB
Al Hirt	If	08/02/1969	116	BB
Al Hudson & The Partners	You Can Do It	25/08/1979	101	BB
Al Jarreau	Never Givin' Up	05/07/1980	102	BB
Al Jarreau And Randy Crawford	Your Precious Love	30/10/1982	102	BB
Al Kasha	Sing (And Tell The Blues "So Long")	31/12/1960	111	CB
Al Kent	Finders Keepers	25/11/1967	104	CB
Al King	Think Twice Before You Speak	23/04/1966	123	CB
Al Kooper	You Never Know Who Your Friends Are	19/07/1969	135	CB
Al Martino	Dearest (Cara)	02/04/1960	106	CB
Al Martino	Little Girl, Little Boy	13/03/1961	109	BB
Al Martino	Here In My Heart	15/07/1961	102	CB
Al Martino	Love, Where Are You Now (Toselli Serenade)	26/05/1962	119	BB
Al Martino	Thank You For Loving Me	29/08/1964	118	BB
Al Martino	Silver Bells	26/12/1964	145	CB
Al Martino	With All My Heart	13/03/1965	122	BB
Al Martino	Wake Up To Me Gentle	05/10/1968	125	CB
Al Martino	Wake Up To Me Gentle	19/10/1968	120	BB
Al Martino	Walking In The Sand	20/06/1970	123	BB
Al Martino	True Love Is Greater Than Friendship	07/11/1970	110	CB
Al Martino	Come Into My Life (Lass Das Weinen Sein)	06/03/1971	104	CB
Al Martino	Kentucky Mornin'	20/08/1977	110	CB
Al Wilson	Do What You Gotta Do	06/01/1968	102	BB
Al Wilson	I Stand Accused	22/03/1969	142	CB
Al Wilson	I Stand Accused	12/04/1969	106	BB
Alabama	Old Flame	02/05/1981	103	BB
Alabama	Mountain Music	20/03/1982	101	BB
Alan Copeland	Mission Impossible Theme/Norwegian Wood	21/09/1968	120	BB
Alan Dale	Monday To Sunday	29/05/1961	101	BB
Alan O'day	Soldier Of Fortune	26/11/1977	103	CB

Alan Parsons Project	To One In Paradise	26/03/1977	108	BB
Alan Parsons Project	What Goes Up	09/09/1978	Np6	CB
Alan Parsons Project	You Won't Be There	09/02/1980	105	BB
Alan Price Set	I Put A Spell On You	28/05/1966	105	CB
Alan Price Set	Hi-Lili, Hi-Lo	17/09/1966	143	CB
Albert Hammond	Names, Tags, Numbers & Labels	26/10/1974	107	CB
Albert King	As The Years Go Passing By	22/02/1969	102	CB
Albert King	As The Years Go Passing By	08/03/1969	132	BB
Albert King	Can't You See What You're Doing To Me	18/07/1970	127	BB
Albert King	Everybody Wants To Go To Heaven	23/10/1971	103	BB
Albert King	Angel Of Mercy	01/04/1972	128	CB
Aldo Nova	Always Be Mine	03/12/1983	107	BB
Alex Brown	Love Really Hurts Without You	17/04/1976	107	CB
Alex Call	Just Another Saturday Night	07/05/1983	101	BB
Alex North	Anthony And Cleopatra Theme	29/06/1963	120	CB
Alexadrow Karazov	Castschok (Life Is A Dance)	05/04/1969	104	CB
Alexadrow Karazov	Castschok (Life Is A Dance)	03/05/1969	120	BB
Alexander O'neal	Innocent	30/03/1985	101	BB
Alfie Khan	She's Comin' Back	30/01/1971	118	CB
Alfonso Ribeiro	Dance Baby	08/09/1984	104	BB
Ali Thomson	Foolish Child	14/03/1981	105	BB
Alicia Bridges	Body Heat	24/02/1979	Np6	CB
Alicia Myers	You Get The Best From Me (say, Say, Say)	06/10/1984	105	BB
Alisha	All Night Passion	07/04/1984	103	BB
Alive 'N Kickin'	London Bridge	20/02/1971	107	CB
Allan Clarke	The Passenger	18/03/1978	110	CB
Allan Sherman Boston Pops Orchestra Arthur Fiedler,	The End Of A Symphony - Part 1 [Live]	26/09/1964	113	BB
Allen Wayne	Walkin' My Baby	05/10/1963	144	CB
Alvin Cash & The Crawlers	Un-Wind The Twine	24/07/1965	134	BB
Alvin Robinson	Fever	12/09/1964	115	CB

Alvin Robinson	Fever	19/09/1964	108	BB
Alzo	That's Alright (I Don't Mind It)	12/02/1972	116	BB
Alzo	Don't Ask Me Why	26/08/1972	106	CB
Amadeo & His Indian Harps	The Grasshopper (El Cigarron)	28/12/1963	126	CB
Amazing Rhythm Aces	Lipstick Traces (On A Cigarette)	03/03/1979	Np6	CB
Amazing Rhythm Aces	Lipstick Traces (On A Cigarette)	07/04/1979	104	BB
Ambergris	Forget It, I Got It	06/06/1970	107	CB
Ambrosia	Can't Let A Woman	11/12/1976	102	BB
Ambrosia	If Heaven Could Find Me	07/07/1979	107	BB
Ambrosia	No Big Deal	15/11/1980	105	BB
Ambrosia	Outside	31/01/1981	102	BB
America	Rainbow Song	22/12/1973	102	CB
America	Only Game In Town	25/08/1979	107	BB
America	Special Girl	20/10/1984	106	BB
American Flyer	Let Me Down Easy	09/10/1976	114	CB
American Machine	Snowball	01/03/1969	141	CB
American Tears	Born To Love	25/09/1976	118	CB
Amy Holland	Anytime You Want Me	04/06/1983	110	BB
André Cymone	Kelly's Eyes	05/02/1983	107	BB
André Previn And His Piano And Orchestra	Like Love	30/05/1960	108	BB
Andre Williams	Cadillac Jack	05/10/1968	124	CB
Andrea Carroll	Please Don't Talk To The Lifeguard	12/08/1961	123	CB
Andy & David Williams	I Don't Know How To Say Goodbye	09/11/1974	114	CB
Andy Adams & Egg Cream	Can I Stay	28/05/1977	109	CB
Andy Cory	Hey You, What Are You, Some Kind Of Nut?	01/05/1961	121	BB
Andy Fraser	Fine, Fine Line	28/07/1984	101	BB
Andy Kim	Tricia Tell Your Daddy	22/03/1969	110	BB
Andy Kim	You	21/02/1970	115	CB
Andy Kim	Who Has The Answers?	08/07/1972	118	CB
Andy Kim	Who Has The Answers?	12/08/1972	111	BB

Andy Kim	The Essence Of Joan (Ain't It Funny How Love Can Own You)	29/03/1975	103	CB
Andy Russell	It's Such A Pretty World Today	08/07/1967	119	BB
Andy Stewart	Donald Where's Your Troosers?	09/09/1961	114	CB
Andy Williams	Help Me	03/03/1962	113	CB
Andy Williams	The Wonderful World Of The Young	31/03/1962	139	CB
Andy Williams	The Peking Theme (So Little Time)	15/06/1963	115	BB
Andy Williams	Under Paris Skies	08/08/1964	121	BB
Andy Williams	Bye Bye Blues	12/02/1966	123	CB
Andy Williams	Bye Bye Blues	19/02/1966	127	BB
Andy Williams	How Can I Tell Her It's Over	04/06/1966	109	CB
Andy Williams	How Can I Tell Her It's Over	11/06/1966	109	BB
Andy Williams	Holly	18/11/1967	113	BB
Andy Williams	Live And Learn	26/07/1969	111	CB
Andy Williams	Live And Learn	09/08/1969	119	BB
Andy Williams	A Woman's Way	01/11/1969	109	BB
Andy Williams	Music From Across The Way	22/01/1972	111	CB
Andy Williams	Macarthur Park	05/08/1972	102	BB
Andy Williams	Macarthur Park	05/08/1972	114	CB
Andy Williams & Noelle	Remember	05/01/1974	117	CB
Angel	Flying With Broken Wings (Without You)	01/04/1978	102	CB
Angel City	Marseilles	14/06/1980	109	BB
Angela Bofill	This Time I'll Be Sweeter	12/05/1979	104	BB
Angie & The Chicklettes	Treat Him Tender, Maureen (Now That Ringo Belongs To You)	20/03/1965	112	CB
Anita Bryant	I Can't Do It By Myself	22/04/1961	113	CB
Anita Bryant	Lonesome For You, Mama	03/07/1961	108	BB
Anita Bryant	The Wedding (La Novia)	23/09/1961	136	CB
Anita Bryant	Step By Step, Little By Little	24/02/1962	119	CB
Anita Bryant	Step By Step, Little By Little	03/03/1962	106	BB
Anita Bryant	Welcome, Welcome Home	12/09/1964	130	BB
Anita Harris	Just Loving You	04/11/1967	120	BB

Anita Harris	Just Loving You	11/11/1967	106	CB
Anita Humes	I'm Making It Over	10/10/1964	142	CB
Anita Humes & The Essex	Curfew Lover	22/02/1964	118	CB
Anita Kerr Quartet	Waitin' For The Evening Train	14/12/1963	125	BB
Ann Cole	Don't Stop The Wedding	27/10/1962	144	CB
Ann Marie	Runaround	21/11/1964	140	CB
Ann Peebles	Walk Away	12/04/1969	120	CB
Ann Peebles	Slipped, Tripped And Fell In Love	25/09/1971	113	BB
Ann Peebles	Breaking Up Somebody's Home	26/02/1972	101	BB
Ann Peebles	Somebody's On Your Case	29/07/1972	119	CB
Ann Peebles	Somebody's On Your Case	26/08/1972	117	BB
Ann Peebles	I'm Gonna Tear Your Playhouse Down	03/02/1973	111	BB
Ann Peebles	I'm Gonna Tear Your Playhouse Down	03/02/1973	118	CB
Ann Peebles	(You Keep Me) Hangin' On	04/05/1974	102	BB
Ann Peebles	(You Keep Me) Hanging On	04/05/1974	104	CB
Ann-Margret	Take All The Kisses	20/04/1963	142	CB
Ann-Margret Lee Hazlewood	Sleep In The Grass	18/01/1969	109	CB
Ann-Margret Lee Hazlewood	Sleep In The Grass	25/01/1969	113	BB
Anna King	Mama's Got A Bag Of Her Own	13/11/1965	120	CB
Anna-King	In Between Tears*	27/05/1961	131	CB
Annabelle Fox	Getting Through To Me	08/01/1966	136	CB
Anne Murray	A Stranger In My Place	06/03/1971	115	CB
Anne Murray	A Stranger In My Place	06/03/1971	122	BB
Anne Murray	Cotton Jenny	29/01/1972	102	CB
Anne Murray	Uproar	01/03/1975	101	CB
Anne Murray	Things	30/10/1976	113	CB
Anne Murray	Walk Right Back	01/04/1978	103	BB
Anne Murray	I'm Happy Just To Dance With You	05/07/1980	I101	CB
Anne Murray	That's Not The Way (It's S'posed To Be)	10/03/1984	106	BB
Anne Murray (with Dave Loggins)	Nobody Loves Me Like You Do	13/10/1984	103	BB

Annette	The Truth About Youth	03/03/1962	132	CB
Annette	Teenage Wedding	23/02/1963	144	CB
Annette	Promise Me Anything	05/10/1963	126	CB
Annette	Promise Me Anything	19/10/1963	123	BB
Annette & The Vonnair Sisters	Dreamin' About You	18/11/1961	108	CB
Annette And The Vonnair Sisters	Dreamin' About You	13/11/1961	106	BB
Annette Snell	You Oughta' Be Here With Me	20/10/1973	102	BB
Annette With The Afterbeats	My Heart Became Of Age	10/10/1959	103	CB
Annette With The Afterbeats	Dream Boy	04/02/1961	105	CB
Annette With The Afterbeats Plus Four	Blue Muu Muu	21/08/1961	107	BB
Annette With The Up Beats	Indian Giver	06/05/1961	135	CB
Annie Laurie	If You're Lonely	18/07/1960	104	BB
Annie Laurie	If You're Lonely	30/07/1960	123	CB
Anthony & The Imperials	It's Not The Same	05/11/1966	101	CB
Anthony & The Sophomores	Play Those Oldies, Mr. Dee Jay	30/03/1963	122	CB
Anthony & The Sophomores	Gee (But I'd Give The World)	06/11/1965	138	CB
Anthony And The Imperials	Don't Tie Me Down	04/03/1967	123	BB
Anthony And The Imperials	Hold On (Just A Little Bit Longer)	12/04/1975	106	BB
Anthony Newley	Tribute	04/01/1964	105	BB
Any Trouble	Second Choice	14/03/1981	108	BB
Aphrodites Child	Rain And Tears	03/08/1968	118	CB
April Stevens & Nino Tempo	Paradise	23/02/1963	102	CB
April Stevens & Nino Tempo	Paradise	30/03/1963	126	BB
April Wine	Bad Side Of The Moon	01/07/1972	106	BB
April Wine	Say Hello	12/01/1980	104	BB
April Young	Gonna Make Him My Baby	26/06/1965	129	CB
Aquatones	Crazy For You	28/08/1961	119	BB
Archie Bell & The Drells	Just A Little Closer	19/04/1969	128	BB
Archie Bell & The Drells	A World Without Music	03/01/1970	111	CB
Archie Bell & The Drells	Here I Go Again	31/01/1970	112	BB

Archie Bell & The Drells	Don't Let The Music Slip Away	25/04/1970	113	CB
Archie Campbell	Rindercella [Live]	29/05/1965	132	BB
Aretha Franklin	Are You Sure	13/05/1961	134	CB
Aretha Franklin	Rough Lover	10/02/1962	141	CB
Aretha Franklin	Don't Cry, Baby	30/06/1962	139	CB
Aretha Franklin	Try A Little Tenderness	01/09/1962	126	CB
Aretha Franklin	Just For A Thrill	22/09/1962	111	BB
Aretha Franklin	Trouble In Mind	22/12/1962	124	CB
Aretha Franklin	Here's Where I Came In (Here's Where I Walk Out)	08/06/1963	150	CB
Aretha Franklin	Here's Where I Came In (Here's Where I Walk Out) (b-side)	22/06/1963	125	BB
Aretha Franklin	Say It Isn't So	06/07/1963	113	BB
Aretha Franklin	Skylark	05/10/1963	124	CB
Aretha Franklin	Soulville	09/05/1964	121	BB
Aretha Franklin	Soulville	30/05/1964	135	CB
Aretha Franklin	Little Miss Raggedy Ann	23/01/1965	103	CB
Aretha Franklin	Can't You Just See Me	06/02/1965	101	CB
Aretha Franklin	One Step Ahead	10/04/1965	122	CB
Aretha Franklin	One Step Ahead	15/05/1965	119	BB
Aretha Franklin	(No, No) I'm Losing You	17/07/1965	114	BB
Aretha Franklin	You Made Me Love You	18/12/1965	109	BB
Aretha Franklin	Tighten Up Your Tie, Button Up Your Jacket (Make It For The Door)	19/02/1966	141	CB
Aretha Franklin	Cry Like A Baby	19/11/1966	113	BB
Aretha Franklin	My Song	28/12/1968	108	CB
Aretha Franklin	Tracks Of My Tears	22/03/1969	102	CB
Aretha Franklin	Today I Sing The Blues	11/10/1969	101	BB
Aretha Franklin	April Fools	08/07/1972	117	CB
Aretha Franklin	Almighty Fire (Woman Of The Future)	13/05/1978	103	BB
Aretha Franklin	Almighty Fire (Woman Of The Future)	10/06/1978	104	CB
Aretha Franklin With The Dixie Flyers	The Thrill Is Gone	20/06/1970	103	CB
Argent	Sweet Mary	17/04/1971	102	BB

Argent	Tragedy	04/11/1972	106	BB
Argent	God Gave Rock And Roll To You	21/04/1973	117	CB
Argent	God Gave Rock And Roll To You	28/04/1973	114	BB
Arkade	Sing Out The Love (In My Heart)	15/08/1970	101	CB
Arlo Guthrie	Alice's Rock & Roll Restaurant	20/12/1969	102	CB
Arlo Guthrie	Valley To Pray	24/10/1970	102	BB
Arlo Guthrie	Gypsy Davy	09/06/1973	105	BB
Arlo Guthrie	Gypsy Davy	16/06/1973	101	CB
Arrival	I Will Survive	01/08/1970	114	CB
Arrows	Touch Too Much	19/10/1974	123	CB
Art Garfunkel	Crying In My Sleep	12/11/1977	101	CB
Art Garfunkel	In A Little While (I'll Be On My Way)	24/03/1979	Np6	CB
Art Mooney And His Orchestra	Smile	08/06/1959	107	BB
Art Mooney And His Orchestra	I Ain't Down Yet	31/12/1960	108	BB
Arthur Alexander	Go Home Girl	12/01/1963	102	BB
Arthur Alexander	Go Home Girl	12/01/1963	120	CB
Arthur Alexander	Pretty Girls Everywhere	10/08/1963	118	BB
Arthur Conley	Run On	12/04/1969	115	BB
Arthur Conley	God Bless	18/04/1970	107	BB
Arthur Conley	Rita	19/08/1972	108	CB
Arthur Lyman Group	Cotton Fields (The Cotton Song)	20/04/1963	129	BB
Arthur Lyman Group	Jungle Drums	24/08/1963	133	CB
Arthur Prysock	Our Love Will Last	02/03/1963	128	BB
Arthur Prysock	Stella By Starlight	28/09/1963	145	CB
Arthur Prysock	Close Your Eyes	27/06/1964	124	BB
Arthur Prysock	Close Your Eyes	04/07/1964	134	CB
Arthur Prysock	Without The One You Love	03/10/1964	126	BB
Arthur Prysock	Only A Fool Breaks His Own Heart	25/09/1965	140	CB
Arthur Prysock	Open Up Your Heart	09/10/1965	109	CB
Arthur Prysock	Only A Fool Breaks His Own Heart	09/10/1965	125	BB

Arthur Prysock	Let It Be Me (Je T'appartiens)	02/07/1966	124	BB
Arthur Prysock	You Don't Have To Say You Love Me	31/12/1966	141	CB
Arthur Prysock	You Don't Have To Say You Love Me	28/01/1967	120	BB
Arthur Prysock	Mamam	20/04/1968	127	CB
Arthur Prysock	Mamam	27/04/1968	134	BB
Arthur Prysock	In The Rain	03/11/1973	110	BB
Arthur Prysock	Colour My World	09/03/1974	117	CB
Arthur, Hurley & Gottlieb	Part Of You	07/07/1973	125	CB
Artist	Title	DOE	Peak	Chart
Artistics	Get My Hands On Some Lovin'	22/08/1964	132	CB
Ashford & Simpson	Main Line	06/07/1974	111	CB
Ashford & Simpson	Send It	03/12/1977	104	CB
Ashford & Simpson	Outta The World	02/02/1985	102	BB
Ashford & Simpson	Babies	08/06/1985	102	BB
Astrud Gilberto	A Time For Us	19/07/1969	114	CB
Atlanta Rhythm Section	Crazy	22/11/1975	111	CB
Atlanta Rhythm Section	Back Up Against The Wall	15/12/1979	103	BB
Atlanta Rhythm Section	I Ain't Much	11/10/1980	101	BB
Atlanta Rhythm Section	Silver Eagle	20/12/1980	101	BB
Atlantic & Pacific Featuring Peter Gormann	The Hands Of Time (Brian's Song)	12/04/1975	113	CB
Atlantic Starr	When Love Calls	11/04/1981	101	BB
Atlantic Starr	Cool, Calm, Collected	20/07/1985	110	BB
Audrey Arno & The Hazy Osterwald Sextet	La Pachanga	15/04/1961	106	CB
Aussie Band	Somebody Wants You	08/11/1980	109	BB
Austin Roberts	The Last Thing On My Mind	02/06/1973	101	CB
Austin Roberts	The Last Thing On My Mind	02/06/1973	120	BB
Austin Roberts	One Word	01/09/1973	121	CB
Austin Roberts	Children Of The Rain	27/12/1975	114	CB
Ava Cherry	Love Is Good News	15/03/1980	107	BB
Avant Garde	Fly With Me!	14/12/1968	130	BB

Average White Band	Nothing You Can Do	21/09/1974	102	CB
Average White Band	For You, For Love	18/10/1980	106	BB
Awb	A Love Of Your Own	15/01/1977	101	BB
Axe	Rock 'N' Roll Party In The Streets	18/09/1982	109	BB
Axe	Heat In The Street	27/08/1983	109	BB
B. Bumble & The Stingers	Boogie Woogie	24/06/1961	101	CB
B. Bumble & The Stingers	Near You	24/06/1961	139	CB
B.B. King	My Own Fault	04/06/1960	113	CB
B.B. King	Peace Of Mind	26/06/1961	119	BB
B.B. King	Gonna Miss You Around Here	17/03/1962	129	CB
B.B. King	Tomorrow Night	10/11/1962	106	BB
B.B. King	Help The Poor	23/05/1964	111	CB
B.B. King	You're Gonna Miss Me	08/08/1964	107	BB
B.B. King	Let Me Love You (b-side)	15/08/1964	110	BB
B.B. King	Never Trust A Woman	07/11/1964	132	CB
B.B. King	Christmas Celebration	26/12/1964	140	CB
B.B. King	The Worst Thing In My Life	06/02/1965	128	CB
B.B. King	I Don't Want You Cuttin' Off Your Hair	13/05/1967	126	CB
B.B. King	Heartbreaker	02/12/1967	136	CB
B.B. King	The Woman I Love	10/08/1968	123	CB
B.B. King	Please Send Me Someone To Love	30/11/1968	102	BB
B.B. King	Please Send Me Someone To Love	30/11/1968	102	CB
B.B. King	Don't Waste My Time	01/02/1969	113	BB
B.B. King	I Want You So Bad	09/08/1969	127	BB
B.B. King	Never Make A Move Too Soon	12/08/1978	102	BB
B.B. King	Better Not Look Down	15/09/1979	110	BB
B.B. King	Into The Night	11/05/1985	107	BB
B.B. King & His Orchestra	Waitin' On You	14/01/1967	109	CB
B.B. King And His Orchestra	Waitin' On You	14/01/1967	112	BB
B.E. Taylor Group	Reggae Rock N Roll	20/04/1985	102	BB

B.J. Thomas	Plain Jane	26/11/1966	126	CB
B.J. Thomas	Plain Jane	17/12/1966	129	BB
B.J. Thomas	Songs	14/07/1973	126	CB
B.T. Express	Energy To Burn	11/09/1976	101	CB
B.W. Stevenson	Say What I Feel	01/07/1972	114	BB
B.W. Stevenson	Say What I Feel	15/07/1972	109	CB
B.W. Stevenson	Don't Go To Mexico	24/02/1973	118	CB
B.W. Stevenson	Look For The Light	06/04/1974	111	CB
B.W. Stevenson	Little Bit Of Understanding	10/08/1974	108	CB
Babies	You Make Me Feel Like Someone	08/07/1967	122	BB
Babs Tino	Too Late To Worry	16/06/1962	150	CB
Babs Tino	Forgive Me (For Giving You Such A Bad Time)	25/08/1962	117	BB
Baby Washington	Work Out	15/02/1960	105	BB
Baby Washington	Work Out	27/02/1960	109	CB
Baby Washington	Handful Of Memories	25/08/1962	116	BB
Baby Washington	Hush Heart	15/12/1962	102	BB
Baby Washington	Hey Lonely One	19/10/1963	131	CB
Baby Washington	Run My Heart	30/01/1965	121	BB
Baby Washington	Run My Heart	06/02/1965	135	CB
Baby Washington	No Time For Pity	20/11/1965	125	CB
Baby Washington	No Time For Pity	27/11/1965	125	BB
Baby Washington & Don Gardner	Forever	02/06/1973	105	CB
Baby Washington & Don Gardner	Forever	07/07/1973	119	BB
Back Porch Majority	Honey And Wine	25/06/1966	133	CB
Bad Habits	My Baby Specializes	01/08/1970	137	CB
Badfinger	Apple Of My Eye	09/02/1974	102	BB
Badge	Gettin' In Over My Head	06/03/1971	110	CB
Badge	Getting' In Over My Head	20/03/1971	119	BB
Baja Marimba Band	Moonglow / Picnic Theme	21/03/1964	121	BB
Baja Marimba Band	Moonglow/Picnic Theme	04/04/1964	142	CB

Baja Marimba Band	Yours	18/06/1966	122	CB
Baja Marimba Band	The Portuguese Washerwomen	22/10/1966	126	BB
Baja Marimba Band	The Cry Of The Wild Goose	04/02/1967	130	CB
Baja Marimba Band	The Cry Of The Wild Goose	18/02/1967	113	BB
Baja Marimba Band	Georgy Girl	06/05/1967	110	CB
Ballin' Jack	Super Highway	23/01/1971	102	CB
Bananarama	He Was Really Sayin' Somethin'	13/11/1982	108	BB
Bananarama	Na Na Hey Hey Kiss Him Goodbye	07/05/1983	101	BB
Bar-Kays	Shine	14/04/1979	102	BB
Bar-Kays	Hit And Run	12/12/1981	101	BB
Barbara & Brenda	Hurtin' Inside	31/10/1964	120	CB
Barbara & The Browns	Big Party	02/05/1964	103	CB
Barbara Acklin	I Did It	17/10/1970	121	BB
Barbara Acklin	Raindrops	20/07/1974	112	CB
Barbara Chandler	It Hurts To Be Sixteen*	13/07/1963	114	CB
Barbara Chandler	It Hurts To Be Sixteen	27/07/1963	114	BB
Barbara Dickson	Who Was It Stole Your Heart Away	23/07/1977	110	BB
Barbara Evans	Souvenirs	01/06/1959	111	BB
Barbara Evans	Charlie Wasn't There	29/05/1961	109	BB
Barbara Evans	Charlie Wasn't There	03/06/1961	110	CB
Barbara Fairchild	Kid Stuff	08/09/1973	106	CB
Barbara George	If You Think	21/07/1962	114	BB
Barbara George	Send For Me (If You Need Some Lovin')	25/08/1962	113	CB
Barbara Jean English	I'm Living A Lie	22/07/1972	125	CB
Barbara Jean English	I'm Sorry	03/02/1973	120	CB
Barbara Lewis	If You Love Her	24/08/1963	131	BB
Barbara Lewis	Someday We're Gonna Love Again (b-side)	09/05/1964	124	BB
Barbara Lewis	Someday We're Gonna Love Again	16/05/1964	126	CB
Barbara Lewis	Spend A Little Time	23/05/1964	119	BB
Barbara Lewis	Pushin' A Good Thing Too Far	31/10/1964	113	BB

Barbara Lewis	Pushin' A Good Thiing Too Far	07/11/1964	140	CB
Barbara Lewis	Don't Forget About Me	05/02/1966	103	CB
Barbara Lewis	I'll Make Him Love Me	15/04/1967	103	CB
Barbara Lewis	Rock And Roll Lullaby	28/04/1973	115	CB
Barbara Lynn	You're Gonna Need Me	22/12/1962	114	CB
Barbara Lynn	To Love Or Not To Love	15/06/1963	135	BB
Barbara Lynn	Don't Spread It Around	10/10/1964	102	CB
Barbara Lynn	It's Better To Have It	19/12/1964	105	CB
Barbara Lynn	I'm A Good Woman	23/07/1966	129	BB
Barbara Lynn	You Left The Water Running	08/10/1966	110	BB
Barbara Mandrell	Do Right Woman - Do Right Man	20/03/1971	128	BB
Barbara Mandrell	Tonight	22/07/1978	103	BB
Barbara Mandrell	Sleeping Single In A Double Bed	18/11/1978	102	BB
Barbara Mandrell	Years	01/03/1980	102	BB
Barbara Mandrell	Crackers	12/07/1980	105	BB
Barbara Mason	You Got What It Takes	30/10/1965	126	CB
Barbara Mason	If You Don't (Love Me, Tell Me So)	13/11/1965	141	CB
Barbara Mason	Is It Me?	29/01/1966	116	CB
Barbara Mason	Poor Girl In Trouble	03/12/1966	129	CB
Barbara Mason	(I Can Feel Your Love) Slipping Away	21/09/1968	101	CB
Barbara Mason	Raindrops Keep Fallin' On My Head	23/05/1970	112a	BB
Barbara Mason	If You Knew Him Like I Do	30/05/1970	112b	BB
Barbara Mason	If You Knew Him Like I Do	13/06/1970	107	CB
Barbara Mason	Yes, I'm Ready (73 Version)	21/04/1973	101	CB
Barbara Mason	Yes, I'm Ready (new Version)	09/06/1973	125	BB
Barbara Mcnair	You're Gonna' Love My Baby	04/12/1965	106	CB
Barbara Mcnair	Here I Am Baby	13/05/1967	125	BB
Barbara Mcnair	Here I Am Baby	10/06/1967	144	CB
Barbara Mcnair	You Could Never Love Him (Like I Love Him)	19/10/1968	120	CB
Barbara Pennington	Twenty-Four Hours A Day	30/04/1977	107	BB

Barbara Randolph	I Got A Feeling	14/10/1967	116	BB
Barbara Randolph	Can I Get A Witness	19/10/1968	135	CB
Barbi Benton	Staying Power	18/09/1976	104	CB
Barbi Benton	Staying Power	02/10/1976	108	BB
Barbra Streisand	My Coloring Book*	15/12/1962	112	CB
Barbra Streisand	I Am Woman	15/02/1964	108	CB
Barbra Streisand	I Am Woman	28/03/1964	114	BB
Barbra Streisand	Absent Minded Me	19/09/1964	105	CB
Barbra Streisand	Absent Minded Me	26/09/1964	123	BB
Barbra Streisand	Stout-Hearted Men	12/08/1967	108	CB
Barbra Streisand	Our Corner Of The Night	16/03/1968	107	BB
Barbra Streisand	My Man (68 Version)	28/12/1968	107	CB
Barbra Streisand	Sing A Song/Make Your Own Kind Of Music (Live)	21/10/1972	120	CB
Barbra Streisand	Shake Me, Wake Me (When It's Over)	31/01/1976	104	CB
Barbra Streisand, Backed By Fanny	Space Captain	11/12/1971	107	CB
Barbra Streisand, Backed By Fanny	Space Captain	18/12/1971	105	BB
Barclay James Harvest	Titles	28/02/1976	113	CB
Barclay James Harvest	Titles	20/03/1976	107	BB
Barefoot Jerry	You Can't Get Off With Your Shoes On	19/04/1975	102	CB
Barefoot Jerry	You Can't Get Off With Your Shoes On	31/05/1975	109	BB
Barnaby Bye	I Think I'm Gonna Like It	29/12/1973	113	CB
Barnaby Bye	Can't Live This Way	26/07/1975	101	CB
Barrabas	Hi-Jack	12/07/1975	104	BB
Barry Allen	Love Drops	02/07/1966	140	CB
Barry And The Tamerlanes	Roberta	01/02/1964	127	BB
Barry Darvell	How Will It End	28/12/1959	110	BB
Barry Darvell	How Will It End?	09/01/1960	101	CB
Barry Darvell	Fountain Of Love	29/04/1961	122	CB
Barry Darvell	I Found A Daisy (In The City)	26/06/1965	128	CB
Barry Devorzon & Perry Botkin Jr.	Bless The Beasts And Children	29/01/1977	102	CB

Barry Goldberg Reunion	Hole In My Pocket	28/09/1968	103	BB
Barry Goudreau	Dreams	25/10/1980	103	BB
Barry Lee Show	I Don't Want To Love You	16/03/1968	142	CB
Barry Mann	Little Miss U.S.A.	13/11/1961	109	BB
Barry Mann	Hey Baby I'm Dancin'	01/09/1962	146	CB
Barry Mann	Talk To Me Baby	21/11/1964	106	CB
Barry Mann	Angelica	30/07/1966	111	BB
Barry Mann	When You Get Right Down To It	15/01/1972	105	BB
Barry Mann	When You Get Right Down To It	15/01/1972	114	CB
Barry Mcguire	Upon A Painted Ocean	23/10/1965	103	CB
Barry Mcguire	Upon A Painted Ocean	30/10/1965	117	BB
Barry Mcguire	This Precious Time	04/12/1965	108	CB
Barry Mcguire	There's Nothing Else On My Mind	22/10/1966	129	CB
Barry Mcguire	Masters Of War	16/09/1967	137	CB
Barry White	Don't Make Me Wait Too Long	29/01/1977	105	BB
Barry White	Playing Your Game, Baby	11/02/1978	101	BB
Barry White	Just The Way You Are	03/02/1979	102	BB
Barry Winslow	The Smallest Astronaut (A Race To The Moon With The Red Baron)	26/07/1969	113	CB
Barry Young	Nashville, Tennessee	05/02/1966	120	CB
Barry Young	Since You Have Gone From Me	05/02/1966	130	BB
Bataan	The Bottle (La Botella)	29/03/1975	102	BB
Bay City Rollers	Bye Bye Baby	07/06/1975	104	CB
Beautiful Bend	Boogie Motion	31/03/1979	110	BB
Beckett	Disco Calypso	20/08/1977	108	BB
Bee Gees	Charade	16/11/1974	102	CB
Bee Gees	Charade	16/11/1974	103	BB
Bell & James	You Never Know What You've Got	12/05/1979	Np6	CB
Bell & James	You Never Know What You've Got	02/06/1979	103	BB
Ben & Bea	Gee Baby	03/03/1962	103	CB
Ben Aiken	Stay Together Young Lovers	09/10/1965	115	CB

Ben Aiken	Stay Together Young Lovers	23/10/1965	121	BB
Ben And Bea	Gee Baby	31/03/1962	119	BB
Ben Blur	The Chariot Race	22/10/1960	116	CB
Ben Colder	Hello Wall No. 2	16/03/1963	131	BB
Ben Colder	Detroit City No. 2	28/09/1963	130	CB
Ben E. King	I'm Standing By	03/11/1962	111	BB
Ben E. King	I'm Standing By	03/11/1962	123	CB
Ben E. King	Tell Daddy	19/01/1963	122	BB
Ben E. King	Tell Daddy	02/02/1963	138	CB
Ben E. King	I Could Have Danced All Night	26/10/1963	112	CB
Ben E. King	What Now My Love	25/01/1964	102	BB
Ben E. King	What Now My Love	01/02/1964	132	CB
Ben E. King	Around The Corner	21/03/1964	125	BB
Ben E. King	What Can A Man Do	04/07/1964	113	BB
Ben E. King	What Can A Man Do	11/07/1964	106	CB
Ben E. King	Let The Water Run Down	12/09/1964	144	CB
Ben E. King	The Record (Baby, I Love You)	10/04/1965	105	CB
Ben E. King	She's Gone Again	05/06/1965	128	BB
Ben E. King	What Is Soul?	17/12/1966	113	CB
Ben E. King	Tears, Tears, Tears	25/03/1967	105	CB
Ben E. King	Katherine	17/06/1967	113	CB
Ben E. King	Don't Take Your Love From Me	27/04/1968	117	BB
Ben E. King	Til I Can't Take It Anymore	07/12/1968	135	CB
Ben E. King	Til I Can't Take It Anymore	21/12/1968	134	BB
Ben E. King	I Had A Love	27/12/1975	104	CB
Ben E. King & Dee Dee Sharp	We Got A Thing Going On	24/02/1968	122	CB
Ben E. King & Dee Dee Sharp	We Got A Thing Going On	02/03/1968	127	BB
Benny Joy	Sincerely, Your Friend	18/03/1961	130	CB
Benny Mardones	Hometown Girls	01/11/1980	103	BB
Benny Spellman	The Word Game	26/06/1965	137	CB

Bent Fabric And His Piano	That Certain Party	05/01/1963	117	BB
Bent Fabric And His Piano	The Happy Puppy	03/08/1963	102	BB
Bergen White	Duke Of Earl	30/10/1976	102	CB
Berlin Philharmonic	Theme Music For The Film "2001 A Space Odyssey" (Also Sprach	13/12/1969	110	CB
Bern Elliot & The Fenmen	New Orleans	04/07/1964	101	CB
Bernadette Carroll	My Heart Stood Still	22/09/1962	111	CB
Bernadette Castro	His Lips Get In The Way	26/09/1964	123	BB
Bernadette Castro	His Lips Get In The Way	26/09/1964	130	CB
Bernadette Peters	Wait Johnny For Me	05/06/1965	127	CB
Bernie Leighton Piano & Orchestra	Don't Break The Heart That Loves You	28/07/1962	101	BB
Bernie Leighton Piano & Orchestra	Don't Break The Heart That Loves You	28/07/1962	115	CB
Bert Kaempfert & His Orchestra	Happy Trumpeter	24/11/1962	128	CB
Bert Kaempfert & His Orchestra	Gentleman Jim	23/02/1963	139	CB
Bert Kaempfert & His Orchestra	The Big Build Up	11/04/1964	150	CB
Bert Kaempfert & His Orchestra	Mister Sandman	08/06/1968	101	CB
Bert Kaempfert And His Orchestra	Echo In The Night	03/02/1962	108	BB
Bert Kaempfert And His Orchestra	Strangers In The Night	07/05/1966	124	BB
Bert Keyes	Do-Do Do Bah-Ah	16/01/1965	114	CB
Bert Keyes	Do-Do Do Bah-Ah	30/01/1965	132	BB
Bessie Banks	Go Now	15/02/1964	146	CB
Bette Midler	Strangers In The Night	20/03/1976	101	CB
Betty Everett	Happy I Long To Be	04/07/1964	126	BB
Betty Everett	It Hurts To Be In Love	29/08/1964	109	BB
Betty Everett	Gonna Be Ready	05/06/1965	117	BB
Betty Everett	Maybe	13/09/1969	116	BB
Betty Everett	Been A Long Time	29/11/1969	105	CB
Betty Everett	Ain't Nothing Gonna Change Me	01/05/1971	113	BB
Betty Everett & Jerry Butler	Ain't That Loving You Baby	12/09/1964	108	BB
Betty Everett & Jerry Butler	Love Is Strange	19/12/1964	118	CB
Betty Harris	Mean Man	16/03/1968	123	CB

Betty Johnson	Slipping Around	12/09/1960	109	BB
Betty Johnson And The Johnson Family Singers	There's A Star Spangled Banner Waving Somewhere-1960	04/07/1960	111	BB
Betty Lavett	My Man - He's A Loving Man	24/11/1962	101	BB
Betty Lavette	Let Me Down Easy	24/04/1965	103	BB
Betty Lavette	He Made A Woman Out Of Me	10/01/1970	118	CB
Betty Logan	Are You Sure	31/08/1963	120	CB
Betty Logan	Are You Sure	07/09/1963	132	BB
Betty Wright	He's Bad Bad Bad	09/11/1968	103	BB
Betty Wright	Pure Love	29/08/1970	104	CB
Betty Wright	I Love The Way You Love	14/08/1971	109	BB
Betty Wright	I'm Gettin' Tired Baby	01/04/1972	108	CB
Betty Wright	I'm Gettin' Tired Baby (b-side)	08/04/1972	121	BB
Betty Wright	If You Love Me The Way You Say You Love Me	22/04/1972	104	BB
Betty Wright	Is It You Girl	17/06/1972	101	BB
Betty Wright	Is It You Girl	08/07/1972	104	CB
Betty Wright	Tonight Is The Night	08/02/1975	119	CB
Betty Wright	Ooola La	30/08/1975	106	CB
Betty Wright	If I Ever Do Wrong	11/09/1976	102	CB
Bettye Lavette	Right In The Middle (Of Falling In Love)	06/02/1982	103	BB
Bettye Swann	Don't Wait Too Long	16/01/1965	149	CB
Bettye Swann	Don't Wait Too Long	03/04/1965	131	BB
Bettye Swann	I'm Lonely For You	24/08/1968	123	CB
Bettye Swann	Angel Of The Morning	21/06/1969	109	BB
Bettye Swann	Don't You Ever Get Tired (Of Hurting Me)	15/11/1969	102	BB
Bettye Swann	Little Things Mean A Lot	07/02/1970	114	BB
Beverly Bremers	Heaven Help Us All	30/12/1972	110	BB
Big Al Downing	The Story Of My Life	26/05/1962	117	BB
Big Brother & The Holding Company	Blindman	23/09/1967	122	CB
Big Brother & The Holding Company	Coo Coo	23/11/1968	107	CB
Big Brother And The Holding Company	Blindman	09/09/1967	110	BB

Big Brother And The Holding Company	Bye, Bye Baby	09/09/1967	118	BB
Big Dee Irwin	Soul Waltzin'	24/08/1963	146	CB
Big Mac	Rough Dried Woman Part 1	15/04/1967	133	CB
Big Maybelle	Don't Pass Me By	19/11/1966	111	CB
Big Maybelle	That's Life	24/12/1966	134	CB
Big Wha-Koo	Love's Been Known	30/07/1977	107	CB
Bill Anderson	Five Little Fingers	22/02/1964	118	BB
Bill Anderson	Me	18/07/1964	121	CB
Bill Anderson	Always Remember	17/04/1971	111	BB
Bill Black's Combo	Dry Bones	11/06/1960	115	CB
Bill Black's Combo	Honky Train	16/09/1961	102	CB
Bill Black's Combo	My Babe	28/04/1962	137	CB
Bill Black's Combo	Joey's Song	15/12/1962	114	BB
Bill Black's Combo	Raunchy	06/06/1964	118	BB
Bill Black's Combo	Come On Home	06/02/1965	124	BB
Bill Black's Combo	Come On Home	13/02/1965	134	CB
Bill Black's Combo	Spootin'	14/08/1965	135	BB
Bill Black's Combo	Hey, Good Lookin'	11/06/1966	124	BB
Bill Carlisle	What Kinda Deal Is This	25/12/1965	140	CB
Bill Coday	Get Your Lie Straight	13/02/1971	105	BB
Bill Coday	Get Your Lie Straight	20/03/1971	117	CB
Bill Cosby	Funky North Philly	24/02/1968	109	CB
Bill Cosby With The Bunions Bradford Band	Hikky Burr - Part One	24/01/1970	124	BB
Bill Deal & The Rhondels	It's Too Late	19/08/1972	108	BB
Bill Haley And His Comets	Tamiami	29/02/1960	101	BB
Bill Haley And His Comets	Rock Around The Clock	15/06/1968	118	BB
Bill Justis	Tamoure'	11/05/1963	101	BB
Bill Justis & His Orchestra	Cloud Nine	03/10/1959	113	CB
Bill Justis & Orchestra	Tamoure'	11/05/1963	116	CB
Bill Labounty	Lie To Me	19/06/1976	109	BB

Bill Labounty	Never Gonna Look Back	26/06/1982	110	BB
Bill Mcelhiney & Orchestra Featuring Bob Johnson On Banjo	Down Yonder	07/09/1963	138	CB
Bill Medley	This Is A Love Song	22/02/1969	110	CB
Bill Medley	This Is A Love Song	22/02/1969	112	BB
Bill Medley (Of The Righteous Brothers)	That Lucky Old Sun (Just Rolls Around Heaven All Day)	02/12/1967	132	CB
Bill Minin As Senator BoBBy	Sock It To Me, Baby	15/06/1968	128	BB
Bill Pursell	Loved	04/05/1963	130	CB
Bill Pursell	Loved	25/05/1963	121	BB
Bill Robinson & The Quails	The Cow	18/01/1964	126	CB
Bill Robinson And The Quails	The Cow	18/01/1964	103	BB
Bill Snyder & Dick Manning	Cimarron	18/03/1961	123	CB
Bill Spivery	Mr. John	28/03/1964	108	CB
Bill Summers And Summers Heat	Call It What You Want	23/05/1981	103	BB
Bill Withers	You	03/08/1974	118	CB
Bill Withers	Oh Yeah!	25/05/1985	106	BB
Billie Daye	When A Girl Gives Her Heart To A Boy*	01/07/1961	141	CB
Billie Sans	Solo	25/09/1971	102	CB
Billie Sans	Bicycle Morning	09/02/1974	103	BB
Billy "Crash" Craddock	Knock Three Times	03/04/1971	113	BB
Billy And The Essentials	Maybe You'll Be There	19/01/1963	117	BB
Billy Bland	Pardon Me	04/07/1960	102	BB
Billy Bland	Harmony	22/10/1960	123	CB
Billy Bland	Do The Bug With Me	04/11/1961	129	CB
Billy Butler	(I've Got A Feeling) You're Gonna Be Sorry	28/08/1965	109	CB
Billy Butler	(I've Got A Feeling) You're Gonna Be Sorry	04/09/1965	103	BB
Billy Butler & The Chanters	Can't Live Without Her	26/09/1964	130	BB
Billy Butler & The Chanters	Nevertheless	28/11/1964	127	CB
Billy Butler & The Chanters	Nevertheless	05/12/1964	102	BB
Billy Butler & The Enchanters	Gotta Get Away	16/05/1964	101	BB
Billy Butler & The Enchanters	Gotta Get Away	23/05/1964	139	CB

Billy Butler & The Four Enchanters	Found True Love	02/11/1963	134	BB
Billy Carr	What's Come Over This World?	27/11/1965	116	BB
Billy Duke	Walking Cane	20/01/1962	142	CB
Billy Duke	Walking Cane	03/02/1962	120	BB
Billy Duke	(Oooh Looka There) Ain't She Pretty	07/04/1962	117	CB
Billy Eckstine	It Isn't Fair	30/09/1961	120	CB
Billy Harner	Sally Sayin' Somethin'	12/08/1967	103	CB
Billy Harner	Sally Sayin' Somethin'	19/08/1967	118	BB
Billy Harner	She's Almost You	25/01/1969	121	BB
Billy Harner	She's Almost You	08/02/1969	109	CB
Billy Harner	I Struck It Rich	03/05/1969	143	CB
Billy Idol	Mony Mony	26/09/1981	107	BB
Billy Idol	White Wedding	27/11/1982	108	BB
Billy Idol With Gen X	Dancing With Myself	10/09/1983	102	BB
Billy J. Kramer With The Dakotas	I Know	01/08/1964	122	CB
Billy J. Kramer With The Dakotas	Twilight Time	16/10/1965	119	CB
Billy Joe Royal	Steal Away	18/09/1965	111	CB
Billy Joe Royal	It's A Good Time	26/02/1966	104	BB
Billy Joe Royal	It's A Good Time	26/02/1966	124	CB
Billy Joe Royal	Yo-Yo	10/12/1966	111	CB
Billy Joe Royal	Yo-Yo	10/12/1966	117	BB
Billy Joe Royal	Everything Turned Blue	18/03/1967	121	CB
Billy Joe Royal	These Are Not My People	13/05/1967	134	CB
Billy Joe Royal	These Are Not My People	03/06/1967	113	BB
Billy Joe Royal	The Greatest Love (b-side)	10/06/1967	117	BB
Billy Joe Royal	The Greatest Love	17/06/1967	125	CB
Billy Joe Royal	Storybook Children	10/08/1968	117	BB
Billy Joe Royal	Storybook Children	17/08/1968	108	CB
Billy Joe Royal	Me Without You	21/03/1970	112	CB
Billy Joe Royal	Every Night	05/09/1970	103	CB

Billy Joe Royal	Every Night	26/09/1970	113	BB
Billy Joe Royal	Poor Little Pearl	03/07/1971	103	CB
Billy Joe Royal	Poor Little Pearl	10/07/1971	111	BB
Billy Larkin And The Delegates	Hold On! I'm A Comin'	10/09/1966	130	BB
Billy Lee Riley	Midnite Hour	22/04/1967	145	CB
Billy Maxted & His Manhattan Jazz Band	Satin Doll	23/09/1961	116	CB
Billy Maxted And His Manhattan Jazz Band	Satin Doll	25/09/1961	117	BB
Billy Meshel	Today Has Been Cancelled	28/06/1969	144	CB
Billy Mitchell Group	Oh Happy Day	14/06/1969	134	CB
Billy Mitchell Group	Oh Happy Day	28/06/1969	115	BB
Billy Mure	Maria Elena	10/08/1963	140	CB
Billy Ocean	L.O.D. (Love On Delivery)	14/08/1976	102	CB
Billy Ocean	L.O.D. (Love On Delivery)	14/08/1976	106	BB
Billy Ocean	Night (Feel Like Getting Down)	20/06/1981	103	BB
Billy Preston	All That I've Got (I'm Gonna Give It To You)	21/03/1970	108	BB
Billy Preston	The Bus	01/04/1972	117	CB
Billy Preston	Blackbird	17/02/1973	122	CB
Billy Preston & Syreeta	Go For It	12/05/1979	108	BB
Billy Preston & Syreeta	Searchin'	15/08/1981	106	BB
Billy Shields	I Was A Boy (When You Needed A Man)	12/04/1969	109	BB
Billy Stewart	Why Am I Lonely	07/05/1966	113	CB
Billy Stewart	Love Me	28/05/1966	119	CB
Billy Storm	Love Theme From "EL Cid"	10/02/1962	104	CB
Billy Storm	Love Theme From "El Cid"	24/02/1962	105	BB
Billy Thorpe & The Aztecs	Over The Rainbow	17/04/1965	107	CB
Billy Thorpe And The Aztecs	Over The Rainbow	01/05/1965	130	BB
Billy Vaughn & His Orchestra	You're The Only Star (In My Blue Heaven)	06/02/1960	118	CB
Billy Vaughn & His Orchestra	Old Cape Cod	01/10/1960	102	CB
Billy Vaughn & His Orchestra	Red Wing	10/06/1961	112	CB
Billy Vaughn & His Orchestra	Everybody's Twisting Down In Mexico	02/12/1961	124	CB

Billy Vaughn & His Orchestra	Chapel By The Sea	17/03/1962	107	CB
Billy Vaughn & His Orchestra	One Love, One Heartache (O Sole Mio)	17/03/1962	112	CB
Billy Vaughn & His Orchestra	Blue Flame	20/10/1962	123	CB
Billy Vaughn & His Orchestra	Happy Cowboy	25/05/1963	131	CB
Billy Vaughn And His Orchestra	All Nite Long	06/07/1959	102	BB
Billy Vaughn And His Orchestra	(It's No) Sin	16/11/1959	105	BB
Billy Vaughn And His Orchestra	You're The Only Star (In My Blue Heaven) (b-side)	18/01/1960	110	BB
Billy Vaughn And His Orchestra	Chop Sticks	01/02/1960	103	BB
Billy Vaughn And His Orchestra	Old Cape Cod	19/09/1960	111	BB
Billy Vaughn And His Orchestra	Everybody's Twisting Down In Mexico	11/12/1961	119	BB
Billy Vaughn And His Orchestra	Blue Flame	27/10/1962	107	BB
Billy Vaughn And His Orchestra	Someone (b-side)	03/11/1962	115	BB
Billy Vaughn And His Orchestra	Happy Cowboy	22/06/1963	131	BB
Billy Vaughn And His Orchestra	Pearly Shells (Popo O Ewa)	02/01/1965	120	BB
Billy Vaughn And His Orchestra	Tiny BuBBles	05/11/1966	131	BB
Billy Vera	I've Been Loving You Too Long	28/09/1968	121	BB
Billy Vera	Julie	04/01/1969	135	CB
Billy Vera	The Bible Salesman	03/05/1969	110	CB
Billy Vera	The Bible Salesman	17/05/1969	112	BB
Billy Vera & Judy Clay	When Do We Go	08/06/1968	107	BB
Billy Walker	Charlie's Shoes	10/03/1962	146	CB
Billy Walker	Cross The Brazos At Waco	30/01/1965	128	BB
Bing Crosby	I'll Be Home For Christmas (If Only In My Dreams)	12/12/1960	102	BB
Bing Day	Mama's Place	01/06/1959	104	BB
Bionic Boogie	Dance Little Dreamer	22/07/1978	105	BB
Björn & Benny (with Svenska Flicka)	People Need Love	04/11/1972	114	CB
Black Ivory	Don't Turn Around	06/11/1971	104	CB
Black Ivory	You And I	08/04/1972	111	BB
Black Ivory	Time Is Love	03/03/1973	114	CB
Black Oak Arkansas	Lord Have Mercy On My Soul	28/08/1971	105	CB

Black Oak Arkansas	Hey Ya'll	19/10/1974	120	CB
Black Oak Arkansas	Back Door Man	02/08/1975	101	CB
Black Oak Arkansas	Strong Enough To Be Gentle	17/01/1976	102	CB
Black Oak Arkansas	Great Balls Of Fire	17/04/1976	113	CB
Black SaBBath	SaBBath, Bloody SaBBath	09/02/1974	108	CB
Blackfoot	Searchin'	26/09/1981	108	BB
Blackfoot	Teenage Idol	30/07/1983	103	BB
Blinky	I Wouldn't Change The Man He Is	15/02/1969	128	BB
Blizzard	Keep A Knockin'/Get Back/Etc.	28/03/1970	137	CB
Blizzard	Baby Blue	24/04/1971	106	BB
Blood, Sweat & Tears	I Can't Move No Mountains	30/12/1972	103	BB
Blood, Sweat & Tears	Tell Me That I'm Wrong	13/07/1974	101	CB
Blood, Sweat & Tears	You're The One	23/10/1976	106	CB
Blood, Sweat & Tears	You're The One	27/11/1976	106	BB
Bloodstone	I Need Time	09/11/1974	108	BB
Bloodstone	Give Me Your Heart	08/11/1975	103	CB
Bloodstone	Do You Wanna Do A Thing	05/06/1976	101	BB
Blue Cheer	Fool	26/09/1970	136	CB
Blue Magic	Grateful	17/04/1976	104	BB
Blue Magic	Summer Snow	01/01/1977	101	CB
Blue Mink	By The Devil I Was Tempted	28/04/1973	111	CB
Blue Steel	No More Lonely Nights	20/10/1979	110	BB
Blues Brothers	Going Back To Miami [Live]	07/03/1981	108	BB
Blues Magoos	I Wanna Be There	12/08/1967	135	CB
Blues Magoos	I Wanna Be There	26/08/1967	133	BB
Blues Magoos	Never Goin' Back To Georgia	17/01/1970	113	CB
Blues Magoos	Never Goin' Back To Georgia	24/01/1970	113	BB
Bo Diddley	She's Alright	21/11/1959	125	CB
Bo Diddley	Say Man, Back Again	30/11/1959	106	BB
Bo Diddley	Crawdad	11/06/1960	117	CB

Bo Diddley	Crawdad	13/06/1960	111	BB
Bo Diddley	Gun Slinger	07/01/1961	115	CB
Bo Diddley	Ooh Baby	31/12/1966	104	CB
Bo Donaldson & The Heywoods	Deeper And Deeper	19/01/1974	107	CB
Boatz	It Was Only The Radio	07/07/1979	107	BB
Bob & Earl	Don't Ever Leave Me	25/08/1962	133	CB
Bob & Earl	Puppet On A String	11/04/1964	141	CB
Bob & Earl	Baby, It's Over	02/07/1966	142	CB
Bob And Earl	Puppet On A String	28/03/1964	111	BB
Bob Beckham	Beloved	16/01/1960	118	CB
Bob Beckham	Mais Oui	18/06/1960	102	CB
Bob Beckham	Mais Oui	20/06/1960	105	BB
Bob Beckham	How Soon (Will I Be Seeing You)	02/09/1961	128	CB
Bob Beckham	Building Memories	10/11/1962	140	CB
Bob Brady & The Con Chords	More, More, More Of Your Love	27/05/1967	102	CB
Bob Brady & The Con Chords	More, More, More Of Your Love	17/06/1967	104	BB
Bob Brady & The Con Chords	Illusion	30/03/1968	125	CB
Bob Brady & The Con Chords	Everybody's Goin' To The Love-In	27/07/1968	135	CB
Bob Braun	Our Anniversary Of Love	03/11/1962	119	BB
Bob Braun	Our Anniversary Of Love	03/11/1962	144	CB
Bob Braun	Sweet Violets	15/02/1964	124	CB
Bob Conrad	Bye Bye Baby	25/12/1961	113	BB
Bob Crewe	Sweetie Pie	27/07/1959	111	BB
Bob Crewe	The Whiffenpoof Song	09/01/1960	101	CB
Bob Crewe	Water Boy	05/03/1960	111	CB
Bob Crewe	After The Ball	18/03/1967	126	BB
Bob Crewe	After The Ball	25/03/1967	136	CB
Bob Darin	Jive	23/08/1969	122	CB
Bob Darin	Jive	06/09/1969	111	BB
Bob Dylan	One Of Us Must Know (Sooner Or Later)	12/03/1966	135	CB

Bob Dylan	One Of Us Must Know (Sooner Or Later)	26/03/1966	119	BB
Bob Dylan	Something There Is About You	18/05/1974	107	BB
Bob Dylan	Rita May	15/01/1977	110a	BB
Bob Dylan	Stuck Inside Of Mobile With The Memphis Blues Again [Live]	15/01/1977	110b	BB
Bob Dylan	Tight Connection To My Heart (Has Anybody Seen My Love)	20/07/1985	103	BB
Bob James	Feel Like Making Love	16/11/1974	115	CB
Bob James	I Feel A Song (In My Heart)	12/07/1975	105	BB
Bob Lind	I Just Let It Take Me	25/06/1966	116	CB
Bob Lind	I Just Let It Take Me	16/07/1966	123	BB
Bob Lind	San Francisco Woman	03/09/1966	107	CB
Bob Lind	San Francisco Woman	10/09/1966	135	BB
Bob Luman	Oh, Lonesome Me	05/12/1960	105	BB
Bob Luman	Why, Why, Bye, Bye (b-side)	19/12/1960	106	BB
Bob Luman	Oh, Lonesome Me	07/01/1961	108	CB
Bob Luman	Private Eye	12/08/1961	142	CB
Bob Luman	The File	28/03/1964	139	CB
Bob Luman & Sue Thompson	I Like Your Kind Of Love	07/09/1963	142	CB
Bob Marley & The Wailers	Exodus	06/08/1977	103	CB
Bob Marley And The Wailers	Exodus	13/08/1977	103	BB
Bob Moore & His Orchestra	(Theme From) My Three Sons	25/03/1961	132	CB
Bob Moore & His Orchestra	Skokiaan	25/12/1965	117	CB
Bob Moore & His Orchestra & Chorus	Auf Wiedersehen Marlene	24/03/1962	108	CB
Bob Moore And His Orchestra	Kentucky	08/06/1963	101	BB
Bob Morrison	I Fall To You	16/04/1966	138	CB
Bob Seger	Beautiful Loser	24/05/1975	103	BB
Bob Seger & The Last Heard	East Side Story	15/10/1966	111	CB
Bob Seger & The Last Heard	Persecution Smith	18/03/1967	118	CB
Bob Seger & The Last Heard	Heavy Music (Part I)	09/09/1967	103	BB
Bob Seger System	Ivory	03/05/1969	101	CB
Bob Shane	Honey	23/03/1968	104	BB

Bob Summers	When I'm Dead And Gone	23/01/1971	118	BB
Bob Summers	When I'm Dead And Gone	30/01/1971	113	CB
Bob Welch	Two To Do	28/11/1981	107	BB
Bob Willow	The One Rose (That's Left In My Heart)	24/11/1962	129	CB
BoBBi Humphrey	Chicago, Damn	30/03/1974	108	CB
BoBBi Humphrey	Chicago, Damn	04/05/1974	106	BB
BoBBi Martin	I Don't Want To Live (Without Your Love)	31/07/1965	115	BB
BoBBi Martin	I Don't Want To Live (Without Your Love)	31/07/1965	138	CB
BoBBi Martin	Don't Take It Out On Me	05/02/1966	119	BB
BoBBi Martin	It's A Sin To Tell A Lie	02/07/1966	125	CB
BoBBi Martin	Oh, Lonesome Me	03/09/1966	134	BB
BoBBi Martin	Harper Valley, P.T.A.	31/08/1968	114	BB
BoBBi Martin	No Love At All	06/03/1971	123	BB
BoBBi Martin	Tomorrow	06/11/1971	112	CB
BoBBie Gentry	Touch 'Em With Love	31/05/1969	113	BB
BoBBie Gentry	Touch 'EM With Love	31/05/1969	125	CB
BoBBy (Boris) Pickett	Me And My Mummy	29/09/1973	118	CB
BoBBy Arvon	From Now On	01/07/1978	104	BB
BoBBy Bare	Book Of Love	29/05/1961	106	BB
BoBBy Bare	Brooklyn Bridge	27/01/1962	132	CB
BoBBy Bare	To Whom It May Concern	10/11/1962	141	CB
BoBBy Bare	I Don't Believe I'll Fall In Love Today	17/11/1962	118	BB
BoBBy Bare	Dear Waste Basket	02/03/1963	130	CB
BoBBy Bare	Have I Stayed Away Too Long	16/05/1964	122	CB
BoBBy Bare	He Was A Friend Of Mine	08/08/1964	134	BB
BoBBy Bare	Times Are Gettin' Hard	27/02/1965	126	CB
BoBBy Bare	It's Alright	29/05/1965	122	BB
BoBBy Bare	In The Same Old Way	19/03/1966	131	BB
BoBBy Bare	The Streets Of Baltimore	02/07/1966	124	BB
BoBBy Bare	Come Sundown	23/01/1971	122	BB

BoBBy Bare	Dropkick Me, Jesus	23/10/1976	114	CB
BoBBy Bland	The Feeling Is Gone	23/11/1963	111	CB
BoBBy Bland	I Can't Stop Singing	21/12/1963	106	BB
BoBBy Bland	After It's Too Late	13/06/1964	111	BB
BoBBy Bland	Black Night	09/01/1965	131	CB
BoBBy Bland	Ain't No Telling	03/04/1965	102	CB
BoBBy Bland	Dust Got In Daddy's Eyes	15/05/1965	125	BB
BoBBy Bland	Back In The Same Old Bag Again	03/12/1966	102	BB
BoBBy Bland	Back In The Same Old Bag Again	31/12/1966	127	CB
BoBBy Bland	I'm Sorry	26/06/1971	121	CB
BoBBy Bland	Yolanda	28/06/1975	104	BB
BoBBy Bland	Today I Started Loving You Again	03/04/1976	111	CB
BoBBy Bland	Today I Started Loving You Again	10/04/1976	103	BB
BoBBy Bland	It Ain't The Real Thing	19/06/1976	101	CB
BoBBy Bland & B.B. King	Let The Good Times Roll [Live]	24/07/1976	101	BB
BoBBy Bloom	Love, Don't Let Me Down	08/04/1967	130	CB
BoBBy Bloom	We're All Goin' Home	15/05/1971	105	CB
BoBBy Bloom	Sha La Boom Boom	17/02/1973	123	BB
BoBBy Byrd	I'm Just A Nobody (Part I)	07/03/1964	128	CB
BoBBy Byrd	I Love You So	06/06/1964	141	CB
BoBBy Byrd	We Are In Love	13/02/1965	107	CB
BoBBy Byrd	We Are In Love	27/02/1965	120	BB
BoBBy Byrd	I Know You Got Soul	26/06/1971	117	BB
BoBBy Byrd	I Know You Got Soul	24/07/1971	123	CB
BoBBy Byrd	If You Got A Love You Better (Hold On To It)	13/05/1972	103	CB
BoBBy Byrd & James Brown	You've Got To Change Your Mind	16/03/1968	102	BB
BoBBy Caldwell	Can't Say Goodbye	26/05/1979	103	BB
BoBBy Caldwell	Jamaica	27/03/1982	105	BB
BoBBy Callender	Little Star	16/02/1963	112	CB
BoBBy Comstock & The Counts	Jambalaya	19/03/1960	102	CB

BoBBy Darin	Look For My True Love	10/06/1961	131	CB
BoBBy Darin	Sorrow Tomorrow	02/09/1961	149	CB
BoBBy Darin	You Know How	29/09/1962	135	CB
BoBBy Darin	A True, True Love	13/10/1962	105	BB
BoBBy Darin	A True, True Love	27/10/1962	133	CB
BoBBy Darin	I Found A New Baby	29/12/1962	133	CB
BoBBy Darin	Hello, Dolly!	13/02/1965	114	CB
BoBBy Darin	Venice Blue (Que C'est Triste Venise)	24/04/1965	133	BB
BoBBy Darin	We Didn't Ask To Be Brought Here	09/10/1965	117	BB
BoBBy Darin	Darling Be Home Soon	15/07/1967	140	CB
BoBBy Darin	She Knows	02/09/1967	120	CB
BoBBy Darin	She Knows	09/09/1967	105	BB
BoBBy Darin	Me & Mr. Hohner	26/04/1969	119	CB
BoBBy Darin	Me & Mr. Hohner	10/05/1969	123	BB
BoBBy Darin And His Orchestra	Theme From "Come September"	17/07/1961	113	BB
BoBBy Day	Gee Whiz	14/11/1960	103	BB
BoBBy Dixon	Woman, You Made Me	08/02/1969	128	CB
BoBBy Freeman	I'll Never Fall In Love Again	17/04/1965	131	BB
BoBBy Freeman	Everybody's Got A Hang Up	19/07/1969	122	BB
BoBBy Fuller Four	Let Her Dance	07/08/1965	133	BB
BoBBy Fuller Four	Let Her Dance	28/08/1965	113	CB
BoBBy Fuller Four	The Magic Touch	02/07/1966	138	CB
BoBBy Fuller Four	The Magic Touch	16/07/1966	117	BB
BoBBy Gee & The Celestials	Blue Jean	28/11/1959	121	CB
BoBBy Goldsboro	I Don't Know You Anymore	07/11/1964	105	BB
BoBBy Goldsboro	I Don't Know You Anymore	07/11/1964	136	CB
BoBBy Goldsboro	Take Your Love	16/07/1966	123	CB
BoBBy Goldsboro	Take Your Love	23/07/1966	114	BB
BoBBy Goldsboro	Goodbye To All You Women	01/04/1967	103	CB
BoBBy Goldsboro	Goodbye To All You Women	08/04/1967	102	BB

BoBBy Goldsboro	Love Is	01/07/1967	122	CB
BoBBy Goldsboro	Jo Jo's Place	25/11/1967	111	BB
BoBBy Goldsboro	Pledge Of Love (b-side)	23/12/1967	118	BB
BoBBy Goldsboro	Pledge Of Love	03/02/1968	109	CB
BoBBy Goldsboro	It's Gonna Change	01/08/1970	108	BB
BoBBy Goldsboro	My God And I	26/09/1970	116	CB
BoBBy Goldsboro	Danny Is A Mirror To Me	13/11/1971	107	BB
BoBBy Goldsboro	Danny Is A Mirror To Me	20/11/1971	119	CB
BoBBy Goldsboro	A Poem For My Little Lady	12/02/1972	130	CB
BoBBy Goldsboro	California Wine	15/04/1972	108	BB
BoBBy Goldsboro	California Wine	22/04/1972	113	CB
BoBBy Goldsboro	Brand New Kind Of Love	17/02/1973	104	CB
BoBBy Goldsboro	Brand New Kind Of Love	03/03/1973	116	BB
BoBBy Goldsboro	Marlena	19/01/1974	101	CB
BoBBy Goldsboro	Hello Summertime	31/08/1974	112	CB
BoBBy Goldsboro	A Butterfly For Bucky	05/06/1976	102	CB
BoBBy Goldsboro	A Butterfly For Bucky	26/06/1976	101	BB
BoBBy Goldsboro	Me And The Elephants	19/03/1977	104	BB
BoBBy Gregg	Scarlet O'hara	06/07/1963	112	BB
BoBBy Gregg & His Friends	Potato Peeler	09/06/1962	121	CB
BoBBy Gregg And His Friends	The Hullabaloo	06/02/1965	133	BB
BoBBy Harris	We Can't Believe You're Gone	06/02/1965	107	BB
BoBBy Harris	Sticky, Sticky	03/09/1966	101	BB
BoBBy Hart	Lovers For The Night	20/12/1980	110	BB
BoBBy Hatfield	My Prayer	03/05/1969	124	CB
BoBBy HeBB	I Love Everything About You	22/04/1967	140	CB
BoBBy HeBB	You Want To Change Me	24/08/1968	129	CB
BoBBy Helms	Fraulein (new Version)	20/07/1963	127	BB
BoBBy Helms	Jingle Bell Rock	28/12/1963	118	CB
BoBBy Lee	I Was Born A Loser	20/08/1966	114	CB

BoBBy Lewis	Mamie In The Afternoon	27/01/1962	110	BB
BoBBy Lewis	Mamie In The Afternoon	27/01/1962	118	CB
BoBBy Lewis	I'm Tossin' And Turnin' Again	14/07/1962	122	CB
BoBBy Marchan	I've Got A Thing Going On	15/08/1964	116	BB
BoBBy Marchan	Shake Your Tambourine	01/10/1966	106	CB
BoBBy Moore	(Call Me Your) Anything Man	16/08/1975	118	CB
BoBBy Nunn	She's Just A Groupie	02/10/1982	104	BB
BoBBy Paris	Who Needs You	18/01/1964	128	BB
BoBBy Paris	Per-So-Nal-Ly	21/09/1968	129	BB
BoBBy Peterson Quintet	Rockin' Charlie Part I	12/03/1960	108	CB
BoBBy Pickett & Peter Ferrara	King Kong (Your Song)	18/12/1976	101	CB
BoBBy Pickett And Peter Ferrara	King Kong (Your Song)	18/12/1976	107	BB
BoBBy Pickett And The Rolling Bones	The Monster Swim	28/11/1964	135	BB
BoBBy Powell	Do Something For Yourself	05/03/1966	117	CB
BoBBy Powell	Do Something For Yourself	23/04/1966	120	BB
BoBBy Powell (with Jackie Johnson)	Done Got Over	29/10/1966	127	CB
BoBBy Rush	Chicken Heads	24/07/1971	107	CB
BoBBy Russell	Carlie	25/01/1969	115	BB
BoBBy Russell	Carlie	25/01/1969	120	CB
BoBBy Russell	Then She's A Lover	29/03/1969	115	CB
BoBBy Russell	Better Homes And Gardens	19/07/1969	110	CB
BoBBy Rydell	Don't Be Afraid (To Fall In Love)	13/05/1961	101	CB
BoBBy Rydell	Gee, It's Wonderful	26/05/1962	109	BB
BoBBy Rydell	Gee, It's Wonderful	26/05/1962	112	CB
BoBBy Rydell	Will You Be My Baby	01/06/1963	114	BB
BoBBy Rydell	Little Queenie	24/08/1963	142	CB
BoBBy Rydell	Love, Love Go Away	02/11/1963	144	CB
BoBBy Rydell	A World Without Love	09/05/1964	103	CB
BoBBy Rydell	I Just Can't Say Goodbye	28/11/1964	119	CB
BoBBy Rydell	Diana	06/02/1965	110	CB

BoBBy Rydell	Side Show	03/07/1965	131	CB
BoBBy Rydell	Sway (Disco Version)	06/03/1976	115	CB
BoBBy Rydell ChuBBy Checker	Teach Me To Twist	05/05/1962	109	BB
BoBBy Sherman	It Hurts Me	27/02/1965	110	CB
BoBBy Sherman	It Hurts Me	06/03/1965	118	BB
BoBBy Sherman	Early In The Morning	14/04/1973	113	BB
BoBBy Sherman	Our Last Song Together	05/07/1975	103	CB
BoBBy Skel	Kiss And Run	28/11/1964	108	CB
BoBBy Skel	Sheila Ann	29/06/1968	117	CB
BoBBy Vee	One Last Kiss	23/05/1960	112	BB
BoBBy Vee	Baby Face	08/05/1961	119	BB
BoBBy Vee	Never Love A Robin	02/11/1963	101	CB
BoBBy Vee	Cross My Heart	30/01/1965	101	CB
BoBBy Vee	Run Like The Devil	11/09/1965	106	CB
BoBBy Vee	Run Like The Devil	25/09/1965	124	BB
BoBBy Vee	A Girl I Used To Know	26/02/1966	133	BB
BoBBy Vee	I'm Gonna Make It Up To You	23/08/1969	132	CB
BoBBy Vee	In And Out Of Love	31/01/1970	105	CB
BoBBy Vee	In And Out Of Love	28/02/1970	111	BB
BoBBy Vee	Signs	20/03/1971	125	CB
BoBBy Vee & The Crickets	Someday (When I'm Gone From You)	29/09/1962	129	CB
BoBBy Vee With The Johnny Mann Singers	In My Baby's Eyes	26/05/1962	121	CB
BoBBy Vee With The Johnny Mann Singers	Anonymous Phone Call	01/12/1962	108	CB
BoBBy Vee With The Johnny Mann Singers	Anonymous Phone Call	12/01/1963	110	BB
BoBBy Vee, Vocal Background By The Eligibles	Where Is She	12/09/1964	120	BB
BoBBy Vinton	Imagination Is A Magic Dream	08/08/1964	140	CB
BoBBy Vinton	Careless	25/12/1965	111	BB
BoBBy Vinton	Why Don't They Understand	19/09/1970	109	BB
BoBBy Vinton	I'll Make You My Baby	03/04/1971	101	BB
BoBBy Vinton	I'll Make You My Baby	03/04/1971	122	CB

BoBBy Vinton	Hurt	19/05/1973	117	CB
BoBBy Vinton	Hurt	09/06/1973	106	BB
BoBBy Vinton	Moonlight Serenade	10/04/1976	113	CB
BoBBy Vinton	Save Your Kisses For Me	22/05/1976	105	CB
BoBBy Vinton	Only Love Can Break A Heart	14/05/1977	105	CB
BoBBy Vinton	Let Me Love You Goodbye	28/03/1981	108	BB
BoBBy Whiteside	Say It Softly	22/05/1965	137	CB
BoBBy Whitlock	Song For Paula	20/05/1972	121	CB
BoBBy Womack	I Left My Heart In San Francisco	15/03/1969	119	BB
BoBBy Womack	I Left My Heart In San Francisco	22/03/1969	104	CB
BoBBy Womack	It's Gonna Rain	16/08/1969	121	CB
BoBBy Womack	Arkansas State Prison	14/02/1970	135	CB
BoBBy Womack	The Preacher (Part 2)/More Than I Can Stand	29/05/1971	111	BB
BoBBy Womack	I'm Through Trying To Prove My Love To You	20/10/1973	101	BB
BoBBy Womack	Where There's A Will, There's A Way	10/01/1976	107	CB
BoBBy Womack	If You Think You're Lonely Now	06/03/1982	101	BB
BoBBy Womack & Bill Withers	It's All Over Now	05/07/1975	101	CB
BoBBy Wood	That's All I Need To Know	10/10/1964	120	CB
BoBBy Wood	That's All I Need To Know	17/10/1964	130	BB
BoBBy Wood	I'd Do It Again	12/12/1964	142	CB
BoBBy Wood	Fool's Paradise	28/08/1965	132	CB
BoBBy Wood	Break My Mind	06/01/1968	110	BB
Bond	Dancin' (On A Saturday Night)	08/03/1975	119	CB
Boney M.	Dancing In The Streets	03/03/1979	103	BB
Bonnie Brooks	Bring Back The Beatles (To Me)	28/03/1964	147	CB
Bonnie Guitar	Candy Apple Red	05/12/1959	103	CB
Bonnie Guitar	Get Your Lie The Way You Want It	21/05/1966	125	CB
Bonnie Raitt	Keep This Heart In Mind	13/03/1982	104	BB
Bonnie Raitt	Me And The Boys	05/06/1982	109	BB
Bonnie Tyler	If I Sing You A Love Song	19/08/1978	103	BB

Bonnie Tyler	My Guns Are Loaded	24/02/1979	107	BB
Booker T	Evergreen	26/10/1974	103	CB
Booker T. & The Mg's	Mo-Onions	08/02/1964	137	CB
Booker T. & The Mg's	Tic-Tac-Toe	29/02/1964	109	BB
Booker T. & The Mg's	Soul Dressing	01/08/1964	112	CB
Booker T. & The Mg's	Can't Be Still	26/12/1964	119	CB
Booker T. & The Mg's	Booker-Loo	12/11/1966	131	CB
Boones Farm	If You Can't Be My Woman	29/07/1972	114	CB
Boots Randolph	Big Daddy	16/12/1967	107	CB
Boots Randolph	Big Daddy	30/12/1967	105	BB
Boots Randolph	Gentle On My Mind	17/08/1968	113	CB
Boots Randolph	Games People Play	08/02/1969	131	CB
Boots Randolph	Anna	02/05/1970	108	CB
Boots Randolph	Anna	16/05/1970	111	BB
Boots Randolph & His Combo	Windy And Warm	31/08/1963	117	CB
Boots Walker	They're Here	17/06/1967	140	CB
Bootsy's RuBBer Band	PhychotiCBumpschool	25/12/1976	104	BB
Bootsy's RuBBer Band	Can't Stay Away	09/07/1977	104	BB
Bow Wow Wow	Baby, Oh No	02/10/1982	103	BB
Boy's Brigade	Melody	11/02/1984	104	BB
Boz Scaggs	Near You	19/06/1971	108	CB
Boz Scaggs	Dinah Flo	16/09/1972	106	CB
Boz Scaggs	You Make It So Hard (To Say No)	13/04/1974	104	CB
Boz Scaggs	You Make It So Hard (To Say No)	29/03/1975	108	CB
Boz Scaggs	You Make It So Hard (To Say No)	12/04/1975	107	BB
Bram Tchaikovsky	Shall We Dance?	27/06/1981	109	BB
Brandon Wade	Letter From A Teenage Son	16/12/1967	120	BB
Brass Construction	Ha Cha Cha (Funktion)	22/01/1977	102	CB
Brass Construction	L-O-V-E-U	11/02/1978	104	BB
Bread	Dismal Day	27/09/1969	120	CB

Break Machine	Street Dance	28/04/1984	105	BB
Brenda & The Tabulations	Stay Together Young Lovers	27/05/1967	126	CB
Brenda & The Tabulations	That's In The Past	07/09/1968	128	CB
Brenda & The Tabulations	That's The Price You Have To Pay	14/06/1969	125	CB
Brenda & The Tabulations	A Child No One Wanted	23/01/1971	120	BB
Brenda & The Tabulations	Why Didn't I Think Of That	08/01/1972	107	BB
Brenda Holloway	I'll Always Love You	01/08/1964	102	CB
Brenda Holloway	You Can Cry On My Shoulder	25/09/1965	116	BB
Brenda Holloway	You Can Cry On My Shoulder	25/09/1965	123	CB
Brenda Holloway	Together 'Til The End Of Time	26/02/1966	125	BB
Brenda Jo Harris	Standing On The Outside	05/10/1968	131	BB
Brenda Lee	It's Never Too Late	01/05/1961	101	BB
Brenda Lee	He's So Heavenly	13/04/1963	119	CB
Brenda Lee	Lonely Lonely Lonely Me	28/12/1963	125	CB
Brenda Lee	The Waiting Game	07/03/1964	101	BB
Brenda Lee	My Dreams	06/06/1964	112	CB
Brenda Lee	He's Sure To Remember Me	15/08/1964	135	BB
Brenda Lee	Too Little Time	12/03/1966	102	CB
Brenda Lee	Time And Time Again (b-side)	12/03/1966	126	BB
Brenda Lee	Too Little Time	26/03/1966	123	BB
Brenda Lee	Take Me	08/04/1967	126	BB
Brenda Lee	Born To Be By Your Side (b-side)	22/04/1967	134	BB
Brenda Lee	Where Love Is	12/08/1967	134	BB
Brenda Lee	Where's The Melody?	04/11/1967	105	BB
Brenda Lee	Where's The Melody?	11/11/1967	128	CB
Brenda Lee	That's All Right	13/01/1968	123	CB
Brenda Lee	That's All Right	27/01/1968	118	BB
Brenda Lee	Bring Me Sunshine	17/05/1969	107	CB
Brenda Lee	If This Is Our Last Time	14/08/1971	106	CB
Brenda Lee & Pete Fountain	Mood Indigo	13/04/1968	112	CB

Brent Fabric & His Piano	Goofus	04/07/1964	109	CB
Brenton Wood	Lovey Dovey Kinda Lovin'	23/03/1968	127	CB
Brenton Wood	Me And You	10/08/1968	121	BB
Brenton Wood	Me And You	24/08/1968	125	CB
Brenton Wood	A Change Is Gonna Come	15/03/1969	131	BB
Brenton Wood	Come Softly To Me	15/10/1977	107	CB
Brian Cadd	Let Go	05/10/1974	112	CB
Brian Gari	The Ashville Union Rescue Mission	14/02/1976	116	CB
Brian Gari	Better Than Average	31/07/1976	116	CB
Brian Hyland	I Gotta Go ('Cause I Love You)	24/12/1960	105	CB
Brian Hyland	I Gotta Go ('Cause I Love You)	31/12/1960	101	BB
Brian Hyland	Lop-Sided Over-Loaded (And It Wiggled When We Rode It) (b-	31/12/1960	105	BB
Brian Hyland	The Night I Cried	11/11/1961	128	CB
Brian Hyland	Let Us Make Our Own Mistakes	09/11/1963	123	BB
Brian Hyland	Here's To Our Love	14/03/1964	131	CB
Brian Hyland	Here's To Our Love	21/03/1964	129	BB
Brian Hyland	Devoted To You	29/08/1964	140	CB
Brian Hyland	(That's The Way Our Love Goes) One Step Forward, Two Steps	14/11/1964	137	CB
Brian Hyland	Get The Message	05/08/1967	109	CB
Brian Hyland	Apologize	11/11/1967	139	CB
Brian Hyland	So Long, Marianne	26/06/1971	120	BB
Brick	All The Way	21/06/1980	106	BB
Bridge	Love Is There	27/06/1970	104	CB
Broadway	You To Me Are Everything	17/07/1976	104	CB
Brook Benton	I Want You Forever	10/10/1959	103	CB
Brook Benton	Your Eyes	20/05/1961	115	CB
Brook Benton	Thanks To The Fool	05/05/1962	106	BB
Brook Benton	With The Touch Of Your Hand	18/08/1962	120	BB
Brook Benton	With The Touch Of Your Hand	01/09/1962	126	CB
Brook Benton	Please, Please Make It Easy	05/12/1964	119	BB

Brook Benton	The Special Years	06/03/1965	109	CB
Brook Benton	The Special Years	20/03/1965	129	BB
Brook Benton	Only A Girl Like You	05/03/1966	122	BB
Brook Benton	Only A Girl Like You	12/03/1966	102	CB
Brook Benton	Too Much Good Lovin' (No Good For Me)	28/05/1966	126	BB
Brook Benton	Do Your Own Thing	12/10/1968	128	CB
Brook Benton	If You Got The Time	07/10/1972	104	BB
Brook Benton	Lay Lady Lay	29/12/1973	107	CB
Brook Benton & Damita Jo	Stop Foolin'	09/11/1963	108	BB
Brook Benton & Damita Jo	Baby, You've Got It Made (b-side)	16/11/1963	111	BB
Brook Benton & Damita Jo	Baby, You've Got It Made	23/11/1963	133	CB
Brook Benton With The Dixie Flyers	Heaven Help Us All	10/04/1971	120	CB
Brooklyn Bridge	Down By The River	06/06/1970	103	CB
Brooks Arthur	The Birthday Card	17/12/1960	110	CB
Brooks Brothers	Warpaint	03/06/1961	130	CB
Brooks O'dell	You Better Make Up Your Mind	05/06/1965	134	CB
Brother Jack Mcduff	Grease Monkey [Live]	28/03/1964	116	BB
Brother Jack Mcduff	Hot Barbecue	25/12/1965	133	CB
Brother Jack Mcduff	A Change Is Gonna Come	10/09/1966	112	CB
Brotherhood Of Man	Sweet Lady From Georgia	18/09/1976	104	CB
Brothers Of Soul	I Guess That Don't Make Me A Loser	30/03/1968	126	CB
Brown Sugar	Loneliness (Will Bring Us Together Again)	14/07/1973	107	BB
Brown Sugar	Loneliness (Will Bring Us Together Again)	04/08/1973	109	CB
Browns Featuring Jim Edward Brown	Whiffenpoof Song	22/08/1960	112	BB
Browns Featuring Jim Edward Brown	Buttons And Bows	07/04/1962	104	BB
Browns Featuring Jim Edward Brown	The Old Master Painter	01/09/1962	118	BB
Browns Featuring Jim Edward Brown	Everybody's Darlin', Plus Mine	03/10/1964	135	BB
Browns Featuring Jim Edward Brown	You Can't Grow Peaches On A Cherry Tree	10/07/1965	120	BB
Bruce "Baby Man" Baum W/Little Roger & The Goosebumps	Marty Feldman Eyes	08/08/1981	1103	CB
Bruce & Terry	Custom Machine	01/02/1964	126	CB

Bruce & Terry	Summer Means Fun	18/07/1964	105	CB
Bruce & Terry	Carmen	20/03/1965	111	CB
Bruce And Terry	Carmen	27/03/1965	107	BB
Bruce Bruno	Hey Little One	11/09/1961	103	BB
Bruce Channel	Come On Baby	14/07/1962	113	CB
Bruce Channel	Somewhere In This Town	29/09/1962	132	CB
Bruce Channel	Somewhere In This Town	13/10/1962	117	BB
Bruce Cockburn	Rumours Of Glory	25/10/1980	104	BB
Bruce Johnston	Do The Surfer Stomp Part One	17/03/1962	121	CB
Bruce Johnston	Pipeline	24/09/1977	109	BB
Bryan Ferry	Heart On My Sleeve	20/11/1976	102	CB
Bryan Ferry	Slave To Love	15/06/1985	109	BB
Bryan Loren	Lollipop Luv	07/04/1984	105	BB
Buchanan & Greenfield	The Invasion	12/09/1964	134	CB
Buchanan And Greenfield	The Invasion	03/10/1964	120	BB
Buck Owens	Foolin' Around	13/03/1961	113	BB
Buck Owens	My Heart Skips A Beat	11/07/1964	130	CB
Buck Owens	Don't Let Her Know	22/08/1964	130	BB
Buck Owens	(I Want) No One But You	15/05/1965	101	CB
Buck Owens	Only You (Can Break My Heart)	31/07/1965	120	BB
Buck Owens	Santa Looked A Lot Like Daddy	18/12/1965	101	CB
Buck Owens And The Buckaroos	Where Does The Good Times Go	18/02/1967	114	BB
Buck Owens And The Buckaroos	It Takes People Like You (To Make People Like Me)	28/10/1967	114	BB
Buck Owens And The Buckaroos	Who's Gonna Mow Your Grass	08/02/1969	106	BB
Buck Owens And The Buckaroos	Johnny B. Goode [Live]	24/05/1969	114	BB
Buck Owens And The Buckaroos	I Wouldn't Live In New York City (If They Gave Me The Whole Dang	05/12/1970	110	BB
Buck Owens And The Buckaroos	Bridge Over Troubled Water	20/03/1971	119	BB
Buck Owens And The Buckaroos	Ruby (Are You Mad)	12/06/1971	106	BB
Buckner & Garcia	Do The Donkey Kong	29/05/1982	103	BB
Buckwheat	Movin' On (Part 2)	27/11/1971	105	CB

Buckwheat	Hey Little Girl	30/09/1972	108	CB
Bud Dashiell & The Kinsmen	I Talk To The Trees	09/09/1961	110	CB
Buddy Clinton	Take Me To Your Ladder (I'll See Your Leader Later)	31/12/1960	115	BB
Buddy Greco	Around The World	10/07/1961	109	BB
Buddy Greco	Around The World	22/07/1961	146	CB
Buddy Greco	Jambalaya (On The Bayou)	30/01/1965	127	CB
Buddy Greco	I Can't Begin To Tell You	14/08/1965	132	BB
Buddy Greco	That Darn Cat	27/11/1965	136	CB
Buddy Greco	Put Yourself In My Place	30/07/1966	132	CB
Buddy Holly	Bo Diddley	27/04/1963	102	CB
Buddy Holly	Bo Diddley	27/04/1963	116	BB
Buddy Holly	True Love Ways	27/04/1963	124	CB
Buddy Holly	Brown-Eyed Handsome Man	05/10/1963	113	BB
Buddy Holly	Love Is Strange	26/04/1969	105	BB
Buddy Knox And The Rhythm Orchids	Hitchhike Back To Georgia	22/02/1964	114	BB
Buddy Miles	Dreams	10/10/1970	101	CB
Buddy Miles	Life Is What You Make It (Part 1)	20/05/1972	107	CB
Buddy Miles	We Got Love	23/11/1974	108	BB
Buddy Miles Express	Memphis Train	26/07/1969	123	CB
Buddy Starcher	Day Of Decision	18/06/1966	131	BB
Buffy Sainte-Marie	The Circle Game	15/08/1970	109	BB
Buffy Sainte-Marie	The Circle Game	15/08/1970	112	CB
Buffy Sainte-Marie	Until It's Time For You To Go	28/11/1970	122	CB
Buffy Sainte-Marie	He's An Indian Cowboy In The Rodeo	08/07/1972	104	CB
Buffy Sainte-Marie	Generation	28/12/1974	119	CB
Bulldog	Are You Really Happy Together	10/03/1973	112	BB
Bullet	Little Bit O' Soul	17/06/1972	107	BB
Bunny Paul	We're Only Young Once	15/06/1963	126	CB
Bunny Sigler	Tossin' And Turnin'	06/10/1973	101	CB
Bunny Sigler	Love Train (Part One)	15/06/1974	111	CB

Bunny Sigler	That's How Long I'll Be Loving You	27/09/1975	102	BB
Buoys	Timothy	18/04/1970	128	CB
Burl Ives	How Do You Fall Out Of Love	27/10/1962	143	CB
Burl Ives	The Same Old Hurt	19/01/1963	103	CB
Burl Ives	Baby Come Home To Me	30/03/1963	125	CB
Burl Ives	Baby Come Home To Me	13/04/1963	131	BB
Burl Ives	I'm The Boss	08/06/1963	110	CB
Burl Ives	I'm The Boss	06/07/1963	111	BB
Burl Ives	It Comes And Goes	12/10/1963	124	BB
Burl Ives	It Comes And Goes	19/10/1963	121	CB
Burl Ives	(I Hear You) Call My Name	23/01/1965	118	CB
Burl Ives	My Gal Sal	23/01/1965	122	BB
Burl Ives	My Gal Sal	30/01/1965	105	CB
Burl Ives	Chim Chim Cheree	10/04/1965	120	BB
Burl Ives	Salt Water Guitar	17/07/1965	138	CB
Burl Ives	I'll Be Your Baby Tonight	06/07/1968	133	BB
Burl Ives	One More Time Billy Brown	25/07/1970	134	CB
Burt Bacharach	I'll Never Fall In Love Again	14/06/1969	105	CB
Burt Bacharach	All Kinds Of People	30/01/1971	120	CB
Burt Bacharach	All Kinds Of People	06/02/1971	116	BB
Burt Bacharach & His Orchestra Featuring Tony Middleton	My Little Red Book (All I Do Is Talk About You)*	03/07/1965	132	CB
Burton Cummings	My Own Way To Rock	24/09/1977	105	CB
Buster Brown	John Henry (The Steel Driving Man)	02/05/1960	105	BB
Buster Brown	John Henry (The Steel Driving Man)	14/05/1960	112	CB
Buster Brown	Sugar Babe	10/02/1962	139	CB
Buster Brown	Falling Out Of Love	26/10/1974	111	CB
Butch Patrick	I.O.I.O.	22/07/1972	114	CB
Buzz And Bucky	Tiger-A-Go-Go	01/05/1965	107	BB
Buzz Clifford	Three Little Fishes	10/04/1961	102	BB
Buzz Clifford	Moving Day	25/11/1961	139	CB

Buzz Clifford	Magic Circle	14/04/1962	147	CB
Byron Mcnaughton & His All News Orchestra	Right From The Shark's Jaws (The Jaws Interview)	13/09/1975	106	BB
C & The Shells	You Are The Circus	05/04/1969	101	CB
C.J. & Co.	Big City Sidewalk	22/07/1978	106	BB
C.L. & The Pictures	I'm Asking Forgiveness	17/02/1962	109	CB
C.W. Mccall	Classified	17/05/1975	102	CB
C.W. Mccall	Classified	28/06/1975	101	BB
C.W. Mccall	Round The World With The RuBBer Duck	18/12/1976	101	BB
C.W. Mccall	ROUND The World With The RuBBer Duck	01/01/1977	105	CB
Café Créme	Discomania (Part I)	29/07/1978	105	BB
Cal Tjader Quartet	Cool	24/02/1962	148	CB
Camel	Another Night	24/07/1976	109	BB
Cameo	Rigor Mortis	05/03/1977	103	BB
Cameo	Funk Funk	17/09/1977	104	BB
Cameo	It's Serious	06/05/1978	106	CB
Cameo	Freaky Dancin'	04/07/1981	102	BB
Cameo	Just Be Yourself	24/04/1982	101	BB
Cameos	I Remember When	27/02/1960	121	CB
Canada Goose	Higher & Higher	11/07/1970	121	CB
Candi Staton	Never In Public	20/09/1969	124	BB
Candi Staton	Mr. And Mrs. Untrue	24/04/1971	109	BB
Candi Staton	Something's Burning	02/06/1973	108	CB
Candi Staton	Nights On Broadway	03/09/1977	102	BB
Canned Heat	Rollin' And Tumblin'	15/07/1967	139	CB
Canned Heat	Rollin' And Tumblin'	29/07/1967	115	BB
Canned Heat	Poor Moon	16/08/1969	119	BB
Canned Heat	Wooly Bully	30/01/1971	101	CB
Canned Heat	Wooly Bully	06/03/1971	105	BB
Canned Heat	Rockin' With The King	25/03/1972	102	CB
Cannibal & The Headhunters	Nau Ninny Nau	19/06/1965	132	CB

Cannibal And The Headhunters	Nau Ninny Nau	26/06/1965	133	BB
Cannibal And The Headhunters	Land Of A Thousand Dances	03/09/1966	106	BB
Capt. Groovy & His BuBBlegum Army	Capt. Groovy And His BuBBlegum Army	28/06/1969	131	CB
Capt. Groovy And His BuBBlegum Army	Capt. Groovy And His BuBBlegum Army	14/06/1969	128	BB
Captain & Tennille	This Is Not The First Time	20/12/1980	106	BB
Captain Beefheart & His Magic Band	Diddy Wah Diddy	14/05/1966	131	CB
Captain Milk (Edwin HuBBard)	Hey Jude	13/09/1969	120	CB
Captain Sky	Dr. Rock	18/08/1979	105	BB
Caravan	Stuck In A Hole	27/09/1975	110	BB
Caravan	Stuck In A Hole	18/10/1975	112	CB
Carillo	I Wanna Live Again	19/08/1978	101	BB
Carl Belew	Hello Out There	20/10/1962	120	BB
Carl Carlton	I Won't Let That Chump Break Your Heart	06/01/1973	119	CB
Carl Carlton	Smokin' Room	01/03/1975	104	CB
Carl Carlton	Baby I Need Your Loving	23/10/1982	103	BB
Carl Douglas Band	Blue Eyed Soul (PT. I)	05/04/1975	110	CB
Carl Graves	The Next Best Thing	05/04/1975	103	BB
Carl Henderson	Sharing You	05/03/1966	126	BB
Carl James & Jackie Irvin	Dance Party Music	06/07/1974	105	CB
Carl Mann	Some Enchanted Evening	06/02/1960	119	CB
Carl Smith	If The World Don't End Tomorrow I'm Comin' After You	18/07/1960	107	BB
Carl Smith	If The World Don't End Tomorrow (I'm Comin' After You)*	06/08/1960	101	CB
Carl Stevens	Baby Elephant Walk*	16/06/1962	102	CB
Carl Wilson	Heaven	22/08/1981	107	BB
Carla Thomas	What A Fool I've Been	29/06/1963	118	CB
Carla Thomas	How Do You Quit (Someone You Love)	20/02/1965	126	CB
Carla Thomas	Comfort Me	29/01/1966	112	CB
Carla Thomas	Unchanging Love	22/04/1967	102	CB
Carla Thomas	A Dime A Dozen	18/05/1968	114	BB
Carla Thomas	Where Do I Go	19/10/1968	103	CB

Carla Thomas	I've Fallen In Love	23/08/1969	117	BB
Carla Thomas	Guide Me Well	11/04/1970	107	CB
Carla Thomas	Guide Me Well	06/06/1970	107	BB
Carla Thomas	I Loved You Like I Love My Very Life	31/10/1970	104	CB
Carlene Carter	Do It In A Heartbeat	01/12/1979	108	BB
Carlo	Baby Doll	02/03/1963	123	BB
Carlos Santana	Watch Your Step	11/06/1983	107	BB
Carly Simon	Take Me As I Am	13/12/1980	102	BB
Carly Simon	Hurt	19/12/1981	106	BB
Carmen Mcrae	What Has She Got	30/04/1960	125	CB
Carmen Mcrae & Herbie Mann	Live For Life	18/11/1967	101	BB
Carol Douglas	Midnight Love Affair	05/02/1977	102	BB
Carol Douglas	Dancing Queen	19/02/1977	110	BB
Carol Douglas	We Do It	17/09/1977	108	BB
Carol Douglas	Night Fever	25/02/1978	106	BB
Carol Hughes	Let Me Go Lover	01/02/1960	114	BB
Carol Lynn Townes	Believe In The Beat	16/03/1985	109	BB
Carol Lynn Townes	I Freak For You	27/07/1985	106	BB
Carol Shaw	Jimmy Boy	28/12/1963	132	BB
Carol Williams	More	27/03/1976	102	BB
Carole Bayer Sager	It's The Falling In Love	19/08/1978	102	CB
Carole King	School Bells Are Ringing	17/11/1962	123	BB
Carole King	Smackwater Jack	11/09/1971	112	CB
Carole King	Bitter With The Sweet	18/11/1972	105	CB
Carole Quinn	What's So Sweet About Sweet Sixteen	29/08/1964	124	CB
Carolyn Crawford	Forget About Me	30/11/1963	119	CB
Carolyn Franklin	It's True I'm Gonna Miss You	16/08/1969	119	BB
Carolyn Franklin	All I Want To Be Is Your Woman	29/08/1970	117	CB
Carolyn Franklin	All I Want To Be Is Your Woman	12/09/1970	108	BB
Carpenters	Bless The Beasts And Children	11/12/1971	113	CB

Carpenters	Make Believe It's Your First Time	19/11/1983	101	BB
Carter Brothers	Booze In The Bottle	22/01/1966	139	CB
Casey Kasem	Letter From Elaina	03/10/1964	103	BB
Casey Kasem	Letter From Elaina	03/10/1964	120	CB
Casey Kelly	You Can't Get There From Here	06/01/1973	110	BB
Cash Mc Call	When You Wake Up	23/07/1966	102	BB
Cash Mccall	You Can't Take Love	24/09/1966	141	CB
Cash Mccall	That Lucky Old Sun	19/11/1966	130	CB
Cashman, Pistilli & West	Goodbye Jo	11/04/1970	105	BB
Cashman, Pistilli & West	Goodbye Jo	18/04/1970	104	CB
Cass Elliot	(If You're Gonna) Break Another Heart	02/09/1972	120	CB
Cassius Clay	Stand By Me	21/03/1964	102	BB
Cassius Clay	I Am The Greatest [Live]	21/03/1964	113	BB
Castle Creek	I Can Make It Better	31/07/1971	112	CB
Cat Mother And The All Night Newsboys	Can You Dance To It?	27/09/1969	115	BB
Cat Stevens	I Love My Dog	10/12/1966	106	CB
Cat Stevens	I Love My Dog	17/12/1966	118	BB
Cat Stevens	Matthew And Son	11/03/1967	115	BB
Cat Stevens	Matthew And Son	22/05/1971	109	CB
Cat Stevens	Bad Brakes	23/12/1978	Np6	CB
Catfish Hodge	Boogie Man	25/08/1973	109	CB
Cathy Carr	Little Sister	06/02/1960	102	CB
Cathy Carr	Little Sister	15/02/1960	106	BB
Cathy Carr	Nein Nein Fraulein	09/12/1961	132	CB
Cathy Carr	Sailor Boy	08/12/1962	120	CB
Cathy Carr	Sailor Boy	29/12/1962	103	BB
Cathy Carroll	Poor Little Puppet	30/06/1962	102	CB
Cathy Jean	Make Me Smile Again	10/06/1961	111	CB
Central Park West	Sweets For My Sweet	21/12/1968	104	CB
Chad & Jeremy	September In The Rain	04/09/1965	112	CB

Chad & Jeremy	Should I	23/10/1965	128	BB
Chad & Jeremy	Teenage Failure	05/02/1966	131	BB
Chad & Jeremy	You Are She	08/10/1966	103	CB
Chad & Jill Stuart	The Cruel War	16/04/1966	110	BB
Chad Allan & The Expressions (The Guess Who)	Hey Ho What You Do To Me	04/09/1965	125	BB
Chad Allen	Little Lonely	04/11/1961	107	CB
Chad Allen	Little Lonely	13/11/1961	112	BB
Chairmen Of The Board	Hanging On (To) A Memory	15/05/1971	110	BB
Chairmen Of The Board	Hanging On (To) A Memory	22/05/1971	102	CB
Chairmen Of The Board	Try On My Love For Size	09/10/1971	103	BB
Chairmen Of The Board	Men Are Getting Scarce	11/12/1971	104	BB
Chaka Khan	Clouds	17/05/1980	103	BB
Chambers Brothers	Wake Up	21/06/1969	101	CB
Champaign	Off And On Love	10/11/1984	104	BB
Change, Lead Vocal By Luther Vandross	Searching	23/08/1980	1103	CB
Chantay's	Pipeline	01/10/1966	106	BB
Charade	And You Do	29/08/1970	128	CB
Charade	And You Do	12/09/1970	116	BB
Charlene	Freddie	21/05/1977	108	CB
Charlene	It Ain't Easy Comin' Down	24/07/1982	109	BB
Charles Albertine	The Long Ships, Part 1	18/07/1964	101	CB
Charles Albertine	The Long Ships, Part 1	15/08/1964	112	BB
Charles Boyer	Where Does Love Go	14/08/1965	148	CB
Charles Brown	Please Come Home For Christmas	22/12/1962	108	BB
Charles Christy & The Crystals	Cherry Pie	22/01/1966	124	CB
Charles Mccullough & The Silks	My Girl	02/12/1961	140	CB
Charles Randolph Green Sounde	The Masterpiece	13/05/1972	124	CB
Charles Wright & The Watts 103rd Street Rhythm Band	Comment	11/10/1969	113	CB
Charles Wright & The Watts 103rd Street Rhythm Band	Must Be Your Thing	08/11/1969	126	CB
Charles Wright And The Watts 103rd Street Rhythm Band	Comment (b-side)	11/10/1969	109	BB

Charles Wright And The Watts 103rd Street Rhythm Band	Must Be Your Thing	22/11/1969	103	BB
Charley Pride	Kaw-Liga [Live]	15/02/1969	120	BB
Charley Pride	(I'm So) Afraid Of Losing You Again	13/12/1969	102	CB
Charley Pride	Wonder Could I Live There Anymore	11/07/1970	122	CB
Charley Pride	I'd Rather Love You	20/03/1971	113	CB
Charley Pride	Let Me Live	29/05/1971	104	BB
Charley Pride	It's Gonna Take A Little Bit Longer	22/07/1972	113	CB
Charley Pride	It's Gonna Take A Little Bit Longer	05/08/1972	102	BB
Charley Pride	A Shoulder To Cry On	17/02/1973	112	CB
Charley Pride	A Shoulder To Cry On	10/03/1973	101	BB
Charley Pride	Don't Fight The Feelings Of Love	07/07/1973	101	BB
Charley Pride	Mississippi Cotton Picking Delta Town	23/11/1974	105	CB
Charley Pride	I Ain't All Bad	31/05/1975	101	BB
Charley Pride	The Happiness Of Having You	14/02/1976	103	CB
Charley Pride	I'll Be Leaving Alone	30/07/1977	101	CB
Charlie	Fool For Your Love	23/01/1982	I103	CB
Charlie Allen & Pacific Gas & Electric	Gumbo Jones	16/02/1974	113	CB
Charlie Calello	Dance, Dance, Dance	13/03/1976	104	BB
Charlie Daniels Band	Sweet Home Alabama (Live)	11/07/1981	I101	CB
Charlie Daniels Band	Sweet Home Alabama [Live]	18/07/1981	110	BB
Charlie Daniels Band	Ragin' Cajun	17/07/1982	109	BB
Charlie Hoss & The Ponies	The Madison Twist	19/11/1960	124	CB
Charlie Mccoy	Cherry Berry Wine	18/02/1961	104	CB
Charlie Mccoy	Orange Blossom Special	31/03/1973	124	CB
Charlie Mccoy	Orange Blossom Special	21/04/1973	101	BB
Charlie Rich	On My Knees	15/10/1960	105	CB
Charlie Rich	Who Will The Next Fool Be	08/04/1961	102	CB
Charlie Rich	Just A Little Bit Sweet	04/11/1961	129	CB
Charlie Rich	Just A Little Bit Sweet	13/11/1961	111	BB
Charlie Rich	Big Boss Man	30/11/1963	108	BB

Charlie Rich	Big Boss Man	21/12/1963	146	CB
Charlie Rich	Nice And Easy	12/09/1964	131	BB
Charlie Rich	I Can't Go On	11/12/1965	109	CB
Charlie Rich	I Can't Go On	11/12/1965	132	BB
Charlie Rich	Hawg Jaw	12/03/1966	125	BB
Charlie Rich	Rollin' With The Flow	30/07/1977	101	BB
Charlie Rich With Gene Lowery Singers	Gonna Be Waitin'	30/07/1960	116	CB
Charlie Van Dyke	The Flag	12/06/1976	106	CB
Charlie Whitehead	Love Being Your Fool	12/07/1975	106	BB
Charo With The Salsoul Orchestra	Dance A Little Bit Closer	28/01/1978	104	BB
Chas Jankel	Glad To Know You	20/02/1982	102	BB
Chase	I Can Feel It	20/05/1972	105	BB
Chase	I Can Feel It	27/05/1972	129	CB
Chase Webster	Sweethearts In Heaven	04/12/1961	116	BB
Cheap Trick	California Man	23/12/1978	Np6	CB
Cheap Trick	Day Tripper	02/08/1980	I102	CB
Cheeks	Boney Moronie	12/07/1980	110	BB
Cher	Magic In The Air	19/11/1966	119	CB
Cher	Mama (When My Dollies Have Babies)	17/12/1966	124	BB
Cher	For What It's Worth	13/09/1969	125	BB
Cher	Am I Blue	12/05/1973	111	BB
Cher	Carousel Man	02/11/1974	104	CB
Cherokee	Girl, I've Got News For You	07/08/1971	116	BB
Cherokee	Girl, I've Got News For You	25/09/1971	111	CB
Cheryl Lynn	Instant Love	24/07/1982	105	BB
Cheryl Lynn (with Luther Vandross)	If This World Were Mine	16/10/1982	101	BB
Chet Atkins	One Mint Julep	09/01/1960	101	CB
Chet Atkins	Theme From "The Dark At The Top Of The Stairs"	17/10/1960	103	BB
Chet Atkins	The Slop	11/03/1961	135	CB
Chet Atkins	Windy And Warm	24/06/1961	132	CB

Chet Atkins	Jingle-Bell Rock	25/12/1961	106	BB
Chet Atkins	From Nashville With Love	02/04/1966	132	BB
Chet Baker & The Mariachi Brass	Flowers On The Wall	05/02/1966	115	BB
Chet Baker & The Mariachi Brass	Flowers On The Wall	05/02/1966	129	CB
Cheyne	Call Me Mr. 'Telephone' (Answering Service)	15/06/1985	106	BB
Chi Coltrane	Go Like Elijah	13/01/1973	107	BB
Chi-Lites	Let Me Be The Man My Daddy Was	26/07/1969	107	CB
Chic	My Feet Keep Dancing	12/01/1980	101	BB
Chic	Stage Fright	30/01/1982	105	BB
Chilliwack	Last Day Of December	24/01/1976	109	BB
Chilliwack	Baby Blue	10/12/1977	110	BB
Chilliwack	Secret Information	12/03/1983	110	BB
Chilly	For Your Love	12/05/1979	Np6	CB
Chilly	For Your Love	19/05/1979	108	BB
Chip Taylor	Here I Am	17/11/1962	113	BB
Chip Taylor	Here I Am	24/11/1962	102	CB
Chip Taylor	Angel Of The Morning	25/11/1972	102	CB
Chocolate Chips	There You Are (I See You)	25/11/1972	127	CB
Chocolate Milk	Comin'	23/10/1976	112	CB
Chocolate Milk	Girl Callin'	10/06/1978	103	BB
Chocolate Syrup	Stop Your Cryin'	01/05/1971	107	CB
Chris & Cathy	All You Had To Do (Was Tell Me)	07/03/1964	111	CB
Chris And Kathy (Chris Montez) (Kathy Young)	All You Had To Do (Was Tell Me)	11/04/1964	125	BB
Chris Bartley	Baby It's Wonderful	21/10/1967	118	CB
Chris Bartley	Baby It's Wonderful	04/11/1967	125	BB
Chris Christian	Make It Last	27/02/1982	I103	CB
Chris Clark	Love's Gone Bad	01/10/1966	105	BB
Chris Clark	Love's Gone Bad	01/10/1966	125	CB
Chris Clark	I Want To Go Back There Again	08/04/1967	113	CB
Chris Clark	I Want To Go Back There Again	08/04/1967	114	BB

Chris Clark	From Head To Toe	07/10/1967	108	CB
Chris Crosby	Tomorrow	02/05/1964	124	BB
Chris De Burgh	The Traveller	13/09/1980	106	BB
Chris Farlowe	Out Of Time	17/09/1966	125	CB
Chris Farlowe	Out Of Time	12/11/1966	122	BB
Chris Glendon	My Fellow Americans	02/03/1974	102	CB
Chris Kenner	A Very True Story	04/09/1961	103	BB
Chris Kenner	Packin' Up	09/09/1961	104	CB
Chris Kenner	A Very True Story	23/09/1961	123	CB
Chris Kenner	Something You Got	30/12/1961	124	CB
Chris Montan	Let's Pick It Up (Where We Left Off)	07/02/1981	I103	CB
Chris Montan	Let's Pick It Up (Where We Left Off)	28/02/1981	106	BB
Chris Montez	All You Had To Do (Was Tell Me)	17/03/1962	114	CB
Chris Montez	All You Had To Do (Was Tell Me)	07/04/1962	108	BB
Chris Montez	(Let's Do) The Limbo	09/03/1963	142	CB
Chris Montez	My Baby Loves To Dance	24/08/1963	129	BB
Chris Montez	Foolin' Around	29/07/1967	135	BB
Christian Morandi	Dear Gesu Bambino (Caro Gesu Bambino)	30/12/1961	125	CB
Christine Cooper	S.O.S. (Heart In Distress)	12/02/1966	101	BB
Christine Kittrell	Sittin' And Drinking	30/12/1961	144	CB
Christopher Cloud	Zip A Dee Doo Dah	07/04/1973	102	CB
Christopher Paul & Shawn	For Your Love	16/08/1975	115	CB
ChuBBy Checker	Good, Good Lovin'	29/04/1961	129	CB
ChuBBy Checker	La Paloma Twist	24/03/1962	114	CB
ChuBBy Checker	Rosie	20/06/1964	116	BB
ChuBBy Checker	Reggae My Way	04/08/1973	112	CB
ChuBBy Checker	Harder Than Diamond	29/05/1982	104	BB
ChuBBy Checker BoBBy Rydell	Jingle Bell Imitations	25/12/1961	115	BB
Chuck Berry	Broken Arrow	28/09/1959	108	BB
Chuck Berry	Childhood Sweetheart	03/10/1959	105	CB

Chuck Berry	Broken Arrow	10/10/1959	111	CB
Chuck Berry	Jaguar And Thunderbird	07/11/1960	109	BB
Chuck Berry	Little Star	01/04/1961	134	CB
Chuck Berry	Go, BoBBy Soxer	24/10/1964	147	CB
Chuck Berry	It Wasn't Me	13/11/1965	138	CB
Chuck Brooks	Love's Gonna Tear Your Playhouse Down Part I	18/04/1970	126	CB
Chuck Howard	A Thing Called Sadness	13/06/1964	115	CB
Chuck Jackson	The Breaking Point	28/10/1961	108	CB
Chuck Jackson	What'cha Gonna Say Tomorrow	27/01/1962	142	CB
Chuck Jackson	Who's Gonna Pick Up The Pieces	11/08/1962	119	BB
Chuck Jackson	Getting Ready For The Heartbreak	03/11/1962	101	CB
Chuck Jackson	Tears Of Joy	25/05/1963	116	CB
Chuck Jackson	I Will Never Turn My Back On You	01/06/1963	110	BB
Chuck Jackson	Somebody New	12/09/1964	106	CB
Chuck Jackson	Good Things Come To Those Who Wait	04/12/1965	105	BB
Chuck Jackson	Good Things Come To Those Who Wait	11/12/1965	109	CB
Chuck Jackson	All In My Mind	07/05/1966	143	CB
Chuck Jackson	These Chains Of Love (Are Breaking Me Down)	30/07/1966	127	CB
Chuck Jackson	Are You Lonely For Me Baby	12/04/1969	107	BB
Chuck Jackson	Are You Lonely For Me	19/04/1969	108	CB
Chuck Jackson	Honey Come Back	25/10/1969	107	CB
Chuck Jackson	Let Somebody Love Me	13/06/1970	133	CB
Chuck Jackson	I Only Get This Feeling	14/07/1973	117	BB
Chuck Jackson & Maxine Brown	I Need You So	16/10/1965	125	CB
Chuck Jackson & Maxine Brown	I'm Satisfied	12/02/1966	112	BB
Chuck Jackson & Maxine Brown	Please Don't Hurt Me	26/02/1966	138	CB
Chuck Mangione	Children Of Sanchez	11/11/1978	104	BB
Chuck Reed	Just Plain Hurt	07/04/1962	126	CB
Chuck Trois & The Amazing Maze	Call On You	13/04/1968	123	CB
Chuck Wood	Seven Days Too Long	23/09/1967	119	BB

Chylds	Psychedelic Soul	09/12/1967	129	CB
Cilla Black	It's For You	05/09/1964	105	CB
Cilla Black	Is It Love?	13/03/1965	133	BB
Cilla Black	Alfie	10/09/1966	139	CB
Cilla Black	What The World Needs Now Is Love	30/11/1968	107	CB
Cilla Black	Without Him	22/03/1969	134	CB
Cilla Black	I'll Take A Tango	22/11/1975	114	CB
Cindy Ellis	Do You Think Of Me (Denkst Du Noch An Mich)	21/05/1960	124	CB
Cissy Houston	He - I Believe	04/04/1970	134	CB
Cissy Houston	I'll Be There	02/05/1970	124	CB
Cissy Houston	I'll Be There	20/06/1970	125	BB
Cissy Houston	Midnite Train To Georgia	10/03/1973	115	CB
Cissy Houston	Think It Over	14/10/1978	106	BB
Clarence "Frogman" Henry	Have You Ever Been Lonely	05/12/1964	135	BB
Clarence Ashe	Trouble I've Had	16/05/1964	101	CB
Clarence Carter	Scratch My Back (And Mumble In My Ear)	11/12/1971	101	BB
Clarence Carter	Back In Your Arms	20/01/1973	117	CB
Clarence Carter	Put On Your Shoes And Walk	17/03/1973	112	BB
Clarence Carter	I'm The Midnight Special	24/11/1973	101	BB
Clarence Henry	Little Suzy	10/06/1961	148	CB
Clarence Henry	Why Can't You	12/08/1961	135	CB
Clarence Henry	Standing In The Need Of Love	20/11/1961	109	BB
Clarence Henry	Dream Myself A Sweetheart	19/05/1962	149	CB
Clarence Henry	Dream Myself A Sweetheart	26/05/1962	112	BB
Clarence Reid	I'm Gonna Tear You A New Heart	08/11/1969	120	BB
Classics	Cinderella	08/10/1960	123	CB
Classics	Cinderella	28/11/1960	109	BB
Claude "Fats" Greene Orch.	"FATS" Shake 'M Up - Pt. 1	25/06/1966	141	CB
Claude King	Big River, Big Man	29/07/1961	114	CB
Claude King	I've Got The World By The Tail	08/12/1962	111	BB

Claude King	I've Got The World By The Tail	22/12/1962	105	CB
Claude King	Scarlet O'hara	17/08/1963	114	CB
Claude King	Tiger Woman	10/07/1965	110	BB
Claude King	Tiger Woman	10/07/1965	129	CB
Claudine Clark	Walkin' Through A Cemetery	24/11/1962	122	CB
Claudine Clark	The Telephone Game	01/12/1962	141	CB
Claudine Longet	Meditation (Meditacao)	15/10/1966	107	CB
Claudine Longet	Here, There And Everywhere	25/02/1967	126	CB
Claudine Longet	Here, There And Everywhere	04/03/1967	126	BB
Claudine Longet	Hello, Hello	27/05/1967	113	CB
Claudine Longet	Good Day Sunshine	05/08/1967	131	CB
Claudine Longet	Small Talk	30/09/1967	118	CB
Claudine Longet	I Love How You Love Me	03/02/1968	122	CB
Claudine Longet	Love Is Blue (L'Amour Est Bleu)	24/02/1968	110	CB
Claudine Longet	White Horses	08/06/1968	127	CB
Clebanoff & His Orchestra	Prelude From King Of Kings*	11/11/1961	111	CB
Clefs Of Lavender Hill	One More Time	08/10/1966	114	BB
Cleveland Crochet & Hill Billy Ramblers	Sugar Bee	10/12/1960	103	CB
Clif Newton	The Rest Of The Night	06/09/1980	101	BB
Cliff Nobles	This Feeling Of Loneliness	19/05/1973	108	CB
Cliff Richard	Dynamite	19/12/1959	115	CB
Cliff Richard	I Only Have Eyes For You	18/04/1964	109	BB
Cliff Richard	I Only Have Eyes For You	18/04/1964	127	CB
Cliff Richard	I Don't Wanna Love You	28/11/1964	120	CB
Cliff Richard	The Twelfth Of Never	11/09/1965	129	CB
Cliff Richard	Power To All Our Friends	19/05/1973	109	BB
Cliff Richard	Power To All Our Friends	26/05/1973	119	CB
Cliff Richard & The Shadows	Theme For A Dream	13/05/1961	112	CB
Cliff Richard & The Shadows	Bachelor Boy	27/06/1964	103	CB
Clifford Scott + 6 Stars	Lavender Sax	06/06/1964	149	CB

Climax Blues Band	Reap What I've Sowed	03/07/1971	128	CB
Climax Blues Band	Using The Power	01/11/1975	104	CB
Climax Blues Band	Using The Power	15/11/1975	110	BB
Climax Featuring Sonny Geraci	Caroline This Time	10/02/1973	123	CB
Climax Featuring Sonny Geraci	Rock And Roll Heaven	07/07/1973	102	CB
Clint Ballard Jr.	The Secret	18/02/1961	119	CB
Clint Holmes	Shiddle-Ee-Dee	15/09/1973	101	CB
Clint Holmes	Shiddle-Ee-Dee	15/09/1973	106	BB
Clint Holmes	Goodbye Maria	01/06/1974	122	CB
Clodagh Rodgers	Jack In The Box	26/06/1971	116	CB
Clyde And The Blue Jays	The Big Jerk - Pt. I	14/11/1964	134	BB
Clyde Brown	You Call Me Back	28/09/1974	101	CB
Clyde Mcphatter	Deep Sea Ball	07/05/1960	123	CB
Clyde Mcphatter	I Ain't Givin' Up Nothin' (If I Can't Get Somethin' From You)	13/08/1960	122	CB
Clyde Mcphatter	Before I Fall In Love Again (I'll Count To Ten)	17/12/1960	106	CB
Clyde Mcphatter	One More Chance	17/12/1960	117	CB
Clyde Mcphatter	Tomorrow Is A-Comin'	20/02/1961	103	BB
Clyde Mcphatter	Tomorrow Is A-Comin'	04/03/1961	116	CB
Clyde Mcphatter	I'll Love You Til The Cows Come Home (b-side)	06/03/1961	110	BB
Clyde Mcphatter	I'll Love You Till The Cows Come Home	11/03/1961	112	CB
Clyde Mcphatter	You're Movin' Me	06/05/1961	120	CB
Clyde Mcphatter	Maybe	15/09/1962	108	CB
Clyde Mcphatter	I Do Believe	15/09/1962	110	CB
Clyde Mcphatter	The Best Man Cried	03/11/1962	118	BB
Clyde Mcphatter	The Best Man Cried	10/11/1962	107	CB
Clyde Mcphatter	From One To One	24/08/1963	143	CB
Clyde Mcphatter	From One To One	21/09/1963	127	BB
Clyde Mcphatter	Crying Won't Help You Now	01/05/1965	104	CB
Clyde Mcphatter	Crying Won't Help You Now	01/05/1965	117	BB
Cold Blood	I'm A Good Woman	28/03/1970	125	BB

Cold Blood	Too Many People	03/10/1970	107	BB
Cold Blood	Down To The Bone	03/06/1972	108	CB
Colours	Love Heals	31/08/1968	106	BB
Commuter	Young Hearts	25/08/1984	101	BB
Company Front	I'm So Happy Now	12/10/1968	139	CB
Comparsa Universitaria De La Laguna	Magic Trumpet (Trompeta Magica)	24/04/1965	102	CB
Comparsa Universitaria De La Laguna	Magic Trumpet (Trompeta Magica)	08/05/1965	107	BB
Con Funk Shun	Confunkshunizeya	01/04/1978	103	BB
Con Funk Shun	Got To Be Enough	03/05/1980	101	BB
Con Funk Shun	Don't Let Your Love Grow Cold	07/04/1984	103	BB
Con Funk Shun	Electric Lady	04/05/1985	102	BB
Connie Francis	Somebody Else's Boy	22/04/1961	109	CB
Connie Francis	Gonna Git That Man	12/05/1962	117	CB
Connie Francis	The Biggest Sin Of All	28/07/1962	116	BB
Connie Francis	Baby's First Christmas	22/12/1962	113	BB
Connie Francis	Waiting For Billy	09/03/1963	127	BB
Connie Francis	You're The Only One Can Hurt Me	18/05/1963	116	CB
Connie Francis	Mala Femmena	10/08/1963	114	BB
Connie Francis	Mala Femmena	17/08/1963	101	CB
Connie Francis	Whatever Happened To Rosemarie	19/10/1963	132	CB
Connie Francis	Tommy	27/06/1964	136	CB
Connie Francis	We Have Something More (Than A Summer Love)	31/10/1964	128	BB
Connie Francis	It's A Different World	28/05/1966	134	BB
Connie Francis	It's A Different World	04/06/1966	142	CB
Connie Francis	A Letter From A Soldier (Dear Mama)	09/07/1966	105	BB
Connie Francis	A Letter From A Soldier (Dear Mama)	16/07/1966	119	CB
Connie Francis	So Nice (Summer Samba)	10/09/1966	121	CB
Connie Francis	Another Page	04/02/1967	121	BB
Connie Francis	Time Alone Will Tell (Non Pensare A Me)	01/04/1967	114	CB
Connie Francis	My Heart Cries For You	12/08/1967	118	BB

Connie Francis	Why Say Goodbye (A Comme Amour)	06/04/1968	103	CB
Connie Francis	Why Say Goodbye (A Comme Amour)	27/04/1968	132	BB
Connie Francis	Should I Tie A Yellow RiBBon Round The Ole Oak Tree? "The	30/06/1973	104	BB
Connie Smith	Once A Day	03/10/1964	101	BB
Connie Smith	Then And Only Then	16/01/1965	116	BB
Connie Smith	I Can't Remember	24/04/1965	130	BB
Connie Smith	Just One Time	26/06/1971	119	BB
Connie Stevens	The Greenwood Tree	23/09/1961	148	CB
Connie Stevens	Hey, Good Lookin'	10/11/1962	134	CB
Connie Stevens	Hey, Good Lookin'	24/11/1962	104	BB
Connie Stevens With The Buddy Cole Trio	Little Sister*	20/02/1960	102	CB
Conway Twitty	Star Spangled Heaven	09/01/1960	104	CB
Conway Twitty	She's Mine	02/07/1960	119	CB
Conway Twitty	What A Dream	12/09/1960	106	BB
Conway Twitty	A Million Teardrops	03/06/1961	106	CB
Conway Twitty	Sweet Sorrow	23/09/1961	134	CB
Conway Twitty	Sweet Sorrow	16/10/1961	107	BB
Conway Twitty	Portrait Of A Fool	30/12/1961	113	CB
Conway Twitty	Comfy 'N Cozy	12/05/1962	133	CB
Conway Twitty	Unchained Melody	25/08/1962	138	CB
Conway Twitty	The Pickup	29/12/1962	136	CB
Conway Twitty	How Much More Can She Stand	17/04/1971	105	BB
Conway Twitty	I Wonder What She'll Think About Me Leaving	31/07/1971	112	BB
Conway Twitty	(Lost Her Love) On Our Last Date	27/05/1972	112	BB
Cook E. Jarr	Red Balloon	01/02/1969	113	CB
Cookie & The Cupcakes	Matilda Has Finally Come Back	04/02/1961	109	CB
Copper N' Brass	Does Anybody Know What Time It Is	14/03/1970	103	BB
Copper N' Brass	Does Anybody Know What Time It Is	21/03/1970	102	CB
Cornbread & Biscuits	The Big Time Spender, Parts 1 & 2	22/10/1960	109	CB
Cornbread & Jerry	Lil' Ole Me	13/05/1961	138	CB

Cornelius Brothers & Sister Rose	I Just Can't Stop Loving You	06/10/1973	104	BB
Cornelius Brothers & Sister Rose	Big Time Lover	09/02/1974	109	CB
Cornelius Brothers & Sister Rose	Since I Found My Baby	04/01/1975	105	CB
Cornell Blakely	You Ain't Gonna Find	04/09/1961	116	BB
Cornerstone	Holly Go Softly	21/03/1970	104	BB
Cory Wells	Starlight	11/02/1978	105	CB
Count Basie & His Orchestra	The Basie Twist	02/12/1961	143	CB
Count Five	Peace Of Mind	10/12/1966	125	BB
Country Funk	Apart Of Me	22/08/1970	117	CB
Country Joe & The Fish	Not So Sweet Martha Lorraine	24/06/1967	103	CB
Country Joe & The Fish	Who Am I	10/02/1968	147	CB
Country Joe & The Fish	Here I Go Again	21/06/1969	103	CB
Country Joe And The Fish	Who Am I	03/02/1968	114	BB
Country Joe And The Fish	Here I Go Again	12/07/1969	106	BB
Country Joe Mcdonald	Breakfast For Two	22/11/1975	103	CB
Country Stone	To Love You	27/12/1969	112	CB
Country Stone	To Love You	10/01/1970	103	BB
Country Store	Days Of Icy Fingers	19/09/1970	117	CB
Coyote Mccloud	Nitty Gritty Rock And Roll	21/08/1976	109	CB
Cozy Cole	Big Noise From Winnetka Part I	01/12/1962	105	CB
Cozy Cole	Big Noise From Winnetka Part I	26/01/1963	121	BB
CraBBy Appleton	Lucy	10/10/1970	103	CB
CraBBy Appleton	Lucy	07/11/1970	114	BB
Crack The Sky	(We Don't Want Your Money) We Want Mine	11/12/1976	108	BB
Craig Ruhnke	Summer Girl	24/08/1974	107	BB
Crazy Elephant	Sunshine, Red Wine	28/06/1969	104	BB
Crazy Elephant	Gimme Some More	13/09/1969	116	BB
Crazy Elephant	Gimme Some More	20/09/1969	135	CB
Crazy Elephant	There Ain't No Umbopo	18/04/1970	135	CB
Crazy Joe And The Variable Speed Band	Eugene	21/02/1981	105	BB

Crazy Paving	Anytime Sunshine	06/03/1971	126	CB
Crazy Paving	Anytime Sunshine	13/03/1971	103	BB
Cream	I Feel Free	16/12/1967	116	BB
Creative Source	You Can't Hide Love	13/10/1973	114	BB
Creative Source	You're Too Good To Be True	19/01/1974	108	BB
Crème Caramel	My Idea	25/10/1969	109	CB
Crème Caramel	My Idea	25/10/1969	128	BB
Crispian St. Peters	Your Ever Changin' Mind	26/11/1966	106	BB
Crispian St. Peters	Your Ever Changin' Mind	03/12/1966	116	CB
Crispian St. Peters	Look Into My Teardrops	05/10/1968	133	BB
Crossroads	Here I Stand	05/09/1970	115	BB
Crow	Time To Make A Turn	09/08/1969	123	BB
Crow	Slow Down	21/03/1970	103	BB
Crow	Watching Can Waste Up The Time	27/02/1971	110	CB
Crow	Something In Your Blood	03/07/1971	115	CB
Crowfoot	California Rock'n Roll	06/06/1970	133	CB
Crown Heights Affair	You Gave Me Love	19/04/1980	1102	CB
Crown Heights Affair	You Gave Me Love	26/04/1980	102	BB
Cryan' Shames	First Train To California	01/03/1969	103	CB
Crystal Gayle	I'll Get Over You	19/06/1976	109	CB
Crystal Grass	Crystal World	26/04/1975	102	BB
Curly Putman	My Elusive Dreams	08/07/1967	134	BB
Curly Putman	My Elusive Dreams	15/07/1967	149	CB
Curtis Knight	That's Why	28/08/1961	109	BB
Curtis Lee	Pledge Of Love	06/02/1961	110	BB
Curtis Lee	Just Another Fool	10/03/1962	112	CB
Curtis Lee	Just Another Fool	07/04/1962	110	BB
Curtis Mayfield	We Got To Have Peace	19/02/1972	115	BB
Curtis Mayfield	She Don't Let Nobody (But Me)	31/10/1981	103	BB
Cy Coleman	Russian Roulette	03/01/1970	138	CB

Cy Coleman	Chloe	31/01/1976	107	CB
Cymande	Bra	30/06/1973	102	BB
Cynthia Manley	Back In My Arms Again	15/01/1983	109	BB
D.A.	Ready "N" Steady	16/06/1979	102	BB
Dale & Grace	Darling It's Wonderful	01/08/1964	114	BB
Dale & Grace	Cool Water	20/02/1965	123	CB
Dale Hawkins	Liza Jane	17/10/1959	112	CB
Dallas	Take You Where The Music's Playing	04/09/1971	114	CB
Dallas Frazier	Just A Little Bit Of You	02/07/1966	108	BB
Dallas Frazier	Just A Little Bit Of You	02/07/1966	119	CB
Dallas Frazier	The Conspiracy Of Homer Jones	15/03/1969	120	BB
Damita Jo	Dance With A Dolly (With A Hole In Her Stocking)	02/10/1961	105	BB
Damita Jo	Dance With A Dolly (With A Hole In Her Stocking)	07/10/1961	123	CB
Damita Jo	Silver Dollar	27/03/1965	104	CB
Damita Jo	Tomorrow Night	27/03/1965	124	BB
Damita Jo	Gotta Travel On	08/05/1965	119	BB
Damita Jo Featuring The Mike Stewart Singers	Do What You Want	15/04/1961	114	CB
Damita Jo With The Merry Melody Singers	Tennessee Waltz	04/08/1962	128	CB
Damnation Of Adam Blessing	Morning Dew	06/12/1969	109	CB
Damnation Of Adam Blessing	Back To The River	21/11/1970	102	BB
Damon Shawn	Feel The Need	22/04/1972	105	BB
Damon Shawn	Feel The Need	29/04/1972	103	CB
Dan Fogelberg	Next Time	29/11/1975	116	CB
Dan Fogelberg	Below The Surface	21/02/1976	115	CB
Dan Hartman	Relight My Fire	08/03/1980	104	BB
Dan Hartman	All I Need	26/09/1981	110	BB
Dan Seals	Can't Get You Out Of My Mind	03/04/1982	110	BB
Daniel Boone	Sunshine Lover	17/03/1973	112	CB
Daniel Boone	Run Tell The People	31/05/1975	117	CB
Daniel Moore	Follow The Spirit	16/02/1974	120	CB

Danny & The Juniors	Cha Cha Go Go (Chicago Cha Cha)	06/05/1961	114	CB
Danny & The Juniors	The Charleston Fish	09/09/1961	123	CB
Danny & The Juniors With Freddy Cannon	Twistin' All Night Long	09/12/1961	106	CB
Danny Bonaduce	Dreamland	10/02/1973	106	CB
Danny Davis & The Nashville Brass	Wabash Cannon Ball	03/01/1970	107	CB
Danny Davis And The Nashville Brass	Wabash Cannon Ball	24/01/1970	131	BB
Danny Hutton	Big Bright Eyes	01/01/1966	112	CB
Danny Hutton	Big Bright Eyes	08/01/1966	102	BB
Danny Hutton	Funny How Love Can Be	21/05/1966	133	CB
Danny Hutton	Funny How Love Can Be	28/05/1966	120	BB
Danny Kaye	D-O-D-G-E-R-S Song (Oh, Really? No, O'malley)	15/09/1962	113	CB
Danny Michaels	Angel Of The Morning	27/01/1968	145	CB
Danny O'keefe	The Road	30/12/1972	102	BB
Danny O'keefe	The Road	20/01/1973	120	CB
Danny O'keefe	Angel Spread Your Wings	20/10/1973	110	BB
Danny Peppermint	One More Time	03/02/1962	148	CB
Danny Peppermint & The Jumping Jacks	The Peppermint Twist	18/11/1961	115	CB
Danny Valentino	(You Gotta Be A) Music Man	16/01/1960	123	CB
Danny White	Kiss Tomorrow Goodbye	10/11/1962	120	BB
Danny White	Kiss Tomorrow Goodbye	12/01/1963	123	CB
Danny White	Taking Inventory	26/11/1966	113	CB
Danny Williams	More*	22/06/1963	113	CB
Danny Williams	More (From The Film "Mondo Cane)	27/06/1964	117	CB
Danny Williams	More	04/07/1964	110	BB
Danté And The Evergreens	What Are You Doing New Year's Eve	31/12/1960	107	BB
Danté And The Evergreens	Yeah Baby	07/01/1961	112	CB
Danté And The Evergreens	Yeah Baby (b-side)	09/01/1961	104	BB
Darin D. Anna	We Were Lovers	27/02/1965	115	CB
Darin D. Anna	Bimbo	29/05/1965	136	CB
Darlene Mccrea	You	24/08/1959	103	BB

Darrell Banks	Here Comes The Tears	01/04/1967	124	BB
Darrow Fletcher	My Young Misery	23/04/1966	129	CB
Daryl Hall & John Oates	Alone Too Long	29/11/1975	123	CB
Daryl Hall & John Oates	Don't Change	24/12/1977	103	CB
Daryl Hall & John Oates	Who Said The World Was Fair	22/03/1980	110	BB
Das Jochen Brauer - Sextett	Sombrero	07/10/1961	132	CB
Dave "Baby" Cortez	Piano Shuffle	26/10/1959	103	BB
Dave "Baby" Cortez	Hurricane	12/11/1960	111	CB
Dave "Baby" Cortez	Fiesta	13/10/1962	111	CB
Dave "Baby" Cortez	Hot Cakes! 1st Serving	20/04/1963	125	CB
Dave "Baby" Cortez	Popping Popcorn	02/01/1965	132	BB
Dave "Baby" Cortez	Tweetie Pie	02/10/1965	122	CB
Dave "Baby" Cortez	Tweetie Pie	02/10/1965	135	BB
Dave & Ansell Collins	Monkey Spanner	18/09/1971	109	CB
Dave Appell And His Orchestra	Happy Jose	13/01/1962	104	BB
Dave Clark Five	I'm Thinking	17/04/1965	128	BB
Dave Clark Five	Look Before You Leap	04/06/1966	101	BB
Dave Clark Five	Please Stay	18/05/1968	115	BB
Dave Clark Five	Paradise (Is Half As Nice)	24/05/1969	104	CB
Dave Dee, Dozy, Beaky, Mick & Tich	The Legend Of Xanadu	30/03/1968	113	CB
Dave Dee, Dozy, Beaky, Mick And Tich	Bend It	31/12/1966	110	BB
Dave Dee, Dozy, Beaky, Mick And Tich	The Legend Of Xanadu	13/04/1968	123	BB
Dave Dudley	Under Cover Of The Night	06/10/1962	141	CB
Dave Dudley	Cowboy Boots	21/09/1963	106	CB
Dave Dudley	Last Day In The Mines	14/12/1963	125	BB
Dave Dudley	Last Day In The Mines	21/12/1963	138	CB
Dave Dudley	Truck Drivin' Son-Of-A-Gun	07/08/1965	106	CB
Dave Dudley	Truck Drivin' Son-Of-A-Gun	07/08/1965	125	BB
Dave Dudley	Viet Nam Blues	02/04/1966	127	BB
Dave Edmunds	Blue Monday	04/09/1971	104	BB

Dave Edmunds	Information	24/09/1983	106	BB
Dave Ford & The Hollywood Flames	Elizabeth	25/08/1962	120	CB
Dave Mason	Waitin' On You	13/02/1971	122	CB
Dave Mason	A Heartache, A Shadow, A Lifetime (I'll Be Home)	22/01/1972	117	CB
Dave Mason	To Be Free	29/04/1972	121	BB
Dave Mason	Bring It On Home To Me	28/12/1974	119	CB
Dave York & The Beachcombers	(Let's Have A) Beach Party	01/09/1962	119	CB
David & Jimmy Ruffin	When My Love Hand Comes Down	22/05/1971	104	CB
David & Jonathan	Speak Her Name	23/04/1966	109	BB
David & Jonathan	Speak Her Name	23/04/1966	138	CB
David & Jonathan	Lovers Of The World Unite	20/08/1966	138	CB
David & Jonathan	She's Leaving Home	24/06/1967	123	BB
David Allan Coe	Longhaired Redneck	03/01/1976	117	CB
David Bowie	Space Oddity	16/08/1969	124	BB
David Bowie	Let's Spend The Night Together	25/08/1973	109	BB
David Bowie	Changes	16/03/1974	119	CB
David Bowie	Tvc 15	05/06/1976	101	CB
David Bowie	D.J.	28/07/1979	106	BB
David Bowie	Ashes To Ashes	25/10/1980	101	BB
David Box	Little Lonely Summer Girl	22/08/1964	112	CB
David Bromberg	Sharon	24/02/1973	117	BB
David Carroll	Waltzing Matilda	04/01/1960	112	BB
David Carroll & His Orchestra	Mexican Joe	04/11/1961	133	CB
David Carroll And His Orchestra	Big Girls Don't Cry Limbo	22/12/1962	102	BB
David Cassidy	Get It Up For Love	09/08/1975	108	CB
David Cassidy	Gettin' It In The Street	04/12/1976	105	BB
David Clayton Thomas	Sing A Song	01/04/1972	112	BB
David Clayton-Thomas	Anytime...Babe	20/07/1974	107	CB
David Crosby	Orleans	31/07/1971	101	CB
David Crosby/Graham Nash	Take The Money And Run	28/02/1976	103	CB

David Crosby/Graham Nash	Spotlight	09/10/1976	109	BB
David Essex	America	07/09/1974	101	BB
David Essex	America	07/09/1974	106	CB
David Essex	Gonna Make You A Star	07/12/1974	105	BB
David Essex	Rolling Stone	25/10/1975	120	CB
David Frizzell & Shelly West	You're The Reason God Made Oklahoma	25/04/1981	I101	CB
David Houston	Mountain Of Love	02/11/1963	147	CB
David Houston	Mountain Of Love	23/11/1963	132	BB
David Houston	Livin' In A House Full Of Love	04/09/1965	117	BB
David Houston	Where Could I Go? (But To Her)	10/12/1966	133	BB
David Houston	A Loser's Cathedral (b-side)	31/12/1966	135	BB
David Huff	Glory Hallelujah	25/08/1973	125	CB
David Idema	House On Holly Road	06/05/1972	116	CB
David Martin	Can't Smile Without You	25/10/1975	114	CB
David Matthews	Theme From Star Wars	16/07/1977	102	BB
David Matthews	Theme From Star Wars	23/07/1977	103	CB
David Mccallum	Communication	19/02/1966	117	BB
David Mcwilliams	Days Of Pearly Spencer	30/03/1968	122	CB
David Mcwilliams	Days Of Pearly Spencer	01/06/1968	134	BB
David Parton	Isn't She Lovely	23/04/1977	105	BB
David Porter	Can't See You When I Want To	06/06/1970	105	BB
David Rockingham Trio	Midnight	07/03/1964	119	BB
David Rose & His Orchestra	Lefty Louie	27/06/1964	142	CB
David Ruffin	Don't Stop Loving Me	20/02/1971	103	CB
David Ruffin	Don't Stop Loving Me	06/03/1971	112	BB
David Ruffin	Just Let Me Hold You For A Night	01/10/1977	108	BB
David Sanborn	Love & Happiness	23/03/1985	103	BB
David Shire	Manhattan Skyline	17/06/1978	105	CB
David T. Walker	My Baby Loves Me	20/12/1969	128	BB
David T. Walker	Love Vibrations	09/01/1971	117	BB

David T. Walker	Love Vibrations	09/01/1971	118	CB
David T. Walker	Hot Fun In The Summertime	01/07/1972	104	BB
David T. Walker	Press On	22/09/1973	118	CB
David Thorne	The Alley Cat Song	27/10/1962	104	CB
David Werner	What's Right	06/10/1979	104	BB
Davie Allan & The Arrows	Theme From The Wild Angels	29/10/1966	112	CB
Davie Allen & The Arrows	Devil's Angels	17/06/1967	110	CB
Davy Jones	I Really Love You	23/10/1971	107	BB
Dazz Band	Invitation To Love	04/04/1981	109	BB
Dazz Band	Heartbeat	23/03/1985	110	BB
Dean & Jean	Thread Your Needle	20/06/1964	114	CB
Dean And Jean	Thread Your Needle	13/06/1964	123	BB
Dean Barlow	Third Window From The Right	24/02/1962	118	CB
Dean Martin	Love Me, My Love	18/01/1960	107	BB
Dean Martin	Love Me, My Love	30/01/1960	110	CB
Dean Martin	Face In A Crowd*	16/03/1963	136	CB
Dean Martin	Face In A Crowd	30/03/1963	128	BB
Dean Martin	Every Minute Every Hour	10/10/1964	123	BB
Dean Martin	Every Minute Every Hour	10/10/1964	140	CB
Dean Martin	I'll Be Seeing You	27/02/1965	148	CB
Dean Martin	Bumming Around	21/08/1965	141	CB
Dean Martin	You're The Reason I'm In Love	06/11/1965	136	CB
Dean Martin	Bouquet Of Roses	07/05/1966	116	CB
Dean Martin	That Old Time Feelin'	10/08/1968	104	BB
Dean Martin	April Again (b-side)	10/08/1968	105	BB
Dean Martin	5 Card Stud	14/09/1968	107	BB
Dean Martin	Gentle On My Mind	22/02/1969	103	BB
Dean Martin	One Cup Of Happiness (And One Peace Of Mind)	25/10/1969	107	BB
Dean Martin	Come On Down	07/03/1970	121	CB
Dean Martin	For The Love Of A Woman	23/05/1970	122	CB

Dean Martin	For The Love Of A Woman	04/07/1970	123	BB
Dean Martin	My Woman, My Woman, My Wife	01/08/1970	110	BB
Dean Martin	Detroit City	31/10/1970	101	BB
Dean Martin	Georgia Sunshine	02/01/1971	117	CB
Dean Martin	Georgia Sunshine	23/01/1971	118	BB
Dean Martin	She's A Little Bit Country	01/05/1971	121	CB
Dean Martin	What's Yesterday	29/01/1972	115	CB
Dean Parrish	Turn On Your Lovelight	29/10/1966	120	CB
Deardorff & Joseph	Never Have To Say Goodbye Again	19/03/1977	109	BB
DeBBie Campbell	Please Tell Him That I Said Hello	26/07/1975	112	CB
DeBBie Dawn	Hands	28/07/1973	102	CB
DeBBie Dean	Don't Let Him Shop Around	18/02/1961	103	CB
DeBBie Harry	Rush, Rush	21/01/1984	105	BB
DeBBie Jacobs	Don't You Want My Love	29/09/1979	106	BB
DeBBie Rollins	He Really Loves Me	08/02/1964	136	CB
DeBBie Taylor	Check Yourself	30/03/1968	127	CB
DeBBy Boone	God Knows	17/06/1978	107	CB
December's Children	Backwards And Forwards	18/05/1968	123	BB
Dee Clark	Blues Get Off My Shoulder	30/11/1959	109	BB
Dee Clark	Blues Get Off My Shoulder	12/12/1959	118	CB
Dee Clark	Because I Love You	09/01/1961	105	BB
Dee Clark	Don't Walk Away From Me	30/10/1961	104	BB
Dee Clark	Don't Walk Away From Me	25/11/1961	107	CB
Dee Clark	You're Telling Our Secrets	25/11/1961	136	CB
Dee Clark	You Are Like The Wind	31/03/1962	139	CB
Dee Clark	I'm A Soldier Boy	02/03/1963	133	CB
Dee Clark	Shook Up Over You	16/03/1963	125	BB
Dee Clark	Nobody But Me	17/08/1963	148	CB
Dee Clark	Come Closer	23/05/1964	140	CB
Dee Clark	Heartbreak	22/08/1964	119	BB

Dee Clark	Heartbreak	29/08/1964	122	CB
Dee Clark	T.C.B.	20/03/1965	130	CB
Dee Clark	T.C.B. (Take Care Off Business)	10/04/1965	132	BB
Dee Dee Sharp	Willyam, Willyam	01/02/1964	102	CB
Dee Dee Sharp	Never Pick A Pretty Boy	25/07/1964	143	CB
Dee Dee Sharp	Never Pick A Pretty Boy	08/08/1964	131	BB
Dee Dee Sharp	Good	10/10/1964	142	CB
Dee Dee Sharp	It's A Funny Situation	19/03/1966	126	BB
Dee Dee Sharp	What Kind Of Lady	05/10/1968	149	CB
Dee Dee Warwick	You're No Good	09/11/1963	117	BB
Dee Dee Warwick	Do It With All Your Heart	13/03/1965	124	BB
Dee Dee Warwick	Gotta Get A Hold Of Myself	30/10/1965	141	CB
Dee Dee Warwick	That's Not Love	31/05/1969	106	BB
Dee Dee Warwick	It's Not Fair	31/05/1969	148	CB
Dee Dee Warwick	Ring Of Bright Water	12/07/1969	105	CB
Dee Dee Warwick	Ring Of Bright Water	19/07/1969	113	BB
Dee Dee Warwick	I Who Have Nothing	11/10/1969	107	CB
Dee Dee Warwick	Cold Night In Georgia	13/02/1971	118	CB
Dee Edwards	Too Careless With My Love	20/11/1965	139	CB
Dee Irwin & Mamie Galore	By The Time I Get To Phoenix/I Say A Little Prayer (Medley)	14/12/1968	114	BB
Dee Mullins	The Continuing Story Of Harper Valley P.T.A.	02/11/1968	117	CB
Dee Mullins	The Continuing Story Of Harper Valley P.T.A.	23/11/1968	111	BB
Deep Purple	Emmaretta	22/03/1969	128	BB
Deep Purple	Hallelujah (I Am The Preacher)	02/08/1969	108	BB
Deep Purple	Hallelujah (I Am The Preacher)	02/08/1969	123	CB
Deep Purple	Fireball	30/10/1971	120	CB
Deep Purple	Burn	01/06/1974	105	BB
Deep Purple	Burn	08/06/1974	115	CB
Def Leppard	Rock Brigade	05/07/1980	106	BB
Defranco Family Featuring Tony Defranco	Write Me A Letter	28/09/1974	104	BB

Defranco Family Featuring Tony Defranco	Write Me A Letter	05/10/1974	120	CB
Del Shannon	Ginny In The Mirror	10/03/1962	123	CB
Del Shannon	I Won't Be There	17/03/1962	113	BB
Del Shannon	Ginny In The Mirror (b-side)	17/03/1962	117	BB
Del Shannon	Mary Jane	29/02/1964	124	CB
Del Shannon	That's The Way Love Is	14/03/1964	133	BB
Del Shannon	That's The Way Love Is	21/03/1964	122	CB
Del Shannon	Move It On Over	21/08/1965	121	CB
Del Shannon	Move It On Over	28/08/1965	128	BB
Del Shannon	Under My Thumb	10/09/1966	128	BB
Del Shannon	She	11/02/1967	131	BB
Del Shannon	Runaway [Live]	09/09/1967	112	BB
Del Shannon	Runaway (Live)	23/09/1967	105	CB
Del Shannon	Comin' Back To Me	21/06/1969	127	BB
Delaney & Bonnie	Where There's A Will There's A Way	06/05/1972	110	CB
Delaney & Bonnie & Friends	Free The People	30/05/1970	101	CB
Delaney & Bonnie & Friends	They Call It Rock & Roll Music	24/10/1970	119	BB
Delaney Bramlett	Guess I Must Be Dreamin'	20/05/1967	126	CB
Delbert Mcclinton	Sandy Beaches	21/11/1981	101	BB
Delfonics	Lying To Myself	08/06/1974	118	CB
Delia Gartrell	See What You Done, Done (Hymn #9)	15/01/1972	120	CB
Delia Gartrell	See What You've Done, Done (Hymn #9)	22/01/1972	101	BB
Della Humphrey	Don't Make The Good Girls Go Bad	02/11/1968	135	CB
Della Reese	Years From Now	21/11/1959	115	CB
Della Reese	In The Still Of The Night	21/11/1959	116	CB
Della Reese	Won'cha Come Home, Bill Bailey	08/04/1961	105	CB
Della Reese	A Far Far Better Thing	05/08/1961	101	CB
Della Reese	A Far Far Better Thing	14/08/1961	115	BB
Della Reese	More (Theme From "Mondo Cane")*	15/06/1963	113	CB
Della Reese	And That Reminds Me	02/10/1965	126	CB

Della Reese	Compared To What (b-side)	03/01/1970	128	BB
Della Reese	Games People Play	10/01/1970	118	CB
Della Reese	Games People Play	10/01/1970	121	BB
Della Reese	The Troublemaker	10/04/1971	110	CB
Della Reese With The BoBBy Bryant Quintet	It Was A Very Good Year	24/09/1966	136	CB
Demetriss Tapp	Lipstick Paint A Smile On Me	02/11/1963	116	CB
Demetriss Tapp	Lipstick Paint A Smile On Me	16/11/1963	112	BB
Deni Lynn	The Lights Of Night	13/09/1969	132	CB
Deniece Williams	That's What Friends Are For	13/08/1977	103	BB
Deniece Williams	I Found Love	27/10/1979	105	BB
Deniece Williams	Waiting By The Hotline	31/07/1982	103	BB
Deniece Williams	Do What You Feel	25/06/1983	102	BB
Denise Lasalle	Don't Nobody Live Here (By The Name Of Fool)	02/02/1974	116	CB
Denise Lasalle	Married, But Not To Each Other	24/04/1976	101	CB
Denise Lasalle	Married, But Not To Each Other	19/06/1976	102	BB
Denise Mccann	Tattoo Man	09/04/1977	106	BB
Dennis Regor	Toys In The Attic	12/10/1963	115	BB
Dennis Regor & Paulette Sisters	Toys In The Attic	28/09/1963	137	CB
Dennis Yost & The Classics Iv	God Knows I Loved Her	18/07/1970	128	BB
Dennis Yost & The Classics Iv	It's Time For Love	17/04/1971	111	CB
Denny Doherty	You'll Never Know	01/06/1974	114	CB
Denny Laine	It's So Easy/Listen To Me	06/11/1976	108	BB
Denny Provisor	Mickey Mouse	18/07/1964	138	CB
Denny Reed	A Teenager Feels It Too	20/08/1960	108	CB
Deodato/Airto	Do It Again (Live)	06/04/1974	105	CB
Deon Jackson	I Can't Do Without You	01/10/1966	111	BB
Deon Jackson	Ooh Baby	25/11/1967	101	CB
Derek & The Dominos	Why Does Love Got To Be So Bad	17/03/1973	106	CB
Derek & The Dominos	Why Does Love Got To Be So Sad	31/03/1973	120	BB
Derek Martin	Your Daddy Wants His Baby Back	23/10/1965	135	CB

Derik Roberts	There Won't Be Any Snow (Christmas In The Jungle)	15/01/1966	105	BB
Desmond Dekker & The Aces	You Can Get It If You Really Want	21/11/1970	103	BB
Detroit Emeralds	Feel The Need In Me	11/11/1972	110	BB
Detroit Emeralds	You're Gettin' A Little Too Smart	14/07/1973	101	BB
Detroit Featuring Mitch Ryder	Rock 'N' Roll	01/01/1972	107	BB
Devo	Freedom Of Choice	20/12/1980	103	BB
Devo	Beautiful World	14/11/1981	102	BB
Devo	Through Being Cool	24/04/1982	107	BB
Devo	Peek • A • Boo!	06/11/1982	106	BB
Devo	That's Good	15/01/1983	104	BB
Devotions	Rip Van Winkle	14/10/1961	145	CB
Dey & Knight	I'm Gonna Love You Tomorrow	25/12/1965	134	CB
Diamond Head	If That's The Way You Want It	05/05/1973	106	BB
Diamond Reo	Rock And Roll Till I Die	10/05/1975	115	CB
Diamond Reo	Work Hard Labor	16/08/1975	108	BB
Diana Ross	To Love Again	21/03/1981	l103	CB
Diana Ross	My Old Piano	16/01/1982	109	BB
Diana Trask	I Fall To Pieces	06/12/1969	114	BB
Diana Trask	Lean It All On Me	01/06/1974	101	BB
Diane Emond	I Wanna Be Your Lover	02/03/1963	140	CB
Diane Gilland	The Serenade That We Played	16/08/1975	116	CB
Diane Ray	Snow Man	04/01/1964	112	CB
Diane Renay	Tender	01/06/1963	143	CB
Diane Renay	Growin' Up Too Fast	20/06/1964	124	BB
Diane Renay	It's In Your Hands	22/08/1964	131	BB
Diane Renay	Watch Out, Sally!	28/11/1964	101	BB
Dick & Deedee	Life's Just A Play	21/07/1962	142	CB
Dick & Deedee	The River Took My Baby	24/11/1962	138	CB
Dick & Deedee	Love Is A Once In A Lifetime Thing	22/06/1963	103	BB
Dick & Deedee	Love Is A Once In A Lifetime Thing	22/06/1963	121	CB

Dick & Deedee	Where Did The Good Times Go	14/09/1963	137	CB
Dick & Deedee	All My Trials	08/02/1964	115	CB
Dick & Deedee	Some Things Just Stick In Your Mind	15/05/1965	141	CB
Dick Caruso	Pretty Little Dancin' Doll	17/09/1960	125	CB
Dick Dale	The Wedge	28/12/1963	122	CB
Dick Dale & The Del-Tones	Miserlou	29/12/1962	102	CB
Dick Dale & The Del-Tones	King Of The Surf Guitar	11/05/1963	110	CB
Dick Dale And The Del-Tones	King Of The Surf Guitar	08/06/1963	124	BB
Dick Dodd	Little Sister	30/11/1968	136	CB
Dick Feller	Biff, The Friendly Purple Bear	24/11/1973	105	CB
Dick Feller	Biff, The Friendly Purple Bear	29/12/1973	101	BB
Dick Feller	The Credit Card Song	23/11/1974	105	BB
Dick Haiman (At The Organ) & The Dial Tones	Blue Moon Of Kentucky	07/10/1961	106	CB
Dick Hyman	Aquarius (b-side)	16/08/1969	126	BB
Dick Hyman	Green Onions	06/09/1969	109	BB
Dick Hyman & "The Group"	In The Heat Of The Night	24/02/1968	105	CB
Dick Hyman And "The Group"	In The Heat Of The Night	09/03/1968	106	BB
Dick Jacobs And His Orchestra	Theme From "Come September"	10/07/1961	104	BB
Dick Jensen	Jealous Feeling	29/11/1969	120	CB
Dick Lee	I Never Knew (Till Now)	10/09/1960	113	CB
Dick Lee	Oh Mein Papa	25/03/1961	134	CB
Dick Lee	One (Two Hearts Are One)	08/04/1967	135	CB
Dick Lee The Golden Boy	All I Want Is A Chance	19/08/1961	143	CB
Dick Miles	The Last Goodbye	30/03/1968	114	BB
Dick Roman	Please Remember Me	13/10/1962	126	CB
Dick Roman	Changing World	23/02/1963	146	CB
Dick Stewart	I Believe	19/01/1963	126	CB
Dick Van Dyke With The Jack Halloran Singers	Chim Chim Cheree	22/05/1965	123	BB
Dick Whittinghill	The Square	10/04/1965	129	CB
Dickey Lee	The Day The Saw-Mill Closed Down	21/09/1963	104	BB

Dickey Lee	The Day The Saw-Mill Closed Down	28/09/1963	124	CB
Dickey Lee	Big Brother	21/11/1964	101	BB
Dickey Lee	Red, Green, Yellow And Blue	27/01/1968	107	BB
Dickey Lee	Red, Green, Yellow And Blue	27/01/1968	108	CB
Dickie Goodman	Berlin Top Ten	23/10/1961	116	BB
Dickie Goodman	Santa And The Touchables	23/12/1961	123	CB
Dickie Goodman	Senate Hearing	02/11/1963	116	BB
Dickie Goodman	The Purple People Eater	15/09/1973	119	BB
Diesel	Goin' Back To China	16/01/1982	105	BB
Dinah Shore	I Ain't Down Yet	26/12/1960	103	BB
Dinah Shore	I Ain't Down Yet	21/01/1961	105	CB
Dinah Washington	Do You Want It That Way	11/03/1961	121	CB
Dinah Washington	Such A Night	21/04/1962	109	CB
Dinah Washington	I Want To Be Loved	04/08/1962	109	CB
Dinah Washington	Am I Blue	04/08/1962	110	CB
Dinah Washington	I Wouldn't Know (What To Do)	18/08/1962	112	CB
Dinah Washington	Cold, Cold Heart	17/11/1962	140	CB
Dinah Washington	Soulville	04/05/1963	126	CB
Dinah Washington	A Stranger On Earth	25/01/1964	136	CB
Dino, Desi & Billy	If You're Thinkin' What I'm Thinkin'	25/02/1967	128	BB
Dino, Desi & Billy	If You're Thinkin' What I'm Thinkin'	04/03/1967	117	CB
Dino, Desi & Billy	Kitty Doyle	16/09/1967	108	BB
Dion	Somebody Nobody Wants	03/07/1961	103	BB
Dion	Little Girl	10/11/1962	107	CB
Dion	King Without A Queen	22/06/1963	143	CB
Dion	Lonely World	24/08/1963	101	BB
Dion	Lonely World	31/08/1963	136	CB
Dion	Shout	11/04/1964	108	BB
Dion	Sanctuary	11/12/1971	103	BB
Dion	Born To Be With You	05/06/1976	108	BB

Dion	Midtown American Main Street Gang	17/06/1978	102	CB
Dion Di Muci	I'm The Hoochie Cooche Man	07/03/1964	113	BB
Dion Di Muci	Sweet, Sweet Baby	30/01/1965	109	CB
Dionne Warwick	Make The Music Play	13/07/1963	114	CB
Dionne Warwick	Who Can I Turn To	06/03/1965	110	CB
Dionne Warwick	Only Love Can Break A Heart	16/04/1977	109	BB
Dionne Warwick	All The Love In The World	16/07/1983	101	BB
Dionne Warwicke	Amanda	07/08/1971	101	CB
Dionne Warwicke	The Love Of My Man	04/12/1971	117	CB
Dionne Warwicke	The Love Of My Man	11/12/1971	107	BB
Dionne Warwicke	Raindrops Keep Falling On My Head	06/05/1972	108	CB
Dionne Warwicke	I'm Your Puppet	26/08/1972	113	BB
Dionne Warwicke	I Think You Need Love	27/01/1973	103	CB
Dionne Warwicke	Take It From Me	17/05/1975	110	CB
Dire Straits	Twisting By The Pool	16/04/1983	105	BB
Dixie Dregs	Take It Off The Top	24/06/1978	102	BB
Dobie Gray	Look At Me	22/12/1962	114	CB
Dobie Gray	In Hollywood	29/05/1965	103	CB
Dobie Gray	Rose Garden	03/05/1969	119	BB
Dobie Gray	Good Old Song	10/11/1973	104	CB
Dobie Gray	Good Old Song	01/12/1973	103	BB
Dobie Gray	Lovin' The Easy Way	02/03/1974	110	CB
Dobie Gray	Watch Out For Lucy	21/09/1974	107	BB
Dobie Gray	If Love Must Go	21/02/1976	102	CB
Dobie Gray	Find 'EM, Fool 'EM & Forget 'EM	18/09/1976	106	CB
Doc Severinsen	The Last Tango In Paris	24/03/1973	106	BB
Doc Severinsen	The Last Tango In Paris	31/03/1973	118	CB
Doc Severinsen & His Orchestra	It Ain't Necessarily So (From "Porgy And Bess")	15/05/1965	149	CB
Doc Severinsen & His Orchestra	"LOVE Theme" From Is Paris Burning	05/11/1966	139	CB
Dodie Stevens	Miss Lonely Hearts	24/08/1959	111	BB

Dodie Stevens	Steady Eddy	12/12/1959	117	CB
Dodie Stevens	Mairzy Doats	12/12/1959	119	CB
Dodie Stevens	Amigo's Guitar	09/04/1960	123	CB
Dodie Stevens	Turn Around	27/05/1961	129	CB
Dokken	Just Got Lucky	16/02/1985	105	BB
Dolly Parton	Happy, Happy Birthday Baby	11/09/1965	122	CB
Dolly Parton	Happy, Happy Birthday Baby	02/10/1965	108	BB
Dolly Parton	Joshua	09/01/1971	108	BB
Dolly Parton	Love Is Like A Butterfly	14/09/1974	102	CB
Dolly Parton	Love Is Like A Butterfly	28/09/1974	105	BB
Dolly Parton	The Seeker	23/08/1975	105	BB
Dolly Parton	Light Of A Clear Blue Morning	11/06/1977	101	CB
Dolly Parton	The House Of The Rising Sun	05/09/1981	1102	CB
Dolly Parton Willie Nelson	Everything's Beautiful (In It's Own Way)	12/02/1983	102	BB
Don & Alleyne Cole	Something's Got A Hold Of Me [Live]	15/08/1964	117	BB
Don & Juan	Two Fools Are We	05/05/1962	118	CB
Don & Juan	Magic Wand	27/10/1962	103	CB
Don & The Goodtimes	Little Sally Tease	18/09/1965	128	CB
Don & The Goodtimes	Happy And Me	15/07/1967	125	CB
Don Cherry	I Love You Drops	30/04/1966	112	BB
Don Cherry	After I'm Number One	23/07/1966	139	CB
Don Cherry	Married	05/11/1966	145	CB
Don Cherry	There Goes My Everything	07/01/1967	113	BB
Don Cherry	Whippoorwill	10/05/1969	119	CB
Don Cherry	To Think You've Chosen Me	17/05/1969	112	CB
Don Costa & His Orchestra	Sugar Blues	03/03/1962	142	CB
Don Costa & His Orchestra & Chorus	That's The Way With Love (Viggio Nell' Infikito)	06/05/1961	104	CB
Don Costa And His Orchestra	Sugar Blues	24/03/1962	112	BB
Don Costa Orchestra And Chorus	The Misfits	09/01/1961	116	BB
Don Covay	Take This Hurt Off Me	05/12/1964	107	CB

Don Covay	Shingaling '67	11/02/1967	133	BB
Don Covay & Jefferson Lemon Blues Band	Ice Cream Man (The Gimme Game)	17/01/1970	124	CB
Don Covay & The Goodtimers	Please Do Something	19/06/1965	109	CB
Don Covay & The Goodtimers	Watching The Late Late Show	12/03/1966	101	BB
Don Covay & The Goodtimers	Watching The Late Late Show	19/03/1966	140	CB
Don Covay & The Goodtimers	Somebody's Got To Love You	22/10/1966	127	BB
Don Covay & The Goodtimers	40 Days - 40 Nights	10/06/1967	137	CB
Don Downing	Lonely Days, Lonely Nights	21/07/1973	121	CB
Don Everly	Warmin' Up The Band	20/07/1974	110	BB
Don Felder	Bad Girls	10/12/1983	104	BB
Don Gardner	My Baby Likes To Boogaloo	24/12/1966	126	BB
Don Gibson	Big Hearted Me	26/12/1959	119	CB
Don Gibson	The World Is Waiting For The Sunrise	18/02/1961	104	CB
Don Gibson	The World Is Waiting For The Sunrise	06/03/1961	108	BB
Don Gibson	The Same Old Trouble	02/12/1961	150	CB
Don Gibson	I Can Mend Your Broken Heart	12/05/1962	135	CB
Don Gibson	I Can Mend Your Broken Heart	26/05/1962	105	BB
Don Grady With The Windupwatchband	The Children Of St. Monica	17/12/1966	131	CB
Don Grady With The Windupwatchband	The Children Of St. Monica	31/12/1966	132	BB
Don Ho	All That's Left Is The Lemon Tree	06/05/1967	118	CB
Don Imus	Son Of Checkers (The Watergate Case)	23/06/1973	122	CB
Don Kirshner Introducing Joe & Bing	Alaska Bloodline	11/01/1975	105	CB
Don Mclean	Fool's Paradise	09/02/1974	112	CB
Don Mclean	Fool's Paradise	16/02/1974	107	BB
Don Mclean	La La Love You	07/12/1974	111	CB
Don Potter	Just Leave Me Alone	07/12/1974	109	CB
Don Randi	Mexican Pearls	03/04/1965	113	BB
Don Reed	She's My Lady (She's All I Need)	09/03/1974	107	CB
Don Robertson	Tennessee Waltz	15/07/1961	135	CB
Don Robertson	Tennessee Waltz	24/07/1961	117	BB

Don Rondo	The King Of Holiday Island	19/11/1960	108	CB
Don Shirley	Lonesome Road	25/12/1961	116	BB
Don Shirley	Drown In My Own Tears	20/01/1962	127	CB
Don Williams	She Never Knew Me	30/10/1976	103	BB
Don Williams	Some Broken Hearts Never Mend	14/05/1977	108	BB
Don Williams	I'm Just A Country Boy	17/09/1977	110	BB
Don Williams	Tulsa Time	20/01/1979	106	BB
Don Young	She Lets Her Hair Down (Early In The Morning)	20/12/1969	112	CB
Don Young	She Let Her Hair Down (Early In The Morning)	27/12/1969	104	BB
Donald Austin	Crazy Legs	03/02/1973	121	BB
Donald Byrd	Think Twice	14/06/1975	104	BB
Donald Height	Can't Help Falling In Love	11/09/1965	139	CB
Donald Height	My Baby's Gone	26/11/1966	132	CB
Donald Height	Three Hundred And Sixty Five Days	11/02/1967	131	CB
Donna Fargo	U.S. Of A	16/11/1974	102	CB
Donna Fargo	It Do Feel Good	29/03/1975	101	CB
Donna Lynn	My Boyfriend Got A Beatle Haircut	22/02/1964	101	CB
Donna Lynn	Java Jones (Java)	02/05/1964	129	BB
Donnie Brooks	Round Robin	05/12/1960	115	BB
Donnie Brooks	Wishbone	03/06/1961	128	CB
Donnie Elbert	Will You Ever Be Mine	19/03/1960	107	CB
Donnie Elbert	Run Little Girl	30/05/1964	122	CB
Donnie Elbert	Run Little Girl	06/06/1964	130	BB
Donnie Iris	The Rapper (Live)	08/08/1981	I101	CB
Donny Gerrard	(Baby) Don't Let It Mess Your Mind	12/07/1975	104	BB
Donny Hathaway	Little Ghetto Boy (Live)	25/03/1972	104	CB
Donny Hathaway	Little Ghetto Boy [Live]	08/04/1972	109	BB
Donny Hathaway & June Conquest	I Thank You	20/05/1972	105	CB
Donny Hathaway With Margie Joseph	Come Back Charleston Blue	02/09/1972	102	BB
Donny Osmond	Lonely Boy	23/09/1972	114	CB

Donny Osmond	You've Got Me Dangling On A String	10/09/1977	109	BB
Donovan	Summer Day Reflection Song	05/08/1967	135	BB
Donovan	Rock 'N Roll With Me	05/10/1974	116	CB
Dore Alpert	Dina	10/08/1963	105	CB
Doris Day	Anyway The Wind Blows	05/03/1960	109	CB
Doris Day	Please Don't Eat The Daisies	02/05/1960	102	BB
Doris Day	Please Don't Eat The Daisies	07/05/1960	102	CB
Doris Day	A Perfect Understanding	11/07/1960	111	BB
Doris Day	Send Me No Flowers	12/12/1964	135	BB
Doris Duke	Feet Start Walking	30/05/1970	109	BB
Doris Troy	Tomorrow Is Another Day (b-side)	19/10/1963	118	BB
Doris Troy	Tomorrow Is Another Day	19/10/1963	127	CB
Doris Troy	What'cha Gonna Do About It	02/11/1963	102	BB
Doris Troy	What'cha Gonna Do About It	09/11/1963	120	CB
Doris Troy	Please Little Angel	14/03/1964	145	CB
Doris Troy	Please Little Angel	28/03/1964	128	BB
Dorothy Collins	Everything I Have Is Yours	03/10/1959	113	CB
Dorothy Jones	It's Unbearable	02/09/1961	140	CB
Dorothy Moore	With Pen In Hand	14/01/1978	103	CB
Dorothy Moore	With Pen In Hand	21/01/1978	101	BB
Dorothy Morrison	All God's Children Got Soul	20/09/1969	118	CB
Dorothy Morrison	Border Song (Holy Moses)	15/08/1970	114	BB
Dorothy Morrison	Spirit In The Sky	24/10/1970	101	CB
Dorsey Burnette	Big Rock Candy Mountain	04/06/1960	118	CB
Dorsey Burnette	Big Rock Candy Mountain	06/06/1960	102	BB
Dorsey Burnette	The Ghost Of Billy Malloo	05/09/1960	103	BB
Dorsey Burnette	The Ghost Of Billy Malloo	17/09/1960	102	CB
Dorsey Burnette	Great Shakin' Fever	20/05/1961	132	CB
Dorsey Burnette	Feminine Touch	06/11/1961	117	BB
Dorsey Burnette	The Boys Kept Hangin' Around	14/07/1962	127	CB

Dottie And Ray	I Love You Baby	30/01/1965	126	BB
Dotty Clark	It's Been A Long Long Time	02/09/1961	132	CB
Double Exposure	My Love Is Free	26/02/1977	104	BB
Double Exposure	Newsy Neighbors	09/12/1978	107	BB
Doucette	Nobody	11/08/1979	108	BB
Doug GiBBs	I'll Always Have You There	16/09/1972	116	CB
Doug Sahm And Band	(Is Anybody Going To) San Antone	03/03/1973	115	BB
Doug Warren & The Rays	If The World Don't End Tomorrow (I'm Comin' After You)	23/07/1960	101	CB
Doug Warren And The Rays	If The World Don't End Tomorrow (I'm Comin' After You)	11/07/1960	107	BB
Dougie & The Dudes	Settle Down	14/10/1961	139	CB
Dr. Feelgood & The Interns	Right String But The Wrong Yo-Yo	25/08/1962	107	CB
Dr. Hook & The Medicine Show	The Ballad Of Lucy Jordan	19/10/1974	102	CB
Dr. John The Night Tripper	Wash, Mama, Wash	20/06/1970	108	BB
Dreamboy	I Promise (I Do Love You)	17/11/1984	106	BB
Driver	(I've Been Lookin' For) A New Way To Say I Love You	10/09/1977	109	BB
Duane Eddy	Gidget Goes Hawaiian	01/04/1961	135	CB
Duane Eddy	Gidget Goes Hawaiian	03/04/1961	101	BB
Duane Eddy	Guitar Child	02/05/1964	144	CB
Duane Eddy	Water Skiing	04/07/1964	122	CB
Duane Eddy	Freight Train	03/01/1970	110	BB
Duane Eddy & The Rebels	The Avenger	02/12/1961	102	CB
Duane Eddy & The Rebels	Runaway Pony	16/06/1962	141	CB
Duane Eddy And The Rebels	The Avenger	06/01/1962	101	BB
Duane Eddy And The Rebels	The Battle	10/02/1962	114	BB
Duke Jupiter	Rescue Me	04/08/1984	101	BB
Dusk	Treat Me Like A Good Piece Of Candy	27/11/1971	106	BB
Dusty Springfield	Guess Who?	26/12/1964	109	BB
Dusty Springfield	Live It Up (b-side)	09/01/1965	128	BB
Dusty Springfield	In The Middle Of Nowhere	03/07/1965	123	CB
Dusty Springfield	In The Middle Of Nowhere	10/07/1965	108	BB

Dusty Springfield	I Close My Eyes And Count To Ten	28/09/1968	122	BB
Dusty Springfield	I Don't Want To Hear It Anymore	26/04/1969	105	BB
Dusty Springfield	In The Land Of Make Believe	04/10/1969	113	BB
Dusty Springfield	I Wanna Be A Free Girl	16/05/1970	105	BB
Dusty Springfield	Lost	29/08/1970	123	CB
Dusty Springfield	What Good Is I Love You	06/02/1971	116	CB
Dusty Springfield	Who Gets Your Love	24/03/1973	121	BB
Dusty Springfield	Mama's Little Girl	28/04/1973	113	CB
Dusty Springfield	Mama's Little Girl	19/05/1973	118	BB
Dusty Springfield	Let Me Love You Once Before You Go	25/06/1977	105	CB
Dusty Springfield	Let Me Love You Once Before You Go	09/07/1977	110	BB
Dwight Twilley	Somebody To Love	27/03/1982	106	BB
Dwight Twilley Band	You Were So Warm	01/11/1975	103	BB
Dyke & The Blazers	So Sharp	24/06/1967	135	CB
Dyke & The Blazers	Runaway People	04/07/1970	101	CB
Dyke And The Blazers	So Sharp	17/06/1967	130	BB
Dyke And The Blazers	Funky Bull Pt. I	28/09/1968	102	BB
Dyke And The Blazers	You Are My Sunshine	10/01/1970	121	BB
Dyke And The Blazers	Uhh	11/04/1970	118	BB
Dyke And The Blazers	Runaway People	25/07/1970	119	BB
Dynamic Superiors	Leave It Alone	05/04/1975	102	BB
Dynasty	Do Me Right	29/11/1980	103	BB
Earl Gaines	The Best Of Luck To You	13/08/1966	128	CB
Earl Gains	The Best Of Luck To You	27/08/1966	133	BB
Earl Grant	Sermonette	22/07/1961	150	CB
Earl Grant	Without A Song	20/03/1965	113	CB
Earl Grant	I Can't Stop Loving You	12/02/1966	135	CB
Earl Grant	I'll Drown In My Tears	19/02/1966	117	CB
Earl Harrison	Humphrey Stomp	28/01/1967	110	CB
Earl Klugh	Doc	16/08/1980	105	BB

Earl Royce & The Olympics	Que Sera, Sera	05/06/1965	141	CB
Earl Van Dyke	Runaway Child, Running Wild	19/04/1969	124	CB
Earl Van Dyke	Runaway Child, Running Wild	03/05/1969	114	BB
Earl-Jean	Randy	17/10/1964	147	CB
Earle Hagen	Nancy's Theme	19/09/1964	128	CB
Earth Opera	Home To You	29/03/1969	106	CB
Earth, Wind & Fire	I Think About Lovin' You	12/02/1972	115	CB
Earth, Wind & Fire	Mom	17/02/1973	104	BB
Earth, Wind & Fire	Mom	24/02/1973	102	CB
Earth, Wind & Fire	Where Have All The Flowers Gone	17/03/1973	103	CB
Earth, Wind & Fire	Touch	28/01/1984	103	BB
Ecstasy, Passion & Pain	I Wouldn't Give You Up	30/03/1974	102	BB
Ecstasy, Passion & Pain	I Wouldn't Give You Up	30/03/1974	105	CB
Ed Ames	Timeless Love	15/07/1967	109	CB
Ed Ames	All My Love's Laughter	03/08/1968	106	CB
Ed Ames	All My Love's Laughter	10/08/1968	122	BB
Ed Ames	Changing, Changing	22/02/1969	130	BB
Ed Ames	Changing, Changing	01/03/1969	112	CB
Ed Ames	A Thing Called Love	10/01/1970	115	CB
Ed Bruce	See The Big Man Cry	09/11/1963	109	BB
Ed Bruce	See The Big Man Cry	16/11/1963	145	CB
Ed Townsend	Hold On	03/08/1959	106	BB
Ed Townsend	And Then Came Love	16/12/1961	148	CB
Ed Townsend	And Then Came Love	18/12/1961	114	BB
Ed Townsend	There's No End	16/03/1963	129	CB
Ed Townsend With The Townsmen	Stay With Me (A Little While Longer)	15/10/1960	108	CB
Ed Townsend With The Townsmen	Stay With Me (A Little While Longer)	24/10/1960	101	BB
Edd "Kookie" Byrnes & The Mary Kaye Trio	Kookie's Love Song (While Dancing)	14/11/1959	108	CB
Eddie & Ernie	Time Waits For No One	13/02/1965	133	CB
Eddie & Ernie	Outcast	04/12/1965	148	CB

Eddie & The Starlites	To Make A Long Story Short	21/04/1962	120	CB
Eddie Albert	Fall Away	09/01/1965	119	BB
Eddie Albert	Fall Away	16/01/1965	124	CB
Eddie Bishop	Call Me	02/07/1966	134	CB
Eddie Bo	Tell It Like It Is	28/05/1960	101	CB
Eddie Bo	It Must Be Love	18/02/1961	131	CB
Eddie Bo	Dinky Doo	10/06/1961	119	CB
Eddie Bo	Now Let's Popeye (Part Ii)	10/02/1962	112	CB
Eddie Cano	A Taste Of Honey*	07/07/1962	101	CB
Eddie Cochran	Three Steps To Heaven	06/06/1960	108	BB
Eddie Drennon & B.B.S. Unlimited	Let's Do The Latin Hustle	08/11/1975	104	CB
Eddie Fisher	Shalom	04/11/1961	105	CB
Eddie Fisher	Tonight	04/11/1961	109	CB
Eddie Fisher	Milk And Honey	18/11/1961	104	CB
Eddie Fisher	Arrivederci, Roma	12/05/1962	142	CB
Eddie Fisher	Arrivederci, Roma	19/05/1962	112	BB
Eddie Fisher	Sunrise, Sunset	12/06/1965	119	CB
Eddie Fisher	Sunrise, Sunset	19/06/1965	119	BB
Eddie Fisher	Now I Know	20/05/1967	135	CB
Eddie Fisher	Now I Know	03/06/1967	131	BB
Eddie Floyd	Love Is A Doggone Good Thing	09/09/1967	132	CB
Eddie Floyd	Big Bird	09/03/1968	132	BB
Eddie Floyd	I've Got To Have Your Love	08/02/1969	102	BB
Eddie Floyd	My Girl	18/07/1970	116	BB
Eddie Floyd	The Best Years Of My Life	03/10/1970	105	CB
Eddie Floyd	The Best Years Of My Life	17/10/1970	118	BB
Eddie Floyd	Yum Yum Yum (I Want Some)	26/02/1972	122	BB
Eddie Floyd Mavis Staples	Never, Never Let You Go	12/07/1969	107	BB
Eddie Harris	God Bless The Child	28/10/1961	148	CB
Eddie Harris	My Buddy	13/11/1961	114	BB

Eddie Harris	God Bless The Child (b-side)	13/11/1961	119	BB
Eddie Harris	Is It In	09/11/1974	107	BB
Eddie Hodges	Halfway	07/09/1963	118	BB
Eddie Hodges	Halfway	07/09/1963	148	CB
Eddie Hodges	Love Minus Zero	23/10/1965	130	CB
Eddie Hodges	Love Minus Zero	06/11/1965	134	BB
Eddie Holland	If It's Love (It's Alright)	15/09/1962	129	CB
Eddie Holman	Don't Stop Now	23/04/1966	104	BB
Eddie Holman	Don't Stop Now	23/04/1966	104	CB
Eddie Holman	Am I A Loser (from The Start)	29/10/1966	101	BB
Eddie Holman	I Love You	06/09/1969	106	CB
Eddie Holman	Since I Don't Have You	11/04/1970	107	CB
Eddie Holman	I'll Be There	20/06/1970	101	CB
Eddie Holman	I'll Be There	20/06/1970	115	BB
Eddie Holman	Cathy Called	17/10/1970	102	CB
Eddie Holman	This Will Be A Night To Remember	04/06/1977	102	CB
Eddie Kendricks	Can I	20/11/1971	101	BB
Eddie Kendricks	Let Me Run Into Your Lonely Heart	15/04/1972	103	CB
Eddie Kendricks	Get It While It's Hot	10/07/1976	112	CB
Eddie Money	Maureen	14/07/1979	Np4	CB
Eddie Powers	Gypsy Woman Told Me	02/05/1964	112	CB
Eddie Quinteros	Come Dance With Me	28/03/1960	101	BB
Eddie Rambeau	Skin Divin'	05/08/1961	129	CB
Eddie Rambeau	Summertime Guy	04/08/1962	112	CB
Eddie Rambeau	My Name Is Mud	10/07/1965	116	CB
Eddie Rambeau	My Name Is Mud	17/07/1965	112	BB
Eddie Rambeau	The Train	06/11/1965	129	BB
Eddie Rambeau	Clock	22/10/1966	122	BB
Eddie-"D"	BackstaBBin'	13/04/1985	103	BB
Eddy Arnold	Before This Day Ends	12/11/1960	113	CB

Eddy Arnold	One Grain Of Sand	23/09/1961	117	CB
Eddy Arnold	One Grain Of Sand	23/10/1961	107	BB
Eddy Arnold	Tears Broke Out On Me	24/02/1962	127	CB
Eddy Arnold	Tears Broke Out On Me	03/03/1962	102	BB
Eddy Arnold	A Little Heartache	16/06/1962	143	CB
Eddy Arnold	A Little Heartache	23/06/1962	103	BB
Eddy Arnold	After Loving You (b-side)	06/10/1962	112	BB
Eddy Arnold	Does He Mean That Much To You?	01/12/1962	136	CB
Eddy Arnold	A Million Years Or So	03/08/1963	144	CB
Eddy Arnold	I'm Letting You Go	07/08/1965	135	BB
Eddy Arnold	Please Don't Go	29/03/1969	129	BB
Eddy Arnold	Please Don't Go	19/04/1969	130	CB
Eddy Arnold	But For Love	14/06/1969	117	CB
Eddy Arnold	But For Love	21/06/1969	125	BB
Eddy Arnold	You Fool	13/09/1969	127	CB
Eddy Arnold	Since December	15/11/1969	150	CB
Eddy Arnold & The Needmore Creek Singers	Molly	01/02/1964	111	CB
Eddy Giles	Losin' Boy	17/06/1967	127	BB
Eddy Senay	Hot Thang	01/04/1972	101	CB
Eddy Senay	Hot Thang	08/04/1972	104	BB
Eden Kane	Well, I Ask You	09/09/1961	104	CB
Eden Kane	Well, I Ask You	02/10/1961	119	BB
Edgar Winter Group	Round & Round	18/11/1972	126	CB
Edgar Winter's White Trash Featuring Jerry La Croix	Where Would I Be (Without You)	26/06/1971	128	BB
Edison Lighthouse	She Works In A Woman's Way	01/08/1970	105	CB
Edith Piaf	Milord	25/02/1961	121	CB
Edith Piaf	Exodus	15/05/1961	116	BB
Edward Bear	Walking On Back	01/09/1973	115	BB
Edward Bear	Same Old Feeling	26/01/1974	108	CB
Edwin Hawkins Singers	Ain't It Like Him	09/08/1969	101	BB

Edwin Hawkins Singers	Ain't It Like Him	16/08/1969	145	CB
Edwin Hawkins Singers	Blowin' In The Wind	08/11/1969	129	CB
Edwin Hawkins Singers	Blowin' In The Wind	15/11/1969	109	BB
Edwin Starr	I Want My Baby Back	04/11/1967	120	BB
Edwin Starr	I Am The Man For You Baby	20/04/1968	112	BB
Edwin Starr	Way Over There	19/10/1968	107	CB
Edwin Starr	Way Over There	16/11/1968	119	BB
Edwin Starr	Time	14/02/1970	112	CB
Edwin Starr	Time	07/03/1970	117	BB
Edwin Starr	Who Is The Leader Of The People	09/09/1972	120	CB
Edwin Starr	Ain't It Hell Up In Harlem	09/02/1974	112	CB
Edwin Starr	Ain't It Hell Up In Harlem	23/03/1974	110	BB
Edwin Starr	Abyssinia Jones	14/02/1976	113	CB
Effie Smith	Dial That Telephone Part I	09/01/1965	127	CB
Egyptian Combo	Gale Winds	10/10/1964	101	CB
Egyptian Combo	Gale Winds	17/10/1964	103	BB
El Chicano	Eleanor Rigby	04/07/1970	115	BB
El Chicano	Dancin' Mama	30/10/1976	108	BB
El Clod	Tijuana Border (Wolverton Mountain)	08/09/1962	111	BB
El Clod	Tijuana Border (Wolverton Mountain)	15/09/1962	135	CB
Electric Light Orchestra	Ma-Ma-Ma Belle	16/03/1974	102	CB
Elena	Evening Time	03/04/1965	138	CB
Elephant's Memory	Skyscrapter Commando	06/03/1971	110	CB
Elephants Memory	Rock 'N' Roll Streaker	01/06/1974	110	CB
Ella Fitzgerald	But Not For Me	10/10/1959	118	CB
Ella Fitzgerald	(You'll Have To Swing It) Mr. Paganini (Live)	12/08/1961	103	CB
Ella Fitzgerald	(You'll Have To Swing It) Mr. Paganini [Live]	14/08/1961	103	BB
Ella Fitzgerald	Desafinado (Slightly Out Of Tune)*	27/10/1962	111	CB
Ella Fitzgerald	Desafinado (Slightly Out Of Tune)	17/11/1962	102	BB
Ella Fitzgerald	Stardust Bossa Nova (b-side)	15/12/1962	129	BB

Ella Fitzgerald	Bill Bailey, Won't You Please Come Home (Live)	13/04/1963	113	CB
Ella Fitzgerald	Hello, Dolly!	27/06/1964	125	BB
Ella Fitzgerald	Ringo Beat	02/01/1965	127	BB
Ella Fitzgerald	Get Ready	27/09/1969	106	CB
Ella Fitzgerald	Get Ready	04/10/1969	126	BB
Ella Fitzgerald With The Count Basie Orchestra	Shiny Stockings	26/10/1963	130	CB
Ellie Greenwich	Maybe I Know	26/05/1973	122	BB
Ellie Greenwich	Maybe I Know	02/06/1973	115	CB
Elliott Evans	Concerto For The X-15 "A Tribute To The X-15"	17/02/1962	111	CB
Elliott Evans	Concerto For The X-15 "A Tribute To The X-15" "A Tribute To The X-	24/02/1962	110	BB
Elmer Bernstein & Orchestra	Walk On The Wild Side	21/04/1962	102	BB
Elmer Bernstein & Orchestra	Walk On The Wild Side	28/04/1962	112	CB
Elmo & Almo	When The Good Sun Shines	10/06/1967	136	CB
Elmore James	It Hurts Me Too	08/05/1965	105	CB
Elmore James	It Hurts Me Too	22/05/1965	106	BB
Elmore James & His Broomdusters	The Sky Is Crying	07/05/1960	123	CB
Elo	Rain Is Falling	30/01/1982	101	BB
Elo	Stranger	19/11/1983	105	BB
Eloise Laws	I'd Do It All Again	15/02/1969	127	CB
Eloise Laws	Number One	25/03/1978	106	CB
Elton Anderson With Sid Lawrence Combo	Secret Of Love	06/02/1960	111	CB
Elton John	Lady Samantha	15/02/1969	139	CB
Elton John	Song For Guy	07/04/1979	110	BB
Elvin Bishop	Struttin' My Stuff	31/07/1976	101	CB
Elvis Costello	Watching The Detectives	25/03/1978	108	BB
Elvis Costello	Accidents Will Happen	10/03/1979	Np7	CB
Elvis Costello	Accidents Will Happen	14/04/1979	101	BB
Elvis Presley	Viva Las Vegas (EP)	25/07/1964	102	CB
Elvis Presley	Wooden Heart	28/11/1964	111	CB
Elvis Presley	Blue Christmas	28/11/1964	143	CB

Elvis Presley	Wooden Heart	05/12/1964	107	BB
Elvis Presley	Wooden Heart	13/11/1965	110	BB
Elvis Presley	Edge Of Reality	30/11/1968	112	BB
Elvis Presley	For Ol' Times Sake	22/09/1973	104	CB
Elvis Presley	Softly, As I Leave You [Live]	20/05/1978	109	BB
Elvis Presley With The Jordanaires	Where Do You Come From	27/10/1962	128	CB
Elvis Presley With The Jordanaires	Suspicion	02/05/1964	127	CB
Elvis Presley With The Jordanaires	Suspicion	09/05/1964	103	BB
Elvis Presley With The Jordanaires	Never Ending	25/07/1964	111	BB
Elvis Presley With The Jordanaires	You'll Be Gone	27/02/1965	124	CB
Elvis Presley With The Jordanaires	You'll Be Gone	06/03/1965	121	BB
Elvis Presley With The Jordanaires	(It's A) Long Lonely Highway	28/08/1965	112	BB
Elvis Presley With The Jordanaires	Come What May	02/07/1966	109	BB
Elvis Presley With The Jordanaires	Fools Fall In Love	28/01/1967	102	BB
Elvis Presley With The Jordanaires	Fools Fall In Love	11/02/1967	113	CB
Elvis Presley With The Jordanaires	We Call On Him	20/04/1968	106	BB
Elvis Presley With The Jordanaires	You'll Never Walk Alone	27/04/1968	116	CB
Elvis Presley With The Jordanaires	(Let Me Be Your) Teddy Bear	26/08/1978	105	BB
Elvis Presley With The Jordanaires And The Imperials Quartet	How Great Thou Art	26/04/1969	101	BB
Elyse Weinberg	Oh, Deed I Do	26/04/1969	120	CB
Emanuel Lasky	Lucky To Be Loved (By You)	03/04/1965	130	CB
Emitt Rhodes	Live Till You Die	03/04/1971	103	CB
Emitt Rhodes	Really Wanted You	04/12/1971	108	CB
Emmylou Harris	Sweet Dreams (Live)	15/01/1977	101	CB
Emmylou Harris	Making Believe	25/06/1977	101	CB
Emmylou Harris	To Daddy	04/03/1978	102	BB
Emmylou Harris	I Don't Have To Crawl	13/06/1981	106	BB
Enchantment	If You're Ready (Here It Comes)	08/07/1978	104	CB
Enchantment	Anyway You Want It	31/03/1979	109	BB
Endgames	Love Cares	24/03/1984	105	BB

Engelbert Humperdinck	Free As The Wind	26/01/1974	103	CB
Engelbert Humperdinck	This Is What You Mean To Me	06/12/1975	102	BB
England Dan & John Ford Coley	New Jersey	04/09/1971	103	BB
England Dan & John Ford Coley	If The World Ran Out Of Love Tonight	19/08/1978	106	CB
English Beat	I Confess	09/04/1983	104	BB
English Beat	Save It For Later	21/05/1983	106	BB
Eric & The Serenaders	Natasha	23/11/1963	136	CB
Eric & The Vikings	Vibrations (Made Us Fall In Love)	18/07/1970	104	CB
Eric Burdon & War	Home Cookin'	10/04/1971	119	CB
Eric Burdon And War	Home Cookin'	10/04/1971	108	BB
Eric Clapton	Knockin' On Heaven's Door	30/08/1975	109	CB
Eric Clapton & His Band	Blues Power (Live)	08/11/1980	1103	CB
Eric Quincy Tate	No Rollin' Boogie	27/09/1975	114	CB
Erma Franklin	What Kind Of Girl Do You Think I Am	30/09/1961	141	CB
Erma Franklin	Hello Again	27/01/1962	102	CB
Erma Franklin	Don't Wait Too Long	02/02/1963	132	CB
Erma Franklin	Open Up Your Soul	18/05/1968	107	BB
Ernest Ashworth	Talk Back Trembling Lips	24/08/1963	110	CB
Ernest Ashworth	Talk Back Trembling Lips	14/09/1963	101	BB
Ernestine Anderson	A Lover's Question	18/02/1961	108	CB
Ernie Freeman	Rockin' Red Wing	28/03/1960	106	BB
Ernie Freeman	Rockin' Red Wing	09/04/1960	101	CB
Ernie Freeman	Swamp Meeting	22/04/1961	140	CB
Ernie Freeman	The Twist	06/01/1962	123	CB
Ernie Heckscher And His Orchestra	The Girl From Ipanema	12/09/1964	125	BB
Ernie K-Doe	Hello My Lover	24/09/1960	102	CB
Ernie K-Doe	Real Man	17/06/1961	144	CB
Ernie K-Doe	A Certain Girl	28/10/1961	103	CB
Ernie K-Doe	Beating Like A Tom Tom	18/08/1962	145	CB
Ernie K-Doe	Later For Tomorrow	01/04/1967	141	CB

Ernie K-Doe	Later For Tomorrow	15/04/1967	122	BB
Ernie K. Doe	(It Will Have To Do) Until The Real Thing Comes Along	28/10/1967	133	CB
Ernie Maresca	Down On The Beach	30/06/1962	103	CB
Ernie Maresca	Mary Jane	30/06/1962	106	CB
Ernie Tucker	Can She Give You Fever	12/11/1960	104	CB
Errol Sober	What Do You Say To A Naked Lady	30/05/1970	106	BB
Errol Sober	What Do You Say To A Naked Lady	30/05/1970	130	CB
Errol Sober	I Did What I Did For Maria	05/10/1974	113	CB
Errol Sober	I Did What I Did For Maria	12/10/1974	108	BB
Erroll Garner	Mack The Knife	29/06/1963	139	CB
Esther Phillips	Am I That Easy To Forget	09/02/1963	112	BB
Esther Phillips	Moonglow & Theme From Picnic	17/07/1965	111	CB
Esther Phillips	Moonglow & Theme From Picnic	24/07/1965	115	BB
Esther Phillips	Let Me Know When It's Over	02/10/1965	102	CB
Esther Phillips	Let Me Know When It's Over	30/10/1965	129	BB
Esther Phillips	Too Late To Worry, Too Blue To Cry	15/02/1969	121	BB
Esther Phillips	Too Late To Worry, Too Blue To Cry	15/02/1969	121	CB
Esther Phillips	Home Is Where The Hatred Is	22/04/1972	122	BB
Esther Phillips	Baby, I'm For Real	01/07/1972	118	CB
Esther Phillips	I've Never Found A Man (To Love Me Like You Do)	09/12/1972	106	BB
Esther Phillips With The Dixie Flyers	Set Me Free	25/07/1970	118	BB
Esther Phillips With The Dixie Flyers	Set Me Free	01/08/1970	111	CB
Eternity's Children	Sunshine Among Us	14/09/1968	117	BB
Etta James	How Do You Speak To An Angel	15/12/1962	146	CB
Etta James	How Do You Speak To An Angel	05/01/1963	109	BB
Etta James	I Worry Bout You	12/10/1963	118	CB
Etta James	I Worry Bout You	23/11/1963	118	BB
Etta James	Baby What You Want Me To Do (Live)	04/01/1964	101	CB
Etta James	Look Who's Blue	04/04/1964	140	CB
Etta James	Mellow Fellow	12/12/1964	127	CB

Etta James	You Got It	28/09/1968	113	BB
Etta James	Miss Pitiful	04/10/1969	131	CB
Etta James	Tighten Up Your Own Thing	21/02/1970	119	CB
Etta James	I Found A Love	03/06/1972	108	BB
Etta James	All The Way Down	13/10/1973	101	BB
Etta Jones	When I Fall In Love	11/02/1961	118	CB
Etta Jones	Sweethearts On Parade	27/03/1961	115	BB
Euclid Beach Band	There's No Surf In Cleveland	19/08/1978	103	CB
Eugene Church	Jack Of All Trades	26/12/1959	117	CB
Eugene Church	Good News	14/11/1960	106	BB
Eugene Pitt & The Jyve Fyve	Come Down In Time	05/06/1971	126	CB
Eugene Wallace	Rock Me On The Water	02/03/1974	103	CB
Evelyn "Champagne" King	Music Box	09/06/1979	Np5	CB
Evelyn "Champagne" King	Shake Down	21/04/1984	107	BB
Evelyn "Champagne" King	Just For The Night	01/12/1984	107	BB
Everly Brothers	Love Of The Common People	28/10/1967	127	CB
Every Mother's Son	No One Knows	27/01/1968	101	CB
Everyday Hudson	Laugh, Funny Funny	14/03/1970	141	CB
Evie Sands	Take Me For A Little While	14/08/1965	114	BB
Evie Sands	Take Me For A Little While	28/08/1965	124	CB
Evie Sands	Billy Sunshine	06/04/1968	115	CB
Evie Sands	Billy Sunshine	27/04/1968	133	BB
Evie Sands	Crazy Annie	03/01/1970	116	BB
Evie Sands	Crazy Annie	31/01/1970	123	CB
Evie Sands	But You Know I Love You	21/03/1970	110	BB
Evie Sands	But You Know I Love You	28/03/1970	130	CB
Evie Sands	Take Me For A Little While	27/06/1970	138	CB
Exile	You're Good For Me	26/07/1980	105	BB
Exile	Take Me Down	18/10/1980	102	BB
Exile	Heart And Soul	03/10/1981	102	BB

Exuma	Exuma, The Obeah Man	27/06/1970	130	CB
Exuma	Brown Girl	07/10/1972	119	CB
Eydie Gorme	The Friendliest Thing	29/02/1964	133	BB
Eydie Gorme	Can't Get Over (The Bossa Nova)	22/08/1964	122	CB
Eydie Gorme	Do I Hear A Waltz?	13/03/1965	116	CB
Eydie Gorme	Do I Hear A Waltz?	10/04/1965	122	BB
Eydie Gorme	Just Dance On By	22/05/1965	140	CB
Eydie Gorme	Just Dance On By	05/06/1965	124	BB
Eydie Gorme	What Did I Have That I Don't Have?	02/04/1966	138	CB
Eydie Gorme	If He Walked Into My Life	18/06/1966	120	BB
Eydie Gorme	Softly, As I Leave You	28/01/1967	117	BB
Eydie Gorme	Life Is But A Moment (Canta Ragazzina)	10/02/1968	115	BB
Fabian	Grapevine	15/04/1961	118	CB
Fabian	Break Down And Cry	17/11/1962	144	CB
Fabian With The Fabulous Four	Wild Party	18/11/1961	128	CB
Fabulous Continentals	Undertow	24/08/1963	102	CB
Fabulous Continentals	Undertow	12/10/1963	128	BB
Faces	Ooh-La-La	30/06/1973	106	CB
Faith, Hope & Charity	Baby Don't Take Your Love	12/09/1970	113	CB
Faith, Hope & Charity With The Choice Four	A Time For Celebration	12/06/1976	107	BB
Fallen Angels	Just Like Romeo And Juliet	26/04/1975	116	CB
Fallen Angels	Just Like Romeo And Juliet	03/05/1975	106	BB
Fallenrock	Mary Anne	14/06/1975	111	CB
Fandango	Headliner	04/02/1978	110	BB
Fantastic Four	As Long As I Live (I Live For You)	29/07/1967	116	CB
Fantastic Four	I've Got To Have You	15/06/1968	115	CB
Fantastic Four	On The Brighter Side Of A Blue World	23/05/1970	102	CB
Fantastic Four	I'm Falling In Love (I Feel Good All Over)	02/03/1974	109	CB
Fantasy	You're Too Late	11/04/1981	104	BB
Faron Young	It's Four In The Morning	11/03/1972	119	CB

Faron Young With The Merry Melody Singers	The Yellow Bandana	02/03/1963	114	BB
Fat Boys	Jail House Rap	22/12/1984	105	BB
Fat Boys	Can You Feel It	16/03/1985	101	BB
Fatback	I Like Girls	09/09/1978	101	BB
Fats Domino	If You Need Me	30/01/1960	113	CB
Fats Domino	I Just Cry	27/05/1961	132	CB
Fats Domino	Good Hearted Man	22/07/1961	121	CB
Fats Domino	I Hear You Knocking	09/12/1961	109	CB
Fats Domino	Ida Jane	24/02/1962	118	CB
Fats Domino	Nothing New (Same Old Thing)	30/06/1962	104	CB
Fats Domino	Dance With Mr. Domino	30/06/1962	108	CB
Fats Domino	Stop The Clock	29/09/1962	118	CB
Fats Domino	Stop The Clock	13/10/1962	103	BB
Fats Domino	Hands Across The Table	08/12/1962	141	CB
Fats Domino	Those Eyes	16/02/1963	105	CB
Fats Domino	Hum Diddy Doo	02/03/1963	124	BB
Fats Domino	You Always Hurt The One You Love	27/04/1963	102	BB
Fats Domino	Trouble Blues	04/05/1963	144	CB
Fats Domino	Can't Go On Without You	01/06/1963	123	BB
Fats Domino	When I'm Walking (Let Me Walk)	03/08/1963	126	CB
Fats Domino	I've Got A Right To Cry	03/08/1963	135	CB
Fats Domino	When I'm Walking (Let Me Walk)	10/08/1963	114	BB
Fats Domino	I've Got A Right To Cry (b-side)	10/08/1963	128	BB
Fats Domino	I Can't Give You Anything But Love	30/11/1963	114	BB
Fats Domino	Just A Lonely Man	21/12/1963	108	BB
Fats Domino	Lazy Lady	07/03/1964	116	CB
Fats Domino	Your Cheatin' Heart	14/03/1964	112	BB
Fats Domino	I Don't Want To Set The World On Fire	21/03/1964	122	BB
Fats Domino	Something You Got, Baby	09/05/1964	147	CB
Fats Domino	Mary, Oh Mary	04/07/1964	131	CB

Fats Domino	Mary, Oh Mary	25/07/1964	127	BB
Fats Domino	Sally Was A Good Old Girl	19/09/1964	128	CB
Fats Domino	Heartbreak Hill	17/10/1964	112	CB
Fats Domino	Why Don't You Do It Right	06/03/1965	128	CB
Fats Domino	I Left My Heart In San Francisco	31/07/1965	111	CB
Fay Simmons	Everybody's Doin' The Pony	27/03/1961	107	BB
Felix Cavaliere	Good To Have Love Back	07/06/1980	105	BB
Felix Slatkin	Theme From King Of Kings	04/11/1961	111	CB
Felix Slatkin	Theme From King Of Kings	20/11/1961	120	BB
Ferlin Husky	The Waltz You Saved For Me	16/12/1961	140	CB
Ferrante & Teicher	Tara's Theme From Gone With The Wind	18/03/1961	110	CB
Ferrante & Teicher	Street Of Palms (Via Margalene)	17/03/1962	133	CB
Ferrante & Teicher	Lida Rose	18/08/1962	144	CB
Ferrante & Teicher	Theme From Taras Bulba (The Wishing Star)*	01/12/1962	107	CB
Ferrante & Teicher	Theme From Taras Bulba (The Wishing Star)	08/12/1962	116	BB
Ferrante & Teicher	Theme From Lawrence Of Arabia	02/02/1963	102	CB
Ferrante & Teicher	Antony And Cleopatra Theme	29/06/1963	115	CB
Ferrante & Teicher	Crystal Fingers	30/11/1963	132	CB
Ferrante & Teicher	Crystal Fingers	14/12/1963	127	BB
Ferrante & Teicher	The Seventh Dawn	18/07/1964	124	BB
Ferrante & Teicher	The Greatest Story Ever Told	20/02/1965	143	CB
Ferrante & Teicher	The Greatest Story Ever Told	27/02/1965	101	BB
Ferrante & Teicher	Love Theme From "THE Godfather"	08/04/1972	110	CB
Ferrante & Teicher	Last Tango In Paris	26/05/1973	115	CB
Fever Tree	What Time Did You Say It Is In Salt Lake City?	23/11/1968	105	CB
Finders Keepers	(We Wear) Lavender Bleu	22/10/1966	123	BB
Finky Fuzz	Here Come The Judge (Part 1)	15/06/1968	126	CB
Fire & Rain	Hello Stranger	15/12/1973	104	CB
Firefall	Runaway Love	05/11/1983	103	BB
First Choice	Guilty	07/12/1974	103	BB

First Choice	Guilty	11/01/1975	103	CB
First Choice	Double Cross	12/05/1979	104	BB
Fish 'N' Chips	Four Times Faster	05/06/1965	129	CB
Five By Five	Apple Cider	01/02/1969	112	CB
Five By Five	Apple Cider	08/03/1969	133	BB
Five By Five	15 Going On 20	01/11/1969	136	CB
Five Discs	Never Let You Go	22/12/1962	141	CB
Five Satins	Your Memory	27/06/1960	107	BB
Five Satins	Your Memory	23/07/1960	117	CB
Five Stairsteps	The Touch Of You	12/08/1967	118	CB
Five Stairsteps & Cubie	Baby Make Me Feel So Good	15/02/1969	101	BB
Flaming Embers	Hey Mama (What'cha Got Good For Daddy)	04/11/1967	119	CB
Flash Cadillac & The Continental Kids	Hot Summer Girls	19/07/1975	101	CB
Flash Cadillac & The Continental Kids	Time Will Tell	06/09/1975	113	CB
Flash Cadillac And The Continental Kids	Hot Summer Girls	19/07/1975	102	BB
Flatt & Scruggs	Like A Rolling Stone	21/09/1968	125	BB
Flavor	Heart - Teaser	21/12/1968	123	CB
Fleetwood Mac	Albatross	22/03/1969	104	BB
Fleetwood Mac	Heroes Are Hard To Find	14/12/1974	122	CB
Flesh Gordon & The Nude Hollywood Argyles	Superstreaker	06/04/1974	118	CB
Florraine Darlin	Johnny Loves Me	04/07/1964	121	BB
Florraine Darlin	Johnny Loves Me	04/07/1964	128	CB
Floyd & Jerry	Dusty	22/10/1966	145	CB
Floyd & Jerry With The Counterpoints	Summer Kisses	30/07/1966	116	CB
Floyd Cramer	Mood Indigo	18/03/1961	126	CB
Floyd Cramer	Let's Go	03/02/1962	123	CB
Floyd Cramer	Lovesick Blues	14/04/1962	118	CB
Floyd Cramer	Swing Low	22/09/1962	101	CB
Floyd Cramer	Swing Low	29/09/1962	110	BB
Floyd Cramer	Losers Weepers (b-side)	20/10/1962	127	BB

Floyd Cramer	(These Are) The Young Years	04/05/1963	129	BB
Floyd Cramer	How High The Moon	27/07/1963	109	CB
Floyd Cramer	How High The Moon	17/08/1963	121	BB
Floyd Cramer	Heartless Heart	21/12/1963	124	BB
Floyd Cramer	Naomi	14/03/1964	138	CB
Floyd Cramer	Stood Up	28/01/1967	128	CB
Floyd Cramer	Dallas	03/05/1980	104	BB
Floyd Dakil Combo	Dance, Franny, Dance	11/07/1964	142	CB
Fludd	What An Animal	19/07/1975	118	CB
Flying Burrito Brothers	Building Fires	15/11/1975	108	CB
Foghat	I Just Want To Make Love To You	25/11/1972	107	CB
Foghat	Live Now-Pay Later	15/08/1981	102	BB
Fontella Bass	I Can't Rest	23/04/1966	108	CB
Fontella Bass	Safe And Sound	03/09/1966	124	CB
Fontella Bass & BoBBy Mcclure	Don't Jump	29/05/1965	110	CB
Force M.D.'s	Tears	15/12/1984	102	BB
Force M.D.'s	Itchin' For A Scratch	15/06/1985	105	BB
Fotomaker	The Other Side (So When I See You Again)	22/07/1978	110	BB
Four Gents	Soul Sister	17/12/1966	139	CB
Four Gents	Soul Sister	31/12/1966	133	BB
Four Jacks And A Jill	Mister Nico	27/07/1968	108	CB
Four Jacks And A Jill	Hey Mister	09/11/1968	130	BB
Four Seasons	Long Lonely Nights	13/06/1964	102	BB
Four Tops	In These Changing Times	19/06/1971	102	CB
Four Tops	I Can't Quit Your Love	06/05/1972	108	CB
Four Tops	I Can't Quit Your Love	20/05/1972	102	BB
Four Tops	Mama You're All Right With Me	17/01/1976	107	BB
France Joli	This Time (I'm Giving All I've Got)	26/07/1980	103	BB
Frank Chacksfield & His Orchestra	Theme From "A New Kind Of Love"	05/10/1963	126	CB
Frank Gari	Lil' Girl	21/11/1959	102	CB

Frank Ifield	The Wayward Wind	16/03/1963	125	CB
Frank Ifield	The Wayward Wind	30/03/1963	104	BB
Frank Ifield	Don't Blame Me	14/03/1964	146	CB
Frank Ifield	Don't Blame Me	21/03/1964	128	BB
Frank Ifield	Out Of Nowhere	27/05/1967	103	CB
Frank Ifield	Out Of Nowhere	01/07/1967	132	BB
Frank Mills	Poor Little Fool	27/05/1972	106	BB
Frank Pourcel And His Orchestra	Milord	06/03/1961	112	BB
Frank Sinatra	It's Over, It's Over, It's Over	20/06/1960	111	BB
Frank Sinatra	My Blue Heaven	08/04/1961	108	CB
Frank Sinatra	Sentimental Baby	15/04/1961	101	CB
Frank Sinatra	American Beauty Rose	09/09/1961	118	CB
Frank Sinatra	I've Heard That Song Before	20/01/1962	139	CB
Frank Sinatra	The Moon Was Yellow	27/01/1962	131	CB
Frank Sinatra	Stardust	17/03/1962	108	CB
Frank Sinatra	Goody Goody	14/07/1962	136	CB
Frank Sinatra	I Love Paris	18/08/1962	148	CB
Frank Sinatra	Come Blow Your Horn	15/06/1963	108	BB
Frank Sinatra	Love Isn't Just For The Young	12/10/1963	118	CB
Frank Sinatra	Love Isn't Just For The Young	26/10/1963	111	BB
Frank Sinatra	Stay With Me	18/01/1964	107	CB
Frank Sinatra	My Kind Of Town	30/05/1964	120	CB
Frank Sinatra	My Kind Of Town (Chicago Is)	13/06/1964	110	BB
Frank Sinatra	When Somebody Loves You	04/09/1965	102	BB
Frank Sinatra	When Somebody Loves You	04/09/1965	104	CB
Frank Sinatra	Ev'rybody Has The Right To Be Wrong! (At Least Once)	16/10/1965	101	CB
Frank Sinatra	Everybody Has The Right To Be Wrong! (At Least Once)	06/11/1965	131	BB
Frank Sinatra	Moment To Moment	25/12/1965	115	BB
Frank Sinatra	I Would Be In Love (Anyway)	14/03/1970	118	CB
Frank Sinatra	What's Now Is Now	13/06/1970	123	BB

Frank Sinatra	Lady Day	05/12/1970	104	CB
Frank Sinatra	Bein' Green	02/01/1971	115	CB
Frank Sinatra	You Will Be My Music	09/02/1974	107	CB
Frank Sinatra	Bad, Bad Leroy Brown	23/03/1974	106	CB
Frank Sinatra	You Turned My World Around	20/07/1974	104	CB
Frank Sinatra & His Orchestra	The Look Of Love	13/10/1962	118	CB
Frank Sinatra And His Orchestra	The Look Of Love	03/11/1962	101	BB
Frank Slay & His Orchestra	Bei Mir Bist Du Schoen	31/03/1962	142	CB
Frank Stallone	Case Of You	27/09/1980	I103	CB
Frank Stallone	If We Ever Get Back	15/09/1984	105	BB
Frank Zappa	Disco Boy	19/03/1977	105	BB
Frank Zappa	I Don't Wanna Get Drafted	24/05/1980	103	BB
Frankie Avalon	Don't Let Love Pass Me By	01/10/1960	124	CB
Frankie Avalon	Call Me Anytime	13/02/1961	102	BB
Frankie Avalon	Call Me Anytime	04/03/1961	120	CB
Frankie Avalon	Voyage To The Bottom Of The Sea	03/07/1961	101	BB
Frankie Avalon	Voyage To The Bottom Of The Sea	08/07/1961	113	CB
Frankie Avalon	Summer Of '61	15/07/1961	118	CB
Frankie Avalon	Married	23/09/1961	109	CB
Frankie Avalon	Married	16/10/1961	112	BB
Frankie Avalon	After You've Gone	27/01/1962	117	BB
Frankie Avalon	After You've Gone	27/01/1962	141	CB
Frankie Avalon	Don't Let Me Stand In Your Way	14/07/1962	117	CB
Frankie Avalon	Don't Let Me Stand In Your Way	21/07/1962	111	BB
Frankie Avalon	Welcome Home	08/12/1962	129	BB
Frankie Avalon	Welcome Home	08/12/1962	136	CB
Frankie Avalon	Cleopatra	04/05/1963	139	CB
Frankie Avalon	New Fangled, Jingle Jangle, Swimming Suit From Paris	08/08/1964	133	CB
Frankie Avalon	Beauty School Dropout	29/07/1978	110	CB
Frankie Calen	Joanie	17/06/1961	134	CB

Frankie Fanelli	Laurie Don't Worry	15/05/1965	144	CB
Frankie Ford	Blue Monday	18/05/1974	118	CB
Frankie Karl & The Dreams	Don't Be Afraid (Do As I Say)	18/01/1969	119	CB
Frankie Laine	Johnny Willow	02/07/1966	133	CB
Frankie Laine	I Found You	06/04/1968	118	BB
Frankie Laine	Take Me Back	29/06/1968	111	CB
Frankie Laine	Take Me Back	06/07/1968	115	BB
Frankie Laine	Please Forgive Me	28/09/1968	124	CB
Frankie Laine	On The Sunny Side Of The Street	13/06/1970	120	CB
Frankie Love	First Star	19/01/1963	140	CB
Frankie Miller	Darlin'	03/03/1979	103	BB
Frankie Randall	Yellow Haired Woman	19/06/1965	114	CB
Frankie Valli	The Sun Ain't Gonna Shine (Anymore)	09/10/1965	141	CB
Frankie Valli	The Sun Ain't Gonna Shine (Anymore)	30/10/1965	128	BB
Frankie Valli	You're Ready Now	30/04/1966	112	BB
Frankie Valli	Circles In The Sand	20/06/1970	108	CB
Frankie Valli	Easily	30/04/1977	108	BB
Frankie Valli	Fancy Dancer	27/01/1979	Np6	CB
Frankie Vaughan	Hercules	20/10/1962	141	CB
Fraternity Of Man	Don't Bogart Me	07/09/1968	113	CB
Fraternity Of Man	Don't Bogart Me	21/09/1968	133	BB
Fred Darian	Battle Of Gettysburg	11/03/1961	127	CB
Fred Knoblock	Memphis	15/08/1981	102	BB
Fred Wesley & The J.B.'s	If You Don't Get It The First Time, Back Up And Try It Again, Party	03/11/1973	114	CB
Fred Wesley & The J.B.'s	If You Don't Get It The First Time, Back Up And Try It Again, Party	17/11/1973	104	BB
Freda Payne	The Unhooked Generation	03/01/1970	127	CB
Freda Payne	The Road We Didn't Take	15/01/1972	101	CB
Freddie & The Dreamers	Send A Letter To Me	25/09/1965	120	CB
Freddie And The Dreamers	Send A Letter To Me	02/10/1965	123	BB
Freddie Cannon	Rock Around The Clock	15/06/1968	118	CB

Freddie Cannon	Rock Around The Clock	22/06/1968	121	BB
Freddie Fender	Holy One	09/05/1960	107	BB
Freddie Gelfand	It's Getting Better	26/04/1969	130	CB
Freddie Hart	My Hang-Up Is You	08/04/1972	121	CB
Freddie Houston	Soft Walkin'	14/07/1962	134	CB
Freddie Houston	I Gotta Move	28/12/1963	111	CB
Freddie Lennon	That's My Life (My Love And My Home)	05/03/1966	133	CB
Freddie North	You And Me Together Forever	12/02/1972	116	BB
Freddie North	Sweeter Than Sweetness	13/05/1972	107	CB
Freddie Scott	Lost The Right	08/04/1961	129	CB
Freddie Scott	Lonely Man	30/01/1965	136	CB
Freddie Scott	He Will Break Your Heart	12/08/1967	120	BB
Freddie Scott	I Shall Be Released	23/05/1970	112	CB
Freddy Cannon	Opportunity	22/04/1961	105	CB
Freddy Cannon	Opportunity	24/04/1961	114	BB
Freddy Cannon	Four Letter Man	26/01/1963	117	CB
Freddy Cannon	Four Letter Man	09/02/1963	121	BB
Freddy Cannon	In The Night	24/04/1965	125	CB
Freddy Cannon	In The Night	01/05/1965	132	BB
Freddy Cannon	Let Me Show You Where It's At	30/10/1965	115	CB
Freddy Cannon	Let Me Show You Where It's All	06/11/1965	127	BB
Freddy Cannon	The Greatest Show On Earth	07/05/1966	150	CB
Freddy Cannon	The Laughing Song	16/07/1966	111	BB
Freddy Cannon	The Laughing Song	23/07/1966	149	CB
Freddy Cannon	Rock N' Roll A-B-C's	24/08/1974	121	CB
Freddy Fender	Talk To Me	05/08/1978	103	BB
Freddy King	Lonesome Whistle Blues	20/05/1961	117	CB
Freddy King	San-Ho-Zay	19/08/1961	114	CB
Freddy King	The Bossa Nova Watusi Twist	02/02/1963	103	BB
Freddy King	Play It Cool	04/01/1969	127	BB

Freddy Weller	These Are Not My People	26/07/1969	113	BB
Freddy Weller	The Promised Land	13/03/1971	125	BB
Freddy Weller	Indian Lake	17/07/1971	108	BB
Frederick	Gentle (Calling Your Name)	18/05/1985	108	BB
Frederick Knight	Trouble	16/09/1972	102	BB
Frederick Knight	I Betcha Didn't Know That	14/06/1975	113	CB
Free	The Highway Song	27/03/1971	129	CB
Free	Little Bit Of Love	03/06/1972	119	BB
Free	Little Bit Of Love	24/06/1972	116	CB
Free	Wishing Well	03/03/1973	101	CB
Free	Wishing Well	10/03/1973	112	BB
Free 'N' Easy	Are You Goin' My Way?	24/07/1971	130	CB
Freeez	I.O.U.	24/09/1983	104	BB
Freeez	Pop Goes My Love	28/01/1984	104	BB
Fresh Aire	Flying Over America	08/07/1978	108	BB
Fresh Start	Free	10/08/1974	104	BB
Frida & Phil Collins	Here We'll Stay	07/05/1983	102	BB
Frijid Pink	Tell Me Why	22/03/1969	109	CB
Frijid Pink	Lost Son	20/11/1971	113	CB
Frijid Pink	Earth Omen	10/06/1972	123	CB
Frummox	There You Go	24/01/1970	129	CB
Fugi	Mary Don't Take Me On No Bad Trip	11/10/1969	130	CB
Funkadelic	Loose Booty	17/03/1973	118	BB
Funkadelic	Cosmic Slop	08/09/1973	104	CB
Funkadelic	Cosmic Slop	06/10/1973	102	BB
Funkadelic	Standing On The Verge Of Getting It On	07/09/1974	105	CB
Funkadelic	Undisco Kidd	23/10/1976	102	BB
Fuzzy Bunnies	The Sun Ain't Gonna Shine Anymore	31/08/1968	115	BB
G.L. Crockett	Every Good-Bye Ain't Gone	30/10/1965	140	CB
Gabor Szabo/BoBBy Womack	Breezin'	03/07/1971	103	CB

Gale Garnett	I'll Cry Alone	24/04/1965	108	BB
Gale Garnett	I'll Cry Alone	24/04/1965	144	CB
Gallagher & Lyle	Every Little Teardrop	05/03/1977	106	BB
Gallery Featuring Jim Gold	Rest In Peace	12/05/1973	110	CB
Gallery Featuring Jim Gold	Maybe Baby	14/07/1973	118	BB
Gallery Featuring Jim Gold	Maybe Baby	14/07/1973	125	CB
Gamma Goochee Himself	(You Got) The Gamma Goochee (Live)	30/10/1965	131	CB
Garfunkel	Traveling Boy	20/04/1974	102	BB
Garland Green	Don't Think That I'm A Violent Guy	20/12/1969	108	CB
Garland Green	Don't Think That I'm A Violent Guy	27/12/1969	113	BB
Garland Green	Plain And Simple Girl	17/04/1971	109	BB
Garland Jeffreys	Wild In The Streets	15/12/1973	106	CB
Garland Jeffreys	Wild In The Streets	26/01/1974	115	BB
Garland Jeffreys	What Does It Take (To Win Your Love)	09/04/1983	107	BB
Garland Jeffreys And Phoebe Snow	Reelin'	17/06/1978	107	BB
Garnell Cooper & The Kinfolks	Green Monkey	06/07/1963	139	CB
Garnell Cooper & The Kinfolks	Green Monkey	03/08/1963	132	BB
Garnet Mimms	It Was Easier To Hurt Her	24/04/1965	124	BB
Garnet Mimms	That Goes To Show You	17/07/1965	115	BB
Garnet Mimms	That Goes To Show You	24/07/1965	119	CB
Garnet Mimms	It's Been Such A Long Way Home	16/07/1966	125	BB
Garnet Mimms	My Baby	10/09/1966	119	CB
Garnet Mimms	My Baby	01/10/1966	132	BB
Garnet Mimms & The Enchanters	A Little Bit Of Soap	02/01/1965	108	CB
Garry Sherman And His Orchestra	Alice's Restaurant Massacree	13/12/1969	112	BB
Gary (U.S.) Bonds	Copy Cat	18/08/1962	101	CB
Gary (U.S.) Bonds	I Dig This Station	20/10/1962	108	CB
Gary (U.S.) Bonds	I Dig This Station	27/10/1962	101	BB
Gary (U.S.) Bonds	What A Dream	27/04/1963	145	CB
Gary (U.S.) Bonds	Take Me Back To New Orleans	16/04/1966	117	CB

Gary (U.S.) Bonds	Take Me Back To New Orleans	07/05/1966	121	BB
Gary & Dave	I Fell In Love With You Sometime	11/05/1974	117	CB
Gary & The Hornets	Kind Of Hush	04/02/1967	114	CB
Gary & The Hornets	Kind Of Hush	11/02/1967	127	BB
Gary & The Hornets	Baby It's You	27/05/1967	138	CB
Gary Criss	Our Favorite Melodies	16/06/1962	126	CB
Gary Lewis	Then Again Maybe	19/08/1972	110	CB
Gary Lewis & The Playboys	Something Is Wrong	22/11/1969	126	CB
Gary Lewis And The Playboys	Ice Melts In The Sun	04/03/1967	121	BB
Gary Lewis And The Playboys	Main Street	02/11/1968	101	BB
Gary Moore	Always Gonna' Love You	28/05/1983	103	BB
Gary Moore	Falling In Love With You	23/07/1983	110	BB
Gary Myrick	Message Is You	06/08/1983	103	BB
Gary Numan	I Die: You Die	27/09/1980	102	BB
Gary Numan & Tubeway Army	Are 'Friends' Electric?	28/06/1980	105	BB
Gary Stites	Little Tear	29/10/1960	112	CB
Gary Stites	Little Lonely One	25/03/1961	109	CB
Gary Stites	Hurting	08/10/1966	123	BB
Gary Stites	Hurting	08/10/1966	140	CB
Gary Toms	Stand Up And Shout	16/10/1976	109	BB
Gary Walker	You Don't Love Me	07/05/1966	131	CB
Gary Walker	You Don't Love Me	28/05/1966	129	BB
Gary Wright	Touch And Gone	28/01/1978	104	CB
Gary Wright	Heartbeat	31/10/1981	107	BB
Gato Barbieri	I Want You (Part I)	09/10/1976	110	BB
Gato Barbieri	Fiesta	26/02/1977	104	BB
Gayle Harris	Here Comes The Hurt	23/03/1963	142	CB
Gayle Mccormick	You Really Got A Hold On Me	15/01/1972	109	CB
Gemini	Take Her Back	20/12/1969	108	CB
Gemini	Take Her Back	17/01/1970	119	BB

Gene "Duke Of Earl" Chandler	Tear For Tear	22/09/1962	114	CB
Gene "Duke Of Earl" Chandler	Tear For Tear	20/10/1962	114	BB
Gene & DeBBe	Make A Noise Like Love	02/11/1968	137	CB
Gene & DeBBe	Make A Noise Like Love	16/11/1968	127	BB
Gene & DeBBe	Memories Are Made Of This	01/02/1969	116	CB
Gene & DeBBe	Memories Are Made Of This	15/02/1969	114	BB
Gene & Jerry	Ten And Two (Take This Woman Off The Corner)	29/05/1971	123	CB
Gene & Jerry	Ten And Two (Take This Woman Off The Corner)	03/07/1971	126	BB
Gene & Ruth	It Shouldn't Happen To A Dog	25/02/1961	130	CB
Gene & Tommy	Richard & Me	21/10/1967	122	BB
Gene & Wendell With The Sweethearts	The Roach	11/11/1961	111	CB
Gene Ammons Quartet	Canadian Sunset	05/11/1960	115	CB
Gene And Wendell	The Roach	30/10/1961	117	BB
Gene Chandler	Check Yourself	04/05/1963	146	CB
Gene Chandler	Check Yourself	25/05/1963	119	BB
Gene Chandler	Think Nothing About It	15/02/1964	101	CB
Gene Chandler	Think Nothing About It	29/02/1964	107	BB
Gene Chandler	Everybody Let's Dance	20/02/1965	106	CB
Gene Chandler	Good Times	07/08/1965	106	CB
Gene Chandler	Here Come The Tears	18/09/1965	102	BB
Gene Chandler	Here Come The Tears	16/10/1965	106	CB
Gene Chandler	You're A Lady	26/06/1971	116	BB
Gene Chandler	Does She Have A Friend?	14/06/1980	101	BB
Gene Chandler & Barbara Acklin	Little Green Apples	19/04/1969	130	CB
Gene Dozier & The Brotherhood	A Hunk Of Funk	28/10/1967	132	CB
Gene Dozier And The Brotherhood	A Hunk Of Funk	07/10/1967	121	BB
Gene Mcdaniels	Chapel Of Tears	21/04/1962	104	CB
Gene Mcdaniels	Funny	21/04/1962	134	CB
Gene Mcdaniels	Anyone Else	09/11/1963	143	CB
Gene Page	All Our Dreams Are Coming True	08/02/1975	104	BB

Gene Pitney	Take Me Tonight	15/04/1961	123	CB
Gene Pitney	Teardrop By Teardrop	30/03/1963	130	BB
Gene Pitney	Who Needs It	01/02/1964	131	BB
Gene Pitney	Nessuno Mi Puo' Giudcare	19/03/1966	115	BB
Gene Pitney	(In The) Cold Light Of Day	10/09/1966	115	BB
Gene Pitney	Animal Crackers (In Cellophane Boxes)	11/03/1967	106	BB
Gene Pitney	Animal Crackers (In Cellophane Boxes)	11/03/1967	129	CB
Gene Pitney	Something's Gotten Hold Of My Heart	23/09/1967	138	CB
Gene Pitney	Something's Gotten Hold Of My Heart	07/10/1967	130	BB
Gene Pitney	A Street Called Hope	20/06/1970	132	CB
Gene Pitney	Shady Lady	19/09/1970	139	CB
Gene Summers	The Clown	27/08/1966	112	CB
General Crook	Gimme Some (Part I)	05/09/1970	119	CB
General Crook	The Best Years Of My Life	03/11/1973	118	CB
General Crook	The Best Years Of My Life	08/12/1973	108	BB
General Public	Never You Done That	16/03/1985	105	BB
Genesis	Journey To The Moon Part I	09/08/1969	148	CB
George "Bad" Benson	Supership	21/06/1975	105	BB
George And Gene George Jones & Gene Pitney	I'm A Fool To Care	26/06/1965	115	BB
George Baker Selection	I Wanna Love You	05/09/1970	103	BB
George Baker Selection	I Wanna Love You	05/09/1970	105	CB
George Benson	My Woman's Good To Me	06/09/1969	113	BB
George Benson	My Woman's Good To Me	13/09/1969	131	CB
George Benson	Everything Must Change	04/06/1977	106	BB
George Benson	Turn Out The Lamplight	27/12/1980	109	BB
George Benson	I Just Wanna Hang Around You	06/04/1985	102	BB
George Chakiris	Maria	13/10/1962	110	BB
George Chakiris	Maria	27/10/1962	142	CB
George Clinton	Atomic Dog	05/03/1983	101	BB
George Clinton	Double Oh-Oh	15/06/1985	101	BB

George Duke	Dukey Stick (Part One)	27/05/1978	110	CB
George Goodman & His Headliners	Let Me Love You	29/05/1965	121	CB
George Hamilton	Don't Envy Me	09/11/1963	110	CB
George Hamilton	Don't Envy Me	30/11/1963	134	BB
George Hamilton Iv	Before This Day Ends	22/10/1960	113	CB
George Hamilton Iv	There's More Pretty Girls Than One	02/11/1963	137	CB
George Hamilton Iv	There's More Pretty Girls Than One	09/11/1963	116	BB
George Hamilton Iv	Fort Worth, Dallas Or Houston	25/07/1964	116	CB
George Harrison	Teardrops	15/08/1981	102	BB
George Jackson	When I Stop Lovin' You	18/02/1967	135	CB
George Jones	Tender Years	24/06/1961	110	CB
George Jones	Ain't It Funny What A Fool Will Do	13/07/1963	124	BB
George Jones	The Race Is On	02/01/1965	114	CB
George Jones	I'll Share My World With You	31/05/1969	124	BB
George Jones	A Good Year For The Roses	09/01/1971	112	BB
George Kerr	3 Minutes 2 - Hey Girl	25/04/1970	130	CB
George Kerr	3 Minutes 2 - Hey Girl	09/05/1970	124	BB
George Kranz	Trommeltanz (Din Daa Daa)	25/02/1984	110	BB
George Maharis	After The Lights Go Down Low	05/05/1962	104	BB
George Maharis	They Knew About You	14/07/1962	111	BB
George Maharis	They Knew About You	21/07/1962	137	CB
George Maharis	Don't Fence Me In	02/03/1963	121	CB
George Maharis	Where Can You Go (For A Broken Heart)	29/06/1963	102	BB
George Maharis	A World Without Sunshine	30/10/1965	133	CB
George Martin & His Orchestra	I Should Have Known Better	03/10/1964	122	CB
George Martin And His Orchestra	And I Love Her	01/08/1964	105	BB
George Martin And His Orchestra	I Should Have Known Better	03/10/1964	111	BB
George Martin And His Orchestra	A Hard's Day Night (b-side)	03/10/1964	122	BB
George Mccannon Iii	Birds Of All Nations	06/06/1970	111	BB
George Mccrae	Kiss Me (The Way I Like It)	19/11/1977	110	BB

George Scott	The Matador	12/06/1961	104	BB
George Stone	Hole In The Wall	20/11/1965	145	CB
George Thorogood & The Destroyers	Nobody But Me	11/09/1982	106	BB
George Tindley	Wan-Tu-Wah-Zuree	28/02/1970	106	CB
George, Johnny & The Pilots	Flying Blue Angels	09/12/1961	102	CB
Georgia GiBBs	Let Me Cry On Your Shoulder	29/05/1965	132	BB
Georgie Fame & The Blue Flames	In The Meantime	17/04/1965	103	CB
Geraldine Stevens	Billy, I've Got To Go To Town	23/08/1969	117	BB
Gerard	Hello, Operator	12/06/1976	109	BB
Gerri Granger	Can't Take My Eyes Off You	20/12/1975	108	BB
Gerry & The Pacemakers	How Do You Do It?	22/06/1963	132	CB
Gerry & The Pacemakers	I'm The One	18/04/1964	132	CB
Gerry & The Pacemakers	Walk Hand In Hand	27/11/1965	137	CB
Gerry And The Pacemakers	You're The Reason	21/08/1965	117	BB
Gerry And The Pacemakers	Walk Hand In Hand	11/12/1965	103	BB
Gerry And The Pacemakers	Don't Let The Sun Catch You Crying	12/12/1970	112	BB
Gerry Granahan	Unchained Melody	08/05/1961	109	BB
Giant Sunflower	February Sunshine	03/06/1967	106	BB
Giant Sunflower	February Sunshine	30/09/1967	110	CB
Giant Sunflower	What's So Good About Good-Bye	14/10/1967	116	BB
Gideon	Oh! Sweet Love	05/07/1969	134	CB
Gil & Johnny	Come On Sunshine	13/08/1966	130	CB
Gil & Johnny	Come On Sunshine	20/08/1966	112	BB
Gilbert O'sullivan	Nothing Rhymed	23/01/1971	106	CB
Gilbert O'sullivan	Nothing Rhymed	06/03/1971	114	BB
Gilbert O'sullivan	A Woman's Place	31/08/1974	109	CB
Gilbert O'sullivan	I Don't Love You But I Think I Like You	20/09/1975	107	CB
Ginny Arnell	I Wish I Knew What Dress To Wear	18/04/1964	130	BB
Ginny Tiu & The Few	Let Me Get Through To You, Baby	14/12/1968	136	CB
Gino Soccio	Try It Out	30/05/1981	103	BB

Gino Soccio	It's Alright	03/07/1982	108	BB
Gino Vannelli	Powerful People	01/03/1975	102	CB
Gino Vannelli	Love Me Now	13/09/1975	103	CB
Gino Vannelli	Mama Coco	03/01/1976	105	CB
Gino Vannelli	The Longer You Wait	27/02/1982	I102	CB
Gino Washington	Gino Is A Coward	09/05/1964	145	CB
Gino Washington	Gino Is A Coward	11/07/1964	121	BB
Gino Washington & The Rochelles With The Atlantics	Out Of This World	08/02/1964	115	CB
Gino Washington And The Rochelles With The Atlantics	Out Of This World	07/03/1964	120	BB
Giorgio	From Here To Eternity	29/10/1977	109	BB
Gladstone	Marietta Station	20/01/1973	117	CB
Gladys Knight & Pips	Lovers Always Forgive	22/08/1964	148	CB
Gladys Knight & The Pips	Guess Who	05/08/1961	125	CB
Gladys Knight & The Pips	Either Way I Lose	07/11/1964	119	BB
Gladys Knight & The Pips	Either Way I Lose	21/11/1964	120	CB
Gladys Knight & The Pips	Stop And Get A Hold Of Myself	13/03/1965	123	BB
Gladys Knight & The Pips	Stop And Get A Hold Of Myself	20/03/1965	125	CB
Gladys Knight & The Pips	Who Knows (b-side)	24/04/1965	129	BB
Gladys Knight & The Pips	Just Walk In My Shoes	16/07/1966	129	BB
Gladys Knight & The Pips	Hero (Wind Beneath My Wings)	03/12/1983	104	BB
Gladys Knight & The Pips	My Time	16/02/1985	102	BB
Glass Moon	(I Like) The Way You Play	19/07/1980	108	BB
Glassmoon	Cold Kid	30/06/1984	103	BB
Glen Campbell	Prima Donna	23/03/1963	103	BB
Glen Campbell	Prima Donna	23/03/1963	141	CB
Glen Campbell	Tomorrow Never Comes	17/04/1965	118	BB
Glen Campbell	Private John Q	04/12/1965	114	BB
Glen Campbell	Gentle On My Mind	21/09/1968	103	CB
Glen Campbell	Oklahoma Sunday Morning	08/01/1972	102	CB
Glen Campbell	Oklahoma Sunday Morning	08/01/1972	104	BB

Glen Campbell	Manhattan Kansas	01/04/1972	114	BB
Glen Campbell	Wherefore And Why	20/10/1973	110	CB
Glen Campbell	Wherefore And Why	20/10/1973	111	BB
Glenn Yarbrough	Honey And Wine	07/10/1967	142	CB
Gloria Dennis	Richie	01/09/1962	105	CB
Gloria Dennis	Richie	15/09/1962	115	BB
Gloria Gaynor	Honey Bee	01/06/1974	103	BB
Gloria Gaynor	Walk On By	14/06/1975	104	CB
Gloria Gaynor	(If You Want It) Do It Yourself	13/09/1975	103	CB
Gloria Gaynor	Substitute	28/10/1978	107	BB
Gloria Gaynor	Anybody Wanna Party?	23/06/1979	105	BB
Gloria Gaynor	I Am What I Am	17/12/1983	102	BB
Gloria Jones	Heartbeat Part 1	23/10/1965	112	CB
Gloria Jones	Heartbeat Part 1	13/11/1965	128	BB
Gloria Lynne	The Jazz In You	24/12/1960	103	CB
Gloria Lynne	The Jazz In You	30/01/1961	109	BB
Gloria Lynne	He Needs Me	08/05/1961	111	BB
Gloria Lynne	This Little Boy Of Mine	15/07/1961	129	CB
Gloria Lynne	Impossible	26/08/1961	105	CB
Gloria Lynne	You Don't Have To Be A Tower Of Strength	16/12/1961	110	CB
Gloria Lynne	Don't Take Your Love From Me	20/06/1964	132	CB
God's Children	Hey, Does Somebody Care	13/03/1971	112	BB
Godspell	Beautiful City	05/05/1973	105	CB
Golden Earring	Sleep Walkin'	03/04/1976	109	BB
Goliath	If Johnny Comes Marching Home	04/07/1970	122	CB
Gonzalez	Haven't Stopped Dancing Yet	18/11/1978	106	BB
Gonzalez	Haven't Stopped Dancing Yet (78 Mix)	23/12/1978	Np6	CB
Good & Plenty	Living In A World Of Make Believe	23/12/1967	111	BB
Good & Plenty	Living In A World Of Make Believe	30/12/1967	116	CB
Googie Rene	The Slide Part I	17/12/1960	104	CB

Googie Rene	The Slide (Part 1)	26/12/1960	105	BB
Googie Rene & His Combo	Flapjacks - Part I	19/01/1963	123	CB
Gordon Jenkins & His Orchestra	This Is All I Ask	27/04/1963	139	CB
Gordon Lightfoot	If I Could	03/04/1971	111	BB
Gordon Lightfoot	If I Could	10/04/1971	112	CB
Gordon Lightfoot	Summer Side Of Life	28/08/1971	116	CB
Gordon Lightfoot	That Same Old Obsession (b-side)	02/12/1972	102	BB
Gordon Lightfoot	That Same Old Obsession	09/12/1972	108	CB
Gordon Lightfoot	You Are What I Am	27/01/1973	126	CB
Gordon Lightfoot	You Are What I Am	24/02/1973	101	BB
Gq	Sitting In The Park	14/06/1980	101	BB
Gq	Sad Girl	06/02/1982	I103	CB
Grace Jones	La Vie En Rose	14/01/1978	109	BB
Grace Jones	Pull Up To The Bumper	06/06/1981	101	BB
Grace Jones	Nipple To The Bottle	13/11/1982	103	BB
Grace Slick	Seasons	29/03/1980	I102	CB
Grace Slick	Dreams	26/07/1980	104	BB
Graduates	What Good Is Graduation	01/06/1959	110	BB
Grady Martin & His Guitar	The Fuzz	11/03/1961	120	CB
Graf	Come To My Arms	14/03/1981	110	BB
Graham Nash	I Used To Be A King	27/11/1971	111	BB
Graham Nash & David Crosby	Southbound Train	29/07/1972	101	CB
Graham Parker	I Want You Back (Alive)	28/07/1979	103	BB
Graham Parker And The Rumour	(Let Me Get) Sweet On You (b-side)	02/04/1977	107b	BB
Grand Funk Railroad	People, Let's Stop The War	06/11/1971	105	CB
Grand Funk Railroad	Stuck In The Middle	28/11/1981	I101	CB
Grand Funk Railroad	Stuck In The Middle	12/12/1981	108	BB
Grandmaster & Melle Mel	White Lines (Don't Don't Do It)	19/11/1983	101	BB
Grapefruit	Dear Delilah	20/01/1968	107	CB
Grapefruit	Elevator	04/05/1968	113	BB

Grapefruit	Elevator	11/05/1968	118	CB
Grateful Dead	U.S. Blues	21/09/1974	109	CB
Gravy	We Can Make The World (A Whole Lot Brighter)	09/01/1971	107	CB
Greg Allman	Don't Mess Up A Good Thing	20/04/1974	106	BB
Greg Kihn	Sheila	11/04/1981	1103	CB
Greg Kihn	Sheila	02/05/1981	102	BB
Greg Kihn	The Girl Most Likely	03/10/1981	104	BB
Greg Kihn	Boy's Won't (Leave The Girls Alone)	08/06/1985	110	BB
Greg Kihn Band	Remember	04/11/1978	105	BB
Greg Kihn Band	Reunited	09/06/1984	101	BB
Greg Kihn Band	Rock	04/08/1984	107	BB
Greg Perry	Come On Down (Get Your Head Out Of The Clouds)	17/05/1975	124	CB
Gregg Diamond	Star Cruiser	27/01/1979	102	BB
Grey And Hanks	You Fooled Me	25/11/1978	104	BB
Griffin	Mississippi Lady	04/11/1972	114	BB
Grin	We All Sung Together	10/10/1970	108	BB
Grin	We All Sung Together	07/11/1970	114	CB
Grinder's Switch Featuring Garland Jeffreys	And Don't Be Late	02/05/1970	128	CB
Groove Holmes	What Now My Love	24/09/1966	102	CB
Groove Holmes	The More I See You	17/12/1966	131	BB
Group Therapy	Magic In The Air	04/11/1967	132	CB
Grover Washington Jr.	Jamming	10/04/1982	102	BB
Grover Washington Jr. With Patti Labelle	The Best Is Yet To Come	25/12/1982	104	BB
Grover Washington, Jr.	Inner City Blues	18/03/1972	120	BB
Guido Sarducci	A European (Speaks Up For The U.S.)	02/03/1974	103	CB
Gus Backus	Wooden Heart (Muss I Denn Zum Stadtele Hinaus)	01/07/1961	109	CB
Gus Backus	Wooden Heart (Muss I Denn Zum Stadtele Hinaus)	03/07/1961	102	BB
Gus Backus	Auf Wiederseh'n	18/09/1961	118	BB
Gus Backus	Auf Wiederseh'n	30/09/1961	125	CB
Gus Jenkins	Chittlins	14/11/1964	119	CB

Gus Jenkins	Chittlins	28/11/1964	113	BB
Guy Mitchell	The Same Old Me	05/03/1960	103	CB
Guy Mitchell	My Shoes Keep Walking Back To You	13/08/1960	106	CB
Guy Mitchell	Your Goodnight Kiss (Ain't What It Used To Be)	20/03/1961	106	BB
Guy Mitchell	Charlie's Shoes	30/06/1962	110	BB
Guy Mitchell	Charlie's Shoes	30/06/1962	143	CB
Guy Mitchell	Go Tiger, Go!	01/12/1962	101	BB
Guy Mitchell	Go Tiger, Go!	01/12/1962	123	CB
Guy Shannon	Naughty Girl	04/08/1973	115	CB
Gwen Guthrie	Love In Moderation	09/02/1985	110	BB
Gwen Guthrie	Padlock	06/07/1985	102	BB
Gwen Mccrae	Lead Me On	14/11/1970	102	BB
Gwen Mccrae	Lead Me On	14/11/1970	120	CB
H.B. Barnum	The Record	10/04/1965	105	CB
Haircut One Hundred	Favourite Shirts (Boy Meets Girl)	28/08/1982	101	BB
Hal Miller & The Rays	An Angel Cried	06/01/1962	135	CB
Hal Willis	The Lumberjack	24/10/1964	106	CB
Hal Willis	The Lumberjack	31/10/1964	120	BB
Hamilton Bohannon	Let's Start The Dance	16/09/1978	101	BB
Hamilton, Joe Frank & Dennison	Light Up The World With Sunshine	17/07/1976	101	CB
Hamilton, Joe Frank & Dennison	Don't Fight The Hands (That Need You)	04/12/1976	108	CB
Hamilton, Joe Frank & Reynolds	One Good Woman	18/03/1972	110	CB
Hamilton, Joe Frank & Reynolds	One Good Woman	18/03/1972	113	BB
Hank Ballard	Do You Know How To Twist	10/02/1962	101	CB
Hank Ballard & The Midnighters	Cute Little Ways	03/10/1959	118	CB
Hank Ballard & The Midnighters	The Float	24/06/1961	102	CB
Hank Ballard & The Midnighters	Nothing But Good	19/08/1961	119	CB
Hank Ballard And The Midnighters	Cute Little Ways	07/09/1959	106	BB
Hank Cochran	Sally Was A Good Old Girl	28/07/1962	128	CB
Hank Leeds	One More For The Road	19/12/1959	111	CB

Hank Leeds	One More For The Road	04/01/1960	103	BB
Hank Levine & Orchestra	Image - Part I	02/12/1961	136	CB
Hank Locklin	You're The Reason	04/09/1961	107	BB
Hank Marr	The Greasy Spoon	18/01/1964	101	BB
Hank Marr	Silver Spoon	27/03/1965	134	BB
Hank Mobley	The Turnaround, Part I	31/07/1965	118	CB
Hank Snow	Miller's Cave	27/06/1960	101	BB
Hank Snow	Miller's Cave	09/07/1960	104	CB
Hank Snow	Ninety Miles An Hour (Down A Dead End Street)	05/10/1963	124	BB
Hank Thompson	Pick Me Up On Your Way Down	23/04/1966	134	BB
Hank Thompson & The Brazos Valley Boys	Oklahoma Hills	13/05/1961	149	CB
Hank Thompson And His Brazos Valley Boys	A Six Pack To Go	21/03/1960	102	BB
Hank Williams	I'm So Lonesome I Could Cry	23/04/1966	109	BB
Hank Williams Jr.	Standing In The Shadows	02/07/1966	120	CB
Hank Williams Jr.	Cajun Baby	24/05/1969	107	BB
Hank Williams Jr.	I've Got A Right To Cry	12/06/1971	102	BB
Hank Williams Jr.	Family Tradition	15/09/1979	104	BB
Hank Williams, Jr. With The Mike Curb Congregation	Rainin' In My Heart	16/01/1971	108	BB
Hansie	Automobile	12/01/1980	109	BB
Harmonica Fats	Tore Up	23/02/1963	111	CB
Harmonica Fats	Tore Up	23/03/1963	103	BB
Harold Burrage	Got To Find A Way	28/08/1965	103	CB
Harold Burrage	Got To Find A Way	25/09/1965	128	BB
Harold Dorman	River Of Tears	30/07/1960	119	CB
Harold Dorman	Moved To Kansas City	15/10/1960	111	CB
Harold Melvin & The Blue Notes, Featuring Sharon Page	After You Love Me, Why Do You Leave Me	11/06/1977	102	BB
Harold Melvin And The Blue Notes	Get Out (And Let Me Cry)	30/01/1965	125	BB
Harpers Bizarre	Cotton Candy Sandman (Sandman's Coming)	09/03/1968	131	CB
Harpers Bizarre	Both Sides Now	01/06/1968	133	CB
Harpers Bizarre	Both Sides Now	15/06/1968	123	BB

Harpers Bizarre	Battle Of New Orleans	21/09/1968	111	CB
Harry Belafonte	A Strange Song	07/10/1967	137	CB
Harry Chapin	Better Place To Be	13/01/1973	101	CB
Harry Chapin	Better Place To Be	03/02/1973	118	BB
Harry Chapin	Story Of A Life	29/08/1981	105	BB
Harry Charles	My Laura	24/08/1963	107	BB
Harry Charles	My Laura	31/08/1963	143	CB
Harry Simeone Chorale	Do You Hear What I Hear?	15/12/1962	106	CB
Harry Simeone Chorale	The Little Drummer Boy	19/12/1964	123	CB
Harry Simeone Chorale	O' Bambino (One Cold And Blessed Winter)	26/12/1964	136	CB
Harry Simeone Chorale	O' Bambino (One Cold And Blessed Winter)	09/01/1965	105	BB
Harry Simeone Orchestra & Chorus	La Dolce Vita (The Sweet Life)*	27/05/1961	113	CB
Harvey (Formerly Of The Moonglows)	Any Way You Wanta	23/03/1963	131	BB
Harvey Russell & The Rogues	Shake Sherry	17/09/1966	123	CB
Harvey Russell & The Rogues	Shake Sherry	24/09/1966	131	BB
Hawkshaw Hawkins	Lonesome 7-7203	06/04/1963	108	BB
Hawkshaw Hawkins	Lonesome 7-7203	27/04/1963	110	CB
Hayley Mills	Ching - Ching And A Ding Ding Ding	16/06/1962	137	CB
Hayley Mills	Ching-Ching And A Ding Ding Ding	07/07/1962	118	BB
Hayley Mills	Castaway	02/02/1963	111	CB
Head East	Got To Be Real	26/01/1980	103	BB
Heart	Bebe Le Strange	14/06/1980	109	BB
Heartsfield	As I Look Into The Fire	27/09/1975	113	CB
Heatwave	Gangsters Of The Groove	22/11/1980	110	BB
Heaven 17	We Live So Fast	09/07/1983	102	BB
Heaven Bound With Tony Scotti	Breaking Up Is Hard To Do	01/07/1972	101	BB
Heaven Bound With Tony Scotti	Breaking Up Is Hard To Do	08/07/1972	101	CB
Hector Rivera	At The Party	31/12/1966	104	BB
Hedgehoppers Anonymous	Don't Push Me	19/03/1966	110	BB
Hedgehoppers Anonymous	Don't Push Me	26/03/1966	113	CB

Heintje	Mama	02/01/1971	112	BB
Helen Shapiro	You Don't Know	04/11/1961	147	CB
Helen Shapiro	Walkin' Back To Happiness	02/12/1961	112	CB
Helene Smith	A Woman Will Do Wrong	24/06/1967	128	BB
Helene Smith	A Woman Will Do Wrong	22/07/1967	126	CB
Helix	Rock You	01/09/1984	101	BB
Helmut Zacharias	Tokyo Melody*	12/12/1964	128	CB
Henry Booth And The Midnighters	Every Beat Of My Heart	15/05/1961	113	BB
Henry Gross	Come On Say It	20/07/1974	109	BB
Henry Gross	Someday (I Didn't Want To Have To Be The One)	13/11/1976	104	CB
Henry Gross	Painting My Love Song	23/04/1977	110	BB
Henry Gross	What A Sound	02/07/1977	110	BB
Henry Mancini & His Orchestra	High Time	15/10/1960	125	CB
Henry Mancini & His Orchestra	Experiment In Terror	07/04/1962	119	CB
Henry Mancini & His Orchestra	A Shot In The Dark	18/07/1964	102	CB
Henry Mancini & His Orchestra	La Raspa	29/05/1965	134	CB
Henry Mancini & His Orchestra	Theme From "Z" ("Life Goes On" To Yelasto Pedi)	28/03/1970	112	CB
Henry Mancini & His Orchestra	Theme From The Molly Maguires	18/04/1970	123	CB
Henry Mancini And His Orchestra	Theme From "Z" (Life Goes On)	07/03/1970	115	BB
Henry Mancini And His Orchestra	Ravel's Bolero	09/02/1980	101	BB
Henry Mancini, His Orchestra & Chorus	The Sweetheart Tree	17/07/1965	117	BB
Henry Mancini, His Orchestra & Chorus	Moment To Moment	29/01/1966	126	CB
Henry Mancini, His Orchestra & Chorus	A Man, A Horse, And A Gun	26/10/1968	120	CB
Henry Mancini, His Orchestra & Chorus	Theme From Nicholas And Alexandra	05/02/1972	121	CB
Henry Paul Band	Longshot	13/09/1980	103	BB
Henry Paul Band	Brown Eyed Girl	06/03/1982	105	BB
Henry Thome	Scotch And Soda (Live)	12/05/1962	141	CB
Herb Alpert	Street Life	29/03/1980	104	BB
Herb Alpert	Magic Man	01/08/1981	1102	CB
Herb Alpert & The T.J.B.	Coney Island	17/05/1975	101	CB

Herb Alpert & The T.J.B.	El Bimbo	12/07/1975	110	CB
Herb Alpert & The T.J.B. Featuring Lani Hall	Save The Sunlight	20/07/1974	113	CB
Herb Alpert & The Tijuana Brass	Mae	29/05/1965	116	BB
Herb Alpert & The Tijuana Brass	Mae	10/07/1965	130	CB
Herb Alpert & The Tijuana Brass	Slick	27/04/1968	119	BB
Herb Alpert & The Tijuana Brass	She Touched Me	18/01/1969	108	CB
Herb Alpert & The Tijuana Brass	Ob-La-Di, Ob-La-Da	09/08/1969	109	CB
Herb Alpert & The Tijuana Brass	Ob-La-Di, Ob-La-Da	16/08/1969	118	BB
Herb Alpert & The Tijuana Brass	Marjorine	23/08/1969	129	CB
Herb Alpert & The Tijuana Brass	You Are My Life	22/11/1969	109	BB
Herb Alpert & The Tijuana Brass	The Maltese Melody	24/01/1970	110	CB
Herb Alpert & The Tijuana Brass	The Maltese Melody	31/01/1970	108	BB
Herb Alpert & The Tijuana Brass	Summertime	05/06/1971	117	CB
Herb Alpert & The Tijuana Brass	Summertime	12/06/1971	114	BB
Herb Alpert's Tijuana Brass	Struttin' With Maria	23/03/1963	102	BB
Herb Alpert's Tijuana Brass	Mexican Drummer Man	21/03/1964	111	CB
Herbie Hancock	Watermelon Man	23/03/1963	121	BB
Herbie Hancock	Watermelon Man	06/07/1974	105	CB
Herbie Hancock	Palm Grease	09/11/1974	115	CB
Herbie Hancock	Doin' It	02/10/1976	104	BB
Herbie Hancock	Mega-Mix (Includes: Rockit, Autodrive, Future Shock, Tfs,	02/06/1984	105	BB
Herbie Mann	Comin' Home Baby	18/08/1962	101	BB
Herbie Mann	Comin' Home Baby	01/09/1962	128	CB
Herbie Mann	Right Now	13/10/1962	111	BB
Herbie Mann	Philly Dog	15/10/1966	144	CB
Herbie Mann	It's A Funky Thing - Right On (pt. 1)	04/10/1969	122	CB
Herman's Hermits	The End Of The World	17/07/1965	113	CB
Herman's Hermits	Sea Cruise	09/10/1965	108	CB
Herman's Hermits	Sunshine Girl	10/08/1968	101	BB
Herman's Hermits	The Most Beautiful Thing In My Life	12/10/1968	131	BB

Herman's Hermits	Something's Happening	01/03/1969	123	CB
Herman's Hermits	Something's Happening	01/03/1969	130	BB
Herman's Hermits	My Sentimental Friend	21/06/1969	109	CB
Hernando And The Orchestra	A Very Precious Love	29/06/1959	103	BB
Herschel Bernardi	If I Were A Rich Man	04/02/1967	134	CB
Herschel Bernardi	Pencil Marks On The Wall	20/02/1971	105	CB
Herschel Bernardi	Pencil Marks On The Wall	27/02/1971	107	BB
Hidden Strength	Hustle On Up (Do The Bump)	06/03/1976	105	CB
Hidden Strength	Hustle On Up (Do The Bump)	13/03/1976	105	BB
High Inergy	Shoulda Gone Dancin'	16/06/1979	101	BB
High Inergy	Back In My Arms Again	06/08/1983	105	BB
Hoagy Lands	Baby Come On Home	15/02/1964	124	BB
Hollies	Gasoline Alley Bred	28/11/1970	113	CB
Hollies	Don't Let Me Down	21/09/1974	114	CB
Holly Penfield	Only His Name	16/08/1980	105	BB
Holly Sherwood	Day By Day (Godspell Medley)	18/09/1971	104	BB
Holly Sherwood	Yesterday And You	12/05/1973	114	CB
Holly Sherwood	Yesterday And You	19/05/1973	117	BB
Homar Jackson	Sea Trip	11/03/1972	122	CB
Homer And Jethro	Please Help Me, I'm Falling	03/10/1960	101	BB
Honey Ltd.	Come Down	23/03/1968	104	CB
Honeyman	Brother Bill (The Last Clean Shirt)	22/08/1964	130	CB
Hong Kong White Sox	Cholley-Oop	06/08/1960	103	CB
Horatio	Age (Where I Started Again)	26/07/1969	119	BB
Horatio	Age (Where I Started Again)	02/08/1969	121	CB
Horatio	I Gotta Have You	15/11/1969	111	CB
Horst Jankowski	Zabadak	20/07/1968	133	CB
Horst Jankowski, His Orchestra & Chorus	Heide	23/10/1965	135	CB
Horst Jankowski, Piano & Orchestra	Play A Simple Melody	15/01/1966	139	CB
Hot Butter	Tequila	16/12/1972	103	CB

Hot Butter	Tequila	20/01/1973	105	BB
Hot Butter	Percolator	21/04/1973	106	BB
Hot Butter	Slag Solution	15/09/1973	123	CB
Hot Tuna	Keep On Truckin'	22/04/1972	108	CB
Hounds	Under My Thumb	08/12/1979	110	BB
Houston Person	Disco Sax	24/01/1976	116	CB
Howard Johnson	So Fine	25/09/1982	105	BB
Howard Jones	Pearl In The Shell	25/08/1984	108	BB
Howard Tate	Get It While You Can	08/04/1967	119	CB
Howard Tate	Get It While You Can	08/04/1967	134	BB
Howard Tate	Baby, I Love You	10/06/1967	127	CB
Howard Tate	These Are The Things That Make Me Know You're Gone	21/06/1969	123	CB
Howard Tate	These Are The Things That Make Me Know You Are Gone	20/09/1969	120	BB
Hoyt Axton	Nashville	08/02/1975	106	BB
Hoyt Axton	Speed Trap	15/03/1975	105	BB
Hudson	Leavin' It's Over	18/03/1972	110	BB
Hudson Brothers	Coochie Coochie Coo	11/01/1975	104	CB
Hudson Brothers	Coochie Coochie Coo	25/01/1975	108	BB
Hudson Brothers	Spinning The Wheel (With The Girl You Love)	06/03/1976	109	CB
Hugh Masekela	Son Of Ice Bag (Live)	16/12/1967	146	CB
Hugh Masekela	Do Me So La So So	21/09/1968	141	CB
Hugh Masekela	A Long Ways From Home	29/03/1969	140	CB
Hugh Masekela	A Long Ways From Home	12/04/1969	107	BB
Hugo & Luigi With Their Children's Chorus	La Pachanga*	15/04/1961	112	CB
Hugo Montenegro	Love Theme From "THE Godfather"	22/04/1972	108	CB
Hugo Montenegro & His Orchestra	Theme From The Motion Picture The Young Savages	01/07/1961	139	CB
Hugo Montenegro & His Orchestra	Tarantella Twist	28/04/1962	149	CB
Hugo Montenegro, His Orchestra & Chorus	For A Few Dollars More	04/11/1967	130	CB
Hugo Montenegro, His Orchestra & Chorus	Good Vibrations	18/01/1969	125	CB
Hugo Montenegro, His Orchestra & Chorus	Happy Together	06/09/1969	117	CB

Hugo Montenegro, His Orchestra And Chorus	For A Few Dollars More	04/11/1967	102	BB
Hugo Montenegro, His Orchestra And Chorus	Good Vibrations	15/02/1969	112	BB
Hugo Montenegro, His Orchestra And Chorus	Happy Together	31/05/1969	112	BB
Humble Pie	Black Coffee	31/03/1973	107	CB
Humble Pie	Black Coffee	07/04/1973	113	BB
Humble Pie	Get Down To It	19/05/1973	112	CB
Humble Pie	Rock And Roll Music	02/08/1975	105	BB
Hutch Davie & His Honky Tonkers	Sweet Georgia Brown	28/11/1959	117	CB
Hypnotics	Beware Of The Stranger	21/04/1973	115	BB
I.A.P. Co. (The Italian Asphalt & Pavement Company)	Check Yourself	28/03/1970	103	CB
Ian & Sylvia	Four Strong Winds	05/10/1963	122	CB
Ian & The Zodiacs	So Much In Love With You	03/07/1965	125	CB
Ian & The Zodiacs	So Much In Love With You	31/07/1965	131	BB
Ian And Sylvia	Lovin' Sound	08/07/1967	101	BB
Ian Hunter	When The Daylight Comes	02/06/1979	108	BB
Ian Hunter	We Gotta' Get Out Of Here	05/07/1980	108	BB
Ian Matthews	Da Doo Ron Ron (When He Walked Me Home)	26/02/1972	105	CB
Ian Whitcomb	Fizz	23/10/1965	138	CB
Ian Whitcomb	Good Hard Rock	18/12/1965	108	CB
Ian Whitcomb & His Seaside Syncopators	Where Did Robinson Crusoe Go With Friday On Saturday Night?	26/11/1966	118	CB
Ian Whitcomb And His Seaside Syncopators	Where Did Robinson Crusoe Go With Friday On Saturday Night?	26/11/1966	101	BB
Idris Muhammad	Turn This Mutha Out (Part 1)	27/08/1977	102	BB
Ike & Tina And The Ikettes	So Fine	30/03/1968	117	BB
Ike & Tina Turner	You're My Baby	25/02/1961	111	CB
Ike & Tina Turner	I'm Jealous	27/02/1961	117	BB
Ike & Tina Turner	You Should'a Treated Me Right	30/06/1962	105	CB
Ike & Tina Turner	You Can't Miss Nothing That You Never Had	08/02/1964	122	BB
Ike & Tina Turner	You Can't Miss Nothing That You Never Had	07/03/1964	105	CB
Ike & Tina Turner	A Fool For A Fool	23/05/1964	142	CB
Ike & Tina Turner	I Can't Believe What You Say (For Seeing What You Do)	10/10/1964	134	CB

Ike & Tina Turner	Tell Her I'm Not Home	27/02/1965	108	BB
Ike & Tina Turner	Tell Her I'm Not Home	06/03/1965	135	CB
Ike & Tina Turner	Good Bye, So Long	15/05/1965	120	CB
Ike & Tina Turner	Good Bye, So Long	05/06/1965	107	BB
Ike & Tina Turner	I Don't Need	07/08/1965	134	BB
Ike & Tina Turner	Two Is A Couple	23/10/1965	113	CB
Ike & Tina Turner	Can't Chance A Break Up	15/01/1966	142	CB
Ike & Tina Turner	River Deep - Mountain High	21/05/1966	105	CB
Ike & Tina Turner	I'll Never Need More Than This	01/07/1967	114	BB
Ike & Tina Turner	The Hunter	21/06/1969	114	CB
Ike & Tina Turner	River Deep-Mountain High	18/10/1969	112	BB
Ike & Tina Turner	I Know	18/10/1969	126	BB
Ike & Tina Turner	River Deep - Mountain High	18/10/1969	129	CB
Ike & Tina Turner	Workin' Together	07/11/1970	105	BB
Ike & Tina Turner	I've Been Loving You Too Long	31/07/1971	120	BB
Ike & Tina Turner	I've Been Loving You Too Long	07/08/1971	121	CB
Ike & Tina Turner	I'm Yours (Use Me Anyway You Wanna)	13/11/1971	104	BB
Ike & Tina Turner	Feel Good	13/05/1972	101	CB
Ike & Tina Turner	Sweet Rhode Island Red	06/04/1974	109	CB
Ike & Tina Turner	Sweet Rhode Island Red	04/05/1974	106	BB
Imagination	Just An Illusion	03/07/1982	102	BB
Impact	Give A Broken Heart A Break	14/08/1976	102	BB
Impact	One Last Memory	06/11/1976	107	BB
Impressions	Loving Power	07/02/1976	103	BB
In Transit	Turn On Your Light	02/08/1980	107	BB
Indeep	Last Night A D.J. Saved My Life	26/02/1983	101	BB
Inez & Charlie Foxx	La De Da I Love You	29/08/1964	124	BB
Inez & Charlie Foxx	La De Da I Love You	12/09/1964	113	CB
Inez & Charlie Foxx	Tightrope	18/03/1967	124	CB
Inez & Charlie Foxx	I Stand Accused	06/05/1967	117	CB

Inez & Charlie Foxx	I Stand Accused	03/06/1967	127	BB
Inez Foxx	He's The One You Love	12/10/1963	113	BB
Inez Foxx	Broken Hearted Fool	19/10/1963	133	CB
Inez Foxx	Hi Diddle Diddle	09/11/1963	108	CB
Inez Foxx With Charlie Foxx	Come By Here	17/12/1966	138	CB
Innervision	Honey Baby (Be Mine)	31/05/1975	106	BB
Instant Funk	Bodyshine	02/02/1980	103	BB
Invictus	New Babe (Since I Found You)	05/04/1969	105	CB
Irish Rovers	Did She Mention My Name	09/08/1969	115	CB
Irma Thomas	Don't Mess With My Man	12/03/1960	124	CB
Irma Thomas	Ruler Of My Heart	03/08/1963	141	CB
Irma Thomas	Time Is On My Side	27/06/1964	129	CB
Irma Thomas	You Don't Miss A Good Thing (Until It's Gone)	06/03/1965	109	BB
Irma Thomas	You Don't Miss A Good Thing (Until It's Gone)	06/03/1965	116	CB
Irma Thomas	I'm Gonna Cry Till My Tears Run Dry	01/05/1965	138	CB
Irma Thomas	I'm Gonna Cry Till My Tears Run Dry	15/05/1965	130	BB
Irma Thomas	Take A Look	13/11/1965	118	BB
Irma Thomas	It's A Man's-Woman's World - Part I	18/06/1966	119	BB
Iron Butterfly	I Can't Help But Deceive You Little Girl	11/10/1969	118	BB
Iron Butterfly	Beyond The Milky Way	27/12/1975	108	BB
Isaac Hayes	Rolling Down A Mountainside	21/04/1973	104	BB
Isaac Hayes	Rolling Down A Mountainside	21/04/1973	105	CB
Isaac Hayes	Wonderful	11/05/1974	101	CB
Isaac Hayes	Juicy Fruit (Disco Freak) Pt. I	28/08/1976	102	BB
Isaac Hayes	Out Of The Ghetto	21/01/1978	107	BB
Isaac Hayes	It's All In The Game	23/08/1980	107	BB
Isley Brothers	Warpath	03/04/1971	111	BB
Israel "Popper Stopper" Tolbert	Shake Your Big Hips	20/02/1971	120	CB
It's A Beautiful Day	White Bird	20/09/1969	110	CB
It's A Beautiful Day	White Bird	04/10/1969	118	BB

J. Frank Wilson & The Cavaliers	Hey Little One	05/12/1964	103	CB
J. Frank Wilson And The Cavaliers	Six Boys	23/01/1965	101	BB
J. Gardner	99 Plus 1	10/07/1965	104	CB
J. Gardner	99 Plus 1	14/08/1965	102	BB
J. Geils Band	Did You No Wrong	16/02/1974	104	BB
J.C. Cunningham	The Pyramid Song	05/07/1980	104	BB
J.D. Souther	White Rhythm And Blues	09/02/1980	105	BB
J.D. Souther	Go Ahead And Rain	21/07/1984	104	BB
J.J. Barnes	Poor-Unfortunate-Me (I Ain't Got Nobody)	23/01/1965	129	CB
J.J. Jackson	Four Walls (Three Windows And Two Doors)	15/07/1967	123	BB
J.R. Bailey	Love Won't Wear Off (As The Years Wear On)	28/12/1968	133	CB
J.R. Bailey	Love, Love, Love	27/05/1972	107	CB
J.R. Bailey	The Entertainer (If They Could Only See Me Now)	12/07/1975	119	CB
Jack B. Nimble & The Quicks	(The Original) Nut Rocker*	10/02/1962	125	CB
Jack B. Nimble And The Quicks	Nut Rocker	17/03/1962	115	BB
Jack Blanchard & Misty Morgan	Big Black Bird (Spirit Of Our Love)	03/05/1969	127	CB
Jack Eubanks, His Orchestra & Singers	What'd I Say	18/02/1961	114	CB
Jack Greene	There Goes My Everything	21/01/1967	136	CB
Jack Greene	All The Time	27/05/1967	103	BB
Jack Greene	Statue Of A Fool	05/07/1969	116	CB
Jack Jones	Gift Of Love	26/05/1962	108	CB
Jack Jones	Poetry	04/08/1962	110	CB
Jack Jones	Toys In The Attic	28/09/1963	115	CB
Jack Jones	Travellin' On	12/06/1965	132	BB
Jack Jones	The True Picture	23/10/1965	109	CB
Jack Jones	The True Picture	23/10/1965	134	BB
Jack Jones	The Weekend	05/02/1966	123	BB
Jack Jones	Open For Business As Usual	07/10/1967	104	CB
Jack Jones	Open For Business As Usual	28/10/1967	130	BB
Jack Jones	Oh How Much I Love You (Dio Come Ti Amo)	16/12/1967	129	CB

Jack Jones	The Gypsies, The Jugglers And The Clowns	23/03/1968	134	CB
Jack Jones	Follow Me	11/05/1968	117	BB
Jack Jones	L.A. Break Down (And Take Me In)	07/12/1968	106	BB
Jack Kittel	Psycho	07/09/1974	114	CB
Jack Laforge, His Piano & Orchestra	Our Crazy Affair	01/05/1965	137	CB
Jack Mcduff	Rock Candy [Live]	02/11/1963	109	BB
Jack Mcduff	Rock Candy (Live)	11/01/1964	134	CB
Jack Nitzsche	Rumble	09/11/1963	111	CB
Jack Nitzsche	Senorita From Detroit	22/05/1965	123	CB
Jack Nitzsche Orchestra	Theme From One Flew Over The Cuckoo's Nest	15/05/1976	109	BB
Jack Reno	Blue	06/04/1963	115	CB
Jack Scott	Strange Desire	29/07/1961	129	CB
Jack Scott	My Dream Come True	12/08/1961	120	CB
Jack Scott	Cry, Cry, Cry	03/03/1962	150	CB
Jack Scott	Laugh And The World Laughs With You	09/03/1963	130	CB
Jack Scott	All I See Is Blue	18/05/1963	102	CB
Jack Scott	Blue Skies (Moving In On Me)	15/02/1964	147	CB
Jack Wagner	Premonition	02/03/1985	101	BB
Jack Wild	Wait For Summer	15/08/1970	115	BB
Jack Wild	Wait For Summer	12/09/1970	101	CB
Jack Wild	(Holy Moses!) Everything's Coming Up Roses	28/08/1971	107	BB
Jackie Brenston	Trouble Up The Road	13/03/1961	118	BB
Jackie Deshannon	The Prince	28/04/1962	108	BB
Jackie Deshannon	You Won't Forget Me	27/10/1962	104	CB
Jackie Deshannon	Faded Love	26/01/1963	144	CB
Jackie Deshannon	Little Yellow Roses	24/08/1963	108	CB
Jackie Deshannon	Little Yellow Roses	14/09/1963	110	BB
Jackie Deshannon	Oh Boy	14/03/1964	133	CB
Jackie Deshannon	Oh Boy	04/04/1964	112	BB
Jackie Deshannon	When You Walk In The Room	24/10/1964	131	CB

Jackie Deshannon	Windows And Doors	29/10/1966	108	BB
Jackie Deshannon	Windows And Doors	12/11/1966	147	CB
Jackie Deshannon	Come On Down (From The Top Of That Hill)	11/02/1967	147	CB
Jackie Deshannon	Come On Down (From The Top Of That Hill)	18/02/1967	121	BB
Jackie Deshannon	It's All In The Game	30/09/1967	110	BB
Jackie Deshannon	Me About You	09/03/1968	119	BB
Jackie Deshannon	Me About You	16/03/1968	113	CB
Jackie Deshannon	You Keep Me Hangin' On/Hurt So Bad	16/05/1970	101	CB
Jackie Deshannon	Paradise	21/10/1972	110	BB
Jackie Hairston	Hijack	08/04/1967	144	CB
Jackie Lee	Your P-E-R-S-O-N-A-L-L-T-Y	05/03/1966	111	BB
Jackie Lee	Do The Temptation Walk	23/04/1966	113	BB
Jackie Lee	Do The Temptation Walk	07/05/1966	139	CB
Jackie Lee	African Boo-Ga-Loo	23/03/1968	121	BB
Jackie Lomax	Sour Milk Sea	28/09/1968	117	BB
Jackie Lomax	The Eagle Laughs At You (b-side)	26/10/1968	125	BB
Jackie Lomax	New Day	21/06/1969	120	CB
Jackie Moore	Willpower	17/10/1970	129	CB
Jackie Moore	Darling Baby	25/03/1972	106	BB
Jackie Moore	Both Ends Against The Middle	17/11/1973	102	BB
Jackie Paine	Go Go Train	25/06/1966	103	CB
Jackie Ross	Haste Makes Waste	05/12/1964	126	BB
Jackie Ross	Haste Makes Waste	26/12/1964	142	CB
Jackie Ross	Take Me For A Little While	24/07/1965	147	CB
Jackie Shane	Any Other Way	19/01/1963	124	BB
Jackie Shane	In My Tenement	06/07/1963	122	CB
Jackie Trent	If You Love Me, Really Love Me	25/04/1964	106	BB
Jackie Trent	If You Love Me Really Love Me	25/04/1964	112	CB
Jackie Wilson	Only You, Only Me	21/11/1959	119	CB
Jackie Wilson	Lonely Life	17/06/1961	114	CB

Jackie Wilson	Forever And A Day	08/09/1962	103	CB
Jackie Wilson	Baby, That's All	06/10/1962	119	BB
Jackie Wilson	What Good Am I Without You?	22/12/1962	103	CB
Jackie Wilson	What Good Am I Without You?	05/01/1963	121	BB
Jackie Wilson	I'm Travelin' On	15/02/1964	121	CB
Jackie Wilson	I'm Travelin' On	29/02/1964	123	BB
Jackie Wilson	Call Her Up	11/04/1964	135	CB
Jackie Wilson	Call Her Up	18/04/1964	110	BB
Jackie Wilson	Big Boss Line	23/05/1964	104	CB
Jackie Wilson	Squeeze Her - Tease Her (But Love Her)	15/08/1964	108	CB
Jackie Wilson	Give Me Back My Heart	22/08/1964	113	CB
Jackie Wilson	She's All Right	10/10/1964	102	BB
Jackie Wilson	Watch Out	10/10/1964	115	CB
Jackie Wilson	She's All Right	17/10/1964	129	CB
Jackie Wilson	Danny Boy	20/02/1965	113	CB
Jackie Wilson	3 Days 1 Hour 30 Minutes	19/02/1966	106	CB
Jackie Wilson	Just Be Sincere	18/02/1967	103	CB
Jackie Wilson	I Still Love You	22/03/1969	105	BB
Jackie Wilson	Helpless	13/09/1969	108	BB
Jackie Wilson	You Got Me Walking	29/01/1972	112	CB
Jackie Wilson & Lavern Baker	Please Don't Hurt Me (I've Never Been In Love Before)	01/01/1966	128	BB
Jackie Wilson & Linda Hopkins	I Found Love	14/04/1962	136	CB
Jackson Browne	Walking Slow	08/02/1975	114	CB
Jackson Browne	You Love The Thunder	02/12/1978	109	BB
Jackson Browne	Hold On, Hold Out	24/01/1981	103	BB
Jacky Ward	A Lover's Question	29/04/1978	106	BB
Jacqui Brookes	Lost Without Your Love	11/02/1984	105	BB
Jake Holmes	How Are You? - Part One	20/09/1969	109	CB
James & BoBBy Purify	Untie Me	28/12/1968	128	CB
James And BoBBy Purify	Do Your Thing	04/01/1975	101	BB

James Anderson	Mama Mama	14/11/1970	106	BB
James Brown	New Breed (Part 1) (The Boo-Ga-Loo)	07/05/1966	102	BB
James Brown	Hey America	12/12/1970	105	BB
James Brown	Hey America	26/12/1970	126	CB
James Brown	Think	01/09/1973	101	CB
James Brown	Sex Machine (Part I)	24/05/1975	102	CB
James Brown	Bodyheat (Part 1)	05/02/1977	110	CB
James Brown & His Orchestra	Caldonia	25/04/1964	104	CB
James Brown & His Orchestra	Maybe The Last Time	22/08/1964	119	CB
James Brown & The Famous Flames	Good Good Lovin'	24/10/1959	113	CB
James Brown & The Famous Flames	Baby, You're Right	19/08/1961	131	CB
James Brown & The Famous Flames	Mashed Potatoes U.S.A.	22/09/1962	138	CB
James Brown & The Famous Flames	Three Hearts In A Tangle	24/11/1962	128	CB
James Brown & The Famous Flames	I've Got To Change	28/12/1963	120	CB
James Brown & The Famous Flames	Again	25/04/1964	150	CB
James Brown & The Famous Flames	So Long	20/06/1964	148	CB
James Brown & The Famous Flames	Have Mercy Baby	02/01/1965	102	CB
James Brown & The Famous Flames	Lost Someone (Live)	12/02/1966	144	CB
James Brown & The Famous Flames	Sweet Little Baby Boy (Part 1)	03/12/1966	104	CB
James Brown & The Famous Flames	The Soul Of J.B.	02/12/1967	125	CB
James Brown & The Famous Flames	Shhhhhhhh (For A Little While)	11/05/1968	108	CB
James Brown And His Orchestra	Maybe The Last Time	10/10/1964	107	BB
James Brown And The Famous Flames	Again	25/04/1964	107	BB
James Brown And The Famous Flames	In The Wee Wee Hours (Of The Night)	25/04/1964	125	BB
James Brown And The Famous Flames	How Long Darling (b-side) [Live]	06/06/1964	134	BB
James Brown And The Famous Flames	So Long	27/06/1964	132	BB
James Brown And The Famous Flames	Shhhhhhhh (For A Little While)	15/06/1968	104	BB
James Brown At The Organ	Our Day Will Come	03/12/1966	105	CB
James Brown At The Organ & His Orchestra	Devil's Hideaway	27/03/1965	107	CB
James Brown At The Organ And His Orchestra	Devil's Hideaway	24/04/1965	114	BB

James Brown Plays & Directs	Soul Pride (Part 1)	05/04/1969	117	BB
James Brown Presents His Band	Hold It	13/02/1961	109	BB
James Brown With The Famous Flames	Please, Please, Please	21/11/1960	105	BB
James Carr	Let It Happen	10/06/1967	106	BB
James Carr	I'm A Fool For You	09/09/1967	112	CB
James Carr	Life Turned Her That Way	03/08/1968	112	BB
James Cleveland And The Cleveland Singers	Without A Song (Part 1)	06/08/1966	129	BB
James Crawford	Strung Out	05/12/1964	124	CB
James Darren	Hail To The Conquering Hero	08/09/1962	113	CB
James Darren	They Should Have Given You The Oscar	13/04/1963	114	CB
James Darren	Since I Don't Have You	22/04/1967	123	BB
James Darren	Mammy Blue	30/10/1971	107	BB
James Darren	I Think Somebody Loves Me	22/04/1972	122	CB
James Davis	Blue Monday	02/11/1963	110	CB
James Davis	Blue Monday	23/11/1963	113	BB
James Ingram	Party Animal	22/10/1983	101	BB
James Last	Music From Across The Way	08/01/1972	103	CB
James Last	Love For Sale	19/07/1975	106	BB
James Macarthur	(The Story Of) The In-Between Years	17/11/1962	132	CB
James O'gwynn	My Name Is Mud	21/04/1962	128	CB
James Stewart	The Legend Of Shenandoah	10/07/1965	133	BB
James Stewart	The Legend Of Shenandoah	17/07/1965	144	CB
James Taylor	Carolina In My Mind	28/03/1969	128	CB
James Taylor	Carolina In My Mind	12/04/1969	118	BB
James Taylor	Hymn	21/04/1973	118	CB
James Walsh Gypsy Band	Love Is For The Best In Us	09/06/1979	103	BB
Jamie Coe	How Low Is Low	10/02/1962	128	CB
Jamie Coe	The Fool	16/03/1963	101	CB
Jamie Coe & The Gigolo's	Close Your Eyes	11/07/1964	120	CB
Jamie Horton	Robot Man	27/08/1960	112	CB

Jamie Horton	They're Playing Our Song	04/11/1961	118	CB
Jamul	Tobacco Road	25/04/1970	137	CB
Jan & Dean	Gee	03/12/1960	119	CB
Jan & Dean	Wanted, One Girl	09/10/1961	104	BB
Jan & Dean	Wanted, One Girl	21/10/1961	130	CB
Jan & Dean	A Sunday Kind Of Love	16/12/1961	109	CB
Jan & Dean	Freeway Flyer	27/02/1965	114	CB
Jan & Dean	A Beginning From An End	01/01/1966	109	BB
Jan & Dean	A Beginning From An End	01/01/1966	110	CB
Jan & Dean	Yellow Balloon	25/02/1967	116	CB
Jan & Dean	Yellow Balloon	18/03/1967	111	BB
Jan & Dean	Sidewalk Surfin' (76 Version)	03/07/1976	119	CB
Jan & Dean	Sidewalk Surfin' (new Version)	24/07/1976	107	BB
Jan Bradley	These Tears	20/04/1963	133	CB
Jan Burgens & His New Orleans Syncopators	Midnight In Moscow	17/02/1962	111	BB
Jan Davis	Fugitive*	25/04/1964	121	CB
Jan Davis	Fugitive	09/05/1964	129	BB
Jan Rhodes	Mom (Can I Talk To You?)	21/09/1968	118	CB
Jane Morgan	I Can't Begin To Tell You	27/07/1959	113	BB
Jane Morgan	In Jerusalem	06/02/1961	115	BB
Jane Morgan	In Jerusalem	18/02/1961	102	CB
Jane Morgan	(Theme From Carnival) Love Makes The World Go 'ROUND	10/06/1961	124	CB
Jane Morgan	Bless 'EM All	30/11/1963	119	CB
Jane Morgan	Bless 'Em All	28/12/1963	131	BB
Jane Morgan	Side By Side	16/10/1965	141	CB
Jane Morgan	1-2-3	18/06/1966	135	BB
Jane Morgan	Kiss Tomorrow Goodbye (Capri C'est Fini)	28/01/1967	121	BB
Jane Morgan	Kiss Tomorrow Goodbye (Capri C'est Fini)	11/02/1967	125	CB
Jane Morgan	The Three Bells (The Jimmy Brown Song)	20/05/1967	139	CB
Jane Olivor	Stay The Night	29/07/1978	102	CB

Jane Olivor	Don't Let Go Of Me	05/04/1980	108	BB
Janet Jackson	Don't Stand Another Chance	08/09/1984	101	BB
Janet Lawson	Two Little Rooms	04/07/1970	109	CB
Janet Lawson	Two Little Rooms	11/07/1970	124	BB
Janice Harper	'TIL Tomorrow	02/04/1960	121	CB
Janice Ward	When A Girl Gives Her Heart (To A Boy)	01/07/1961	140	CB
Janie Black	Lonely Sixteen	06/11/1961	116	BB
Janie Grant	Romeo	19/08/1961	118	CB
Janie Grant With Hutch Davie Orch.	Oh Johnny	03/03/1962	127	CB
Janis Ian	Society's Child (Baby I've Been Thinking)	29/10/1966	120	CB
Janis Ian	Insanity Comes Quietly To The Structured Mind	09/12/1967	109	BB
Janis Ian	The Man You Are In Me	22/06/1974	105	CB
Janis Ian	The Man You Are In Me	13/07/1974	104	BB
Janis Ian	When The Party's Over	26/04/1975	112	CB
Janis Joplin	Try (Just A Little Bit Harder)	07/02/1970	103	BB
Janis Joplin	Try (Just A Little Bit Harder)	07/02/1970	103	CB
Janis Joplin	Maybe	18/04/1970	110	BB
Jay & The Americans	Tonight	27/11/1961	120	BB
Jay & The Americans	This Is It	14/07/1962	109	BB
Jay & The Americans	When It's All Over	22/05/1965	129	BB
Jay & The Americans	(We'll Meet In The) "Yellow Forest"	19/08/1967	131	BB
Jay & The Americans	No Other Love	16/03/1968	114	BB
Jay & The Americans	No Other Love	30/03/1968	119	CB
Jay & The Americans	(I'd Kill) For The Love Of A Lady	27/09/1969	113	CB
Jay & The Americans	Do I Love You?	13/06/1970	123	CB
Jay & The Techniques	Singles Game	10/08/1968	116	BB
Jay & The Techniques	Change Your Mind	26/04/1969	106	CB
Jay & The Techniques	Change Your Mind	26/04/1969	107	BB
Jay & The Techniques	Robot Man	13/01/1973	112	CB
Jay Bentley & The Jet Set	Watusi '64	23/01/1965	141	CB

Jay Bentley And The Jet Set	Watusi '64	30/01/1965	128	BB
Jay Black	What Will My Mary Say	28/01/1967	119	CB
Jay Wiggins	Sad Girl	31/08/1963	110	CB
Jay Wiggins	Sad Girl	21/09/1963	116	BB
Jaye P. Morgan	That Funny Feeling	21/11/1959	112	CB
Jaye P. Morgan	A Heartache Named Johnny	16/06/1962	119	BB
Jaye P. Morgan	A Song For You	21/08/1971	105	BB
Jaye P. Morgan	A Song For You	28/08/1971	108	CB
Jean Jacques Perrey	Passport To The Future	27/06/1970	106	BB
Jean Shepard	Slippin' Away	20/01/1973	105	CB
Jean-Claude Borelly And His Orchestra	Dolannes Melodie	24/01/1976	106	BB
Jean-Luc Ponty	As	06/03/1982	108	BB
Jeanette "Baby" Washington	There You Go Again	28/10/1961	133	CB
Jeanie Greene	Only The Children Know	30/10/1971	114	BB
Jeannie C. Riley	The Rib	21/06/1969	111	CB
Jeannie C. Riley	The Rib	05/07/1969	111	BB
Jeannie C. Riley	Things Go Better With Love	27/09/1969	117	CB
Jeannie C. Riley	Things Go Better With Love	04/10/1969	111	BB
Jeannie C. Riley	Country Girl	10/01/1970	150	CB
Jeannie C. Riley	Country Girl	07/02/1970	106	BB
Jeannie C. Riley	Roses And Thorns	06/11/1971	115	CB
Jeannie Seely	It's Only Love	10/09/1966	143	CB
Jeff Barry	I'll Still Love You	22/05/1965	120	CB
Jeff Beck	Hi-Ho Silver Lining	13/05/1967	119	CB
Jeff Beck	Hi-Ho Silver Lining	20/05/1967	123	BB
Jeff Lorber Featuring Audrey Wheeler	Step By Step	06/04/1985	105	BB
Jeff Perry	Love Don't Come No Stronger (Than Yours And Mine)	13/09/1975	108	BB
Jeff Perry	Love Don't Come No Stronger (Than Yours And Mine)	25/10/1975	103	CB
Jefferson Airplane	My Best Friend	04/02/1967	103	BB
Jefferson Airplane	Two Heads	23/09/1967	114	CB

Jefferson Airplane	Two Heads	30/09/1967	124	BB
Jefferson Airplane	Crown Of Creation	02/11/1968	122	CB
Jefferson Airplane	Plastic Fantastic Lover (Live)	10/05/1969	104	CB
Jefferson Airplane	Plastic Fantastic Lover [Live]	31/05/1969	133	BB
Jefferson Airplane	Mexico	04/07/1970	102a	BB
Jefferson Airplane	Have You Seen The Saucers (b-side)	04/07/1970	102b	BB
Jefferson Airplane	Long John Silver	07/10/1972	104	BB
Jefferson Starship	Caroline	22/02/1975	101	CB
Jefferson Starship	Save Your Love	31/10/1981	104	BB
Jennifer	Easy To Be Hard	10/05/1969	128	BB
Jennifer	Do It For Me	18/06/1977	110	BB
Jennifer Holliday	Just Let Me Wait	24/12/1983	103	BB
Jennifer Warnes	Come To Me	03/04/1982	107	BB
Jennifer Warnes	Nights Are Forever	02/07/1983	105	BB
Jenny Burton	Bad Habits	09/03/1985	101	BB
Jerry Butler	I Was Wrong	14/11/1959	118	CB
Jerry Butler	Aware Of Love	02/10/1961	105	BB
Jerry Butler	Aware Of Love	07/10/1961	118	CB
Jerry Butler	Isle Of Sirens	03/03/1962	130	CB
Jerry Butler	Theme From Taras Bulba (The Wishing Star)	01/12/1962	107	CB
Jerry Butler	Whatever You Want	06/04/1963	114	CB
Jerry Butler	I Almost Lost My Mind	22/06/1963	146	CB
Jerry Butler	I Don't Want To Hear Anymore	13/06/1964	142	CB
Jerry Butler	I Can't Stand To See You Cry	03/07/1965	120	CB
Jerry Butler	I Can't Stand To See You Cry	10/07/1965	122	BB
Jerry Butler	Believe In Me	30/10/1965	136	CB
Jerry Butler	For Your Precious Love (1966 Version)	12/02/1966	126	CB
Jerry Butler	Love (Oh, How Sweet It Is)	23/07/1966	103	BB
Jerry Butler	Love (Oh, How Sweet It Is)	06/08/1966	123	CB
Jerry Butler	A Brand New Me	01/11/1969	109	BB

Jerry Butler	Special Memory	07/11/1970	109	BB
Jerry Fuller	Shy Away	29/04/1961	132	CB
Jerry Fuller	First Love Never Dies	26/08/1961	141	CB
Jerry Fuller	Dear Teresa	18/05/1963	135	CB
Jerry Hudson	Gillian Frank	10/02/1973	117	BB
Jerry Jackson	Time	08/07/1961	138	CB
Jerry Jackson	Turn Back	23/03/1963	115	CB
Jerry Jackson	Shrimp Boats (Jamaican Ska)	25/07/1964	134	BB
Jerry Jackson	Tell Her Johnny Said Goodbye	14/11/1964	109	CB
Jerry Jackson	Tell Her Johnny Said Goodbye	05/12/1964	114	BB
Jerry Jaye	Let The Four Winds Blow	29/07/1967	107	BB
Jerry Jaye	Let The Four Winds Blow	29/07/1967	122	CB
Jerry Jaye	Long Black Veil	30/11/1968	149	CB
Jerry Keller	Be Careful How You Drive Young Joey	23/10/1961	112	BB
Jerry Knight	Overnight Sensation	03/05/1980	103	BB
Jerry Landis	The Lone Teen Ranger	19/01/1963	119	CB
Jerry Lee Lewis	Sweet Little Sixteen	25/08/1962	147	CB
Jerry Lee Lewis	How's My Ex Treating You	22/09/1962	114	BB
Jerry Lee Lewis	How's My Ex Treating You	22/09/1962	125	CB
Jerry Lee Lewis	Good Golly Miss Molly	05/01/1963	140	CB
Jerry Lee Lewis	Hit The Road Jack	23/11/1963	103	BB
Jerry Lee Lewis	Pen And Paper	23/11/1963	145	CB
Jerry Lee Lewis	High Heel Sneakers (Live)	17/10/1964	130	CB
Jerry Lee Lewis	Baby, Hold Me Close	27/02/1965	129	BB
Jerry Lee Lewis	Touching Home	22/05/1971	110	BB
Jerry Lee Lewis	Lonely Weekends	29/07/1972	129	CB
Jerry Lee Lewis	No Headstone On My Grave	11/08/1973	104	BB
Jerry Lee Lewis	Rockin' My Life Away	05/05/1979	101	BB
Jerry Lee Lewis & His Pumping Piano	Little Queenie	17/10/1959	106	CB
Jerry Lee Lewis & His Pumping Piano	It Won't Happen With Me	05/08/1961	150	CB

Jerry Lee Lewis & His Pumping Piano	Save The Last Dance For Me	30/09/1961	131	CB
Jerry Lee Lewis With Gene Lowery Singers	Old Black Joe	23/04/1960	121	CB
Jerry Mccain	Red Top	02/06/1962	142	CB
Jerry Mcgee & The Cajuns	Walkin'	14/04/1962	147	CB
Jerry Murad's Harmonicats	Theme From "HIPPODROME"	22/04/1961	119	CB
Jerry Murad's Harmonicats	Peg O' My Heart	01/07/1961	148	CB
Jerry O	(Funky) Four Corners	26/10/1968	109	CB
Jerry Reed	Soldier's Joy	27/07/1959	115	BB
Jerry Reed	Love And War (Ain't Much Difference In The Two)	31/07/1961	117	BB
Jerry Reed	You Got A Lock On Me	04/10/1975	104	BB
Jerry Reed	East Bound And Down	17/09/1977	103	BB
Jerry Reed	East Bound And Down	08/10/1977	107	CB
Jerry Ross Symposium	Let Me Love You One More Time (Un Poquito Mas)	04/07/1970	117	CB
Jerry Ross Symposium	Let Me Love You One More Time (Un Poquito Mas)	11/07/1970	123	BB
Jerry Smith	Drivin' Home	04/07/1970	125	BB
Jerry Vale	Old Cape Cod	20/07/1963	114	CB
Jerry Vale	Old Cape Cod	10/08/1963	118	BB
Jerry Vale	On And On	25/01/1964	116	CB
Jerry Vale	On And On	15/02/1964	123	BB
Jerry Vale	Deep In Your Heart	16/10/1965	118	BB
Jerry Vale	It'll Take A Little Time	23/07/1966	120	BB
Jerry Vale	Dommage, Dommage (Too Bad, Too Bad)	24/09/1966	113	CB
Jerry Vale	I've Lost My Heart Again	24/12/1966	123	CB
Jerry Vale	I've Lost My Heart Again	07/01/1967	132	BB
Jerry Vale	Time Alone Will Tell (Non Pensare A Me)	22/04/1967	126	BB
Jerry Vale	Stay Awhile	10/01/1970	127	CB
Jerry Wallace	You're Singing Our Love Song To Somebody Else	02/05/1960	115	BB
Jerry Wallace	Lonesome	16/10/1961	110	BB
Jerry Wallace	You'll Never Know	28/07/1962	117	CB
Jerry Wallace	On A Merry-Go-Round	20/04/1963	150	CB

Jerry Wallace	Just Walking In The Rain	01/06/1963	139	CB
Jerry Wallace	Auf Wiedersehen	21/12/1963	121	CB
Jerry Wallace	Spanish Guitars (b-side)	17/10/1964	132	BB
Jerry Wallace	Spanish Guitars	24/10/1964	137	CB
Jerry Wallace	Even The Bad Times Are Good	31/10/1964	114	BB
Jerry Washington	Right Here Is Where You Belong	24/02/1973	120	BB
Jesse Anderson	I Got A Problem	09/05/1970	127	CB
Jesse Colin Young	Light Shine	13/07/1974	102	CB
Jesse Colin Young	Songbird	05/07/1975	115	CB
Jesse Colin Young	Higher & Higher	02/07/1977	109	BB
Jesse Gee	Don't Mess With My Money	21/10/1967	122	CB
Jesse James	Believe In Me Baby - Part I	07/10/1967	116	CB
Jesse James	Don't Nobody Want To Get Married (Part Ii)	29/08/1970	117	BB
Jesse James	I Need You Baby	10/04/1971	118	CB
Jesse Johnson's Revue	Can You Help Me	01/06/1985	110	BB
Jet	Stranded In The Moonlight	17/10/1981	105	BB
Jet Harris & Tony Meehan	Scarlet O'hara	03/08/1963	147	CB
Jethro Tull	Living In The Past	13/09/1969	111	CB
Jethro Tull	A Passion Play (Edit #10)	29/09/1973	105	BB
Jethro Tull	Minstrel In The Gallery	23/08/1975	102	CB
Jethro Tull	Fallen On Hard Times	12/06/1982	108	BB
Jewel Akens	It's The Only Way To Fly	14/08/1965	120	BB
Jewel Akens	It's The Only Way To Fly	21/08/1965	136	CB
Jewell & The Rubies	Kidnapper	30/11/1963	107	CB
Jill Corey	Have I Told You Lately That I Love You?	07/11/1959	107	CB
Jim & Jean	What's That Got To Do With Me	18/03/1967	123	BB
Jim & Monica	Slipin' And Slidin'	28/12/1963	108	CB
Jim Campbell	The Lights Of Tucson	20/06/1970	106	CB
Jim Capaldi	Eve	25/03/1972	111	CB
Jim Capaldi	It's All Up To You	31/05/1975	118	CB

Jim Capaldi	It's All Up To You	21/06/1975	110	BB
Jim Capaldi	I'll Keep Holding On	15/09/1984	106	BB
Jim Carroll Band	People Who Died	29/11/1980	103	BB
Jim Croce	Mississippi Lady	24/04/1976	110	BB
Jim Ford	Harlan County	13/09/1969	106	BB
Jim Lowe	Hootenanny Granny	21/09/1963	103	BB
Jim Lowe	Hootenanny Granny	21/09/1963	131	CB
Jim Messina	Do You Want To Dance	19/01/1980	110	BB
Jim Messina With Pauline Wilson	Stay The Night	29/08/1981	110	BB
Jim Nabors	Love Me With All Your Heart (Cuando Calienta El Sol)	07/05/1966	111	CB
Jim Photoglo	More To Love	22/08/1981	1103	CB
Jim Reeves	Losing Your Love	04/11/1961	108	CB
Jim Reeves	I'm Gonna Change Everything	18/08/1962	114	CB
Jim Reeves	Is This Me?	02/02/1963	103	BB
Jim Reeves	Guilty	22/06/1963	122	CB
Jim Reeves	Welcome To My World	25/01/1964	102	BB
Jim Reeves	Welcome To My World	01/02/1964	119	CB
Jim Reeves	I Won't Forget You	26/12/1964	132	CB
Jim Reeves	I Won't Come In While He's There	21/01/1967	112	BB
Jim Reeves	I Won't Come In While He's There	21/01/1967	131	CB
Jim Reeves & Dottie West	Look Who's Talking (b-side)	21/03/1964	121	BB
Jim Reeves & Dottie West	Love Is No Excuse	04/04/1964	115	BB
Jim Stafford	Cow Patti	31/01/1981	1103	CB
Jim Stafford	Cow Patti	07/02/1981	102	BB
Jim Valley	Try, Try, Try	12/08/1967	106	BB
Jim Weatherly	Loving You Is Just An Old Habit	06/01/1973	116	BB
Jimi Hendrix	No Such Animal Part I	28/11/1970	115	CB
Jimmie Beaumont	Ev'rybody's Cryin'	25/11/1961	122	CB
Jimmie Mack	It's Gonna Hurt	27/12/1980	1103	CB
Jimmie Rodgers	Wistful Willie	21/12/1959	112	BB

Jimmie Rodgers	Waltzing Matilda	30/01/1960	103	CB
Jimmie Rodgers	Four Little Girls In Boston	09/07/1960	116	CB
Jimmie Rodgers	Woman From Liberia	05/11/1960	108	CB
Jimmie Rodgers	John Brown's Baby	08/07/1961	141	CB
Jimmie Rodgers	A Little Dog Cried	26/08/1961	106	CB
Jimmie Rodgers	Afraid	26/01/1963	143	CB
Jimmie Rodgers	Face In A Crowd	23/02/1963	129	BB
Jimmie Rodgers	Face In A Crowd	09/03/1963	136	CB
Jimmie Rodgers	Mama Was A Cotton Picker	21/12/1963	131	BB
Jimmie Rodgers	Together	11/01/1964	136	CB
Jimmie Rodgers	Love Me, Please Love Me	26/11/1966	118	CB
Jimmie Rodgers	What A Strange Town (The People Had No Faces)	16/12/1967	141	CB
Jimmie Rodgers	Today	26/10/1968	104	BB
Jimmie Rodgers	The Windmills Of Your Mind	03/05/1969	123	BB
Jimmy "Bo" Horn	Gimme Some (Part One)	06/09/1975	112	CB
Jimmy "Bo" Horne	You Get Me Hot	06/10/1979	101	BB
Jimmy Beaumont	I Feel Like I'm Falling In Love	18/12/1965	123	BB
Jimmy Beaumont & The Skyliners	Where Have They Gone	25/01/1975	103	CB
Jimmy Bing	Gabrielle	17/04/1965	142	CB
Jimmy Buffett	Grapefruit - Juicy Fruit	25/08/1973	106	CB
Jimmy Buffett	Saxophones	02/03/1974	110	CB
Jimmy Buffett	Saxophones	16/03/1974	105	BB
Jimmy Buffett	Pencil Thin Mustache	05/10/1974	101	BB
Jimmy Buffett	Pencil Thin Mustache	12/10/1974	119	CB
Jimmy Buffett	A Pirate Looks At Forty	05/04/1975	101	BB
Jimmy Buffett	Door Number Three	02/08/1975	102	BB
Jimmy Buffett	Door Number Three	02/08/1975	109	CB
Jimmy Buffett	Mañana	09/12/1978	Np4	CB
Jimmy Castor Bunch	Luther The Anthropoid (Ape Man)	12/08/1972	105	BB
Jimmy Castor Bunch	Luther The Anthropoid (Ape Man)	12/08/1972	113	CB

Jimmy Castor Bunch	Space Age	12/03/1977	101	BB
Jimmy Castor Bunch	I Love A Mellow Groove	11/06/1977	108	BB
Jimmy Clanton	Wait	20/08/1960	111	CB
Jimmy Clanton	Red Don't Go With Blue	21/12/1963	115	BB
Jimmy Clanton	Red Don't Go With Blue	18/01/1964	147	CB
Jimmy Clanton	I'll Step Aside	18/04/1964	121	CB
Jimmy Clanton	If I'm A Fool For Loving You	01/08/1964	118	CB
Jimmy Clanton	A Million Drums	08/08/1964	110	CB
Jimmy Clanton	Curly	01/11/1969	106	CB
Jimmy Cliff	Wild World	26/09/1970	132	CB
Jimmy Dean	Sing Along	08/06/1959	106	BB
Jimmy Dean	Little Bitty Big John	23/06/1962	110	CB
Jimmy Dean	Gonna Raise A Rukus Tonight	01/12/1962	105	CB
Jimmy Dean	This Ole House	06/04/1963	126	CB
Jimmy Dean	This Ole House	06/04/1963	128	BB
Jimmy Dean	Mind Your Own Business	18/01/1964	138	CB
Jimmy Dean	The First Thing Ev'ry Morning (And The Last Thing Ev'ry Night)	19/06/1965	112	CB
Jimmy Dean	Sweet Misery	15/04/1967	116	CB
Jimmy Druiett	Is There Anyone Home	10/06/1972	102	CB
Jimmy Durante	One Of Those Songs	19/02/1966	135	BB
Jimmy Edwards	Rosie Lee	04/06/1960	116	CB
Jimmy George	It Was Fun While It Lasted	26/10/1968	121	CB
Jimmy Gilmer	Look At Me	23/05/1964	133	BB
Jimmy Gilmer	What Kinda Love?	08/08/1964	148	CB
Jimmy Gilmer	What Kinda Love?	29/08/1964	133	BB
Jimmy Gilmer	Cinnamon Cindy	23/01/1965	143	CB
Jimmy Gordon	Buzzzzzz	19/11/1966	121	BB
Jimmy Gordon	Buzzzzzz	26/11/1966	146	CB
Jimmy Gray Hall	Be That Way	11/05/1974	120	CB
Jimmy Griffin	All My Loving	28/03/1964	118	BB

Jimmy Griffin	All My Loving	04/04/1964	140	CB
Jimmy Holiday	Poor Boy	22/06/1963	124	BB
Jimmy Holiday	The New Breed	27/11/1965	115	BB
Jimmy Holiday	Baby I Love You	02/07/1966	122	CB
Jimmy Holiday	Everybody Needs Help	01/04/1967	116	BB
Jimmy Holiday	Everybody Needs Help	22/04/1967	119	CB
Jimmy Holiday	I Wanna Help Hurry My Brothers Home	29/07/1967	132	BB
Jimmy Holiday	We Got A Good Thing Goin'	16/11/1968	113	CB
Jimmy Holiday	I'm Gonna Use What I Got (To Get What I Need)	23/11/1968	110	CB
Jimmy Huff	I'd Love Making Love To You	02/05/1970	130	CB
Jimmy Hughes	It Was Nice	20/03/1965	148	CB
Jimmy Hughes	I Worship The Ground You Walk On	20/08/1966	115	CB
Jimmy Hughes	Don't Lose Your Good Thing	08/07/1967	121	BB
Jimmy Hughes	Hi-Heel Sneakers	19/08/1967	130	CB
Jimmy James & The Vagabonds	Come To Me Softly	30/03/1968	103	CB
Jimmy James & The Vagabonds	Red Red Wine	25/01/1969	105	CB
Jimmy James & The Vagabonds	Red Red Wine	15/02/1969	127	BB
Jimmy Johnson & His Band Featuring Hank Alexander	Don't Answer The Door (Part 1)	02/01/1965	113	CB
Jimmy Johnson And His Band Featuring Hank Alexander	Don't Answer The Door (Part 1)	13/02/1965	128	BB
Jimmy Jones	Ee-I Ee-I Oh! (Sue Macdonald)	12/09/1960	102	BB
Jimmy Jones	Itchin' (b-side)	03/10/1960	106	BB
Jimmy Jones	Ee-I, Ee-I Oh! (Sue Macdonald)	08/10/1960	117	CB
Jimmy Jones	Holler Hey	23/12/1961	119	CB
Jimmy Jones	Mr. Fix-It	20/04/1963	143	CB
Jimmy Justice	When My Little Girl Is Smiling	22/09/1962	119	CB
Jimmy Justice	When My Little Girl Is Smiling	13/10/1962	127	BB
Jimmy Mccracklin	Arkansas (Part 1)	24/07/1965	132	BB
Jimmy Mccracklin	Dog (Part I)	01/07/1967	112	BB
Jimmy Mccracklin	Get Together	27/01/1968	114	BB
Jimmy Mcgriff	M.G. Blues	05/01/1963	102	CB

Jimmy Mcgriff	The Last Minute (Pt. I)	18/05/1963	110	CB
Jimmy Mcgriff	Topkapi	14/11/1964	133	BB
Jimmy Mcgriff	I Cover The Waterfront	17/09/1966	135	BB
Jimmy Mcgriff	I Can't Get No Satisfaction	13/05/1967	141	CB
Jimmy Mcgriff	I Can't Get No Satisfaction	20/05/1967	130	BB
Jimmy Mcgriff	The Worm	21/12/1968	119	CB
Jimmy Norman	Here Comes The Night - Part I	22/04/1961	118	CB
Jimmy Norman	Can You Blame Me	22/10/1966	121	CB
Jimmy Radcliffe	My Ship Is Comin' In	14/08/1965	128	CB
Jimmy Reed	Going By The River (Part Ii)	19/09/1960	104	BB
Jimmy Reed	I'm Mr. Luck	02/09/1961	121	CB
Jimmy Reed	Mary-Mary	21/09/1963	119	BB
Jimmy Reed	A New Leaf	23/01/1965	136	CB
Jimmy Reed	Two Ways To Skin (A Cat)	14/01/1967	125	BB
Jimmy Ricks	Trouble In Mind	05/09/1964	115	BB
Jimmy Robins	I Can't Please You	24/12/1966	131	BB
Jimmy Roselli	Mala Femmina	27/07/1963	101	CB
Jimmy Roselli	Mala Femmina	10/08/1963	135	BB
Jimmy Roselli	Anema E Core (With All My Heart And Soul)	19/12/1964	125	CB
Jimmy Roselli	Just Say I Love Her	13/02/1965	140	CB
Jimmy Roselli	All The Time	30/09/1967	107	CB
Jimmy Roselli	Please Believe Me	09/12/1967	125	CB
Jimmy Roselli	O Surdato 'NNAMMURATO (Soldiers Sweetheart)	24/02/1968	122	CB
Jimmy Roselli	Oh What It Seemed To Be	11/05/1968	134	CB
Jimmy Roselli	My Heart Cries For You	25/01/1969	123	CB
Jimmy Ruffin	As Long As There Is L-O-V-E Love	20/11/1965	137	CB
Jimmy Ruffin	As Long As There Is L-O-V-E Love	01/01/1966	120	BB
Jimmy Ruffin	Lonely Lonely Man Am I	13/07/1968	126	CB
Jimmy Ruffin	Don't Let Him Take Your Love From Me	31/08/1968	113	BB
Jimmy Ruffin	Farewell Is A Lonely Sound	13/12/1969	104	BB

Jimmy Sedlar & His Orchestra	Thunderball	11/12/1965	144	CB
Jimmy Smith	Midnight Special, Part 1	06/01/1962	144	CB
Jimmy Smith	Jumpin' The Blues	21/04/1962	145	CB
Jimmy Smith	One O'clock Jump	26/05/1962	103	BB
Jimmy Smith	Everybody Loves My Baby	01/09/1962	130	CB
Jimmy Smith	Everybody Loves My Baby	15/09/1962	107	BB
Jimmy Smith	Theme From "ANY Number Can Win"	05/10/1963	102	CB
Jimmy Smith	Who's Afraid Of Virginia Woolf? (Part I)	25/04/1964	107	CB
Jimmy Smith	Pork Chop, Part I	11/07/1964	145	CB
Jimmy Smith	Prayer Meetin', Part I	29/08/1964	135	CB
Jimmy Smith	Goldfinger (Part 1)	06/03/1965	105	BB
Jimmy Smith	Respect	12/08/1967	119	CB
Jimmy Smith	Chain Of Fools (Part 1)	09/03/1968	107	CB
Jimmy Soul	Treat Em' Tough	27/07/1963	108	BB
Jimmy Soul	Go 'WAY Christina	28/09/1963	136	CB
Jimmy Spheeris	Hold Tight	02/08/1980	110	BB
Jimmy Spheeris	Hold Tight	30/08/1980	I101	CB
Jimmy Velvet	To The Aisle	28/03/1964	118	BB
Jimmy WeBB	One Of The Nicer Things	21/09/1968	118	CB
Jimmy WeBB	If You See Me Getting Smaller I'm Leaving	02/07/1977	103	CB
Jimmy Witter	A Cross Stands Alone	20/05/1961	117	CB
Jive Five	Rain	20/04/1963	128	BB
Jive Five Featuring Eugene Pitt	Sugar (Don't Take Away My Candy)	01/06/1968	119	BB
Jive Five With Eugene Pitt	Hully Gully Callin' Time	17/03/1962	135	CB
Jive Five With Eugene Pitt	Hully Gully Callin' Time	31/03/1962	105	BB
Jive Five With Eugene Pitt	These Golden Rings	22/12/1962	130	CB
Jive Fyve	If You Let Me Make Love To You Then Why Can't I Touch You?	02/05/1970	134	CB
Jivin' Gene	Go On, Go On	25/04/1960	101	BB
Jivin' Gene	Go On, Go On	07/05/1960	121	CB
Jo Ann Campbell	Let Me Do It My Way	08/12/1962	131	CB

Jo Armstead	A Stone Good Lover	18/05/1968	128	CB
Jo Armstead	A Stone Good Lover	25/05/1968	129	BB
Jo Mama	Sailin'	24/04/1971	107	CB
Jo Stafford	Pine Top's Boogie	14/09/1959	105	BB
Joan Armatrading	Show Some Emotion	07/01/1978	110	BB
Joan Baez	We Shall Overcome (Live)	09/11/1963	101	CB
Joan Baez	Be Not Too Hard	12/08/1967	126	CB
Joan Baez	Will The Circle Be Unbroken	19/02/1972	115	CB
Joan Baez	Forever Young	29/06/1974	117	CB
Joan Jett And The Blackhearts	I Love You Love	15/12/1984	105	BB
Joanie Sommers	Be My Love*	29/10/1960	112	CB
Joanie Sommers	When The Boys Get Together	29/09/1962	104	CB
Joanie Sommers	Little Girl Bad	20/07/1963	125	CB
Joanie Sommers	Little Girl Bad	24/08/1963	132	BB
Joanie Taylor & The Tabs	You Lied	03/03/1962	123	CB
Joann Bon & The Coquettes	I'll Release You	09/09/1967	105	BB
Joanne Engel	The Dum-De-Dum Song (The Boy I Love)	20/06/1964	144	CB
Jody Miller	He Walks Like A Man	15/02/1964	109	CB
Jody Miller	Magic Town	13/11/1965	120	CB
Jody Miller	Magic Town	04/12/1965	125	BB
Jody Miller	There's A Party Goin' On	01/07/1972	115	BB
Jody Miller	There's A Party Goin' On	22/07/1972	120	CB
Jody Miller	The House Of The Rising Sun	01/12/1973	120	CB
Jody Moreing	All Girls Want It	15/08/1981	103	BB
Jody Moreing	All Girls Want It	15/08/1981	I102	CB
Joe & Ann	Gee Baby	31/12/1960	108	BB
Joe & Eddie	There's A Meetin' Here Tonite	09/11/1963	112	CB
Joe & Eddie	There's A Meetin' Here Tonite	22/02/1964	101	BB
Joe & Eddie	Depend On Yourself	26/06/1965	149	CB
Joe Barry	You Don't Have To Be A Baby To Cry	23/12/1961	123	CB

Joe Bataan	My Cloud	27/12/1969	137	CB
Joe Bennett And The Sparkletones	Boys Do Cry	14/09/1959	105	BB
Joe Chemay Band	Love Is A Crazy Feeling	13/06/1981	105	BB
Joe Cocker	Threw It Away	18/06/1983	104	BB
Joe Cuba Sextet	El Pito (I'll Never Go Back To Georgia)	06/08/1966	115	BB
Joe Dowell	A Kiss For Christmas (O Tannenbaum)	25/12/1961	110	BB
Joe Dowell	A Kiss For Christmas (O Tannenbaum)	30/12/1961	111	CB
Joe Dowell	The Thorn On The Rose	20/01/1962	138	CB
Joe Dowell With The Stephen Scott Singers	Poor Little Cupid	29/09/1962	109	CB
Joe Harnell	The Mighty Quinn	20/07/1968	122	CB
Joe Harnell & His Orchestra	My One And Only Love	15/06/1963	119	CB
Joe Harnell & His Orchestra	Nature Boy	07/01/1967	117	CB
Joe Henderson	Baby Don't Leave Me	30/12/1961	102	CB
Joe Henderson	Baby Don't Leave Me	17/02/1962	106	BB
Joe Henderson	The Searching Is Over	10/11/1962	149	CB
Joe Henderson	You Take One Step (I'll Take Two)	30/05/1964	128	BB
Joe Hinton	Better To Give Than Receive	21/09/1963	109	CB
Joe Hinton	There's No In Between	05/10/1963	127	CB
Joe Hinton	A Thousand Cups Of Happiness	31/10/1964	111	BB
Joe Hinton	I Want A Little Girl	23/01/1965	135	CB
Joe Hinton	I Want A Little Girl	06/02/1965	132	BB
Joe Hinton	Darling Come Talk To Me	01/05/1965	111	CB
Joe Jackson	It's Different For Girls	17/11/1979	101	BB
Joe Jeffrey	Dreamin' Till Then	11/10/1969	108	BB
Joe Jeffrey	Hey Hey Woman	29/11/1969	111	CB
Joe Jeffrey	Hey Hey Woman	27/12/1969	109	BB
Joe Jeffrey	My Baby Loves Lovin'	11/04/1970	115	BB
Joe Leahy	Life	28/08/1965	118	CB
Joe London	It Might Have Been	02/11/1959	112	BB
Joe Odom	It's In Your Power	31/05/1969	109	BB

Joe Perry Project	Let The Music Do The Talking	17/05/1980	110	BB
Joe Quarterman & Free Soul	(I Got) So Much Trouble In My Mind Pt. 1	25/11/1972	109	CB
Joe Sentieri (Ricordi Orchestra)	Chariot (I Will Follow You)	18/05/1963	115	CB
Joe Sherman & The Arena Brass	Feeling Good	12/02/1966	140	CB
Joe Simon	My Adorable One	12/09/1964	102	BB
Joe Simon	Let's Do It Over	18/09/1965	111	CB
Joe Simon	What Makes A Man Feel Good	10/09/1966	148	CB
Joe Simon	Put Your Trust In Me (Depend On Me)	05/08/1967	129	BB
Joe Simon	San Francisco Is A Lonely Town	13/09/1969	109	CB
Joe Simon	To Lay Down Beside You	17/04/1971	102	CB
Joe Simon	To Lay Down Beside You	24/04/1971	117	BB
Joe Simon	The Best Time Of My Life	22/06/1974	106	CB
Joe Simon	Come Get To This	11/09/1976	102	BB
Joe South	Same Old Song	22/06/1963	133	CB
Joe South	Birds Of A Feather	13/01/1968	106	BB
Joe South	Leanin' On You	10/05/1969	108	CB
Joe South	Leanin' On You	17/05/1969	104	BB
Joe South	Birds Of A Feather	12/07/1969	140	CB
Joe South	Why Does A Man Do What He Has To Do	03/10/1970	118	BB
Joe Sun	Shotgun Rider	07/06/1980	1102	CB
Joe Tex	All I Could Do Was Cry (Part 2)	15/08/1960	102	BB
Joe Tex	All I Could Do Was Cry Part 1	27/08/1960	117	CB
Joe Tex	What Should I Do	19/08/1961	149	CB
Joe Tex	Someone To Take Your Place	27/07/1963	113	CB
Joe Tex	I Wanna Be Free	28/12/1963	139	CB
Joe Tex	I'd Rather Have You	04/07/1964	135	CB
Joe Tex	It Ain't Sanitary	04/10/1969	117	BB
Joe Tex	It Ain't Sanitary	18/10/1969	101	CB
Joe Tex	(When Johnny Comes Marching Home Again) I Can't See You No	15/11/1969	105	BB
Joe Tex	Bad Feet	19/06/1971	124	CB

Joe Tex	Give The Baby Anything The Baby Wants	09/10/1971	102	BB
Joe Tex	A Mother's Prayer	15/01/1972	113	CB
Joe Tex	Woman Stealer	03/03/1973	103	BB
Joe Turner	Chains Of Love	02/04/1960	118	CB
Joe Turner	My Little Honey Dripper	02/05/1960	102	BB
Joe Vitale	Roller Coaster Weekend	23/11/1974	116	CB
Joe Vitale	Shoot 'EM Up	12/04/1975	109	CB
Joe Walsh	Walk Away [Live]	05/06/1976	105	BB
Joe Walsh	Over And Over	11/11/1978	106	BB
Joe Walsh	Turn To Stone	13/01/1979	109	BB
Joey & Danny With Ali Baba & 4 Thieves	Rats In My Room (Part I)	27/07/1963	141	CB
Joey Dee	Help Me Pick Up The Pieces	12/01/1963	148	CB
Joey Dee	Baby, You're Driving Me Crazy	19/01/1963	143	CB
Joey Dee & The Starliters	Face Of An Angel	14/01/1961	122	CB
Joey Dee And The Starliters	Everytime (I Think About You) - Part I	16/06/1962	105	BB
Joey Gregorash	Down By The River	30/10/1971	113	BB
Joey Heatherton	Crazy	03/03/1973	104	CB
Joey Porrello	Fools Rush In	17/01/1976	108	BB
Joey Powers	Billy Old Buddy	29/02/1964	129	CB
Joey Powers	You Comb Her Hair	30/05/1964	128	CB
John & Anne Ryder	A Sign For Love	27/12/1969	105	CB
John & Paul	People Say	07/08/1965	135	CB
John Barry And His Orchestra	Midnight Cowboy	11/10/1969	116	BB
John Beland	Baby You Come Rollin' 'CROSS My Mind	11/10/1969	115	CB
John Beland	Baby You Come Rollin' 'Cross My Mind	08/11/1969	110	BB
John Cougar	A Little Night Dancin'	19/04/1980	105	BB
John Cowsill	The Path Of Love	09/11/1968	111	CB
John Cowsill	The Path Of Love	09/11/1968	132	BB
John Culliton Mahoney	The Ballad Of Evel Knievel	14/09/1974	105	BB
John D. Loudermilk	Callin' Doctor Casey	21/07/1962	137	CB

John D. Loudermilk	Angela Jones	08/12/1962	137	CB
John D. Loudermilk	Blue Train (Of The Heartbreak Line)	15/02/1964	127	CB
John D. Loudermilk	Blue Train (Of The Heartbreak Line)	11/04/1964	132	BB
John Davis And The Monster Orchestra	Night And Day	10/04/1976	109	BB
John Deer	The Battle Hymn Of Lt. Calley	24/04/1971	114	BB
John Denver	Hard Life, Hard Times (Prisoners)	30/09/1972	103	BB
John Denver	Hard Life, Hard Times (Prisoners)	07/10/1972	105	CB
John Denver	Downhill Stuff	03/03/1979	106	BB
John Denver	What's On Your Mind	21/04/1979	107	BB
John Edwards	Careful Man	16/11/1974	109	BB
John Entwistle	Too Late The Hero	07/11/1981	101	BB
John Fogerty	You Got The Magic	17/04/1976	101	CB
John Fred & His Playboy Band	Agnes English	08/07/1967	126	CB
John Fred & His Playboy Band	Agnes English	29/07/1967	125	BB
John Fred & His Playboy Band	We Played Games	18/05/1968	122	CB
John Fred & His Playboy Band	We Played Games	25/05/1968	130	BB
John Gary	Warm And Willing	08/08/1964	137	CB
John Gary	Soon I'll Wed My Love	12/09/1964	111	CB
John Gary	Don't Throw The Roses Away	16/10/1965	132	BB
John Gary	Hang On To Me	11/03/1967	145	CB
John Kay	Moonshine (Friend Of Mine)	02/06/1973	105	BB
John Kay	Easy Evil	25/08/1973	102	BB
John Kongos	Tokoloshe Man	05/02/1972	106	CB
John Kongos	Tokoloshe Man	19/02/1972	111	BB
John Lennon	Borrowed Time	09/06/1984	108	BB
John Lester & Mello-Queens	Getting Nearer	01/06/1959	105	BB
John Livigni	Gimme Some Lovin'	05/07/1975	120	CB
John Mayall	Room To Move [Live]	10/01/1970	102	BB
John Palumbo	Blowing Up Detroit	30/03/1985	109	BB
John Roberts	To Be My Girl	13/01/1968	133	CB

John Sebastian	Magical Connection	16/05/1970	109	CB
John Stewart	Survivors	10/05/1975	108	CB
John Stewart	(Odin) Spirit Of The Water	24/05/1980	l103	CB
John Tipton	Spring	07/06/1969	118	BB
John Travolta	(Feel So Good) Slow Dancing	03/09/1977	106	BB
John Williams	Theme From E.T. (The Extra-Terrestrial)	17/07/1982	103	BB
John's Children	Smashed! Blocked!	31/12/1966	102	BB
Johnathan Edwards	Train Of Glory	18/03/1972	101a	BB
Johnathan Edwards	Everybody Knows Her (b-side)	18/03/1972	106b	BB
Johnathan Edwards	Stop And Start It All Again	17/02/1973	112	BB
Johnnie Mae Matthews	My Little Angel	28/04/1962	148	CB
Johnnie Mae Matthews	Baby What's Wrong	02/01/1965	114	CB
Johnnie Mae Matthews	My Man (Sweetest Man In The World)	15/05/1965	121	CB
Johnnie Taylor	Rome (Wasn't Built In A Day)	09/06/1962	122	CB
Johnnie Taylor	Rome (Wasn't Built In A Day)	23/06/1962	112	BB
Johnnie Taylor	Dance What You Wanna	30/03/1963	140	CB
Johnnie Taylor	I Had A Dream	09/04/1966	115	CB
Johnnie Taylor	Stop Doggin' Me	30/09/1972	101	BB
Johnnie Taylor	Your Love Is Rated X	25/06/1977	101	CB
Johnnie Taylor	Keep On Dancing	22/04/1978	101	BB
Johnnie Taylor (The Soul Philosopher)	Doing My Own Thing (Part 1)	08/04/1972	109	BB
Johnnie Taylor, Carla Thomas	Just Keep On Loving Me	02/08/1969	115	BB
Johnny "Guitar" Watson	I Need It	14/08/1976	101	BB
Johnny "Guitar" Watson	Superman Lover	13/11/1976	101	BB
Johnny & The Expressions	Shy Girl	07/05/1966	126	CB
Johnny & The Hurricanes	You Are My Sunshine	26/11/1960	112	CB
Johnny & The Hurricanes	Old Smokie	24/06/1961	109	CB
Johnny & The Tokens	The Taste Of A Tear	07/08/1961	112	BB
Johnny Adams	Closer To You	04/02/1961	120	CB
Johnny Adams	A Losing Battle	24/03/1962	122	CB

Johnny Adams	Part Of Me	06/06/1964	117	CB
Johnny Adams	Release Me	09/11/1968	112	CB
Johnny Adams	Proud Woman	27/12/1969	129	CB
Johnny Adams	Proud Woman	03/01/1970	121	BB
Johnny Adams	I Won't Cry	22/08/1970	109	CB
Johnny And The Hurricanes	Old Smokie	19/06/1961	116	BB
Johnny Bristol	Leave My World	12/04/1975	104	BB
Johnny Bristol	You Turned Me On To Love	12/03/1977	106	BB
Johnny Burnette	Ballad Of The One Eyed Jacks	22/04/1961	126	CB
Johnny Burnette	I've Got A Lot Of Things To Do	31/07/1961	109	BB
Johnny Burnette	Clown Shoes	03/03/1962	113	BB
Johnny Burnette	I Wanna Thank Your Folks	25/08/1962	117	BB
Johnny Burnette With The Johnny Mann Singers	Girls	22/07/1961	112	CB
Johnny Burnette With The Johnny Mann Singers	The Fool Of The Year	19/05/1962	147	CB
Johnny Cash	Smiling Bill Mccall	23/05/1960	110	BB
Johnny Cash	Honky-Tonk Girl	02/07/1960	108	CB
Johnny Cash	Oh Lonesome Me	07/01/1961	108	CB
Johnny Cash	The Rebel - Johnny Yuma	06/05/1961	109	CB
Johnny Cash	The Rebel-Johnny Yuma	29/05/1961	108	BB
Johnny Cash	In The Jailhouse Now	09/06/1962	131	CB
Johnny Cash	Bonanza!	25/08/1962	150	CB
Johnny Cash	Dark As A Dungeon	08/02/1964	119	BB
Johnny Cash	Dark As A Dungeon	15/02/1964	145	CB
Johnny Cash	The Streets Of Laredo	03/07/1965	124	BB
Johnny Cash	The Sons Of Katie Elder	28/08/1965	119	BB
Johnny Cash	Happy To Be With You	06/11/1965	127	CB
Johnny Cash	Boa Constrictor	03/09/1966	107	BB
Johnny Cash	Boa Constrictor	10/09/1966	128	CB
Johnny Cash	Singing In Viet Nam Talking Blues	19/06/1971	124	BB
Johnny Cash	Oney	09/09/1972	101	BB

Johnny Cash & The Evangel Temple Choir	A Thing Called Love	19/02/1972	120	CB
Johnny Cash & The Tennessee Two	Goodbye Little Darlin'	14/11/1959	106	CB
Johnny Cash & The Tennessee Two	Straight A's In Love	27/02/1960	115	CB
Johnny Cash & The Tennessee Two	Sugartime	12/08/1961	146	CB
Johnny Cash And The Evangel Temple Choir	Papa Was A Good Man	23/10/1971	104	BB
Johnny Cash And The Evangel Temple Choir	A Thing Called Love	29/01/1972	103	BB
Johnny Cash And The Tennessee Two	The Story Of A Broken Heart	04/07/1960	107	BB
Johnny Caswell	At The Shore	20/07/1963	106	CB
Johnny Cooper	Bonnie Do	19/01/1963	129	CB
Johnny Copeland	Down On Bending Knees	14/09/1963	105	BB
Johnny Copeland	Dedicated To The Greatest	28/05/1966	108	CB
Johnny Crawford	Cry On My Shoulder	20/04/1963	126	BB
Johnny Crawford	When I Fall In Love	11/05/1963	129	CB
Johnny Crawford	What Happened To Janie	10/08/1963	132	CB
Johnny Crawford	Judy Loves Me	28/12/1963	120	CB
Johnny Crawford	Sandy	22/02/1964	135	CB
Johnny Crawford	Sandy	07/03/1964	108	BB
Johnny Cymbal	Always, Always	15/10/1960	118	CB
Johnny Cymbal	The Water Was Red	25/03/1961	133	CB
Johnny Cymbal	The Water Was Red	27/03/1961	108	BB
Johnny Dankworth & His Orchestra	African Waltz	10/04/1961	101	BB
Johnny Darrell	With Pen In Hand	27/04/1968	112	CB
Johnny Darrell	With Pen In Hand	25/05/1968	126	BB
Johnny Duncan	Stranger	17/07/1976	111	CB
Johnny Duncan	A Song In The Night	13/08/1977	105	BB
Johnny Gatewood	Pocketful Of Rainbows	16/09/1961	119	CB
Johnny George And The Pilots	Flying Blue Angels	11/09/1961	108	BB
Johnny Griffith, Inc.	Grand Central Shuttle	30/12/1972	116	CB
Johnny Guitar Watson	I Need It	28/08/1976	101	CB
Johnny Hallyday With The Merry Melody Singers	Shake The Hand Of A Fool	31/03/1962	110	CB

Johnny Horton	They'll Never Take Her Love From Me	20/05/1961	146	CB
Johnny Horton	Ole Slew-Foot	19/08/1961	105	CB
Johnny Horton	Ole Slew-Foot	04/09/1961	110	BB
Johnny Horton	Honky-Tonk Man	31/03/1962	119	CB
Johnny Lee	One In A Million	22/11/1980	102	BB
Johnny Lytle	The Snapper	02/04/1966	114	CB
Johnny Madara	Vacation Time	09/09/1961	149	CB
Johnny Maestro With The Crests	Heartburn	16/07/1966	140	CB
Johnny Mann Singers	Cinnamint Shuffle (Mexican Shuffle)	23/04/1966	126	BB
Johnny Mann Singers	Up-Up And Away	03/06/1967	111	CB
Johnny Mathis	You Are Everything To Me	15/06/1959	109	BB
Johnny Mathis	The Story Of Our Love	03/10/1959	104	CB
Johnny Mathis	All Is Well	05/03/1960	106	CB
Johnny Mathis	You Set My Heart To Music	10/04/1961	107	BB
Johnny Mathis	Jenny (b-side)	10/04/1961	118	BB
Johnny Mathis	Wasn't The Summer Short?	07/10/1961	117	CB
Johnny Mathis	Marianna	26/05/1962	113	CB
Johnny Mathis	That's The Way It Is	18/08/1962	135	CB
Johnny Mathis	Sooner Or Later	17/08/1963	105	CB
Johnny Mathis	The Little Drummer Boy	14/12/1963	108	CB
Johnny Mathis	I'll Search My Heart	04/01/1964	111	CB
Johnny Mathis	The Fall Of Love	18/04/1964	120	BB
Johnny Mathis	The Fall Of Love	25/04/1964	114	CB
Johnny Mathis	Taste Of Tears	20/06/1964	125	CB
Johnny Mathis	Take The Time	12/06/1965	104	BB
Johnny Mathis	Sweetheart Tree	07/08/1965	108	BB
Johnny Mathis	Venus	22/06/1968	111	BB
Johnny Mathis	I'll Never Fall In Love Again	31/05/1969	122	CB
Johnny Mathis	Wherefore And Why	20/06/1970	126	CB
Johnny Mathis	Pieces Of Dreams	05/09/1970	129	CB

Johnny Mathis	Evil Ways	07/11/1970	118	CB
Johnny Mathis	Make It Easy On Yourself	05/08/1972	103	BB
Johnny Mathis	Sweet Child	01/06/1974	117	CB
Johnny Mathis (with Deniece Williams)	Love Won't Let Me Wait	31/03/1984	106	BB
Johnny Nash	Take A Giant Step	10/10/1959	119	CB
Johnny Nash	Some Of Your Lovin'	13/02/1961	104	BB
Johnny Nash	Don't Take Away Your Love	05/05/1962	129	CB
Johnny Nash	Ol' Man River	15/09/1962	120	BB
Johnny Nash	I'm Leaving	15/02/1964	103	CB
Johnny Nash	I'm Leaving	28/03/1964	120	BB
Johnny Nash	Love Ain't Nothin'	06/06/1964	133	CB
Johnny Nash	Somewhere	14/05/1966	118	CB
Johnny Nash	Somewhere	21/05/1966	120	BB
Johnny Nash	Lovey Dovey	15/02/1969	130	BB
Johnny Nash	Love And Peace	09/08/1969	132	BB
Johnny Nash	(What A) Groovey Feeling	28/03/1970	102	BB
Johnny Nash	(What A) Groovey Feeling	18/04/1970	131	CB
Johnny Nash	Ooh What A Feeling	29/09/1973	103	BB
Johnny Nash	You Can't Go Halfway	09/11/1974	105	BB
Johnny Nash	(What A) Wonderful World	15/05/1976	103	BB
Johnny October	Growin' Prettier	03/10/1959	113	CB
Johnny October	Growin' Prettier	26/10/1959	106	BB
Johnny Preston	Charming Billy	24/10/1960	105	BB
Johnny Preston	Willy Walk	29/04/1961	111	CB
Johnny Restivo	Dear Someone	17/10/1959	120	CB
Johnny Rivers	Oh What A Kiss	11/07/1964	120	BB
Johnny Rivers	Oh What A Kiss	25/07/1964	134	CB
Johnny Rivers	Moody River	07/11/1964	148	CB
Johnny Rivers	Medley: Searchin'/So Fine	21/07/1973	113	BB
Johnny Rivers	Six Days On The Road	08/06/1974	110	CB

Johnny Rivers	Six Days On The Road	15/06/1974	106	BB
Johnny Rivers	Get It Up For Love	18/01/1975	111	CB
Johnny Rivers	Can I Change My Mind	25/10/1975	120	CB
Johnny Rivers	Ashes And Sand	29/01/1977	107	CB
Johnny Rivers	Romance (Give Me A Chance)	31/05/1980	1103	CB
Johnny Rodriguez	Something	18/05/1974	102	CB
Johnny Sea	My Baby Walks All Over Me	09/05/1964	121	BB
Johnny Sea	My Baby Walks All Over Me	06/06/1964	128	CB
Johnny Thunder	The Rosy Dance	16/03/1963	104	CB
Johnny Thunder	The Rosy Dance	30/03/1963	122	BB
Johnny Thunder	Jailer, Bring Me Water	01/06/1963	132	CB
Johnny Thunder	Hey Child	26/10/1963	118	BB
Johnny Thunder	More, More, More Love, Love, Love	25/07/1964	116	CB
Johnny Thunder	Send Her To Me	12/12/1964	121	BB
Johnny Thunder	My Prayer	12/03/1966	106	BB
Johnny Thunder	I'm Alive	05/04/1969	122	BB
Johnny Tillotson	What'll I Do	29/09/1962	106	BB
Johnny Tillotson	Please Don't Go Away	08/02/1964	112	BB
Johnny Tillotson	Please Don't Go Away	15/02/1964	122	CB
Johnny Tillotson	I'm Watching My Watch	02/05/1964	125	CB
Johnny Tillotson	Hello Enemy	29/01/1966	104	CB
Johnny Tillotson	Hello Enemy	05/02/1966	128	BB
Johnny Tillotson	Apple Bend	19/06/1971	127	BB
Johnny Tillotson With The Jimmy Bowen Orchestra & Chorus	Tears On My Pillow	07/06/1969	119	BB
Johnny Van Zant Band	634-5789	25/10/1980	105	BB
Johnny Walsh	Girl Machine	29/04/1961	131	CB
Johnny Wells	Lonely Moon	24/10/1959	123	CB
Johnny Williams	He Will Break Your Heart	22/04/1972	104	BB
Johnny Williams & His Orchestra	Theme From "CHECKMATE"	18/02/1961	135	CB
Johnny Winter	Rollin' And Tumblin'	03/05/1969	129	BB

Johnny Winter	Johnny B. Goode	17/01/1970	103	CB
Johnny Winter	Jumpin' Jack Flash (Live)	01/05/1971	101	CB
Johnny Winter	Silver Train	09/06/1973	112	CB
Johnny Winter	Stone County	02/03/1974	106	CB
Johnny Winter	Boney Moroney	27/04/1974	103	CB
Johnny Winter	Raised On Rock	25/01/1975	108	BB
Johnny Winter	Raised On Rock	01/02/1975	107	CB
Jon & Robin	Drums	29/07/1967	102	CB
Jon & Robin	You Got Style	06/07/1968	110	BB
Jon & Robin & The In Crowd	I Want Some More	04/11/1967	111	CB
Jon & Robin And The In Crowd	I Want Some More	04/11/1967	108	BB
Jon Anderson	Some Are Born	17/01/1981	109	BB
Jon St. James	Oogity Boogity	03/03/1984	105	BB
Jon Thomas	Hey, Hey, Baby!	24/09/1960	121	CB
Jonathan Edwards	Stop And Start It All Again	27/01/1973	110	CB
Jonathan King	Round, Round	13/05/1967	122	BB
Jonathan King	Round, Round	13/05/1967	126	CB
Jonathan King	It's A Tall Order For A Short Guy	14/10/1972	116	CB
Jonathan, David & Elbert	Three Kids	10/04/1965	135	CB
Joni James	Are You Sorry?	28/09/1959	102	BB
Joni James	Are You Sorry?	03/10/1959	106	CB
Joni James	I Laughed At Love	30/11/1959	108	BB
Joni James	I Laughed At Love	12/12/1959	123	CB
Joni James	We Know	06/08/1960	124	CB
Joni James	Be My Love	29/10/1960	112	CB
Joni James	Somebody Else Is Taking My Place	23/09/1961	123	CB
Joni James	Anyone But Her	26/01/1963	126	CB
Joni Mitchell	Why Do Fools Fall In Love [Live]	04/10/1980	102	BB
Jorgen Ingmann & His Guitar	Cherokee	03/06/1961	140	CB
José Feliciano	Hitchcock Railway	19/10/1968	110	CB

José Feliciano	She's A Woman	02/08/1969	101	CB
José Feliciano	She's A Woman	02/08/1969	103	BB
José Feliciano	Wichita Lineman	21/03/1970	111	CB
José Feliciano	Susie-Q	27/06/1970	137	CB
José Feliciano	Life Is That Way	21/11/1970	101	CB
José Feliciano	Shake A Hand	27/03/1971	106	CB
José Feliciano	I Only Want To Say (Gethsemane)	22/05/1971	119	CB
José Feliciano	I Only Want To Say (Gethsemane)	29/05/1971	122	BB
José Feliciano	Chico And The Man (Main Theme)	18/01/1975	104	CB
Journey	Anytime	03/06/1978	101	CB
Joyce CoBB	How Glad I Am	16/08/1980	107	BB
Jr. Walker & All Stars	Groove Thang	05/08/1972	104	CB
Jr. Walker & The All Stars	Carry Your Own Load	20/02/1971	117	BB
Jr. Walker & The All Stars	Gimme That Beat (Part 1)	10/02/1973	109	CB
Jr. Walker & The All Stars	Gimme That Beat (Part 1)	24/02/1973	101	BB
Jr. Walker All Stars	Cleo's Mood	03/11/1962	145	CB
Ju-Par Universal Orchestra	Funky Music	16/07/1977	101	BB
Jud Strunk	Next Door Neighbor's Kid	07/07/1973	117	CB
Judi Pulver	Dancing On The Moon	06/10/1973	118	BB
Judie Tzuke	Stay With Me Till Dawn	22/12/1979	101	BB
Judy Clay	Greatest Love	18/04/1970	122	BB
Judy Collins	Hard Lovin' Loser	10/12/1966	114	CB
Judy Collins	Secret Gardens	09/06/1973	122	BB
Judy Garland	Rock-A-Bye Your Baby (With A Dixie Melody) (Live)*	30/09/1961	112	CB
Judy Lynn	My Father's Voice	27/04/1963	136	CB
Judy Lynn	Married To A Memory	10/04/1971	109	CB
Judy Lynn	Married To A Memory	24/04/1971	104	BB
Judy, Johnny & Billy	Beautiful Brown Eyes	30/01/1960	110	CB
Judy, Johnny And Billy	Beautiful Brown Eyes	18/01/1960	110	BB
Juicy	Beat Street Strut	18/08/1984	107	BB

Jules Farmer	Love Me Now	03/08/1959	112	BB
Julie Driscoll, Brian Auger & The Trinity	This Wheel's On Fire	13/07/1968	106	BB
Julie Driscoll, Brian Auger & Trinity	This Wheel's On Fire	06/07/1968	108	CB
Julie London	Slightly Out Of Tune (Desafinado)	27/10/1962	110	BB
Julie London	Desafinado (Slightly Out Of Tune)*	27/10/1962	111	CB
Julie London	I'm Coming Back To You	31/08/1963	118	BB
Julie London	I'm Coming Back To You	31/08/1963	123	CB
Julie London	Yummy, Yummy, Yummy	23/11/1968	125	BB
Juliet: Olivia Hussey, Romeo: Leonard Whiting, Nurse: Pat	Farewell Love Scene	23/08/1969	117	CB
Julio Iglesias	Amor	30/04/1983	105	BB
Julio Iglesias	Moonlight Lady	20/10/1984	102	BB
Julius Wechter & The Baja Marimba Band	Yes Sir, That's My Baby	22/06/1968	109	BB
Julius Wechter & The Baja Marimba Band	Do You Know The Way To San Jose	14/09/1968	129	CB
Julius Wechter & The Baja Marimba Band	Flyin' High	25/01/1969	125	BB
Julius Wechter & The Baja Marimba Band	I Don't Want To Walk Without You	26/07/1969	121	BB
Juluka	Scatterlings Of Africa	16/07/1983	106	BB
June Jackson	Little Dog Heaven	22/04/1972	105	CB
June Valli	Guess Things Happen That Way	21/01/1961	104	CB
Junior	Too Late	12/06/1982	102	BB
Junior And The Classics	The Dog	26/09/1964	134	BB
Junior Parker	Someone Somewhere	12/01/1963	136	CB
Junior Parker	If You Don't Love Me	04/05/1963	101	BB
Junior Parker	If You Don't Love Me	11/05/1963	140	CB
Junior Parker	Things I Used To Do	30/05/1964	130	CB
Junior Parker	These Kind Of Blues (Pt. 1)	27/11/1965	133	CB
Junior Parker	Goodbye Little Girl	28/05/1966	128	BB
Junior Parker	Drownin' On Dry Land	06/02/1971	114	BB
Junior Wells	Little By Little	14/05/1960	119	CB
Junior Wells	You're Tuff Enough	27/07/1968	120	CB
Just Us	I Keep Changing My Mind	27/08/1966	131	CB

Just Us	What Are We Gonna Do	14/10/1967	113	CB
Just Us	Used To Be	09/10/1971	103	BB
Justine Washington	I Can't Wait Until I See My Baby	18/01/1964	111	CB
Justine Washington	Who's Going To Take Care Of Me	29/02/1964	125	BB
Kagny & The Dirty Rats	At 15	20/08/1983	110	BB
Kai Winding	The Lonely One	12/10/1963	116	CB
Kai Winding	Mondo Cane #2	21/03/1964	134	CB
Kai Winding & His Orchestra	Baby Elephant Walk*	30/06/1962	102	CB
Kai Winding & Orchestra	Mondo Cane #2	14/03/1964	120	BB
Kai Winding With Vocal Group	Time Is On My Side	23/11/1963	143	CB
Kalyan	Disco Reggae (Tony's Groove) Part 1	02/04/1977	102	BB
Kane's Cousins	Take Your Love (And Shove It)	14/06/1969	116	BB
Karen Alexander	Isn't It Always Love	21/06/1975	112	CB
Karen Small	Boys Are Made To Love	30/04/1966	133	CB
Karen Small	Boys Are Made To Love	11/06/1966	123	BB
Karla Bonoff	Someone To Lay Down Beside Me	03/06/1978	101	CB
Karla Bonoff	When You Walk In The Room	15/12/1979	101	BB
Karla Bonoff	Somebody's Eyes	14/07/1984	109	BB
Karla Devito	Midnight Confession	07/11/1981	109	BB
Kasenetz-Katz "Super Cirkus"	Dong-Dong-Diki-Di-Ki-Dong	04/10/1969	142	CB
Kasenetz-Katz Singing Orchestral Circus	Down In Tennessee	13/07/1968	124	BB
Kasenetz-Katz Super Circus	I'm In Love With You	04/01/1969	105	BB
Kashif	I Just Gotta Have You (Lover Turn Me On)	26/03/1983	103	BB
Kashif	Baby Don't Break Your Baby's Heart	04/08/1984	108	BB
Kate Bush	Wuthering Heights	04/11/1978	108	BB
Kate Bush	The Man With The Child In His Eyes	27/01/1979	Np5	CB
Kathy Young With The Innocents	Our Parents Talked It Over	27/05/1961	101	CB
Kathy Young With The Innocents	Magic Is The Night	02/09/1961	120	CB
Kathy Young With The Innocents	Great Pretender	03/02/1962	141	CB
Kay Starr	Riders In The Sky	21/11/1959	125	CB

Kay Starr	Well, I Ask Ya	16/09/1961	104	CB
Kay Starr	Four Walls	20/10/1962	119	CB
Kay Starr With The California Dreamers	When The Lights Go On Again (All Over The World)	25/11/1967	120	CB
Kayak	Keep The Change	17/02/1979	Np5	CB
Kc	Are You Ready	05/05/1984	104	BB
Kc & The Sunshine Band (with Teri Desario)	Don't Run (Come Back To Me)	02/04/1983	103	BB
Keely Smith	I'd Climb The Highest Mountain	14/11/1959	116	CB
Keith	Sugar Man	26/08/1967	104	CB
Keith	I'm So Proud	04/11/1967	147	CB
Keith	I'm So Proud	11/11/1967	135	BB
Keith Colley	Queridita Mia (Little Darlin')	28/12/1963	122	BB
Keith Everett	Don't You Know	23/04/1966	119	CB
Keith Hampshire	Forever And Ever (Baby I'm Gonna Be Yours)	21/09/1974	113	CB
Keith Sykes	Love To Ride	06/12/1980	108	BB
Keith Textor Singers	Measure The Valleys	10/10/1970	112	BB
Keith West	Excerpt From "A Teenage Opera" (Grocer Jack)	21/10/1967	109	BB
Kelly Marie	Feels Like I'm In Love	25/07/1981	I103	CB
Ken Dodd	Tears (For Souvenirs)	18/12/1965	107	BB
Ken Dodds	Tears (For Souvenirs)	18/12/1965	108	CB
Ken Jones His Piano & Orchestra	Chicken Pot Pie	14/12/1963	137	CB
Ken Jones His Piano & Orchestra	Chicken Pot Pie	04/01/1964	125	BB
Ken Stella	I Wanna Spend My Whole Life Loving You	14/06/1969	133	CB
Kenni Woods	Can't He Take A Hint?	07/09/1963	109	CB
Kenny Ball & His Jazzmen	Heartaches	23/11/1963	138	CB
Kenny Ball & His Jazzmen	From Russia With Love*	18/04/1964	116	CB
Kenny Ball And His Jazzmen	Heartaches	30/11/1963	119	BB
Kenny Burrell	Chittlins Con Carne, Part I	25/05/1963	144	CB
Kenny Burrell & Jimmy Smith	What'd I Say?	28/09/1963	122	CB
Kenny Burrell And Jimmy Smith	What'd I Say	21/09/1963	113	BB
Kenny Chandler	Drums	26/08/1961	124	CB

Kenny Chandler	Drums	04/09/1961	112	BB
Kenny Nolan	My Eyes Get Blurry	01/10/1977	102	CB
Kenny O'dell	Happy With You	18/05/1968	118	BB
Kenny O'dell	My Honky Tonk Ways	21/06/1975	105	BB
Kenny Price	The Sheriff Of Boone County	30/01/1971	119	BB
Kenny Rankin	On And On	21/05/1977	110	BB
Kenny Rogers	Love Lifted Me	21/02/1976	101	CB
Kenny Rogers & Dottie West	Every Time Two Fools Collide	18/03/1978	101	BB
Kenny Rogers & Dottie West	All I Ever Need Is You	21/04/1979	Np4	CB
Kenny Rogers & Dottie West	All I Ever Need Is You	19/05/1979	102	BB
Kenny Rogers & The First Edition	Take My Hand	03/07/1971	103	CB
Kenny Rogers & The First Edition	School Teacher	08/04/1972	104	CB
Kenny Rogers & The First Edition	Lady, Play Your Symphony	02/12/1972	110	CB
Kenny Rogers And The First Edition	Lady, Play Your Symphony	02/12/1972	105	BB
Kenny Williams	Sugar Lump	13/10/1962	137	CB
Ketty Lester	You Can't Lie To A Liar	15/09/1962	111	CB
Ketty Lester	This Land Is Your Land*	10/11/1962	102	CB
Ketty Lester	Some Things Are Better Left Unsaid	04/04/1964	127	BB
Ketty Lester	Some Things Are Better Left Unsaid	04/04/1964	135	CB
Kid Creole & The Coconuts	My Male Curiosity	07/07/1984	110	BB
Kiki Dee	Super Cool	13/07/1974	108	BB
Kim Weston	A Thrill A Moment	05/06/1965	143	CB
Kim Weston	Lift Ev'ry Voice And Sing	30/05/1970	120	BB
Kim Weston Johnny Nash	We Try Harder	10/05/1969	135	BB
King Curtis	Hide Away	24/10/1964	112	BB
King Curtis	Hide Away	31/10/1964	133	CB
King Curtis	Tanya	02/01/1965	130	BB
King Curtis	Spanish Harlem	22/01/1966	139	CB
King Curtis	Something On Your Mind	28/01/1967	120	CB
King Curtis	Jump Back	29/04/1967	111	CB

King Curtis	You Don't Miss Your Water	01/07/1967	105	BB
King Curtis	La Jeanne	26/07/1969	133	CB
King Curtis	La Jeanne	09/08/1969	128	BB
King Curtis	Changes (Part I)	09/10/1971	109	CB
King Curtis & Noble Knights	WoBBle Twist	21/07/1962	127	CB
King Curtis & The Kingpins	For What It's Worth	18/11/1967	107	CB
King Curtis & The Kingpins	(Sittin' On) The Dock Of The Bay	09/03/1968	101	CB
King Curtis & The Kingpins	Valley Of The Dolls	01/06/1968	125	CB
King Curtis & The Kingpins	I Heard It Thru The Grapevine	27/07/1968	123	CB
King Curtis & The Kingpins	Harper Valley P.T.A.	21/09/1968	118	CB
King Curtis & The Kingpins	Games People Play	22/03/1969	116	BB
King Curtis & The Kingpins	Games People Play	22/03/1969	144	CB
King Curtis & The Kingpins	Foot Pattin', Part Ii (b-side)	12/04/1969	123	BB
King Curtis & The Kingpins	Instant Groove	24/05/1969	101	CB
King Curtis & The Kingpins	Instant Groove	31/05/1969	127	BB
King Curtis & The Kingpins	Changes - Part Ii	05/12/1970	116	CB
King Curtis And The Noble Knights	WoBBle Twist	11/08/1962	119	BB
King Curtis With Delaney Bramlett, Eric Clapton & Friends	Teasin'	11/04/1970	128	BB
King Floyd	Got To Have Your Lovin'	14/08/1971	101	BB
King Hannibal	The Truth Shall Make You Free (St. John 8:32)	13/01/1973	105	BB
King Richard's Fleugel Knights	Cabaret	21/01/1967	112	CB
King Richard's Fluegel Knights	Everybody Loves My Baby	29/04/1967	131	CB
King Richard's Fluegel Knights	Everybody Loves My Baby	13/05/1967	126	BB
King Richard's Fluegel Knights	Camelot	30/12/1967	124	CB
King Richard's Fluegel Knights	Camelot	13/01/1968	107	BB
Kinsman Dazz	I Might As Well Forget About Loving You	06/01/1979	104	BB
Kip & Ken	Trouble With A Woman	16/10/1965	123	CB
Kip Anderson	That's When The Crying Begins	19/09/1964	130	BB
Kiss	Nothin' To Lose	20/04/1974	106	CB
Kiss	Shout It Out Loud (Live)	31/12/1977	101	CB

Kiss	I Love It Loud	22/01/1983	102	BB
Kiss Inc.	Hey, Mr. Holy Man	14/11/1970	122	CB
Kit & The Outlaws	Midnight Hour	31/12/1966	123	CB
Kit And The Outlaws	Midnight Hour	21/01/1967	131	BB
Kitty Kallen	Summertime Lies	08/07/1961	118	CB
Kitty Kallen	It Wasn't God Who Made Honky Tonk Angels	17/02/1962	137	CB
Kitty Kallen	It Wasn't God Who Made Honky Tonk Angels	03/03/1962	101	BB
Kitty Kallen	Please Don't	30/03/1963	121	BB
Kix	Body Talk	14/05/1983	104	BB
Kleeer	Keep Your Body Workin	17/03/1979	101	BB
Klymaxx	The Men All Pause	02/02/1985	105	BB
Koffie & James	Different Shades	28/06/1969	130	CB
Kokomo	Humorous	27/05/1961	113	CB
Kokomo	I Can Understand It	16/08/1975	101	BB
Kool & The Gang	Kool It (Here Comes The Fuzz)	28/02/1970	134	CB
Kool & The Gang	Who's Gonna Take The Weight (Part One)	16/01/1971	113	BB
Kool & The Gang	I Want To Take You Higher [Live]	19/06/1971	105	BB
Kool & The Gang	I Want To Take You Higher (Live)	10/07/1971	115	CB
Kool & The Gang	Love The Life You Live (Part Ii)	26/02/1972	107	BB
Kool & The Gang	Love The Life You Live (Part I)	11/03/1972	126	CB
Kool & The Gang	Good Times	30/09/1972	116	CB
Kool & The Gang	Love And Understanding (Come Together)	27/03/1976	101	CB
Kool & The Gang	Universal Sound	04/07/1976	101	BB
Kool & The Gang	Super Band	07/05/1977	101	BB
Kool & The Gang	Slick Superchick	29/04/1978	102	BB
Kool & The Gang	Hangin' Out	17/05/1980	103	BB
Kool & The Gang	Straight Ahead	30/06/1984	103	BB
Kracker	Because Of You (The Sun Don't Set)	02/12/1972	104	BB
Kracker	Because Of You (The Sun Don't Set)	02/12/1972	104	CB
Kraftwerk	Pocket Calculator	06/06/1981	102	BB

Kraftwerk	Pocket Calculator	06/06/1981	I101	CB
Kraftwerk	Numbers	12/12/1981	103	BB
Kris Jensen	Don't Take Her From Me	12/01/1963	112	BB
Kris Jensen	Big As I Can Dream	09/11/1963	130	CB
Kris Kristofferson	The Pilgrim: Chapter 33	18/12/1971	101	CB
Kris Kristofferson & Rita Coolidge	Lover Please	01/02/1975	113	CB
Kyle	She Brings Sunshine	15/09/1973	102	CB
L.A. Boppers	Is This The Best (Bop-Doo-Wah)	08/03/1980	103	BB
L.J. Reynolds & Chocolate Syrup	Let One Hurt Do	18/12/1971	104	BB
L.T.D.	We Both Deserve Each Other's Love	20/01/1979	107	BB
L.T.D.	Kickin' Back	05/12/1981	102	BB
L.T.D.	Kickin' Back	12/12/1981	I103	CB
Labelle	Messin' With My Mind	13/09/1975	101	CB
Labelle	Get You Somebody New	16/10/1976	102	BB
Labelle	Isn't It A Shame	22/01/1977	104	CB
Lacy J. Dalton	Slow Down	05/06/1982	106	BB
Lainie Kazan	Kiss Tomorrow Goodbye	28/01/1967	123	BB
Lakeside	It's All The Way Live (Part 1)	28/04/1979	102	BB
Lakeside	I Want To Hold Your Hand	13/02/1982	102	BB
Lakeside	Something About That Woman	22/05/1982	110	BB
Lakeside	Outrageous	28/07/1984	101	BB
Lally Stott	Chirpy Chirpy, Cheep Cheep	13/03/1971	110	CB
Lamont Dozier	All Cried Out	03/05/1975	101	BB
Lani Hall	Never Say Never Again	22/10/1983	103	BB
Larry Finnegan	Pretty Suzy Sunshine	02/06/1962	127	CB
Larry Finnegan	The Other Ringo (A Tribute To Ringo Starr)	19/12/1964	130	BB
Larry Finnegan	A Tribute To Ringo Starr The Other Ringo	02/01/1965	149	CB
Larry Gatlin	Delta Dirt	21/09/1974	118	CB
Larry Gatlin And The Gatlin Brothers	Taking Somebody With Me When I Fall	31/05/1980	108	BB
Larry Gatlin With Family & Friends	Broken Lady	21/02/1976	101	CB

Larry Graham	When We Get Married	11/10/1980	I102	CB
Larry Graham	Don't Stop When You're Hot	29/05/1982	102	BB
Larry Graham	Sooner Or Later	31/07/1982	110	BB
Larry Jon Wilson	Through The Eyes Of Little Children	13/12/1975	119	CB
Larry Lurex	I Can Hear Music	08/09/1973	115	BB
Larry Marks	L.A. Break Down (And Take Me In)	07/09/1968	102	CB
Larry Marks	L.A. Break Down (And Take Me In)	05/10/1968	129	BB
Larry Santos	Now That I Have Found You	19/12/1970	103	CB
Larry Santos	Now That I Have Found You	02/01/1971	114	BB
Larry Santos	Long, Long Time	06/11/1976	109	CB
Larry Santos	Long, Long Time	11/12/1976	109	BB
Larry Verne	Abdul's Party	29/04/1961	135	CB
Larry Verne	Abdul's Party	08/05/1961	113	BB
Larry Williams	My Baby's Got Soul	03/10/1959	110	CB
Larry Williams	I Hear My Baby	15/10/1960	114	CB
Latimore	Stormy Monday	26/01/1974	102	BB
Latimore	I Get Lifted	16/07/1977	104	BB
Latoya Jackson	If You Feel The Funk	15/11/1980	103	BB
Laura Lee	As Long As I Got You	27/04/1968	123	BB
Laura Lee	Love And Liberty	25/12/1971	101	CB
Laura Lee	Crumbs Off The Table	23/12/1972	107	BB
Laura Lee	I Need It Just As Bad As You	03/08/1974	121	CB
Laura Nyro	Wedding Bell Blues	22/10/1966	103	BB
Laura Nyro	It's Gonna Take A Miracle	05/02/1972	120	CB
Laura Nyro	It's Gonna Take A Miracle	12/02/1972	103	BB
Lavell Hardy	Don't Lose Your Groove	02/12/1967	139	CB
Lavern Baker	Shadows Of Love	14/05/1960	104	CB
Lavern Baker	Hurtin' Inside	05/08/1961	130	CB
Lavern Baker	You'd Better Find Yourself Another Fool	18/07/1964	128	BB
Lavern Baker	Fly Me To The Moon	30/01/1965	109	CB

Lavern Baker	Batman To The Rescue	27/08/1966	135	BB
Lavern Baker & Ben E. King	A Help-Each-Other Romance	06/08/1960	105	CB
Lavern Baker & Jimmy Ricks	I'll Never Be Free	16/01/1961	103	BB
Lawrence Welk & His Orchestra	Out Of A Clear Blue Sky	08/04/1961	128	CB
Lawrence Welk & His Orchestra	Theme From The Brothers Grimm	26/05/1962	130	CB
Lawrence Welk & His Orchestra	Breakwater	29/06/1963	101	CB
Lawrence Welk & His Orchestra	Fiesta	05/10/1963	111	CB
Lawrence Welk & His Orchestra	Stockholm	29/02/1964	115	CB
Lawrence Welk & His Orchestra Featuring Frank Scott On Piano	Last Date	29/10/1960	103	CB
Lawrence Welk And His Orchestra	Blue Velvet	28/09/1963	103	BB
Lawrence Welk And His Orchestra	Fiesta (b-side)	05/10/1963	106	BB
Lawrence Welk And His Orchestra	The Beat Goes On	08/04/1967	104	BB
Lawrence Welk, His Orchestra & Chorus	My Love For You	30/09/1961	141	CB
Lawrence Welk, His Orchestra And Chorus	A-One A-Two A-Cha Cha Cha	04/12/1961	117	BB
Le Roux	Let Me Be Your Fantasy	27/09/1980	105	BB
Lea Roberts	Laughter In The Rain	21/09/1974	125	CB
Lea Roberts	Laughter In The Rain	02/11/1974	109	BB
Lea Roberts	All Right Now	19/04/1975	101	CB
Leapy Lee	Here Comes The Rain	01/02/1969	128	CB
Lee Allen	Cat Walk	19/10/1959	102	BB
Lee Allen	Cat Walk	07/11/1959	107	CB
Lee Andrews	I'm Sorry, Pillow	02/02/1963	113	CB
Lee Dorsey	Eenie-Meenie-Minee-Mo	31/03/1962	149	CB
Lee Dorsey	Can You Hear Me	09/10/1965	114	CB
Lee Dorsey	Work, Work, Work	09/10/1965	121	BB
Lee Dorsey	Confusion	30/04/1966	130	CB
Lee Dorsey	Rain Rain Go Away	04/02/1967	105	BB
Lee Dorsey	Rain Rain Go Away	04/02/1967	126	CB
Lee Dorsey & Betty Harris	Love Lots Of Lovin'	23/12/1967	110	BB
Lee Greenlee	Starlight	31/08/1959	102	BB

Lee Hazlewood	Trouble Maker	13/12/1969	116	BB
Lee Lamont	The Crying Man	06/02/1965	142	CB
Lee Merril & The Golden Horns	The Ballad Of The Green Hornet	10/09/1966	136	CB
Lee Michaels	Heighty Hi	06/09/1969	106	BB
Lee Michaels	Hold On To Freedom	29/04/1972	104	CB
Lee Morgan	The Sidewinder, Part 1	02/01/1965	132	CB
Lee Moses	Time And Place	16/05/1970	122	CB
Lee Rogers	I Want You To Have Everything	28/11/1964	114	BB
Lee Rogers	You're The Cream Of The Crop	20/02/1965	110	CB
Lee Rogers	Boss Love	03/07/1965	106	CB
Lee Rogers	I'm A Practical Guy	02/07/1966	106	CB
Leer Brothers	Love Fever	15/11/1969	129	CB
Len Barry	I Struck It Rich	17/09/1966	114	CB
Len Barry	The Moving Finger Writes	29/04/1967	124	BB
Len Barry	4 5 6 (Now I'm Alone)	13/07/1968	122	CB
Lena Horne	Watch What Happens	30/05/1970	119	BB
Lena Horne	Watch What Happens	20/06/1970	124	CB
Lenny Damon & The Bah Humbug Band	Tippicaw Calley	21/03/1970	107	BB
Lenny Damon & The Bah Humbug Band	Tippicaw Calley	28/03/1970	132	CB
Lenny Miles	In Between Tears	27/05/1961	131	CB
Lenny Welch	If You See My Love	04/07/1964	101	CB
Lenny Welch	Rags To Riches	12/03/1966	102	BB
Lenny Welch	Since I Fell For You	18/03/1967	134	BB
Lenny Welch	The Right To Cry	25/03/1967	128	BB
Lenny Welch	Until The Real Thing Comes Along	08/04/1967	146	CB
Lenny Welch	Darling Stay With Me	17/02/1968	112	BB
Lenny Welch	To Be Loved/Glory Of Love	18/04/1970	110	BB
Lenny Welch	Since I Don't Have You	25/08/1973	111	CB
Lenny Williams	Shoo Doo Fu Fu Ooh! [Live]	17/09/1977	105	BB
Lenny Williams	Shoo Doo Fu Fu Ooh! (Live)	08/10/1977	105	CB

Lenny Williams	Choosing You	10/12/1977	101	CB
Lenny Williams	Choosing You	14/01/1978	108	BB
Lenny Williams	You Got Me Running	19/08/1978	104	BB
Lenny Williams	Midnight Girl	25/11/1978	102	BB
Lenny Williams	Ooh Child	04/10/1980	109	BB
Leo & Libra With The Mystic Moods	Get It While The Gettin' Is Good	20/12/1975	109	BB
Leo Sayer	One Man Band	13/07/1974	103	BB
Leo Sayer	One Man Band	14/06/1975	101	CB
Leo Sayer	Moonlighting	01/11/1975	102	CB
Leon Ashley	Laura What's He Got That I Ain't Got	26/08/1967	120	BB
Leon Haywood	Mellow Moonlight	02/12/1967	105	CB
Leon Haywood	Sugar Lump	24/08/1974	108	BB
Leon Haywood	Believe Half Of What You See (And None Of What You Hear)	15/02/1975	120	CB
Leon Haywood	Just Your Fool	17/01/1976	102	CB
Leon Haywood	Just Your Fool	31/01/1976	102	BB
Leon Haywood	Strokin' (Pt. Ii)	19/06/1976	101	BB
Leon Haywood	The Streets Will Love You To Death - Part I	16/10/1976	107	BB
Leon Mcauliff	Cozy Inn	16/09/1961	135	CB
Leon Mcauliffe	Shape Up Or Ship Out	21/12/1963	142	CB
Leon Peels	A Casual Kiss	11/07/1964	120	CB
Leon Peels	A Casual Kiss	25/07/1964	135	BB
Leon Russell	Roll Away The Stone	20/06/1970	109	BB
Leon Russell	A Hard Rain's A Gonna Fall	25/09/1971	105	BB
Leon Russell	Leaving Whipporwhill	17/08/1974	104	CB
Leonard Nimoy	A Visit To A Sad Planet	23/09/1967	114	CB
Leonard Nimoy	A Visit To A Sad Planet	23/09/1967	121	BB
Leroy Holmes & His Orchestra	Alice Blue Gown	24/10/1959	113	CB
Leroy Hutson	So In Love With You	17/03/1973	101	CB
Leroy Van Dyke	You Couldn't Get My Love Back (If You Tried)	30/04/1966	120	BB
Leroy Van Dyke With The Merry Melody Singers	Dim Dark Corner	16/06/1962	129	CB

Leroy Van Dyke With The Merry Melody Singers	I Sat Back And Let It Happen	08/09/1962	112	CB
Leroy Van Dyke With The Merry Melody Singers	Black Cloud	17/11/1962	125	CB
Les Brown & His Band Of Renown	La Bomba	29/02/1964	150	CB
Les Compagnons De La Chanson	Down By The Riverside (Qu'il Fait Bon Vivre)	19/03/1960	107	CB
Les Cooper & The Soulrockers	Garbage Can	20/04/1963	144	CB
Les Mccann	The Shampoo	20/04/1963	122	BB
Les Paul And Mary Ford	It's Been A Long, Long Time	17/04/1961	105	BB
Les Variations	Superman Superman	28/06/1975	103	CB
Lesley Gore	Sometimes I Wish I Were A Boy	24/10/1964	102	CB
Lesley Gore	Off And Running	28/05/1966	108	BB
Lesley Gore	Treat Me Like A Lady	17/09/1966	115	BB
Lesley Gore	Magic Colors	16/12/1967	125	CB
Lesley Gore	Small Talk	16/03/1968	124	BB
Lesley Gore	He Gives Me Love (La La La)	08/06/1968	119	BB
Lesley Miller	He Wore The Green Beret	19/03/1966	101	BB
Lesley Miller	He Wore The Green Beret	19/03/1966	129	CB
Leslie Uggams	A House Built On Sand	13/01/1968	121	CB
Leslie Uggams	River Deep, Mountain High	27/07/1968	127	CB
Leslie West	Dreams Of Milk And Honey	13/09/1969	114	CB
Leslie West	Long Red	20/09/1969	108	CB
Lester Flatt, Earl Scruggs & Foggy Mountain Boys	Pearl Pearl Pearl	04/05/1963	119	CB
Lester Flatt, Earl Scruggs And The Foggy Mountain Boys	Pearl Pearl Pearl	27/04/1963	113	BB
Lew Courtney	The Man With The Cigar	14/12/1963	135	CB
Life	Hands Of The Clock	19/07/1969	120	BB
Life	Cool Down	02/05/1981	106	BB
Lighthouse	You Girl	27/01/1973	107	CB
Lighthouse	You Girl	17/02/1973	114	BB
Lightin' Hopkins	Mojo Hand	18/02/1961	109	CB
Lillo Thomas	Your Love's Got A Hold On Me	18/08/1984	102	BB
Lincoln Mayorga	You've Lost That Lovin' Feelin'	08/05/1965	120	CB

Linda Brannon	Don't Cross Over (To My Side Of The Street)	04/01/1964	115	BB
Linda Brannon	Don't Cross Over (To My Side Of The Street)	11/01/1964	111	CB
Linda Clifford	If My Friends Could See Me Now	26/08/1978	109	CB
Linda Hall	Hugo	05/09/1964	143	CB
Linda Jones	I Who Have Nothing	21/12/1968	116	BB
Linda Laine With The Sinners	Low Grades And High Fever	12/12/1964	141	CB
Linda Lewis	The Old Schoolyard	29/03/1975	124	CB
Linda Lewis	It's In His Kiss	26/07/1975	107	BB
Linda Lloyd	I'm Gonna Love That Guy (Like He's Never Been)	04/04/1964	122	BB
Linda Ronstadt	Will You Love Me Tomorrow?	04/04/1970	111	BB
Linda Ronstadt	Rock Me On The Water	26/02/1972	101	CB
Linda Ronstadt	Desperado	20/07/1974	105	CB
Linda Ronstadt	Colorado	20/07/1974	108	BB
Linda Ronstadt	Alison	19/05/1979	Np7	CB
Linda Ronstadt	Skylark	22/12/1984	101	BB
Linda Scott	Town Crier	17/02/1962	116	BB
Linda Scott	The Loneliest Girl In Town	22/12/1962	145	CB
Linda Scott	Let's Fall In Love	07/09/1963	108	BB
Linda Scott	Let's Fall In Love	14/09/1963	105	CB
Linda Scott	Who's Been Sleeping In My Bed?	25/01/1964	110	CB
Linda Scott	Patch It Up	30/01/1965	138	CB
Linda Scott	Patch It Up	13/02/1965	135	BB
Lindsey Buckingham	It Was I	20/03/1982	110	BB
Lindsey Buckingham	Slow Dancing	24/11/1984	106	BB
Linus & The Little People	Lovin' La La	02/05/1970	123	CB
Lister Shaw	Theme From Northern Lights	10/11/1962	134	CB
Little Anthony & The Imperials	Please Say You Want Me	11/03/1961	102	CB
Little Anthony & The Imperials	You Better Take It Easy Baby	06/08/1966	111	CB
Little Anthony & The Imperials	Gonna Fix You Good (Every Time You're Bad)	27/08/1966	141	CB
Little Anthony And The Imperials	Please Say You Want Me	06/03/1961	104	BB

Little Anthony And The Imperials	You Better Take It Easy Baby	20/08/1966	125	BB
Little Anthony And The Imperials	Don't Get Close	14/02/1970	116	BB
Little Anthony And The Imperials	World Of Darkness	20/06/1970	121	BB
Little Caesar & The Romans	Hully Gully Again	19/08/1961	124	CB
Little Caesar & The Romans	Memories Of Those Oldies But Goodies	16/09/1961	126	CB
Little Caesar And The Romans	Memories Of Those Oldies But Goodies	18/09/1961	101	BB
Little Carl Carlton 14 Year Old Sensation	46 Drums-1 Guitar	12/10/1968	105	BB
Little Esther	Hello Walls	04/04/1964	126	CB
Little Esther Phillips & Big Al Downing	If You Want It (I've Got It)	30/03/1963	129	BB
Little Esther Phillips & Big Al Downing	You Never Miss Your Water (Till The Well Runs Dry)	04/05/1963	120	CB
Little Eva	What I Gotta Do (To Make You Jealous)	27/07/1963	101	BB
Little Eva	Let's Start The Party Again	16/11/1963	123	BB
Little Eva	Mama Said	04/04/1970	120	CB
Little Eva Harris	Get Ready-Uptight	10/08/1968	128	CB
Little Jerry Williams	I'm The Lover Man	21/11/1964	102	BB
Little Jerry Williams	I'm The Lover Man	28/11/1964	107	CB
Little Jerry Williams	Baby, You're My Everything	04/12/1965	102	CB
Little Jerry Williams	Baby, You're My Everything	15/01/1966	122	BB
Little Jimmy Dickens	When The Ship Hits The Sand	12/02/1966	103	BB
Little Jimmy Osmond	Mother Of Mine	15/04/1972	101	BB
Little Jimmy Osmond	Mother Of Mine	15/04/1972	107	CB
Little Jimmy Rivers & The Tops	Puppy Love	03/02/1962	128	CB
Little Joe Blue	Dirty Work Going On	02/07/1966	102	CB
Little Joe Blue	Dirty Work Going On	30/07/1966	111	BB
Little Johnny Taylor	You'll Need Another Favor	04/05/1963	125	BB
Little Johnny Taylor	You'll Need Another Favor	18/05/1963	117	CB
Little Johnny Taylor	First Class Love	28/03/1964	102	CB
Little Johnny Taylor	If You Love Me (Like You Say) (b-side)	11/04/1964	101	BB
Little Johnny Taylor	First Class Love	11/04/1964	107	BB
Little Johnny Taylor	If You Love Me (Like You Say)	02/05/1964	138	CB

Little Johnny Taylor	Nightingale Melody	04/07/1964	111	CB
Little Johnny Taylor	Nightingale Melody	18/07/1964	109	BB
Little Johnny Taylor	Somebody's Got To Pay	01/05/1965	125	CB
Little Jr. Parker	Strange Things Happening	08/02/1964	119	CB
Little Junior Parker	In The Dark	28/10/1961	120	CB
Little Milton	So Mean To Me	20/01/1962	150	CB
Little Milton	Sacrifice	19/09/1964	138	CB
Little Milton	Without My Sweet Baby	28/08/1965	126	CB
Little Milton	Your People	18/12/1965	106	BB
Little Milton	Man Loves Two	13/08/1966	115	CB
Little Milton	Man Loves Two	13/08/1966	127	BB
Little Milton	Feel So Bad	14/01/1967	104	CB
Little Milton	Just A Little Bit	12/04/1969	102	CB
Little Milton	Poor Man	11/10/1969	103	BB
Little Milton	I Play Dirty	27/03/1971	109	CB
Little Milton	Before The Honeymoon	29/04/1972	117	CB
Little Milton	Behind Closed Doors	18/05/1974	120	CB
Little Milton Campbell	Somebody's Changin' My Sweet Baby's Mind	05/12/1970	110	CB
Little Nat	Do This Do That	27/01/1962	102	CB
Little Peggy March	My Teenage Castle (Is Tumblin' Down)	01/06/1963	121	CB
Little Peggy March	(I'm Watching) Every Little Move You Make	25/01/1964	112	CB
Little Richard	He Got What He Wanted (But He Lost What He Had)	26/05/1962	134	CB
Little Richard	Crying In The Chapel	06/04/1963	119	BB
Little Richard	Crying In The Chapel	27/04/1963	141	CB
Little Richard	Annie Is Back	04/07/1964	138	CB
Little Richard	Bama Lama Bama Loo	11/07/1964	109	CB
Little Richard	Whole Lotta Shakin' Goin' On	05/09/1964	126	BB
Little Richard	Goodnight Irene (b-side)	05/09/1964	128	BB
Little Richard	A Whole Lotta Shakin' Goin' On	19/09/1964	143	CB
Little Richard	Poor Dog (Who Can't Wag His Own Tail)	23/07/1966	121	BB

Little Richard	Poor Dog (Who Can't Wag His Own Tail)	06/08/1966	150	CB
Little Richard	Call My Name	10/01/1976	106	BB
Little Richard "King Of The Gospel Singers"	He's Not Just A Soldier	18/12/1961	113	BB
Little Stevie Wonder	Contract On Love	16/03/1963	137	CB
Little Stevie Wonder	I Call It Pretty Music, But The Old People Call It The Blues - Pt. I	31/08/1963	101	BB
Little Stevie Wonder	I Call It Pretty Music, But The Old People Call It The Blues - Pt. I	07/09/1963	125	CB
Little Walter And His Jukes	My Babe	27/06/1960	106	BB
Little Willie John	Let Nobody Love You	13/07/1959	108	BB
Little Willie John	The Very Thought Of You	25/03/1961	121	CB
Little Willie John	(I've Got) Spring Fever	27/05/1961	111	CB
Little Willie John	Now You Know	29/07/1961	116	CB
Little Willie John	Take My Love (I Want To Give It All To You)	29/07/1961	117	CB
Little Willie John	Until Again My Love	12/05/1962	141	CB
Little Willie John	I Wish I Could Cry	30/06/1962	116	BB
Little Willie John	Big Blue Diamonds	20/10/1962	148	CB
Liv Maessen	Knock Knock Who's There	12/09/1970	118	CB
Livingston Taylor	Carolina Day	06/02/1971	104	CB
Livingston Taylor	Get Out Of Bed	05/02/1972	101	CB
Livingston Taylor	Somewhere Over The Rainbow	01/12/1973	124	CB
Liz Anderson	If The Creek Don't Rise	06/09/1969	120	CB
Liza Minnelli	Theme From "New York, New York"	13/08/1977	104	BB
Lloyd Price	Under Your Spell Again	17/11/1962	119	CB
Lloyd Price	Under Your Spell Again	17/11/1962	123	BB
Lloyd Price	Billie Baby	21/12/1963	102	CB
Lloyd Price	I Love You (I Just Love You)	31/10/1964	123	BB
Lloyd Price	Amen	26/12/1964	124	BB
Lloyd Price	If I Had My Life To Live Over	10/07/1965	107	BB
Lloyd Price	If I Had My Life To Live Over	31/07/1965	126	CB
Lloyd Price	Peeping And Hiding	19/02/1966	119	CB
Lloyd Price	Bad Conditions	22/11/1969	118	CB

Lloyd Price	Love Music	24/03/1973	108	CB
Lloyd Price	Love Music	21/04/1973	102	BB
Lloyd Price & His Great Orchestra	Mary And Man-O	10/06/1961	136	CB
Lloyd Price & His Orchestra	Never Let Me Go	26/03/1960	124	CB
Lloyd Price & His Orchestra	If I Look A Little Blue	02/07/1960	111	CB
Lloyd Price & His Orchestra	One Hundred Percent	08/04/1961	125	CB
Lloyd Price And His Great Orchestra	Mary And Man-O	12/06/1961	110	BB
Lloyd Price And His Orchestra	Who Coulda' Told You (They Lied)	05/09/1960	103	BB
Lobo	We'll Make It - I Know We Will	15/04/1972	108	CB
Lobo	The Albatross	15/04/1972	128	CB
Lobo	Love Me For What I Am	15/09/1973	114	CB
Loggins & Messina	Peacemaker	10/04/1976	113	CB
Lolita	Theme From "A Summer Place" (Wenn Der Sommer Kommt)	06/02/1961	112	BB
Lolita	Theme From "A Summer Place" (Wenn Der Sommer Kommpt)	11/02/1961	105	CB
Lonette	Stop! (Don't Worry About It)	13/07/1968	141	CB
Lonnie Mack	Where There's A Will	23/11/1963	112	CB
Lonnie Mack	Where There's A Will	30/11/1963	113	BB
Lonnie Mack	Baby, What's Wrong	07/12/1963	118	CB
Lonnie Mack	Lonnie On The Move	29/02/1964	136	CB
Lonnie Mack	Lonnie On The Move	07/03/1964	117	BB
Lonnie Mack	I've Had It	02/05/1964	128	BB
Lonnie Mack	I've Had It	02/05/1964	134	CB
Lonnie Mack	Sa-Ba-Hoola	29/08/1964	147	CB
Lonnie Sattin And Orchestra	I'll Fly Away	04/07/1960	103	BB
Looking Glass	Rainbow Man	03/03/1973	104	BB
Loretta Lynn	Coal Miner's Daughter	02/01/1971	107	CB
Loretta Lynn	Love Is The Foundation	08/09/1973	102	BB
Lorne Greene	Five Card Stud	19/02/1966	112	BB
Lorraine Ellison	I Dig You Baby	22/01/1966	103	BB
Lorraine Ellison	A Good Love	24/12/1966	121	CB

Lorraine Ellison	A Good Love	31/12/1966	131	BB
Lorraine Ellison	If I Had A Hammer (The Hammer Song)	18/02/1967	144	CB
Lorraine Ellison	Heart Be Still	09/09/1967	106	CB
Lorraine Ellison	I Want To Be Loved	25/11/1967	137	CB
Los Bravos	I'm All Ears	08/07/1967	107	CB
Los Canarios	Get On Your Knees	30/11/1968	122	CB
Los Diablos	Un Rayo De Sol	29/08/1970	110	CB
Los Indios Tabajaras	Marta	05/09/1964	133	CB
Lou Christie	You And I (Have A Right To Cry)	13/07/1963	119	CB
Lou Christie	Shy Boy	19/10/1963	119	BB
Lou Christie	Shy Boy	19/10/1963	135	CB
Lou Christie	Guitars And Bongos	22/08/1964	123	BB
Lou Christie	Guitars And Bongos	19/09/1964	131	CB
Lou Christie	If My Car Could Only Talk	17/09/1966	118	BB
Lou Christie	Since I Don't Have You	26/11/1966	101	CB
Lou Christie	Since I Don't Have You	03/12/1966	102	BB
Lou Christie	Self Exprression (The Kids On The Street Will Never Give In)	08/07/1967	127	CB
Lou Christie	Gina	05/08/1967	139	CB
Lou Christie	Indian Lady	28/11/1970	106	BB
Lou Christie	Blue Canadian Rocky Dream	02/06/1973	102	CB
Lou Christie	Summer Days	30/08/1975	120	CB
Lou Courtney	You Ain't Ready	01/07/1967	141	CB
Lou Courtney	Hey Joyce	09/12/1967	105	CB
Lou Courtney	It's Love Now	17/02/1968	147	CB
Lou Johnson	It Ain't No Use	15/02/1964	126	CB
Lou Johnson	It Ain't No Use	07/03/1964	117	BB
Lou Johnson	Kentucky Bluebird (Send A Message To Martha)	24/10/1964	104	BB
Lou Johnson	Kentucky Bluebird (Send A Message To Martha)	31/10/1964	126	CB
Lou Johnson	Please, Stop The Wedding	24/04/1965	131	CB
Lou Lawton	Doing The Philly Dog	09/04/1966	133	BB

Lou Lawton	Doing The Philly Dog	23/04/1966	118	CB
Lou Monte	Dominick The Donkey (The Italian Christmas Donkey)	26/12/1960	114	BB
Lou Monte	Please Mr. Columbus (Turn The Ship Around)	02/06/1962	104	CB
Lou Monte	Please Mr. Columbus (Turn The Ship Around)	09/06/1962	109	BB
Lou Monte	Bossa Nova Italiano	18/05/1963	115	CB
Lou Monte	Bossa Nova Italiano	01/06/1963	128	BB
Lou Monte	Hello, Dolly! (Italian Style)	06/06/1964	130	CB
Lou Monte	Hello Dolly (Italian Style)	20/06/1964	131	BB
Lou Rawls	Three O'clock In The Morning	22/05/1965	103	CB
Lou Rawls	My Ancestors	10/02/1968	113	CB
Lou Rawls	My Ancestors	17/02/1968	113	BB
Lou Rawls	You're Good For Me	11/05/1968	103	BB
Lou Rawls	The Split	16/11/1968	104	CB
Lou Rawls	The Split	23/11/1968	123	BB
Lou Rawls	You've Made Me So Very Happy	14/02/1970	102	CB
Lou Rawls	His Song Shall Be Sung	12/02/1972	105	BB
Lou Rawls	Walk On In	04/11/1972	106	BB
Lou Rawls	Walk On In	18/11/1972	116	CB
Lou Rawls	She's Gone	28/09/1974	115	CB
Lou Rawls With The Onzy Matthews Band	Tobacco Road (Live)	26/10/1963	121	CB
Lou Reed	Satellite Of Love	09/06/1973	119	BB
Lou Reed	Satellite Of Love	16/06/1973	118	CB
Lou Reed	Sweet Jane (Live)	23/03/1974	118	CB
Lou Reed	Sally Can't Dance	02/11/1974	118	CB
Lou Reed	Sally Can't Dance	09/11/1974	103	BB
Lou Zerato	Louie - Part I	24/11/1973	121	CB
Loudon Wainwright Iii	Down Drinking At The Bar	08/12/1973	101	CB
Louis Armstrong	The Life Of The Party	13/04/1968	146	CB
Louis Armstrong	What A Wonderful World	06/07/1968	116	BB
Louis Armstrong	What A Wonderful World	20/07/1968	134	CB

Louis Armstrong & Dave Brubeck	Nomad	09/05/1964	142	CB
Louis Armstrong And Dave Brubeck	Nomad	09/05/1964	122	BB
Louis Jordan And His Tympany Five	Hard Head	04/05/1963	128	BB
Louis Prima & Keely Smith	I'm Confessin' (That I Love You)	31/08/1959	115	BB
Louisiana Red	I'm Too Poor To Die	08/08/1964	115	CB
Louisiana Red	I'm Too Poor To Die	12/09/1964	117	BB
Louisiana's Le Roux	Take A Ride On A Riverboat	02/12/1978	109	BB
Love	Alone Again Or	04/05/1968	123	BB
Love	Alone Again Or	12/09/1970	111	CB
Love Affair	Mama Sez	27/09/1980	109	BB
Love Childs Afro Cuban Blues Band	Life And Death In G&A	05/07/1975	105	CB
Love Sculpture	Sabre Dance	01/03/1969	118	CB
Love Society	Do You Wanna Dance	10/08/1968	108	BB
Love Society	Do You Wanna Dance	24/08/1968	106	CB
Love Unlimited	Is It Really True Boy - Is It Really Me	12/08/1972	122	CB
Love Unlimited	Is It Really True Boy-Is It Really Me	19/08/1972	101	BB
Love Unlimited	Yes, We Finally Made It	18/08/1973	101	BB
Love Unlimited Orchestra	Baby Blues	21/12/1974	102	BB
Love Unlimited Orchestra	Midnight Groove	08/05/1976	108	BB
Loverboy	Jump	11/12/1982	101	BB
Lowell Fulsom	Make A Little Love	15/04/1967	119	CB
Lowell Fulsom	I'm A Drifter	07/10/1967	118	BB
Luba	Everytime I See Your Picture	22/09/1984	105	BB
Lucille Starr	Yours	08/08/1964	149	CB
Lucky Peterson Blues Band	1-2-3-4	10/07/1971	112	CB
Lucky Peterson Blues Band	1-2-3-4	21/08/1971	102	BB
Lulu	I'll Come Running	26/12/1964	105	BB
Lulu	I'll Come Running	16/01/1965	111	CB
Lulu	The Boat That I Row	01/07/1967	115	BB
Lulu	The Boat That I Row	22/07/1967	138	CB

Lulu	Shout	09/12/1967	108	CB
Lulu	Boy	22/06/1968	105	CB
Lulu	Boy	29/06/1968	108	BB
Lulu	Without Him	02/11/1968	141	CB
Lulu	I'm A Tiger	07/12/1968	141	CB
Lulu	Who's Foolin' Who	10/04/1982	106	BB
Lulu With The Dixie Flyers	After The Feeling Is Gone	04/07/1970	117	BB
Luther Ingram	To The Other Man	07/11/1970	110	BB
Luther Ingram	Missing You	26/02/1972	108	BB
Luther Randolph & Johnny Stiles	Cross Roads (Part 1)	06/07/1963	109	BB
Luther Randolph & Johnny Stiles	Cross Roads (Part 1)	13/07/1963	114	CB
Luther Vandross	It's Good For The Soul - Pt. I	29/05/1976	102	BB
Luther Vandross	Don't You Know That?	16/01/1982	107	BB
Luther Vandross	I'll Let You Slide	14/01/1984	102	BB
Luther Vandross	It's Over Now	29/06/1985	101	BB
Lyn Collins (The Female Preacher)	Mama Feelgood	21/04/1973	103	CB
Lyn Collins (The Female Preacher)	How Long Can I Keep It Up Part I	14/07/1973	119	CB
Lyn Earlington With Sherman Conrad & His Bourbon Street	D.D.T. And The Boll Weevil	02/09/1961	117	CB
Lynn Anderson	I'm Alright	05/12/1970	112	BB
Lynn Anderson	Listen To A Country Song	17/06/1972	111	CB
Lynn Anderson	Listen To A Country Song	01/07/1972	107	BB
Lynn Anderson	Fool Me	11/11/1972	112	CB
Lynn Anderson	Fool Me	18/11/1972	101	BB
Lynn Anderson	Keep Me In Mind	03/03/1973	104	BB
Lynn Anderson	Sing About Love	24/11/1973	110	CB
Lynyrd Skynyrd	Down South Jukin'	04/11/1978	103	BB
Mac Davis	I'll Paint You A Song	18/07/1970	110	BB
Mac Davis	I'll Paint You A Song	01/08/1970	125	CB
Mac Davis	I Believe In Music	24/10/1970	117	BB
Mac Davis	Kiss It And Make It Better	01/09/1973	105	BB

Mac Davis	Kiss It And Make It Better	29/09/1973	105	CB
Mac Davis	Forever Lovers	17/04/1976	106	CB
Mac Davis	Every Now And Then	27/11/1976	104	CB
Mac Davis	Picking Up The Pieces Of My Life	04/06/1977	105	CB
Mac Davis	Hooked On Music	07/03/1981	102	BB
Mac Davis	Hooked On Music	14/03/1981	1102	CB
Mac Davis	You're My Bestest Friend	21/11/1981	106	BB
Mac Mcanally	Bad Boy	24/09/1977	104	CB
Maceo & The Macks	Parrty - Part I	19/05/1973	114	CB
Maceo & The Macks	Soul Power 74 (Part I)	15/12/1973	119	CB
Maceo And The Macks	Soul Power 74 (Part I)	19/01/1974	109	BB
Mack Rice	Coal Man	22/02/1969	135	BB
Mad Lads	So Nice	28/09/1968	122	CB
Madeline Bell	Step Inside Love	11/01/1969	121	CB
Madonna	Everybody	25/12/1982	107	BB
Maggie Bell	Caddo Queen	06/07/1974	110	CB
Maggie Thrett	Soupy	29/05/1965	130	CB
Magic Disco Machine	Control Tower	30/08/1975	106	BB
Magic Lanterns	Let The Sun Shine In	24/04/1971	103	BB
Magna Carta	Airport Song	12/12/1970	111	BB
Mahalia Jackson	In The Summer Of His Years	21/12/1963	116	BB
Mai Tai	History	10/08/1985	109	BB
Major Lance	Everybody Loves A Good Time	13/11/1965	102	CB
Major Lance	Everybody Loves A Good Time	13/11/1965	109	BB
Major Lance	Investigate	18/06/1966	132	BB
Major Lance	It's The Beat	27/08/1966	128	BB
Major Lance	It's The Beat	10/09/1966	111	CB
Major Lance	Ain't No Soul (In These Old Shoes)	31/12/1966	134	CB
Major Lance	Follow The Leader	24/05/1969	111	CB
Major Lance	Follow The Leader	21/06/1969	125	BB

Major Lance	Must Be Love Coming Down	02/01/1971	103	CB
Major Lance	Must Be Love Coming Down	23/01/1971	119	BB
Mal	Mighty Mighty And Roly Poly	13/05/1972	108	BB
Mal	Mighty Mighty And Roly Poly	27/05/1972	124	CB
Malo	Café	24/06/1972	102	CB
Malo	Café	08/07/1972	101	BB
Malo	Latin Bugaloo	11/11/1972	109	CB
Malo	Latin Bugaloo	02/12/1972	103	BB
Mama Cass Elliot	A Song That Never Comes	08/08/1970	104	CB
Mamas Cass Elliot	The Good Times Are Coming	24/10/1970	104	BB
Mamas Cass Elliot	The Good Times Are Coming	24/10/1970	121	CB
Mamas Cass Elliot	Don't Let The Good Life Pass You By	05/12/1970	124	CB
Mamas Cass Elliot	Don't Let The Good Life Pass You By	19/12/1970	110	BB
Mamie Galore	It Ain't Necessary	23/04/1966	132	BB
Mamie Galore	It Ain't Necessary	23/04/1966	142	CB
Mancini & Fox	(But I Could) Reach The Wisdom Of Soloman	07/10/1972	115	CB
Mandrill	Git It All	19/08/1972	104	CB
Mandrill	Mango Meat	20/10/1973	125	CB
Mandrill	Mango Meat	17/11/1973	107	BB
Mandrill	Love Song	02/02/1974	111	CB
Manfred Mann	My Little Red Book	26/06/1965	124	BB
Manfred Mann	My Little Red Book	03/07/1965	132	CB
Manfred Mann	She Needs Company	30/04/1966	125	CB
Manfred Mann	Just Like A Woman	20/08/1966	101	BB
Manfred Mann	My Name Is Jack	13/07/1968	104	BB
Manfred Mann	Fox On The Run	21/12/1968	108	CB
Manfred Mann	Ragamuffin Man	17/05/1969	126	CB
Manfred Mann	Please Mrs. Henry	16/10/1971	108	CB
Manfred Mann	Please Mrs. Henry	30/10/1971	108	BB
Manfred Mann's Earth Band	I'm Up And I'm Leaving	22/07/1972	112	BB

Manfred Mann's Earth Band	For You	21/03/1981	106	BB
Manny Kellem, His & Voices	Love Is Blue (L'Amour Est Bleu)	27/01/1968	111	CB
Mantovani	The Bowery	30/11/1963	129	CB
Mantovani And His Orchestra	Games That Lovers Play	12/11/1966	122	BB
Manu Dibango	Dangwa	22/09/1973	115	CB
Manu Dibango	Dangwa	20/10/1973	109	BB
Manuel & The Renegades	Rev-Up	21/09/1963	108	CB
Mar-Keys	Foxy	13/01/1962	116	CB
Mar-Keys	Pop-Eye Stroll	07/04/1962	115	CB
Mar-Keys	Banana Juice	03/04/1965	121	BB
Mar-Keys	Grab This Thing (Pt 1)	04/12/1965	111	BB
Mara Lynn Brown	Salty Tears	27/01/1973	108	CB
Mara Lynn Brown	Salty Tears	10/02/1973	118	BB
Marc Allen Trujillo	(Everybody's Goin') Hollywood	03/04/1976	102	CB
Marc Anthony Thompson	So Fine	13/10/1984	101	BB
Marcia Strassman	The Flower Children	22/04/1967	105	BB
Marcie Blane	You Gave My Number To Billy	14/09/1963	143	CB
Marcy Jo	Lover's Medley "The More I See You"/"When I Fall In Love"	17/08/1963	132	BB
Marcy Jo & Eddie Rambeau	Lover's Medley "The More I See You"/"When I Fall In Love"	20/07/1963	142	CB
Marcy Joe	Since Gary Went In The Navy	15/07/1961	101	CB
Margaret Whiting	Just Like A Man	11/02/1967	104	CB
Margaret Whiting	Just Like A Man	04/03/1967	132	BB
Margaret Whiting	I Almost Called Your Name	21/10/1967	108	BB
Margaret Whiting	It Keeps Right On A Hurtin'	24/02/1968	115	BB
Margaret Whiting	I Hate To See Me Go (b-side)	09/03/1968	127	BB
Margaret Whiting	Faithfully	27/04/1968	103	CB
Margaret Whiting	Faithfully	18/05/1968	117	BB
Margaret Whiting	Can't Get You Out Of My Mind	28/09/1968	124	BB
Margaret Whiting	Can't Get You Out Of My Mind	28/09/1968	139	CB
Margie Joseph	That Other Woman Got My Man And Gone	03/07/1971	109	CB

Margie Joseph	Let's Stay Together	14/04/1973	116	CB
Margie Joseph	Words (Are Impossible)	04/01/1975	115	CB
Margie Joseph	Hear The Words, Feel The Feeling	26/06/1976	111	CB
Margie Singleton	Magic Star (Tel-Star)	12/01/1963	110	CB
Margie Singleton	Magic Star (Tel-Star)	26/01/1963	124	BB
Margo Smith	Don't Break The Heart That Loves You	11/03/1978	104	BB
Maria Muldaur	Gringo En Mexico	26/04/1975	103	CB
Marian Love	I Believe In Music	06/03/1971	111	BB
Marianne Faithfull	Counting	27/08/1966	138	CB
Marianne Faithfull	Is This What I Get For Loving You?	11/03/1967	125	BB
Marie Knight	Cry Me A River	10/04/1965	124	BB
Marie Osmond	In My Little Corner Of The World	21/09/1974	102	BB
Marilyn Maye	Cabaret	29/10/1966	116	CB
Marilyn Michaels	Tell Tommy I Miss Him	05/09/1960	110	BB
Marilyn Michaels	Tell Tommy I Miss Him	10/09/1960	102	CB
Marion	Happy Lonesome	27/07/1959	102	BB
Marion Black	Go On Fool	20/03/1971	124	BB
Marion Worth	Are You Willing, Willie	06/02/1960	125	CB
Marion Worth	That's My Kind Of Love	25/06/1960	110	CB
Marion Worth	Crazy Arms	20/04/1963	122	CB
Marjoe	Lo And Behold!	25/11/1972	109	BB
Mark Dinning	All Of This For Sally	31/03/1962	129	CB
Mark James	Roller Coaster	16/06/1973	125	CB
Mark Johnson	Ode To Otis Redding	03/02/1968	122	BB
Mark Lindsay	Sing Your Own Song	14/08/1976	103	CB
Mark Murphy	Fly Me To The Moon (In Other Words)	19/01/1963	123	BB
Mark Radice	If You Can't Beat 'Em, Join 'Em	18/09/1976	110	BB
Mark-Almond	The City	03/07/1971	122	CB
Marlena Shaw	It's Better Than Walkin' Out	22/05/1976	103	BB
Marshall Crenshaw	There She Goes Again	23/10/1982	110	BB

Marshall Crenshaw	Whenever You're On My Mind	18/06/1983	103	BB
Martha Reeves & The Vandellas	Taking My Love (And Leaving Me)	13/09/1969	102	BB
Martha Reeves & The Vandellas	In And Out Of My Life	19/02/1972	102	BB
Martha Reeves & The Vandellas	Tear It On Down	17/06/1972	103	BB
Martin Denny	Paradise Cove*	17/03/1962	143	CB
Martin Denny	Cast Your Fate To The Wind	01/12/1962	124	BB
Martin Denny	More, Theme From "MONDO Cane"	01/06/1963	113	CB
Martin Denny	Hawaii Tattoo	12/12/1964	132	BB
Martin Denny & His Orchestra	Cast Your Fate To The Wind*	01/12/1962	104	CB
Martin Mull & Orchestra	Dueling Tubas	01/09/1973	107	CB
Marty Balin	Do It For Love	07/05/1983	102	BB
Marty Hill With Bill Ramal	Summer Job	01/07/1961	106	CB
Marty RoBBins	Five Brothers	17/09/1960	112	CB
Marty RoBBins	Sometimes I'm Tempted	13/01/1962	109	BB
Marty RoBBins	Teenager's Dad	09/03/1963	106	CB
Marty RoBBins	I'm Not Ready Yet	11/05/1963	140	CB
Marty RoBBins	No Signs Of Loneliness Here	01/06/1963	132	CB
Marty RoBBins	Not So Long Ago	24/08/1963	140	CB
Marty RoBBins	Not So Long Ago	21/09/1963	115	BB
Marty RoBBins	Girl From Spanish Town	22/02/1964	106	BB
Marty RoBBins	The Cowboy In The Continental Suit	13/06/1964	108	CB
Marty RoBBins	The Cowboy In The Continental Suit	27/06/1964	103	BB
Marty RoBBins	Up In The Air	07/11/1964	127	CB
Marty RoBBins	One Of These Days	14/11/1964	105	BB
Marty RoBBins	RiBBon Of Darkness	15/05/1965	103	BB
Marty RoBBins	RiBBon Of Darkness	05/06/1965	139	CB
Marty RoBBins	Private Wilson White	05/02/1966	145	CB
Marty RoBBins	Tonight Carmen	03/06/1967	114	BB
Marty RoBBins	Jolie Girl	03/10/1970	115	CB
Marty RoBBins	Jolie Girl	24/10/1970	108	BB

Marty RoBBins	Padre	09/01/1971	113	BB
Marty RoBBins	The Chair	03/07/1971	121	BB
Marty RoBBins	I Don't Know Why (I Just Do)	25/06/1977	108	BB
Marv Johnson	Don't Leave Me	03/10/1959	120	CB
Marv Johnson	How Can We Tell Him	08/07/1961	112	CB
Marv Johnson	I'm Not A Plaything	11/09/1965	133	CB
Marv Meredith & His Orchestra	Salvation Rock	10/12/1960	103	CB
Marva Whitney	Things Got To Get Better	12/07/1969	103	CB
Marva Whitney	Things Got To Get Better (Get Together)	23/08/1969	110	BB
Marvin Gaye	I'm Crazy 'BOUT My Baby	26/10/1963	143	CB
Marvin Gaye	Gonna Give Her All The Love I've Got	21/02/1970	103	CB
Marvin Gaye	A Funky Space Reincarnation (Part I)	17/02/1979	106	BB
Marvin Gaye	Praise	21/03/1981	101	BB
Marvin Gaye	Sanctified Lady	11/05/1985	101	BB
Marvin Gaye & Kim Weston	It's Got To Be A Miracle (This Thing Called Love)	04/03/1967	144	CB
Marvin Gaye & Tammi Terrell	The Onion Song	11/04/1970	122	CB
Marvin Rainwater	I Can't Forget	18/09/1961	119	BB
Mary Ann Fisher	Can't Take The Heartbreaks	09/12/1961	106	CB
Mary Hopkin	Think About Your Children	28/11/1970	104	CB
Mary Hopkin	Water, Paper & Clay	01/01/1972	113	BB
Mary Jane Girls	Candy Man	04/06/1983	101	BB
Mary Jane Girls	All Night Long	13/08/1983	101	BB
Mary Jane Girls	Boys	29/10/1983	102	BB
Mary Jane Girls	Jealousy	18/02/1984	106	BB
Mary Love	You Turned My Bitter Into Sweet	29/05/1965	133	BB
Mary Macgregor	The Wedding Song (There Is Love)	25/11/1978	Np4	CB
Mary Travers	The Song Is Love	28/08/1971	118	CB
Mary Travers	Too Many Mondays	10/03/1973	122	BB
Mary Wells	Stop Takin' Me For Granted	31/10/1964	116	CB
Mary Wells	Why Don't You Let Yourself Go	06/03/1965	106	CB

Mary Wells	Why Don't You Let Yourself Go	06/03/1965	107	BB
Mary Wells	I'm Learnin'	12/06/1965	106	CB
Mary Wells	(Hey You) Set My Soul On Fire	25/03/1967	120	CB
Mary Wells	(Hey You) Set My Soul On Fire	01/04/1967	122	BB
Mary Wells	Dig The Way I Feel	07/02/1970	115	BB
Mason & Cass	Something To Make You Happy	09/01/1971	110	CB
Mason Proffit	Hope	27/11/1971	108	BB
Mason Proffit	Hope	27/11/1971	110	CB
Mason Williams	Saturday Night At The World	07/12/1968	101	CB
Mason Williams	A Gift Of Song	26/07/1969	118	BB
Matt Monro	Softly As I Leave You	14/07/1962	116	BB
Matt Monro	Softly As I Leave You*	29/08/1964	115	CB
Matt Monro	Softly As I Leave You (shorter Version)	12/09/1964	121	BB
Matt Monro	For Mama	27/02/1965	135	BB
Matt Monro	Without You (I Cannot Live)	01/05/1965	101	BB
Matt Monro	Born Free	26/11/1966	126	BB
Matt Monro	Born Free	24/12/1966	132	CB
Matthews' Southern Comfort	Mare, Take Me Home	24/07/1971	101	CB
Matthews' Southern Comfort	Tell Me Why	30/10/1971	114	CB
Mattie Moultrie	That's How Strong My Love Is	21/01/1967	132	BB
Mauds	Man Without A Dream	26/09/1970	138	CB
Maureen Gray	Dancin' The Strand	26/05/1962	110	CB
Maureen Mcgovern	Nice To Be Around	23/03/1974	101	BB
Maurice & Mac	Oh What A Time	21/02/1970	124	CB
Maurice Mcalister & The Radiants	Shy Guy	23/11/1963	104	BB
Maurice Mcalister & The Radiants	Shy Guy	23/11/1963	112	CB
Maurice Williams & The Zodiacs	Come Along	08/04/1961	104	CB
Mavis Staples	Endlessly	28/10/1972	109	BB
Max Frost & The Troopers	Fifty Two Per Cent	07/12/1968	113	CB
Max Frost And The Troopers	Fifty Two Per Cent	14/12/1968	123	BB

Maxine Brown	I Don't Need You No More	08/07/1961	126	CB
Maxine Brown	Heaven In Your Arms	15/07/1961	132	CB
Maxine Brown	After All We've Been Through	28/10/1961	112	CB
Maxine Brown	After All We've Been Through	30/10/1961	102	BB
Maxine Brown	My Life	18/11/1961	122	CB
Maxine Brown	I Got A Funny Kind Of Feeling	20/01/1962	104	CB
Maxine Brown	I Got A Funny Kind Of Feeling	27/01/1962	104	BB
Maxine Brown	Coming Back To You	23/11/1963	108	CB
Maxine Brown	We Can Work It Out	30/07/1966	109	CB
Maxine Brown	I Don't Need Anything	10/12/1966	129	BB
Maxine Brown	Love In Them There Hills	25/01/1969	130	CB
Maxine Starr	Theme From Taras Bulba (The Wishing Star)*	08/12/1962	107	CB
Maxus	Nobody's Business	13/02/1982	I101	CB
Maxus	Nobody's Business	13/03/1982	109	BB
Maynard Ferguson	Main Title (From The 20th Century-Fox Film "Star Wars")	03/09/1977	107	BB
Maze Featuring Frankie Beverly	Lady Of Magic	13/08/1977	108	BB
Maze Featuring Frankie Beverly	Too Many Games	15/06/1985	103	BB
Mc 5	Tonight	08/11/1969	101	CB
Mcguinn, Clark & Hillman	Surrender To Me	07/07/1979	104	BB
Mcguinness Flint	Friends Of Mine	25/09/1971	117	CB
Mckendree Spring	Because It's Time	16/01/1971	105	BB
Mckendree Spring	Because It's Time	30/01/1971	108	CB
Mckendree Spring	Too Young To Feel This Old	27/03/1976	110	BB
Mckendree Spring	Too Young To Feel This Old	27/03/1976	118	CB
Mckinley Mitchell	The Town I Live In	31/03/1962	115	BB
Mckinley Mitchell	The Town I Live In	14/04/1962	145	CB
Meat Loaf	I'm Gonna Love Her For Both Of Us	12/09/1981	I102	CB
Meco	Love Theme From Shogun (Mariko's Theme)	11/10/1980	I101	CB
Meco	Blue Moon	05/09/1981	I101	CB
Meco	Blue Moon	19/09/1981	106	BB

Meco	Big Band Medley	12/06/1982	101	BB
Medical Missionaries Of Mary Choral Group	Angels (Watching Over Me)	22/01/1966	131	CB
Medical Missionaries Of Mary Choral Group	Angels (Watching Over Me)	05/02/1966	117	BB
Megan Mcdonough	No Return	05/05/1973	124	CB
Mel & Tim	Feeling Bad	16/05/1970	129	CB
Mel & Tim	Mail Call Time	06/06/1970	120	CB
Mel And Tim	Feeling Bad	09/05/1970	106	BB
Mel And Tim	I May Not Be What You Want	03/03/1973	113	BB
Mel Carter	The Richest Man Alive	26/12/1964	116	CB
Mel Carter	The Richest Man Alive	23/01/1965	104	BB
Mel Carter	I Wish I Didn't Love You So	05/02/1966	143	CB
Mel Carter	As Time Goes By	04/03/1967	111	BB
Mel Carter	Be My Love	21/10/1967	132	BB
Mel Carter	Be My Love	21/10/1967	138	CB
Mel Carter	I Only Have Eyes For You	11/05/1974	119	CB
Mel Carter	I Only Have Eyes For You	18/05/1974	104	BB
Mel Tillis	Life Turned Her That Way	03/06/1967	128	BB
Mel Tillis And Sherry Bryce With The Statesiders	Take My Hand	17/07/1971	110	BB
Mel Tillis And The Statesiders	The Arms Of A Fool	13/03/1971	114	BB
Mel Torme	Lover's Roulette	23/09/1967	122	CB
Mel Wynn Trend	That's When The World Really Began	25/07/1970	127	CB
Melanie	Beautiful People	08/11/1969	104	CB
Melanie	Stop! I Don't Wanna' Hear It Anymore	17/10/1970	112	BB
Melanie	Some Day I'll Be A Farmer	27/05/1972	106	BB
Melanie	Steppin'	22/07/1972	108	CB
Melanie	Do You Believe	30/12/1972	108	CB
Melanie	Do You Believe	13/01/1973	115	BB
Melanie	Seeds	07/07/1973	102	CB
Melanie	Lover's Cross	17/08/1974	109	BB
Melanie	You're Not A Bad Ghost, Just An Old Song	15/02/1975	116	CB

Melanie	One More Try	21/03/1981	110	BB
Melba Moore	I Got Love	30/05/1970	111	BB
Melba Moore	This Is It	15/05/1976	102	CB
Melba Moore	The Way You Make Me Feel	05/03/1977	108	BB
Melba Moore	Pick Me Up, I'll Dance	28/04/1979	103	BB
Melba Moore	Love's Comin' At Ya	06/11/1982	104	BB
Melba Moore	Livin' For Your Love	17/03/1984	108	BB
Melba Moore	Read My Lips	13/04/1985	104	BB
Melba Moore	When You Love Me Like This	29/06/1985	106	BB
Melissa Manchester	O Heaven (How You've Changed To Me)	04/05/1974	112	CB
Melissa Manchester	Rescue Me	31/07/1976	108	CB
Melissa Manchester	If This Is Love	20/09/1980	I103	CB
Melissa Manchester	If This Is Love	18/10/1980	102	BB
Menudo	If You're Not Here (By My Side)	05/05/1984	102	BB
Menudo	Please Be Good To Me	27/07/1985	104	BB
Merle Haggard & Strangers	Okie From Muskogee	08/11/1969	105	CB
Merle Haggard And The Strangers	Street Singer	25/04/1970	124	BB
Merle Haggard And The Strangers	Jesus, Take A Hold	13/06/1970	107	BB
Merle Haggard And The Strangers	I Can't Be Myself	17/10/1970	106a	BB
Merle Haggard And The Strangers	Sidewalks Of Chicago (b-side)	24/10/1970	106b	BB
Merle Haggard And The Strangers	Someday We'll Look Back	31/07/1971	119	BB
Merrilee Rush	Everyday Livin' Days	17/05/1969	127	CB
Merrilee Rush	Everyday Livin' Days	24/05/1969	130	BB
Merrilee Rush	Sign On For The Good Times	13/09/1969	119	CB
Merrilee Rush	Sign On For The Good Times	04/10/1969	125	BB
Merrilee Rush	Angel On My Shoulder	10/01/1970	122	BB
Merrill Staton Choir	Waltzing Matilda*	30/01/1960	103	CB
Merry Clayton	Country Road	10/10/1970	103	BB
Merv Griffin	Banned In Boston	27/02/1961	101	BB
Merv Griffin With Sid Bass Orchestra	You Came A Long Way From St. Louis	17/06/1961	150	CB

Metropolis	I Love New York	06/05/1978	105	BB
Mfsb	The Zip	06/12/1975	115	CB
Mia Farrow	Lullaby From "ROSEMARY'S Baby" Part 1	29/06/1968	114	CB
Mia Farrow	Lullaby From "Rosemary's Baby" Part 1	03/08/1968	111	BB
Miami	Kill That Roach	07/08/1976	102	BB
Michael & The Messengers	Midnight Hour	22/04/1967	116	BB
Michael & The Messengers	Romeo & Juliet	22/07/1967	129	BB
Michael & The Messengers	Romeo And Juliet	05/08/1967	121	CB
Michael Allen	I Was A Boy When You Needed A Man	19/12/1970	109	CB
Michael Allen	The Big Parade	12/08/1972	111	CB
Michael Allen	When Mabel Comes In The Room	09/11/1974	104	CB
Michael Clark	Work Out	23/03/1963	130	BB
Michael Clark	Work Out	23/03/1963	132	CB
Michael Dinner	The Promised Land	08/11/1975	111	CB
Michael Furlong	Use It Or Lose It	29/09/1984	103	BB
Michael Henderson	Be My Girl	25/12/1976	101	BB
Michael Henderson	Be My Girl	15/01/1977	103	CB
Michael Henderson	I Can't Help It	06/08/1977	103	BB
Michael Johnson	On The Road	21/04/1973	118	BB
Michael Johnson	The Very First Time	02/02/1980	101	BB
Michael Kenny	Morning	23/08/1975	112	CB
Michael Murphey	Don't Count The Rainy Days	22/10/1983	106	BB
Michael Parks	Tie Me To Your Apron Strings Again	03/01/1970	117	BB
Michael Parks	Sally (Was A Gentle Woman)	01/08/1970	109	CB
Michael Rabon & The Five Americans	Virginia Girl	15/03/1969	111	CB
Michael Rabon And The Five Americans	Virginia Girl	01/03/1969	133	BB
Mick Ronson	Love Me Tender	23/03/1974	117	CB
Mickey Gilley	I Overlooked An Orchid	24/08/1974	104	CB
Mickey Gilley	Bring It On Home To Me	28/08/1976	101	BB
Mickey Gilley	That's All That Matters	15/11/1980	101	BB

Mickey Gilley	Talk To Me	08/01/1983	106	BB
Mickey Newbury	Heaven Help The Child	03/03/1973	103	BB
Micky Denne/Ken Gold	Let's Put Our Love Back Together	08/04/1978	105	CB
Midnight Star	Hot Spot	18/09/1982	108	BB
Midnight String Quartet	Classical Gas	29/06/1968	107	CB
Mighty Clouds Of Joy	Time	05/10/1974	102	BB
Mighty Clouds Of Joy	Time	26/10/1974	107	CB
Mighty Sam	Sweet Dreams (Of You)	23/07/1966	117	CB
Mighty Sam	Fannie Mae	24/09/1966	120	BB
Mike Clifford	Uh Huh	01/04/1961	130	CB
Mike Clifford	Bombay	30/12/1961	140	CB
Mike Clifford	All The Colors Of The Rainbow (Turn To Blue)	25/07/1964	143	CB
Mike Curb Congregation	Sweet Gingerbread Man	14/08/1971	115	BB
Mike Curb Congregation	Monday Man	30/10/1971	105	CB
Mike Curb Congregation	Take Up The Hammer Of Hope	08/04/1972	114	CB
Mike Curb Congregation	See You In September	24/06/1972	108	BB
Mike Douglas	Here's To My Jenny	19/03/1966	116	CB
Mike Douglas	Cabaret	29/10/1966	129	BB
Mike Douglas	Cabaret	12/11/1966	133	CB
Mike Kennedy	The Livin' I'm Doin' (Ain't Worth The Lovin' I'm Getting')	20/05/1972	115	CB
Mike Minor	Silver Dollar	11/07/1964	126	CB
Mike Quatro Jam Band	Circus	08/07/1972	108	BB
Millicent Martin	In The Summer Of His Years	28/12/1963	104	BB
Millie Jackson	A Child Of God (It's Hard To Believe)	13/11/1971	102	BB
Millie Jackson	A Child Of God (It's Hard To Believe)	13/11/1971	107	CB
Millie Jackson	Breakaway	21/04/1973	110	BB
Millie Jackson	I Got To Try It One Time	16/02/1974	101	CB
Millie Jackson	Loving Arms	22/11/1975	110	CB
Millie Jackson	All The Way Lover	18/03/1978	102	BB
Ministry	I Wanted To Tell Her	20/08/1983	106	BB

Miquel Brown	So Many Men, So Little Time	08/10/1983	107	BB
Miracles	I Need A Change	03/12/1960	114	CB
Miracles	If Your Mother Only Knew	29/09/1962	143	CB
Miriam Makeba	What Is Love	23/03/1968	116	CB
Miriam Makeba	What Is Love	23/03/1968	123	BB
Miss Abrams & The Strawberry Point School Third Grade Class	Mill Valley	11/07/1970	109	CB
Mitch Miller & The Gang	The Guns Of Navarone*	08/07/1961	112	CB
Mitch Miller With His Orchestra & Chorus	Tunes Of Glory*	11/02/1961	102	CB
Mitch Miller With His Orchestra And Chorus	The Longest Day	01/12/1962	109	BB
Mitch Ryder	I'd Rather Go To Jail	08/07/1967	140	CB
Mitch Ryder	Ruby Baby & Peaches On A Cherry Tree	18/05/1968	106	BB
Mitch Ryder	Ruby Baby & Peaches On A Cherry Tree	01/06/1968	130	CB
Mitch Ryder	The Lights Of Night	15/06/1968	122	BB
Mitch Ryder & Detroit Wheels	Takin' All I Can Get	23/07/1966	110	CB
Mitch Ryder And The Detroit Wheels	Come See About Me	16/12/1967	113	BB
Mitch Ryder And The Spirit Feel	Ring Your Bell	04/01/1969	125	BB
Mitchell Torok	Mexican Joe	02/11/1959	102	BB
Mitty Collier	I Got To Get Away From It All	26/08/1961	139	CB
Mitty Collier	I'm Your Part Time Love	21/09/1963	104	CB
Mitzi Gaynor	I Don't Regret A Thing	27/02/1960	124	CB
Moby Grape	Hey Grandma	15/07/1967	127	BB
Mocedades	Dime Senor	18/05/1974	107	CB
Modern Folk Quintet	Night Time Girl	09/04/1966	122	BB
Moe Koffman Quartette	Swingin' Shepherd Blues Twist	14/04/1962	130	CB
Moe Koffman Quartette	Swingin' Shepherd Blues Twist (twist Version)	28/04/1962	110	BB
Mojo	I Can't Let Go	31/05/1969	112	CB
Molly Bee	She's New To You	30/03/1963	129	CB
Molly Bee	She's New To You	30/03/1963	130	BB
Molly Hatchet	Dreams I'll Never See	12/05/1979	Np6	CB
Molly Hatchet	Dreams I'll Never See	16/06/1979	106	BB

Molly Hatchet	Beatin' The Odds	01/11/1980	107	BB
Moments	With You	11/12/1976	102	CB
Monday After	Merry-Go-Round Pt. I	06/03/1976	106	BB
Mongo Santamaria	El Pussy Cat	05/12/1964	123	CB
Mongo Santamaria	We Got Latin Soul	18/10/1969	132	BB
Mongo Santamaria Orchestra	Yeh-Yeh!	15/06/1963	114	CB
Monk Higgins	Who-Dun-It?	06/08/1966	117	BB
Monk Higgins & The Specialties	Gotta Be Funky	10/06/1972	105	BB
Monk Montgomery	A Place In The Sun	25/10/1969	109	CB
Montrose	Paper Money	08/02/1975	122	CB
Moon Martin	Love Gone Bad	31/01/1981	105	BB
Moon People	Land Of Love	21/09/1968	123	CB
Moonlion	The Little Drummer Boy	27/12/1975	116	CB
Morning Mist	California On My Mind	31/07/1971	102	CB
Mort Garson & His Orchestra	Early Sunday	20/01/1962	126	CB
Morty Jay & The Surferin' Cats	Salt Water Taffy	12/10/1963	129	CB
Mother's Finest	Fire	04/09/1976	108	CB
Motherlode	Memories Of A Broken Promise (b-side)	08/11/1969	116	BB
Motherlode	What Does It Take (To Win Your Love)	29/11/1969	111	BB
Mountain	For Yasgur's Farm	12/09/1970	107	BB
Mountain	Roll Over Beethoven	08/01/1972	111	CB
Mouse	A Public Execution	26/02/1966	121	BB
Mouse	A Public Execution	12/03/1966	127	CB
Mouse And The Traps	Sometimes You Just Can't Win	08/06/1968	125	BB
Mr. Acker Bilk	Dardanella (Part 1)	23/06/1962	105	BB
Mr. Acker Bilk	Only You (And You Alone)	26/01/1963	114	CB
Mr. Acker Bilk And His Paramount Jazz Bandmr. Acker Bilk And His	The Harem	08/02/1964	125	BB
Mr. Acker Bilk And His Paramount Jazz Bandmr. Acker Bilk And His	Summer Set	22/02/1960	104	BB
Mr. Acker Bilk With The Leon Young String Chorale	Underneath The Arches	01/06/1963	129	CB
Mr. Acker Bilk With The Leon Young String Chorale	The Good Life	21/11/1964	134	CB

Mr. Danny Pearson	What's Your Sign Girl?	14/04/1979	106	BB
Mr. Jim & The Rhythm Machine	(Do The) Hot Pants	20/03/1971	102	CB
Mtume	C.O.D. (I'll Deliver)	17/11/1984	104	BB
Mungo Jerry	Johnny B. Badde	21/11/1970	103	CB
Mungo Jerry	Baby Jump	06/02/1971	116	CB
Murry Kellum	Red Ryder	04/04/1964	121	CB
Muscle Shoals Horns	Born To Get Down (Born To Mess Around)	20/03/1976	105	BB
My Friends	I'm An Easy Rider	25/09/1971	102	CB
Myrna March	I Can't Say No	26/10/1963	150	CB
Nana Mouskouri	The White Rose Of Athens	17/02/1962	114	CB
Nancy Ames	Cu Cu Rru Cu Cu Paloma	27/04/1963	120	CB
Nancy Ames	The Funny Thing About It	02/10/1965	119	BB
Nancy Ames	The Funny Thing About It	02/10/1965	125	CB
Nancy Ames	Friends And Lovers Forever	11/12/1965	140	CB
Nancy Ames	Friends And Lovers Forever	15/01/1966	123	BB
Nancy Ames	He Wore The Green Beret	19/03/1966	118	CB
Nancy Sinatra	To Know Him Is To Love Him	10/03/1962	141	CB
Nancy Sinatra	Tony Rome	18/11/1967	101	CB
Nancy Sinatra	Here We Go Again	10/05/1969	128	CB
Nancy Sinatra & Lee Hazlewood	Sand	28/10/1967	107	BB
Nancy Sinatra And Lee Hazlewood	Down From Dover	19/02/1972	120	BB
Nancy Sinatra With Lee Hazlewood	Summer Wine	18/03/1967	105	CB
Nancy Wilson	My Foolish Heart	04/03/1961	132	CB
Nancy Wilson	That's What I Want For Christmas	14/12/1963	128	CB
Nancy Wilson	And Satisfy	21/11/1964	106	BB
Nancy Wilson	And Satisfy	28/11/1964	117	CB
Nancy Wilson	Take What I Have	26/12/1964	150	CB
Nancy Wilson	Welcome, Welcome	08/05/1965	125	BB
Nancy Wilson	Welcome, Welcome	08/05/1965	129	CB
Nancy Wilson	Uptight (Everything's Alright)	02/07/1966	104	CB

Nancy Wilson	In A Long White Room	14/12/1968	117	BB
Nancy Wilson	You'd Better Go	08/03/1969	137	CB
Nancy Wilson	You'd Better Go	15/03/1969	111	BB
Nancy Wilson	Got It Together	26/07/1969	131	CB
Nancy Wilson	Got It Together	02/08/1969	114	BB
Nancy Wilson	Now I'm A Woman	23/01/1971	101	CB
Napoleon Xiv	They're Coming To Take Me Away, Ha-Haaa!	21/04/1973	101	CB
Napoli & Glasson	Ii Est Toujours Temps Pour Partir (Never Can Say Goodbye)	04/10/1975	106	BB
Nappy Brown	I Cried Like A Baby	28/11/1959	117	CB
Narada Michael Walden (with Patti Austin)	Gimme, Gimme, Gimme	23/02/1985	106	BB
Narvel Felts	Honey Love	20/02/1960	117	CB
Nat "King" Cole	That's You	18/04/1960	101	BB
Nat "King" Cole	Step Right Up (And Say You Love Me)	20/01/1962	106	BB
Nat "King" Cole	The Right Thing To Say	31/03/1962	110	BB
Nat "King" Cole	Looking Back	11/12/1965	123	BB
Nat King Cole	That's You	30/04/1960	104	CB
Nat King Cole	If I Knew	07/01/1961	109	CB
Nat King Cole	The World In My Arms	07/01/1961	125	CB
Nat King Cole	Illusion	25/02/1961	122	CB
Nat King Cole	Illusion	06/03/1961	108	BB
Nat King Cole	Make It Last	01/07/1961	149	CB
Nat King Cole	Let True Love Begin	23/09/1961	102	CB
Nat King Cole	Cappuccina	09/10/1961	115	BB
Nat King Cole	Step Right Up (And Say You Love Me)	06/01/1962	107	CB
Nat King Cole	More And More Of Your Amor	18/07/1964	102	BB
Nat King Cole	L-O-V-E	26/09/1964	105	CB
Nat King Cole & StuBBy Kaye	The Ballad Of Cat Ballou	15/05/1965	136	CB
Nat Stuckey	Sweet Thang	29/10/1966	114	CB
Natalie Cole	Annie Mae	10/06/1978	102	CB
Natalie Cole	Stand By	24/03/1979	108	BB

Natalie Cole	Sorry	23/06/1979	109	BB
Natalie Cole & Peabo Bryson	Gimme Some Time	22/12/1979	102	BB
Nathaniel Mayer & His Fabulous Twilights	I Had A Dream	30/11/1963	146	CB
Natural Four	Love That Really Counts	27/04/1974	102	CB
Navajo	Frisco Bay	11/03/1972	116	CB
Nazareth	Razamanaz	29/09/1973	115	CB
Nazareth	Love Leads To Madness	31/07/1982	105	BB
Nazz	Open My Eyes	03/08/1968	104	CB
Nazz	Open My Eyes	21/09/1968	112	BB
Neal Dover	Mr. Bus Driver	31/01/1970	128	CB
Neal Hefti, His Orchestra & Chorus	The Odd Couple	06/07/1968	132	CB
Ned Miller	One Among The Many	13/04/1963	111	CB
Ned Miller	Invisible Tears	18/04/1964	136	CB
Ned Miller	Invisible Tears	25/04/1964	131	BB
Neil Sedaka	Crying My Heart Out For You	01/06/1959	111	BB
Neil Sedaka	The Closest Thing To Heaven	18/04/1964	111	CB
Neil Sedaka	The Closest Thing To Heaven	25/04/1964	107	BB
Neil Sedaka	I Hope He Breaks Your Heart	31/10/1964	104	BB
Neil Sedaka	I Hope He Breaks Your Heart	31/10/1964	112	CB
Neil Sedaka	Let The People Talk	06/03/1965	124	CB
Neil Sedaka	Let The People Talk	13/03/1965	107	BB
Neil Sedaka	We Can Make It If We Try	10/12/1966	135	CB
Neil Sedaka	We Can Make It If We Try	07/01/1967	121	BB
Neil Sedaka	Rainy Jane	12/07/1969	131	CB
Neil Sedaka	Alone At Last	27/08/1977	104	BB
Neil Sedaka	Letting Go	06/09/1980	107	BB
Neil Young	Time Fades Away [Live]	22/12/1973	108	BB
Neil Young	Time Fades Away (Live)	29/12/1973	111	CB
Nektar	Astral Man	26/04/1975	111	CB
Nella Dodds	Finders Keepers, Losers Weepers	02/01/1965	104	CB

Nella Dodds	P's And Q's	17/04/1965	123	CB
Nelson Riddle	Lolita Ya Ya*	18/08/1962	104	CB
Nelson Riddle	Naked City Theme	29/09/1962	114	CB
Nelson Riddle	Naked City Theme	20/10/1962	130	BB
Nena	Just A Dream	05/05/1984	102	BB
New Edition	Popcorn Love	21/01/1984	101a	BB
New Edition	Jealous Girl (b-side)	21/01/1984	101b	BB
New Edition	My Secret (Didja Gitit Yet?)	03/08/1985	103	BB
New England	Ddt	04/07/1981	I103	CB
New Holidays	Maybe So Maybe No	14/02/1970	133	CB
New Order	The Perfect Kiss	27/07/1985	109	BB
New Riders Of The Purple Sage	I Don't Need No Doctor	03/06/1972	104	CB
New Riders Of The Purple Sage	Dead Flowers	21/08/1976	105	BB
New York Citi Peech Boys	Life Is Something Special	19/02/1983	108	BB
New York City	Love Is What You Make It	11/01/1975	104	BB
New York City	Got To Get You Back In My Life	05/04/1975	105	BB
New York Dolls	Trash	29/09/1973	111	CB
New York Dolls	Stranded In The Jungle	08/06/1974	105	CB
Newbeats	I Know (You Don't Want Me No More)	21/12/1974	113	CB
Nick Lowe	So It Goes	22/07/1978	109	BB
Nick Lowe	Switch Board Susan	24/11/1979	107	BB
Nick Lowe	Half A Boy And Half A Man	04/08/1984	110	BB
Nick Noble	They Call Me The Fool	03/06/1961	142	CB
Nick Noble	Main Theme From The Cardinal (Stay With Me)*	25/01/1964	107	CB
Nicky Como	Look For A Star	20/06/1960	110	BB
Nicolette Larson	Give A Little	25/08/1979	104	BB
Nicolette Larson	Ooo-Eee	28/02/1981	110	BB
Nicolette Larson	Fool Me Again	07/11/1981	I103	CB
Nicolette Larson	Fool Me Again	21/11/1981	105	BB
Nielsen/Pearson	Two Lonely Nights	31/01/1981	110	BB

Nigel Olsson	Something Lacking In Me	11/10/1975	111	CB
Nigel Olsson	A Girl Like You	24/01/1976	107	BB
Nigel Olsson	Rainy Day	06/05/1978	105	CB
Nik Kershaw	The Riddle	13/04/1985	107	BB
Nikita The K And The Friends Of Ed Labunski	Go Go Radio Moscow	25/03/1967	105	BB
Nikki Wills	Some Guys Have All The Luck	05/12/1981	1103	CB
Nikki Wills	Some Guys Have All The Luck	19/12/1981	109	BB
Nils Lofgren	Night Fades Away	24/10/1981	109	BB
Nilsson	You Can't Do That	26/08/1967	122	BB
Nilsson	Everybody's Talkin'	10/08/1968	113	BB
Nilsson	Down To The Valley	11/07/1970	114	CB
Nilsson	Many Rivers To Cross	03/08/1974	109	BB
Nilsson	Subterranean Homesick Blues	12/10/1974	108	CB
Nilsson	Kojak Columbo	22/03/1975	104	CB
Nina Simone	He Needs Me	24/10/1959	107	CB
Nina Simone	Little Girl Blue	31/10/1959	117	CB
Nina Simone	Nobody Knows You When You're Down And Out	15/10/1960	115	CB
Nina Simone	Gin House Blues	11/09/1961	113	BB
Nina Simone	Don't Let Me Be Misunderstood	05/12/1964	131	BB
Nina Simone	I Put A Spell On You	19/06/1965	107	CB
Nina Simone	I Put A Spell On You	26/06/1965	120	BB
Nina Simone	Four Women	15/10/1966	138	CB
Nina Simone	(You'll) Go To Hell	04/11/1967	133	BB
Nina Simone	I Wish I Knew How It Would Feel To Be Free	25/11/1967	118	CB
Nina Simone	Do What You Gotta Do	26/10/1968	101	CB
Nina Simone	Ain't Got No; I Got Life	07/12/1968	107	CB
Nini Rosso	Ii Silenzio	16/10/1965	101	BB
Nino & April	Put It Where You Want It	07/07/1973	122	BB
Nino Tempo & April Stevens	I Surrender Dear	25/07/1964	132	CB
Nino Tempo & April Stevens	Ooh La La	12/09/1964	113	BB

Nino Tempo & April Stevens	Swing Me	05/06/1965	127	BB
Nino Tempo & April Stevens	The Habit Of Lovin' You Baby	31/12/1966	149	CB
Nino Tempo & April Stevens	You'll Be Needing Me Baby	21/01/1967	133	BB
Nino Tempo & April Stevens	My Old Flame	08/04/1967	104	CB
Nino Tempo & April Stevens	My Old Flame	15/04/1967	101	BB
Nino Tempo & April Stevens	I Can't Go On Living Baby Without You	29/07/1967	118	CB
Nino Tempo & April Stevens	Let It Be Me	25/05/1968	127	BB
Nino Tempo & April Stevens	Yesterday I Heard The Rain (Esta Tarde Vi Llover)	29/03/1969	136	CB
Nino Tempo & April Stevens	Love Story	09/12/1972	113	BB
Nitty Gritty Dirt Band	Truly Right	05/08/1967	141	CB
Nitty Gritty Dirt Band	Some Of Shelly's Blues	18/10/1969	106	BB
Nitty Gritty Dirt Band	Cosmic Cowboy - Part 1	30/06/1973	123	BB
Noel Harrison	In A Dusty Old Room	03/12/1966	130	CB
Noel Harrison	The Windmills Of Your Mind	03/08/1968	103	CB
Nolan Strong	Mind Over Matter (I'm Gonna Make You Mine)	03/11/1962	112	BB
Nolan Thomas	One Bad Apple	15/06/1985	105	BB
Norma Jean	Go Cat Go	03/10/1964	134	BB
Norma Jean	Saturday	26/08/1978	110	CB
Norma Jean Wright	Saturday	09/09/1978	103	BB
Norma Tanega	A Street That Rhymes At Six A.M.	14/05/1966	120	CB
Norma Tanega	A Street That Rhymes At Six A.M.	21/05/1966	129	BB
Norma Tracey & The Cinderella Kids	Leroy	09/01/1965	108	CB
Norma Tracey And The Cinderella Kids	Leroy	30/01/1965	107	BB
Norman Connors	We Both Need Each Other	31/07/1976	101	BB
Norman Connors Featuring Phyllis Hyman	Betcha By Golly Wow	15/01/1977	102	BB
Norman Greenbaum	California Earthquake	22/05/1971	105	CB
Norman Warren & The Warrentones	The Puerto Rican Pedlar	13/02/1960	121	CB
Nova's Nine	Pain	09/11/1968	145	CB
Novo Combo	Tattoo	06/02/1982	103	BB
Nrbq	Stomp	31/05/1969	106	CB

Nrbq	Stomp	28/06/1969	122	BB
Nrbq	I Love Her, She Loves Me	15/04/1978	105	CB
O.C. Smith	That's Life	21/01/1967	127	BB
O.C. Smith	Main Street Mission	13/07/1968	124	CB
O.C. Smith	Main Street Mission	27/07/1968	105	BB
O.C. Smith	Me And You	22/11/1969	103	BB
O.C. Smith	Moody	21/02/1970	114	BB
O.C. Smith	I've Been There	27/03/1971	120	CB
O.C. Smith	Help Me Make It Through The Night	20/11/1971	120	CB
O.C. Smith	Don't Misunderstand	18/11/1972	102	BB
O.C. Smith	Don't Misunderstand	30/12/1972	102	CB
O.V. Wright	Poor Boy	13/11/1965	129	CB
O.V. Wright	Heartaches-Heartaches	22/07/1967	136	CB
O.V. Wright	Love The Way You Love	25/04/1970	139	CB
O.V. Wright	When You Took Your Love From Me	06/03/1971	118	BB
O.V. Wright	A Nickel And A Nail	25/09/1971	103	BB
O.V. Wright	Drowning On Dry Land	10/02/1973	119	CB
O.V. Wright With The Keys	That's How Strong My Love Is	08/08/1964	127	CB
O.V. Wright With The Keys	That's How Strong My Love Is	29/08/1964	109	BB
O'bryan	Lovelite	09/06/1984	101	BB
O'jays	Work On Me	13/08/1977	106	CB
O'kaysions	Watch Out Girl	03/10/1970	130	CB
Oak	Draw The Line	05/01/1980	108	BB
Oak	Set The Night On Fire	13/12/1980	l101	CB
Oak Ridge Boys	I'll Be True To You	22/07/1978	102	BB
Oak Ridge Boys	Cryin' Again	07/10/1978	107	BB
Oak Ridge Boys	Heart Of Mine	20/09/1980	105	BB
Oak Ridge Boys	Fancy Free	03/10/1981	104	BB
Odia Coates & Paul Anka	Make It Up To Me In Love	06/11/1976	101	CB
Odyssey	Single Again/What Time Does The Balloon Go Up	04/11/1978	107	BB

Odyssey	Don't Tell Me, Tell Her	28/06/1980	105	BB
Odyssey	Inside Out	07/08/1982	104	BB
Ohio Express	Cowboy Convention	22/11/1969	101	BB
Ohio Express	Love Equals Love	14/02/1970	138	CB
Ohio Players	Far East Mississippi	04/12/1976	101	CB
Ohio Players	Body Vibes	07/05/1977	101	CB
Ohio Players	Good Luck Charm (Part I)	07/01/1978	101	BB
Ohio Players	Funk-O-Nots	23/09/1978	105	BB
Ohta-San	Song For Anna (Chanson D' Anna)	03/08/1974	104	BB
Oliver	Early Mornin' Rain	03/04/1971	118	CB
Oliver	Early Mornin' Rain	01/05/1971	124	BB
Oliver Sain	She's A Disco Queen	27/03/1976	103a	BB
Oliver Sain	Party Hearty (b-side)	27/03/1976	103b	BB
Olivia Newton-John	Take Me Home, Country Roads	26/05/1973	119	BB
Ollie & The Nightingales	I Got A Sure Thing	13/04/1968	105	CB
Ollie Nightingale	It's A Sad Thing	29/05/1971	121	BB
Olympic Runners	Do It Over	01/06/1974	115	CB
Olympic Runners	Do It Over	20/07/1974	107	BB
Olympic Runners	Put The Music Where Your Mouth Is	20/07/1974	111	CB
Olympic Runners	Put The Music Where Your Mouth Is	24/08/1974	103	BB
Olympic Runners	Grab It	11/01/1975	103	BB
Olympic Runners	Drag It Over Here	26/07/1975	117	CB
Olympic Runners	Drag It Over Here	16/08/1975	109	BB
One G Plus Three	Poquito Soul	24/10/1970	122	BB
Orchestra Del Oro, Score By Don Costa	Theme From Lolita	28/04/1962	116	CB
Originals	Keep Me	04/09/1971	103	CB
Orleans	One Of A Kind	18/09/1982	110	BB
Orlons	My Best Friend	15/06/1963	112	CB
Orlons	Goin' Places	19/09/1964	125	CB
Ornadel & The Starlight Symphony Orchestra	Theme From "KING Of Kings"*	18/11/1961	111	CB

Orpheus	Can't Find The Time	09/03/1968	111	BB
Oscar Peterson Trio	Hymn To Freedom	28/09/1963	109	BB
Oscar Peterson Trio	Mumbles	24/10/1964	101	BB
Oscar Peterson Trio	Mumbles	31/10/1964	105	CB
Oscar Toney Jr.	You Can Lead Your Woman To The Altar	14/10/1967	120	BB
Oscar Weathers	You Wants To Play	20/03/1971	125	BB
Oscar Weathers	Tell It Like It Is - Part 2	23/06/1973	115	CB
Oscar Weathers	Tell It Like It Is-Part 1	28/07/1973	113	BB
Osibisa	Sunshine Day	24/04/1976	108	BB
Otis & Carla	When Somethiing Is Wrong With My Baby	26/04/1969	101	CB
Otis And Carla	When Something Is Wrong With My Baby	26/04/1969	109	BB
Otis Clay	I'm Satisfied	16/04/1966	105	BB
Otis Clay	That's How It Is (When You're In Love)	02/09/1967	131	BB
Otis Clay	Trying To Live My Life Without You	06/01/1973	102	BB
Otis Leavill	Let Her Love Me	27/02/1965	116	BB
Otis Leavill	To Be Or Not To Be	24/04/1965	115	CB
Otis Leavill	To Be Or Not To Be	08/05/1965	128	BB
Otis Redding	That's What My Heart Needs	20/07/1963	133	CB
Otis Redding	Security	16/05/1964	106	CB
Otis Redding	Direct Me	18/01/1969	111	CB
Otis Redding	Free Me	02/08/1969	103	BB
Otis Redding	(You're Love Has Lifted Me) Higher And Higher (b-side)	16/08/1969	110	BB
Otis Redding	(Your Love Has Lifted Me) Higher And Higher	30/08/1969	116	CB
Otis Redding	Demonstration	04/04/1970	105	BB
Otis Redding	I've Been Loving You Too Long (Live)	23/01/1971	122	CB
Otis Redding	I've Been Loving You Too Long [Live]	06/02/1971	110	BB
Outlaws	Breaker - Breaker	29/05/1976	107	CB
Outlaws	Green Grass And High Tides	20/11/1976	101	CB
Outlaws	I Can't Stop Loving You	18/04/1981	102	BB
Owen B.	Never Goin' Home	06/06/1970	119	CB

Ozark Mountain Daredevils	Look Away	05/10/1974	101	BB
Ozark Mountain Daredevils	Thin Ice	27/09/1975	109	CB
Ozone	Li'l Suzy	28/08/1982	109	BB
Ozzy Osbourne	Crazy Train	04/07/1981	106	BB
Ozzy Osbourne	Crazy Train	11/07/1981	1103	CB
Ozzy Osbourne	Bark At The Moon	11/02/1984	109	BB
Ozzy Osbourne	So Tired	10/03/1984	104	BB
P. J. Proby	Together	05/12/1964	117	BB
P. J. Proby	I Can't Make It Alone	12/11/1966	131	BB
P. J. Proby	Work With Me Annie	10/06/1967	119	BB
P. J. Proby	Just Holding On	23/09/1967	130	BB
P. J. Proby	I Apologize Baby	18/05/1968	135	BB
P.F. Sloan	Halloween Mary	20/11/1965	110	CB
P.F. Sloan	From A Distance	26/02/1966	142	CB
P.F. Sloan	From A Distance	02/04/1966	109	BB
P.J. Proby	I Apologize	03/04/1965	117	CB
P.J. Proby	Let The Water Run Down	17/07/1965	134	CB
P.R. Battle	Radio Loves You	29/10/1977	110	CB
Pablo Cruise	Island Woman	28/06/1975	115	CB
Pablo Cruise	Island Woman	26/07/1975	104	BB
Pablo Cruise	Will You, Won't You	01/10/1983	107	BB
Pacific Gas & Electric	Father Come On Home	12/09/1970	102	CB
Pamala Stanley	This Is Hot	10/11/1979	108	BB
Pamala Stanley	Coming Out Of Hiding	16/06/1984	106	BB
Panhandle	Hey Girl	22/11/1969	122	BB
Panhandle	Hey Girl	20/12/1969	122	CB
Panic Buttons	O-Wow	26/04/1969	123	CB
Papa Doo Run Run	Be True To Your School	04/10/1975	116	CB
Papa Joe's Music Box	Papa Joe's Thing	22/11/1969	126	CB
Parker Mcgee	A Little Love And Understanding	30/04/1977	103	CB

Parliament	Breakdown	14/08/1971	107	BB
Parliament	Star Child (Mothership Connection)	16/10/1976	110	CB
Parliament	Dr. Funkenstein	05/03/1977	102	BB
Parliament	Bop Gun (Endangered Species)	03/12/1977	102	BB
Pastors	She Lets Her Hair Down	10/03/1973	119	CB
Pat & Lolly Vegas	Robot Walk	12/09/1964	149	CB
Pat & Shirley Boone	Blues Stay Away From Me	17/11/1962	142	CB
Pat Boone	Brightest Wishing Star	03/10/1959	112	CB
Pat Boone	That's My Desire	12/08/1961	126	CB
Pat Boone	(If I'm Dreaming) Just Let Me Dream	06/11/1961	114	BB
Pat Boone	(If I'm Dreaming) Just Let Me Dream	11/11/1961	132	CB
Pat Boone	Willing And Eager	12/05/1962	113	BB
Pat Boone	Mexican Joe	15/12/1962	112	CB
Pat Boone	Days Of Wine And Roses	09/03/1963	117	BB
Pat Boone	Rosemarie	11/04/1964	120	CB
Pat Boone	Rosemarie	25/04/1964	129	BB
Pat Boone	Five Miles From Home (Soon I'll See Mary)	11/06/1966	127	BB
Pat Daisy	Everybody's Reaching Out For Someone	26/02/1972	101	CB
Pat Daisy	Everybody's Reaching Out For Someone	11/03/1972	112	BB
Pat Johnson	Love Brought You Here	11/03/1972	116	CB
Pat Shannon	Back To Dreamin' Again	24/01/1970	103	BB
Pat Thomas	Desafinado (Slightly Out Of Tune)	27/10/1962	111	CB
Pat Wilson	Bop Girl	07/04/1984	104	BB
Patrice Rushen	Look Up	24/01/1981	102	BB
Patsy Cline	I Can't Forget	07/07/1962	149	CB
Patsy Cline	You're Stronger Than Me	21/07/1962	107	BB
Patsy Cline	Why Can't He Be You	06/10/1962	104	CB
Patsy Cline	Why Can't He Be You	27/10/1962	103	BB
Patsy Cline	Walkin' After Midnight	30/03/1963	108	BB
Patsy Cline	Back In Baby's Arms	20/04/1963	113	CB

Patsy Cline	Faded Love	17/08/1963	112	CB
Patsy Cline	Someday You'll Want Me To Want You	14/03/1964	123	BB
Patti Austin	A Most Unusual Boy	22/01/1966	116	CB
Patti Drew	Hard To Handle	09/11/1968	101	CB
Patti Drew	The Love That A Woman Should Give To A Man	12/07/1969	119	BB
Patti La Belle & The Bluebelles	He's My Man	14/09/1968	143	CB
Patti Labelle & Her Bluebells	Danny Boy	12/12/1964	103	CB
Patti Labelle & The Blue Belles	Always Something There To Remind Me	01/04/1967	125	BB
Patti Labelle & The Bluebelles	Over The Rainbow	19/02/1966	142	CB
Patti Page	Little Donkey	26/12/1959	105	CB
Patti Page	Two Thousand, Two Hundred, Twenty-Three Miles	19/03/1960	103	CB
Patti Page	A City Girl Stole My Country Boy	25/03/1961	102	CB
Patti Page	Broken Heart And A Pillow Filled With Tears	30/09/1961	102	CB
Patti Page	Pretty Boy Lonely	16/02/1963	101	CB
Patti Page	Just A Simple Melody	23/02/1963	109	CB
Patti Page	Just A Simple Melody	23/02/1963	114	BB
Patti Page	I'm Walkin'	01/06/1963	127	BB
Patti Page	Nobody	05/10/1963	147	CB
Patti Page	I Adore You	08/02/1964	139	CB
Patti Page	I Adore You	29/02/1964	131	BB
Patti Page	Custody	26/02/1966	126	BB
Patti Page	Till You Come Back To Me	26/02/1966	127	CB
Patti Page	Till You Come Back To Me (b-side)	26/02/1966	130	BB
Patti Page	Almost Persuaded	01/10/1966	116	CB
Patti Page	Almost Persuaded	08/10/1966	113	BB
Patti Page	Little Green Apples	22/06/1968	110	CB
Patti Page	Stand By Your Man	09/11/1968	121	BB
Patti Page	I Wish I Had A Mommy Like You	13/06/1970	114	BB
Patti Page With The Merry Melody Singers	Three Fools	28/07/1962	110	CB
Patty Lace & The Petticoats	Sneaky Sue	21/12/1963	101	CB

Patty Lace And The Petticoats	Sneaky Sue	28/12/1963	104	BB
Paul & Paula	Flipped Over You	17/08/1963	119	CB
Paul & Paula	A Perfect Pair	28/09/1963	124	CB
Paul & Paula	Holiday Hootenanny	14/12/1963	105	CB
Paul & Paula	We'll Never Break Up For Good	28/03/1964	112	CB
Paul And Paula	Flipped Over You	24/08/1963	108	BB
Paul And Paula	A Perfect Pair	28/09/1963	105	BB
Paul And Paula	We'll Never Break Up For Good	04/04/1964	105	BB
Paul Anka	Rudolph, The Red-Nosed Reindeer	12/12/1960	104	BB
Paul Anka	Don't Say You're Sorry	09/01/1961	108	BB
Paul Anka	The Bells At My Wedding	04/12/1961	104	BB
Paul Anka	Loveland (b-side)	04/12/1961	110	BB
Paul Anka	Loveland	09/12/1961	101	CB
Paul Anka	The Fools Hall Of Fame	27/01/1962	103	BB
Paul Anka	The Fools Hall Of Fame	03/02/1962	107	CB
Paul Anka	I'd Never Find Another You	07/04/1962	106	BB
Paul Anka	I Never Knew Your Name	26/05/1962	104	CB
Paul Anka	Did You Have A Happy Birthday?	07/12/1963	110	CB
Paul Anka	My Baby's Comin' Home	02/05/1964	113	BB
Paul Anka	The Loneliest Boy In The World	26/06/1965	113	CB
Paul Davis	Can't You	05/12/1970	106	CB
Paul Davis	Can't You	19/12/1970	118	BB
Paul Delicato	Ice Cream Sodas And Lollipops And A Red Hot Spinning Top	13/09/1975	106	CB
Paul Delicato	Cara Mia	20/03/1976	108	BB
Paul Delicato	Cara Mia	27/03/1976	112	CB
Paul Desmond	Ob-La-Di, Ob-La-Da	31/05/1969	120	CB
Paul Evans	Hushabye Little Guitar	12/11/1960	116	CB
Paul Hampton	Echoes From The Thunder	04/02/1967	139	CB
Paul Humphrey & His Cool Aid Chemists	Funky L.A.	14/08/1971	109	BB
Paul Kantner - Jefferson Starship	A Child Is Coming	17/04/1971	121	CB

Paul Kelly	Chills And Fever	11/12/1965	123	BB
Paul Kelly	Sweet Sweet Lovin'	24/06/1967	126	BB
Paul Kelly	Don't Burn Me	09/06/1973	125	CB
Paul Martin	Snake In The Grass	01/05/1965	116	CB
Paul Mauriat & His Orchestra	Hey Jude	08/03/1969	124	CB
Paul Mauriat And His Orchestra	San Francisco (Wear Some Flowers In Your Hair)	10/08/1968	103	BB
Paul Mauriat And His Orchestra	Hey Jude	15/03/1969	119	BB
Paul Mauriat And His Orchestra	Love Is Still Blue	22/01/1977	109	BB
Paul Mccartney	Waterfalls	16/08/1980	1103	CB
Paul Mccartney	Waterfalls	30/08/1980	106	BB
Paul Peek	Pin The Tail On The Donkey	02/04/1966	108	CB
Paul Petersen	Poorest Boy In Town	22/02/1964	123	CB
Paul Petersen	A Little Bit For Sandy	05/10/1968	117	CB
Paul Revere & The Raiders	Louie Louie	26/10/1963	118	CB
Paul Revere & The Raiders	Louie - Go Home	11/04/1964	106	CB
Paul Revere & The Raiders	Over You	17/10/1964	132	CB
Paul Revere & The Raiders	Your Love (Is The Only Love)	07/06/1975	123	CB
Paul Revere & The Raiders Featuring Mark Lindsey	Do Unto Others	09/12/1967	118	CB
Paul Revere And The Raiders	Louie, Louie	02/11/1963	103	BB
Paul Revere And The Raiders	Louie - Go Home	02/05/1964	118	BB
Paul Revere And The Raiders	Over You	03/10/1964	133	BB
Paul Revere And The Raiders	Sometimes	15/05/1965	131	BB
Paul Revere And The Raiders Featuring Mark Lindsey	Do Unto Others	02/12/1967	102	BB
Paul Rodgers	Cut Loose	26/11/1983	102	BB
Paul Simon & Arthur Garfunkel	That's My Story	23/04/1966	123	BB
Paul Vance	Dommage, Dommage (Too Bad, Too Bad)	10/09/1966	108	CB
Paul Williams	I Won't Last A Day Without You	10/03/1973	106	BB
Paul Williams	Inspiration	08/12/1973	108	BB
Pawnee Drive	Break My Mind	07/06/1969	130	CB
Peabo Bryson	Reaching For The Sky	10/06/1978	102	BB

Peabo Bryson	I'm So Into You	27/01/1979	109	BB
Peaches & Herb	It's Just A Game, Love	23/05/1970	110	BB
Peaches & Herb	We're Still Together	09/04/1977	107	BB
Pearl Bailey	I'd Rather Be Rich	19/09/1964	132	BB
Pearl Harbor & The Explosions	You Got It (Release It)	16/02/1980	108	BB
PeBBles & Bamm Bamm Of The Flintstones	Daddy	09/07/1966	122	CB
Pee Wee Spitelera	Tansy	24/07/1965	142	CB
Peggy Lee	Hey, Look Me Over	02/09/1961	129	CB
Peggy Lee	A Doodlin' Song	27/07/1963	135	CB
Peggy Lee	In The Name Of Love	29/08/1964	132	BB
Peggy Lee	In The Name Of Love	12/09/1964	138	CB
Peggy Lee	Sneakin' Up On You	15/05/1965	145	CB
Peggy Lee	Whistle For Happiness	13/12/1969	104	CB
Peggy Lee	Love Story	31/01/1970	105	BB
Peggy Lee	Love Story	14/02/1970	113	CB
Peggy Lipton	Stoney End	28/12/1968	121	BB
Peggy Lipton	Stoney End	25/01/1969	136	CB
Peggy Lipton	Red Clay County Line	03/05/1969	134	CB
Peggy Lipton	Lu	07/02/1970	102	BB
Peggy Lipton	Wear Your Love Like Heaven	20/06/1970	108	BB
Peggy Lipton	Wear Your Love Like Heaven	27/06/1970	129	CB
Peggy March	Losin' My Touch	17/04/1965	127	CB
Peggy March	If You Loved Me (Soul Coaxing-Ame Caline)	06/04/1968	107	CB
Peggy Scott	Every Little Bit Hurts	12/04/1969	126	BB
Penny Mclean	Smoke Gets In Your Eyes	22/05/1976	108	BB
People	Apple Cider	07/09/1968	111	BB
Peppino Di Capri	Roberta	10/08/1963	148	CB
Percy Faith & His Orchestra	Sons And Lovers	30/07/1960	110	CB
Percy Faith & His Orchestra	The Sound Of Surf	31/08/1963	122	CB
Percy Faith And His Orchestra	Sons And Lovers	08/08/1960	111	BB

Percy Faith And His Orchestra	Theme From "The Dark At The Top Of The Stairs"	10/10/1960	101	BB
Percy Faith And His Orchestra	The Sound Of Surf	21/09/1963	111	BB
Percy Faith, His Orchestra & Chorus	Theme From "A Summer Place" (vocal Version)	26/07/1969	111	BB
Percy Mayfield	River's Invitation	22/06/1963	109	CB
Percy Mayfield	To Live The Past	07/03/1970	113	CB
Percy Sledge	You're All Around Me	19/10/1968	109	BB
Percy Sledge	My Special Prayer	25/01/1969	102	CB
Percy Sledge	The Angels Listened In	31/05/1969	126	BB
Percy Sledge	Kind Woman	02/08/1969	104	CB
Percy Sledge	Kind Woman	09/08/1969	116	BB
Percy Sledge	Too Many Rivers To Cross	28/03/1970	125	CB
Percy Sledge	Help Me Make It Through The Night	17/04/1971	115	CB
Perez Prado & His Orchestra	Patricia - Twist	31/03/1962	109	CB
Perry Como	Meet Me At The Altar	25/12/1965	120	CB
Perry Como	Coo Coo Roo Coo Coo Paloma	11/06/1966	128	BB
Perry Como	Here Comes My Baby	07/01/1967	124	BB
Perry Como	Happy Man	15/06/1968	134	BB
Perry Como	Love Don't Care (Where It Grows)	06/10/1973	102	CB
Perry Como	Love Don't Care (Where It Grows)	13/10/1973	106	BB
Perry Como	Beyond Tomorrow (Love Theme From "Serpico")	09/02/1974	118	CB
Perry Como	Just Out Of Reach	11/10/1975	110	CB
Perry Como With Anita Kerr Quartet	Here Comes My Baby	10/12/1966	109	CB
Persuaders	Peace In The Valley Of Love	11/11/1972	104	BB
Pervis Herder	Soul City	22/06/1963	131	CB
Pete Antell	The Times They Are A-Changing	06/11/1965	135	BB
Pete Bennett & The Embers	Fever	13/11/1961	105	BB
Pete Drake & His Talking Steel Guitar	I'm Sorry	04/07/1964	108	CB
Pete Drake And His Talking Steel Guitar	I'm Sorry	11/07/1964	122	BB
Pete Fountain	A Closer Walk	23/01/1960	101	CB
Pete Fountain	Columbus Stockade Blues	25/06/1960	118	CB

Pete Fountain	Licorice Stick	11/07/1964	115	BB
Pete Fountain	Humbug	29/08/1964	129	CB
Pete Fountain	Gotta Travel On	29/05/1965	129	CB
Pete Fountain	Mae	29/05/1965	130	CB
Pete Fountain	Mae	26/06/1965	129	BB
Pete Klint Quintet	Walkin' Proud	07/10/1967	103	CB
Pete Townshend	Face Dances Part Two	07/08/1982	105	BB
Pete Wingfield	Lovin' As You Wanna Be	14/02/1976	108	BB
Peter & Gordon	If You Wish	10/04/1965	101	CB
Peter & Gordon	The Jokers	03/06/1967	104	CB
Peter & Gordon	You've Had Better Times	29/06/1968	128	CB
Peter Allen	The More I See You	21/08/1976	101	CB
Peter Allen	The More I See You	28/08/1976	108	BB
Peter And Gordon	Stranger With A Black Dove	14/05/1966	130	BB
Peter And Gordon	You've Had Better Times	31/08/1968	118	BB
Peter Antell	The Times They Are A-Changing	16/10/1965	112	CB
Peter Brown	Baby Gets High	12/02/1983	104	BB
Peter Brown	They Only Come Out At Night	28/04/1984	102	BB
Peter Brown	Zie Zie Won't Dance	18/05/1985	108	BB
Peter Courtney	The Loser	11/02/1967	131	CB
Peter Courtney	The Loser	04/03/1967	121	BB
Peter Criss	Don't You Let Me Down	09/12/1978	Np4	CB
Peter Dean	Four Or Five Times	23/11/1974	108	CB
Peter Duchin His Piano With Orchestra & Chorus	Star Dust	30/05/1964	143	CB
Peter Foldy	Bondi Junction	01/09/1973	113	BB
Peter Gabriel	I Don't Remember	29/11/1980	107	BB
Peter Godwin	Images Of Heaven	02/04/1983	105	BB
Peter Nero	Theme From "LOVE Story"	23/01/1971	112	CB
Peter Nero	Brian's Song	19/02/1972	105	BB
Peter Nero	Brian's Song	26/02/1972	105	CB

Peter Noone	Meet Me On The Corner Down At Joe's Café	14/09/1974	101	BB
Peter Sarstedt	Frozen Orange Juice	05/07/1969	103	CB
Peter Sarstedt	Frozen Orange Juice	12/07/1969	116	BB
Peter Skellern	Hold On To Love	18/10/1975	106	BB
Peter Tosh	(You Got To Walk And) Don't Look Back	04/11/1978	Np4	CB
Peter Yarrow	Don't Ever Take Away My Freedom	01/04/1972	120	CB
Peter Yarrow	Weave Me The Sunshine [Live]	27/05/1972	110	BB
Peter, Paul & Mary	Oh, Rock My Soul (Part I) (Live)	13/06/1964	105	CB
Peter, Paul & Mary	The Other Side Of This Life	10/09/1966	134	CB
Peter, Paul & Mary	Hurry Sundown	24/12/1966	116	CB
Peter, Paul & Mary	Hurry Sundown	07/01/1967	123	BB
Peter, Paul & Mary	Love City (Postcards To Duluth)	19/10/1968	113	BB
Peter, Paul & Mary	The Marvelous Toy	20/12/1969	120	CB
Peters And Lee	Welcome Home	01/09/1973	119	BB
Petula Clark	The Song Is Love	19/09/1970	106	CB
Petula Clark	Natural Love	30/01/1982	I102	CB
Phil Collins	In The Air Tonight	20/10/1984	102	BB
Phil Flowers	Cry On My Shoulder	24/02/1968	136	CB
Phil Flowers	The Man, The Wife And The Little Baby Daughter	31/10/1970	108	CB
Phil Flowers	The Man, The Wife, & The Little Baby Daughter	12/12/1970	106	BB
Phil Flowers & The Flower Shop	Like A Rolling Stone	11/10/1969	104	BB
Phil Garland	You Are The One	19/03/1983	109	BB
Phil Gentili	Mama Lied	22/08/1981	110	BB
Phil Ochs	Outside Of A Small Circle Of Friends	24/02/1968	118	BB
Phil Phillips	Verdi Mae	07/11/1959	114	CB
Phil Phillips	What Will I Tell My Heart	18/04/1960	108	BB
Phil Phillips	What Will I Tell My Heart	30/04/1960	117	CB
Phil Seymour	Let Her Dance	16/05/1981	110	BB
Philippe' Wynn	Hats Off To Mama	14/05/1977	102	CB
Philly Devotions	I Just Can't Make It (Without You)	20/09/1975	106	BB

Photoglo	When Love Is Gone	09/08/1980	106	BB
Phyllis Hyman	Loving You-Losing You	21/05/1977	103	BB
Phyllis Hyman	You Know How To Love Me	02/02/1980	101	BB
Pia Zadora	Rock It Out	05/11/1983	110	BB
Pic & Bill	All I Want Is You	13/05/1967	147	CB
Pieces Of A Dream	Fo-Fi-Fo	18/02/1984	107	BB
Piero Soffici	That's The Way With Love	06/05/1961	104	CB
Pigmeat Markham	Sock It To 'Em Judge	16/11/1968	103	BB
Ping-Ping And The Al Verlane Orchestra	Sucu Sucu	01/05/1961	103	BB
Pink Floyd	Us And Them	02/03/1974	101	BB
Pink Floyd	Have A Cigar	06/12/1975	119	CB
Pinkerton's 'Assort'. Colors	Mirror, Mirror	26/03/1966	130	CB
Piper	Can't Wait	22/10/1977	105	CB
Player	Givin' It All	06/09/1980	105	BB
Pockets	Take It On Up	18/11/1978	106	BB
Poco	Just For Me And You	13/11/1971	110	BB
Poco	Good Feeling To Know	22/07/1972	119	CB
Poco	Legend	15/09/1979	103	BB
Poco	Sea Of Heartbreak	10/04/1982	109	BB
Poco	Ghost Town	09/10/1982	108	BB
Point Blank	Let Me Stay With You Tonight	11/04/1981	107	BB
Point Blank	Let Her Go	01/05/1982	109	BB
Pointer Sisters	Steam Heat	06/04/1974	108	BB
Pointer Sisters	You Gotta Believe	11/12/1976	103	BB
Pointer Sisters	Blind Faith	03/11/1979	107	BB
Pointer Sisters	Who Do You Love	24/11/1979	106	BB
Pointer Sisters	Where Did The Time Go?	21/02/1981	1101	CB
Ponderosa Twins	Why Do Fools Fall In Love	10/06/1972	102	BB
Ponderosa Twins + One	Bound	15/01/1972	102	BB
Pookie Hudson	I Know I Know	25/05/1963	117	CB

Pookie Hudson	Miracles	21/09/1963	127	CB
Popcorn Wylie	Funky RuBBer Band	09/10/1971	105	CB
Popcorn Wylie	Funky RuBBer Band	23/10/1971	109	BB
Porgy & The Monarchs	Stay	31/08/1963	136	CB
Porter Wagoner	Charley's Picture	03/07/1971	116	BB
Porter Wagoner And Dolly Parton	The Right Combination	21/08/1971	106	BB
Posse	Don't Take Away The Music	10/03/1973	115	CB
Potliquor	Beyond The River Jordan	03/06/1972	132	CB
Pousette-Dart Band	Stand By Me	01/07/1978	103	CB
Pozo Seco	Strawberry Fields/Something	28/11/1970	115	BB
Pozo-Seco Singers	I'll Be Gone	04/06/1966	120	CB
Pozo-Seco Singers	Excuse Me Dear Martha	11/03/1967	102	BB
Pozo-Seco Singers	Excuse Me Dear Martha	11/03/1967	122	CB
Pozo-Seco Singers	I Believed It All	13/05/1967	112	CB
Pratt & Mcclain	Devil With A Blue Dress	17/07/1976	105	CB
Premiers	Annie Oakley	26/09/1964	141	CB
Prince	Uptown	25/10/1980	101	BB
Prince	Let's Work	30/01/1982	104	BB
Prince Harold	Forget About Me	19/11/1966	123	CB
Prince Harold	Forget About Me	10/12/1966	114	BB
Prince La La	She Put The Hurt On Me	09/09/1961	105	CB
Prince La La	She Put The Hurt On Me	20/11/1961	119	BB
Procol Harum	Grand Hotel	02/06/1973	120	CB
Procol Harum	Grand Hotel	16/06/1973	117	BB
Professor Longhair	Big Chief - Part 2	27/02/1965	144	CB
Punch	Fallin', Lady	02/10/1971	110	BB
Pure Love & Pleasure	All In My Mind	04/04/1970	104	BB
Pure Love & Pleasure	All In My Mind	11/04/1970	117	CB
Pure Prairie League	That'll Be The Day	12/06/1976	106	BB
Pure Prairie League	You're Mine Tonight	18/07/1981	I102	CB

Q	Sweet Summertime	16/07/1977	108	BB
Q-Feel	Dancing In Heaven (Orbital Be-Bop)	26/03/1983	110	BB
Queen	Keep Yourself Alive	05/01/1974	112	CB
Quicksilver Messenger Service	Dino's Song	29/06/1968	133	CB
Quicksilver Messenger Service	Stand By Me	23/11/1968	110	BB
Quicksilver Messenger Service	Who Do You Love	09/08/1969	102	CB
Quincy Jones	Ironside (Theme From "IRONSIDE" - Nbc-Tv)*	11/03/1972	120	CB
Quincy Jones	Summer In The City	11/08/1973	102	BB
Quincy Jones	If I Ever Lose This Heaven	17/08/1974	110	CB
Quincy Jones	Boogie Joe, The Grinder	21/12/1974	114	CB
Quincy Jones	Midnight Soul Patrol	20/11/1976	104	BB
Quincy Jones & His Orchestra	A Taste Of Honey*	14/07/1962	101	CB
R. Dean Taylor	Candy Apple Red	31/07/1971	104	BB
R.B. Greaves	Margie, Who's Watching The Baby	28/10/1972	115	BB
R.B. Hudmon	How Can I Be A Witness	13/03/1976	107	CB
R.E.M.	Can't Get There From Here	17/08/1985	110	BB
R.E.O. Speedwagon	Sophisticated Lady	19/02/1972	115	CB
R.J.'S Latest Arrival	Swing Low	20/07/1985	107	BB
Rachel Sweet	Spellbound	07/06/1980	107	BB
Radiants	Whole Lot Of Woman	14/08/1965	129	CB
Raiders Vocal By: Mark Lindsay	Gone Movin' On	09/05/1970	120	BB
Rainbow	Open Up Your Heart	25/03/1972	105	CB
Rainbow	Open Up Your Heart	15/04/1972	114	BB
Rainbow	All Night Long	08/03/1980	110	BB
Rainbow	I Surrender	18/04/1981	105	BB
Raintree	Keep The Candle Burning	23/01/1971	115	CB
Ral Donner	So Close To Heaven	12/08/1961	128	CB
Ral Donner	Loveless Life	16/06/1962	142	CB
Ral Donner	Loveless Life	23/06/1962	117	BB
Ral Donner	To Love	17/11/1962	140	CB

Ral Donner	I Got Burned	16/03/1963	139	CB
Ral Donner	I Got Burned	30/03/1963	124	BB
Ralfi Pagan	Make It With You	03/07/1971	104	CB
Ralfi Pagan	Make It With You	24/07/1971	104	BB
Ralph Carter	When You're Young And In Love	06/09/1975	107	CB
Ralph Marterie	Bacardi	22/05/1961	115	BB
Ralph Marterie	Bacardi	27/05/1961	123	CB
Ramsey Lewis	Ain't That Peculiar	09/07/1966	129	BB
Ramsey Lewis	Day Tripper	31/12/1966	106	CB
Ramsey Lewis	Function At The Junction	06/05/1967	108	CB
Ramsey Lewis	Bear Mash	24/02/1968	123	BB
Ramsey Lewis	Do What You Wanna	29/03/1969	148	CB
Ramsey Lewis	Slipping Into Darkness	22/07/1972	101	BB
Randy & The Rainbows	Why Do Kids Grow Up	07/12/1963	130	CB
Randy & The Rainbows	Little Star	05/12/1964	114	CB
Randy & The Rainbows	Joyride	31/07/1965	138	CB
Randy And The Rainbows	Little Star	19/12/1964	133	BB
Randy Crawford	One Hello	05/06/1982	110	BB
Randy Crawford	Imagine [Live]	29/01/1983	108	BB
Randy Edelman	Isn't It A Shame	24/05/1975	109	BB
Randy Edelman	Concrete And Clay	10/04/1976	108	BB
Randy Meisner	Gotta Get Away	30/05/1981	104	BB
Randy Newman	I Love L.A.	16/04/1983	110	BB
Randy Sparks	Julie Knows	07/11/1964	111	CB
Randy Sparks	Julie Knows	05/12/1964	126	BB
Ranji	It's So Easy (To Be Bad)	20/05/1972	109	BB
Rare Bird	Sympathy	11/04/1970	121	BB
Rare Bird	Birdman-Part One (Title No. 1 Again)	11/08/1973	104	CB
Rare Bird	Birdman - Part One (Title No. 1 Again)	01/09/1973	122	BB
Rare Earth	We're Gonna Have A Good Time	27/01/1973	118	CB

Rare Earth	"Ma"	14/04/1973	108	BB
Rare Earth	"MA"	14/04/1973	121	CB
Rare Earth	Hum Along And Dance	29/09/1973	110	BB
Rare Earth	It Makes You Happy (But It Ain't Gonna Last Too Long)	08/11/1975	106	BB
Raspberries	Ecstacy	23/03/1974	116	CB
Ray & Bob	Air Travel	26/05/1962	101	CB
Ray Adams	(Hear My Song) Violetta	05/05/1962	119	BB
Ray Adams & Orchestra	(Hear My Song) Violetta	21/04/1962	127	CB
Ray Anthony	Let Me Entertain You	08/12/1962	113	CB
Ray Anthony	I Get The Blues When It Rains	28/09/1968	124	BB
Ray Barretto & His Orchestra	Mr. Blah Blah	06/07/1963	147	CB
Ray Bryant	Shake A Lady	14/11/1964	108	BB
Ray Bryant Combo	Sack O' Woe	25/02/1961	127	CB
Ray Charles	I'm Gonna Move To The Outskirts Of Town	24/06/1961	105	CB
Ray Charles	Carrying That Load	19/01/1963	145	CB
Ray Charles	Feelin' Sad	02/02/1963	113	BB
Ray Charles	The Cincinnati Kid	25/09/1965	115	BB
Ray Charles	The Cincinnati Kid	02/10/1965	109	CB
Ray Charles	I Want To Talk About You	18/02/1967	119	CB
Ray Charles	Somebody Ought To Write A Book About It	13/05/1967	105	BB
Ray Charles	Understanding	06/07/1968	108	CB
Ray Charles	When I Stop Dreaming	11/01/1969	112	BB
Ray Charles	I Didn't Know What Time It Was	08/03/1969	105	BB
Ray Charles	We Can Make It	13/09/1969	101	BB
Ray Charles	Claudie Mae	20/12/1969	108	CB
Ray Charles	Claudie Mae	20/12/1969	111	BB
Ray Charles	Hey Mister	18/11/1972	101	CB
Ray Charles	Hey Mister	23/12/1972	115	BB
Ray Charles	Every Saturday Night	27/01/1973	103	CB
Ray Charles	America The Beautiful	10/04/1976	102	CB

Ray Charles & Betty Carter	Baby It's Cold Outside	17/02/1962	122	CB
Ray Charles & His Orchestra	Just For A Thrill	30/04/1960	123	CB
Ray Charles & His Orchestra	The Brightest Smile In Town	23/02/1963	108	CB
Ray Charles & His Orchestra	Ol' Man Time	14/12/1963	137	CB
Ray Charles & His Orchestra	I Don't Need No Doctor	19/11/1966	102	CB
Ray Charles And His Orchestra	No Letter Today	13/04/1963	105	BB
Ray Charles And His Orchestra	Teardrops From My Eyes	06/02/1965	112	BB
Ray Charles With Orchestra & Chorus	Without A Song (Part 1)	01/05/1965	117	CB
Ray Charles With Orchestra & Chorus	Without A Song-Part 1	15/05/1965	112	BB
Ray Charles With String Orchestra & Chorus	Making Believe	07/09/1963	102	BB
Ray Charles, Ray Charles Orchestra	Something Inside Me	11/03/1967	112	BB
Ray Conniff	Cabaret	04/02/1967	140	CB
Ray Conniff	Cabaret	11/02/1967	118	BB
Ray Conniff	The World Will Smile Again	08/04/1967	148	CB
Ray Conniff & Billy Butterfield & The Ray Conniff Sextet	Sweet Sue, Just You	16/11/1963	136	CB
Ray Conniff & His Orchestra & Chorus	Blue Moon	08/02/1964	138	CB
Ray Conniff & The Singers	Lookin' For Love	01/10/1966	126	CB
Ray Conniff And His Orchestra And Chorus	Blue Moon	29/02/1964	119	BB
Ray Ellis & His Orchestra	La Dolce Vita (The Sweet Life)	27/05/1961	113	CB
Ray Godfrey	I Gotta Get Away (From My Own Self)	04/07/1970	120	CB
Ray Hildebrand	The Way Of The D.J.	11/09/1965	135	CB
Ray Hildebrand	Mr. Balloon Man	16/05/1970	106	CB
Ray Kennedy	Starlight	30/08/1980	109	BB
Ray Parker Jr.	It's Our Own Affair	23/10/1982	106	BB
Ray Peterson	What Do You Want To Make Those Eyes At Me For?	29/02/1960	104	BB
Ray Peterson	I'm Tired	06/02/1961	104	BB
Ray Peterson	You Thrill Me	17/06/1961	115	CB
Ray Peterson	I'm Not Jimmy	02/03/1963	113	CB
Ray Peterson	Promises (You Made Now Are Broken)	11/01/1964	108	BB
Ray Peterson	Promises (You Made Now Are Broken)	25/01/1964	150	CB

Ray Peterson	Oh No!	12/09/1964	128	BB
Ray Peterson	Across The Street (It's A Million Miles Away)	19/12/1964	106	BB
Ray Pollard	Darling Take Me Back (I'm Sorry)*	22/05/1965	114	CB
Ray Price	Soft Rain	02/10/1961	115	BB
Ray Price	Burning Memories	25/04/1964	132	CB
Ray Price	That's All That Matters	23/05/1964	136	CB
Ray Price	The Lonesomest Lonesome	29/04/1972	109	BB
Ray Sawyer	I Want Johnny's Job	14/07/1979	Np4	CB
Ray Sharpe With The King Curtis Orchestra	Help Me - Part I (Get The Feeling)	05/03/1966	126	CB
Ray Smith	That's All Right	10/10/1959	123	CB
Ray Smith	One Wonderful Love	08/08/1960	103	BB
Ray Stevens	Sergeant Preston Of The Yukon	08/08/1960	108	BB
Ray Stevens	Sergeant Preston Of The Yukon	13/08/1960	112	CB
Ray Stevens	Scratch My Back (I Love It)	02/12/1961	147	CB
Ray Stevens	Butch Babarian	25/04/1964	117	CB
Ray Stevens	Party People	18/12/1965	130	BB
Ray Stevens	Party People	25/12/1965	130	CB
Ray Stevens	Funny Man	22/06/1968	121	CB
Ray Stevens	Funny Man	20/07/1968	122	BB
Ray Stevens	The Great Escape	02/11/1968	114	BB
Ray Stevens	Have A Little Talk With Myself	06/12/1969	115	CB
Ray Stevens	Have A Little Talk With Myself	13/12/1969	123	BB
Ray Stevens	I'll Be Your Baby Tonight	28/02/1970	117	CB
Ray Stevens	I'll Be Your Baby Tonight	07/03/1970	112	BB
Ray Stevens	Turn Your Radio On	30/10/1971	102	CB
Ray Stevens	You Are So Beautiful	22/05/1976	101	BB
Ray Stevens	Lady Of Spain	24/07/1976	108	BB
Ray Stevens	Shriner's Convention	01/03/1980	101	BB
Ray Thomas	High Above My Head	26/07/1975	117	CB
Raydio	Honey I'm Rich	12/08/1978	102	BB

Raydio	Honey I'm Rich	19/08/1978	107	CB
Raydio	More Than One Way To Love A Woman	20/10/1979	103	BB
Raymond Lefevre & His Orchestra	La La La (He Gives Me Love)	29/06/1968	139	CB
Raymond Lefevre And His Orchestra	La La La (He Gives Me Love)	18/05/1968	110	BB
Rcr	Give It To You	26/07/1980	108	BB
Ready For The World	Tonight	23/02/1985	103	BB
Realistic's	Please Baby Please	25/07/1970	119	CB
Rebecca Hall	Who Says Girls Can't Rock & Roll	06/08/1983	109	BB
Red Rider	Don't Fight It	07/06/1980	103	BB
Red Saunders & His Orchestra With Dolores Hawkins & The	Hambone	16/03/1963	103	CB
Red Sovine	Little Joe	25/09/1976	102	BB
Redbone	Light As A Feather	10/04/1971	105	CB
Redbone	When You Got Trouble	01/04/1972	111	BB
Redbone	Wovoka	22/06/1974	113	CB
Redbone	Wovoka	06/07/1974	101	BB
Redbone	Suzie Girl	31/08/1974	108	BB
Redbone	One More Time	02/11/1974	110	CB
Redwing	California Blues	17/04/1971	108	BB
Reggie Garner	Teddy Bear	24/04/1971	117	BB
Reggie Hall	The Joke	24/03/1962	137	CB
Rejoice!	November Snow	08/02/1969	105	CB
Rejoice!	November Snow	08/03/1969	126	BB
René & Angela	Save Your Love (For #1)	29/06/1985	101	BB
Rene & Rene	Las Cosas	08/03/1969	113	CB
Rene & Rene	Las Costas	15/03/1969	128	BB
Rene & Rene	Love Is For The Two Of Us	24/01/1970	120	CB
Renee Roberts	I Want To Love You (So Much It Hurts Me)	17/02/1962	109	CB
Renee Roberts	I Want To Love You (So Much It Hurts Me)	07/04/1962	112	BB
Reo Speedwagon	Sophisticated Lady	04/03/1972	122	BB
Reo Speedwagon	Ridin' The Storm Out	02/02/1974	102	CB

Reparata & The Delrons	I Can Tell	18/12/1965	110	CB
Reparata & The Delrons	I'm Nobody's Baby Now	21/05/1966	128	CB
Reparata & The Delrons	Captain Of Your Ship	10/02/1968	111	CB
Reparata And The Delrons	Captain Of Your Ship	03/02/1968	127	BB
Reparata With Hash Brown & His Orchestra	A Summer Thought	12/06/1965	144	CB
Reunion	Disco-Tekin	01/02/1975	101	BB
Reunion	They Don't Make 'EM Like That Anymore	19/04/1975	101	CB
Rev. Maceo Woods And The Christian Tabernacle Baptist	Hello Sunshine	20/12/1969	121	BB
Revelation	You To Me Are Everything, Part I	10/07/1976	110	CB
Rex Garvin (& The Mighty Cravers)	Sock It To 'EM J.B. - Part I	06/08/1966	117	CB
Rex Garvin (and The Mighty Cravers)	Sock It To 'Em J.B. - Part I	25/06/1966	110	BB
Rex Smith	Simply Jessie (From The Movie "Sooner Or Later")	07/07/1979	Np4	CB
Rex Smith	Sooner Or Later	20/10/1979	109	BB
Rhetta Hughes	Light My Fire	18/01/1969	102	BB
Rhinoceros	I Need Love	05/07/1969	132	CB
Rhinoceros	Better Times	08/08/1970	109	BB
Rhinoceros	Better Times	15/08/1970	127	CB
Rhythm Heritage	Disco-Fied	14/08/1976	101	BB
Rich Little	President Rap's [Live]	26/06/1982	105	BB
Richard "Groove" Holmes	Secret Love	01/10/1966	119	CB
Richard "Popcorn" Wylie	Come To Me	10/11/1962	108	CB
Richard "Popcorn" Wylie	Come To Me	29/12/1962	109	BB
Richard & The Young Lions	Nasty	31/12/1966	136	CB
Richard Berry & The Pharaohs	Have Love Will Travel	20/02/1960	122	CB
Richard Chamberlain	True Love	22/06/1963	102	CB
Richard Chamberlain	Georgia On My Mind	07/03/1964	123	CB
Richard Chamberlain	Stella By Starlight	14/03/1964	134	CB
Richard Chamberlain	Rome Will Never Leave You	12/12/1964	109	CB
Richard Harris	The Hive	04/01/1969	130	CB
Richard Harris	There Are Too Many Saviours On My Cross	21/10/1972	102	CB

Richard Harris	There Are Too Many Saviors On My Cross	28/10/1972	107	BB
Richard Harris	I Don't Have To Tell You	17/02/1973	106	BB
Richard Harris	I Don't Have To Tell You	17/02/1973	108	CB
Richard Hayman & His Orchestra	Night Train	30/09/1961	136	CB
Richard Landis	A Man Who Sings	19/02/1972	106	CB
Richard Landis	A Man Who Sings	26/02/1972	102	BB
Richard Spencer & The Winstons	Say Goodbye To Daddy	03/01/1970	107	BB
Richie Allen	Stranger From Durango	24/09/1960	112	CB
Richie Furay	This Magic Moment	17/06/1978	101	BB
Richie Havens	Handsome Johnny	20/06/1970	115	BB
Richie Havens	Eyesight To The Blind	24/02/1973	111	BB
Richie Havens	Eyesight To The Blind	03/03/1973	101	CB
Richie Havens	I'm Not In Love	04/12/1976	102	BB
Rick Coyne	Someone Else's Arms	13/05/1967	129	CB
Rick Cunha	Jesse James (Is An Outlaw, Honey)	17/08/1974	102	CB
Rick Dees	Get Nekked	01/12/1984	104	BB
Rick Dees And His Cast Of Idiots	Bigfoot	05/08/1978	110	BB
Rick James	High On Your Love Suite	10/03/1979	Np6	CB
Rick James	Ghetto Life	30/01/1982	102	BB
Rick James	U Bring The Freak Out	12/11/1983	101	BB
Rick James	Glow	27/07/1985	106	BB
Rick Nelson	Summertime	03/03/1962	111	CB
Rick Nelson	I've Got My Eyes On You (And I Like What I See)	11/08/1962	130	CB
Rick Nelson	I've Got My Eyes On You (And I Like What I See)	25/08/1962	105	BB
Rick Nelson	A Long Vacation	22/06/1963	107	CB
Rick Nelson	A Long Vacation	29/06/1963	120	BB
Rick Nelson	There's Not A Minute	17/08/1963	149	CB
Rick Nelson	There's Not A Minute	07/09/1963	127	BB
Rick Nelson	Down Home	14/09/1963	131	CB
Rick Nelson	Down Home	19/10/1963	126	BB

Rick Nelson	Congratulations	14/03/1964	104	CB
Rick Nelson	Lucky Star	04/07/1964	127	BB
Rick Nelson	Lucky Star	11/07/1964	142	CB
Rick Nelson	Lonely Corner	15/08/1964	105	CB
Rick Nelson	Lonely Corner	29/08/1964	113	BB
Rick Nelson	Come Out Dancin'	19/06/1965	131	CB
Rick Nelson	Come Out Dancin'	03/07/1965	130	BB
Rick Nelson	Love And Kisses	25/09/1965	124	CB
Rick Nelson	You Just Can't Quit	18/06/1966	108	BB
Rick Nelson & The Stone Canyon Band	Life	06/03/1971	110	CB
Rick Nelson & The Stone Canyon Band	Lifestream	13/10/1973	105	CB
Rick Nelson & The Stone Canyon Band	Windfall	16/02/1974	116	CB
Rick Nelson And The Stone Canyon Band	I Shall Be Released	16/05/1970	102	BB
Rick Nelson And The Stone Canyon Band	Life	27/02/1971	109	BB
Ricky Allen	Cut You A-Loose	14/09/1963	107	CB
Ricky Allen	Cut You A-Loose	21/09/1963	126	BB
Ricky Dee & The Embers	Workout (Part 1)	19/05/1962	109	CB
Ricky Dee & The Embers	Work Out (Part 1)	02/06/1962	103	BB
Ricky Lyons	Shim Sham Shuffle	17/10/1960	104	BB
Ricky Nelson	Songs By Ricky Ep	30/07/1960	105	CB
Ricky Nelson	Milk Cow Blues	17/12/1960	101	CB
Ricky Page	Yes, I'm Lonesome Tonight*	31/12/1960	122	CB
Ringo Starr	Snookeroo	08/02/1975	105	CB
Ringo Starr	Lipstick Traces (On A Cigarette)	20/05/1978	102	CB
Ripple	Willie Pass The Water	09/03/1974	108	BB
Rita Coolidge	Turn Around And Love You	05/04/1969	107	CB
Rita Coolidge	Crazy Love	17/04/1971	129	CB
Rita Coolidge	Whiskey, Whiskey	28/04/1973	106	BB
Rita Coolidge	The Closer You Get	19/09/1981	103	BB
Rita Pavone	Just Once More	13/06/1964	116	CB

Rita Pavone	Just Once More	27/06/1964	123	BB
Rita Pavone	Wait For Me	03/10/1964	104	BB
Rita Pavone	Eyes Of Mine (Occi Mici)	03/04/1965	113	CB
Ritchie Adams	Back To School	17/09/1960	108	CB
Ritchie Dean	Goodbye Girl	03/10/1964	134	CB
Ritchie Hart	The Great Duane	14/11/1959	124	CB
Rob Hegel	New York City Girl	04/05/1974	106	CB
Rob Hegel	Tommy, Judy & Me	16/08/1980	109	BB
Robert & Johnny	We Belong Together	23/01/1961	104	BB
Robert Byrne	Baby Fat	09/06/1979	101	BB
Robert Cobert Orchestra	Shadows Of The Night (Quentin's Theme)	16/08/1969	125	BB
Robert Davie	The Gypsy	03/10/1964	132	CB
Robert Goulet	Two Different Worlds	14/04/1962	144	CB
Robert Goulet	Two Of Us	13/04/1963	132	BB
Robert Goulet	I'd Rather Be Rich	03/10/1964	131	BB
Robert Goulet	Begin To Love (Cominciamo Ad Amarci)	27/02/1965	110	BB
Robert Goulet	Come Back To Me, My Love	25/09/1965	107	CB
Robert Goulet	Come Back To Me, My Love	02/10/1965	118	BB
Robert Goulet	On A Clear Day You Can See Forever (b-side)	16/10/1965	119	BB
Robert Goulet	Crazy Heart Of Mine	22/01/1966	133	CB
Robert Hazard	Change Reaction	18/06/1983	106	BB
Robert John	Don't Leave Me	05/10/1968	108	BB
Robert John	Don't Leave Me	12/10/1968	134	CB
Robert John	Only Time	03/11/1979	102	BB
Robert Johnson	I'll Be Waiting	13/01/1979	106	BB
Robert Knight	Blessed Are The Lonely	06/01/1968	101	CB
Robert Knight	The Power Of Love	06/04/1968	147	CB
Robert Knight	Isn't It Lonely Together	28/09/1968	112	CB
Robert Mersey & His Orchestra	Portobello Sunset	27/04/1963	118	CB
Robert Mosley	Goodbye My Lover Goodbye	22/06/1963	123	CB

Robert Palmer	Get Outside	03/01/1976	105	BB
Robert Palmer	Give Me An Inch Girl	17/01/1976	106	BB
Robert Palmer	Jealous	17/11/1979	106	BB
Robert Palmer	Looking For Clues	29/11/1980	105	BB
Robert Parker	All Nite Long (Part 1)	19/10/1959	113	BB
Robert Parker	The Scratch	17/09/1966	128	BB
Robert Parker	The Scratch	24/09/1966	132	CB
Robert Parker	Happy Feet	22/10/1966	115	CB
Robert Parker	Tip Toe	14/01/1967	105	CB
Robert Plant	Too Loud	03/08/1985	108	BB
Robert Winters & Fall	Magic Man	09/05/1981	101	BB
Roberta Flack	Reverend Lee	26/09/1970	125	CB
Roberta Flack	Do What You Gotta Do	01/05/1971	106	CB
Roberta Flack	Do What You Gotta Do	22/05/1971	117	BB
Roberta Flack	Don't Make Me Wait Too Long	27/09/1980	104	BB
Roberta Flack	You Stopped Loving Me	13/06/1981	108	BB
Roberta Quinlan	Merry Go Round Of Love	14/06/1969	140	CB
Robertino	O Sole Mio	28/10/1961	118	CB
Robie Lester	The Miracle Of Life	25/04/1960	107	BB
Robin Clark	Daddy, Daddy (Gotta Get A Phone In My Room)	13/03/1961	120	BB
Robin Clark	Daddy, Daddy (Gotta Get A Phone In My Room)	01/04/1961	121	CB
Robin GiBB	Saved By The Bell	02/08/1969	103	CB
Robin GiBB	Juliet	22/10/1983	104	BB
Robin Luke	Bad Boy*	30/01/1960	105	CB
Robin Mcnamara	Hang In There, Baby	05/12/1970	105	CB
Robin Trower	Man Of The World	21/04/1973	109	BB
Robin Trower	My Love (Burning Love)	13/01/1979	110	BB
Robin Ward	Winter's Here	14/03/1964	123	BB
Robin Williams (Popeye)	I Yam What I Yam	27/12/1980	104	BB
Robin Wilson	The Nervous Auctioneer	22/10/1960	121	CB

Rock Master Scott And The Dynamic Three	Request Line	19/01/1985	103	BB
Rockin' Horse	Dancin' To The Music	21/09/1974	120	CB
Rockin' Horse	Love Do Me Right	12/07/1975	104	BB
Rockwell	He's A Cobra	23/02/1985	108	BB
Rocky Burnette	Fallin' In Love (Bein' Friends)	01/11/1980	109	BB
Rod Bernard	One More Chance	21/11/1959	103	CB
Rod Bernard	Colinda	24/03/1962	102	BB
Rod Lauren	Listen My Love	09/04/1960	103	CB
Rod Stewart	It's All Over Now	18/07/1970	126	BB
Rod Stewart	Mine For Me	21/12/1974	106	CB
Rodge Martin	When She Touches Me "Nothing Else Matters"	09/04/1966	131	BB
Rodger Collins	She's Looking Good	28/01/1967	101	BB
Rodney Allen Rippy	Take Life A Little Easier	20/10/1973	112	BB
Rodney Crowell	Stars On The Water	10/10/1981	105	BB
Roger & The Gypsies	Pass The Hatchet (Part I)	02/07/1966	115	CB
Roger Daltrey	Waiting For A Friend	24/01/1981	104	BB
Roger Glover	The Mask	23/06/1984	102	BB
Roger Mcguinn	Take Me Away	21/08/1976	110	BB
Roger Miller	It Happened Just That Way	17/07/1965	105	BB
Roger Miller	I've Been A Long Time Leavin' (But I'll Be A Long Time Gone)	19/02/1966	103	BB
Roger Miller	The Ballad Of Waterhole #3 (Code Of The West)	21/10/1967	102	BB
Roger Miller	Old Toy Trains	09/12/1967	133	CB
Roger Miller	Me And BoBBy Mcgee	05/07/1969	122	BB
Roger Miller	Me And BoBBy Mcgee	12/07/1969	118	CB
Roger Miller	South	29/08/1970	119	CB
Roger Miller	Tomorrow Night In Baltimore	03/04/1971	128	CB
Roger Miller	Open Up Your Heart	18/08/1973	105	BB
Roger Nichols Trio	Snow Queen	14/01/1967	126	CB
Roger Nichols Trio	Snow Queen	28/01/1967	129	BB
Roger Taylor	Let's Get Crazy	30/05/1981	1103	CB

Roger Waters	5:01 A.M. (The Pros And Cons Of Hitch Hiking)	02/06/1984	110	BB
Roger White	Mystery Of Tallahatchie Bridge	07/10/1967	123	BB
Roger White	Mystery Of Tallahatchie Bridge	07/10/1967	140	CB
Roger Williams	Sunrise Serenade	19/10/1959	106	BB
Roger Williams	Sunrise Serenade	31/10/1959	119	CB
Roger Williams	Marie, Marie	11/02/1961	108	CB
Roger Williams	On The Trail	13/04/1963	140	CB
Roger Williams	On The Trail	04/05/1963	113	BB
Roger Williams	Janie Is Her Name	29/06/1963	118	CB
Roger Williams	Look Again Theme From "Irma La Douce"	17/08/1963	127	CB
Roger Williams	Theme From "THE Cardinal"	30/11/1963	120	CB
Roger Williams	Theme From "The Cardinal"	21/12/1963	109	BB
Roger Williams	Whistl'n	29/08/1964	140	CB
Roger Williams	Autumn Leaves - 1965	06/11/1965	110	CB
Roger Williams	More Than A Miracle	14/10/1967	108	BB
Roger Williams	Only For Lovers	02/11/1968	123	CB
Roger Williams	Only For Lovers	07/12/1968	119	BB
Roger Williams	Love Theme From "LA Strada"	08/03/1969	122	CB
Roger Williams	The Summer Knows (Theme From "Summer Of '42")	05/06/1971	118	CB
Roger Williams	Love Theme From The Godfather	01/04/1972	116	BB
Roger Williams	Love Theme From The Godfather	08/04/1972	115	CB
Roger Williams & The Harry Simeone Chorale	Summer Wind	21/08/1965	109	BB
Rogue	Fallen Angel	01/05/1976	108	BB
Rolf Harris	Nick Teen And Al K. Hall	14/09/1963	120	CB
Rolf Harris	Lost Little Boy	21/12/1963	148	CB
Rolf Harris	The Court Of King Caractacus (Live)	16/05/1964	110	CB
Rolf Harris	The Court Of King Caractacus [Live]	30/05/1964	116	BB
Rolf Harris	Two Little Boys	07/02/1970	108	CB
Rolf Harris	Two Little Boys	21/03/1970	119	BB
Rome & Paris (Bob Feldman & Jerry Goldstein)	Because Of You	02/07/1966	104	BB

Ron Banks & The Dramatics	(I'm Going By) The Stars In Your Eyes	08/11/1975	102	CB
Ron Dante	Let Me Bring You Up	08/08/1970	102	BB
Ron Dante	Let Me Bring You Up	08/08/1970	118	CB
Ron Holden	Gee, But I'm Lonesome	08/08/1960	106	BB
Ronn Price	(I Think You Better) Think About Forgetting Me	22/06/1974	120	CB
Ronnie & The Dirt Riders	Yellow Van	14/08/1976	111	CB
Ronnie & The Hi-Lites	Be Kind	14/07/1962	122	CB
Ronnie & The Hi-Lites	A Slow Dance	10/08/1963	123	CB
Ronnie And The Hi-Lites	Be Kind	21/07/1962	120	BB
Ronnie And The Hi-Lites	A Slow Dance	10/08/1963	116	BB
Ronnie Dove	Sweeter Than Sugar	09/05/1964	141	CB
Ronnie Dove	What's Wrong With My World	01/03/1969	111	CB
Ronnie Dove	What's Wrong With My World	01/03/1969	131	BB
Ronnie Dove	Chains Of Love	07/03/1970	118	CB
Ronnie Dyson	We Can Make It Last Forever	04/05/1974	102	CB
Ronnie Hawkins	Bo Diddley	04/05/1963	117	BB
Ronnie Hawkins	Bo Diddley	04/05/1963	121	CB
Ronnie Hawkins	Bitter Green	18/04/1970	118	BB
Ronnie Hawkins & The Hawks	Ruby Baby	21/05/1960	112	CB
Ronnie Hayden	S.O.S. (I Love You)	17/07/1961	108	BB
Ronnie Mcdowell	Fallin'	18/03/1978	102	CB
Ronnie Milsap	Never Had It So Good	16/10/1965	106	BB
Ronnie Milsap	Denver	12/04/1969	118	CB
Ronnie Milsap	Denver	10/05/1969	123	BB
Ronnie Milsap	Loving You Is A Natural Thing	19/09/1970	104	CB
Ronnie Milsap	A Rose By Any Other Name (Is Still A Rose)	19/12/1970	125	BB
Ronnie Milsap	Too Late To Worry, Too Blue To Cry	14/06/1975	101	BB
Ronnie Milsap	(I'm A) Stand By My Woman Man	25/09/1976	101	CB
Ronnie Milsap	Cowboys And Clowns	09/08/1980	103	BB
Ronnie Milsap	Show Her	07/01/1984	103	BB

Ronnie Walker	Really, Really Love You	07/10/1967	128	BB
Ronny & The Daytonas	Somebody To Love Me	26/03/1966	115	CB
Ronny And The Daytonas	Somebody To Love Me	26/03/1966	115	BB
Ronny And The Daytonas	I'll Think Of Summer	19/11/1966	133	BB
Ronny Douglas	Run, Run, Run	17/06/1961	115	CB
Ronny Douglas	You'll Come Back	09/12/1961	128	CB
Roosevelt Fountain & Pens Of Rhythm	Red Pepper I	15/12/1962	103	CB
Roosevelt Grier	People Make The World	20/07/1968	129	CB
Roosevelt Grier	People Make The World	10/08/1968	126	BB
Rosanne Cash	Blue Moon With Heartache	20/02/1982	104	BB
Roscoe Robinson	How Much Pressure (Do You Think I Can Stand)	12/11/1966	125	BB
Roscoe Robinson	How Much Pressure (Do You Think I Can Stand)	19/11/1966	136	CB
Roscoe Robinson	Oo Wee Baby I Love You	31/05/1969	105	CB
Roscoe Shelton	Strain On My Heart	02/01/1965	119	CB
Roscoe Shelton	Strain On My Heart	30/01/1965	109	BB
Roscoe Shelton	I Know Your Heart Has Been Broken	30/10/1965	135	BB
Roscoe Shelton	Easy Going Fellow	29/01/1966	102	BB
Rose Royce	Wishing On A Star	04/03/1978	101	BB
Rose Royce	Is It Love You're After	29/09/1979	105	BB
Rosemarie & Bo	Close Your Eyes	18/11/1961	142	CB
Rosemary Clooney	Give Myself A Party	04/11/1961	143	CB
Rosemary Clooney	Give Myself A Party	06/11/1961	108	BB
Ross Bagdasarian	I Treasure Thee	25/04/1970	136	CB
Rotary Connection	Paper Castle	12/10/1968	132	BB
Rotary Connection	Aladdin	16/11/1968	113	BB
Round Robin	Land Of A Thousand Dances "The Na Na Song" [Live]	03/04/1965	135	BB
Round Robin & The Parlays	Do The Slauson	28/12/1963	105	CB
Rox	Dddddddance	11/04/1981	109	BB
Roxanne Shanté	Roxanne's Revenge	09/03/1985	109	BB
Roxy Music	Oh Yeah (On The Radio)	04/10/1980	102	BB

Roxy Music	In The Midnight Hour	01/11/1980	I103	CB
Roxy Music	In The Midnight Hour	08/11/1980	106	BB
Roxy Music	Take A Chance With Me	10/07/1982	104	BB
Roxy Music	More Than This	04/06/1983	102	BB
Roy "C"	Shotgun Wedding	02/10/1965	125	CB
Roy "C"	Got To Get Enough (Of Your Sweet Love Stuff)	05/06/1971	120	CB
Roy Clark	Application For Love	05/10/1963	137	CB
Roy Clark	Through The Eyes Of A Fool	04/01/1964	116	CB
Roy Clark	Through The Eyes Of A Fool	25/01/1964	128	BB
Roy Clark	September Song	13/09/1969	103	BB
Roy Clark	Right Or Left At Oak Street	29/11/1969	123	BB
Roy Clark	I Never Picked Cotton	13/06/1970	122	BB
Roy Drusky & Priscilla Mitchell	Yes, Mr. Peters	18/09/1965	122	CB
Roy Hamilton	EBB Tide	30/11/1959	105	BB
Roy Hamilton	I'll Come Running Back To You	14/07/1962	135	CB
Roy Hamilton	I'll Come Running Back To You	21/07/1962	110	BB
Roy Hamilton	Let Go	11/05/1963	129	BB
Roy Hamilton	It's Only Make Believe	06/12/1969	132	CB
Roy Hamilton Orchestra & The Malcolm Dodds Singers	If	09/09/1961	142	CB
Roy Head	Get Back	01/01/1966	112	CB
Roy Head	Wigglin' And Gigglin'	21/05/1966	110	BB
Roy Head	Wigglin' And Gigglin'	04/06/1966	115	CB
Roy Head	To Make A Big Man Cry	24/09/1966	139	CB
Roy Head	Carol	24/03/1973	111	CB
Roy Head	One Night	25/09/1976	101	CB
Roy Milton	Early In The Morning	11/06/1960	119	CB
Roy Orbison	The Actress	10/02/1962	131	CB
Roy Orbison	Mama	26/05/1962	119	CB
Roy Orbison	Distant Drums	08/06/1963	130	CB
Roy Orbison	Beautiful Dreamer	04/01/1964	144	CB

Roy Orbison	So Good	04/03/1967	103	CB
Roy Orbison	So Good	25/03/1967	132	BB
Roy Orbison	She	28/10/1967	119	BB
Roy Orbison	She	25/11/1967	118	CB
Roy Orbison	Walk On	06/07/1968	121	BB
Roy Orbison	Heartache	19/10/1968	104	BB
Roy Orbison	Penny Arcade	30/08/1969	134	CB
Roy Orbison	Penny Arcade	13/09/1969	133	BB
Roy Orbison	So Young (Love Theme From "Zabriskie Point")	25/04/1970	114	CB
Roy Orbison	So Young (Love Theme From "Zabriskie Point")	02/05/1970	122	BB
Roy Orbison	Easy Way Out	30/06/1979	109	BB
Roy Tyson	Oh What A Night For Love	09/11/1963	105	CB
Roy Tyson	Oh What A Night For Love	07/12/1963	106	BB
Royal Teens	Was It A Dream	13/02/1960	108	CB
Rozetta Johnson	A Woman's Way	31/10/1970	119	CB
Rubert's People	Reflections Of Charles Brown	07/10/1967	111	BB
Ruby & The Party Gang	Hey Ruby (Shut Your Mouth)	18/12/1971	117	CB
Ruby & The Romantics	Nevertheless (I'm In Love With You)	20/02/1965	133	CB
Ruby & The Romantics	Your Baby Doesn't Love You Anymore	29/05/1965	103	CB
Ruby & The Romantics	We Can Make It	16/07/1966	136	CB
Ruby & The Romantics	Hurting Each Other	12/04/1969	122	CB
Ruby And The Party Gang	Hey Ruby (Shut Your Mouth)	25/12/1971	105	BB
Ruby And The Romantics	Your Baby Doesn't Love You Anymore	26/06/1965	108	BB
Ruby And The Romantics	We Can Make It	06/08/1966	120	BB
Ruby And The Romantics	Hurting Each Other	12/04/1969	113	BB
Ruby Andrews	Everybody Saw You	30/05/1970	118	BB
Ruby Winters	I Want Action	28/10/1967	109	BB
Ruby Winters	I Want Action	28/10/1967	128	CB
Ruby Winters	Just A Dream	26/04/1969	129	CB
Ruby Winters	Always David	04/10/1969	121	BB

Ruby Winters	I Will	02/02/1974	110	CB
Ruby Wright	Dern Ya	29/08/1964	112	CB
Ruby Wright	Dern Ya	12/09/1964	103	BB
Rudy West & The Five Keys	Out Of Sight Out Of Mind	10/02/1962	130	CB
Rufus	Brand New Day	23/01/1971	121	CB
Rufus	Slip N' Slide	21/04/1973	110	BB
Rufus	Keep It Together (Declaration Of Love)	17/02/1979	109	BB
Rufus (Mr. Soul) Beacham	No Man Is King	14/01/1961	118	CB
Rufus & Carla	Night Time Is The Right Time	23/05/1964	108	CB
Rufus And Chaka	Any Love	08/03/1980	102	BB
Rufus And Chaka Khan	One Million Kisses	11/02/1984	102	BB
Rufus Featuring Chaka Khan	Blue Love	26/08/1978	105	BB
Rufus Thomas	Somebody Stole My Dog	04/04/1964	104	CB
Rufus Thomas	Love Trap	17/06/1972	114	BB
Rufus Thomas	Itch And Scratch (Part I)	23/09/1972	103	BB
Run-A-Rounds	Let Them Talk	22/02/1964	150	CB
Run-D.M.C.	King Of Rock	23/03/1985	108	BB
Run-D.M.C.	You Talk Too Much	08/06/1985	107	BB
Runt-Todd Rundgren	A Long Time, A Long Way To Go	21/08/1971	113	CB
Rupert Holmes	Blackjack	14/02/1981	103	BB
Rupert Holmes	Loved By The One You Love	07/11/1981	103	BB
Rush	Entre Nous	24/05/1980	110	BB
Rush	Subdivisions	15/01/1983	105	BB
Rush	Body Electric	21/07/1984	105	BB
Russ Ballard	Voices	12/05/1984	110	BB
Russ Ballard	Two Silhouettes	04/08/1984	106	BB
Russ Ballard	The Fire Still Burns	13/07/1985	105	BB
Russ Conway	Roulette	03/08/1959	106	BB
Russell Byrd	You'd Better	29/04/1961	107	CB
Russell Morris	The Real Thing (Part I)	09/08/1969	107	BB

Russell Morris	The Real Thing (Part I)	16/08/1969	125	CB
Rusty & Doug	Louisiana Man	13/03/1961	104	BB
Rusty & Doug	Louisiana Man	25/03/1961	104	CB
Rusty Draper	Mule Skinner Blues	13/06/1960	105	BB
Rusty Draper	Luck Of The Irish	27/08/1960	108	CB
Rusty Wier	Don't It Make You Wanna Dance?	20/09/1975	119	CB
Ruth Brown	I Burned Your Letter	09/04/1960	111	CB
Ruth Brown	Taking Care Of Business	29/10/1960	119	CB
Ruth Brown	Anyone But You	22/07/1961	136	CB
Ruth Brown With The Milestone Singers	Mama (He Treats Your Daughter Mean)	18/08/1962	127	CB
S.S.O.	Tonight's The Night	31/01/1976	104	CB
Sad Café	Emptiness	06/10/1979	108	BB
Sad Café	La-Di-Da	01/08/1981	l103	CB
Sade	Hang On To Your Love	08/12/1984	102	BB
Safaris	Kick Out	21/09/1963	129	CB
Safaris	Kick Out	12/10/1963	120	BB
Sagittarius	Another Time	06/01/1968	114	CB
Sagittarius (featuring Gary Usher)	I Guess The Lord Must Be In New York City	04/10/1969	111	CB
Sagittarius (featuring Gary Usher)	I Guess The Lord Must Be In New York City	25/10/1969	135	BB
Sailcat	She Showed Me	28/04/1973	115	BB
Sailor	Runaway	15/11/1980	103	BB
Saint Tropez	Fill My Life With Love	07/07/1979	102	BB
Sajid Khan	Getting To Know You	05/10/1968	114	CB
Sajid Khan	Getting To Know You	12/10/1968	108	BB
Sajid Khan	Dream	25/01/1969	114	CB
Sajid Khan	Dream	01/02/1969	119	BB
Salt Water Taffy	Finders Keepers	04/05/1968	104	CB
Salt Water Taffy	Finders Keepers	11/05/1968	105	BB
Salvatore Bono & Cher Lapiere Aka Caeser & Cleo	Love Is Strange	04/12/1965	131	BB
Salvatore Bono & Cher Lapiere Aka Caeser & Cleo	Love Is Strange	04/12/1965	132	CB

Sam & Bill	Fly Me To The Moon	01/01/1966	103	CB
Sam & Dave	I Got A Thing Going On	28/03/1964	145	CB
Sam & Dave	If You Got The Loving (I Got The Time)	03/09/1966	131	CB
Sam & Dave	Baby-Baby Don't Stop Now	07/03/1970	117	BB
Sam & Dave	Don't Pull Your Love	27/11/1971	102	BB
Sam & Dave With The Dixie Flyers	One Part Love - Two Parts Pain	25/04/1970	123	BB
Sam Cooke	Summertime (Part 2)	24/08/1959	106	BB
Sam Cooke	No One (Can Ever Take Your Place)	11/01/1960	103	BB
Sam Cooke	You Understand Me	30/04/1960	107	CB
Sam Cooke	Love Will Find A Way	27/04/1963	105	BB
Sam Cooke	(Somebody) Ease My Troublin' Mind	10/04/1965	115	BB
Sam Cooke	(Somebody) Ease My Troublin' Mind	10/04/1965	127	CB
Sam Cooke	Feel It	05/02/1966	144	CB
Sam Cooke	Let's Go Steady Again	16/04/1966	110	CB
Sam Cooke & The Stars	Steal Away	24/12/1960	113	CB
Sam Dees	Worn Out Broken Heart	05/10/1974	103	CB
Sam Fletcher	Time Has A Way	22/06/1959	103	BB
Sam Harris	Hearts On Fire	26/01/1985	108	BB
Sam Hawkins	No Time For Tears	07/05/1960	102	CB
Sam Hawkins	Hold On Baby	15/05/1965	104	CB
Sam Hawkins	Hold On Baby	19/06/1965	133	BB
Sam Hawkins	I Know It's All Right	13/11/1965	117	BB
Sam Hawkins	I Know It's All Right	13/11/1965	125	CB
Sam Hutchins	Dang Me	02/11/1968	127	CB
Sam Kimble Orchestra Featuring Henry, Taffy, Gail, Al & Leon	Henry's In (Part 1)	22/02/1964	136	CB
Sam Lazar Trio	Space Flight	09/07/1960	120	CB
Sam Neely	Sadie Take A Lover	25/05/1974	103	BB
Sam Neely	Sadie Take A Lover	25/05/1974	103	CB
Sam The Sham	Banned In Boston	23/09/1967	116	CB
Sam The Sham	Banned In Boston	23/09/1967	117	BB

Sam The Sham	Yakety Yak	09/12/1967	111	CB
Sam The Sham	Yakety Yak	16/12/1967	110	BB
Sam The Sham	I Couldn't Spell !!*@!	14/09/1968	111	CB
Sam The Sham	I Couldn't Spell !!'@!	05/10/1968	120	BB
Sam The Sham & The Pharaohs	Old Macdonald Had A Boogaloo Farm	20/04/1968	124	CB
Sammi Smith	Then You Walk In	15/05/1971	118	BB
Sammi Smith	Then You Walk In	22/05/1971	120	CB
Sammi Smith	Saunders' Ferry Line	02/10/1971	111	CB
Sammy Ambrose	This Diamond Ring	09/01/1965	117	BB
Sammy Davis Jr.	Choose	30/05/1964	112	BB
Sammy Davis Jr.	Choose	06/06/1964	146	CB
Sammy Davis Jr.	Bee-Bom (b-side)	27/06/1964	135	BB
Sammy Davis Jr.	Don't Shut Me Out	24/10/1964	106	BB
Sammy Davis Jr.	Don't Shut Me Out	14/11/1964	118	CB
Sammy Davis Jr.	If I Ruled The World	20/02/1965	135	BB
Sammy Davis Jr.	No One Can Live Forever	22/05/1965	117	BB
Sammy Davis Jr.	No One Can Live Forever	29/05/1965	115	CB
Sammy Davis Jr.	Break My Mind	10/08/1968	106	BB
Sammy Davis Jr.	I Have But One Life To Live	31/05/1969	119	BB
Sammy Davis Jr.	I Have But One Life To Live	14/06/1969	141	CB
Sammy Davis Jr.	(I'd Be) A Legend In My Time	05/05/1973	104	CB
Sammy Davis Jr.	(I'd Be) A Legend In My Time	05/05/1973	116	BB
Sammy Davis Jr.	Singin' In The Rain	16/02/1974	110	CB
Sammy Davis Jr.	Baretta's Theme ("Keep Your Eye On The Sparrow")	08/05/1976	101	BB
Sammy Davis Jr.	Baretta's Theme	08/05/1976	114	CB
Sammy Davis Jr. & Ensemble	Rhythm Of Life	19/04/1969	131	CB
Sammy Davis Jr. And Ensemble	Rhythm Of Life	05/04/1969	124	BB
Sammy Hagar	Turn Up The Music	25/03/1978	101	CB
Sammy Johns	Falling For You	20/09/1980	I102	CB
Sammy Johns	Falling For You	11/10/1980	103	BB

Sammy Masters	Rockin' Red Wing	26/03/1960	101	CB
Sammy Salvo	Afraid	03/10/1959	114	CB
Sandalwood	Lovin' Naturally	09/06/1973	110	CB
Sandalwood	Lovin' Naturally	23/06/1973	111	BB
Sandie Shaw	I'll Stop At Nothing	14/08/1965	123	BB
Sandie Shaw	How Can You Tell	18/12/1965	122	CB
Sandie Shaw	How Can You Tell	25/12/1965	131	BB
Sandy Nelson	Drum Party	21/11/1959	101	CB
Sandy Nelson	The Birth Of The Beat	03/02/1962	101	CB
Sandy Nelson	Drummin' Up A Storm	21/04/1962	110	CB
Sandy Nelson	All Night Long	30/06/1962	108	CB
Sandy Nelson	Rompin' And Stompin'	30/06/1962	108	CB
Sandy Nelson	Live It Up	01/09/1962	128	CB
Sandy Nelson	Live It Up	15/09/1962	101	BB
Sandy Nelson	Day Train	03/11/1962	121	CB
Sandy Nelson	Let The Four Wings Blow	29/12/1962	107	BB
Sandy Nelson	Let The Four Winds Blow	29/12/1962	123	CB
Sandy Nelson	Chop-Chop	06/03/1965	143	CB
Sandy Nelson	Reach For A Star	13/03/1965	133	BB
Sandy Nelson	Let There Be Drums '66 [Live]	22/05/1965	120	BB
Sandy Nelson	Drums A Go-Go	18/09/1965	124	BB
Sandy Nelson	Manhattan Spiritual	31/05/1969	108	CB
Sandy Nelson	Manhattan Spiritual	07/06/1969	119	BB
Sandy Posey	Something I'll Remember	17/02/1968	102	BB
Sandy Salisbury	Do Unto Others	31/05/1969	110	CB
Sandy Stewart	I Know He Needs Her	19/10/1963	145	CB
Sandy Stewart	Saddest Victory	14/04/1984	105	BB
Santa Esmeralda	The House Of The Rising Sun	25/02/1978	106	CB
Santana	When I Look In Your Eyes	16/02/1974	102	BB
Santana	Let It Shine	22/05/1976	102	CB

Santana	Let The Children Play	19/03/1977	102	BB
Santana	I'll Be Waiting	08/04/1978	107	CB
Santana	Well All Right	11/11/1978	Np4	CB
Santana	Searchin'	19/09/1981	l101	CB
Santana	I'm The One Who Loves You	25/05/1985	102	BB
Santo & Johnny	The Breeze And I	30/05/1960	109	BB
Santo & Johnny	The Breeze And I	04/06/1960	102	CB
Santo & Johnny	Birmingham	25/11/1961	129	CB
Santo & Johnny	Twistin' Bells	30/12/1961	150	CB
Santo & Johnny	Spanish Harlem	07/04/1962	110	CB
Santo & Johnny	Spanish Harlem	21/04/1962	101	BB
Santo & Johnny	Manhattan Spiritual	15/06/1963	149	CB
Santo & Johnny	A Thousand Miles Away	04/04/1964	122	BB
Santo & Johnny	A Thousand Miles Away	11/04/1964	135	CB
Sarah Johns	I'm Ready To Love You Now	20/09/1975	122	CB
Sarah Vaughan	Misty	20/07/1959	106	BB
Sarah Vaughan	Maybe It's Because (I Love You Too Much)	31/10/1959	104	CB
Sarah Vaughan	Our Waltz	18/04/1960	103	BB
Sarah Vaughan	Ooh! What A Day!	30/05/1960	111	BB
Sarah Vaughan	Ooh! What A Day!	11/06/1960	107	CB
Sarah Vaughan	One Mint Julep	07/04/1962	143	CB
Sarah Vaughan	Bluesette	18/04/1964	131	BB
Sarah Vaughan	Sole, Sole, Sole	01/08/1964	132	CB
Savage Grace Vocal: Al & Ron	Come On Down	25/07/1970	104	BB
Savoy Brown	Lay Back In The Arms Of Someone	18/07/1981	107	BB
Scat Man Crothers	What's A Nice Kid Like You Doing In A Place Like This?	21/05/1966	134	BB
Scientists Of Soul	Be's That-A-Way Sometime	13/09/1969	128	CB
Scott Bedford Four	Last Exit To Brooklyn	10/04/1965	136	CB
Scott Bedford Four	Last Exit To Brooklyn	08/05/1965	129	BB
Scott Bros.	Stolen Angel	18/04/1960	110	BB

Scott Bros.	Lost Love	23/07/1960	109	CB
Scott Key	Town Cryer	24/04/1976	101	CB
Scott Key	Town Cryer	04/07/1976	110	BB
Scott Mac Kenzie	Look In Your Eyes	05/08/1967	111	BB
Scott Mac Kenzie	Look In Your Eyes	12/08/1967	130	CB
Scott Mckenzie	Holy Man	20/04/1968	126	BB
Scotty Mckay	Mess Around	04/05/1963	134	CB
Scuffy Shew	Reason To Feel	27/10/1973	103	CB
Scuffy Shew	Reason To Feel	10/11/1973	112	BB
Sea Level	Living In A Dream	10/02/1979	101	BB
Seals & Crofts	When I Meet Them	18/12/1971	104	BB
Seals & Crofts	When I Meet Them	25/12/1971	112	CB
Seals & Crofts	Takin' It Easy	19/08/1978	105	CB
Seatrain	Marblehead Messenger	13/11/1971	108	BB
Sergio Mendes	Say A Little Prayer	27/01/1968	106	BB
Sergio Mendes & Brasil '66	The Joker	27/08/1966	120	CB
Sergio Mendes & Brasil '66	Slow Hot Wind	17/12/1966	112	CB
Sergio Mendes & Brasil '66	The Frog	23/09/1967	126	BB
Sergio Mendes & Brasil '66	The Frog	30/09/1967	133	CB
Sergio Mendes & Brasil '66	With A Little Help From My Friends	23/03/1968	137	CB
Sergio Mendes & Brasil '66	Wichita Lineman	22/11/1969	121	CB
Sergio Mendes & Brasil '66	Norwegian Wood	21/02/1970	107	BB
Sergio Mendes & Brasil '66	For What It's Worth	29/08/1970	101	BB
Sergio Mendes & Brasil '77	Love Music	14/04/1973	113	BB
Sergio Mendes & Brazil '66	Norwegian Wood	28/02/1970	125	CB
Serino	Marie, Marie*	11/02/1961	108	CB
Seven Seas	Super "Jaws"	27/09/1975	104	BB
Sha Na Na	Remember Then	03/01/1970	114	CB
Sha Na Na	Only One Song	15/05/1971	110	BB
Sha Na Na	Bounce In Your Buggy	09/09/1972	124	CB

Shack	Too Many Lovers	13/02/1971	118	BB
Shad O'shea & The 18 Wheelers	Colorado Call	20/03/1976	110	BB
Shadow Mann	Come Live With Me	25/01/1969	129	CB
Shalamar	I Can Make You Feel Good	24/07/1982	102	BB
Shalamar	You Can Count On Me	28/01/1984	101	BB
Shalamar	My Girl Loves Me	23/03/1985	106	BB
Shane Martin	You're So Young	05/10/1968	107	CB
Shango	Mescalito	22/02/1969	103	CB
Shango	Mama Lion	17/05/1969	118	CB
Shango	Some Things A Man's Gotta Do	11/07/1970	107	BB
Shannon	Jesamine	15/11/1969	104	CB
Shannon	Stronger Together	17/08/1985	103	BB
Sharpees	Do The "45"	17/07/1965	117	BB
Sharpees	Do The "45"	07/08/1965	119	CB
Sharpees	I've Got A Secret	07/05/1966	133	BB
Shawn Phillips	Anello (Where Are You)	02/06/1973	112	BB
Shawn Phillips	Do You Wonder	25/10/1975	106	BB
Sheb Wooley	Skin Tight, Pin Striped, Purple Pedal Pushers	17/06/1961	105	CB
Shel Silverstein	Sarah Cynthia Sylvia Stout (Would Not Take The Garbage Out)	03/02/1973	107	BB
Shel Silverstein	Stacy Brown Got Two	17/03/1973	118	CB
Shelby Flint	I Will Love You	24/06/1961	147	CB
Shelby Flint	Little Dancing Doll	22/06/1963	102	CB
Shelby Flint	Little Dancing Doll	27/07/1963	103	BB
Shelia E.	Sister Fate	03/08/1985	102	BB
Shelley Fabares	Telephone (Won't You Ring)	19/01/1963	109	BB
Shelley Fabares	My Prayer	17/07/1965	144	CB
Shelley Looney	This Is My Country, Thank You Canada	15/03/1980	109	BB
Shep & The Limelites	What Did Daddy Do	19/05/1962	113	CB
Shep & The Limelites	Gee Baby, What About You	01/09/1962	138	CB
Shep & The Limelites	I'm A Hurting Inside	26/06/1965	119	CB

Shep And The Limelites	Why, Why, Won't You Believe Me	25/01/1964	125	BB
Shepstone & DiBBens	Moment Of Truth	11/11/1972	107	CB
Shepstone & DiBBens	Shady Lady	15/09/1973	111	BB
Sheridan Hollenbeck Orchestra & Chorus	Tokyo Melody	12/12/1964	128	CB
Shirley	I Hear Those Church Bells Ringing/Chapel Of Love	18/01/1975	106	CB
Shirley (And Company)	Cry Cry Cry	21/06/1975	123	CB
Shirley & Alfred	Kid Games And Nursery Rhymes	29/06/1968	134	CB
Shirley & Lee	Well-A, Well-A	02/09/1961	112	CB
Shirley Bassey	Reach For The Stars	16/10/1961	120	BB
Shirley Bassey	You'll Never Know	21/10/1961	110	CB
Shirley Bassey	For All We Know	16/10/1971	108	CB
Shirley Bassey	Davy	27/04/1974	104	CB
Shirley Brown	It Ain't No Fun	17/05/1975	103	CB
Shirley Brown	Blessed Is The Woman (With A Man Like Mine)	23/04/1977	102	BB
Shirley Ellis	Shy One (Live)	18/04/1964	111	CB
Shirley Ellis	Shy One [Live]	09/05/1964	130	BB
Shirley Ellis	I Told You So	07/08/1965	149	CB
Shirley Ellis	Ever See A Diver Kiss His Wife While The BuBBles Bounce About	05/02/1966	135	BB
Shirley Ellis	Sugar, Let's Shing-A-Ling	27/05/1967	138	CB
Shirley Matthews And The Big Town Girls	Big-Town Boy	11/01/1964	104	BB
Shor Patrol	Loverboy	16/07/1983	108	BB
Shorty Long	Devil With The Blue Dress	23/05/1964	101	CB
Shorty Long	Devil With The Blue Dress	30/05/1964	125	BB
Shorty Long	Function At The Junction	07/05/1966	123	CB
Shorty Long	Chantilly Lace	11/03/1967	135	CB
Sid Feller & His Orchestra & Chorus	The Puerto Rican Pedlar*	13/02/1960	121	CB
Sid Feller & His Orchestra & Chorus	Midnight Lace*	22/10/1960	102	CB
Siegel-Schwall Band And San Francisco Symphony Orchestra,	Blues Band, Opus 50, Part I	12/05/1973	105	BB
Silk	Party - Pt. 1	09/07/1977	107	BB
Silver Bird	Save Me	05/04/1975	103	BB

Silver Convention	Dancing In The Aisles (Takes Me Higher)	11/12/1976	102	BB
Silver Convention	Telegram	18/06/1977	103	BB
Silver Hawk	Awaiting On You All	22/05/1971	108	BB
Simon & Garfunkel	For Emily, Whenever I May Find Her	05/11/1966	105	CB
Simon & Garfunkel	Baby Driver	12/04/1969	101	BB
Simon & Garfunkel	Baby Driver	26/04/1969	114	CB
Simon & Garfunkel	America	02/12/1972	105	CB
Simon Scott	Move It Baby	24/10/1964	128	BB
Simon Scott	Move It Baby	31/10/1964	138	CB
Simtec & Wylie	Gotta' Get Over The Hump	21/08/1971	104	CB
Simtec & Wylie	Gotta' Get Over The Hump	11/09/1971	101	BB
Sir Douglas Quintet	The Tracker	17/07/1965	110	CB
Sir Douglas Quintet	The Tracker	24/07/1965	105	BB
Sir Douglas Quintet	Quarter To Three	07/05/1966	133	CB
Sir Douglas Quintet	Quarter To Three	21/05/1966	129	BB
Sir Douglas Quintet	She Digs My Love	29/10/1966	132	BB
Sir Douglas Quintet	It Didn't Even Bring Me Down	17/05/1969	101	CB
Sir Douglas Quintet	It Didn't Even Bring Me Down	17/05/1969	108	BB
Sir Douglas Quintet	At The Crossroads	20/12/1969	104	BB
Sir Douglas Quintet	Nitty Gritty	30/06/1973	113	CB
Sir Mack Rice	Mustang Sally	01/05/1965	111	CB
Sir Mack Rice	Mustang Sally	15/05/1965	108	BB
Sir Raleigh & The Cupons	White Cliffs Of Dover	26/12/1964	145	CB
Sissy Spacek	Lonely But Only For You	27/08/1983	110	BB
Sister Sledge	Love Don't You Go Through No Changes On Me	11/01/1975	103	CB
Sister Sledge	Reach Your Peak	19/04/1980	101	BB
Sisters Love	Now Is The Time	01/08/1970	111	CB
Sisters Love	The Bigger You Love (The Harder You Fall)	15/08/1970	123	CB
Sisters Love	Are You Lonely?	05/06/1971	108	BB
Sisters Love	Are You Lonely?	31/07/1971	121	CB

Skeeter Davis	Something Precious	15/09/1962	136	CB
Skeeter Davis	How Much Can A Lonely Heart Stand	11/01/1964	104	CB
Skeeter Davis	Let Me Get Close To You	01/08/1964	106	BB
Skeeter Davis	Let Me Get Close To You	08/08/1964	117	CB
Skeeter Davis	What Am I Gonna Do With You	07/11/1964	123	BB
Skeeter Davis	I Can't Help It (If I'm Still In Love With You)	17/04/1965	126	BB
Skeeter Davis	Sun Glasses	28/08/1965	120	BB
Skeeter Davis	Sun Glasses	28/08/1965	123	CB
Skeeter Davis	What Does It Take (To Keep A Man Like You Satisfied)	05/08/1967	115	CB
Skeeter Davis	What Does It Take (To Keep A Man Like You Satisfied)	26/08/1967	121	BB
Skeeter Davis	I Can't Believe That It's All Over	22/09/1973	101	BB
Skeeter Davis & BoBBy Bare	A Dear John Letter	20/02/1965	111	CB
Skeeter Davis & BoBBy Bare	A Dear John Letter	13/03/1965	114	BB
Skip & Flip & Their Orchestra	Hully Gully Cha Cha Cha	20/08/1960	123	CB
Skip And Flip And Their Orchestra	Hully Gully Cha Cha Cha	08/08/1960	109	BB
Skip Mchoney And The Casuals	Your Funny Moods	16/03/1974	113	BB
Skipworth & Turner	Thinking About Your Love	18/05/1985	104	BB
Skitch Henderson His Piano And His Orchestra	Green Green Grass Of Home	27/01/1968	110	BB
Sky	Toccata	13/12/1980	I103	CB
Skylark	I'll Have To Go Away	01/09/1973	106	BB
Skyy	High	10/05/1980	102	BB
Slade	Let The Good Times Roll/Feel So Fine	21/07/1973	107	CB
Slade	Let The Good Times Roll/Feel So Fine	01/09/1973	114	BB
Slave	The Party Song	25/02/1978	110	BB
Slave	Just Freak	03/02/1979	110	BB
Slave	Wait For Me	16/01/1982	103	BB
Sleepy Hollow	Sincerely Yours (The Next One's On You)	05/05/1973	122	CB
Slim & Ann	It's A Sin	09/09/1961	138	CB
Slim Harpo	I Love The Life I'm Living	26/10/1963	134	CB
Slim Harpo	Shake Your Hips	23/07/1966	116	BB

Slim Harpo	I'm Your Bread Maker, Baby	31/12/1966	116	BB
Slim Harpo	Tip On In (Part 1)	12/08/1967	127	BB
Slim Harpo	I'm Gonna Keep What I've Got	07/10/1967	124	CB
Slim Harpo	Mohair Sam	12/10/1968	113	CB
Slim Harpo	I've Got My Finger On Your Trigger	25/10/1969	138	CB
Slim Whitman	Valley Of Tears	12/05/1962	148	CB
Slim Whitman	I Remember You	17/09/1966	134	BB
Slim Whitman	Guess Who	23/01/1971	121	BB
Sly & Family Stone	Sing A Simple Song	29/03/1969	123	CB
Sly & The Family Stone	If It Were Left Up To Me	26/01/1974	118	CB
Sly And The Family Stone	Remember Who You Are	03/11/1979	104	BB
Small Faces	Lazy Sunday	04/05/1968	114	BB
Small Faces	Lazy Sunday	04/05/1968	119	CB
Smith	Comin' Back To Me (Ooh Baby)	15/08/1970	101	BB
Smith Connection	(I've Been A Winner, I've Been A Loser) I've Been In Love	13/01/1973	104	CB
Smitty Williams	The Cure	28/07/1962	130	CB
Smokey	If You Think You Know How To Love Me	26/07/1975	125	CB
Smokey & His Sister	Creators Of Rain	10/06/1967	106	CB
Smokey And His Sister	Creators Of Rain	13/05/1967	121	BB
Smokey Robinson	Open	15/05/1976	102	CB
Smokey Robinson	Vitamin U	06/08/1977	101	BB
Smokey Robinson	Yes It's You Lady	31/07/1982	107	BB
Smokey Robinson	I've Made Love To You A Thousand Times	12/03/1983	101	BB
Smokey Robinson	Touch The Sky	14/05/1983	110	BB
Smokey Robinson	Don't Play Another Love Song	03/12/1983	103	BB
Smokey Robinson	And I Don't Love You	19/05/1984	106	BB
Smokey Robinson	I Can't Find	06/10/1984	109	BB
Smokey Robinson & The Miracles	Come Spy With Me	18/02/1967	121	CB
SmuBBs	It Can't Be Too Late	18/05/1968	129	CB
Sneakers & Lace	Skateboardin'	09/10/1976	115	CB

Sniff 'N' The Tears	New Lines On Love	15/12/1979	108	BB
Soeur Sourire (The Singing Nun)	Tous Les Chemins (All The Roads)	08/02/1964	115	BB
Soft Cell	What!	18/09/1982	101	BB
Soft Tones	Can't Help Falling In Love	11/08/1973	120	CB
Solomon Burke	I'm Hanging Up My Heart For You	26/05/1962	112	CB
Solomon Burke	I Really Don't Want To Know	08/09/1962	111	CB
Solomon Burke	Words	09/03/1963	120	CB
Solomon Burke	Words	16/03/1963	121	BB
Solomon Burke	Home In Your Heart	01/06/1963	148	CB
Solomon Burke	Yes I Do	10/10/1964	103	CB
Solomon Burke	I Feel A Sin Coming On	02/04/1966	131	CB
Solomon Burke	Keep Looking	27/08/1966	109	BB
Solomon Burke	Woman How Do You Make Me Love You Like I Do	29/10/1966	133	CB
Solomon Burke	Detroit City	02/12/1967	104	BB
Solomon Burke	Party People	23/03/1968	112	BB
Solomon Burke	Save It	15/06/1968	114	CB
Solomon Burke	Up Tight Good Woman	01/02/1969	140	CB
Solomon Burke	Up Tight Good Woman	22/02/1969	116	BB
Solomon Burke	That Lucky Old Man	12/07/1969	129	BB
Solomon Burke	We're Almost Home	17/06/1972	110	CB
Solomon King	She Wears My Ring	06/04/1968	117	BB
Sonny & Cher	Baby Don't Go	09/01/1965	117	CB
Sonny & Cher	The Letter	23/10/1965	104	CB
Sonny & Cher	Circus	17/02/1968	106	CB
Sonny & Cher	You Gotta Have A Thing Of Your Own	24/08/1968	126	CB
Sonny Charles	It Takes A Little Longer	02/05/1970	119	CB
Sonny Charles	Half As Much	05/09/1970	121	CB
Sonny Charles	Half As Much	03/10/1970	116	BB
Sonny Curtis	My Way Of Life	24/09/1966	134	CB
Sonny Curtis	My Way Of Life	08/10/1966	134	BB

Sonny Curtis	Atlanta Georgia Stray	02/03/1968	120	BB
Sonny Curtis	Atlanta Georgia Stray	09/03/1968	123	CB
Sonny Fulton	Locked Up	15/05/1961	106	BB
Sonny Fulton	Locked Up	24/06/1961	146	CB
Sonny Geraci & Climax	Walking In The Georgia Rain	10/11/1973	107	CB
Sonny James	Pure Love	29/06/1959	107	BB
Sonny James	A Mile And A Quarter	18/08/1962	137	CB
Sonny James	Going Through The Motions (Of Living)	02/11/1963	140	CB
Sonny James	Baltimore	04/04/1964	134	BB
Sonny James	I'll Keep Holding On (Just To Your Love)	03/04/1965	116	BB
Sonny James	I'll Keep Holding On (Just To Your Love)	10/04/1965	133	CB
Sonny James	Behind The Tear	28/08/1965	113	BB
Sonny James	Born To Be With You	14/12/1968	127	CB
Sonny James	When The Snow Is On The Roses	09/09/1972	103	BB
Sonny James	When The Snow Is On The Roses	23/09/1972	113	CB
Sonny James, The Southern Gentleman	A World Of Our Own	27/01/1968	118	BB
Sonny James, The Southern Gentleman	My Love	25/04/1970	125	BB
Sonny James, The Southern Gentleman	Endlessly	24/10/1970	108	BB
Sonny Spencer	Gilee	31/10/1959	102	CB
Sonny Til & Orioles	Come On Home	19/03/1960	110	CB
Sonoma	Love For You	15/12/1973	112	BB
Sons Of Champlin	Sing Me A Rainbow	27/05/1967	139	CB
Sons Of Champlin	Sing Me A Rainbow	03/06/1967	124	BB
Sons Of Champlin	Lookout	27/09/1975	116	CB
Sons Of Champlin	Lookout	11/10/1975	103	BB
Sons Of Champlin	Imagination's Sake	25/09/1976	107	BB
Soul Brothers Six	What Can You Do When You Ain't Got Nobody	27/01/1968	107	BB
Soul Generation	Body And Soul (That's The Way It's Got To Be)	20/05/1972	114	CB
Soul Generation	That's The Way It's Got To Be (Body And Soul)	27/05/1972	115	BB
Soul Runners	Grits 'N Corn Bread	14/01/1967	103	BB

Soul Sisters	Loop De Loop	29/08/1964	107	BB
Soul Survivors	City Of Brotherly Love	05/10/1974	116	CB
Soul Train Gang	Ooh Cha	04/12/1976	107	BB
Sound Foundation	Morning Dew (Walk Me Out In The)	29/11/1969	118	BB
Sounds Orchestral	A Boy And A Girl	13/11/1965	113	CB
Sounds Orchestral	A Boy And A Girl	04/12/1965	104	BB
Sounds, Incorporated	In The Hall Of The Mountain King	19/06/1965	107	CB
South Shore Commission	We're On The Right Track	24/01/1976	115	CB
Southside Johnny & The Asbury Jukes	I Don't Want To Go Home	07/08/1976	105	BB
Southside Johnny & The Jukes	Trash It Up	05/11/1983	108	BB
Southside Johnny & The Jukes	New Romeo	11/08/1984	103	BB
Southwest F.O.B.	Feelin' Groovy	17/01/1970	115	BB
Southwind	Ready To Ride	13/12/1969	127	BB
Southwind	Boogie Woogie Country Girl	25/04/1970	107	CB
Southwind	Boogie Woogie Country Girl	02/05/1970	105	BB
Spandau Ballet	Lifeline	04/06/1983	108	BB
Spanky & Our Gang	Everybody's Talkin' At Me Theme From "Midnight Cowboy"	01/11/1969	126	CB
Sparks	Wonder Girl	04/11/1972	112	BB
Sparks	Achoo	26/04/1975	112	CB
Sparks	With All My Might	28/07/1984	104	BB
Special Delivery	Oh Let Me Know It (pt. 1)	13/08/1977	105	CB
Special Delivery	Oh Let Me Know It (pt. 1)	20/08/1977	107	BB
Spencer Davis Group	Looking Back	11/05/1968	113	BB
Spider	Everything Is Alright	02/08/1980	1101	CB
Spin	Grasshopper	04/09/1976	110	CB
Spinners	Love (I'm So Glad) I Found You	25/11/1961	142	CB
Spinners	Heaven On Earth (So Fine)	08/10/1977	105	CB
Spinners	Easy Come, Easy Go	18/02/1978	104	CB
Spinners	Body Language	03/11/1979	103	BB
Spinners	You Go Your Way (I'll Go Mine)	31/10/1981	110	BB

Spinners	Love Connection (Raise The Window Down)	09/01/1982	107	BB
Spinners	Right Or Wrong	14/04/1984	104	BB
Spiral Starecase	Baby What I Mean	02/03/1968	111	BB
Spirit	Mechanical World	18/05/1968	123	BB
Spirit	Dark Eyed Woman	27/09/1969	118	BB
Spirit	Nature's Way	20/03/1971	111	BB
Spirit Of Us	Simple Song Of Freedom	15/08/1970	106	BB
Split Enz	One Step Ahead	27/06/1981	104	BB
Split Enz	Six Months In A Leaky Boat	05/06/1982	104	BB
Spooky Tooth	Sunshine Help Me	20/01/1968	126	CB
Spooky Tooth	Feelin' Bad	04/10/1969	132	BB
Spooner's Crowd	Two In The Morning	13/08/1966	141	CB
Springers	I Know Why	23/01/1965	143	CB
Spyro Gyra	Percolator	26/07/1980	105	BB
Spyro Gyra	Summer Strut	07/11/1981	108	BB
Squeeze	Black Coffee In Bed	10/07/1982	103	BB
Ssgt. Barry Sadler - U.S Army Special Forces	One Day Nearer Home	15/10/1966	132	CB
Stacey Cane	Who Are You	03/04/1965	119	CB
Stacy Lattisaw	Don't Throw It All Away	31/07/1982	101	BB
Stacy Lattisaw	Hey There Lonely Boy	25/12/1982	108	BB
Stacy Lattisaw & Johnny Gill	Baby It's You	26/05/1984	102	BB
Stairsteps	From Us To You	06/03/1976	110	CB
Stairsteps	From Us To You	13/03/1976	102	BB
Stairsteps	Tell Me Why	04/07/1976	106	BB
Stallion	Magic Of The Music	09/07/1977	108	BB
Stamford Bridge	Roly Poly	05/09/1970	101	CB
Stampeders	Monday Morning Choo-Choo	11/03/1972	103	CB
Stampeders	Wild Eyes	27/05/1972	101	CB
Stampeders	Oh My Lady	24/03/1973	115	BB
Stampeders	Oh My Lady	07/04/1973	117	CB

Stan Getz	Blowin' In The Wind	23/05/1964	110	BB
Stan Getz/Astrud Gilberto	The Telephone Song	20/02/1965	134	CB
Stanley Turrentine	Naked As The Day I Was Born	26/07/1975	105	BB
Starcastle	Lady Of The Lake	22/05/1976	101	BB
Starlites	Valarie	19/11/1960	118	CB
Starpoint	Don't Be So Serious	02/07/1983	107	BB
Stars On 45 Proudly Presents The Star Sisters	The Star Sisters Melody	06/08/1983	107	BB
Starz	Last Night I Wrote A Letter	03/03/1979	104	BB
Statler Brothers	Ruthless	03/06/1967	131	CB
Steam	What I'm Saying Is True	04/04/1970	117	CB
Steel River	Ten Pound Note	07/11/1970	121	CB
Steel River	Ten Pound Note	14/11/1970	109	BB
Steel River	Southbound Train	24/07/1971	106	BB
Steely Dan	Bad Sneakers	20/09/1975	103	BB
Steely Dan	Kid Charlemagne	10/07/1976	101	CB
Steff	Where Did She Go	22/01/1966	124	BB
Stella Parton	I'll Miss You	20/02/1982	1103	CB
Stephanie Mills	You Can Get Over	17/11/1979	101	BB
Stephanie Mills	Last Night	31/07/1982	101	BB
Stephen Bishop	Send A Little Love My Way (Like Always)	11/04/1981	108	BB
Stephen Bishop	If Love Takes You Away	25/09/1982	108	BB
Stephen Bishop & Yvonne Elliman	Your Precious Love	26/07/1980	105	BB
Stephen Monahan	City Of Windows	01/07/1967	101	BB
Stephen Stills & Manassas	Rock And Roll Crazies	29/07/1972	111	CB
Steppenwolf	Get Into The Wind	14/12/1974	111	CB
Steppenwolf	Smokey Factory Blues	15/02/1975	105	CB
Steppenwolf	Smokey Factory Blues	22/03/1975	108	BB
Steve & Eydie	Real True Lovin'	26/04/1969	119	BB
Steve Alaimo	Mashed Potatoes (Part 1)	03/03/1962	124	CB
Steve Alaimo	Don't Let The Sun Catch You Crying	06/07/1963	126	CB

Steve Alaimo	Don't Let The Sun Catch You Crying	17/08/1963	125	BB
Steve Alaimo	Michael - Pt. 1	21/09/1963	105	CB
Steve Alaimo	I Don't Know	05/09/1964	115	CB
Steve Alaimo	I Don't Know	12/09/1964	103	BB
Steve Alaimo	Tomorrow Is Another Day	17/04/1965	109	CB
Steve Alaimo	Cast Your Fate To The Wind	29/05/1965	120	CB
Steve Alaimo	Blowin' In The Wind	18/09/1965	139	CB
Steve Alaimo	You Don't Know Like I Know	29/04/1967	116	CB
Steve Alaimo	New Orleans	16/09/1967	126	BB
Steve Alaimo	Denver	23/03/1968	118	BB
Steve Alaimo	One Woman	06/09/1969	101	BB
Steve Alaimo	One Woman	06/09/1969	132	CB
Steve Alaimo	When My Little Girl Is Smiling	19/06/1971	101	CB
Steve Alaimo & Betty Wright	After The Smoke Is Gone	05/04/1969	126	CB
Steve Allen	How's Your Sister	12/09/1964	111	BB
Steve Allen & His Orchestra With The Copacabana Trio	Cuando Calienta El Sol (When The Sun Is Hot)	21/09/1963	103	CB
Steve Arrington	Feel So Real	27/04/1985	104	BB
Steve Goodman	City Of New Orleans	05/02/1972	113	BB
Steve Goodman	The Dutchman	31/03/1973	110	CB
Steve Greenberg	Big Bruce	21/06/1969	122	CB
Steve Lawrence	Why, Why, Why	04/06/1960	110	CB
Steve Lawrence	Come Back, Silly Girl	01/10/1960	112	CB
Steve Lawrence	Hold Back The Dyke	19/11/1960	122	CB
Steve Lawrence	Somewhere Along The Way	21/10/1961	104	CB
Steve Lawrence	Our Concerto	20/01/1962	116	CB
Steve Lawrence	Our Concerto	03/02/1962	107	BB
Steve Lawrence	The Lady Wants To Twist	05/05/1962	144	CB
Steve Lawrence	The Lady Wants To Twist	19/05/1962	120	BB
Steve Lawrence	House Without Windows	07/07/1962	132	CB
Steve Lawrence	More (Theme From The Film "Mondo Cane")	18/05/1963	113	CB

Steve Lawrence	More (Theme From The Film "Mondo Cane")	22/06/1963	117	BB
Steve Lawrence	My Home Town	04/01/1964	106	BB
Steve Lawrence	My Home Town	11/01/1964	113	CB
Steve Lawrence	A Room Without Windows (b-side)	18/01/1964	120	BB
Steve Lawrence	I Will Wait For You	02/01/1965	113	CB
Steve Lawrence	Bewitched	09/01/1965	103	BB
Steve Lawrence	I Will Wait For You (b-side)	09/01/1965	113	BB
Steve Lawrence	Last Night I Made A Little Girl Cry	05/06/1965	126	BB
Steve Lawrence	Where Can I Go	12/06/1965	106	CB
Steve Lawrence	Millions Of Roses	28/08/1965	106	BB
Steve Lawrence	Millions Of Roses	28/08/1965	118	CB
Steve Lawrence	Only The Young	29/01/1966	128	CB
Steve Lawrence	The Week-End	12/02/1966	117	CB
Steve Lawrence	The Week-End	19/02/1966	131	BB
Steve Lawrence	Sweet Maria	22/04/1967	137	CB
Steve Lawrence & Eydie Gorme	This Could Be The Start Of Something	07/05/1960	113	CB
Steve Miller Band	My Dark Hour	12/07/1969	126	BB
Steve Miller Band	Steve Miller's Midnight Tango	07/11/1970	117	BB
Steve Miller Band	Rock Love	11/12/1971	118	CB
Steve Rowland & The Ring Leaders	Out Ridin'	22/06/1963	141	CB
Steve Wariner	All Roads Lead To You	17/10/1981	I103	CB
Steve Wariner	All Roads Lead To You	14/11/1981	107	BB
Steve Wightman	You Know The Feelin'	15/05/1976	110	BB
Steve Winwood	Night Train	08/08/1981	104	BB
Stevie Wonder	With A Child's Heart	16/07/1966	131	BB
Stonewall Jackson	Greener Pastures	25/03/1961	135	CB
Stoney & Meatloaf	It Takes All Kinds Of People	07/08/1971	108	CB
Stories	Darling	10/02/1973	111	BB
Storm	Bend Me, Shape Me	11/09/1971	105	BB
Storm	This I Find Is Beautiful	22/04/1972	121	CB

Strange Loves	Love, Love (That's All I Want From You)	12/12/1964	122	CB
Strange Loves	Love, Love (That's All I Want From You)	19/12/1964	122	BB
Strawbs	Part Of The Union	21/04/1973	111	BB
Street People	Thank You Girl	02/05/1970	112	CB
Street People	You're My One Weakness Girl	27/03/1976	116	CB
Street People	I Wanna Spend My Whole Life With You	25/09/1976	109	BB
Stu Nunnery	Sally From Syracuse	10/11/1973	101	BB
Stu Nunnery	Madelaine	16/03/1974	107	BB
Stuff 'N' Ramjett	It's Been A Long Long Time	20/03/1976	116	CB
Stutz Bearcat & The Vanity Fair	Lucky Lindy	14/01/1967	150	CB
Styx	Best Thing	19/08/1972	102	CB
Styx	Crystal Ball	14/05/1977	109	BB
Sue Lyon	Lolita Ya Ya*	28/07/1962	104	CB
Sue Raney	Biology	09/05/1960	109	BB
Sue Saad	Looker	05/12/1981	I102	CB
Sue Saad	Looker	12/12/1981	104	BB
Sue Saad And The Next	Won't Give It Up	01/03/1980	107	BB
Sue Thompson	It Has To Be	31/03/1962	150	CB
Sue Thompson	If The Boy Only Knew	09/06/1962	112	BB
Sue Thompson	If The Boy Only Knew	09/06/1962	143	CB
Sue Thompson	What's Wrong Bill	30/03/1963	135	BB
Sue Thompson	Susie	25/05/1963	127	CB
Sue Thompson	True Confession	25/05/1963	148	CB
Sue Thompson	Big Daddy	22/02/1964	132	BB
Sue Thompson	Stop Th' Music	24/04/1965	135	CB
Sue Thompson	Stop Th' Music	08/05/1965	115	BB
Sue Thompson	What Should I Do	30/04/1966	148	CB
Sue Thompson	Put It Back (Where You Found It)	06/08/1966	131	BB
Sugar Bears	Happiness Train	26/08/1972	102	CB
Sugar Billy	Super Duper Love - Part 1 (Are You Diggin' On Me)	18/01/1975	102	CB

Sugarloaf/Jerry Corbetta	Stars In My Eyes	21/06/1975	104	CB
Sugarloaf/Jerry Corbetta	I Got A Song	01/11/1975	110	BB
Summer Wine	Why Do Fools Fall In Love	17/02/1973	103	BB
Sun	Wanna Make Love (Come Flic My Bic)	04/09/1976	109	CB
Sunny & The Sunliners	Out Of Sight - Out Of Mind	22/02/1964	113	CB
Sunny & The Sunliners	Something's Got A Hold On Me	23/01/1965	128	BB
Sunny Gale	Church Bells May Ring	09/07/1960	125	CB
Sunny Gale	Let The Rest Of The World Go By	05/02/1966	139	CB
Survivor	Rebel Girl	14/06/1980	103	BB
Survivor	I Never Stopped Loving You	18/02/1984	104	BB
Susan Hart	Is This A Disco Or A Honky Tonk?	09/05/1981	109	BB
Susan Jacks And The Poppy Family	You Don't Know What Love Is	05/05/1973	116	BB
Susan Summers	Mommy And Daddy Were Twistin'	13/01/1962	106	CB
Susan Wayne	Think Summer	27/03/1965	118	CB
Susann Farrar	Our Town	26/10/1968	146	CB
Suzi Quatro	Your Mama Won't Like Me	29/03/1975	103	CB
Swamp Dogg	Mama's Baby-Daddy's Maybe	30/05/1970	113	BB
Swamp Dogg	Creeping Away	24/04/1971	117	CB
Syl Johnson	One Way Ticket To Nowhere	11/07/1970	125	BB
Syl Johnson	The Love You Left Behind	20/11/1971	108	CB
Syl Johnson	I Only Have Love	01/11/1975	118	CB
Sylvia	Sweet Stuff	30/03/1974	103	BB
Sylvia Robinson	Have You Had Any Lately?	22/08/1970	102	BB
T-Connection	On Fire	17/12/1977	103	BB
T-K-O's	The Fat Man Part 1	12/02/1966	126	CB
T. Rex	Metal Guru	17/06/1972	106	CB
T. Rex	The Slider	07/10/1972	112	CB
T.C. Atlantic	Twenty Years Ago (In Speedy's Kitchen)	15/06/1968	130	CB
T.G. Sheppard	Motels And Memories	07/02/1976	102	BB
T.G. Sheppard	Solitary Man	03/07/1976	101	CB

T.K. Hulin	I'm Not A Fool Anymore	24/08/1963	125	CB
Talking Heads	Once In A Lifetime	07/02/1981	103	BB
Talking Heads	Road To Nowhere	22/06/1985	105	BB
Tammy Montgomery	I Cried	15/06/1963	123	CB
Tammy Wynette	I'll See Him Through	07/02/1970	113	CB
Tammy Wynette	Run, Woman, Run	31/10/1970	114	CB
Tammy Wynette	The Wonders You Perform	05/12/1970	104	BB
Tammy Wynette	We Sure Can Love Each Other	20/03/1971	103	BB
Tammy Wynette	We Sure Can Love Each Other	03/04/1971	125	CB
Tammy Wynette	Good Lovin' (Makes It Right)	31/07/1971	111	BB
Tammy Wynette	Bedtime Story	08/01/1972	114	CB
Tammy Wynette	'TIL I Get It Right	13/01/1973	113	CB
Tammy Wynette	'Til I Get It Right	20/01/1973	106	BB
Tammy Wynette	Kids Say The Darndest Things	26/05/1973	108	CB
Tammy Wynette	Another Lonely Song	12/01/1974	104	CB
Tammy Wynette	You And Me	23/10/1976	101	BB
Tané Cain	My Time To Fly	29/01/1983	108	BB
Tanya Tucker	Delta Dawn	22/07/1972	107	CB
Tanya Tucker	Here's Some Love	16/10/1976	116	CB
Tanya Tucker	Save Me	01/07/1978	105	BB
Tanya Tucker	Lover Goodbye	07/04/1979	103	BB
Tata Vega	You'll Never Rock Alone	16/07/1977	108	BB
Tata Vega	I Need You Now	28/07/1979	107	BB
Tavares	The Love I Never Had	10/04/1976	119	CB
Tax	Loddy	06/09/1969	137	CB
Teardrops	Tears Come Tumbling	25/12/1965	136	CB
Ted Neeley	Paradise	14/06/1975	102	BB
Ted Neeley	Paradise	28/06/1975	112	CB
Ted Nugent	Tied Up In Love	03/03/1984	107	BB
Ted Taylor	Look Out	31/12/1960	105	BB

Ted Taylor	My Darling	06/05/1961	140	CB
Ted Taylor	I'll Release You	23/02/1963	134	BB
Ted Taylor	You Give Me Nothing To Go On	14/09/1963	104	BB
Ted Taylor	So Hard	28/03/1964	130	CB
Ted Taylor	(Love Is Like A) Ramblin' Rose	03/07/1965	132	BB
Ted Taylor	Daddy's Baby	26/03/1966	129	BB
Ted Taylor	It's Too Late	30/08/1969	118	BB
Ted Taylor	It's Too Late	06/09/1969	111	CB
Ted Taylor & His Band	Be Ever Wonderful	11/05/1963	125	CB
Ted Taylor And His Band	Be Ever Wonderful	04/05/1963	123	BB
Teddy & The Pandas	Once Upon A Time (This World Was Mine)	23/04/1966	130	CB
Teddy And The Continentals	Ev'rybody Pony	18/09/1961	101	BB
Teddy And The Pandas	Once Upon A Time (This World Was Mine)	30/04/1966	134	BB
Teddy And The Pandas	We Can't Go On This Way	20/08/1966	103	BB
Teddy Baker	It's Over	10/10/1981	101	BB
Teddy Pendergrass	The Whole Town's Laughing At Me	10/09/1977	102	BB
Teddy Pendergrass	Only You	06/01/1979	106	BB
Teddy Pendergrass	I Can't Live Without Your Love	05/09/1981	103	BB
Teddy Randazzo	Happy Ending	06/05/1961	133	CB
Teddy Randazzo	Let The Sunshine In	22/07/1961	131	CB
Teddy Randazzo	Dear Heart	11/05/1963	131	CB
Teddy Randazzo	Lost Without You	03/10/1964	105	CB
Teddy Randazzo	Lost Without You	07/11/1964	130	BB
Teddy Randazzo & The Dazzlers	Dance To The Locomotion	01/09/1962	148	CB
Teddy Vann	Cindy	07/03/1960	104	BB
Teena Marie	I'm A Sucker For Your Love	04/08/1979	102	BB
Telly Savalas	RuBBer Bands And Bits Of String	16/11/1974	113	CB
Telstars	Keep On Running	24/06/1967	112	CB
Ten Wheel Drive With Genya Ravan	Tightrope	10/01/1970	136	CB
Ten Years After	Cho Choo Mama	30/12/1972	101	CB

Tennessee Ernie Ford	Dark As A Dungeon	08/04/1961	129	CB
Tennison Stephens	Hurry Change (If You're Coming)	29/11/1969	135	CB
Teresa Brewer	Bye Bye Baby Goodbye	13/07/1959	115	BB
Teresa Brewer	Have You Ever Been Lonely (Have You Ever Been Blue)	10/12/1960	120	CB
Teresa Brewer	Whip-Poor-Will	01/04/1961	131	CB
Teresa Brewer	Older And Wiser	22/04/1961	136	CB
Teresa Brewer	Milord	13/05/1961	105	CB
Teresa Brewer	Little Miss Belong To No One	05/08/1961	111	CB
Teresa Brewer	She'll Never Never Love You (Like I Do)	23/02/1963	113	CB
Teresa Brewer	She'll Never Never Love You (Like I Do)	16/03/1963	122	BB
Teresa Brewer	He Understands Me	09/11/1963	130	BB
Teresa Brewer	He Understands Me	09/11/1963	145	CB
Teresa Brewer	Music, Music, Music	07/07/1973	112	CB
Teresa Brewer	Music, Music, Music	14/07/1973	109	BB
Teresa Brewer With The Milestone Singers	The Ballad Of Lover's Hill	24/11/1962	118	CB
Teri Thornton	Somewhere In The Night (Naked City Theme)	29/06/1963	139	CB
Terri Dean	I'm Confessin' (That I Love You)	01/06/1959	107	BB
Terry & The Chain Reaction	Keep Your Cool	09/12/1967	140	CB
Terry Bradshaw	I'm So Lonesome I Could Cry	21/02/1976	101	CB
Terry Dactyl & The Dinosaurs	Sea Side Shuffle	23/09/1972	113	CB
Terry Jacks	I'm Gonna Love You Too	06/01/1973	102	CB
Terry Jacks	I'm Gonna Love You Too	27/01/1973	116	BB
Terry Jacks	Christina	07/06/1975	106	BB
Terry Knight	Lizbeth Peach	24/06/1967	137	CB
Terry Knight	Come Home, Baby	26/08/1967	144	CB
Terry Knight	Saint Paul	28/06/1969	114	BB
Terry Knight & The Pack	One Monkey Don't Stop No Show	25/03/1967	116	CB
Terry Knight & The Pack	Love, Love, Love, Love, Love	13/05/1967	107	CB
Terry Knight And The Pack	Better Man Than I	16/04/1966	125	BB
Terry Knight And The Pack	A Change On The Way	13/08/1966	111	BB

Terry Knight And The Pack	This Precious Time (b-side)	11/02/1967	120	BB
Terry Knight And The Pack	Love, Love, Love, Love, Love	27/05/1967	117	BB
Terry Stafford	Follow The Rainbow	15/08/1964	112	CB
Terry Stafford	Follow The Rainbow	22/08/1964	101	BB
Terry Tyler	A Thousand Feet Below	20/01/1962	127	CB
Terry Williams	Melanie Makes Me Smile	25/11/1972	112	BB
Tex Ritter	The Americans (A Canadian's Opinion)	16/02/1974	111	CB
Textones	Midnight Mission	29/06/1985	109	BB
The "5" Royales	I Know It's Hard But It's Fair	08/06/1959	103	BB
The "5" Royales	I'm With You	27/06/1960	107	BB
The "5" Royales	Please, Please, Please	21/11/1960	114	BB
The 3° Degrees	Close Your Eyes	11/09/1965	105	CB
The 3° Degrees	Close Your Eyes	02/10/1965	126	BB
The 31st Of February	Sandcastles	13/07/1968	105	CB
The 4 Seasons	Peanuts	23/02/1963	131	CB
The 4 Seasons	Peanuts [EP] (Peanuts/Never On Sunday/I Can't Give You Anything	23/03/1963	115	BB
The 4 Seasons	Since I Don't Have You [EP] (Since I Don't Have You/Alone/Why Do	06/04/1963	123	BB
The 4 Seasons	Since I Don't Have You	27/04/1963	106	CB
The 4 Seasons	Peanuts [EP] (Peanuts/Never On Sunday/I Can't Give You Anything	18/01/1964	108	BB
The 4 Seasons	Never On Sunday	16/01/1965	146	CB
The 4 Seasons Featuring Frankie Valli	Something's On Her Mind	22/03/1969	101	CB
The 4 Seasons Featuring The "sound" Of Frankie Valli	Saturday's Father	22/06/1968	103	BB
The 5th Dimension	No Love In The Room	01/03/1975	105	BB
The 5th Dimension	Magic In My Life	04/10/1975	107	CB
The A's	A Woman's Got The Power	08/08/1981	106	BB
The Accents Featuring Sandi	Better Watch Out Boy	08/08/1964	133	BB
The Ad Libs	He Ain't No Angel	24/04/1965	104	CB
The Alan Copeland Singers	Classical Gas/Scarborough Fair	25/01/1969	123	BB
The Alarm	Sixty Eight Guns	14/04/1984	106	BB
The Alarm	The Deceiver	21/07/1984	104	BB

The Allisons	Are You Sure	03/04/1961	102	BB
The Allisons	Surfer Street	09/11/1963	121	CB
The Allman Brothers Band	Revival (Love Is Everywhere)	02/01/1971	119	CB
The Allman Brothers Band	Melissa	19/08/1972	103	CB
The Allman Brothers Band	One Way Out	18/11/1972	103	CB
The Allman Brothers Band	Louisiana Lou And Three Card Monty John	08/11/1975	101	CB
The Allman Brothers Band	Can't Take It With You	07/07/1979	105	BB
The Ambassadors	I Really Love You	15/02/1969	123	BB
The Amboy Dukes	Baby Please Don't Go	02/03/1968	106	BB
The Amboy Dukes	You Talk Sunshine, I Breathe Fire	12/10/1968	114	BB
The Amboy Dukes	For His Namesake	24/05/1969	108	CB
The Amen Corner	The World Of Broken Hearts	04/11/1967	149	CB
The American Breed	I Don't Think You Know Me	01/04/1967	124	CB
The American Breed	Don't Forget About Me	12/08/1967	107	BB
The American Breed	Keep The Faith	23/11/1968	107	CB
The American Breed	Hunky Funky	03/05/1969	107	BB
The American Breed	Hunky Funky	10/05/1969	125	CB
The American Breed	Room At The Top	09/08/1969	127	CB
The Ames Brothers	Take Me Along	28/11/1959	124	CB
The Ames Brothers	Washington Square	26/10/1963	129	BB
The Angels	Everybody Loves A Lover	26/05/1962	103	BB
The Angels	Everybody Loves A Lover	16/06/1962	113	CB
The Angels	Cotton Fields	21/09/1963	119	BB
The Angels	Little Beatle Boy	14/03/1964	130	CB
The Angels	The Boy With The Green Eyes	28/09/1968	140	CB
The Animals	Baby Let Me Take You Home	12/09/1964	102	BB
The Animals	Baby Let Me Take You Home	19/09/1964	123	CB
The Apollas	You're Absolutely Right	20/11/1965	138	CB
The Applejacks	Theme From "THE Untouchables"	02/07/1960	117	CB
The Applejacks	Mexican Hat Twist	25/11/1961	145	CB

The Applejacks	Tell Me When	30/05/1964	146	CB
The Applejacks	Tell Me When	06/06/1964	135	BB
The Arbors	Just Let It Happen	14/01/1967	111	CB
The Arbors	Just Let It Happen	04/02/1967	113	BB
The Arbors	With You Girl	19/08/1967	125	CB
The Archies	Together We Two	26/12/1970	113	CB
The Archies	Together We Two	09/01/1971	122	BB
The Ardells	Eefananny	28/09/1963	109	BB
The Argyles	Vacation Days Are Over	21/09/1959	101	BB
The Art Of Noise	Beat Box	07/04/1984	101	BB
The Art Of Noise	Close (To The Edit)	18/08/1984	102	BB
The Arthur Lyman Group	America	23/06/1962	140	CB
The Artistics	Get My Hands On Some Lovin'	19/09/1964	118	BB
The Artistics	This Heart Of Mine	18/12/1965	115	BB
The Artistics	This Heart Of Mine	25/12/1965	113	CB
The Artistics	Love Song	20/05/1967	111	BB
The Assembled Multitude	Medley From "SUPERSTAR" (A Rock Opera)	23/01/1971	106	CB
The Association	Looking Glass	28/01/1967	113	BB
The Association	Requiem For The Masses	09/09/1967	113	CB
The Association	Under Branches	26/04/1969	117	BB
The Association	Yes, I Will	12/07/1969	101	CB
The Association	Yes, I Will	19/07/1969	120	BB
The Association	Just About The Same	28/02/1970	106	BB
The Association	Darling Be Home Soon	13/05/1972	104	BB
The Astronauts	Baja	29/06/1963	105	CB
The Astronauts	Competition Coupe	15/02/1964	124	BB
The Asylum Choir (lead Vocal: Leon Russell)	Tryin' To Stay 'Live	08/01/1972	115	BB
The Atlanta Disco Band	Do What You Feel	10/04/1976	104	BB
The Avantis	Keep On Dancing	17/08/1963	146	CB
The Babies	You Make Me Feel Like Someone	01/07/1967	123	CB

The Bachelors	Charmaine	25/05/1963	123	CB
The Bachelors	Whispering	30/11/1963	121	CB
The Back Porch Majority	Second-Hand Man [Live]	19/03/1966	104	BB
The Back Porch Majority	Second-Hand Man (Live)	30/04/1966	125	CB
The Bad Boys	Black Olives	28/01/1967	111	CB
The Bad Habits	Night Owl	28/02/1970	121	CB
The Bad Habits	Thank You For The Love	25/09/1971	116	CB
The Balladeers	Roll Call Company "J"	25/04/1960	104	BB
The Balladeers	Roll Call Company "J"	07/05/1960	106	CB
The Baltimore And Ohio Marching Band	Lapland	04/11/1967	101	CB
The Banana Splits	The Tra La La Song (One Banana, Two Banana)	04/01/1969	133	CB
The Band	The Shape I'm In	05/12/1970	104	CB
The Band	The Shape I'm In	02/01/1971	121	BB
The Band	(I Don't Want To) Hang Up My Rock And Roll Shoes	23/12/1972	113	BB
The Band	(I Don't Want To) Hang Up My Rock And Roll Shoes	13/01/1973	117	CB
The Bandwagon	Breakin' Down The Walls Of Heartache	03/08/1968	115	BB
The Bar-Kays	Midnight Cowboy	09/08/1969	120	CB
The Bar-Kays	Montego Bay	21/11/1970	108	CB
The Bar-Kays	Let's Have Some Fun	11/02/1978	102	BB
The Barbarians	What The New Breed Say	20/11/1965	102	BB
The Bards	Never Too Much Love	02/12/1967	134	CB
The Bards	Tunesmith	22/03/1969	135	CB
The Bareback Rockers	Giddyap Girl (Ride Your Horsey Home)	23/08/1975	111	CB
The Barons	Pledge Of A Fool	18/05/1963	138	CB
The Barracuda	The Dance At St. Francis	07/12/1968	113	BB
The Baskerville Hounds	Space Rock - Part 2	01/04/1967	110	CB
The Bay Brothers	Baby Don't Give Up	11/10/1980	108	BB
The Beach Boys	409	25/08/1962	105	CB
The Beach Boys	Why Do Fools Fall In Love	29/02/1964	120	BB
The Beach Boys	She Knows Me Too Well	12/09/1964	101	BB

The Beach Boys	The Man With All The Toys	19/12/1964	116	CB
The Beach Boys	Cottonfields	16/05/1970	101	CB
The Beach Boys	Cottonfields	16/05/1970	103	BB
The Beach Boys	Marcella	08/07/1972	116	CB
The Beach Boys	Marcella	15/07/1972	110	BB
The Beach Boys	California Saga (On My Way To Sunny Californ-I-A)	15/12/1973	110	CB
The Beach Boys	Barbara Ann	12/07/1975	111	CB
The Beach Boys	Barbara Ann	26/07/1975	101	BB
The Beach Boys	Wouldn't It Be Nice	16/08/1975	103	BB
The Beach Boys	Goin' On	05/04/1980	I101	CB
The Beach-Nuts	Out In The Sun (Hey-O)	31/07/1965	106	BB
The Beacon Street Union	South End Incident (I'm Afraid)	09/12/1967	142	CB
The Beatles	From Me To You	13/07/1963	149	CB
The Beatles	From Me To You	03/08/1963	116	BB
The Beatles	The Beatles Souvenir Of Their Visit To America (EP)	28/03/1964	130	CB
The Beatles	Ask Me Why	25/07/1964	139	CB
The Beatles	Yes It Is	01/05/1965	107	CB
The Beatles	I'm Down	07/08/1965	101	BB
The Beatles	I'm Down	07/08/1965	126	CB
The Beatles	Boys	23/10/1965	102	BB
The Beatles With Tony Sheridan	Why	25/04/1964	129	CB
The Bee Gees	I Can't See Nobody	01/07/1967	128	BB
The Bee Gees	The Singer Sang His Song	27/04/1968	116	BB
The Bee Gees	I.O.I.O.	20/06/1970	102	CB
The Bee Gees	Wouldn't I Be Someone	30/06/1973	115	BB
The Bee Gees	Wouldn't I Be Someone	04/08/1973	122	CB
The Beginning Of The End	Monkey Tamarind	02/10/1971	113	CB
The Belairs	Mr. Moto	10/02/1962	150	CB
The Belfast Gipsies	Gloria's Dream (Round And Around)	17/09/1966	124	BB
The Belfast Gipsies	Gloria's Dream (Round And Around)	24/09/1966	120	CB

The Bells	To Know You Is To Love You	11/12/1971	119	CB
The Belmonts	We Belong Together	23/01/1961	108	BB
The Belmonts	We Belong Together	04/02/1961	103	CB
The Belmonts With Pete Bennett Orch.	Hombre	07/04/1962	106	CB
The Berkeley Kites	Hang Up City	17/02/1968	115	CB
The Billy Vaughn Singers	Sweet Maria	28/01/1967	105	BB
The Birdwatchers	Girl I Got News For You	28/05/1966	139	CB
The Birdwatchers	I'm Gonna Love You Anyway	03/09/1966	125	BB
The Blackbyrds	Summer Love (b-side)	17/08/1974	101b	BB
The Blackbyrds	Soft And Easy	07/01/1978	102	BB
The Blackbyrds	Soft And Easy	14/01/1978	102	CB
The Blackbyrds	Supernatural Feeling	22/04/1978	102	BB
The Blackwells	Love Or Money	10/04/1961	107	BB
The Blades Of Grass	Just Another Face	16/09/1967	140	CB
The Blendtones	Lovers	25/05/1963	118	BB
The Blendtones	Lovers	15/06/1963	108	CB
The Blossoms	That's When The Tears Start (b-side)	05/03/1966	128	BB
The Blossoms	That's When The Tears Start	19/03/1966	127	CB
The Blossoms	Good Good Lovin'	02/04/1966	101	BB
The Blossoms	Good Good Lovin'	16/12/1967	115	BB
The Blue Belles	I Found A New Love	13/10/1962	114	CB
The Blue Belles	I Found A New Love	13/10/1962	122	BB
The Blue Belles	Cool Water	26/01/1963	127	BB
The Blue Belles	Cool Water	23/02/1963	119	CB
The Blue Diamonds	In A Little Spanish Town	09/09/1961	115	CB
The Blue Notes	My Hero	15/10/1960	103	CB
The Blue Ridge Rangers	Back In The Hills	13/10/1973	107	BB
The Blues Busters	Baby I'm Sorry	17/01/1976	105	BB
The Bob Crewe Generation	Miniskirts In Moscow Or...	29/04/1967	147	CB
The Bob Crewe Generation	Miniskirts In Moscow Or...	06/05/1967	129	BB

The Bob Crewe Generation	You Only Live Twice	10/06/1967	124	CB
The Bob Crewe Generation	Birds Of Britain	28/10/1967	109	CB
The Bob Crewe Generation Choir	The Battle Hymn Of The Republic - '68	08/06/1968	132	CB
The Bob Seger System	Noah	16/08/1969	114	CB
The Bob Seger System	Noah	23/08/1969	103	BB
The BoBBettes	Dance With Me Georgie	15/10/1960	104	CB
The BoBBettes	Mr. Johhny Q	10/07/1961	120	BB
The BoBBettes	I Don't Like It Like That	09/09/1961	111	CB
The Boogie Boys	A Fly Girl	17/08/1985	102	BB
The Boys In The Band Featuring Herman Griffin	Money Music	12/09/1970	104	CB
The Boys In The Band Featuring Herman Griffin	Money Music	19/09/1970	103	BB
The Bracelets	Waddle, Waddle	25/08/1962	128	CB
The Bracelets	Waddle, Waddle	15/09/1962	113	BB
The Brady Bunch	Time To Change	26/02/1972	116	CB
The Brady Bunch	We'll Always Be Friends	10/06/1972	117	CB
The Brandywine Singers	Summer's Come And Gone	02/11/1963	129	BB
The Brandywine Singers	Summer's Come And Gone	02/11/1963	149	CB
The Brass Ring	Lara's Theme (From Dr. Zhivago)	16/07/1966	138	CB
The Brass Ring	Lara's Theme (from Dr. Zhivago)	23/07/1966	126	BB
The Briarwood Singers	He Was A Friend Of Mine	28/12/1963	126	BB
The Brides Of Funkenstein	Disco To Go	23/12/1978	101	BB
The British Walkers	Shake	08/04/1967	106	BB
The Brooklyn Bridge	Free As The Wind	21/02/1970	109	BB
The Brothers Four	25 Minutes To Go	13/10/1962	114	CB
The Brothers Four	Four Strong Winds	26/10/1963	114	BB
The Brothers Four	Hootenanny Saturday Night (Live)	28/12/1963	127	CB
The Brothers Four	Somewhere	27/02/1965	131	BB
The Brothers Johnson	Free And Single	15/01/1977	103	BB
The Brothers Johnson	Runnin' For Your Lovin'	14/01/1978	107	BB
The Brothers Johnson	Ride-O-Rocket	21/10/1978	104	BB

The Brothers Johnson	Ain't We Funkin' Now	13/01/1979	102	BB
The Brothers Johnson	Treasure	23/08/1980	1102	CB
The Brothers Johnson	You Keep Me Coming Back	21/07/1984	102	BB
The Browns Featuring Jim Edward Brown	Teen-Ex	12/03/1960	114	CB
The Browns Featuring Jim Edward Brown	Lonely Little Robin	04/07/1960	105	BB
The Browns Featuring Jim Edward Brown	Brighten The Corner Where You Are	10/09/1960	114	CB
The Browns Featuring Jim Edward Brown	You Can't Grow Peaches On A Cherry Tree	10/07/1965	134	CB
The BuBBle Puppy	If I Had A Reason	31/05/1969	128	BB
The BuBBle Puppy	If I Had A Reason	21/06/1969	119	CB
The Buchanan Brothers	The Last Time	27/12/1969	106	BB
The Buchanan Brothers	Rosianna	21/02/1970	119	CB
The Buckinghams	I'll Go Crazy	21/05/1966	112	BB
The Buckinghams	I'll Go Crazy	21/05/1966	132	CB
The Buckinghams	I Call Your Name	18/06/1966	102	CB
The Buckinghams	I've Been Wrong	03/09/1966	129	CB
The Buckinghams	Where Did You Come From	02/11/1968	125	CB
The Buckinghams	Where Did You Come From	16/11/1968	117	BB
The Buckinghams	It's A Beautiful Day (For Lovin')	13/09/1969	126	BB
The Buckinghams	It's A Beautiful Day (For Lovin')	27/09/1969	110	CB
The Buena Vistas	Soul Clappin'	10/08/1968	116	CB
The Buena Vistas	Soul Clappin	07/09/1968	126	BB
The Buffalo Springfield	Nowadays Clancy Can't Even Sing	20/08/1966	110	BB
The Buffalo Springfield	Nowadays Clancy Can't Even Sing	03/09/1966	142	CB
The Buffalo Springfield	Un-Mundo	18/05/1968	105	BB
The Buffalo Springfield	Special Care	07/09/1968	107	BB
The Bugaloos	For A Friend	14/11/1970	107	CB
The Bugaloos	For A Friend	19/12/1970	128	BB
The Butterflys	I Wonder	23/01/1965	117	BB
The By Liners	Archie's Melody	06/01/1962	106	CB
The By Liners	Archie's Melody	20/01/1962	117	BB

The Byrds	I'll Feel A Whole Lot Better	24/07/1965	103	BB
The Byrds	I'll Feel A Whole Lot Better	31/07/1965	104	CB
The Byrds	Lay Lady Lay	07/06/1969	132	BB
The Byrds	Wasn't Born To Follow	29/11/1969	125	CB
The Byrds	Jesus Is Just Alright	14/02/1970	121	CB
The Byrds	Chestnut Mare	19/12/1970	121	BB
The Byrds	Glory, Glory	09/10/1971	110	BB
The Byrds	Full Circle	05/05/1973	109	BB
The C.O.D.'s	I'm A Good Guy	02/04/1966	128	BB
The Cadillacs	Romeo	03/08/1959	105	BB
The Cake	You Can Have Him	04/11/1967	124	CB
The California Earthquake	What A Beautiful Feeling	06/12/1969	113	CB
The California Earthquake	What A Beautiful Feeling	20/12/1969	133	BB
The Camel Drivers	Sunday Morning 6 O'clock	20/07/1968	106	CB
The Camelots	Pocahontas	05/09/1964	103	CB
The Candymen	Deep In The Night	30/12/1967	107	CB
The Candymen	Ways	23/03/1968	114	CB
The Cantina Band (featuring Lou Christie)	Summer '81 Medley	25/07/1981	1101	CB
The Capitol Showband	Born To Be With You	12/06/1965	126	BB
The Capitols	Patty Cake	29/04/1967	125	BB
The Capitols	Patty Cake	29/04/1967	144	CB
The Capitols	Soul Brother, Soul Sister	28/12/1968	126	CB
The Capreez	Rosanna	24/09/1966	115	BB
The Capreez	Soulsation	09/09/1967	115	CB
The Capreez	Soulsation	09/09/1967	125	BB
The Carmel	I Can't Shake This Feeling	30/12/1967	126	CB
The Carnival	Son Of A Preacher Man	09/08/1969	119	CB
The Carousels	If You Want To	31/03/1962	117	BB
The Carousels	If You Want To	14/04/1962	102	CB
The Carter Brothers	Southern Country Boy	17/07/1965	123	CB

The Carter Brothers	Southern Country Boy	17/07/1965	133	BB
The Cascades	My First Day Alone	03/08/1963	121	CB
The Cascades	A Little Like Lovin'	17/08/1963	116	BB
The Cascades	A Little Like Lovin'	17/08/1963	128	CB
The Cascades	For Your Sweet Love	14/12/1963	121	CB
The Cascades	Cheryl's Goin' Home	30/04/1966	131	BB
The Cascades	Cheryl's Goin' Home	07/05/1966	142	CB
The Cashelles	Outside City Limits	25/01/1964	129	BB
The Casinos	How Long Has It Been	17/06/1967	121	BB
The Caslons	For All We Know	27/01/1962	120	BB
The Castaways	Goodbye Babe	13/11/1965	101	BB
The Castells	Little Sad Eyes	27/02/1961	101	BB
The Castells	Make Believe Wedding	23/09/1961	104	CB
The Castells	Oh! What It Seemed To Be	28/07/1962	111	CB
The Castells	Echoes In The Night	13/10/1962	142	CB
The Casuals	Mustang 2 + 2 (Big Mule)	05/12/1964	117	BB
The Cavaliers	Funky	11/02/1961	115	CB
The Center Stage	Someday, Someway (You're Gonna Love Me)	15/05/1971	122	CB
The Chambers Brothers	All Strung Out Over You	25/02/1967	120	CB
The Chambers Brothers	Uptown	18/11/1967	126	BB
The Chambers Brothers	Are You Ready	15/03/1969	113	BB
The Chambers Brothers	Are You Ready	15/03/1969	119	CB
The Chambers Brothers	Love, Peace And Happiness	14/02/1970	135	CB
The Chambers Brothers	Let's Do It (Do It Together)	30/05/1970	103	BB
The Chambers Brothers	Let's Do It (Do It Together)	18/07/1970	108	CB
The Chambers Brothers	Funky	19/12/1970	106	BB
The Chambers Brothers	Let's Go, Let's Go, Let's Go	16/03/1974	106	BB
The Chambers Brothers	Let's Go, Let's Go, Let's Go	30/03/1974	116	CB
The Chambers Brothers	1-2-3	03/08/1974	121	CB
The Champs	Double Eagle Rock	03/10/1959	111	CB

The Champs	The Little Matador	14/05/1960	113	CB
The Champs	Hokey Pokey	04/03/1961	125	CB
The Champs	Limbo Dance	15/09/1962	130	CB
The Champs	Mr. Cool	26/01/1963	116	CB
The Champs	Mr. Cool	02/02/1963	111	BB
The Champs' Boys Orchestra	Tubular Bells	15/05/1976	115	CB
The Chancellors	Little Latin Lupe Lu	06/03/1965	122	CB
The Chantay's	Monsoon	06/07/1963	149	CB
The Chantay's	Pipeline	12/11/1966	134	CB
The Chantels	I Love You So	21/01/1961	117	CB
The Chantels	Glad To Be Back	29/07/1961	146	CB
The Chantels	There's Our Song Again	04/11/1961	115	CB
The Chantels	Here It Comes Again	17/03/1962	101	CB
The Chantels	Here It Comes Again	17/03/1962	118	BB
The Chantels	Maybe	06/12/1969	116	BB
The Chants	Respectable	13/05/1961	107	CB
The Chants	Respectable	22/05/1961	101	BB
The Chaperones	Cruise To The Moon	25/06/1960	121	CB
The Chariots	Tiger In The Tank	05/12/1964	110	CB
The Charles Randolph Grean Sounde	Peter And The Wolf	28/02/1970	114	CB
The Charles Randolph Grean Sounde	Peter And The Wolf	14/03/1970	108	BB
The Charlie Daniels Band	Birmingham Blues	29/11/1975	101	BB
The Charlie Daniels Band	Wichita Jail	19/06/1976	101	CB
The Charmaines	What Kind Of Girl (Do You Think I Am)	29/07/1961	126	CB
The Charmaines	What Kind Of Girl (Do You Think I Am)	18/09/1961	117	BB
The Charmettes	Oozi-Oozi-Ooh	01/02/1964	124	CB
The Chartbusters	You're Breakin' My Heart	27/02/1965	135	CB
The Chartbusters	New Orleans [Live]	03/07/1965	134	BB
The Charts	Desiree	05/03/1966	105	CB
The Charts	Desiree (new Version)	26/03/1966	132	BB

The Cherry People	Feelings	01/03/1969	106	CB
The Cherry People	Feelings	15/03/1969	134	BB
The Cherry People	Light Of Love	02/08/1969	113	CB
The Cherry Slush	I Cannot Stop You	10/02/1968	103	CB
The Cherry Slush	I Cannot Stop You	24/02/1968	119	BB
The Chevrons	Come Go With Me	18/06/1960	124	CB
The Chi-Lites	The Twelfth Of Never	06/09/1969	137	CB
The Chi-Lites	The Twelfth Of Never	20/09/1969	122	BB
The Chi-Lites	24 Hours Of Sadness	07/02/1970	105	CB
The Chi-Lites	24 Hours Of Sadness	14/03/1970	119	BB
The Chi-Lites	Are You My Woman? (Tell Me So)	23/01/1971	108	CB
The Chi-Lites	There Will Never Be Any Peace (Until God Is Seated At The	18/05/1974	101	CB
The Chi-Lites	Toby	08/03/1975	104	CB
The Chi-Lites	It's Time For Love	15/11/1975	120	CB
The Chiffons	Tonight's The Night	17/09/1960	103	CB
The Chiffons	Easy To Love (Hard To Get)	21/03/1964	105	BB
The Chiffons	Easy To Love (So Hard To Get)	21/03/1964	118	CB
The Chiffons	Stop, Look And Listen	08/10/1966	133	CB
The Chiffons	My Boyfriend's Back	03/12/1966	117	BB
The Chiffons	My Boyfriend's Back	03/12/1966	133	CB
The Children	From The Very Start	07/11/1970	103	CB
The Children	From The Very Start	07/11/1970	105	BB
The Chipmunks	All My Loving	31/10/1964	139	CB
The Chipmunks	All My Loving	07/11/1964	134	BB
The Chipmunks	You May Be Right	09/08/1980	101	BB
The Chipmunks (Alvin, Simon & Theodore) With David Seville	Eefin' Alvin	19/10/1963	139	CB
The Choice Four	When You're Young And In Love	30/08/1975	103	CB
The Choice Four	Hey, What's That Dance You're Doing	01/05/1976	107	BB
The Choir	No One Here To Play With	19/08/1967	134	CB
The Chordettes	A Broken Vow	06/08/1960	117	CB

The Chordettes	A Broken Vow	08/08/1960	102	BB
The Chordettes	Faraway Star	30/09/1961	123	CB
The Chosen Few	Synthetic Man	22/10/1966	148	CB
The Church Street Five	A Night With Daddy "G" (Part 2)	20/02/1961	111	BB
The Church Street Five	A Night With Daddy "G" (Part 2)	04/03/1961	124	CB
The Cinderellas	Baby, Baby (I Still Love You)	23/05/1964	134	BB
The Cinders	The Cinnamon Cinder (It's A Very Nice Dance)	08/12/1962	108	CB
The Clams	First Time Ever I Saw Your Face	26/10/1974	124	CB
The Classics	Life Is But A Dream Sweetheart	05/06/1961	109	BB
The Classics	Life Is But A Dream Sweetheart	24/06/1961	137	CB
The Classics	P.S. I Love You	21/09/1963	120	BB
The Classics	P.S. I Love You	28/09/1963	141	CB
The Classics	Pollyanna	17/09/1966	106	BB
The Classics Iv	Nothing To Lose	14/01/1967	142	CB
The Clique	Splash 1	07/10/1967	113	BB
The Clovers	Lovey	26/03/1960	102	CB
The Clovers	The Honeydripper	22/05/1961	110	BB
The Clovers Featuring Buddy Bailey	Stop Pretending	03/08/1963	116	CB
The Clovers Featuring Buddy Bailey	Stop Pretending	17/08/1963	134	BB
The Coachmen	Mr. Moon	19/02/1966	114	BB
The Coasters	Bad Blood	18/11/1961	114	CB
The Coasters	(Ain't That) Just Like Me	25/11/1961	109	CB
The Coasters	Bad Detective	06/06/1964	118	CB
The Coasters	Down Home Girl	29/04/1967	133	CB
The Coastliners	She's My Girl	15/10/1966	121	BB
The Coastliners	California On My Mind	08/04/1967	115	BB
The Cobras	La La (Hey Baby)	29/08/1964	135	CB
The Coconuts	If I Only Had A Brain	27/08/1983	108	BB
The Committee	California My Way	28/10/1967	110	BB
The Concords	Again	29/07/1961	122	CB

The Concords	Marlene	09/02/1963	117	CB
The Continental 4	How Can I Pretend	27/11/1971	105	CB
The Contours	You Get Ugly	20/07/1963	109	CB
The Contrails (Vocal By Dick & Jack)	Someone	19/11/1966	130	CB
The Contrasts Featuring Bob Morrison	What A Day	13/04/1968	120	BB
The Controllers	Somebody's Gotta Win, Somebody's Gotta Lose	21/01/1978	102	BB
The Cookies	Softly In The Night	02/03/1963	127	CB
The Coronados	Johnny B. Goode	26/08/1967	128	CB
The Cotillions Feat. Gwen Richards	Sometimes I Get Lonely	11/05/1963	143	CB
The Cousins	St. Louis Blues	17/07/1961	110	BB
The Cowsills	Most Of All	16/07/1966	118	BB
The Cowsills	Most Of All	23/07/1966	119	CB
The Cowsills	The Candy Kid (From The Mission On The Bowery)	07/12/1968	118	BB
The Cowsills	The Candy Kid (From The Mission On The Bowery)	14/12/1968	128	CB
The Cowsills	On My Side	20/03/1971	109	CB
The Cowsills	On My Side	03/04/1971	108	BB
The Craftys	L-O-V-E	21/08/1961	104	BB
The Crawford Brothers (Johnny & BoBBy)	Good Buddies	19/01/1963	140	CB
The Crazy World Of Arthur Brown	Nightmare	30/11/1968	107	BB
The Crazy World Of Arthur Brown	I Put A Spell On You (b-side)	21/12/1968	111	BB
The Creep	Haldeman, Ehrlichman, Mitchell And Dean	01/09/1973	116	BB
The Crestones	She's A Bad Motorcycle	02/05/1964	123	CB
The Crestones	She's A Bad Mototcycle	23/05/1964	135	BB
The Crests	Guilty	29/12/1962	108	CB
The Crests	Guilty	02/02/1963	123	BB
The Crests Featuring Johnny Maestro	Journey Of Love	24/09/1960	111	CB
The Crests With Johnny Mastro	I Remember (In The Still Of The Night)	31/12/1960	102	BB
The Crests With Johnny Mastro	I Remember (In The Still Of The Night)	14/01/1961	116	CB
The Crickets	He's Old Enough To Know Better	02/12/1961	121	CB
The Crickets	He's Old Enough To Know Better	18/12/1961	105	BB

The Crickets	My Little Girl	23/03/1963	133	CB
The Crickets	My Little Girl	23/03/1963	134	BB
The Crickets	(They Call Her) La Bamba	06/06/1964	131	CB
The Critters	Marryin' Kind Of Love	04/02/1967	106	CB
The Critters	Marryin' Kind Of Love	18/02/1967	111	BB
The Critters	Little Girl	14/10/1967	105	CB
The Critters	Little Girl	21/10/1967	113	BB
The Cruisers	If I Knew	14/03/1960	102	BB
The Cruisers	If I Knew	26/03/1960	110	CB
The Crusaders	So Far Away	07/10/1972	102	CB
The Crusaders	So Far Away	11/11/1972	114	BB
The Crusaders	That's How I Feel	11/08/1973	105	CB
The Crusaders	Stomp And Buck Dance	15/02/1975	102	BB
The Cryan' Shames	Mr. Unreliable	25/03/1967	127	BB
The Cryan' Shames	Mr. Unreliable	01/04/1967	106	CB
The Cryan' Shames	Greenburg, Glickstein, Charles, David Smith & Jones	05/10/1968	115	BB
The Crystals	He Hit Me (And It Felt Like A Kiss)	04/08/1962	107	CB
The Crystals	My Place	06/11/1965	117	CB
The Cure	Let's Go To Bed	09/04/1983	109	BB
The Cure	The Love Cats	11/02/1984	107	BB
The Curtain Calls	Sock It To Me Sunshine	25/05/1968	116	BB
The Cy Coleman Co-Op	What Are Heavy?	22/07/1972	122	CB
The Cyrkle	Turn Of The Century	09/12/1967	112	BB
The Daisies	I Wanna Swim With Him	26/09/1964	133	BB
The Daniels	(I Lost My Love In The) Big City	30/07/1966	120	CB
The Dapps Featuring Alfred Ellis	There Was A Time	27/07/1968	103	BB
The Darnells	Too Hurt To Cry, Too Much In Love To Say Goodbye	23/11/1963	117	BB
The Dartells	Dance, Everybody, Dance	17/08/1963	145	CB
The Dartells Featuring Doug & Corky	Convicted	08/02/1964	146	CB
The Dave Clark Five	Here Comes Summer	25/07/1970	135	CB

The Daytrippers	That's Part Of The Game	26/02/1966	129	BB
The Deacons	Sock It To Me Part I	14/12/1968	121	BB
The Deaxville Trio	Shenandoah	30/09/1961	137	CB
The Deele	Material Thangz	08/06/1985	101	BB
The Deep Six	Rising Sun	27/11/1965	122	BB
The Deep Six	Rising Sun	11/12/1965	124	CB
The Deep Six	Counting	28/05/1966	147	CB
The Del Vikings	Bring Back Your Heart	22/05/1961	101	BB
The Del Vikings	Come Go With Me ('72 Version)	30/12/1972	101	CB
The Del Vikings	Come Go With Me (new Version)	27/01/1973	112	BB
The Delcos	Arabia	13/04/1963	123	CB
The Delcos	Arabia	20/04/1963	111	BB
The Delfonics	He Don't Really Love You	18/05/1968	117	CB
The Delfonics	Hey! Love	24/07/1971	124	CB
The Delfonics	Think It Over	27/01/1973	101	BB
The Delfonics	Alfie	04/08/1973	105	CB
The Delfonics	I Told You So	05/01/1974	107	CB
The Delfonics	I Told You So	16/02/1974	101	BB
The Delicates	Ronnie Is My Lover	24/08/1959	105	BB
The Delicates	I Want To Get Married	23/01/1965	148	CB
The Delicates	I Want To Get Married	30/01/1965	120	BB
The Delights Orchestra	Paul's Midnight Ride	26/10/1968	128	BB
The Dells	The (Bossa Nova) Bird	15/12/1962	123	CB
The Dells	Stay In My Corner	22/05/1965	131	CB
The Dells	Stay In My Corner	12/06/1965	122	BB
The Dells	When I'm In Your Arms	01/11/1969	108	BB
The Dells	Walk On By	15/07/1972	102	CB
The Dells	Bring Back The Love Of Yesterday	09/11/1974	123	CB
The Dells	We Got To Get Our Thing Together	20/12/1975	104	BB
The Dells	The Power Of Love	07/02/1976	106	BB

The Dells	Slow Motion	24/07/1976	102	BB
The Dells	Super Woman	09/09/1978	108	BB
The Dells	You Just Can't Walk Away	17/03/1984	107	BB
The Deltairs	Lullaby Of The Bells	17/04/1961	114	BB
The Demensions	Again	29/07/1961	112	CB
The Demensions	Young At Heart	14/07/1962	134	CB
The Diablos Featuring Nolan Strong	The Wind	27/06/1960	114	BB
The Diablos Featuring Nolan Strong	The Wind*	09/07/1960	121	CB
The Dillards	One A.M.	01/07/1972	111	BB
The Dillards	America (The Lady Of The Harbor)	25/11/1972	112	CB
The Dinks	Nina-Kocka-Nina	18/12/1965	125	CB
The Diplomats	Here's A Heart	11/01/1964	105	CB
The Diplomats	Help Me	09/05/1964	129	CB
The Diplomats	Love Ain't What It Used To Be	23/10/1965	137	CB
The Diplomats	I Can Give You Love	26/10/1968	117	BB
The Dirt Band	Badlands	18/10/1980	107	BB
The Disco Sound Of Andre Gagnon	Wow	13/03/1976	102	CB
The Distant Cousins	To Have And To Hold	24/04/1965	123	CB
The Distant Cousins	She Ain't Lovin' You	27/08/1966	102	BB
The Dixie Cups	Gee The Moon Is Shining Bright	03/07/1965	102	BB
The Dixie Cups	Gee The Moon Is Shining Bright	03/07/1965	126	CB
The Dixiebelles	New York Town	16/05/1964	119	BB
The Dixiebelles With Cornbread & Jerry	New York Town	23/05/1964	147	CB
The Dodgers	Don't Let Me Be Wrong	17/07/1976	107	CB
The Donays	Bad Boy	01/09/1962	126	CB
The Doobie Brothers	Nobody	17/07/1971	122	BB
The Doors	Break On Through (To The Other Side)	11/03/1967	104	CB
The Doors	Break On Through (To The Other Side)	08/04/1967	126	BB
The Doors	Light My Fire	28/09/1968	114	CB
The Doors	Get Up And Dance	01/07/1972	115	CB

The Dorians	Help For My Waiting	23/01/1971	112	CB
The Dovells	Dance The Froog	31/08/1963	117	CB
The Dovells	Stop Monkeyin' Aroun'	02/11/1963	108	CB
The Dovells	Be My Girl	15/02/1964	124	CB
The Dovells	Dancing In The Street	24/08/1974	105	BB
The Dramatics	You're Fooling You	24/01/1976	101	CB
The Dramatics	I Can't Get Over You	14/05/1977	101	BB
The Dramatics	Ocean Of Thoughts And Dreams	06/05/1978	106	BB
The Dramatics	Stop Your Weeping	29/07/1978	101	CB
The Dreamers	Teenage Vows Of Love	30/01/1961	104	BB
The Dreamlovers	Let Them Love (And Be Loved)	28/10/1961	104	CB
The Dreamlovers	Let Them Love (And Be Loved)	30/10/1961	102	BB
The Dreamlovers	I Miss You	23/06/1962	115	BB
The Dreamlovers	You Gave Me Somebody To Love	08/05/1965	121	BB
The Dreamlovers	You Gave Me Somebody To Love	05/06/1965	133	CB
The Dregs	Crank It Up	17/04/1982	110	BB
The Drifters	Room Full Of Tears	02/12/1961	102	CB
The Drifters	Stranger On The Shore	12/05/1962	103	CB
The Drifters	Sometimes I Wonder	14/07/1962	118	CB
The Drifters	If You Don't Come Back	06/07/1963	116	CB
The Drifters	If You Don't Come Back	13/07/1963	101	BB
The Drifters	He's Just A Playboy	07/11/1964	115	BB
The Drifters	The Outside World	26/06/1965	112	CB
The Drifters	Follow Me	03/07/1965	111	CB
The Drifters	We Gotta Sing	04/12/1965	130	CB
The Drifters	Up In The Streets Of Harlem	11/06/1966	115	CB
The Drifters	You Can't Love Them All	25/06/1966	127	BB
The Drifters	Ain't It The Truth	19/08/1967	135	CB
The Drifters	Still Burning In My Heart	06/01/1968	111	BB
The Drifters	Kissin' In The Back Row Of The Movies	31/08/1974	114	CB

The Drums Of Earl Palmer	New Orleans Medley: I'm Walkin' / Blueberry Hill / Ain't That A Shame	19/08/1961	132	CB
The Ducanes	I'm So Happy (Tra La La)	17/07/1961	109	BB
The Ducanes	I'm So Happy (Tra La La)	29/07/1961	111	CB
The Duprees	The Exodus Song	30/04/1966	118	CB
The Duprees	Goodnight My Love	16/11/1968	113	BB
The Duprees	Two Different Worlds	26/04/1969	133	CB
The Duprees Featuring Joey Vann	I Gotta Tell Her Now	25/05/1963	141	CB
The Duprees Featuring Joey Vann	Where Are You	04/04/1964	114	BB
The Dutones	The Bird	02/02/1963	117	CB
The Dutones	The Bird	16/02/1963	101	BB
The Dynamics	Chapel On A Hill	02/11/1963	150	CB
The Earls	Life Is But A Dream	05/06/1961	107	BB
The Earls	Never	09/03/1963	119	BB
The Earls	Eyes	22/06/1963	111	CB
The Earls	Eyes	06/07/1963	123	BB
The Earls Featuring Larry Chance	Cry, Cry, Cry	07/09/1963	150	CB
The Earls Featuring Larry Chance	Kissin'	14/09/1963	147	CB
The Easybeats	Falling Off The Edge Of The World (Seeing You With Him)	23/09/1967	138	CB
The Easybeats	Gonna Have A Good Time (Good Times)	22/02/1969	144	CB
The Ebonys	I Believe	18/05/1974	104	CB
The Echoes	Born To Be With You	23/05/1960	101	BB
The Echoes	Sad Eyes (Don't You Cry)	10/06/1961	102	CB
The Echoes	Gee Oh Gee	05/08/1961	127	CB
The Echoes	Gee Oh Gee	21/08/1961	112	BB
The Echoes With The Stephen Scott Singers	Bluebirds Over The Mountain	27/10/1962	112	BB
The Edsels	What Brought Us Together	14/01/1961	125	CB
The Edsels	Three Precious Words	12/08/1961	148	CB
The Edsels	Shake Shake Sherry	24/02/1962	113	CB
The Eighth Day	Hey Boy! (The Girl's In Love With You)	02/12/1967	130	CB
The Electras	Ten Steps To Love	20/01/1962	140	CB

The Electric Indian	Rain Dance	28/03/1970	115	CB
The Electric Prunes	Dr. Do-Good	24/06/1967	105	CB
The Electric Prunes	Dr. Do-Good	01/07/1967	128	BB
The Electric Prunes	The Great Banana Hoax	05/08/1967	142	CB
The Elektras	All I Want To Do Is Run	11/05/1963	125	CB
The Elektras	All I Want To Do Is Run	22/06/1963	126	BB
The Elephants Memory	Crossroads Of The Stepping Stones	07/06/1969	120	BB
The Elephants Memory	Crossroads Of The Stepping Stones	05/07/1969	124	CB
The Eligibles	Car Trouble	01/06/1959	107	BB
The Embers	Solitaire	12/06/1961	103	BB
The Embers	I Won't Cry Anymore	11/11/1961	113	CB
The Embers	Abigail	25/08/1962	104	CB
The Embers	Abigail	25/08/1962	117	BB
The Emotions	L-O-V-E (Love)	23/02/1963	119	CB
The Emotions	A Story Untold	12/10/1963	110	BB
The Emotions	The Best Part Of A Love Affair	13/09/1969	101	BB
The Emotions	Heart Association	29/08/1970	126	CB
The Emotions	My Honey And Me	25/03/1972	113	BB
The Emotions	From Toys To Boys	30/12/1972	116	CB
The Emotions	From Toys To Boys	20/01/1973	112	BB
The Emotions	Shouting Out Love	28/01/1978	105	CB
The Emotions	Smile	12/08/1978	102	BB
The Enchanters	I Wanna Thank You	12/09/1964	121	CB
The English Congregation	Jesahel	22/07/1972	109	BB
The Entertainers Iv	Temptation Walk (People Don't Look No More)	12/02/1966	113	CB
The Escorts	Somewhere	15/12/1962	119	CB
The Escorts	Let's Make Love (At Home Sometime)	03/08/1974	116	CB
The Esquires	You Say	24/02/1968	113	CB
The Esquires	You Say	09/03/1968	126	BB
The Esquires	Why Can't I Stop	27/04/1968	131	CB

The Esquires	Girls In The City	13/03/1971	120	BB
The Eternals	Babalu's Wedding Day	19/12/1959	108	CB
The Everly Brothers	Brand New Heartache	14/11/1960	109	BB
The Everly Brothers	All I Have To Do Is Dream	05/08/1961	133	CB
The Everly Brothers	No One Can Make My Sunshine Smile	20/10/1962	102	CB
The Everly Brothers	No One Can Make My Sunshine Smile	03/11/1962	117	BB
The Everly Brothers	Nancy's Minuet	16/03/1963	116	CB
The Everly Brothers	Nancy's Minuet	30/03/1963	107	BB
The Everly Brothers	(So It Was...So It Is) So It Will Always Be (b-side)	30/03/1963	116	BB
The Everly Brothers	It's Been Nice (Goodnight)	25/05/1963	114	CB
The Everly Brothers	It's Been Nice (Goodnight)	01/06/1963	101	BB
The Everly Brothers	Love Her	19/10/1963	104	CB
The Everly Brothers	Love Her	26/10/1963	117	BB
The Everly Brothers	Ain't That Lovin' You Baby	02/05/1964	133	BB
The Everly Brothers	You're My Girl	06/02/1965	110	BB
The Everly Brothers	You're My Girl	13/02/1965	136	CB
The Everly Brothers	That'll Be The Day	20/03/1965	111	BB
The Everly Brothers	The Price Of Love	15/05/1965	104	BB
The Everly Brothers	The Price Of Love	29/05/1965	118	CB
The Everly Brothers	Love Is Strange	21/08/1965	128	BB
The Everly Brothers	Love Of The Common People	04/11/1967	114	BB
The Everly Brothers	It's My Time	18/05/1968	112	BB
The Everly Brothers	Lord Of The Manor	05/10/1968	121	CB
The Exciters	Get Him	15/06/1963	115	CB
The Exciters	Do-Wah-Diddy	14/12/1963	103	CB
The Exciters	I Want You To Be My Boy	09/01/1965	106	CB
The Exciters	You Better Come Home	02/04/1966	123	CB
The Exiles	Church St. Soul Revival	24/01/1970	104	BB
The Exiles	Church St. Soul Revival	31/01/1970	101	CB
The Exits	Under The Street Lamp	26/08/1967	116	BB

The Exports	Car Hop	12/09/1964	128	CB
The Fabulous Rhinestones	Freewheelin'	08/09/1973	105	CB
The Falcons	You're Mine	05/10/1959	107	BB
The Falcons	Just For Your Love	19/12/1959	125	CB
The Falcons	Standing On Guard	22/10/1966	101	CB
The Falcons	Standing On Guard	05/11/1966	107	BB
The Family	Face The Autumn	18/11/1967	113	CB
The Fantastic Baggys	It Was I	27/03/1965	115	CB
The Fantastic Four	I Feel Like I'm Falling In Love Again	12/04/1969	111	BB
The Fantastic Johnny C	Is There Anything Better Than Making Love?	01/03/1969	129	CB
The Fantastic Johnny C	Is There Anything Better Than Making Love?	22/03/1969	130	BB
The Fantastics	Something Old, Something New	22/05/1971	111	CB
The Fantastics	Something Old, Something New	29/05/1971	102	BB
The Fascinations	Mama Didn't Lie	12/01/1963	108	BB
The Fascinations	(Say It Isn't So) Say You'd Never Go	03/09/1966	142	CB
The Fasinations	Mama Didn't Lie	02/02/1963	125	CB
The Fastest Group Alive	The Bears	26/11/1966	121	CB
The Fastest Group Alive	The Bears	26/11/1966	133	BB
The Fat Albert Orchestra & Chorus	Fat Albert (Hey, Hey, Hey)	20/04/1968	103	CB
The Fat Albert Orchestra And Chorus	Fat Albert (Hey, Hey, Hey)	27/04/1968	120	BB
The Fatback Band	Street Dance	07/07/1973	121	CB
The Fatback Band	Njia (Nija) Walk (Street Walk)	03/11/1973	122	CB
The Fatback Band	Spanish Hustle	27/03/1976	101	BB
The Fawns	Wish You Were Here With Me	04/11/1967	118	CB
The Fendermen	Don't You Just Know It	26/09/1960	110	BB
The Fenways	Walk	27/02/1965	129	CB
The Festivals	Music	29/10/1966	130	BB
The Festivals	You're Gonna Make It	19/09/1970	114	BB
The Festivals	Baby Show It	24/04/1971	116	BB
The Fidelitys	Walk With The Wind	26/03/1960	115	CB

The Fiestas	I Feel Good All Over	24/11/1962	123	BB
The Fifth Estate	Do Drop Inn	16/03/1968	122	BB
The Fifth Estate	Do Drop Inn	23/03/1968	115	CB
The Fifth Order	Goin' Too Far	12/11/1966	127	CB
The Fireballs	Foot-Patter	23/04/1960	111	CB
The First Edition	I Found A Reason	25/11/1967	121	CB
The First Edition	Only Me	04/05/1968	102	CB
The First Edition	Only Me	11/05/1968	133	BB
The First Edition	Are My Thoughts With You	12/10/1968	119	BB
The First Edition	Once Again She's All Alone	17/05/1969	126	BB
The Five Americans	Good Times	16/07/1966	135	CB
The Five Americans	Stop Light	04/11/1967	123	CB
The Five Americans	Stop Light	11/11/1967	132	BB
The Five Americans	7:30 Guided Tour	16/12/1967	103	CB
The Five Americans	Lovin' Is Livin'	21/09/1968	131	CB
The Five Americans	She's Too Good To Me	27/09/1969	137	CB
The Five Counts	Watermelon Walk	01/12/1962	139	CB
The Five Satins	When Your Love Comes Along	01/06/1959	112	BB
The Five Satins	In The Still Of The Nite	28/11/1959	108	CB
The Five Satins	I'll Be Seeing You	09/04/1960	107	CB
The Five Satins	The Masquerade Is Over	09/06/1962	114	CB
The Five Satins	The Masquerade Is Over	21/07/1962	102	BB
The Five Whispers	Midnight Sun	13/10/1962	115	BB
The Fixx	Red Skies	12/03/1983	101	BB
The Flaming Ember	Stop The World And Let Me Off	13/02/1971	101	BB
The Flaming Ember	Sunshine	15/05/1971	108	CB
The Flaming Ember	Sunshine	22/05/1971	117	BB
The Flamingos	When I Fall In Love	12/11/1960	107	CB
The Flamingos	Kokomo	11/03/1961	107	CB
The Flamingos	Golden Teardrops	21/08/1961	108	BB

The Flamingos	Lovers Never Say Goodbye	09/10/1961	117	BB
The Flamingos	I Know Better	04/05/1963	107	BB
The Flamingos	I Know Better	11/05/1963	126	CB
The Flamingos	Dealin' (Groovin' With The Feelin')	13/09/1969	142	CB
The Flares	Make It Be Me	08/09/1962	136	CB
The Flares	The Monkey Walk	09/11/1963	133	BB
The Fleetwoods	Magic Star	15/02/1960	113	BB
The Fleetwoods	Confidential	17/12/1960	111	CB
The Fleetwoods	You Should Have Been There	06/04/1963	107	CB
The Fleetwoods	You Should Have Been There	13/04/1963	114	BB
The Fleetwoods	Ruby Red, Baby Blue	16/05/1964	134	BB
The Fleetwoods	Mr. Sandman	29/08/1964	113	BB
The Fleetwoods	Mr. Sandman	29/08/1964	119	CB
The Flirtations	South Carolina	26/07/1969	111	BB
The Flirtations	South Carolina	02/08/1969	104	CB
The Floaters	You Don't Have To Say You Love Me	05/11/1977	102	CB
The Floaters	I Just Want To Be With You	08/07/1978	103	BB
The Flock	Take Me Back	02/09/1967	131	CB
The Flower Pot Men	In A Moment Of Madness	20/09/1969	129	CB
The Flying Machine	Night Owl	08/07/1967	143	CB
The Flying Machine	Hanging On The Edge Of Sadness	23/05/1970	135	CB
The Fortune Tellers	Song Of The Nairobi Trio	25/09/1961	114	BB
The Foundations	Any Old Time (You're Lonely And Sad)	15/06/1968	117	CB
The Foundations	Stoney Ground	26/02/1972	113	BB
The Four Aces	Always Keep Me In Your Heart	05/04/1969	120	CB
The Four Coachmen	Wintertime	21/12/1959	113	BB
The Four Coins	My First Love	01/06/1959	106	BB
The Four Coquettes	Sparkle And Shine	08/04/1961	103	CB
The Four Coquettes	Sparkle And Shine	01/05/1961	107	BB
The Four Lads	Thanks Mr. Florist	10/04/1965	126	CB

The Four Larks	Rain	04/11/1967	140	CB
The Four Pennies	When The Boy's Happy (The Girl's Happy Too)	02/11/1963	129	CB
The Four Pennies	Juliet	20/06/1964	140	CB
The Four Pennies	Juliet	27/06/1964	116	BB
The Four Preps	Big Surprise	20/07/1959	111	BB
The Four Preps	Madelina	23/07/1960	114	CB
The Four Preps	Once Around The Block	16/12/1961	134	CB
The Four Preps	Alice	14/07/1962	146	CB
The Four Preps	Charmaine	15/06/1963	123	CB
The Four Preps	Charmaine	29/06/1963	116	BB
The Four Seasons	Apple Of My Eye	03/10/1964	117	CB
The Four Seasons	Apple Of My Eye (new Version)	10/10/1964	106	BB
The Four Seasons	Since I Don't Have You	03/04/1965	105	BB
The Four Seasons	Since I Don't Have You	10/04/1965	110	CB
The Four Speeds	R.P.M.	27/04/1963	124	CB
The Four Tops	Tonight I'm Gonna Love You All Over	20/02/1982	1102	CB
The Four Voices	Sealed With A Kiss	09/07/1960	109	CB
The Four-Evers	Everybody South Street	20/04/1963	125	BB
The Four-Evers	(Say I Love You) Doo Bee Dum	05/09/1964	125	CB
The Four-Evers	(Say I Love You) Doo Bee Dum	12/09/1964	119	BB
The Fourmost	Here, There And Everywhere	24/09/1966	120	BB
The Frankie Miller Band	A Fool In Love	20/12/1975	101	CB
The Frantics	Werewolf	12/03/1960	113	CB
The Free Design	Kites Are Fun	11/11/1967	119	CB
The Free Design	Kites Are Fun	23/12/1967	114	BB
The Freeman Brothers	My Baby	24/04/1965	127	CB
The Freewheelers	Walk, Walk	04/04/1964	117	CB
The Freewheelers	Walk, Walk	04/04/1964	119	BB
The Frost	Rock And Roll Music (Live)	31/01/1970	123	CB
The Frost	Rock And Roll Music [Live]	21/02/1970	105	BB

The Furys	Zing! Went The Strings Of My Heart	19/01/1963	108	CB
The G.T.O.'s	She Rides With Me	21/05/1966	105	CB
The Gallahads	Lonely Guy	06/08/1960	103	CB
The Gallahads	Lonely Guy	15/08/1960	111	BB
The Gamblers	Moon Dawg!	21/05/1960	117	CB
The Gants	Little Boy Sad	22/01/1966	125	CB
The Gap Band	Shake	02/06/1979	101	BB
The Gap Band	Steppin' (Out)	02/02/1980	103	BB
The Gap Band	I Don't Believe You Want To Get Up And Dance (Opps, Up Side Your	29/03/1980	102	BB
The Gap Band	Party Train	10/09/1983	101	BB
The Gap Band	Beep A Freak	12/01/1985	103	BB
The Gayletts	Son-Of-A-Preacherman	23/08/1969	138	CB
The Gentrys	Brown Paper Sack	08/01/1966	101	BB
The Gentrys	Brown Paper Sack	08/01/1966	115	CB
The Gentrys	Everyday I Have To Cry	28/05/1966	115	CB
The Gentrys	A Woman Of The World	27/08/1966	119	CB
The Gentrys	A Woman Of The World	03/09/1966	112	BB
The Gentrys	You Make Me Feel So Good	18/03/1967	130	BB
The Gentrys	I Can't Go Back To Denver	11/05/1968	132	BB
The Gentrys	He'll Never Love You	25/07/1970	129	CB
The Gentrys	He'll Never Love You	01/08/1970	116	BB
The Gentrys	Goddess Of Love	21/11/1970	119	BB
The Gentrys	Goddess Of Love	21/11/1970	121	CB
The Gentrys	Little Gold Band	14/09/1974	110	CB
The Gestures	Don't Mess Around	06/03/1965	141	CB
The Giant Sunflower	What's So Good About Good-Bye	14/10/1967	104	CB
The Gilberto Sextet	Good Lovin'	05/11/1966	131	CB
The Glass Bottle	Love For Living	30/05/1970	109	BB
The Glass Bottle	Sorry Suzanne	18/07/1970	130	CB
The Glass House	Stealing Moments From Another Woman's Life	07/11/1970	121	BB

The Glass House	Touch Me Jesus	26/06/1971	118	CB
The Glass House	Look What We've Done To Love	30/10/1971	101	BB
The Glass House	Look What We've Done To Love	13/11/1971	107	CB
The Gleams	You Broke My Heart	04/09/1961	117	BB
The Glencoves	Devil's Waitin' (On Bald Mountain)	16/11/1963	140	CB
The Glories	(I Love You Babe But) Give Me My Freedom	16/09/1967	124	BB
The Goldebriars	Shenandoah	06/06/1964	142	CB
The Golden Gate	Diane	21/02/1970	104	CB
The Golden Gate	Diane	14/03/1970	105	BB
The Good Earth	I Can See A Light	28/09/1968	133	CB
The Good Rats	The Hobo	16/11/1968	116	CB
The Goodtimes	The Hard Life	29/10/1966	145	CB
The Grass Roots	Mr. Jones (A Ballad Of A Thin Man)	09/10/1965	104	CB
The Grass Roots	Mr. Jones (A Ballad Of A Thin Man)	30/10/1965	121	BB
The Grass Roots	A Melody For You	24/02/1968	123	BB
The Grass Roots	A Melody For You	02/03/1968	120	CB
The Grass Roots	Anyway The Wind Blows	07/10/1972	101	CB
The Grass Roots	Anyway The Wind Blows	07/10/1972	107	BB
The Grassroots	Feelings	13/04/1968	118	CB
The Green River Boys Featuring Glen Campbell	Kentucky Means Paradise	15/12/1962	144	CB
The Green River Boys Featuring Glen Campbell	Kentucky Means Paradise	29/12/1962	114	BB
The Groop	A Famous Myth	05/07/1969	110	CB
The Groop	The Jet Song (When The Weekend's Over)	29/11/1969	112	BB
The Gross National Product	Cover Girl	05/07/1969	119	CB
The Guess Who	Rosanne	16/08/1975	103	CB
The Guess Who	Rosanne	30/08/1975	105	BB
The Guess Who	When The Band Was Singin' "Shaking All Over"	08/11/1975	102	BB
The Guides	You Must Try	10/10/1959	103	CB
The Guilloteens	I Don't Believe "Call On Me"	07/08/1965	108	CB
The Guise (& Their Mod Sound)	Long Haired Music	26/11/1966	110	CB

The Guise (and Their Mod Sound)	Long Haired Music	05/11/1966	123	BB
The Gun	Race With The Devil	15/02/1969	129	CB
The Gurus	Blue Snow Night	26/11/1966	126	CB
The Gypsies	Jerk It	01/05/1965	106	CB
The Gypsies	Jerk It	08/05/1965	111	BB
The Handclappers	Three Gassed Rats	02/09/1961	133	CB
The Hands Of Time	Got To Get You Into My Life	15/10/1966	127	CB
The Happenings	Randy	11/05/1968	118	BB
The Happenings	Crazy Rhythm	19/10/1968	111	CB
The Happenings	Crazy Rhythm	26/10/1968	114	BB
The Happenings	Answer Me, My Love	17/01/1970	115	BB
The Happenings	Tomorrow Today Will Be Yesterday	09/05/1970	111	CB
The Happenings	Crazy Love	11/07/1970	113	CB
The Happy Sound Of Johnny Mendell With Gill & His Premiers	Jingle Bell Twist U.S.A.	16/12/1961	115	CB
The Hardtimes	Fortune Teller	17/12/1966	117	CB
The Hardy Boys	Love And Let Love	20/09/1969	103	CB
The Hardy Boys	Love And Let Love	04/10/1969	101	BB
The Harlequins	Everybody Fish - Part Ii	14/10/1961	127	CB
The Harptones	What Will I Tell My Heart	20/05/1961	145	CB
The Hassles	You've Got Me Hummin'	25/11/1967	112	BB
The Hassles	Every Step I Take (Every Move I Make)	02/03/1968	133	CB
The Hawk	In The Mood	12/11/1960	117	CB
The Hello People	(As I Went Down To) Jerusalem	24/08/1968	123	BB
The Hesitations	Soul Superman	10/12/1966	112	CB
The Hesitations	Who Will Answer	06/07/1968	112	BB
The Hesitations	Who Will Answer	06/07/1968	113	CB
The Hi-Lites	Hey Baby	01/05/1965	128	BB
The Highwaymen	Pretoria	02/03/1963	138	CB
The Hillside Singers	Kum Ba Yah	13/05/1972	112	CB
The Hit Parade	Ah, Ha, Ha, Do Your Thing	10/05/1969	131	BB

The Holidays	No Greater Love	13/08/1966	107	CB
The Hollies	Here I Go Again	08/08/1964	107	BB
The Hollies	Here I Go Again	08/08/1964	118	CB
The Hollies	I'm Alive	07/08/1965	103	BB
The Hollies	Do The Best You Can	24/08/1968	133	CB
The Hollies	Listen To Me	09/11/1968	129	BB
The Hollies	Hey Willy	04/09/1971	110	BB
The Hollies	Jesus Was A Crossmaker	26/05/1973	105	CB
The Hollies	Another Night	31/05/1975	101	CB
The Hollies	I'm Down	04/10/1975	104	BB
The Hollyridge Strings	Love Me Do	18/07/1964	134	BB
The Hollyridge Strings	All My Loving	18/07/1964	144	CB
The Hollywood Persuaders	Drums A-Go-Go	04/09/1965	109	BB
The Hollywood Persuaders	Drums A-Go-Go	16/10/1965	143	CB
The Hollywood Stars	All The Kids On The Street	30/04/1977	102	CB
The Holy Modal Rounders	Boobs A Lot	02/02/1974	103	BB
The Hombres	It's A Gas	13/01/1968	113	BB
The Hombres	The Prodigal	04/05/1968	110	CB
The Hombres	Take My Overwhelming Love (And Cram It Up Your Heart)	16/11/1968	115	CB
The Hondells	Sea Cruise	16/10/1965	110	CB
The Hondells	Sea Cruise	16/10/1965	131	BB
The Hondells	Kissin' My Life Away	13/08/1966	118	BB
The Hondells	Kissin' My Life Away	20/08/1966	109	CB
The Honey Cone	Take Me With You	11/04/1970	108	BB
The Honey Cone	When Will It End	05/09/1970	113	CB
The Honey Cone	When Will It End	19/09/1970	117	BB
The Honey Cone	Innocent Til Proven Guilty	07/10/1972	101	BB
The Honeycombs	That's The Way	17/04/1965	143	CB
The Horizons	Hey Now Baby	28/11/1964	147	CB
The HuBBels	Hippy Dippy Funky Monkey Double BuBBle Sitar Man	14/06/1969	112	CB

The Hues Corporation	Miracle Maker (Sweet Soul Shaker)	17/11/1973	112	CB
The Hullaballoos	Did You Ever	20/02/1965	107	CB
The Hullaballoos	Learning The Game	01/05/1965	121	BB
The Human Beings	Because I Love Her	19/06/1965	136	CB
The Hummers	Old Betsy Goes Boing, Boing, Boing	30/06/1973	105	CB
The Hummers	Old Betsy Goes Boing, Boing, Boing	25/08/1973	104	BB
The Hutch Davie Calliope Band	D.W. Washburn/L. David Sloane (A Good Man Is Hard To Find)	31/08/1968	137	CB
The Ideals	The Gorilla	21/09/1963	134	CB
The Ideals	The Gorilla	12/10/1963	127	BB
The Ideals	You Lost And I Won	18/12/1965	148	CB
The Ides Of March	Roller Coaster	17/09/1966	112	CB
The Ides Of March	Melody	03/10/1970	121	CB
The Ides Of March	Melody	03/10/1970	122	BB
The Ides Of March	Tie-Dye Princess	31/07/1971	113	BB
The Ikettes	Troubles On My Mind	12/05/1962	132	CB
The Ikettes	No Bail In This Jail (Prisoner In Love)	11/05/1963	126	BB
The Ikettes	(He's Gonna Be) Fine, Fine, Fine	15/05/1965	106	CB
The Ikettes	(He's Gonna Be) Fine, Fine, Fine	29/05/1965	125	BB
The Ikettes	(Never More) Lonely For You	22/01/1966	122	BB
The Iketts	Camel Walk	13/02/1965	107	BB
The Iketts	Camel Walk	20/02/1965	135	CB
The Illusion	Did You See Her Eyes	15/03/1969	133	CB
The Illusion	How Does It Feel	11/10/1969	108	CB
The Illusion	How Does It Feel	11/10/1969	110	BB
The Illusion	Let's Make Each Other Happy	20/06/1970	118	CB
The Imaginations	Goodnight Baby	27/05/1961	131	CB
The Impressions	Grow Closer Together	27/01/1962	117	CB
The Impressions	Little Young Lover	30/06/1962	130	CB
The Impressions	Minstrel And Queen	29/09/1962	113	CB
The Impressions	Minstrel And Queen	13/10/1962	113	BB

The Impressions	I'm The One Who Loves You	09/02/1963	116	CB
The Impressions	Sad, Sad Girl And Boy	25/05/1963	104	CB
The Impressions	Long, Long Winter	21/11/1964	122	CB
The Impressions	I've Been Trying	20/02/1965	133	BB
The Impressions	You Got Me Runnin'	10/06/1967	120	CB
The Impressions	My Deceiving Heart	22/02/1969	104	BB
The Impressions	Amen (1970)	20/12/1969	110	BB
The Impressions	Wherever She Leadeth Me (b-side)	24/01/1970	128	BB
The Impressions	Love Me	07/08/1971	111	CB
The Impressions	This Love's For Real	22/04/1972	119	CB
The In Crowd	The Girl In The Black Bikini	28/08/1965	121	CB
The In Crowd	Hangin' From Your Lovin' Tree	25/05/1968	131	BB
The Incredible Bongo Band	Let There Be Drums	20/10/1973	107	BB
The Incredibles	I'll Make It Easy (If You'll Come On Home)	10/12/1966	108	BB
The Incredibles	I'll Make It Easy (If You Come On Home)	21/01/1967	143	CB
The Incredibles	Heart And Soul	15/07/1967	116	CB
The Incredibles	Heart And Soul	29/07/1967	122	BB
The Independents	I Just Want To Be There	23/09/1972	114	CB
The Independents	I Just Want To Be There	28/10/1972	113	BB
The Independents	The First Time We Met	19/01/1974	103	BB
The Independents	Arise And Shine (Let's Get It On)	22/06/1974	121	CB
The Inmates	The Walk	16/02/1980	107	BB
The Innocence	All I Do Is Think About You	03/06/1967	140	CB
The Innocents	Beware	24/06/1961	148	CB
The Inspirations	Touch Me, Kiss Me, Hold Me	11/03/1967	130	CB
The Intrigues	Just A Little Bit More	16/05/1970	111	CB
The Intruders	Gonna Be Strong	09/04/1966	108	CB
The Intruders	Devil With An Angel's Smile	26/11/1966	117	CB
The Intruders	It Must Be Love	04/03/1967	127	CB
The Intruders	Give Her A Transplant	08/02/1969	104	BB

The Intruders	Lollipop (I Like You)	14/06/1969	101	BB
The Intruders	Tender (Was The Love We Knew)	28/02/1970	101	CB
The Intruders	Tender (Was The Love We Knew)	28/03/1970	119	BB
The Intruders	Pray For Me	03/07/1971	105	BB
The Intruders	(Win, Place Or Show) She's A Winner	02/09/1972	104	CB
The Invincibles	Heart Full Of Love	06/03/1965	132	CB
The Invitations	Hallelujah	10/07/1965	111	BB
The Invitations	They Say The Girl's Crazy	21/04/1973	101	CB
The Invitations	They Say The Girl's Crazy	16/06/1973	110	BB
The Irish Rovers	Lily The Pink	15/02/1969	113	BB
The Irish Rovers	Lily The Pink	22/03/1969	104	CB
The Irish Rovers	Rhymes And Reasons	07/03/1970	130	CB
The Irish Rovers	Years May Come, Years May Go	22/08/1970	119	CB
The Isley Brothers	Respectable	23/01/1960	123	CB
The Isley Brothers	Shout - Part 1	07/10/1961	138	CB
The Isley Brothers	The Snake	10/02/1962	140	CB
The Isley Brothers	Nobody But Me	12/01/1963	109	CB
The Isley Brothers	Nobody But Me	26/01/1963	106	BB
The Isley Brothers	The Last Girl	20/02/1965	119	CB
The Isley Brothers	Simon Says	13/03/1965	107	CB
The Isley Brothers	Simon Says	27/03/1965	131	BB
The Isley Brothers	Love Is A Wonderful Thing	17/09/1966	110	BB
The Isley Brothers	That's The Way Love Is	22/07/1967	105	CB
The Isley Brothers	That's The Way Love Is	05/08/1967	125	BB
The Isley Brothers	Take Me In Your Arms (Rock Me A Little While)	13/04/1968	121	BB
The Isley Brothers	Bless Your Heart	22/11/1969	101	CB
The Isley Brothers	Bless Your Heart	06/12/1969	105	BB
The Isley Brothers	If He Can, You Can	25/04/1970	113	BB
The Isley Brothers	If He Can, You Can	09/05/1970	110	CB
The Isley Brothers	Between The Sheets	18/06/1983	101	BB

The Ivy League	Funny How Love Can Be	10/04/1965	124	CB
The Ivy League	Our Love Is Slipping Away	04/12/1965	139	CB
The J. Geils Band	Southside Shuffle	22/09/1973	115	CB
The J. Geils Band	Givin' It All Up	22/02/1975	106	BB
The J's With Jamie	Theme From "A Summer Place"	25/07/1964	131	CB
The J's With Jamie	Theme From "A Summer Place"	08/08/1964	115	BB
The Jack Cole Quintet	Sax Fifth Avenue*	02/03/1963	106	CB
The Jagged Edge	Deep Inside	27/08/1966	129	BB
The Jaggerz	What A Bummer	15/08/1970	102	CB
The Jaggerz	2 + 2	29/03/1975	118	CB
The James Gang	Funk No. 48	13/12/1969	126	BB
The James Gang	Looking For My Lady	27/05/1972	108	BB
The James Gang	Looking For My Lady	10/06/1972	108	CB
The James Gang	Had Enough	14/10/1972	123	CB
The James Gang	Had Enough	04/11/1972	111	BB
The James Gang	Standing In The Rain	25/05/1974	101	BB
The Jarmels	Little Lonely One	25/03/1961	109	CB
The Jaynetts	Keep An Eye On Her	09/11/1963	135	CB
The Jaynetts	Keep An Eye On Her	16/11/1963	120	BB
The Jaynetts	Snowman, Snowman, Sweet Potato Nose	21/12/1963	149	CB
The Jazztet Featuring Art Farmer & Benny Golson (Narration: Benny	Killer Joe	06/08/1960	101	CB
The Jerms	Green Door	17/05/1969	115	CB
The Jerms	Green Door	31/05/1969	129	BB
The Jerry Hahn Brotherhood	Captain BoBBy Stout	11/07/1970	135	CB
The Jesters	The Wind	20/06/1960	110	BB
The Jesters	The Wind	09/07/1960	121	CB
The Jet Stream	All's Quiet On West 23rd	10/06/1967	101	BB
The Jet Stream	All's Quiet On West 23rd	17/06/1967	115	CB
The Jewels	But I Do	26/06/1965	130	BB
The Jimi Hendrix Experience	Up From The Skies	09/03/1968	109	CB

The Jimi Hendrix Experience	Stone Free	04/10/1969	113	CB
The Jimi Hendrix Experience	Stone Free	18/10/1969	130	BB
The Jive Five	In My Neighborhood	23/07/1966	134	CB
The Jive Five Featuring Eugene Pitt	A Bench In The Park	16/10/1965	112	CB
The Jive Five Featuring Eugene Pitt	A Bench In The Park	30/10/1965	106	BB
The Jive Five Featuring Eugene Pitt	Goin' Wild	02/04/1966	129	CB
The Jive Five Featuring Eugene Pitt	Crying Like A Baby	29/07/1967	127	BB
The Jive Five Featuring Eugene Pitt	Sugar (Don't Take Away My Candy)	04/05/1968	131	CB
The John Hall Band	You Sure Fooled Me	17/04/1982	109	BB
The Johnny Gibson Trio	Beachcomber	06/06/1964	134	CB
The Johnny Gibson Trio	Beachcomber	13/06/1964	116	BB
The Johnny Harris Orchestra	Footprints On The Moon	13/09/1969	134	CB
The Johnny Mann Singers	Cinnamint Shuffle (Mexican Shuffle)	09/04/1966	102	CB
The Johnson Family	Peace In The Family	20/09/1975	124	CB
The Johnstons	Both Sides Now	19/10/1968	106	CB
The Johnstons	Both Sides Now	09/11/1968	128	BB
The Jones Boys	Impressions	27/08/1966	104	CB
The Jones Boys	Impressions	03/09/1966	101	BB
The Jonzun Crew	Pack Jam (Look Out For The Ovc)	30/10/1982	108	BB
The Jordan Bros.	Gimme Some Lovin'	21/01/1967	129	BB
The Juveniles	Bo Diddley	11/12/1965	140	CB
The Kalin Twins	Why Don't You Believe Me	05/12/1959	105	CB
The Kalin Twins (Herbie & Hal)	Zing! Went The Strings Of My Heart	05/11/1960	103	CB
The Kalin Twins (Herbie & Hal)	Zing! Went The Strings Of My Heart	05/12/1960	112	BB
The Keane Brothers	Sherry	04/12/1976	103	CB
The Keepers Of The Light	And I Don't Want Your Love	01/07/1967	145	CB
The Kenjolairs	Little White Lies	29/12/1962	116	BB
The King Family	The Sweetheart Tree	28/08/1965	147	CB
The King Tones	Goodnight Baby	10/05/1969	114	CB
The Kings	Don't Let Me Know	21/03/1981	109	BB

The Kingsmen	Long Green	02/01/1965	112	CB
The Kingsmen	Louie Louie	17/07/1965	112	CB
The Kingsmen	(You Got) The Gamma Goochee	25/12/1965	122	BB
The Kingsmen	If I Need Someone	29/10/1966	128	CB
The Kingsmen	Bo Diddley Bach	21/10/1967	128	BB
The Kingsmen	Bo Diddley Bach	28/10/1967	139	CB
The Kingston Trio	Home From The Hill	08/02/1960	102	BB
The Kingston Trio	Jane, Jane, Jane	14/04/1962	109	CB
The Kingston Trio	Old Joe Clark	01/09/1962	113	BB
The Kingston Trio	Last Night I Had The Strangest Dream	29/02/1964	124	BB
The Kingston Trio	If You Don't Look Around	25/04/1964	148	CB
The Kingston Trio	If You Don't Look Around	23/05/1964	123	BB
The Kingston Trio	Hope You Understand	14/11/1964	146	CB
The Kingston Trio	My Ramblin' Boy	21/11/1964	101	CB
The Kingston Trio	I'm Going Home	16/01/1965	104	BB
The Kingston Trio	Parchment Farm (Blues)	11/12/1965	114	CB
The Kingston Trio	Scotch And Soda (Live)	26/04/1969	104	CB
The Kingston Trio	Scotch And Soda [Live]	03/05/1969	124	BB
The Kinks	Long Tall Sally	09/01/1965	129	BB
The Kinks	Come On Now	20/03/1965	129	CB
The Kinks	See My Friends	16/10/1965	102	CB
The Kinks	See My Friends	16/10/1965	111	BB
The Kinks	Waterloo Sunset	23/09/1967	141	CB
The Kinks	God's Children	07/08/1971	127	CB
The Kinks	20th Century Man	29/01/1972	113	CB
The Kinks	20th Century Man	12/02/1972	106	BB
The Kinks	Supersonic Rocket Ship	14/10/1972	111	BB
The Kinks	One Of The Survivors	02/06/1973	108	BB
The Kinks	Lola (Live)	09/08/1980	1103	CB
The Kinks	Destroyer	16/01/1982	1103	CB

The Kit-Kats	Let's Get Lost On A Country Road	19/11/1966	144	CB
The Kit-Kats	Let's Get Lost On A Country Road	26/11/1966	119	BB
The Kit-Kats	Sea Of Love	30/09/1967	102	CB
The Kit-Kats	Sea Of Love	07/10/1967	130	BB
The Knack	Time Waits For No One	18/03/1967	130	CB
The Knickerbockers	High On Love	11/06/1966	112	CB
The Knickerbockers	Chapel In The Fields	13/08/1966	106	BB
The Knickerbockers	Love Is A Bird	22/10/1966	133	BB
The Knickerbockers	Love Is A Bird	29/10/1966	140	CB
The Lamp Of Childhood	No More Running Around	10/06/1967	116	BB
The Lamp Sisters	A Woman With The Blues	23/03/1968	116	CB
The Larks	Mickey's East Coast Jerk	20/03/1965	132	BB
The Larry Page Orchestra	Those Were The Days	09/11/1968	139	CB
The Last Word	I Wish I Had Time	30/12/1967	105	BB
The Last Words	I Wish I Had Time	30/12/1967	108	CB
The Latin Quarters	Mira Mira	31/10/1964	137	CB
The Leaves	Too Many People	30/07/1966	136	CB
The Leer Bros. Band	Mystery Of Love	09/05/1970	133	CB
The Left Banke	Ivy, Ivy	29/04/1967	106	CB
The Left Banke	Ivy, Ivy	06/05/1967	119	BB
The Left Banke	She May Call You Up Tonight	24/06/1967	120	BB
The Left Banke	She May Call You Up Tonight	01/07/1967	118	CB
The Left Banke	Desireé	14/10/1967	127	CB
The Legendary Stardust Cowboy	Paralyzed	26/10/1968	127	CB
The Lemon Pipers	Turn Around And Take A Look	23/09/1967	121	CB
The Lemon Pipers	Turn Around And Take A Look	07/10/1967	132	BB
The Lennon Sisters	Sad Movies (Make Me Cry)	16/09/1961	147	CB
The Lettermen	A Song For Young Love	17/02/1962	123	CB
The Lettermen	Turn Around, Look At Me	02/06/1962	105	BB
The Lettermen	Again	10/11/1962	120	BB

The Lettermen	Heartache Oh Heartache	02/03/1963	122	BB
The Lettermen	Allentown Jail	22/06/1963	123	BB
The Lettermen	Put Away Your Tear Drops	01/08/1964	125	CB
The Lettermen	Put Away Your Tear Drops	15/08/1964	132	BB
The Lettermen	Girl With A Little Tin Heart	27/03/1965	112	CB
The Lettermen	Girl With A Little Tin Heart	10/04/1965	135	BB
The Lettermen	Sweet September	08/01/1966	114	BB
The Lettermen	You'll Be Needin' Me	12/02/1966	118	CB
The Lettermen	Chanson D'amour	15/10/1966	117	CB
The Lettermen	Chanson D'amour	05/11/1966	112	BB
The Lettermen	Our Winter Love	14/01/1967	120	CB
The Lettermen	All The Grey Haired Men	01/06/1968	116	CB
The Lettermen	All The Grey Haired Men	08/06/1968	109	BB
The Lettermen	I Have Dreamed	01/03/1969	129	BB
The Lettermen	Hang On Sloopy	21/03/1970	101	CB
The Lettermen	Hey, Girl	17/10/1970	111	CB
The Lettermen	Hey, Girl	07/11/1970	104	BB
The Lewis & Clarke Expedition	Freedom Bird	18/11/1967	104	CB
The Lewis & Clarke Expedition	Chain Around The Flowers	04/05/1968	131	BB
The Link Eddy Combo	Big Mr. C	01/04/1961	106	CB
The Litter	Silly People	26/07/1969	124	CB
The Lonnie Donegan Skiffle Group	Rock Island Line	28/10/1961	138	CB
The Lost Generation	Wait A Minute	21/11/1970	127	BB
The Love Notes	Our Songs Of Love	16/02/1963	127	CB
The Lovin' Spoonful Featuring Joe Butler	(Till I) Run With You	14/09/1968	113	CB
The Lovin' Spoonful Featuring Joe Butler	(Till I) Run With You	21/09/1968	128	BB
The Ly-Dells	Book Of Songs	15/12/1962	146	CB
The M-M & The Peanuts	The Phillie	23/01/1965	144	CB
The Mad Lads	Sugar Sugar	14/05/1966	132	CB
The Mad Lads	I Want A Girl	06/08/1966	119	CB

The Mad Lads	Patch My Heart	08/10/1966	111	CB
The Mad Lads	Seeing Is Believin'	29/08/1970	115	CB
The Magic Mushrooms	It's-A-Happening	05/11/1966	141	CB
The Magic Ring	Do I Love You?	11/05/1968	125	CB
The Magic Touch	Step Into My World (Part 2)	03/07/1971	114	BB
The Magnificent Four	The Closer You Are	07/10/1961	110	CB
The Magnificent Men	Stormy Weather	25/02/1967	105	CB
The Magnificent Men	Stormy Weather	25/02/1967	133	BB
The Magnificent Men	By The Time I Get To Phoenix	09/03/1968	109	CB
The Main Ingredient	I'm Leaving This Time	25/12/1971	108	CB
The Main Ingredient	You Can Call Me Rover	26/05/1973	101	BB
The Main Ingredient	Girl Blue	22/09/1973	119	BB
The Main Ingredient	Girl Blue	29/09/1973	111	CB
The Main Ingredient	California My Way	23/11/1974	108	CB
The Main Ingredient	Shame On The World	17/01/1976	110	CB
The Majic Ship	Hummin'	06/09/1969	127	CB
The Majorettes	White Levis (Tennis Shoes - Surfin' Hat And Big Plaid Pendleton Shirt)	05/01/1963	103	CB
The Majors	Anything You Can Do	23/02/1963	117	BB
The Majors	Tra La La	27/04/1963	118	CB
The Majors	Your Life Begins (At Sweet Sixteen)	28/09/1963	125	BB
The Majors	Your Life Begins (At Sweet Sixtenn)	28/09/1963	139	CB
The Majors	I'll Be There (To Bring You Love)	08/02/1964	113	BB
The Malibu's	A Broken Man	18/01/1969	102	CB
The Malibu's	A Broken Man	25/01/1969	121	BB
The Mamas & The Papas	Step Out	12/02/1972	103	CB
The Mamas And The Papas	Staight Shooter	02/09/1967	130	BB
The Mamas And The Papas	Hey Girl	28/10/1967	134	BB
The Manhattan Transfer	Spies In The Night	16/01/1982	103	BB
The Manhattan Transfer	Mystery	28/04/1984	102	BB
The Manhattans	Searchin' For My Baby	24/04/1965	116	CB

The Manhattans	Searchin' For My Baby	22/05/1965	135	BB
The Manhattans	I'm The One That Love Forgot	03/07/1965	133	CB
The Manhattans	I'm The One That Love Forgot (b-side)	24/07/1965	135	BB
The Manhattans	That New Girl	11/06/1966	101	CB
The Manhattans	I Bet'cha (Couldn't Love Me)	19/11/1966	128	BB
The Manhattans	All I Need Is Your Love	01/04/1967	112	CB
The Manhattans	When We're Made As One	22/07/1967	119	CB
The Manhattans	It's Gonna Take A Lot To Bring Me Back	27/12/1969	137	CB
The Manhattans	From Atlanta To Goodbye	03/10/1970	107	CB
The Manhattans	From Atlanta To Goodbye	07/11/1970	113	BB
The Manhattans	A Million To One	27/05/1972	114	BB
The Manhattans	One Life To Live	21/10/1972	102	BB
The Manhattans	Back Up	03/02/1973	112	CB
The Manhattans	Back Up	24/02/1973	107	BB
The Manhattans	Wish That You Were Mine	05/01/1974	106	CB
The Manhattans	Summertime In The City	27/07/1974	103	CB
The Manhattans	We Never Danced To A Love Song	30/07/1977	104	CB
The Manhattans	Am I Losing You	04/03/1978	101	BB
The Manhattans	I'll Never Find Another (Find Another Like You)	13/12/1980	109	BB
The Mar-Keys	One Degree North	23/12/1961	130	CB
The Mar-Keys	Banana Juice	20/03/1965	102	CB
The Mar. Vels	Go On And Have Yourself A Ball	25/01/1964	115	BB
The Marathons	Tight Sweater	19/08/1961	136	CB
The Marcels	Twistin' Fever	31/03/1962	103	BB
The Marketts	Vanishing Point	04/04/1964	106	CB
The Marketts	Tarzan (Tarzan's Dance)	17/09/1966	139	CB
The Marmalade	My Little One	01/05/1971	123	BB
The Marmalade	My Little One	08/05/1971	125	CB
The Marshall Tucker Band	Can't You See	25/08/1973	114	CB
The Marshall Tucker Band	Can't You See	01/09/1973	108	BB

The Marshall Tucker Band	Take The Highway	20/10/1973	108	CB
The Marshall Tucker Band	This Ol' Cowboy	15/03/1975	101	CB
The Marshall Tucker Band	Searchin' For A Rainbow	28/02/1976	104	BB
The Marshall Tucker Band	This Time I Believe	30/05/1981	106	BB
The Martinels	Baby, Think It Over	09/11/1963	119	CB
The Marvelettes	Too Strong To Be Strung Along	01/12/1962	106	CB
The Marvelettes	What's Easy For Two Is Hard For One	21/09/1968	114	BB
The Marvelettes	A Breath Taking Guy	05/02/1972	118	CB
The Marvellos	Why Do You Want To Hurt The One That Loves You	24/12/1966	141	CB
The Marvellos	Piece Of Silk	29/07/1967	137	CB
The Masked Marauders	Cow Pie	29/11/1969	123	BB
The Masked Marauders	Cow Pie	29/11/1969	125	CB
The Masqueraders	I'm Just An Average Guy	25/01/1969	117	CB
The Masqueraders	Please Take Me Back	23/05/1970	114	CB
The Masqueraders	(Call Me) The Traveling Man	07/02/1976	101	BB
The Matadors (Tony, Vic & Manuel)	Perfidia	31/08/1963	113	CB
The Mauds	Hold On	22/07/1967	105	CB
The Mauds	Hold On	29/07/1967	114	BB
The Mcguire Sisters	Sugartime Twist	10/03/1962	130	CB
The Mcguire Sisters	Sugartime Twist (new Version)	07/04/1962	107	BB
The Megatons	Shimmy, Shimmy Walk, Part 1	30/12/1961	104	CB
The Memos	My Type Of Girl	19/10/1959	105	BB
The Memphis Horns	Get Up And Dance	26/02/1977	108	BB
The Memphis Horns	Just For Your Love	01/10/1977	101	BB
The Memphis Horns	Just For Your Love	12/11/1977	103	CB
The Merging Traffic	Bit By Bit	24/05/1969	115	CB
The Merry-Go-Round	Come Ride, Come Ride	20/01/1968	138	CB
The Merry-Go-Round	Listen, Listen!	18/05/1968	114	CB
The Messengers	Midnight Hour	22/04/1967	148	CB
The Messengers	Window Shopping	14/10/1967	132	BB

The Messengers	Window Shopping	21/10/1967	135	CB
The Metallics	Need Your Love	07/04/1962	136	CB
The Metallics	Need Your Love	14/04/1962	101	BB
The Meters	Dry Spell	25/10/1969	114	CB
The Meters	(The World Is A Bit Under The Weather) Doodle-Oop	05/06/1971	124	CB
The Meters	They All Ask'd For You	15/11/1975	101	CB
The Mgm Singing Strings	Lara's Theme	08/01/1966	127	CB
The Mighty Hannibal	Hymn No. 5	19/11/1966	115	BB
The Mighty Marvelows	In The Morning	02/03/1968	124	CB
The Mighty Marvelows	In The Morning	30/03/1968	105	BB
The Mike Curb Congregation	Sweet Gingerbread Man	08/08/1970	126	CB
The Mike Curb Congregation	It's A Small Small World	01/09/1973	108	BB
The Mills Brothers	Dream	01/02/1969	111	CB
The Mills Brothers	The Jimtown Road	15/03/1969	131	CB
The Mills Brothers	Sally Sunshine	04/03/1972	118	CB
The Miniature Men	Baby Elephant Walk*	02/06/1962	102	CB
The Miracles	Way Over There	03/09/1960	109	CB
The Miracles	Mighty Good Lovin'	08/07/1961	102	CB
The Miracles	Broken Hearted	08/07/1961	121	CB
The Miracles	I've Been Good To You	14/04/1962	103	BB
The Miracles	I've Been Good To You	21/04/1962	143	CB
The Miracles	Way Over There	22/09/1962	129	CB
The Miracles	I Can Take A Hint	30/03/1963	107	BB
The Miracles	I Can Take A Hint	30/03/1963	122	CB
The Miracles	Give Me Just Another Day	22/12/1973	111	BB
The Miracles	Gemini	10/05/1975	101	BB
The Miracles Featuring Billy Griffin	Spy For Brotherhood	05/02/1977	104	BB
The Mission	Together (Body And Soulin')	20/10/1973	108	BB
The Mission	Together (Body And Soulin')	20/10/1973	111	CB
The Mob	Money (That's What I Want)	05/06/1971	112	CB

The Moments	Walk Right In	05/01/1963	110	CB
The Moments	Where	04/10/1969	121	CB
The Moments	Lovely Way She Loves	03/01/1970	132	CB
The Moments	Lovely Way She Loves	24/01/1970	120	BB
The Moments	I Can't Help It	20/02/1971	108	BB
The Moments	That's How It Feels	29/05/1971	118	CB
The Moments	That's How It Feels	05/06/1971	115	BB
The Moments	To You With Love	13/11/1971	106	CB
The Moments	To You With Love	11/12/1971	107	BB
The Moments	I Don't Wanna Go	13/08/1977	108	CB
The Moms And Dads	The Rangers Waltz	11/12/1971	101	BB
The Monarchs	This Old Heart	19/10/1963	143	CB
The Monclairs	Happy Feet Time	10/07/1965	108	BB
The Monitors	Since I Lost You Girl	11/02/1967	117	BB
The Monkees	Goin' Down	18/11/1967	104	BB
The Monkees	As We Go Along	12/10/1968	106	BB
The Monkees	A Man Without A Dream	22/02/1969	127	CB
The Monkees	Mommy And Daddy	20/09/1969	109	BB
The Monkees	Mommy And Daddy	18/10/1969	101	CB
The Monkees	Daydream Believer	09/10/1976	101	CB
The Montanas	I'm Gonna Change	08/06/1968	118	CB
The Montanas	Run To Me	26/10/1968	121	BB
The Montanas	Let's Get A Little Sentimental	06/06/1970	113	CB
The Moods	Rainmaker	12/09/1970	113	BB
The Moody Blues	This Is My House (But Nobody Calls)	09/07/1966	119	BB
The Moody Blues	This Is My House (But Nobody Calls)	30/07/1966	112	CB
The Moody Blues	Nights In White Satin (short Version)	10/02/1968	103	BB
The Moonglows	Sincerely	23/09/1972	101	CB
The Motels	Total Control	08/12/1979	109	BB
The Motley Blues Band Featuring: Bob Eberly Jr.	Little White Lies	24/12/1966	140	CB

The Movers	Birmingham	14/09/1968	104	CB
The Movers	Birmingham	14/09/1968	116	BB
The Mudd Family	Johnny B. Goode	18/06/1966	126	CB
The Mugwumps	Jug Band Music	13/08/1966	102	CB
The Mugwumps	Jug Band Music	03/09/1966	127	BB
The Murmaids	A Heartbreak Ahead	29/02/1964	110	CB
The Murmaids	Heartbreak Ahead	14/03/1964	116	BB
The Music Explosion	We Gotta Go Home	14/10/1967	103	BB
The Music Explosion	We Gotta Go Home	28/10/1967	114	CB
The Music Explosion	What You Want (Baby I Want You)	10/02/1968	119	BB
The Music Explosion	What You Want (Baby I Want You)	10/02/1968	126	CB
The Music Explosion	Yes Sir	06/07/1968	120	BB
The Music Machine	Double Yellow Line	13/05/1967	111	BB
The Mystery Tour	The Ballad Of Paul	29/11/1969	104	BB
The Mystic Moods Orchestra	Sensuous Woman	25/12/1971	106	BB
The Mystics	All Through The Night	29/02/1960	107	BB
The Mystics	All Through The Night	12/03/1960	123	CB
The Mystics	Pain	16/08/1969	121	CB
The Mystics	Pain	23/08/1969	116	BB
The Nashville Brass Featuring Danny Davis	I Saw The Light	15/02/1969	129	BB
The Nashville Teens	Google Eye	05/12/1964	102	CB
The Nashville Teens	Google Eye	12/12/1964	117	BB
The Nashville Teens	Find My Way Back Home	27/02/1965	107	CB
The Nashville Teens	The Little Bird	29/05/1965	119	CB
The Nashville Teens	The Little Bird	12/06/1965	123	BB
The Neighborhood	Laugh	03/10/1970	104	BB
The Neon Philharmonic	No One Is Going To Hurt You	09/08/1969	107	CB
The Neon Philharmonic	No One Is Going To Hurt You	09/08/1969	120	BB
The Neon Philharmonic	Heighdy-Ho Princess	18/04/1970	121	CB
The New Birth	What'll I Do	23/01/1971	120	CB

The New Birth	Until It's Time For You To Go	17/02/1973	120	CB
The New Birth	I Wash My Hands Of The Whole Damn Deal, Part I	07/09/1974	106	CB
The New Christy Minstrels	This Land Is Your Land	10/11/1962	102	CB
The New Christy Minstrels	Denver	02/02/1963	137	CB
The New Christy Minstrels	Denver	02/03/1963	127	BB
The New Christy Minstrels	Silly Ol' Summertime	08/08/1964	116	CB
The New Christy Minstrels	Gotta Get A'goin'	12/12/1964	118	CB
The New Christy Minstrels	Gotta Get A Goin'	02/01/1965	111	BB
The New Christy Minstrels	Se Piangi, Se Ridi	15/05/1965	123	CB
The New Christy Minstrels	A Little Bit Of Happiness	31/07/1965	147	CB
The New Christy Minstrels	If I Could Start My Life Again	21/05/1966	121	CB
The New Christy Minstrels	Chitty Chitty Bang Bang	08/02/1969	114	BB
The New Christy Minstrels	Chitty Chitty Bang Bang	08/02/1969	129	CB
The New Christy Minstrels	Brother	24/04/1971	124	CB
The New Colony Six	I Lie Awake	16/04/1966	111	BB
The New Colony Six	I Lie Awake	23/04/1966	103	CB
The New Colony Six	Cadillac	06/08/1966	140	CB
The New Colony Six	You're Gonna Be Mine	08/04/1967	108	BB
The New Colony Six	I'm Just Waiting (Anticipating For Her To Show Up)	15/07/1967	128	CB
The New Colony Six	I'm Just Waitin' (Anticipatin' For Her To Show Up)	22/07/1967	128	BB
The New Colony Six	Treat Her Groovy	25/11/1967	125	CB
The New Colony Six	People And Me	23/05/1970	103	CB
The New Colony Six	People And Me	23/05/1970	116	BB
The New Colony Six	Long Time To Be Alone	04/12/1971	112	CB
The New Colony Six	Someone, Sometime	15/04/1972	109	BB
The New Establishment	(One Of These Days) Sunday's Gonna' Come On Tuesday	15/11/1969	120	CB
The New Happiness	Winchester Cathedral	29/10/1966	109	CB
The New Happiness	Winchester Cathedral	29/10/1966	112	BB
The New Jersey Mass Choir Featuring Donnie Harper And	I Want To Know What Love Is	23/02/1985	101	BB
The New Marketts	Song From M*A*S*H	05/06/1976	106	CB

The New Order	You've Got Me High	28/05/1966	130	CB
The New Seekers	When There's No Love Left	12/12/1970	101	CB
The New Seekers	Tonight	16/10/1971	107	CB
The New Seekers	Dance, Dance, Dance	07/10/1972	106	CB
The New Vaudeville Band	The Bonnie And Clyde	06/04/1968	122	BB
The New Vaudeville Band (featuring Tristam Vii)	Finchley Central	27/05/1967	106	CB
The New Vaudeville Band (featuring Tristam Vii)	Finchley Central	03/06/1967	102	BB
The New York Rock Ensemble	Beside You	23/01/1971	123	BB
The New Young Hearts	The Young Hearts Get Lonely Too	14/11/1970	123	BB
The Newbeats	Hey-O-Daddy-O	23/01/1965	118	BB
The Newbeats	Crying My Heart Out	07/05/1966	103	CB
The Newbeats	My Yesterday Love	03/12/1966	135	CB
The Newbeats	Thou Shall Not Steal	28/06/1969	128	BB
The Newbeats	Laura (What's He Got That I Ain't Got)	07/03/1970	115	BB
The Newbeats	The Way You Do The Things You Do	08/12/1973	116	CB
The Next Five	Mama Said	17/02/1968	134	CB
The Night Beats	Exotic	11/02/1961	119	CB
The Nightcrawlers	The Little Black Egg	11/12/1965	120	CB
The Nightcrawlers	The Little Black Egg	18/12/1965	135	BB
The Nite-Liters	(We've Got To) Pull Together	18/12/1971	110	CB
The Nitty Gritty Dirt Band	Some Of Shelly's Blues	18/10/1969	106	CB
The Noble Knights	Sing A Simple Song	12/04/1969	132	BB
The Nomads	Bounty Hunter	18/03/1961	107	CB
The Nomads	Bounty Hunter	27/03/1961	116	BB
The North Atlantic Invasion Force	Black On White	23/03/1968	114	CB
The Noteables	Tonto	11/06/1960	122	CB
The O'jays	Stand Tall	01/02/1964	131	BB
The O'jays	Oh, How You Hurt Me	09/01/1965	133	CB
The O'jays	Stand In For Love	01/10/1966	109	CB
The O'jays	The Choice	14/09/1968	103	CB

The O'jays	Don't You Know A True Love	15/03/1969	130	CB
The O'jays	You're The Best Thing Since Candy	06/12/1969	137	CB
The O'jays	Sunshine (Part Ii) (Live)	28/12/1974	101	CB
The O'jays	Sing A Happy Song	27/10/1979	102	BB
The O'jays	I Just Want To Satisfy	08/05/1982	101	BB
The Obsession	Music To My Heart	21/02/1970	130	CB
The October Country	October Country	06/01/1968	122	CB
The Ohio Players	Trespassin'	13/01/1968	117	CB
The Ohio Players	I've Got To Hold On	11/05/1968	137	CB
The Olympics	Dooley	17/06/1961	115	CB
The Ones	You Haven't Seen My Love	03/02/1968	107	CB
The Ones	You Haven't Seen My Love	10/02/1968	117	BB
The Orchids	That Boy Is Messin' Up My Mind	30/11/1963	133	CB
The Original Caste	Mr. Monday	28/03/1970	108	CB
The Original Caste	Mr. Monday	25/04/1970	119	BB
The Original Caste	Nothing Can Touch Me (Don't Worry Baby, It's Alright)	11/07/1970	114	BB
The Original Caste	Ain't That Tellin' You People	19/09/1970	120	CB
The Original Caste	Ain't That Tellin' You People	03/10/1970	117	BB
The Original Caste	When Love Is Near	13/03/1971	128	CB
The Originals	We Can Make It Baby	01/08/1970	112	CB
The Originals	I Like Your Style	22/08/1970	108	CB
The Originals	I'm Someone Who Cares	04/03/1972	113	BB
The Originals	Game Called Love	27/07/1974	105	CB
The Orlons	Them Terrible Boots	23/02/1963	130	CB
The Orlons	Come On Down Baby Baby	06/02/1965	129	CB
The Orlons	I Ain't Comin' Back	06/02/1965	129	BB
The Osmond Brothers	Mary Elizabeth	17/08/1968	103	CB
The Osmond Brothers	I Can't Stop	27/03/1971	119	CB
The Osmonds	I'm Still Gonna Need You	11/10/1975	102	CB
The Outsiders	Gotta Leave Us Alone	29/04/1967	131	CB

The Outsiders	Gotta Leave Us Alone	06/05/1967	121	BB
The Outsiders	Little Bit Of Lovin'	09/12/1967	117	BB
The Outsiders (featuring Sonny Geraci)	Changes	05/09/1970	107	BB
The Outsiders Featuring Sonny Geraci	I'll Give You Time (To Think It Over)	04/03/1967	110	CB
The Outsiders Featuring Sonny Geraci	I'll Give You Time (To Think It Over)	04/03/1967	118	BB
The Outsiders Featuring Sonny Geraci	I'll See You In The Summertime	05/08/1967	117	CB
The Ovations	Touching Me	22/07/1972	111	CB
The Ovations	Touching Me	19/08/1972	104	BB
The Overlanders	Don't It Make You Feel Good	14/11/1964	101	CB
The Oxford 12	Goldfinger*	30/01/1965	134	CB
The Paley Brothers	You're The Best	20/05/1978	109	BB
The Palm Beach Band Boys	I'm Gonna Sit Right Down And Write Myself A Letter	24/12/1966	117	BB
The Palm Beach Band Boys	I'm Gonna Sit Right Down And Write Myself A Letter	07/01/1967	114	CB
The Parade	The Radio Song	24/02/1968	127	BB
The Paragons	Blue Velvet	19/09/1960	103	BB
The Paragons	If	05/08/1961	136	CB
The Parkays	Late Date	16/09/1961	127	CB
The Parliaments	The Goose (That Laid The Golden Egg)	03/02/1968	123	CB
The Parliaments	Look At What I Almost Missed	06/04/1968	101	CB
The Parliaments	Look At What I Almost Missed	13/04/1968	104	BB
The Passions	This Is My Love	27/02/1960	105	CB
The Passions	I Only Want You	14/03/1960	113	BB
The Pastors	I Need You/Isn't Life Strange/Without You	11/08/1973	125	CB
The Pat Boone Family	Please Mr. Postman	26/10/1974	101	CB
The Patty Cakes	I Understand Them (A Love Song To The Beatles)	30/05/1964	112	CB
The Peanut Butter Conspiracy	It's A Happening Thing	25/02/1967	102	CB
The Peanut Butter Conspiracy	I'm A Fool	16/11/1968	125	BB
The Peanut Butter Conspiracy	I'm A Fool	23/11/1968	121	CB
The Peanut Butter Conspiracy	Back In L.A.	13/09/1969	116	CB
The Pearly Gate	Free	08/11/1969	102	CB

The Pearly Gate	Free	06/12/1969	104	BB
The Penguins	Earth Angel	28/12/1959	101	BB
The Penguins	Earth Angel	30/01/1960	105	CB
The Pentagons	I Wonder (If Your Love Will Ever Belong To Me)	21/10/1961	101	CB
The Peoples Choice	Lost And Found	02/08/1969	130	CB
The Peppermint Rainbow	Walking In Different Circles	06/07/1968	136	CB
The Persians	I Don't Know How (To Fall Out Of Love)	16/08/1969	120	CB
The Persians	Your Love	12/02/1972	108	BB
The Persians	Your Love	12/02/1972	120	CB
The Persuaders	Bad, Bold And Beautiful, Girl	26/05/1973	105	BB
The Pete Jolly Trio & Friends	Little Bird	30/03/1963	102	CB
The Pete Jolly Trio And Friends	Little Bird	04/05/1963	112	BB
The Pete King Chorale And Orchestra	Hey! Look Me Over	27/02/1961	108	BB
The Piltdown Men	Goodnight Mrs. Flintstone	11/02/1961	111	CB
The Pin-Ups	Lookin' For Boys	04/07/1964	108	CB
The Pink Floyd	See Emily Play	16/09/1967	134	BB
The Pink Floyd	See Emily Play	23/09/1967	125	CB
The Pinups	Song On The Radio	19/06/1982	110	BB
The Pipkins	Yakety Yak	08/08/1970	101	CB
The Pixies Three	Cold Cold Winter	23/11/1963	106	CB
The Pixies Three	It's Summertime U.S.A.	27/06/1964	106	CB
The Pixies Three	It's Summer Time U.S.A.	04/07/1964	116	BB
The Plastic Cow Goes Moooooog	Lady Jane	01/11/1969	113	BB
The Plastic Cow Goes Moooooog	Lady Jane	08/11/1969	133	CB
The Platters	Song For The Lonely (b-side)	27/11/1961	115	BB
The Platters	Song For The Lonely	02/12/1961	127	CB
The Platters	You'll Never Know	11/12/1961	109	BB
The Platters	Devri	13/08/1966	117	CB
The Platters	Devri	10/09/1966	111	BB
The Platters	How Beautiful Our Love Is	09/12/1967	120	CB

The Platters	Think Before You Walk Away	24/02/1968	137	CB
The Platters	Hard To Get A Thing Called Love	17/08/1968	117	CB
The Platters	Hard To Get A Thing Called Love	24/08/1968	125	BB
The Platters Featuring Tony Williams	(I'll Be With You In) Apple Blossom Time	30/05/1960	102	BB
The Playboys Of Edinburg	Look At Me Girl	16/07/1966	108	BB
The Playboys Of Edinburg	Let's Get Back To Rock And Roll	22/11/1969	130	CB
The Players	He'll Be Back	10/09/1966	107	BB
The Players	I'm Glad I Waited	10/12/1966	130	BB
The Playmates	Keep Your Hands In Your Pockets	23/06/1962	147	CB
The Playmates	She Never Looked Better	24/08/1963	110	CB
The Playmates Donny-Morey-Chic	First Love	31/10/1959	109	CB
The Playmates Donny-Morey-Chic	Tell Me What She Said	08/07/1961	131	CB
The Pleasure Fair	Morning Glory Days	01/07/1967	121	CB
The Pleasure Fair	Morning Glory Days	22/07/1967	134	BB
The Pleasures	Let's Have A Beach Party	31/07/1965	136	CB
The Poets	So Young (And So Innocent)	16/07/1966	121	CB
The Politicians	Free Your Mind	29/04/1972	110	BB
The Politicians	Free Your Mind	06/05/1972	115	CB
The Poor	She's Got The Time (She's Got The Changes)	01/04/1967	111	CB
The Poor	She's Got The Time (She's Got The Changes)	08/04/1967	133	BB
The Pop Explosion	Fill My Soul	31/08/1968	120	CB
The Poppies	He's Ready	28/05/1966	106	BB
The Poppy Family Vocal: Susan Jacks	Good Friends?	26/02/1972	105	BB
The Portraits	Yo-Yo Girl	29/07/1961	138	CB
The Power Plant	I Can't Happen Without You	07/10/1967	134	BB
The Precisions	Why Girl	13/01/1968	146	CB
The Precisions	Instant Heartbreak (Just Add Tears)	09/03/1968	121	CB
The Premeers	Diary Of Our Love	02/03/1963	147	CB
The Preparations	Get-E-Up (The Horse)	13/04/1968	134	BB
The Pretenders	Louie Louie	17/10/1981	110	BB

The Pretty Things	Don't Bring Me Down	28/11/1964	121	CB
The Pretty Things	Honey, I Need	01/05/1965	123	CB
The Princetons	Georgianna	19/02/1966	148	CB
The Producers	What's He Got?	22/08/1981	108	BB
The Pussycats	I Want Your Love	08/05/1965	138	CB
The Quotations	Imagination	27/01/1962	105	BB
The Radiants	Father Knows Best	22/09/1962	141	CB
The Radiants	Whole Lot Of Woman	04/09/1965	116	BB
The Radiants	(Don't It Make You) Feel Kind Of Bad	28/01/1967	139	CB
The Radiants	Hold On	13/07/1968	106	CB
The Raelets	Into Something Fine	29/07/1967	130	CB
The Raeletts Featuring Estella Yarbrough	Here I Go Again	24/07/1971	113	CB
The Raeletts Featuring Estella Yarbrough	Here I Go Again	31/07/1971	101	BB
The Raging Storms	The DriBBle (Twist)	27/01/1962	103	CB
The Raindrops	Let's Go Together	30/05/1964	109	BB
The Raindrops	Let's Go Together	30/05/1964	130	CB
The Raindrops	One More Tear	26/09/1964	142	CB
The Ramadas	Teenage Dream	06/04/1963	141	CB
The Ramrods	Loch Lomand Rock	25/03/1961	119	CB
The Ramsey Lewis Trio	Blueberry Hill	13/10/1962	133	CB
The Ramsey Lewis Trio	My Cherie Amour	17/01/1970	107	CB
The Rance Allen Group	There's Gonna Be A Showdown	23/09/1972	117	CB
The Rare Breed	Beg, Borrow And Steal	25/06/1966	118	CB
The Rascals	Right On	26/12/1970	116	CB
The Rascals	Right On	02/01/1971	119	BB
The Ray Charles Singers	My Love, Forgive Me (Amore, Scusami)	18/09/1965	124	BB
The Ray Charles Singers	One Of Those Songs	29/01/1966	123	CB
The Ray Charles Singers	One Of Those Songs	19/02/1966	134	BB
The Ray Charles Singers	Don't Cry (Una Casa La Cima Al Mondo)	19/11/1966	141	CB
The Ray Charles Singers	Little By Little And Bit By Bit	03/06/1967	135	BB

The Ray Charles Singers	Take Me Along	07/10/1967	113	CB
The Ray Conniff Singers	If I Knew Then	05/12/1964	126	BB
The Ray Conniff Singers	If I Knew Then	19/12/1964	118	CB
The Rays	Mediterranean Moon	26/12/1959	113	CB
The Rebels	Wild Weekend	11/06/1960	115	CB
The Redwoods	Shake Shake Sherry	02/09/1961	146	CB
The Reflections	(I'm Just) A Henpecked Guy	12/09/1964	124	BB
The Reflections	ShaBBy Little Hut	02/01/1965	121	BB
The Regents	Liar	28/10/1961	135	CB
The Reivers	Revolution In My Soul	05/09/1970	112	BB
The Remains	Why Do I Cry	17/04/1965	144	CB
The Remains	Diddy Wah Diddy	23/04/1966	129	BB
The Rev-Lons	Boy Trouble	13/10/1962	127	CB
The Reveres	Beyond The Sea	15/02/1964	144	CB
The Rhodes Kids	Voo-Doo Magic	28/09/1974	105	CB
The Rhodes Kids	Runaway	22/02/1975	107	BB
The Rhodes Kids	Runaway	15/03/1975	119	CB
The Rhodes Kids	Take Good Care Of Her	31/05/1975	107	CB
The Righteous Brothers	Try To Find Another Man	02/05/1964	119	BB
The Righteous Brothers	This Little Girl Of Mine	24/10/1964	114	BB
The Righteous Brothers	My Babe	30/01/1965	107	CB
The Righteous Brothers	My Babe	06/02/1965	101	BB
The Righteous Brothers	Bring Your Love To Me	13/02/1965	116	CB
The Righteous Brothers	Fannie Mae	13/02/1965	117	BB
The Righteous Brothers	Fannie Mae	13/02/1965	119	CB
The Righteous Brothers	For Your Love	09/10/1965	103	BB
The Righteous Brothers	For Your Love	09/10/1965	111	CB
The Righteous Brothers	He Will Break Your Heart	11/06/1966	101	CB
The Righteous Brothers	The White Cliffs Of Dover	15/10/1966	118	BB
The Righteous Brothers	Along Came Jones	11/02/1967	108	BB

The Righteous Brothers	Along Came Jones	11/02/1967	121	CB
The Righteous Brothers	Been So Nice	30/09/1967	128	BB
The Righteous Brothers	Here I Am	03/02/1968	121	BB
The Rinkydinks	Hot Potato (Part 1)	15/06/1963	128	CB
The Rip Chords	One Piece Topless Bathing Suit	25/07/1964	119	CB
The Ritchie Family	Life Is Music	19/03/1977	102	BB
The Rivieras	Our Love	27/07/1959	103	BB
The Rivieras	Since I Made You Cry	09/01/1960	112	CB
The Rivieras	Moonlight Cocktails	13/06/1960	103	BB
The Rivieras	Moonlight Cocktails	25/06/1960	105	CB
The Rivieras	Let's Have A Party	09/05/1964	104	CB
The Rivieras	Rockin' Robin	05/09/1964	105	CB
The Rivingtons	Mama-Oom-Mow-Mow (The Bird)	12/01/1963	106	BB
The Rivingtons	Mama-Oom-Mow-Mow (The Bird)	12/01/1963	111	CB
The Rivingtons	Little Sally Walker	21/09/1963	144	CB
The Rivingtons	Weejee Walk	21/03/1964	125	CB
The Roaches	Beatle Mania Blues	11/04/1964	117	BB
The Road	She's Not There	01/02/1969	114	BB
The Road Apples	Holding On	13/03/1976	110	BB
The Road Apples	Holding On	20/03/1976	106	CB
The Road Home	Keep It In The Family	25/09/1971	113	CB
The Road Home	Keep It In The Family	25/09/1971	120	BB
The RoBBs	Race With The Wind	11/06/1966	101	CB
The RoBBs	Race With The Wind	11/06/1966	103	BB
The RoBBs	Bittersweet	28/01/1967	117	CB
The RoBBs	Rapid Transit	06/05/1967	123	BB
The RoBBs	Rapid Transit	13/05/1967	125	CB
The RoBBs	Movin'	25/10/1969	131	BB
The RoBBs	Last Of The Wine	18/04/1970	112	CB
The RoBBs	Last Of The Wine	02/05/1970	114	BB

The RoBBs	I'll Never Get Enough	12/09/1970	106	BB
The Robins	White Cliffs Of Dover	24/04/1961	108	BB
The Robins	White Cliffs Of Dover	17/06/1961	146	CB
The Rock-A-Teens	Twangy	09/01/1960	109	CB
The Rockin' Ramrods	Don't Fool With Fu Manchu	09/10/1965	119	CB
The Rocky Fellers	Ching-A-Ling Baby	12/10/1963	150	CB
The Rocky Fellers	Bye Bye Baby	18/01/1964	148	CB
The Rogues	Everyday	16/01/1965	112	CB
The Rogues	Everyday	23/01/1965	101	BB
The Rogues	Come On, Let's Go	17/04/1965	140	CB
The Roller Coasters	Rimshot Pt. 1	29/04/1961	108	CB
The Roller Coasters	Spanish Twist	29/12/1962	105	CB
The Rolling Stones	What A Shame	16/01/1965	125	CB
The Rolling Stones	What A Shame	30/01/1965	124	BB
The Rolling Stones	Play With Fire	27/03/1965	137	CB
The Rolling Stones	Child Of The Moon	29/06/1968	138	CB
The Rolling Stones	If I Was A Dancer (Dance Pt. 2)	21/03/1981	l101	CB
The Romeos	The Tiger's Wide Awake (The Lion Sleeps Tonight)	10/02/1962	117	CB
The Romeos	Mucho Soul	26/03/1966	119	CB
The Ron-Dels	Matilda	02/03/1963	143	CB
The Rondels	Satan's Theme	21/10/1961	116	CB
The Rondels	Caldonia	24/02/1962	137	CB
The Ronettes (Featuring The Voice Of Veronica)	You Came, You Saw, You Conquered!	05/04/1969	108	BB
The Ronettes Featuring Veronica	I Can Hear Music	29/10/1966	146	CB
The Roomates	Band Of Gold	31/07/1961	119	BB
The Roosters	Fun House	07/04/1962	123	CB
The Roosters	Love Machine	20/04/1968	106	BB
The Rose Garden Featuring Diane Derose	If My World Falls Through	16/03/1968	104	CB
The Roulettes	Only Heaven Knows	23/05/1981	l103	CB
The Roulettes	Only Heaven Knows	06/06/1981	105	BB

The Routers	Half Time	26/01/1963	103	CB
The Routers	Half Time	16/02/1963	115	BB
The Routers	A-Ooga	17/08/1963	147	CB
The Rowan Brothers	All Together	18/11/1972	124	CB
The Rowan Brothers	All Together	02/12/1972	112	BB
The Royal Guardsmen	Wednesday	26/08/1967	101	CB
The Royal Guardsmen	Snoopy For President	06/07/1968	107	CB
The Royal Guardsmen	Mother Where's Your Daughter	12/04/1969	112	BB
The Royalettes	No Big Thing	25/05/1963	140	CB
The Royalettes	Blue Summer	07/09/1963	121	BB
The Royalettes	You Bring Me Down	05/02/1966	101	CB
The Royalettes	You Bring Me Down	05/02/1966	116	BB
The Royalettes	It's A Big Mistake	28/05/1966	150	CB
The Royalettes	When Summer's Gone	01/10/1966	124	CB
The Royalettes Featuring Sheila Ross	Poor Boy	17/04/1965	113	BB
The Royaltones	Royal Whirl	11/03/1961	119	CB
The Royaltones	The Peppermint Twist	09/12/1961	139	CB
The Royaltones	Our Faded Love	11/04/1964	103	BB
The RuBBer Band	Let Love Come Between Us	10/12/1966	130	CB
The Rubies	A Spanish Boy	25/07/1964	127	CB
The Rugbys	Wendegahl The Warlock	22/11/1969	122	CB
The Rumbles, Ltd.	Jezebel	20/01/1968	106	CB
The Runarounds	You're A Drag	30/04/1966	141	CB
The Runaways	Cherry Bomb	24/07/1976	103	CB
The Runaways	Cherry Bomb	07/08/1976	106	BB
The Runaways	Heartbeat	12/03/1977	110	BB
The S.O.S. Band	No One's Gonna Love You	10/11/1984	102	BB
The Safaris With The Phantom's Band	The Girl With The Story In Her Eyes	15/10/1960	106	CB
The Saints	I'll Be With You	24/01/1970	128	CB
The Salsoul Orchestra	Short Shorts	25/06/1977	106	BB

The Salsoul Orchestra	Getaway	23/07/1977	106	CB
The Salsoul Orchestra	Getaway	30/07/1977	105a	BB
The Salsoul Orchestra	Magic Bird Of Fire (b-side)	30/07/1977	105b	BB
The Salsoul Orchestra Featuring Cognac	How High	10/11/1979	105	BB
The San Remo Golden Strings	Blueberry Hill	06/11/1965	139	CB
The SandpeBBles	If You Didn't Hear Me The First Time (I'll Say It Again)	06/04/1968	122	BB
The SandpeBBles	Never My Love	02/11/1968	121	CB
The Sandpipers	Glass	13/05/1967	104	CB
The Sandpipers	Glass	20/05/1967	112	BB
The Sandpipers	Quando M'innamore	15/06/1968	124	BB
The Sandpipers	Chotto Matte Kudasai (Never Say Goodbye)	07/08/1971	125	CB
The Sapphires	Where Is Johnny Now?	10/08/1963	133	BB
The Sapphires	Thank You For Loving Me	10/10/1964	106	BB
The Sapphires	Thank You For Loving Me	10/10/1964	123	CB
The Satisfactions	One Light Two Lights	10/10/1970	107	CB
The Saturday Morning Cartoon Show	Hayride	30/11/1968	110	CB
The Searchers	Don't You Know Why	09/10/1965	105	CB
The Searchers	Popcorn, Double Feature	25/03/1967	127	CB
The Seashells	(The Best Part Of) Breakin' Up	27/01/1973	115	BB
The Second Time	Listen To The Music	26/10/1968	128	CB
The Secrets	Hey, Big Boy	29/02/1964	138	CB
The Seeds	Mr. Farmer	28/01/1967	109	CB
The Seekers	Chilly Wind	01/05/1965	122	BB
The Seekers	Chilly Wind	15/05/1965	143	CB
The Seekers	Myra (Shake Up The Party)	06/11/1965	138	CB
The Seekers	The Carnival Is Over	20/11/1965	105	BB
The Seekers	Some Day, One Day	16/04/1966	143	CB
The Seekers	On The Other Side	26/08/1967	115	BB
The Seekers	When The Good Apples Fall	14/10/1967	106	CB
The Seekers	Love Is Kind, Love Is Wine	16/03/1968	135	BB

The Senators	There's A New Man In The White House	04/02/1961	117	CB
The Serendipity Singers	Down Where The Winds Blow (Chilly Winds)	01/08/1964	112	BB
The Serendipity Singers	Same Old Reason	31/10/1964	114	CB
The Serendipity Singers	Little Brown Jug	26/12/1964	114	CB
The Serendipity Singers	Little Brown Jug	09/01/1965	124	BB
The Serendipity Singers	My Heart Keeps Following You	27/03/1965	122	CB
The Serendipity Singers	Plastic	27/11/1965	129	CB
The Serendipity Singers	Plastic	04/12/1965	118	BB
The Sex-O-Lettes	Ride A Wild Horse	06/11/1976	105	BB
The Shackelfords	California Sunshine Girl	03/06/1967	115	BB
The Shadows	Wonderful Land	19/05/1962	137	CB
The Shadows Of Knight	I'm Gonna Make You Mine	31/12/1966	129	CB
The Shame	Too Old To Go 'WAY Little Girl	02/12/1967	131	CB
The Shangri-Las	Maybe	26/12/1964	107	CB
The Shangri-Las	Right Now And Not Later	16/10/1965	150	CB
The Shangri-Las	The Sweet Sounds Of Summer	24/12/1966	143	CB
The Shangri-Las	The Sweet Sounds Of Summer	07/01/1967	123	BB
The Sharpees	I've Got A Secret	16/04/1966	141	CB
The Sheep	I Feel Good	21/05/1966	136	CB
The Sheep	I Feel Good	28/05/1966	130	BB
The Sheppards	Island Of Love	24/08/1959	109	BB
The Sherrys	Slop Time	26/01/1963	112	CB
The Sherrys	Saturday Night	11/05/1963	101	CB
The Sherrys	Saturday Night	11/05/1963	116	BB
The Shevelles	I Could Conquer The World	05/09/1964	104	BB
The Shevelles	I Could Conquer The World	05/09/1964	105	CB
The Shieks	Baghdad Rock (Part 1)	14/12/1959	111	BB
The Shillings	Lying And Trying	11/02/1967	136	CB
The Shindogs	Who Do You Think You Are	09/07/1966	106	CB
The Shirelles	I Met Him On A Sunday (Ronde-Ronde)	11/03/1961	127	CB

The Shirelles	The Things I Want To Hear (Pretty Words)	11/12/1961	107	BB
The Shirelles	The Things I Want To Hear (Pretty Words)	30/12/1961	115	CB
The Shirelles	Love Is A Swingin' Thing	17/03/1962	134	CB
The Shirelles	Love Is A Swingin' Thing	07/04/1962	109	BB
The Shirelles	Mama, Here Comes The Bride	23/06/1962	115	CB
The Shirelles	Mama, Here Comes The Bride	14/07/1962	104	BB
The Shirelles	It's Love That Really Counts (In The Long Run)	01/09/1962	103	CB
The Shirelles	It's Love That Really Counts (In The Long Run)	29/09/1962	102	BB
The Shirelles	It's A Mad, Mad, Mad, Mad World	19/10/1963	105	CB
The Shirelles	Maybe Tonight	10/10/1964	102	CB
The Shirelles	Lost Love	10/10/1964	125	BB
The Shirelles	March (You'll Be Sorry)	03/07/1965	108	BB
The Shirelles	March (You'll Be Sorry)	03/07/1965	140	CB
The Shirelles	My Heart Belongs To You	25/09/1965	133	CB
The Shirelles	My Heart Belongs To You	16/10/1965	125	BB
The Shirelles	I Met Him On A Sunday - '66	26/03/1966	139	CB
The Shirelles	Shades Of Blue	08/10/1966	122	BB
The Shirelles	Shades Of Blue	29/10/1966	139	CB
The Shirelles	Don't Go Home (My Little Darlin')	28/01/1967	110	BB
The Shirelles	Last Minute Miracle	15/07/1967	104	CB
The Shirelles	There Goes My Baby/Be My Baby	21/03/1970	121	CB
The Shocking Blue	Never Marry A Railroad Man	26/12/1970	102	BB
The Shocking Blue	Serenade	30/10/1971	110	BB
The Shondells	Wonderful One	08/09/1962	119	CB
The Shondells	Wonderful One	13/10/1962	116	BB
The Short-Kuts	Born On The Bayou	30/08/1969	141	CB
The Short-Kuts	Born On The Bayou	13/09/1969	109	BB
The Show Stoppers	Ain't Nothin' But A House Party	27/05/1967	118	BB
The Show Stoppers	Ain't Nothin' But A House Party	24/06/1967	136	CB
The Show Stoppers	Eeny Meeny	28/09/1968	116	CB

The Showmen	It Will Stand	16/05/1964	101	CB
The Showmen	In Paradise	15/05/1965	138	CB
The Showmen	39-21-46	17/06/1967	101	BB
The Showmen	39-21-46	01/07/1967	126	CB
The Shut Downs	Four In The Floor	09/11/1963	131	BB
The Shy Guys	We Gotta Go	18/06/1966	118	CB
The Sickniks	The Presidential Press Conference (Parts 1 & 2) (Live)	10/06/1961	117	CB
The Sickniks	The Presidential Press Conference (Part 1) [Live]	26/06/1961	105	BB
The Sickniks	The Presidential Press Conference (Part 2) [Live]	26/06/1961	105	BB
The Sidekicks	Fifi The Flea	15/10/1966	125	CB
The Sidekicks	Fifi The Flea	29/10/1966	115	BB
The Sierras	I'll Believe It When I See It	14/09/1963	108	BB
The Silkie	The Keys To My Soul	15/01/1966	111	CB
The Silkie	The Keys To My Soul	22/01/1966	124	BB
The Silkie	Born To Be With You	06/08/1966	133	BB
The Simon Sisters	Winkin', Blinkin' And Nod	18/04/1964	116	CB
The Sister & Brothers	Dear Ike (Remember I'm John's Girl)	15/08/1970	142	CB
The Sister And Brothers	Dear Ike (Remember I'm John's Girl)	18/07/1970	131	BB
The Ska Kings	Jamaica Ska	06/06/1964	123	CB
The Skyliners	Close Your Eyes	18/12/1961	105	BB
The Skyliners	Comes Love	12/01/1963	119	CB
The Skyliners	Comes Love	16/02/1963	128	BB
The Smiths	Now I Taste The Tears	25/05/1968	110	CB
The Smothers Brothers	Jenny Brown	28/09/1963	105	CB
The Soft Machine	Why Are We Sleeping?	07/12/1968	124	CB
The Sonics	You Got Your Head On Backwards	20/08/1966	140	CB
The Sorrows	Take A Heart	04/12/1965	129	BB
The Sorrows	Take A Heart	04/12/1965	134	CB
The Soul Children	Don't Take My Kindness For Weakness	19/08/1972	102	BB
The Soul Children	It Ain't Always What You Do (It's Who You Let See You Do It)	10/03/1973	105	BB

The Soul Children	Love Makes It Right	14/09/1974	120	CB
The Soul Clan	Soul Meeting	20/07/1968	101	CB
The Soul Survivors	Turn Out The Fire	16/11/1968	132	CB
The Soul Survivors	Mama Soul	03/05/1969	131	CB
The Soul Survivors	Mama Soul	10/05/1969	115	BB
The Soul Twins	Just One Look	24/06/1967	123	BB
The Source	It's Me I'm Running From	26/09/1970	120	CB
The Spaniels	100 Years From Today	05/12/1959	123	CB
The Spaniels	I Know	30/07/1960	107	CB
The Spats Featuring Dick Johnson	Gator Tails And Monkey Ribs	05/09/1964	106	CB
The Spectors Three	I Really Do	02/01/1960	121	CB
The Spellbinders	Chain Reaction	26/02/1966	117	CB
The Spellbinders	Chain Reaction	19/03/1966	118	BB
The Spellbinders	We're Acting Like Lovers	04/06/1966	130	BB
The Spellbinders	Help Me (Get Myself Back Together Again)	15/10/1966	146	CB
The Spencer Davis Group	After Tea	27/04/1968	131	CB
The Spike Drivers	Baby Won't You Let Me Tell You How I Lost My Mind	10/12/1966	141	CB
The Spike Drivers	Break Out The Wine	11/03/1967	102	CB
The Spinners	Truly Yours	21/05/1966	111	BB
The Spinners	For All We Know	10/06/1967	137	CB
The Spokesmen	Michelle	08/01/1966	124	CB
The Spokesmen	Michelle	15/01/1966	106	BB
The Spotlights	Batman And Robin	19/02/1966	111	BB
The Springfield Rifle	It Ain't Happened	08/07/1967	123	CB
The Springfields	Gotta Travel On	17/11/1962	114	BB
The Springfields	Island Of Dreams	27/04/1963	129	BB
The Stairsteps	I Love You - Stop	22/01/1972	110	CB
The Stairsteps	I Love You - Stop	12/02/1972	115	BB
The Standells	The Boy Next Door	06/02/1965	102	BB
The Standells	Riot On Sunset Strip	04/03/1967	134	CB

The Standells	Riot On Sunset Strip	25/03/1967	133	BB
The Standells	Try It	01/07/1967	111	CB
The Standells	Animal Girl	24/02/1968	133	CB
The Staple Singers	It's Been A Change	17/12/1966	143	CB
The Staple Singers	Slippery People	27/10/1984	109	BB
The Staples Singers	Why? (Am I Treated So Bad)	02/04/1966	131	CB
The Starlets	P.S. I Love You	11/06/1960	104	CB
The Starlets	P.S. I Love You	20/06/1960	106	BB
The Starlets	My Last Cry	28/10/1961	103	CB
The State Dept.	Wild Honey Part I	25/11/1972	104	CB
The Statler Brothers	My Darling Hildegarde	19/02/1966	105	CB
The Statler Brothers	My Darling Hildegarde	26/02/1966	110	BB
The Statler Brothers	Do You Remember These	22/04/1972	105	BB
The Statler Brothers	Do You Remember These	13/05/1972	120	CB
The Stereos	Sweet Water	16/12/1961	134	CB
The Stills-Young Band	Midnight On The Bay	18/12/1976	105	BB
The Stokes	Whipped Cream*	13/02/1965	113	CB
The Stokes	Young Man, Old Man	16/04/1966	122	CB
The Stompers	One Heart For Sale	29/09/1984	110	BB
The Strangeloves	Hand Jive	25/06/1966	117	CB
The Strangeloves	Honey Do	23/11/1968	120	BB
The Stratfords	Never Leave Me	25/01/1964	112	CB
The Stratfords	Never Leave Me	22/02/1964	124	BB
The Streakers	Streakin'	30/03/1974	103	CB
The Streamliners With Joanne	Frankfurter Sandwiches	03/07/1965	117	BB
The String-A-Longs	Mina Bird	14/10/1961	127	CB
The String-A-Longs	My Blue Heaven	08/09/1962	143	CB
The String-A-Longs	Matilda	15/12/1962	133	BB
The String-A-Longs	Matilda	15/12/1962	144	CB
The Stylistics	Hey Girl, Come And Get It	22/02/1975	101	CB

The Sugar Blues	Look What We Have Joined Together	22/03/1969	113	CB
The Sunglows	Guess Who	18/04/1964	145	CB
The Sunrays	Don't Take Yourself Too Seriously	16/07/1966	130	CB
The Sunshine Company	Let's Get Together	18/05/1968	112	BB
The Sunshine Company	On A Beautiful Day	06/07/1968	114	CB
The Sunshine Company	On A Beautiful Day	27/07/1968	106	BB
The Sunshine Company	Willie Jean	19/10/1968	111	BB
The Sunshine Company	Willie Jean	25/01/1969	126	CB
The Superlatives	I Don't Know How (To Say I Love You) Don't Walk Away	22/02/1969	147	CB
The Supremes	Your Heart Belongs To Me	30/06/1962	105	CB
The Supremes	My Heart Can't Take It No More	06/04/1963	129	BB
The Surfaris	Scatter Shield	18/01/1964	120	CB
The Surfaris	Show Biz	05/11/1966	102	CB
The Surfaris	Wipe Out	08/08/1970	110	BB
The Surfer Girls	Draggin' Wagon	04/04/1964	150	CB
The Surfer Girls	Draggin' Wagon	02/05/1964	134	BB
The Surfmen	Paradise Cove	10/03/1962	143	CB
The Sutherland Brothers	One More Night With You	29/07/1978	105	CB
The Swampseeds	Can I Carry Your Balloon	11/05/1968	124	BB
The Swans	You Better Be A Good Girl Now	07/09/1963	103	CB
The Swans	The Boy With The Beatle Hair	22/02/1964	121	CB
The Swe-Danes (Alice Babs, Ulrich Neumann & Svend Asmussen)	Scandinavian Shuffle	22/02/1960	101	BB
The Swe-Danes (Alice Babs, Ulrich Neumann & Svend Asmussen)	Scandinavian Shuffle	05/03/1960	102	CB
The Sweet	Poppa Joe	18/03/1972	105	CB
The Sweet	Wig-Wam Bam	13/10/1973	114	CB
The Sweet Inspirations	Let It Be Me	05/08/1967	136	CB
The Sweet Inspirations	That's How Strong My Love Is	02/09/1967	131	CB
The Sweet Inspirations	That's How Strong My Love Is	09/09/1967	123	BB
The Sweet Inspirations	Oh! What A Fool I've Been	04/11/1967	104	CB
The Sweet Inspirations	Unchained Melody	24/08/1968	109	CB

The Sweet Inspirations	What The World Needs Now Is Love	30/11/1968	128	BB
The Sweet Inspirations	Crying In The Rain	19/04/1969	112	BB
The Sweet Inspirations	Crying In The Rain	19/04/1969	113	CB
The Sweet Inspirations	(Gotta Find) A Brand New Lover (Part 1)	06/12/1969	128	CB
The Sweet Inspirations	(Gotta Find) A Brand New Lover- Part 1	20/12/1969	117	BB
The Sweet Inspirations	This World	17/10/1970	119	CB
The Sweet Inspirations	This World	31/10/1970	123	BB
The Sweet Inspirations	Love Is On The Way	25/08/1979	104	BB
The Sweet Marie	Stella's Candy Store	03/02/1973	123	BB
The Sweethearts Of Soul Peaches & Herb	So True	04/01/1969	126	BB
The Sweethearts Of Soul: Peaches & Herb	So True	21/12/1968	108	CB
The Swingin' Medallions	I Found A Rainbow	29/04/1967	107	BB
The Swinging Blue Jeans	You're No Good	01/08/1964	101	CB
The Swinging Blue Jeans	Promise You'll Tell Her	03/10/1964	130	BB
The Swinging Blue Jeans	Don't Make Me Over	12/03/1966	138	CB
The Swinging Blue Jeans	Don't Make Me Over	19/03/1966	116	BB
The Sylvers	Fool's Paradise	16/09/1972	109	CB
The System	The Pleasure Seekers	10/08/1985	108	BB
The T-Birds	Green Stamps	18/02/1961	122	CB
The T-Bones	Underwater	04/06/1966	110	CB
The Tabs	Dance Party	03/02/1962	128	CB
The Tams	Silly Little Girl	07/11/1964	112	CB
The Tams	Find Another Love	07/11/1964	129	BB
The Tams	Laugh At The World	14/09/1968	108	CB
The Tams	Trouble Maker	28/09/1968	118	BB
The Tams	Love, Love, Love	18/10/1969	116	CB
The Tams	Too Much Foolin' Around	08/08/1970	133	CB
The Tangeers	This Empty Place	07/02/1970	107	CB
The Tassels	To A Young Lover	10/10/1959	116	CB
The Teen Queens Betty And Rose	There's Nothing On My Mind Part 1	08/10/1960	121	CB

The Tempests	Would You Believe	05/08/1967	127	BB
The Tempests	Would You Believe	09/09/1967	107	CB
The Temprees	A Thousand Miles Away	19/05/1973	119	CB
The Temptations	Paradise	01/12/1962	122	BB
The Temptations	Paradise	08/12/1962	135	CB
The Temptations	I Want A Love I Can See	18/05/1963	124	CB
The Temptations	Farewell My Love	20/07/1963	137	CB
The Temptations	The Girl's Alright With Me	23/05/1964	102	BB
The Temptations	You've Got To Earn It	24/07/1965	109	CB
The Temptations	You've Got To Earn It	31/07/1965	123	BB
The Temptations	I've Been Good To You	05/08/1967	124	BB
The Temptations	I Truly, Truly Believe	30/03/1968	116	BB
The Temptations	Funky Music Sho Nuff Turns Me On	15/07/1972	105	CB
The Temptations	Up The Creek (Without A Paddle)	19/06/1976	102	CB
The Temptations	Who Are You	11/12/1976	103	CB
The Temptations	Oh, What A Night	28/11/1981	104	BB
The Third Rail	Boppa Do Down Down	14/10/1967	119	CB
The Third Rail	It's Time To Say Goodbye	16/03/1968	113	BB
The Thirteenth Floor Elevators	Reverbaration (Doubt)	26/11/1966	129	BB
The Thorndike Pickledish Choir	Ballad Of Walter Wart (Brrriggett)	21/01/1967	136	CB
The Thorndike Pickledish Choir	Ballad Of Walter Wart (Brrriggett)	04/02/1967	131	BB
The Three Dimensions (with The Thing)	Look At Me	20/11/1965	121	CB
The Three Dimensions (with The Thing)	Look At Me Girl	04/12/1965	113	BB
The Three Sounds	It Was A Very Good Year	11/02/1967	138	CB
The Tidal Wave	Sinbad The Sailor	22/06/1968	142	CB
The Tigers	Geeto Tiger	29/05/1965	122	CB
The Tigers	Geeto Tiger	05/06/1965	119	BB
The Tijuana Brass Featuring Herb Alpert	Acapulco 1922	22/12/1962	102	CB
The Time	The Walk	18/12/1982	104	BB
The Time	Ice Cream Castles	18/08/1984	106	BB

The Time Tones	Pretty, Pretty Girl (The New Beat)	31/07/1961	106	BB
The Timetones	In My Heart	22/04/1961	102	CB
The Tokens	When I Go To Sleep At Night	08/07/1961	117	CB
The Tokens	Sincerely	09/09/1961	130	CB
The Tokens	Sincerely	18/09/1961	120	BB
The Tokens	Big Boat	28/04/1962	144	CB
The Tokens	Tonight I Met An Angel	23/03/1963	126	BB
The Tokens	Please Write	12/10/1963	108	BB
The Tokens	Please Write	19/10/1963	146	CB
The Tokens	Swing	02/05/1964	105	BB
The Tokens	Sylvie Sleepin'	06/03/1965	138	CB
The Tokens	The Bells Of St. Mary	04/09/1965	149	CB
The Tokens	The Three Bells (The Jimmy Brown Song)	13/11/1965	112	CB
The Tokens	The Three Bells (The Jimmy Brown Song)	13/11/1965	120	BB
The Tokens	Greatest Moments In A Girl's Life	28/05/1966	102	BB
The Tokens	Greatest Moments In A Girl's Life	28/05/1966	123	CB
The Tokens	Green Plant	21/01/1967	145	CB
The Tokens	Some People Sleep	04/01/1969	146	CB
The Tokens	Go Away Little Girl/Young Girl	26/04/1969	118	BB
The Tokens	Go Away Little Girl/Young Girl	10/05/1969	107	CB
The Tornadoes	Bustin' Surfboards	13/10/1962	102	BB
The Tornadoes	Like Locomotion	23/02/1963	119	BB
The Tornadoes	The Ice Cream Man	20/07/1963	103	CB
The Tourists	I Only Want To Be With You	19/04/1980	I101	CB
The Toy Factory	Sunny Sunny Feeling	26/07/1969	128	CB
The Toys	May My Heart Be Cast Into Stone	26/03/1966	102	CB
The Toys	Silver Spoon	07/05/1966	111	BB
The Toys	Silver Spoon	07/05/1966	111	CB
The Toys	Sealed With A Kiss	06/07/1968	112	BB
The Trade Winds	The Girl From Greenwich Village	01/05/1965	129	BB

The Trade Winds	The Girl From Greenwich Village	22/05/1965	131	CB
The Trade Winds	Catch Me In The Meadow	24/12/1966	132	BB
The Trade Winds	Catch Me In The Meadow	31/12/1966	130	CB
The Trammps	Sixty Minute Man	07/10/1972	108	BB
The Trammps	Sixty Minute Man	14/10/1972	107	CB
The Trammps	Trusting Heart	16/11/1974	101	BB
The Trammps	Ninety-Nine And A Half	20/11/1976	105	BB
The Trammps	I Feel Like I've Been Livin' (On The Dark Side Of The Moon)	02/07/1977	105	BB
The Trammps	The Night The Lights Went Out	24/12/1977	104	BB
The Trashmen	Bad News	25/04/1964	108	CB
The Trashmen	Bad News	16/05/1964	124	BB
The Tremeloes	Helule Helule	25/05/1968	110	CB
The Tremeloes	Helule Helule	01/06/1968	122	BB
The Tremeloes	My Little Lady	26/10/1968	127	BB
The Trend-Els	Don't You Hear Me Calling - Baby	27/05/1961	149	CB
The Triumphs	Burnt Biscuits	20/01/1962	148	CB
The Troggs	Give It To Me	18/03/1967	135	CB
The Troggs	You Can Cry If You Want To	06/07/1968	120	BB
The Troggs	Good Vibrations	12/04/1975	111	CB
The Troggs	Good Vibrations	19/04/1975	102	BB
The Trolls	Every Day And Every Night	24/09/1966	119	CB
The Trolls	I Got To Have Ya	25/05/1968	135	CB
The Trolls	I Got To Have Ya	15/06/1968	129	BB
The Tubes	Talk To Ya Later	10/10/1981	101	BB
The Turbans	When You Dance (61 Version)	15/04/1961	135	CB
The Turbans	When You Dance (new Version)	17/04/1961	114	BB
The Turtles	Come Back	11/06/1966	119	CB
The Turtles	We'll Meet Again	27/08/1966	116	CB
The Turtles	Eve Of Destruction	13/06/1970	105	CB
The Turtles	Me About You	31/10/1970	101	CB

The Turtles	Me About You	07/11/1970	105	BB
The Twentie Grans	Giving Up Your Love Is Like (Giving Up The World)	14/10/1967	140	CB
The Twilights	My Heart Belongs To Only You	06/02/1960	104	CB
The Twisters	Peppermint Twist Time	09/12/1961	115	CB
The Tymes	Wonderland Of Love	21/03/1964	124	BB
The Tymes	The Magic Of Our Summer Love	13/06/1964	115	CB
The Tymes	Pretend	23/07/1966	127	CB
The Tymes	(A Touch Of) Baby	24/12/1966	148	CB
The Tymes	It's Cool	08/05/1976	107	CB
The U.S. Apple Corps	Get High On Jesus	01/05/1971	120	CB
The Unchained Mynds	We Can't Go On This Way	12/04/1969	115	BB
The Underbeats	Sweet Words Of Love	26/09/1964	136	CB
The Underbeats	Book Of Love	02/04/1966	137	CB
The Underdogs	The Man In The Glass	04/12/1965	133	CB
The Underdogs	Love's Gone Bad	28/01/1967	107	CB
The Underdogs	Love's Gone Bad	04/02/1967	122	BB
The Undisputed Truth	Save My Love For A Rainy Day	13/03/1971	111	CB
The Undisputed Truth	Girl You're Alright	18/11/1972	107	BB
The Undisputed Truth	Mama I Got A Brand New Thing (Don't Say No)	24/03/1973	109	BB
The Undisputed Truth	Mama I Got A Brand New Thing (Don't Say No)	31/03/1973	112	CB
The Undisputed Truth	Lil' Red Ridin' Hood	23/11/1974	106	BB
The Undisputed Truth	Sunshine	23/07/1977	109	BB
The Unifics	Toshisumasu	12/07/1969	117	CB
The Uniques	You Ain't Tuff	15/01/1966	127	CB
The Uniques	Run And Hide	08/10/1966	126	BB
The Uniques	Groovin' Out (On Your Good, Good Lovin')	15/04/1967	133	CB
The Uniques	All I Took Was Love	04/05/1968	128	CB
The Uniques	How Lucky (Can One Man Be)	05/10/1968	105	CB
The Uniques	How Lucky (Can One Man Be)	12/10/1968	115	BB
The Uniques	Sha-La Love	05/04/1969	140	CB

The Uniques	Toys Are Made For Children	02/08/1969	105	BB
The Uniques	All These Things	12/09/1970	112	BB
The Universals	Love Bound	21/10/1961	141	CB
The Unrelated Segments	Story Of My Life	22/04/1967	124	CB
The Unrelated Segments	Where You Gonna Go?	28/10/1967	141	CB
The Untouchable Sound Bill Black's Combo	Joey's Song	01/12/1962	101	CB
The Untouchable Sound Bill Black's Combo	Tequila	09/05/1964	113	CB
The Untouchable Sound Bill Black's Combo	Little Queenie	05/09/1964	111	CB
The Untouchables	Poor Boy Needs A Preacher	16/04/1960	103	CB
The Untouchables	Goodnight Sweetheart, Goodnight (Goodnight, Well It's Time To Go)	06/08/1960	102	CB
The Untouchables	60 Minute Man	07/11/1960	104	BB
The Untouchables	Raisin' Sugar Cane	04/03/1961	117	CB
The Uptones	No More	27/10/1962	148	CB
The V.I.P.'S	You Pulled A Fast One	15/08/1964	117	BB
The V.I.P.'S	You Pulled A Fast One	15/08/1964	130	CB
The Vacels	Can You Please Crawl Out Your Window?	09/10/1965	120	CB
The Valadiers	Greetings (This Is Uncle Sam)	11/11/1961	102	CB
The Valentinos	Everybody Wants To Fall In Love	21/11/1964	142	CB
The Valrays	Yo Me Pregunto (I Ask Myself)	18/04/1964	102	CB
The Valrays	Yo Me Pregunto (I Ask Myself)	09/05/1964	121	BB
The Van Dykes	The Bells Are Ringing	12/08/1961	148	CB
The Van Dykes	Stupidity	24/11/1962	133	CB
The Van Dykes	I've Got To Go On Without You	25/06/1966	109	BB
The Van Dykes	Never Let Me Go	12/11/1966	105	CB
The Vejtables	I Still Love You	18/09/1965	109	CB
The Vejtables	The Last Thing On My Mind	27/11/1965	117	BB
The Velvelettes	These Things Will Keep Me Loving You	01/10/1966	102	BB
The Velvellettes	There He Goes	05/10/1963	119	CB
The Velvet Crest	Look Homeward Angel	08/03/1969	110	CB
The Velveteens	Teen Prayer	24/06/1961	101	CB

The Velvets	Let The Good Times Roll	25/08/1962	102	BB
The Ventures	Instant Mashed	02/06/1962	140	CB
The Ventures	Instant Mashed	09/06/1962	104	BB
The Ventures	Skip To M'limbo	30/03/1963	114	BB
The Ventures	Skip To M' Limbo	30/03/1963	120	CB
The Ventures	The Ninth Wave	15/06/1963	122	BB
The Ventures	The Ninth Wave	29/06/1963	144	CB
The Ventures	Fugitive	18/04/1964	121	CB
The Ventures	Fugitive	02/05/1964	126	BB
The Ventures	Rap City	07/11/1964	132	CB
The Ventures	Rap City	21/11/1964	135	BB
The Ventures	Blue Star	11/06/1966	120	BB
The Ventures	Green Hornet Theme	03/09/1966	116	BB
The Ventures	Green Hornet Theme	10/09/1966	131	CB
The Ventures	Wild Thing	29/10/1966	116	BB
The Ventures	Penetration	29/10/1966	121	CB
The Ventures	Theme From "The Wild Angels"	24/12/1966	110	BB
The Ventures	Theme From "THE Wild Angels"	21/01/1967	129	CB
The Ventures	Theme From Endless Summer	01/07/1967	106	BB
The Ventures	Theme From Endless Summer	22/07/1967	111	CB
The Ventures	Flights Of Fantasy	02/03/1968	110	CB
The Ventures	Joy	25/12/1971	109	BB
The Ventures	Main Theme From "THE Young And The Restless"	20/04/1974	118	CB
The Vibrations	So Blue	06/06/1960	110	BB
The Vibrations	So Blue	18/06/1960	105	CB
The Vibrations	Continental With Me, Baby	15/04/1961	111	CB
The Vibrations	The Junkernoo	22/04/1961	109	CB
The Vibrations	The Junkernoo	24/04/1961	112	BB
The Vibrations	Stranded In The Jungle (new Version)	03/07/1961	117	BB
The Vibrations	Let's Pony Again	21/10/1961	133	CB

The Vibrations	Sloop Dance	31/10/1964	109	BB
The Vibrations	Keep On Keeping On	30/01/1965	137	CB
The Vibrations	Keep On Keeping On	13/02/1965	118	BB
The Vibrations	End Up Crying	29/05/1965	130	BB
The Vibrations	Canadian Sunset	26/03/1966	128	CB
The Vibrations	And I Love Her	15/10/1966	118	BB
The Vibrations	And I Love Her	12/11/1966	114	CB
The Vibrations	Pick Me	06/05/1967	133	CB
The Vibrations	Smoke Signals	18/07/1970	116	CB
The Viceroys	Seagrams	02/03/1963	108	CB
The Viceroys	Seagrams	30/03/1963	127	BB
The Victorians	What Makes Little Girls Cry	27/07/1963	120	BB
The Victorians	Move In A Little Closer	22/06/1968	147	CB
The Videls	A Letter From Ann	21/10/1961	143	CB
The Village Stompers	The La-Dee-Da Song	01/02/1964	103	CB
The Village Stompers	The La-Dee-Da Song	01/02/1964	104	BB
The Village Stompers	Oh! Marie	03/10/1964	101	CB
The Village Stompers	Oh! Marie	03/10/1964	132	BB
The Village Stompers	Brother, Can You Spare A Dime?	08/05/1965	137	CB
The Village Stompers	Those Magnificent Men In Their Flying Machines	17/07/1965	130	BB
The Village Stompers	Those Magnificent Men In Their Flying Machines	17/07/1965	146	CB
The Violinaires	I Don't Know	06/04/1968	121	BB
The Virtues	Guitar Boogie Shuffle Twist	10/03/1962	134	CB
The Viscounts	Shadrach	18/03/1961	118	CB
The Viscounts	Night Train	19/02/1966	122	BB
The Visuals	The Submarine Race	17/11/1962	147	CB
The Vogues	That's The Tune	24/12/1966	103	CB
The Vogues	Lovers Of The World Unite	26/08/1967	109	CB
The Vogues	See That Girl	11/10/1969	108	CB
The Vogues	God Only Knows	24/01/1970	114	CB

The Vogues	God Only Knows	31/01/1970	101	BB
The Vogues	Hey, That's No Way To Say Goodbye	02/05/1970	101	BB
The Vogues	Hey, That's No Way To Say Goodbye	02/05/1970	118	CB
The Vogues	Love Song	15/05/1971	101	CB
The Vogues	Love Song	12/06/1971	118	BB
The Vogues	Prisoner Of Love	27/04/1974	107	CB
The Voices Of East Harlem	Right On Be Free	14/11/1970	123	CB
The Volcanos	Storm Warning	07/08/1965	126	CB
The Volumes	Come Back Into My Heart	04/08/1962	139	CB
The Volumes	Come Back Into My Heart	11/08/1962	118	BB
The Volumes	Sandra	13/04/1963	113	CB
The Volumes	Gotta Give Her Love	17/10/1964	108	CB
The Volumes	Gotta Give Her Love	24/10/1964	117	BB
The Vonnair Sisters	Goodbye To Toyland	13/01/1962	115	BB
The Wackers	Hey Lawdy Lawdy	24/03/1973	124	BB
The Wailers	It's You Alone	11/06/1966	118	BB
The Wailers	It's You Alone	18/06/1966	120	CB
The Walker Bros.	(Baby) You Don't Have To Tell Me	30/07/1966	141	CB
The Walker Bros.	Another Tear Falls	29/10/1966	114	CB
The Wanderers	I Could Make You Mine	15/10/1960	102	CB
The Wanderers	I'll Never Smile Again	07/08/1961	107	BB
The Wanted	In The Midnight Hour	08/04/1967	118	BB
The Wanted	Don't Worry Baby	10/06/1967	105	CB
The Watts 103rd Street Rhythm Band	Brown Sugar	16/03/1968	118	CB
The Weather Girls	Well-A-Wiggy	03/08/1985	107	BB
The Webs	This Thing Called Love	02/12/1967	102	BB
The Webs	We Belong Together	09/11/1968	133	CB
The Wheels	Clap Your Hands - Part 1	04/01/1960	102	BB
The Whispers	As I Sit Here	04/09/1965	116	CB
The Whispers	There's A Love For Everyone	05/12/1970	110	CB

The Whispers	There's A Love For Everyone	26/12/1970	116	BB
The Whispers	Can't Help But Love You	11/12/1971	105	CB
The Whispers	Can't Help But Love You	19/02/1972	114	BB
The Whispers	I Only Meant To Wet My Feet	27/05/1972	112	CB
The Whispers	Somebody Loves You	16/12/1972	111	CB
The Whispers	Living Together (In Sin)	30/10/1976	101	BB
The Whispers	(Let's Go) All The Way	03/06/1978	101	BB
The Whispers	I Can Make It Better	16/05/1981	105	BB
The Whispers	In The Raw	13/02/1982	103	BB
The Whispers	This Time	01/10/1983	110	BB
The Whispers	Contagious	08/12/1984	105	BB
The Whispers	Some Kinda Lover	23/03/1985	106	BB
The Who	Anyway Anyhow Anywhere	19/06/1965	112	CB
The Who	The Kids Are Alright	13/08/1966	106	BB
The Who	I'm A Boy	28/01/1967	110	CB
The Who	Substitute	26/08/1967	105	CB
The Who	Young Man (Blues) (Live)	24/10/1970	109	CB
The Who	Trick Of The Light	13/01/1979	107	BB
The Wilburn Brothers	Trouble's Back In Town	21/04/1962	107	CB
The Wilburn Brothers	Trouble's Back In Town	30/06/1962	101	BB
The Wildweeds	Someday Morning	26/08/1967	141	CB
The Wildweeds	I'm Dreaming	22/06/1968	112	CB
The Wildweeds	And When She Smiles	05/06/1971	101	CB
The Wildweeds	And When She Smiles	10/07/1971	113	BB
The Will-O-Bees	Make Your Own Kind Of Music	14/09/1968	126	CB
The Willies	The Willy	08/10/1966	113	BB
The Winstons	The Greatest Love	15/11/1969	135	CB
The Winters Brothers Band	Smokey Mountain Log Cabin Jones	25/06/1977	106	CB
The Womenfolk	The Last Thing On My Mind	07/05/1966	105	BB
The Wonder Who?	On The Good Ship Lollipop	25/06/1966	107	CB

The Wonderettes	I Feel Strange	09/10/1965	117	CB
The Wonders	Say There	24/08/1963	112	CB
The Wooden Nickels	Should I Give My Love Tonight	27/11/1965	128	CB
The Yardbirds	Goodnight Sweet Josephine	18/05/1968	127	BB
The Yellow Balloon	Good Feelin' Time	24/06/1967	101	BB
The Yellow Payges	I'm A Man	23/05/1970	102	BB
The Young World Singers	Ringo For President	22/08/1964	132	BB
The Young World Singers	Ringo For President	29/08/1964	107	CB
The Youngbloods	Merry-Go-Round	08/04/1967	101	CB
The Youngbloods	Quicksand	20/01/1968	131	CB
The Youngbloods	Darkness, Darkness	03/05/1969	121	CB
The Youngbloods	Darkness, Darkness	10/05/1969	124	BB
The Youngbloods	Sunlight	08/11/1969	114	BB
The Youngbloods	Sunlight	12/06/1971	123	BB
The Z-Debs	Changing My Life For You	07/03/1964	132	CB
The Zephyrs	She's Lost You	10/04/1965	112	CB
The Zephyrs	She's Lost You	17/04/1965	109	BB
The Zodiacs	May I	13/08/1966	150	CB
The Zombies	Remember When I Loved Her	26/06/1965	122	CB
The Zombies	Whenever You're Ready	04/09/1965	110	BB
The Zombies	Whenever You're Ready	04/09/1965	114	CB
The Zombies	Just Out Of Reach	06/11/1965	113	BB
The Zombies	Just Out Of Reach	13/11/1965	110	CB
The Zombies	Imagine The Swan	17/05/1969	109	BB
Thee Midniters	Whittier Blvd.	10/07/1965	102	CB
Thee Midniters	Whittier Blvd.	04/09/1965	127	BB
Thee Prophets	Some Kind-A Wonderful	17/05/1969	111	BB
Thee Prophets	Some Kind-A Wonderful	24/05/1969	114	CB
Thelma Houston	If This Was The Last Song	21/06/1969	129	CB
Thelma Houston	Jumpin' Jack Flash	15/11/1969	123	CB

Thelma Houston	You've Been Doing Wrong For So Long	14/09/1974	118	CB
Thelma Jones	The House That Jack Built	13/04/1968	132	BB
Thelma Jones	Salty Tears	23/10/1976	107	CB
Them	Baby, Please Don't Go	13/03/1965	102	BB
Them	Half As Much	28/08/1965	130	CB
Them	Call My Name	19/03/1966	111	CB
Theola Kilgore	He's Coming Back To Me (b-side)	27/06/1964	133	BB
Theola Kilgore	I'll Keep Trying	27/06/1964	139	CB
Theola Kilgore	I'll Keep Trying	25/07/1964	108	BB
Theresa Lindsey	Gotta Find A Way	01/02/1964	129	BB
Thin Lizzy	Cowboy Song	11/09/1976	105	CB
Third World	Try Jah Love	27/03/1982	101	BB
Thp Orchestra	Two Hot For Love	25/02/1978	103	BB
Three Dog Night	Nobody	25/01/1969	116	BB
Thunderclap Newman	Something In The Air	24/10/1970	120	BB
Thundermama	Thundermama	13/05/1972	117	CB
Thundermug	Africa	02/12/1972	102	CB
Thundermug	Africa	16/12/1972	110	BB
Tico & The Triumphs	Motorcycle	23/12/1961	103	CB
Tidal Waves	Farmer John	02/07/1966	123	BB
Tim Goodman	New Romeo	19/09/1981	107	BB
Tim Moore	Strengthen My Love	12/11/1977	109	CB
Tim Tam & The Turn-Ons	Wait A Minute	15/01/1966	105	CB
Tim Tam & The Turn-Ons	Cheryl Ann	04/06/1966	102	CB
Tim Tam & The Turn-Ons	Kimberly	15/10/1966	120	CB
Tim Weisberg	I'm The Lucky One	20/09/1980	106	BB
Timi Yuro	I Apologize	14/10/1961	116	CB
Timi Yuro	She Really Loves You	25/11/1961	123	CB
Timi Yuro	I Know (I Love You)	07/04/1962	147	CB
Timi Yuro	Insult To Injury	30/03/1963	127	CB

Timi Yuro	Permanently Lonely	22/02/1964	136	CB
Timi Yuro	Permanently Lonely	04/04/1964	130	BB
Timi Yuro	If	22/08/1964	120	BB
Timi Yuro	You Can Have Him	20/02/1965	118	CB
Timi Yuro	Teardrops 'TILL Dawn	02/10/1965	146	CB
Timi Yuro	Big Mistake	09/10/1965	135	CB
Timi Yuro	Once A Day	01/01/1966	123	CB
Timi Yuro	Once A Day	08/01/1966	118	BB
Timi Yuro	Turn The World Around The Other Way	12/11/1966	129	CB
Timi Yuro	Southern Lady	18/10/1975	108	BB
Timmy Thomas	Let Me Be Your Eyes	21/07/1973	107	BB
Timmy Thomas	What Can I Tell You	17/11/1973	102	BB
Timmy Thomas	What Can I Tell Her	15/12/1973	107	CB
Timmy Willis	Mr. Soul Satisfaction	03/02/1968	120	BB
Timmy Willis	Mr. Soul Satisfaction	10/02/1968	132	CB
Timothy B. Schmit	Playin' It Cool	27/10/1984	101	BB
Timothy Carr	A Stop Along The Way	06/04/1968	107	CB
Timothy Carr	A Stop Along The Way	20/04/1968	112	BB
Tina Britt	The Real Thing	22/05/1965	103	BB
Tina Britt	The Real Thing	22/05/1965	117	CB
Tina Charles	You Set My Heart On Fire	22/11/1975	104	BB
Tina Robin	Dear Mr. D. J. Play It Again	09/09/1961	117	CB
Tinker's Moon	Shang-A-Lang	03/08/1974	114	CB
Tiny Tim	Hello, Hello	14/09/1968	109	CB
Tiny Tim	Hello, Hello	21/09/1968	122	BB
Titus Turner	Pony Train	10/04/1961	115	BB
Titus Turner	Pony Train	15/04/1961	126	CB
Tnt Band	The Meditation	21/12/1968	106	CB
Tnt Band	The Meditation	25/01/1969	117	BB
Tobin Matthews	Susan	22/09/1962	104	CB

Toby Beau	Into The Night	21/10/1978	Np5	CB
Toby Beau	Into The Night	28/10/1978	108	BB
Today's People	He	18/08/1973	109	CB
Todd Rundgren	Couldn't I Just Tell You	22/07/1972	104	CB
Todd Rundgren	Sometimes I Don't Know What To Feel	21/07/1973	111	CB
Todd Rundgren	Time Heals	28/03/1981	107	BB
Todd Rundgren (featuring Wolfman Jack)	Wolfman Jack	18/01/1975	105	BB
Tom & Jerrio	Great Goo-Ga-Moo-Ga	14/08/1965	123	BB
Tom & Jerrio	Great Goo-Ga-Moo-Ga	14/08/1965	130	CB
Tom & Jerry	Golden Wildwood Flower	11/02/1961	115	CB
Tom Dooley & His Lovelights	My Groovy Baby	19/10/1968	130	CB
Tom Fogerty	Goodbye Media Man Part I	04/09/1971	103	BB
Tom Jones	Chills & Fever	11/12/1965	125	BB
Tom Jones	What A Party	03/09/1966	140	CB
Tom Jones	What A Party	10/09/1966	120	BB
Tom Jones	Pledging My Love	28/12/1974	106	CB
Tom Jones	Take Me Tonight	18/06/1977	101	BB
Tom Jones	Take Me Tonight	25/06/1977	101	CB
Tom Jones	Darlin'	18/04/1981	103	BB
Tom Jones	What In The World's Come Over You	15/08/1981	109	BB
Tom Middleton	It Wouldn't Have Made Any Difference	19/01/1974	103	CB
Tom Northcott	Sunny Goodge Street	29/07/1967	123	BB
Tom Northcott	1941	17/02/1968	117	CB
Tom Paxton	Jimmy Newman	04/04/1970	120	CB
Tom Powers	It Ain't Love	08/10/1977	106	CB
Tom Rush	Urge For Going	29/10/1966	118	CB
Tom Rush	Who Do You Love	27/02/1971	105	BB
Tom Rush	Mother Earth	03/06/1972	111	BB
Tom Rush	Mother Earth	01/07/1972	120	CB
Tom Rush	Ladies Love Outlaws	26/10/1974	117	CB

Tom Scott & The L.A. Express	Strut Your Stuff	11/05/1974	117	CB
Tom Scott & The L.A. Express	Jump Back	27/07/1974	110	CB
Tom Sullivan	Yes, I'm Ready	01/05/1976	103	BB
Tom Sullivan	Yes, I'm Ready	08/05/1976	111	CB
Tom T. Hall	Watergate Blues	23/06/1973	101	BB
Tom Tom Club	Wordy Rappinghood	15/05/1982	105	BB
Tom Tom Club	The Man With The 4-Way Hips	17/09/1983	106	BB
Tommy Adderley With Max Merritt & His Meteors	I Just Don't Understand	24/10/1964	118	CB
Tommy Boyce	Along Came Linda	27/01/1962	103	CB
Tommy Boyce	Along Came Linda	27/01/1962	118	BB
Tommy Boyce	Sunday, The Day Before Monday	10/09/1966	132	BB
Tommy Boyce & BoBBy Hart	Sometimes She's A Little Girl	30/09/1967	110	BB
Tommy Boyce & BoBBy Hart	We're All Going To The Same Place	09/11/1968	124	CB
Tommy Boyce & BoBBy Hart	We're All Going To The Same Place	16/11/1968	123	BB
Tommy Boyce & BoBBy Hart	L.U.V. (Let Us Vote)	15/03/1969	111	BB
Tommy Collins	If You Can't Bite, Don't Growl	05/02/1966	105	BB
Tommy Dee	Here Is My Love	10/01/1981	107	BB
Tommy Duncan	Dance, Dance, Dance	13/06/1964	133	BB
Tommy Edwards	Blue Heartaches	08/10/1960	113	CB
Tommy Edwards	Vaya Con Dios (May God Be With You)	04/03/1961	119	CB
Tommy Edwards	The Golden Chain	13/05/1961	150	CB
Tommy Hunt	I Just Don't Know What To Do With Myself	15/08/1964	119	BB
Tommy Hunt	The Biggest Man	04/02/1967	102	CB
Tommy Hunt	The Biggest Man	18/02/1967	124	BB
Tommy Hunt	I Need A Woman Of My Own	20/01/1968	134	CB
Tommy James	You Got Me	31/05/1980	101	BB
Tommy Leonetti	Soul Dance	04/01/1964	105	BB
Tommy Leonetti	Wasn't It Nice In New York City	26/05/1973	112	CB
Tommy Mclain	Think It Over	15/10/1966	147	CB
Tommy Overstreet	Gwen (Congratulations)	26/06/1971	123	BB

Tommy Overstreet	Heaven Is My Woman's Love	20/01/1973	102	BB
Tommy Overstreet	Heaven Is My Woman's Love	03/02/1973	123	CB
Tommy Quickly	The Wild Side Of Life	09/01/1965	137	CB
Tommy Raye	You Don't Love Me	08/08/1964	141	CB
Tommy Ridgley	In The Same Old Way	25/11/1961	128	CB
Tommy Roe	Piddle De Pat	06/10/1962	118	CB
Tommy Roe	Piddle De Pat	03/11/1962	108	BB
Tommy Roe	Rainbow	15/12/1962	143	CB
Tommy Roe	Town Crier	29/12/1962	121	CB
Tommy Roe	Gonna Take A Chance	19/01/1963	125	CB
Tommy Roe	Don't Cry Donna	19/01/1963	145	CB
Tommy Roe	Kiss And Run	06/07/1963	137	CB
Tommy Roe	Party Girl	12/12/1964	104	CB
Tommy Roe	Kick Me Charlie	21/01/1967	113	CB
Tommy Roe	Melancholy Mood	07/10/1967	129	CB
Tommy Roe	Dottie I Like It	10/02/1968	114	BB
Tommy Roe	Brush A Little Sunshine	14/11/1970	117	BB
Tommy Roe	Brush A Little Sunshine	28/11/1970	102	CB
Tommy Roe	Little Miss Goodie Two Shoes	23/01/1971	104	BB
Tommy Roe	Little Miss Goody Two Shoes	06/02/1971	130	CB
Tommy Roe	Pistol Legged Mama	17/04/1971	124	BB
Tommy Roe	Mean Little Woman, Rosalie	16/09/1972	102	CB
Tommy Roe & The Oremans	Love Me, Love Me	06/03/1965	142	CB
Tommy Sands	A Young Man's Fancy	10/08/1963	129	CB
Tommy Tucker	Long Tall Shorty	02/05/1964	129	CB
Tommy Tucker	Alimony	26/06/1965	129	CB
Tommy Tucker	Alimony	17/07/1965	103	BB
Tommy Tutone	Which Man Are You	24/07/1982	101	BB
Tommy Vann & The Echoes	Too Young	09/04/1966	111	CB
Tommy Vann & The Echoes	Pretty Flamingo	18/06/1966	130	CB

Tommy Vann And The Echoes	Too Young	12/03/1966	103	BB
Tommy Vann And The Echoes	Pretty Flamingo	02/07/1966	125	BB
Tommy Wills (Man With A Horn)	Honky Tonk Ii 66 Style	26/11/1966	145	CB
Tommy Zang	I Can't Stop Loving You	06/08/1960	106	CB
Tommy Zang	I Can't Stop Loving You	15/08/1960	108	BB
Tomorrow's Promise	That's The Way It Will Stay	27/04/1974	112	CB
Tompall	Put Another Log On The Fire (Male Chauvinist National Anthem)	01/11/1975	103	BB
Tompall & Glaser Brothers	California Girl (And The Tennessee Square)	05/04/1969	101	CB
Toni Fisher	The Music From The House Next Door	20/10/1962	115	CB
Toni Jones	Dear (Here Comes My Baby)	27/04/1963	125	CB
Tony & Terri	I Want You	25/12/1965	119	CB
Tony & Tyrone	Turn It On Girl	18/12/1965	147	CB
Tony Bennett	Candy Kisses	26/05/1962	140	CB
Tony Bennett	True Blue Lou	10/08/1963	132	CB
Tony Bennett	The Moment Of Truth	14/12/1963	127	BB
Tony Bennett	Song From "THE Oscar"	05/02/1966	135	CB
Tony Bennett	Song From "The Oscar"	26/02/1966	104	BB
Tony Bennett	A Time For Love	10/09/1966	113	CB
Tony Bennett	A Time For Love	17/09/1966	119	BB
Tony Bennett	What Makes It Happen	31/12/1966	119	CB
Tony Bennett	Keep Smiling At Trouble (Trouble's A BuBBle)	03/06/1967	121	CB
Tony Bennett	A Fool Of Fools	16/03/1968	119	BB
Tony Bennett	Yesterday I Heard The Rain (Esta Tarde Vi Llover)	20/04/1968	114	CB
Tony Bennett	Yesterday I Heard The Rain	27/04/1968	130	BB
Tony Bennett	Hushabye Mountain	13/07/1968	130	CB
Tony Bennett	(Where Do I Begin) Love Story	13/02/1971	114	BB
Tony Bennett With The Mike Curb Congregation	Living Together, Growing Together	09/12/1972	111	BB
Tony Bruno	Hard To Get Thing Called Love	19/11/1966	124	CB
Tony Christie	(Is This The Way To) Amarillo	18/03/1972	126	CB
Tony Christie	(Is This The Way To) Amarillo	25/03/1972	121	BB

Tony Clarke	Poor Boy	03/07/1965	102	CB
Tony Clarke And You, His Audience	Ain't Love Good - Ain't Love Proud (Live)	20/06/1964	130	CB
Tony Conigliaro	Why Don't They Understand	20/03/1965	121	CB
Tony Defranco	Cuore (Don't Suffer My Heart)	09/06/1962	105	CB
Tony Joe White	High Sheriff Of Calhoun Parrish	04/04/1970	112	BB
Tony Joe White	Scratch My Back	28/11/1970	111	CB
Tony Joe White	Scratch My Back	28/11/1970	117	BB
Tony Joe White	It Must Be Love	12/06/1976	119	CB
Tony Joe White	It Must Be Love	10/07/1976	108	BB
Tony Lawrence	You Got To Show Me	05/06/1961	114	BB
Tony Martin	Talkin' To Your Picture	16/01/1965	133	BB
Tony Mason	(We're Gonna) Bring The Country To The City	26/11/1966	125	BB
Tony Mottola	This Guy's In Love With You	24/08/1968	142	CB
Tony Orlando	At The Edge Of Tears	11/08/1962	146	CB
Tony Orlando	Chills	08/09/1962	109	BB
Tony Orlando	Chills	29/09/1962	111	CB
Tony Orlando	Shirley	09/02/1963	109	CB
Tony Orlando	Shirley	23/02/1963	133	BB
Tony Orlando	I'll Be There	26/10/1963	123	CB
Tony Orlando	I'll Be There	09/11/1963	124	BB
Tony Orlando	Tell Me What Can I Do	18/04/1964	147	CB
Tony Orlando	To Wait For Love	26/09/1964	119	CB
Tony Osborne With His Piano & Orchestra	Turkish Coffee	21/04/1962	119	CB
Tony Sandler & Ralph Young	Dominique	07/01/1967	110	CB
Tony Scotti	Come Live With Me	16/03/1968	105	CB
Tony Scotti	Come Live With Me	16/03/1968	126	BB
Tony Scotti	Rose (A Ring To The Name Of Rose)	08/06/1968	104	CB
Tony Scotti	Devil Or Angel	19/04/1969	116	CB
Tony Scotti	Devil Or Angel	03/05/1969	117	BB
Tony Scotti	Those Lazy, Hazy, Crazy Days Of Summer	05/07/1969	119	CB

Tony Scotti	It Won't Hurt To Try It	05/06/1971	106	CB
Tony Scotti	It Won't Hurt To Try It	12/06/1971	118	BB
Tony Williams	Sleepless Nights	02/09/1961	112	CB
Tony Wilson	I Like Your Style	21/05/1977	107	CB
Toronto	Even The Score	13/09/1980	104	BB
Toto	Goodbye Elenore	07/03/1981	107	BB
Tower Of Power	Sparkling In The Sand	01/09/1973	107	BB
Tower Of Power	What Is Hip?	15/12/1973	103	CB
Tower Of Power	Only So Much Oil In The Ground	01/03/1975	102	BB
Tower Of Power	Willing To Learn	12/04/1975	117	CB
Tower Of Power	Lovin' You Is Gonna See Me Thru	22/07/1978	106	BB
Tracey Dey	Hangin' On To My Baby	11/07/1964	107	BB
Tracey Dey	I Won't Tell	03/10/1964	121	CB
Trade Martin	La Mer	16/01/1960	122	CB
Trade Martin	Hula Hula Dancin' Doll	29/12/1962	133	CB
Trade Martin	I Can't Do It For You	08/01/1972	106	BB
Trade Martin	I Can't Do It For You	29/01/1972	119	CB
Traffic	Hole In My Shoe	14/10/1967	122	CB
Traffic	Feelin' Alright?	26/10/1968	109	CB
Traffic	Feelin' Alright?	26/10/1968	123	BB
Traffic	Medicated Goo	01/03/1969	118	CB
Traffic	Rock & Roll Stew...Part 1	08/01/1972	105	CB
Traffic	Walking In The Wind	28/09/1974	101	CB
Trammps	Where Do We Go From Here	22/06/1974	122	CB
Trash	Golden Slumbers/Carry That Weight	15/11/1969	112	BB
Travis & Bob	Little Bitty Johnny	13/07/1959	114	BB
Travis Wammack	Louie Louie	09/04/1966	128	BB
Trella Hart	Two Little Rooms	05/09/1970	120	BB
Tremeloes	(Call Me) Number One	28/02/1970	124	CB
Trini Lopez	La Bamba (Part I) (Live)	06/07/1963	123	CB

Trini Lopez	Lonesome Traveler (Live)	16/11/1963	135	CB
Trini Lopez	Sinner Not A Saint	11/01/1964	103	BB
Trini Lopez	Jailer, Bring Me Water (Live)	29/02/1964	106	CB
Trini Lopez	Are You Sincere	05/06/1965	106	CB
Trini Lopez	Made In Paris	29/01/1966	113	CB
Trini Lopez	Made In Paris	05/02/1966	113	BB
Trini Lopez	Your Ever Changin' Mind	17/12/1966	131	CB
Trini Lopez	Up To Now	27/05/1967	123	BB
Trini Lopez	The Bramble Bush	01/07/1967	117	CB
Trini Lopez	Sally Was A Good Old Girl	17/02/1968	106	CB
Trini Lopez	Come A Little Bit Closer	22/03/1969	121	BB
Trini Lopez	Don't Let The Sun Catch You Cryin'	31/05/1969	133	BB
Triumph	Say Goodbye	13/02/1982	102	BB
Troy Shondell	Na-Ne-No	12/05/1962	103	CB
Troy Shondell	Na-Ne-No	02/06/1962	107	BB
Troy Shondell	Let's Go All The Way	21/12/1968	121	CB
Troy Shondell	Let's Go All The Way	04/01/1969	129	BB
Trudy Pitts & Mr. Carney	I Really Mean It	22/09/1962	135	CB
Turley Richards	I Heard The Voice Of Jesus	11/07/1970	106	CB
Tuxedo Junction	Moonlight Serenade	12/08/1978	103	BB
Twennynine Featuring Lenny White	Kid Stuff	29/11/1980	106	BB
Twice As Much	Sittin' On A Fence	09/07/1966	122	BB
Twiggy & Friends	Zoo De Zoo Zong	28/08/1971	110	CB
Twinkle	Terry	09/01/1965	106	CB
Twinkle	Terry	23/01/1965	110	BB
Twisted Sister	The Price	05/01/1985	107	BB
Ty Hunter	Darling, Darling, Darling	13/07/1963	130	CB
Ty Hunter & The Voice Masters	Free	10/12/1960	113	CB
Ty Hunter & The Voice Masters	Free	16/01/1961	110	BB
Ty Hunter With The Voice Masters	Everything About You	16/07/1960	120	CB

Typically Tropical	Barbados	11/10/1975	108	BB
Tyrone Davis	All The Waiting Is Not In Vain	09/08/1969	125	BB
Tyrone Davis	Come And Get This Ring	26/08/1972	119	BB
Tyrone Davis	If You Had A Change In Mind	21/10/1972	107	BB
Tyrone Davis	What Goes Up (Must Come Down)	13/07/1974	110	CB
Tyrone Davis	This I Swear	30/07/1977	102	BB
Tyrone Davis	Get On Up (Disco)	25/03/1978	102	BB
U.S. Bonds	Not Me	25/02/1961	105	CB
U.S. Bonds	Not Me	06/03/1961	116	BB
U2	Two Hearts Beat As One	02/07/1983	101	BB
Ufo	Too Hot To Handle	20/08/1977	106	BB
Ultravox	Dancing With Tears In My Eyes	07/07/1984	108	BB
Underground Sunshine	Don't Shut Me Out	04/10/1969	114	CB
Underground Sunshine	Don't Shut Me Out	11/10/1969	102	BB
Unit Four Plus Two	You've Never Been In Love Like This Before	03/07/1965	117	CB
Unit Four Plus Two	Hark	02/10/1965	123	CB
Unit Four Plus Two	Hark	09/10/1965	131	BB
Unit Four Plus Two	I Was Only Playing Games	21/01/1967	141	CB
United States Double Quartet: The Tokens The Kirby Stone Four	Life Is Groovy	28/01/1967	110	BB
United States Double Quartet: The Tokens The Kirby Stone Four	Life Is Groovy	11/02/1967	137	CB
Universal Jones	River	02/09/1972	115	BB
Universal Jones	River	16/09/1972	115	CB
Up 'N Adam	Time To Get It Together	06/09/1969	135	CB
Uproar	Drifting Away (I've Been Drifting Away)	24/06/1978	105	BB
Uriah Heep	That's The Way That It Is	25/09/1982	106	BB
Val Doonican	What Would I Be	07/01/1967	142	CB
Val Doonican	If The Whole World Stopped Lovin'	10/02/1968	125	CB
Val Doonican	If The Whole World Stopped Lovin'	02/03/1968	128	BB
Valentinos	I Can Understand It-Part I	14/04/1973	109	BB
Valerie & Nick	I'll Find You	28/03/1964	110	CB

Valerie & Nick	I'll Find You	25/04/1964	117	BB
Valerie Carr	The Way To My Heart	10/10/1959	111	CB
Valerie Carr	I Left There Crying	27/05/1961	106	CB
Valerie Carter	Ooh Child	02/04/1977	103	BB
Van & Titus	Cry Baby Cry	29/06/1968	128	CB
Van Halen	So This Is Love?	01/08/1981	110	BB
Van Mccoy	Mr. D. J.	08/07/1961	105	CB
Van Mccoy	Mr. D.J.	25/09/1961	104	BB
Van Mccoy	Girls Are Sentimental	06/01/1962	149	CB
Van Mccoy	The Shuffle	22/01/1977	105	BB
Van Morrison	Ro Ro Rosey	04/11/1967	107	BB
Van Morrison	Ro Ro Rosey	04/11/1967	115	CB
Van Morrison	Call Me Up In Dreamland	05/06/1971	112	CB
Van Morrison	(Straight To Your Heart) Like A Cannonball	01/04/1972	119	BB
Van Morrison	Redwood Tree	04/11/1972	119	CB
Van Morrison	Gypsy	13/01/1973	101	BB
Van Morrison	Bright Side Of The Road	03/11/1979	110	BB
Van Morrison	Tore Down A La Rimbaud	30/03/1985	101	BB
Van Strickland	Gotta Get A Date	12/03/1960	111	CB
Van Zant	You've Got To Believe In Love	08/06/1985	102	BB
Vanilla Fudge	Some Velvet Morning	24/05/1969	103	BB
Vanilla Fudge	Need Love	23/08/1969	111	BB
Vanity	Mechanical Emotion	12/01/1985	107	BB
Vanity 6	Nasty Girl	02/10/1982	101	BB
Vardi & The Medallion Strings	Theme From King Of Kings*	04/11/1961	111	CB
Vaughn Monroe	Queen Of The Senior Prom	15/05/1965	132	BB
Vee Allen	Can I	03/03/1973	107	BB
Vernon & Jewell	Those Lonely, Lonely Nights	19/12/1964	130	CB
Vernon Burch	Changes (Messin' With My Mind)	01/02/1975	101	BB
Vernon Burch	Changes (Messin' With My Mind)	08/03/1975	119	CB

Vernon Harrel	Do Unto Others	02/03/1963	140	CB
Verrill Keene	Lilly's Back	01/03/1969	109	CB
Vic Damone	What Kind Of Fool Am I?	06/10/1962	131	BB
Vic Damone	Why Don't You Believe Me	10/07/1965	127	BB
Vic Dana	(A Girl Needs) To Love And Be Loved	14/07/1962	102	CB
Vic Dana	The Prisoner's Song	14/12/1963	143	CB
Vic Dana	Frenchy	12/12/1964	129	CB
Vic Dana	Distant Drums	22/10/1966	114	BB
Vic Dana	Grown Up Games	24/12/1966	127	CB
Vic Dana	Fraulein	11/03/1967	138	CB
Vic Dana	You Are My Destiny	01/03/1969	133	CB
Vic Mizzy & His Orchestra	(Main Theme) The Addams Family	16/01/1965	147	CB
Vicki Anderson	Tears Of Joy	23/09/1967	131	BB
Vicki Belmonte	I'm Gonna Get Him	17/11/1962	137	CB
Vicki Britton	Flight 309 To Tennessee	29/06/1974	110	CB
Vicki Lawrence	Ships In The Night	03/11/1973	106	CB
Vicki Sue Robinson	Trust In Me	22/04/1978	110	BB
Vicki Sue Robinson	Nightime Fantasy	31/03/1979	102	BB
Vicki Sue Robinson With The New York Community Choir	Should I Stay/I Won't Let You Go	22/01/1977	104	BB
Vicki Tasso	The Sound Of The Hammer	16/06/1962	118	BB
Victor Feldman Quartet	A Taste Of Honey*	07/07/1962	101	CB
Vikki Carr	He's A Rebel*	08/09/1962	102	CB
Vikki Carr	He's A Rebel	22/09/1962	115	BB
Vikki Carr	My Heart Reminds Me - Part 1	06/08/1966	127	CB
Vikki Carr	Don't Break My Pretty Balloon	08/06/1968	103	CB
Vikki Carr	Don't Break My Pretty Balloon	15/06/1968	114	BB
Vikki Carr	I'll Be Home	06/02/1971	117	CB
Vikki Carr	I Can't Give Back The Love I Feel For You	25/09/1971	103	CB
Vikki Carr	I'd Do It All Again	18/12/1971	102	CB
Vikki Carr	Big Hurt	22/07/1972	108	BB

Village People	San Francisco (You've Got Me)	15/10/1977	102	BB
Vince Hill	Edelweiss	15/04/1967	134	CB
Vince Hill	Edelweiss	22/04/1967	119	BB
Vince Vance & The Valiants	Bomb Iran	01/11/1980	101	BB
Vincent Edwards	Don't Worry 'BOUT Me	21/07/1962	112	CB
Vincent Edwards	No, Not Much	22/05/1965	134	CB
Vincent Edwards	No, Not Much	05/06/1965	108	BB
Vinnie Monte	Follow That Girl	17/06/1961	144	CB
Vinnie Monte	One Of The Guys	03/03/1962	143	CB
Vito & The Salutations	Gloria	19/05/1962	133	CB
Vivian Reed	Yours Until Tomorrow	15/06/1968	113	BB
Vivian Reed	You've Lost That Lovin' Feeling/(You're My) Soul And	14/09/1968	115	BB
Vivian Reed	You've Lost That Lovin' Feeling/(You're My) Soul And	14/09/1968	117	CB
Vivian Reed	Unbelievable	25/10/1969	126	CB
Voggue	Dancin' The Night Away	22/08/1981	109	BB
Voyage	Let's Fly Away	26/05/1979	105	BB
Wade Flemons	Slow Motion	13/07/1959	101	BB
Wade Flemons	What's Happening	16/01/1960	116	CB
Wade Flemons	Welcome Stranger	11/08/1962	149	CB
Wade Ray	Burning Desire	09/03/1963	145	CB
Wallace Brothers	I'll Step Aside	13/02/1965	146	CB
Wallace Brothers (Ervin & Johnny)	Faith	28/03/1964	141	CB
Wallace Brothers (Ervin And Johnny)	Precious Words	16/05/1964	107	BB
Walter Brennan	Houdini	21/07/1962	108	CB
Walter Gates & His Orchestra	My Man	16/05/1964	110	CB
Walter Gates And His Orchestra	My Man	20/06/1964	133	BB
Walter Jackson	That's What Mama Say	04/04/1964	132	CB
Walter Jackson	I'll Keep On Trying	02/10/1965	120	BB
Walter Jackson	Funny (Not Much)	29/01/1966	103	BB
Walter Jackson	Funny (Not Much)	26/03/1966	115	CB

Walter Jackson	After You There Can Be Nothing	03/09/1966	130	BB
Walter Jackson	After You There Can Be Nothing	10/09/1966	138	CB
Walter Jackson	Deep In The Heart Of Harlem	24/06/1967	110	BB
Walter Jackson	My Ship Is Comin' In	21/10/1967	124	BB
Walter Jackson	Any Way That You Want Me	08/11/1969	121	CB
Walter Jackson	Anyway That You Want Me	20/12/1969	111	BB
Walter Jackson	Feelings	18/12/1976	101	CB
Walter Murphy	Rhapsody In Blue	30/04/1977	102	BB
Walter Murphy & The Big Apple Band	California Strut	01/05/1976	116	CB
Walter Vaughn	Down On My Knees	01/07/1961	119	CB
Walter Wanderley	Cheganca	10/12/1966	120	CB
Wanda Jackson	Happy, Happy Birthday	10/12/1960	106	CB
Wanda Jackson	Mean, Mean Man	10/12/1960	108	CB
Wanda Jackson	Riot In Cell Block Number Nine	04/03/1961	134	CB
Wanda Jackson	A Little Bitty Tear	20/01/1962	112	CB
Wanda Jackson	I Misunderstood	14/07/1962	117	BB
Wanda Jackson	Between The Window And The Phone	21/07/1962	141	CB
Wanda Jackson	The Greatest Actor	15/09/1962	134	CB
Wanda Jackson	The Greatest Actor	22/09/1962	117	BB
Wang Chung	Fire In The Twilight	11/05/1985	110	BB
War	Good, Good Feelin'	28/04/1979	101	BB
War Featuring Lonnie Jordan	Lonely Feelin'	03/04/1971	107	BB
Was (Not Was)	Smile	12/11/1983	106	BB
Was (Not Was)	Knocked Down, Made Small (Treated Like A RuBBer Ball)	21/01/1984	109	BB
Washrag	Bang!	21/10/1972	112	BB
Waylon	Clyde	19/07/1980	103	BB
Waylon Jennings	Delia's Gone	21/06/1969	124	CB
Waylon Jennings	Delia's Gone	05/07/1969	124	BB
Waylon Jennings	You Can Have Her	24/03/1973	114	BB
Waylon Jennings	Waymore's Blues	16/08/1975	110	BB

Waylon Jennings	Are You Ready For The Country	25/12/1976	106	CB
Wayne Anthony	A Thousand Miles Away	05/02/1966	136	CB
Wayne Cochran	Harlem Shuffle	25/12/1965	127	BB
Wayne Fontana	Come On Home	09/07/1966	117	BB
Wayne Miran & Rush Release	Oh Baby	27/09/1975	110	CB
Wayne Miran And Rush Release	Oh Baby	11/10/1975	104	BB
Wayne Newton	I'm Looking Over A Four Leaf Clover	22/02/1964	123	BB
Wayne Newton	Only You	04/07/1964	119	CB
Wayne Newton	Only You	08/08/1964	122	BB
Wayne Newton	Comin' On Too Strong	23/01/1965	114	CB
Wayne Newton	Some Sunday Morning	25/12/1965	123	BB
Wayne Newton	After The Laughter	26/02/1966	123	CB
Wayne Newton	Laura Lee	23/04/1966	144	CB
Wayne Newton	Stagecoach To Cheyenne	28/05/1966	113	BB
Wayne Newton	Stagecoach To Cheyenne	04/06/1966	148	CB
Wayne Newton	If I Only Had A Song To Sing	11/03/1967	132	CB
Wayne Newton	Love Of The Common People	28/10/1967	106	BB
Wayne Newton	All The Time	10/02/1968	134	CB
Wayne Newton	Remembering	08/06/1968	128	CB
Wayne Newton	While We're Still Young	31/03/1973	107	BB
Wayne Newton	Pour Me A Little More Wine	29/09/1973	107	CB
Wayne Newton	Lady Lay	16/11/1974	101	BB
Wayne Thomas	I'll Be Yours (Nel Sol)	23/03/1968	117	CB
We Five	Cast Your Fate To The Wind	20/11/1965	133	CB
We Five	You Let A Love Burn Out	19/03/1966	115	CB
We Five	There Stands The Door	28/05/1966	116	BB
We Five	The First Time	12/11/1966	136	CB
We The People	You Made Me (A Brand New World)	14/10/1972	108	CB
Weapons Of Peace	Just Can't Be That Way (Ruth's Song)	02/10/1976	102	CB
WeBB Pierce	Is It Wrong (For Loving You)	19/03/1960	117	CB

WeBB Pierce	Drifting Texas Sand	15/08/1960	108	BB
WeBB Pierce	There's More Pretty Girls Than One	09/01/1961	118	BB
WeBB Pierce	Nobody's Darlin' But Mine	11/05/1963	147	CB
WeBB Pierce	Sands Of Gold	22/06/1963	117	CB
WeBB Pierce	Sands Of Gold	29/06/1963	118	BB
WeBB Pierce	French Rivieria	23/05/1964	126	BB
Webster Lewis	Give Me Some Emotion	03/05/1980	107	BB
Wednesday	Roses Are Red My Love	02/11/1974	116	CB
Weird Al Yankovic	Another One Rides The Bus	21/03/1981	104	BB
Weird Al Yankovic	I Love Rocky Road	06/08/1983	106	BB
Wendy Hill	Without Your Love	23/10/1961	111	BB
Wendy Hill	(Gary, Please Don't Sell) My Diamond Ring	20/03/1965	134	BB
Wendy Rene	After Laughter	10/10/1964	134	BB
Wendy Rene	After Laughter	17/10/1964	150	CB
Wes Montgomery	Wind Song	30/03/1968	103	BB
Wes Montgomery	Georgia On My Mind	13/07/1968	104	CB
Wes Montgomery	Where Have All The Flowers Gone?	04/01/1969	132	CB
Wes Montgomery	Where Have All The Flowers Gone?	25/01/1969	119	BB
Wha-Koo	(You're Such A) Fabulous Dancer	13/05/1978	101	BB
Wha-Koo	(You're Such A) Fabulous Dancer	20/05/1978	101	CB
Whitesnake	Ain't No Love In The Heart Of The City [Live]	14/02/1981	109	BB
Whodini	Freaks Come Out At Night	26/01/1985	104	BB
Wilbert Harrison	Good Bye Kansas City	22/02/1960	102	BB
Wilbert Harrison	Good Bye Kansas City	05/03/1960	101	CB
Wilbert Harrison	Off To Work Again	12/06/1961	114	BB
Wilbert Harrison	Let's Stick Together	12/05/1962	127	CB
Wilbert Harrison	Near To You	02/11/1963	103	CB
Wilbert Harrison	Near To You	16/11/1963	118	BB
Wilbert Harrison	My Heart Is Yours	20/03/1971	116	CB
Wild Butter	Roxanna (Thank You For Getting Me High)	12/09/1970	118	CB

Wild Cherry	1 2 3 Kind Of Love	29/07/1978	104	CB
Wille Nelson & Waylon Jennings	Take It To The Limit	08/10/1983	102	BB
William "Bootsy" Collins	Take A Lickin' And Keep On Kickin'	01/05/1982	103	BB
William Bell	You Don't Miss Your Water	20/01/1962	108	CB
William Bell	Any Other Way	20/10/1962	131	BB
William Bell	Every Man Oughta Have A Woman	06/04/1968	115	BB
William Bell	Happy	26/07/1969	141	CB
William Bell	Happy	09/08/1969	129	BB
William Bell	Lonely Soldier	05/09/1970	107	CB
William Bell	Lovin' On Borrowed Time	07/07/1973	101	BB
William Bell & Judy Clay	My Baby Specializes	28/12/1968	104	BB
William Bell, Carla Thomas	I Need You Woman	12/07/1969	106	BB
William Bell, Mavis Staples	Love's Sweet Sensation	05/07/1969	113	CB
Willie Bobo	Sunshine Superman	10/12/1966	107	BB
Willie Hightower	If I Had A Hammer	29/10/1966	146	CB
Willie Hightower	It's A Miracle	12/04/1969	130	BB
Willie Hightower	Walk A Mile In My Shoes	30/05/1970	107	BB
Willie Hutch	Sunshine Lady	24/11/1973	117	CB
Willie Hutch	Theme Of Foxy Brown	13/04/1974	110	CB
Willie Mitchell	Crawl - Part 2	17/03/1962	144	CB
Willie Mitchell	Sunrise Serenade	10/11/1962	111	CB
Willie Mitchell	Percolatin'	02/01/1965	104	CB
Willie Mitchell	Everything Is Gonna Be Alright	06/11/1965	126	BB
Willie Mitchell	Everything Is Gonna Be Alright	20/11/1965	117	CB
Willie Mitchell	Mercy	15/10/1966	127	BB
Willie Mitchell	Misty	04/02/1967	143	CB
Willie Mitchell	Slippin' And Slidin'	24/06/1967	109	CB
Willie Mitchell	Ooh Baby, You Turn Me On	23/09/1967	131	CB
Willie Mitchell	Take Five	14/12/1968	101	CB
Willie Mitchell	Young People	26/04/1969	112	CB

Willie Mitchell	Young People	07/06/1969	120	BB
Willie Mitchell	My Babe	01/11/1969	125	CB
Willie Mitchell	My Babe	08/11/1969	115	BB
Willie Mitchell	Last Tango In Paris	31/03/1973	111	CB
Willie Nelson	Touch Me	05/05/1962	124	CB
Willie Nelson	Touch Me	23/06/1962	109	BB
Willie Nelson	Half A Man	30/03/1963	129	BB
Willie Nelson	I Gotta Get Drunk [Live]	17/04/1976	101	BB
Willie Nelson	If You Can Touch Her At All	01/04/1978	104	BB
Willie Nile	It's All Over	07/06/1980	106	BB
Willie West	Greatest Love	18/02/1967	134	CB
Willows	Church Bells May Ring	06/03/1961	114	BB
Wilma Burgess	Don't Touch Me	14/05/1966	149	CB
Wilmer & The Dukes	Living In The U.S.A.	23/08/1969	114	BB
Wilson Pickett	I'm Down To My Last Heartbreak	09/11/1963	123	CB
Wilson Pickett	I'm Gonna Cry	27/06/1964	143	CB
Wilson Pickett	I'm Gonna Cry (Cry Baby)	11/07/1964	124	BB
Wilson Pickett	Come Home Baby	13/02/1965	103	CB
Wilson Pickett	My Heart Belongs To You	25/12/1965	109	BB
Wilson Pickett	I've Come A Long Way	23/03/1968	101	BB
Wilson Pickett	International Playboy	21/04/1973	103	CB
Wilson Pickett	International Playboy	19/05/1973	104	BB
Wilson Pickett	Soft Soul Boogie Woogie	08/12/1973	103	BB
Wilson Pickett	Soft Soul Boogie Woogie	15/12/1973	105	CB
Wilson Pickett	Take Your Pleasure Where You Find It	29/06/1974	106	CB
Wilton Felder Featuring BoBBy Womack And Introducing Alltrina	(No Matter How High I Get) I'll Still Be Lookin' Up To You	16/02/1985	102	BB
Wind	I'll Hold Out My Hand	27/12/1969	114	CB
Wink Martindale	Giddyup Go	12/03/1966	114	BB
Wishbone Ash	No Easy Road	23/06/1973	112	CB
Witches & The Warlock	No Where To Run No Where To Hide	13/04/1968	138	CB

Wolfman Jack	I Ain't Never Seen A White Man	09/09/1972	106	CB
Wolfman Jack	I Ain't Never Seen A White Man	23/09/1972	106	BB
Wolfman Jack	My Girl	03/11/1973	118	CB
World Of Oz	The Muffin Man	24/08/1968	128	CB
World Of Oz	King Croesus	30/11/1968	126	BB
Wright's Wonderwheel	I Know	07/10/1972	119	CB
Wyatt (Earp) Mcpherson	Here's My Confession	13/05/1961	121	CB
Wynton Kelly	Comin' In The Back Door	28/12/1963	112	CB
Wynton Kelly	Little Tracy	18/04/1964	103	CB
Wynton Kelly	Little Tracy	09/05/1964	113	BB
Xavier	Work That Sucker To Death	24/04/1982	104	BB
Xavion	Eat Your Heart Out	08/09/1984	103	BB
Xtc	Generals And Majors	24/01/1981	104	BB
Xtc	Generals And Majors	07/02/1981	1102	CB
Yarbrough & Peoples	Heartbeats	15/01/1983	101	BB
Yello	I Love You	16/07/1983	103	BB
Yellow Hand	Down To The Wire	05/12/1970	120	BB
Yellowstone & Voice	Well Hello	05/05/1973	117	BB
Yes	Into The Lens (I Am A Camera)	25/10/1980	104	BB
Yonah	After The First One	15/09/1979	102	BB
Young Hearts	Oh, I'll Never Be The Same	27/04/1968	109	BB
Young-Holt Unlimited	Just A Melody	24/05/1969	110	CB
Young-Holt Unlimited	Straight Ahead	02/08/1969	110	BB
Young-Holt Unlimited	Horoscope	18/10/1969	116	CB
Young-Holt Unlimited	Horoscope	01/11/1969	115	BB
Young-Holt Unlimited	Mellow Dreaming	26/09/1970	106	BB
Young-Holt Unlimited	Mellow Dreaming	03/10/1970	121	CB
Yvonne Baker & The Sensations	Party Across The Hall	08/09/1962	127	CB
Yvonne Caroll And The Roulettes	Gee What A Guy	31/08/1963	115	BB
Yvonne Carroll & The Roulettes	Gee What A Guy	10/08/1963	101	CB

Yvonne Elliman	Walk Right In	10/01/1976	107	CB
Yvonne Elliman	Walk Right In	10/01/1976	109	BB
Yvonne Elliman	Moment By Moment	30/12/1978	Np7	CB
Yvonne Fair	Funky Music Sho Nuff Turns Me On	03/08/1974	117	CB
Z.Z. Hill	Hey Little Girl	14/08/1965	134	BB
Z.Z. Hill	Happiness Is All I Need	26/02/1966	126	CB
Z.Z. Hill	You Got What I Need	05/10/1968	129	BB
Z.Z. Hill	You Got What I Need	12/10/1968	145	CB
Z.Z. Hill	Don't Make Promises (You Can't Keep)	25/01/1969	141	CB
Z.Z. Hill	Chokin' Kind	23/10/1971	108	BB
Z.Z. Hill	Second Chance	17/06/1972	117	CB
Z.Z. Hill	Ain't Nothing You Can Do	09/06/1973	114	BB
Z.Z. Hill	I Keep On Lovin' You	26/10/1974	104	BB
Z.Z. Hill	I Created A Monster	09/08/1975	109	BB
Z.Z. Hill	Love Is So Good When You're Stealing It	17/09/1977	102	BB
Zagar & Evans	Mr. Turnkey	11/10/1969	106	BB
Zager & Evans	Help One Man Today	21/03/1970	104	CB
Zalman Yanovsky (Zally)	As Long As You're Here	07/10/1967	101	BB
Zapp	Dance Floor (Part I)	17/07/1982	101	BB
Zapp	Doo Wa Ditty (Blow That Thing)	06/11/1982	103	BB
Zapp	I Can Make You Dance (Part I)	20/08/1983	102	BB
Zapp	Heartbreaker (Part I)	12/11/1983	107	BB
Zebra	Tell Me What You Want	10/09/1983	107	BB
Zip & The Zippers	Where You Goin', Little Boy?	06/04/1963	145	CB
Zorro	Somebody Cares	14/08/1961	118	BB
Zz Top	Enjoy And Get It On	04/06/1977	105	BB
Zz Top	Tube Snake Boogie	12/12/1981	1102	CB
Zz Top	Tube Snake Boogie	26/12/1981	103	BB

Made in United States
Troutdale, OR
06/03/2024

20304072R00379